THE ROMAN FORUM

A SURVEY OF ANCIENT HISTORY

TO THE DEATH OF CONSTANTINE

BY

M. L. W. LAISTNER

PROFESSOR OF ANCIENT HISTORY
IN CORNELL UNIVERSITY

D. C. HEATH AND COMPANY

BOSTON   NEW YORK   CHICAGO
ATLANTA   SAN FRANCISCO   DALLAS
LONDON

TO

CAPTAIN PHILIP HEMINGWAY

IN

FRIENDSHIP AND GRATITUDE

Tot nos praeceptoribus, tot exemplis instruxit antiquitas, ut possit videri nulla sorte nascendi aetas felicior quam nostra, cui docendae priores elaborarunt. — Quintilian, *Inst. Orat.* xii, 11, 22

PREFACE

For some years it has been one of my academic duties to deliver throughout the session an introductory course of lectures on Ancient History. Whatever other reading may be done by students in connection with such a course, it is desirable, indeed necessary, that they should have a textbook or survey to guide them. The absence of a work in one volume, in which the treatment of the subject is sufficiently mature for university students, and in which at the same time the important features of Ancient History and Civilization have been brought out with detail sufficient to justify the historical generalizations, led me to essay the composition of such a book. Much has had to be omitted; much had needs to be compressed into a paragraph. Yet, in the process of selection and arrangement, I have striven to secure clarity and balance, and to avoid assigning a disproportionate amount of space to any particular topic or period. That some epochs or subjects have nevertheless been treated more fully than others is due either to the existence of ampler source material or to the fact that their significance was greater and that they exerted a more lasting influence.

At the same time it is perhaps not too much to hope that this book, which has been written as a continuous narrative and in which the sections, subsections, and leaded paragraph headings of the typical textbook have been avoided, may also be found interesting by a wider class of readers who may desire to make or to renew acquaintance with the Ancient World.

My sincerest thanks are due to Professor Nathaniel Schmidt of this University who, with characteristic kindness, read Chapters I to V, VII, and part of VIII in manuscript, and made a number of valuable criticisms and suggestions. While his aid saved me from perpetrating some errors in detail, the views expressed and any inaccuracies which may still remain must be laid solely to my charge. I also have to thank the authorities

v

of the Metropolitan Museum in New York for leave to reproduce Plates 9, 11, 12, and 16*a;* the Trustees of the British Museum for similar permission in respect of Plate 21; and the University of Chicago Press for allowing me to quote considerable portions from R. F. Harper's edition of the Code of Hammurabi.

The publishers desire me to make acknowledgments to Professor Hutton Webster for the preparation of Maps 3 to 15.

M. L. W. L.

CORNELL UNIVERSITY
Ithaca, N.Y.
April, 1929

CONTENTS

CONTENTS   ix

LIST OF PLATES

LIST OF MAPS

A SURVEY OF ANCIENT HISTORY

INTRODUCTION

SOURCES AND CHRONOLOGY

THE sources from which the modern historian reconstructs the history of the Ancient World are of the most varied character. There are formal histories like the masterpieces of Thucydides and of Livy. There is a great body of other Greek and Latin writings in prose and verse, which, insofar as they illustrate or are expressions of Hellenic and Roman civilization, must be regarded as historical material. These literatures have been transmitted through centuries and have not been appreciably increased by modern discoveries. He would be a sanguine man indeed who looked forward with any confidence to the recovery of a considerable body of Greek and Roman literature now lost.[1] On the other hand, the archæological and epigraphic material continues steadily to increase.

While the beginnings of serious epigraphic studies reach back to the eighteenth century, scientific excavation of historic and prehistoric sites dates only from the middle of the nineteenth. Especially during the last fifty years a mass of monumental and inscriptional evidence has accumulated; with its help many aspects of ancient civilization, on which the surviving literatures of Greece and Rome, or such monuments as have remained

---

[1] In spite of the recovery from the rubbish heaps of Egypt of Aristotle's *Constitution of Athens*, a portion of an important Greek historical work of the early fourth century B.C., some pæans of Pindar, poems by Bacchylides, the *Mimes* of Herondas, and some other literary fragments hitherto unknown, the vast number of *papyri* from Egypt have added singularly little to our knowledge of Greek literature and thought. On the other hand, they have immensely increased our knowledge of the economic and legal and administrative history of the Hellenistic and Græco-Roman periods.

1

above ground through the ages, throw little or no light, have been at least partially illumined. Yet there would seem to be a danger in the very wealth of this new material, and in its too exclusive use. It is possible to be so overawed by the quantity of pottery unearthed on an unimportant site, or by a mass of *papyri* illustrating but one human activity during a short period and in a restricted area, as to attribute to these a historical significance out of all proportion to the information that they offer. Again, it will rarely be possible to write a continuous history of a state or of a long epoch, if the material available for their reconstruction is wholly or mainly archæological and epigraphic. Such material may be abundant for one era and most scanty for another. Thus, while there is plentiful evidence for Egyptian history during the fourth, fifth, sixth, and twelfth dynasties, and again for the eighteenth and those that follow, the intervening ages are still extremely obscure. What greater contrast could one find than between Greek history during the fifth and fourth centuries B.C. on the one hand and during the third century on the other? Or, between the two centuries from Cicero to Hadrian and the century and a half that follow? In the former instances the historian has both abundant literature and archæological material from which to fashion his mosaic of ancient history; in the latter the literature is either non-existent or so poor in quantity or quality as to make any reconstruction largely a matter of guess-work.

A further danger, which is one of method, is more radical. There are extensive periods of Greek and Roman history for which the student has the guidance of historical works. But the accounts of the ancient historians are in the main concerned with political, military, and constitutional history. The speeches of the Attic orators or of Cicero deal primarily with political affairs or judicial business; and even Cicero's voluminous correspondence, invaluable historical source though it be, chiefly illustrates the public and the social life of the governing class at Rome between 65 and 44 B.C. To a less degree we learn also about the equestrian or financial class. Cicero's interests scarcely pass beyond those limits, and we look in vain for information about the life and activities of the mass of the people in Rome and Italy. This being the character of the most important literary sources available at that time, it was inevitable that the older generation of modern writers on Greek and Roman history — men like Niebuhr, Thirlwall, Grote — should treat mainly of political, military, and intellectual history. The accumulation of archæological and epigraphic material has enabled more recent scholars to enlarge the picture of the Greek and Roman world, by adding to their narrative sections on economic development, or on social history and institutions. Yet the new method of reconstructing the past sometimes seems in danger of being carried too far. Political, military, and constitutional history is relegated to second place, and page after page is devoted to the treatment of social or economic history.

The more brilliant the reconstruction of these aspects from the recently found material, the greater the danger that the picture of Greek and Roman history is out of focus. For, ultimately, where ancient histories have survived, they must necessarily form the framework on which the modern student has to build up his reconstruction of ancient history. In view of the character of those histories a properly balanced reconstruction should give first place to those aspects of the ancient world which they illuminate. Besides, while in the case of the ancient kingdoms of the Near and Middle East political history is synonymous with the history of dynasts and dynasties, so that a certain distaste on the part of the modern reader for the continual rivalries, the endless wars, the egotistical aggrandizement of eastern potentates, is intelligible and excusable, in the case of the Greeks and Romans — at any rate during a great part of their history — political affairs, both at home and abroad, were the concern of the citizen body as a whole. Thus, to give but one example, an account of the Greek city-states from the sixth to the fourth century B.C., which relegates to a secondary place the political history and institutions of that period, can only be radically false and one-sided. In fine, the disproportion between political and social history, and the gross overemphasis of the latter in more than one recent publication on ancient history, necessitate the repetition of a truism, that it is impossible for a student to understand the social institutions and life of any people until he has a clear grasp of that people's political development and history.

Whereas some consideration will subsequently be given in their proper chronological place to the more noteworthy historical and other writers of Greece and Rome, it is convenient at this point to offer some remarks on the materials which have been broadly designated archæological sources. By these are meant the remains of ancient cities and buildings, objects of art of most divers kinds, implements of domestic use or from the workshop, coins, pottery, and inscriptions. Utensils made of baked clay are cheap; unless they are meant for ornament and are therefore elaborately decorated, they can be easily and inexpensively replaced; and, though they may be broken, the fragments are almost imperishable. Broken pottery will be thrown aside by the inhabitants of a settlement, so that in time a dump or rubbish heap will accumulate. And, even if the settlement be abandoned, the dump will remain as a record of the site's former occupation. Again, it was a common practice among ancient peoples to bury with their dead articles such as these had used during their earthly life. Pottery is not only the commonest form of such grave furniture, it is also the most important to the modern student of ancient civilization. In the prehistoric period of any country, or in any era of which written records are meagre or absent, potsherds are indeed precious historical material. If pottery be present in any quantity at a given site, the stratification will enable the excavator to establish some form of chronological scheme. It may provide evidence, too, for commercial, or for less friendly, intercourse between the inhabitants of different regions; and something may be learnt from it of the culture and conditions of life of its makers. The depth of such deposits is sometimes very considerable; in the mound of Tell-el-Hesy, in southern Palestine, the different strata together totalled a depth of some sixty feet; at Cnossus in Crete the Neolithic deposit amounted on an average to twenty-six feet, representing many centuries of human occupation.

Many kinds of substance have been used for the recording of inscriptions, while their content is of almost infinite variety. The material is mainly determined by the natural resources of a country. In Mesopotamia, where both stone and wood were scarce, clay was usually employed; in Egypt, stone and papyrus.

But wood, wooden tablets smeared with wax, leather, and skins, in short, any substance presenting a reasonably smooth surface, have been used at various times and places as writing material. The contents of an inscription — using the latter word in its widest sense — may be almost anything. It may be no more than a person's name, it may be a letter, a bill, a curse, a chronicle, an official document, a funeral éloge.

Apart from late writers like Manetho and Berossus (both lived in the third century B.C.), and foreigners like Herodotus and Ctesias, no formal histories of the great oriental kingdoms and dynasties have survived. The epigraphic records on the other hand are abundant for some periods, scanty or lacking for others. Doubtless chance and the ravages of time have operated very greatly to effect this unequal preservation of written sources. But warfare and the accompanying destruction of material things are no less the cause of many gaps in our knowledge; and, in addition, we must not leave out of sight the possibility that a people might deliberately seek to suppress, or at least take no trouble to preserve, the memory of some part of its history. Modern ignorance concerning the period of Hyksos domination in Egypt is due not merely to the material factors already noted, but to the desire of the Egyptians of the eighteenth and later dynasties to forget this unhappy period of their national growth. Conversely, the deliberate act of one of Assyria's last kings, Ashurbanipal, in collecting a great library of cuneiform tablets, which modern excavation has retrieved, has put at our disposal exceptionally full material for studying the latest and most glorious centuries of Assyrian history.

But in Greek and Roman history, too, there are periods of considerable length for whose political history the existing literary evidence is restricted in amount and inferior in quality. This is the case, for example, with Greece in the third century B.C., and with the Roman Empire in the second century A.D.; but in either case the epigraphic material is fortunately abundant. Finally, there are aspects of Greek and Roman civilization about which we should be almost wholly ignorant, save for the preservation of numerous inscriptions. But for these, to give but two instances, the development of school and higher education in the Greek world of the last three centuries B.C., or the elaborate machinery of municipal government which developed during the early Roman Empire, would be alike obscure.

An introductory chapter to a general survey of ancient history must necessarily include some reference to the methods of reckoning time used by the ancients, and to the general principles on which the chronology of ancient states has been reconstructed. The modern reader is so accustomed to seeing the birth of the Founder of Christianity taken as the starting point for reckoning historical events both forward and backward, that he tends to forget that, while there was a certain unity due to the fact that ultimately all time-reckoning depends on observation of the heavenly bodies, in detailed practice there was great diversity. The use of both the lunar year and of the solar is extremely ancient. Babylonia and Egypt may be said to share the honor of evolving systems of time-reckoning and methods of expressing conveniently the intervals between, and the succession of, events, on which all subsequent chronological schemes are based. The contribution of Babylonia was the greater, for the familiar divisions into years and months, and of the day into two sets of twelve hours each, appear to have originated there. The Babylonians, however, followed the lunar year, so that frequent intercalary periods were necessary to keep the months in proper relation to the seasons. It is remarkable that their method of expressing successive events in official documents was for centuries so primitive and cumbersome; for we can hardly call otherwise a system in which a particular year is named after some important event, or else the year after such and such an occurrence. In Egypt the reckoning by a solar year of exactly 365 days was in use from earliest times. As it was not the practice to intercalate a day every four years, the months in time lost all relation to the seasons, and corrections do not appear to have been made in the calendar with any regularity or frequency. Again, the dating of events as occurring in such and such a year of King X was clumsy; it has also caused much difficulty to the modern student of Egyptian history. For there is often great uncertainty about the length of a particular king's reign. The system followed by the Assyrians marks a great advance on earlier usage. They, in their official documents and computation of events, followed the more convenient method of naming each year after an official or magistrate. It was a method analogous to that in use at a much later date in the majority of Greek city-states and in Rome. Many such lists of Assyrian magistrates (*limmu* lists) have been preserved; they are invaluable not only for dating events in Assyrian history, but for reconstructing the chronology of other countries, for example, of Egypt. It must be admitted that the dating of reigns and events in Egyptian and Mesopotamian history prior to the middle of the second millennium B.C. is still attended by many uncertainties, and the dates, reckoned in terms of years B.C., which are given in modern histories, must therefore be regarded as approximate rather than precise.

Both in the Greek city-states and in Rome the lunar year formed the basis of the calendar, with the inevitable result that some inaccuracy in the relation between calendar and seasons was more or less constant. In Greece the lunar year was reckoned as 354 days, and it was therefore 11 days short of the solar. In order to bring the two into harmony, an intercalary month was inserted every two or three years. Thus, in Athens, to the last quarter of the fifth century, a lunar-solar cycle of eight years with three intercalary months was in force. For a time this cycle was superseded by a nineteen-year cycle, devised by the astronomer Meton; though this gave a somewhat more accurate computation it was still short of exact. Later, the Athenians reverted once more to the eight-year cycle. So far as we know, no other Greek state devised a more efficient calendar. The usual method of dating events was by reference to the chief magistrate in a given year (*e.g.* at Athens, the senior archon, at Sparta, the senior ephor); but, even on official inscriptions, we do not find such indications of date before the middle of the fifth century. The dating by Olympiads, that is to say, by a four-year period computed on the celebration of the Olympian festival (Traditional date of the first Olympiad, 776 B.C.), was never used in public or private business, or in official documents. And, though relatively a far more convenient system of reckoning, it was not even adopted by historical writers before the third century B.C.

The Roman lunar year was computed at 355 days; to keep this year and the seasons in harmony various methods of adjust-

ment and intercalation were tried at different times. But less
care seems to have been taken than in Greece to keep the equation reasonably accurate. In the stress of the later years of the
Republic adjustment was so long neglected that, at the time of
Cæsar's reform of the calendar, based on the solar year of 365
days with an intercalary day every four years, there was a dis-
crepancy of no less than three months. The Cæsarian calendar
is still followed in the Greek Orthodox Church, and the countries where her authority holds good; while our own calendar
is the same, with a slight modification introduced at the end of
the sixteenth century by Gregory XIII. Events in Republican
Rome were dated by indicating the two chief magistrates (consuls) in a given year. This method continued under the Empire,
but on official documents is frequently accompanied by what is
in effect, if not in form, the regnal year of the emperor, indicated
in several ways. It need scarcely be added that such double
indication of date is of the greatest possible value to the student
of Roman imperial history.

The Jewish calendar, which is still in use among that people
for religious purposes, is likewise lunar. The year is divided into
twelve months of twenty-nine and thirty days. To make up the
difference between the lunar and the solar year a thirteenth
month is periodically inserted, usually every three years.

Finally, we must note the practice of reckoning in eras, that is
to say, dating the history of a country by the years after some
event of outstanding importance. Thus Roman antiquarians
might take as the starting point of their calculations the foundation of Rome, and indicate an occurrence as happening in such
and such a year after the foundation of the city. Of such eras
a goodly number were introduced at different times, but for the
most part their use was restricted to comparatively small areas.
Of the few which were widely adopted, and existed for a prolonged period, one instance will suffice. The so-called Seleucid
era, which began in the autumn of 312 B.C., was followed for
many centuries in the countries included in the one-time Syrian
empire. Among many of the Jews of the Near East its use continued at least as late as the eleventh century A.D.; and it survives to the present day among some Christian sects and their
Mohammedan neighbors in Syria.

CHAPTER I

MAN IN THE STONE AGE

I would then that I lived not among the fifth race of men, but either had died before or had been afterward. For now verily is a race of iron. Neither by day shall they ever cease from weariness and woe, neither in the night from wasting, and sore cares shall the gods give them. Howbeit even for them shall good be mingled with evil. Hesiod, *Works and Days*, 174–179. (Mair's translation.)

A VERY old myth, once perhaps current among many peoples though varying in details, teaches that mankind, since man's creation, has passed through several stages, each of considerable length. According to the commonest form of the legend there were four such eras, but the early Greek poet Hesiod, adding one to the number, describes successively five: the Golden, the Silver, the Bronze, the Heroic, and the Iron Ages. The idea underlying this myth is one of the progressive degeneration of mankind, the story of man's gradual decline from a god-like character and existence. Modern archæological science, too, distinguishes a number of stages in the history of man; but, reversing the pessimism of legendary fancy, traces man's continuous advance in material culture, and his social and political evolution. These stages or periods of material progress have been conveniently named after the substances which men have in each case used to fashion the implements on which they chiefly depended for their means of subsistence. Thus it has become customary to refer to the Early Stone (Palæolithic) Age and the Late Stone (Neolithic) Age, the Copper and Bronze Ages, and, finally, the Iron Age. But it should be noted at the outset that, though such a classification is very convenient for defining the general course of man's material progress, and for distinguishing very approximately the main stages of a long journey, it would be a serious error to assume that these epochs were sharply marked off one from the other. On the contrary, the more evidence accumulates, the clearer it becomes that there was no break in continuity between the Palæolithic and the Neolithic, or between the Neolithic and the Copper-Bronze Ages. Rather, one merged gradually into the other, so that, for example, the earliest users of copper or bronze tools in a given area continued side by side with these to use stone implements or arms.

The remains of the Palæolithic Age have been found in river drifts and valley deposits, in caves, and in rock shelters, over a very wide geographic area; namely, in Syria, North Africa and Egypt, central Europe as far as Bulgaria, South Russia; above all, in England, France, and the Spanish peninsula. So far no finds of Palæolithic objects are attested for Macedonia and Greece or for the islands of the eastern Mediterranean. By far the densest distribution is in France and Spain; it is from the Early Stone Age remains brought to light in those two countries that the slow evolution, representing the passage of many thousands of years, of Palæolithic man, his tools, and his art, can best be studied in unbroken continuity from the first beginnings down to the advent of the Neolithic Age. Very slowly man learnt to improve with his hands the rough stones and flints which at first he had used much as he found them in nature. These flints are of various types, serving as knives, cleavers, scrapers, and axes. Even in the earliest period of the Palæolithic Age man acquired the art of chipping pieces from a flint core and fashioning them into sharp-edged tools. Excavators have in different areas discovered what may be called Palæolithic workshops, that is to say, Palæolithic deposits of flints with the cores from which they had been flaked. A further stage of development is reached with the use of animal bones for making implements. At last, with the greater diversity and immensely improved character of their tools, men were enabled to advance culturally with relatively much greater speed. It is to the latest period of the Palæolithic Age that belong numerous and most varied examples of earliest man's artistic skill. Carving or sculpture in the round, incised drawing, low relief, and painting — all these methods of portraying human or animal figures he learnt to master. In all probability he modelled or carved rude figurines in the round before trying his hand at reproducing figures and objects on a flat surface, whether by incision or by painting. For the latter processes demand a somewhat greater measure of skill. Yet it is precisely in these that Palæolithic man attained to the greatest degree of success. The paintings, drawings, or engravings of reindeer, bison, horses, wild goats, and other animals, which are to be seen in the caves of the Dordogne in France or in the Altamira cave in northern Spain, show an astonishing realism or naturalism, and testify to the keen powers of observation possessed by the artists who made them. No less striking is the minute skill displayed in engraving figure designs on reindeer horns and bones, which were either used as implements or intended as votive offerings.[1] In either case we may suppose that the representations of wild animals on them were believed to be, as it were, good magic, in one case insuring success to the hunter who used a spear point or harpoon so engraved, and in the case of votive gifts to procure in a more general way a plentiful supply of game. Human figures, especially in paintings and drawings, are much rarer, and the surviving examples show that Palæolithic man failed to display the same artistic aptitude in portraying his fellows. Probably, indeed, he had less skill in this respect because less practice, if we are right in assuming that his primary impulse in drawing and engraving was utilitarian rather than artistic. One discovery of immense importance in the history of human progress can now be said with certainty to have been made in the last period of the Palæolithic Age, the art of making fire. Momentous as was this new knowledge, it does not appear to have been at all fully utilized. For it is only in the Later Stone Age that those crafts for which the use of fire is essential began to be developed.

Compared with the slow cultural advance of man in the Palæolithic period progress in the Neolithic Age is rapid. Man of the Late Stone Age used more varied materials; he showed greater constructive ability in fashioning and constantly improving his implements; he displayed an inventive genius and a social sense, which led to far-reaching developments. The dis-

[1] There is a magnificent collection of such decorated reindeer horns in the museum at St. Germain-en-Laye, about twelve miles from Paris.

tribution of Neolithic remains is extremely wide; it extends from Scandinavia and England to North Africa and Egypt; from France and Spain in the West to Anau in central Asia (West Turkestan).[1] Though there are certain characteristics common to all this widely diffused culture, there are also many variations and differences in the material objects found in various Neolithic stations and graves. Hence archæologists have been enabled to distinguish some nine or ten regional groups, besides making various classifications, especially of the ceramic fabrics. Thus we can distinguish between the Neolithic culture of the Alpine and of the Danubian area, or the western from the eastern Mediterranean type. Other phases, again, are found in Egypt, Syria, Susa, and Anau.

The making of clay vessels, which is one of Neolithic man's important inventions, may well have been, up to a point, due to an accidental discovery. In a general way it is true that the earliest pot fabrics are imitations of more primitive containers; for example, in the western Mediterranean region, wooden bowls and vessels made from matted rushes, in eastern countries, the gourd. To procure greater density, or to protect the pots from the action of fire while the contents were being heated, a coating of clay might be applied. This, when exposed to the action of fire, hardened, and it was but one step further to fashion an all-clay pot in imitation of a gourd or rush vessel. The principle of reinforcing rush-work with clay is also found in late Neolithic building. Although it must be admitted that the Neolithic period has no naturalistic paintings or drawings to show, to match the best of the Palæolithic cave pictures, Neolithic man was by no means devoid of an æsthetic sense, which he manifested in other ways. Much of the later Neolithic pottery shows great diversity of shapes, precision of form, fineness of texture, and equal firing, to a truly remarkable degree. For, at that time neither the potter's wheel nor the kiln had yet been invented. Again, we can trace a gradual evolution of design; at first it is quite primitive, finger impressions made on the wet clay, which, on being baked, left a rude pattern on the surface of the vase. Then, simple linear ornaments began to be incised or painted in

[1] For completeness be it added that both the older and the younger Stone Age can be illustrated by finds in China and Japan.

more regular designs on the vessels. In the latest stage the whole pot may be covered with regular, and often very elaborate, geometric or spiral decoration. To Neolithic man's accomplishments as a maker of stone implements far in advance of Palæolithic tools, and as a potter, we may further add his skill in textile work, using this term in a wide sense to include spinning, weaving, netting, and basket making. Examples of such work have been preserved, but they are necessarily scarce owing to the perishable nature of the material.

Of far-reaching importance, too, was the domestication of animals (horse, ass, ox, sheep, pig, goat, dog), and of plants, which was now first effected. Yet the most striking characteristic of Neolithic man was his gradual realization that, to use Aristotle's famous phrase, man is a political being. In other words, not only did men by degrees abandon the nomadic and hunting modes of life, but they learnt to join together in groups and form communities, and to lead a more stationary existence. Indeed, the immense advance in material progress, which has already been outlined, was only possible because men realized the need of coalescing into settled communities and of collaborating in the satisfaction of their daily wants. Corporate action was especially manifested in Neolithic building. In such villages and stations as have been unearthed the ground plans of the huts show that these were sometimes square or rectangular, sometimes circular. They were built of branches and flexible twigs bound together by clay. Especially noteworthy are the lake-dwellings found in Switzerland, northern Italy, and some other districts. They are formed of square huts built on artificially constructed platforms, which in turn were supported by wooden piles driven into the bed of the lake. Some of these belong to the latest period of the Neolithic Age, but continued to be inhabited in the early Bronze Age; the lake-dwellings of Italy, however, do not appear to have been formed before the conclusion of the Stone Age.

But the most remarkable examples of engineering skill in the Neolithic epoch are to be found in the megalithic monuments. These occur in many places, but are most numerous in western Europe, especially in France. The names given in Brittany to these structures have been taken into general use by prehistoric archæologists. *Menhirs* are single large stones set on end; sometimes a number of such are arranged in a circular or oval formation (*cromlech*), sometimes they occur set up in a series of parallel rows (*alinement*). A *dolmen* is composed of several vertical stones surmounted by a single flat slab placed horizontally. The enormous size and weight of these stones fill the spectator with wonder how Neolithic men performed the feat of setting them on end, or — still greater feat — of transporting them for considerable distances from the place where they were originally found.[1] While the dolmens were certainly burial chambers, the purpose of the other types of megalithic monuments is still obscure. It is now definitely established that regular inhumation was already practiced in the late Palæolithic Age, but it was earth-interment of the simplest character. Neolithic burials, on the other hand, were often far more elaborate. They were made in caves, both natural and artificial, under large boulders, or cut into the solid rock, in stone cists, or in the more elaborate stone chamber of a dolmen.

It has been convenient to portray the chief characteristics of the Neolithic area as a whole, but it is important to bear in mind that the duration of the Neolithic Age in different regions within that era varied enormously. Broadly speaking, it is in the South and East that men first learnt the use of metal, and in the North and Northwest that the Later Stone Age lasted longest. Thus, in Elam copper was in use perhaps as far back as 5000 B.C., and the earliest traces of man in southern Mesopotamia show that he was already familiar with metal. In Egypt copper was known by the middle of the fourth millennium and in Crete not much later. On the other hand, in Britain and in Scandinavia the Stone Age lasted to approximately 2000 B.C. The transition from one to the other, at whatever period it occurred, was very gradual. In some areas, as in Egypt and Crete, the transitional process can be traced with fair completeness; hence it has become convenient to dub the age, during which the use of stone and metal tools went on side by side, Sub-Neo-

---

[1] For example, several of the Breton menhirs attain to a height of from thirty to thirty-five feet; the enormous fallen monolith at Locmariaquer, now broken into several pieces, when intact was nearly seventy feet long. The largest of the menhirs in southern France do not exceed about fifteen feet.

lithic, Eneolithic, or Chalcolithic. That there was considerable commercial intercourse between the inhabitants of different regions during the Neolithic Age has been proved beyond question. The discovery in Neolithic graves in western Germany of necklaces made of Mediterranean shells, or the presence of the volcanic glass, called obsidian, coming from the island of Melos, in different parts of the eastern Mediterranean, are but two instances of such early trade relations. At the same time, owing to the chronological reasons given above, the Neolithic Age cannot be satisfactorily separated from the Copper-Bronze Age in a matter affecting different geographic areas at the same date. At this point it is enough to allude to the facts, since a fuller treatment of the topic may be reserved for a survey of the Bronze Age civilization of the Mediterranean area.

CHAPTER II

THE LAND OF THE TWO RIVERS

As for the land of Sumer and Akkad, I collected the scattered peoples thereof, and I procured food and drink for them. In abundance and plenty I pastured them, and I caused them to dwell in a peaceful habitation. — From an inscription of King Hammurabi. (L. W. King, *Letters and Inscriptions of Hammurabi,* iii, p. 191.)

1. POLITICAL DEVELOPMENT AND HISTORY TO *c.* 1900 B.C.

IT was convenient in the previous chapter to sacrifice chronological order and to sketch as a whole the general character of Stone Age culture. We must now revert to a more detailed consideration of those regions of the Near and Middle East in which the earliest historic kingdoms took their rise. We must begin with that district of Asia, lying between the rivers Euphrates and Tigris, which is itself but a part of that larger area to which the name, the Fertile Crescent, has sometimes been applied.[1] The two great streams which enclose this land of the two rivers both rise in the Armenian highlands, and at no great distance from one another. The Euphrates, after a tortuous course through the Taurus and Anti-Taurus ranges, enters the north Syrian plain by Samosata. From here to the Persian Gulf the length of the river is almost twelve hundred miles at the present day, but at the beginning of the historic period was much less. For the process of silting-up has been so extensive through the centuries that the sites of ancient cities, which *c.* 3000 B.C. were on or close to the sea, are now a hundred miles inland. The Tigris, whose upper course is much shorter, passes through the hill-country of Assyria, and emerges into the plain

[1] By the Fertile Crescent is meant that wide semi-circular area bounded on the south by the Persian Gulf and Indian Ocean, on the east by the Iranian mountains, on the north by the Armenian highlands, and on the west by the Mediterranean and Red sea.

near Tekrit. The two streams gradually converge, so that on the thirty-fourth parallel of latitude they are only a little more than a hundred miles apart, while in the neighborhood of Baghdad the width of the intervening plain narrows down to twenty miles. Since in ancient times the Euphrates followed a slightly more easterly course, the narrowest part of the plain may not have been more than fifteen miles from river to river. Below this point the interfluvial land widens again, and it is this region, with its rich alluvial soil, which corresponded to the kingdom of Babylonia, and, earlier still, to the lands of Akkad and Sumer. Only a very few cities belonging to this political area lay a little further to the north.

The hilly and mountainous country situated to the east of the lower Tigris was the land of Elam, corresponding roughly to the modern Persian provinces of Luristan and north Khuzistan. Its mountains are the southern extension of the ancient Zagros range, the central portion of which formed the eastern boundary of Assyria. Excavations conducted on two Elamitic sites, Susa and Musyan, have shown that the region was inhabited at a very early date (before 4000 B.C.) by a people whose earliest remains seem to show that they were at the end of the Neolithic and the beginning of the Chalcolithic Ages. Though there are certain affinities between the early Elamitic pottery and the earliest wares found in Mesopotamia on the one hand, and those unearthed at Anau in west Turkestan on the other, the evidence does not at present warrant any definite ethnological conclusions being drawn from these remains. It is, however, abundantly clear that, from very early times, the inhabitants of Elam and Mesopotamia were in close contact, which, more often than not, took the form of warlike relations.

At the earliest date of which we have any record Babylonia had become the home of two peoples who were racially quite distinct, the Semites and the Sumerians. Which of these two races first settled in this region is still a disputed question; nor does the existing evidence permit us to draw any certain conclusions about the earlier home of the Mesopotamian Semites, though both Arabia and Asia Minor have been suggested. Again, several theories have been put forward regarding the original home of the Sumerians. The regions about and beyond the Caspian,

central Asia, and India have all been so proposed, but none of
these hypotheses is free from difficulties. Recent discoveries in
Sind and in the Punjab have revealed ruins of a civilization
which bears marked resemblance to the Sumerian. Tentatively
the earliest of these Indian remains may be assigned to the beginning of the third millennium; we are warned, however, that
the differences between the two cultures are by no means negligible.[1] The balance of probability seems to be slightly in favor
of an original central Asiatic home, from whence several migrations took place. The earliest may have brought the Sumerians
to Mesopotamia, while a later wave of peoples, akin to them,
found its way to the Indus valley. At all events it is certain
that when we first meet the Sumerians in Mesopotamia they are
culturally far ahead of the earliest Semitic settlers.

Of the surviving lists of early Sumerian kings some at least
belong to a very early date. Much later (end of the third millennium) are accounts of early Sumeria, which were composed
by scholars and poets at a time when the Sumerians had lost
their political independence and had been merged in a Semitic
kingdom. Such writings, however good as literature, depict the
realm of legend not of history. There are stories of a great deluge
and of a very early unified kingdom of Babylon, as well as of
various dynasties in city-states, of which the chief were at Kish
in the North and at Erech in the South. The mythical king of
Erech, Gilgamesh, became the central figure in many Sumerian
legends, and the hero of a Sumerian, and later of a Semitic, epic.
Even though these poems and tales are legendary, there can be
no doubt that, underlying them, is a sound, if rather shadowy,
historical tradition of a Sumerian occupation of southern Mesopotamia, extending over many centuries. Indeed, in more than
one instance recent discoveries have shown the names of very
early kings, hitherto regarded as quite mythical, to have been in
fact historical. But, apart from isolated examples like this, the
latest archæological explorations as a whole give startling sup-

---

[1] Cf. the warning in *Antiquity*, ii (1928), p. 82: "Recent excavation,
whilst confirming the previous evidence of close connexion with the Sumerian civilization of Mesopotamia, has also revealed striking differences,
and it is proposed to recognize this fact by substituting for the name
Indo-Sumerian, formerly given to the newly discovered culture, that of
Indus."

port to the belief that those legends enclose a very solid kernel
of historic truth.   In the most recent excavations at Ur graves
were opened up, which certainly antedate the first dynasty of
Ur, and may do so by several centuries.   Not only were some of
these burials in vaulted chambers of limestone and brick, showing a most advanced architectural technique, but the funeral
furniture laid with the dead is even more remarkable.   Gold,
silver, and copper vessels, silver lamps, jewelry of gold, lapis,
and carnelian, ostrich shells encrusted with mother of pearl and
lapis lazuli, delicately modelled figurines of gold, and beautifully
worked daggers — all these are convincing proof of two important historic facts.   In the first place, by the second half of the
fourth millennium B.C. the Sumerians had developed a material
culture far in advance of any contemporary civilization, not excepting Egypt;   secondly, the artistry and craftsmanship revealed in these objects presuppose centuries of previous cultural
development.   To cite the words of the fortunate discoverer of
these treasures, C. L. Woolley, "The earliest of the graves . . .
bear witness in their contents to a civilization already old and
with centuries of apprenticeship and development behind it." [1]
If then these objects may be dated about 3500 B.C. — and they
cannot be much later — the beginnings of Sumerian occupation
of Mesopotamia must be placed well back in the fifth millennium.

When, from about 3200 B.C., historical data for Mesopotamian history begin to be more definite and rapidly become fuller,
we find a great number of city-states in both the northern half
(Akkad) and the southern half (Sumer) of this region.   In
Akkad the Semitic element is already becoming strong and continues to increase steadily.   The history of the next twelve
hundred years in Mesopotamia is both a chronicle of almost
continuous warfare and political rivalry, in which the ruler of
first one, and then another, city temporarily subjugates one or
more of his neighbors, and also it is a record of a racial struggle,
in which the more vigorous, though less artistic, Semitic stock
ultimately triumphs, and the Sumerian is submerged.   The
Semites learnt much from their neighbors; they took over the

[1] *Antiquity*, ii (1928), p. 17.   The reports of the excavations at Ur are
to be found in the *Antiquaries Journal*.

Sumerian method of writing and adapted it to their own Semitic tongue. The Sumerian language, save as a vehicle of religious ideas and ritual, by degrees passed out of use.

Existing records are too few and too sporadic to enable one to give anything like a consecutive account of early Sumero-Akkadian history. Ur, Erech, Adab, Lagash, Umma, Kish, Opis, seem to have been the politically more powerful or culturally more advanced cities (Cf. Map 1). The ambitions of their rulers (*patesis*) made fighting an almost continuous occupation for at least a goodly portion of their subjects. From time to time the *patesi* of one city, being endowed with greater ability or ampler material resources, succeeded in bringing under his control one or more adjacent or rival communities. He would emphasize the greater power and dignity that he had won, by assuming the more impressive title *lugal*, which may be rendered king. What methods were adopted to administer his enlarged territories is quite obscure. We may suppose that the conquered cities were obliged to pay tribute, and their governors forced to swear fealty to the *lugal* as overlord. The death of the *lugal* was generally the signal for the subject cities to reassert their political independence. The *patesis* of Lagash appear to have exercised power in Mesopotamia for an unusually long period. King Ur-nina, the founder of a dynasty about 2900 B.C., is known from reliefs, on which he is pictured in the midst of his family. He is credited with improving the irrigation in his territories by building canals, and is known for his religious zeal, which took the form of numerous dedications to the gods. The character of the third ruler of Lagash, Eannatum, was more warlike. He claimed to have conquered the peoples of Umma, Opis, Erech, and Ur, to have laid low the powerful city of Kish, and even to have warred successfully against the Elamites. It has been questioned whether he was really as remarkable a conqueror as his inscriptions record. At all events a sculptured slab survives as a memorial of his prowess. On it several scenes are depicted: we see the king setting out to war at the head of his army, and the formal burial of his slain troops. We see, too, the enemy's dead, who are left unburied, and vultures are shown devouring them and carrying off their heads. From this grim piece of realism the slab has been dubbed the "Stele of the Vultures."

Information about the successors of Eannatum is at present very scanty; but it seems clear that Eannatum's wide conquests, even if his account thereof be strictly accurate, were not lasting, and, further, that the relations between Lagash and her near neighbor, Umma, were a source of constant anxiety. Situated on the opposite side of a canal, the men of Umma could

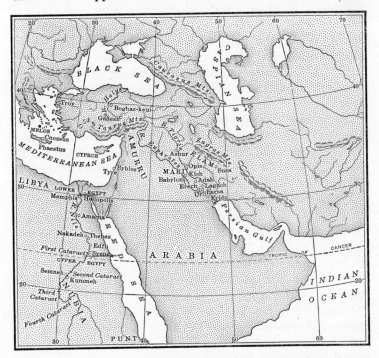

EGYPT AND THE NEAR EAST IN THE THIRD MILLENNIUM B.C.

interfere with the water supply of Lagash, and we now know that the feud between the two communities was old-standing. For, perhaps a century before Ur-nina's time, the king of Kish, Mesilim, who was then (about 3000 B.C.) a power in the land, had acted as arbitrator and had delimited the boundaries of the two cities. The "Stele of the Vultures" had also been set up as a boundary-stone. For about a century after Eannatum periods of peace and war alternated in the political history of Lagash and Umma, and the last independent *patesi* of Lagash was des-

tined to be overthrown by the ruler of Umma. It happens that
a goodly number of documents from the time of Urukagina of
Lagash (about 2700 B.C.) have been recovered. They show him
to have been, not indeed a man of war, but a would-be social
reformer. He aimed at improving the status of the laboring
population, more especially by restraining the priestly and official classes, of whose greed and exactions many instances are
quoted. These well-meant reforms naturally brought him the
hostility of the more powerful among his subjects, and perhaps
his rapid defeat at the hands of the ruler of Umma, Lugalzaggisi,
and the reduction of Lagash, might at least have been postponed, if Urukagina could have relied on the full loyalty of all
his subjects.

Lugalzaggisi's warlike progress was meteoric. He conquered
Erech and made it his capital. When, somewhat later, he styled
himself "king of the land of Sumer," it was no idle boast, for he
really had brought city after city under his political control.
His ambition did not end here, for he next turned his attention
to the land of Amurru (*i.e.* Syria). "When he conquered from
the rising to the setting sun, (the god) Enlil smoothed his path
from the lower sea (*i.e.* the Persian Gulf) across the Tigris and
Euphrates as far as the upper sea (*i.e.* the Mediterranean)," is
the impressive statement of an inscription, in the later part of
which is a list of important Sumerian cities who had acknowledged his overlordship.

Though there can be no doubt that for several centuries
Semitic influence and power had been steadily growing in the
northern district of Akkad, no Semitic dynasty had hitherto succeeded in winning a dominant position comparable to that held
by Lugalzaggisi for a quarter of a century, or even to that enjoyed by the ablest of the rulers of Ur. With the arrival of
Sharru-kin (Sargon) of Agade and Kish we enter on the first
period of Semitic domination in Mesopotamia. Sargon's career
of conquest was remarkable and his reign a long one (about
2637–2581 B.C.). The systematic reduction of the Sumerian
cities, and the winning of undisputed mastery over the two
lands of Sumer and Akkad, were followed by a series of foreign
expeditions of which unhappily no detailed accounts have survived. It is clear, however, that he invaded the mountainous

country of Elam, and, besides laying siege to and capturing Susa, occupied also some of the lesser Elamite towns. Even more ambitious were his campaigns in the Northwest. Sargon claims to have brought all the western lands as far as the Mediterranean sea under his sway, and to have penetrated as far as the Taurus mountains; indeed, there is now reason to believe that he conducted an expedition even further northward, into central Asia Minor, the region which at a later date was to become the centre of the Hittite empire. For fifty-five years Sargon ruled over his dominions, though the peace of his later years was disturbed by rebellions. On his death, as on that of his successor, Urumush, many of his subjects rose in revolt, and the new king was faced at once with the difficult task of reinforcing obedience to his commands. Such disturbances were but too common in the oriental monarchies, especially during the earlier period, and they show the dangers inherent in the quasi-feudal system of government, in which, on the death of the ruler, each or any prince of a dependent city might see an opportunity for his own advancement by force of arms.

After the relatively brief reigns of Urumush and Manishtusu, the kingdom passed to one who was to show himself an even greater conqueror than the founder of the dynasty. The relationship of Naram-sin to Sargon is disputed; probably he was Sargon's grandson. Like his grandfather, Naram-sin ruled over his people for more than half a century; again our records are scanty and not free from difficulties. He had to put down serious risings in the kingdom that he inherited, on the first occasion soon after his succession, and again after one of his foreign expeditions. Thus we see how a fairly prolonged absence from his seat of government might jeopardize entirely the safety of his throne. His foreign campaigns took him into the Zagros mountains in the East and as far as Kurdistan in the North. Whether Naram-sin's overlordship extended to northern Syria and the Mediterranean, as Sargon's had done, is not clear. There is no doubt about a great expedition to the southeast, for it is referred to on the base of a diorite statue of Naram-sin: "Naram-sin, the mighty, king of the four regions of the earth, conqueror of nine armies in one year . . . He conquered Magan and defeated Mani(um), prince of Magan. In their mountains he quarried

stones and bore them to his city of Akkad. And he made thereof
a statue of himself and dedicated it to the god . . ." By the
land of Magan is probably meant the eastern or southeastern
portion of the Arabian peninsula. The best-known monument
of Naram-sin is the so-called Stele of Victory, on which is commemorated the king's defeat of King Satuni in the latter's kingdom situated in the Zagros mountains. Naram-sin is seen
ascending a steep mountain followed by his army; he has just
slain his opponent, who lies wounded on the ground. Naram-
sin himself is armed with spear, bow and arrow, and battle-axe,
and wears a helmet on his head, but apparently no body armor.
His men are armed with bows and arrows and spears (Plate 1).

Naram-sin's successor, Shargali-sharri, seems to have maintained his authority successfully over his wide kingdom; but
after his time the dynasty of Akkad rapidly declined in power,
and the work of Sargon and Naram-sin was undone. Already in
the days of Shargali-sharri the mountain tribes of Gutium had
caused trouble to the more peaceful inhabitants of the plains.
Under the later kings of Akkad such raids became more frequent
and more destructive. Finally, these rude mountaineers overran Sumer and Akkad, where they appear to have exercised control for more than a century. For a while a dynasty at Erech
seems to have ruled in Sumer, only to be ultimately overthrown
by the men of Gutium. The *patesis* of Lagash were more fortunate and more powerful. Even in the time of the kings of
Akkad, the rulers of Lagash, though vassals of the former, had
enjoyed considerable independence and power. They seem to
have maintained their position even when the oppression of the
rest of the land by the kings of Gutium was at its worst. It
happens that exceptionally full records have been recovered illustrating the reign of one of the later *patesis* of Lagash, Gudea.
His numerous inscriptions bear witness to his great piety, which
manifested itself in the erection of temples and dedications to
the gods. For this purpose he imported building-stone, cedar
and other costly woods, gold and copper, from distant lands.
Incidentally these statements afford an indication of extensive
commerce at this period, extending to the Taurus mountains and
Syria in the West, and to Arabia in the Southeast. Gudea's rule
lasted for many (forty?) years; it appears to have been marked

not only by piety to the gods but by justice and care for his subjects.

It was a prince of Erech, Utukhegal, who brought the oppression of the Gutium dynasty over Sumer and Akkad to an end; but information about these countries is extremely sparse until, about 2300 B.C., a new dynasty arose at Ur. Its founder was Ur-engur, to whose importance as a law-giver we shall have occasion to refer later. Otherwise he is somewhat overshadowed in the existing records by his successor, Dungi, who is reputed to have reigned for fifty-eight years. His rule marks the last great Sumerian revival in Mesopotamia; at the same time it was a period during which Sumer and Akkad were once more under the ultimate control of a single ruler. Dungi styled himself both "king of the four regions of the earth" and "king of Sumer and Akkad"; as a conqueror he sought to rival Sargon and Naramsin. He waged war against the Elamites and the mountain tribes of the Zagros range, and northern Mesopotamia and Assyria were effectively controlled by him. That his empire extended over Syria and as far as the Mediterranean is possible, but cannot in the present state of our knowledge be regarded as certain. That a part of Asia Minor was under the political control of Dungi, as has recently been suggested, must for the present be regarded as pure speculation. The empire of Ur-engur and Dungi fell to pieces under their successors; more than that, no Sumerian dynasty ever again attained to political power, and the Sumerian element in the population of Mesopotamia, which seems to have been growing steadily less for several centuries before this time, gradually disappeared or was merged in the Semitic.

Toward the end of the third millennium very important political developments occurred which radically altered the whole situation in Mesopotamia, and culminated in the establishment of the first Babylonian empire. The two main factors which operated so powerfully to change the political situation were the increased power of the Elamites and the appearance in the land of the two rivers of a new wave of Semites. Hostilities between Elam and the cities of Sumer and Akkad go back almost to the beginning of Mesopotamian history, and we have had occasion to refer more than once to wars between these neighboring countries. Hitherto, however, the advantage, so far as our very imperfect records allow us to form certain conclusions, seems generally to have been on the side of the Sumerian or Semitic princes. Of the growth of Elamite power in the second half of the third millennium nothing is known, but it was sufficient ultimately to give the Elamites a permanent hold on Sumer for a century. The last king of the Ur dynasty, Ibi-sin, was defeated by a coalition of the Elamite king and the chief of Mari, a considerable principality on the western side of the middle Euphrates. The Mari prince, Ishbi-irri, then established himself at Isin, and was the founder of a Semitic dynasty which endured for nearly two hundred years. A rival Semitic dynasty at Larsa came to the fore about the same time; for a while the two, whose relations seem at first to have been unusually harmonious, controlled most of the land. Later, Isin in alliance with the Elamites attacked Larsa, and a Semitic was replaced by an Elamite ruler there. But these new allies did not remain on good terms permanently; some forty years after they had made common cause against Larsa, the king of Isin himself succumbed to his Elamite neighbor.

But the most momentous occurrence during these two centuries, between the fall of the Ur dynasty and the establishment of the first Babylonian empire, was the settlement of a body of west Semitic (Amorite) invaders in Babylon. Geographically Babylon was situated on the western borders of Akkad, being on the western bank of the Euphrates a little below the point where the two rivers approach to within twenty miles of one another. Though inhabited from early times, Babylon was politically unimportant in the Sumero-Akkadian period. Maintaining at first a precarious existence in face of the powerful princes of Isin and Larsa, the new Amorite rulers of Babylon preserved their independence and in time began to encroach on the territories adjacent to their city. Even so, at the accession of the sixth in the line of Babylonian kings, Hammurabi (1947–1905 B.C.), the greatest power in the land was the Elamite king of Larsa, Rim-sin, who destroyed Isin and made himself master of all Sumer and at least a part of Akkad. Hammurabi was king of Babylon for over forty years; but, though he seems to have captured Isin and Erech early in his reign, it was not until he had been on the throne for thirty years that the great and final clash with the Elamites came. From this war (about 1918 B.C.) Hammurabi emerged triumphant. Rim-sin was captured, his Elamite allies were defeated, and the whole of Sumer and Akkad was brought under the sway of the Babylonian monarch. In the North Hammurabi's authority extended as far as Assyria; for in a military despatch reference is made to "two hundred and forty men of the king's company . . . who have left the land of Ashur and the district of Shitullum." Hammurabi's son and successor, Samsu-iluna, ruled almost as long as his father, but his kingdom was disturbed and even threatened by foreign peoples, who under his successors encroached more and more, and finally, about 1750 B.C., brought the Babylonian dynasty to an end. These new political developments in Mesopotamia and the adjacent countries, since they to some extent inaugurate a new era, must be postponed to a later chapter.

2. Mesopotamian Civilization

Social and economic life in Mesopotamia at the time of the first Babylonian dynasty can be reconstructed with considerable fullness, thanks to the copious documentary material which has been recovered by the excavator's spade. Thus, there are available numerous letters of Hammurabi and his successors, as well as a substantial body of inscriptions. Above all, in 1901 the French archæologist De Morgan discovered at Susa in Elam a large slab inscribed with the now famous code of laws which has made Hammurabi's name immortal (Plate 2). For Mesopotamian civilization prior to Hammurabi's time the available material is far less abundant and much more scattered. Nevertheless, though it is often very hazardous to use the evidence of one age to illustrate the history of another, the risk in the present case is relatively slight. For, where the life and habits of a people were so largely determined by geographical and climatic conditions, which in the land of the two rivers have varied little through the ages, it is safe to assume that many of the conditions which are well attested for c. 2000 B.C. had existed with little change for centuries before. This would be especially true of what was by far the most important occupation in that region, agriculture.

As far back as our records go, we find allusions to irrigation and to the building and upkeep of canals, which branched off from, or connected, the two rivers, and formed a perfect network of waterways. The snows melting in Armenia in the early spring cause an enormous increase in the volume of water carried down toward the sea by the Euphrates and Tigris. In April and May the rivers are at their highest, and cause heavy inundations in the plains; in June the waters gradually fall. The plain-dwellers from earliest times had two problems to face; on the one hand, they must prevent the flood-waters from standing and converting large tracts of territory into marsh land, unfit for cultivation. On the other hand, they must so husband their resources that there would be enough water available for the fields during the hot summer months, when the rivers were at their lowest. It causes no surprise, therefore, that, even in the earliest epigraphic records, we meet with allusions to canal-building and to proper irrigation, which was of such vital importance to every Mesopotamian community. We have already seen how the question of the water-supply was a constant anxiety to the rulers of Lagash, and involved them in frequent hostilities with the neighboring city of Umma. The inscriptions of both Ur-nina and Urukagina record the construction of canals, while a similar attention to irrigation is found in documents of Ur-engur, the founder of the third dynasty at Ur. The letters of the Babylonian dynasty have numerous allusions to this same topic, and the code of Hammurabi contains many ordinances which testify to a careful supervision of all waterways. Nor must it be forgotten that the larger canals, like the rivers, were extensively used for purposes of navigation and transport. Occasionally, in spite of every care being taken, disasters might occur. In the twenty-sixth, and again in the thirty-eighth, year of Hammurabi serious floods devastated the land, and doubtless caused much misery. The task of keeping the canals themselves clear by dredging, as well as seeing that the canal-banks were in good repair, entailed constant attention and much labor. For the upkeep of the banks the farmers through whose plots the canal flowed were responsible. If a cultivator was careless in keeping his portion of a dike in proper condition, and his negligence caused loss to others, the code provides that he must make good the loss. On the other hand, such a regulation as this, "if a man owe a debt and (the god) Adad inundate his field and carry away the produce, or through lack of water, grain have not grown in the field, in that year he shall not make any return of grain to the creditor, he shall alter his contract tablet, and he shall not pay the interest for that year," [1] shows that there was a good deal of sound equity in the code.

The population of Babylonia, as we find it in Hammurabi's day, was made up of three groups: an upper class, a lower class of free men, and a servile class. The barrier between the first and second seems to have been rather rigid. The upper class must have been a very heterogeneous one, including not only the landed nobility and the priests, but the numerous public officials and the wealthier traders and merchants. The lower class was made up of small farmers, craftsmen, artisans, and so forth. In the sense that these seem to have had no political influence they may be regarded as half-free; but, inasmuch as they were liable to some military service, and could own property and slaves, they are almost as sharply separated from the servile class as from their superiors. That slavery was a very ancient institution is beyond doubt; what is remarkable is that the slaves had certain privileges which we do not find in other ancient slave-holding societies. For example, a male slave might marry a free woman; the children of such a marriage would be free. Again, slaves, though legally regarded as chattels, could nevertheless acquire some property of their own, which, on the death of a married slave, would pass to his wife and children. One remarkable feature of Hammurabi's code has never been satisfactorily explained. The punishments are extremely severe and framed on the principle of exact retributive justice, best expressed in the Biblical phrase, "an eye for an eye, a tooth for a tooth." Nevertheless, there are two scales of punishment, one for the upper class, one for the humbler folk, and members of the former are punished more severely than the latter. It has been suggested that the distinction indicates an original difference of race, but this explanation creates as many difficulties as it solves, and the problem must for the present be regarded as unsolved.

Of a great part of the land the monarch himself was the owner;

---

[1] Code of Hammurabi, § 48.

much, too, was "owned" by one or other of the gods, that is to say, for practical and mundane purposes, it was under the control of the priests. Thus it is probable that a relatively small portion of all the territory suitable for cultivation was privately owned. The actual agricultural work, whether the land was royal domain, temple property, or privately owned, was carried on partly by slaves, partly by the poorer class of free men, who were in effect small tenant farmers. Their living was at all times precarious, since the tithes or payments to the landlord were heavy; and in addition they were, as we have seen, liable for the upkeep of the canals, on which the success of their crops depended. The field crops that were most extensively grown were wheat, barley, and spelt. Hardly less important than these for the essential food-supply was the cultivation of the date-palm. Cattle- and especially sheep-rearing, was carried on intensively; for wool, together with grain and the produce of the date-palm, formed the most important articles of export. Cattle were also used for plowing and for draught purposes, but the universal beast of burden was the donkey. Recent discoveries have shown that the horse and the war-chariot were already known in Mesopotamia at the beginning of the third millennium; but probably the horse was used only for military and not for domestic needs. One special class of agriculturists in the time of the first Babylonian dynasty is of peculiar interest. The military forces were made up partly of a standing army, partly of a citizen militia, levied as need for it arose. To the members of the standing force, the professional soldiery, the king regularly assigned lots of land. These their sons inherited, but with the liability to serve in the army as their fathers had done. Thus it is in Babylonia that we first meet with such military occupiers, a class found in later centuries, for instance, in Egypt and in the Roman empire.

The official class was very numerous. In the earlier period of Mesopotamian history a quasi-feudal system obtained; consequently, the *lugal's* officials were relatively few in number, because the government of cities conquered by him was left to the local chiefs or *patesis*, after they had made their submission to him. The efforts of Sargon and Naram-sin, and later of Urengur and Dungi, to form a more unified state out of Akkad and

Sumer, must have resulted in an increase in the number of royal officials, who to a great extent replaced the local chiefs or magistrates. Under the Babylonian dynasty this process was carried much further. Hammurabi or Samsu-iluna governed their dominion through their own officials, and the monarch concerned himself not only with their conduct but with that of their subordinates. The most numerous body of officials was those charged with the collection of taxes and tribute. All classes had to pay tribute to the king; in Hammurabi's time even temple lands were not exempt. The payment of tribute was either in kind or else in gold, silver, or copper. The ingots of metal were stamped to guarantee their weight and purity. Remission of taxation was a very exceptional reward, which the monarch sometimes bestowed on specially deserving officials.

The conditions under which the lower class lived in the towns were a good deal better than those endured by the small-farming population. The craftsmen seem regularly to have been organized in associations or gilds; at the head of each was a kind of president or master, who acted as intermediary between the members of his craft and the officials in such matters as taxation or recruiting for the army, in a manner curiously reminiscent of the professional corporations and their *magistri* in the Roman empire.

The most recent excavations at Ur have revealed a part of the town-site; even after the loss of its political independence Ur must have continued to be one of the more important cities in Babylonia. The remains of houses and streets thus laid bare belong to the period of the first Babylonian dynasty. The houses were carefully built in such a way that the lower courses of the walls were of burnt bricks, and the upper courses of mud brick, very accurately joined together. They were roomy, too, for there can be little doubt that many of them had an upper story. The ground floor contained a general living-room, domestic offices, and, sometimes at least, a private chapel; a staircase led to the more private rooms above. Thus, we are at liberty to deduce that the standard of comfort enjoyed by the town-dwellers was reasonably high, a conclusion that is also borne out by the material objects, and by the evidence of numerous private letters of this age, recovered from various Mesopotamian sites.

Nothing is more remarkable than the highly centralized and carefully organized administration under which the subjects of Hammurabi lived, as illustrated particularly by the careful administration of justice. These Babylonians seem to have been as fond of litigation as the Greeks of the fourth century B.C. are said to have been. Thus we may properly conclude this chapter with some further remarks on the code of Hammurabi and on judicial affairs in general. When the code was first deciphered, Hammurabi was hailed as one of the world's great legislators. Though further discoveries have shown that he hardly deserves such a title, his claim to be regarded as an administrator of undoubted eminence is beyond dispute. Since the code was discovered considerable remains of an earlier Sumerian law-code have been recovered; a comparison of the two codes makes it clear that Hammurabi's legal ordinances were based on the earlier Sumerian laws. For these the founder of the third dynasty of Ur, Ur-engur, may be largely responsible, for he was noted for his attention to justice and good order. Yet much that the Sumerian code contained was, in all likelihood, not so much express legislation by a particular ruler, as a codification and writing down of custom and customary law, existing long before and till then handed down by oral tradition. Hammurabi's code contains nearly three hundred headings, but most of them are very brief. They deal with a great variety of topics.[1] Some citations will best make clear the strange contrast between the crudest application of the *lex talionis* and a civil law of considerable juristic refinement, which we find side by side in the code. Thus, on the one hand we find the retributive principle carried to extreme lengths:[2]

195 If a son strike his father, they shall cut off his fingers.
196 If a man destroy the eye of another man, they shall destroy his eye.

[1] The following is a brief summary of the contents: §§ 1–5, penalties for false witness and unjust judge; §§ 6–25, criminal offenses; §§ 26–41, regulations respecting military service; §§ 42–126, civil law, especially as governing contracts of various kinds; §§ 127–194, the law of the family and divorce regulations; §§ 195–227, punishments; §§ 228–277, ordinances regulating prices, hire of labor, and building operations; §§ 278–282, slaves.

[2] The citations that follow are taken from *The Code of Hammurabi* by R. F. Harper (University of Chicago Press; 1904). The numbers refer to the sections.

STELE OF NARAM–SIN

Plate 1

STELE CONTAINING THE CODE OF HAMMURABI

Plate 2

202 If a man strike the person of a man who is his superior, he shall receive sixty strokes with an ox-tail whip in public.

218 If a physician operate on a man for a severe wound with a bronze lancet and cause the man's death; or open an abscess (in the eye) of a man with a bronze lancet and destroy the man's eye, they shall cut off his fingers.

229 If a builder build a house for a man and do not make its construction firm, and the house which he has built collapse and cause the death of the owner of the house, that builder shall be put to death.

230 If it cause the death of a son of the owner of the house, they shall put to death a son of that builder.

It is difficult to believe that the law was ever fully enforced, or that the savage punishments for criminal offenses were regularly carried out. It is more reasonable to suppose that the code lays down the maximum penalty, leaving it to the discretion of the judges to fix a lighter punishment in specific cases. On the other hand, it was the mark of an enlightened government to hold the towns and their magistrates responsible for the maintenance of law and order in their respective communities, as exemplified in paragraph 23:

23 If the brigand be not captured, the man who has been robbed, shall, in the presence of God, make an itemized statement of his loss, and the city and the governor, in whose province and jurisdiction the robbery was committed, shall compensate him for whatever was lost.

Again, the provisions of the code, as well as contemporary letters, make it clear that the position of women was juridically more favorable than in other ancient communities. The laws governing marriage and divorce seem less to the woman's disadvantage than the provisions of the Greek or earlier Roman law. The following quotations are a fair sample of this part of the code:

138 If a man would put away his wife who has not borne him children, he shall give her money to the amount of her marriage settlement, and he shall make good to her the dowry which she brought from her father's house, and then he may put her away.

141 If the wife of a man who is living in his house, set her face to go out and play the part of a fool, neglect her house, belittle her husband, they shall call her to account; if her husband

say "I have put her away," he shall let her go. On her departure nothing shall be given to her for her divorce. If her husband say, "I have not put her away," her husband may take another woman. The first woman shall dwell in the house of her husband as a maidservant.

142 If a woman hate her husband, and say, "Thou shalt not have me," they shall inquire into her antecedents for her defects; and if she have been a careful mistress and be without reproach and her husband have been going about and greatly belittling her, that woman has no blame. She shall receive her dowry and shall go to her father's house.

We may conclude with one or two citations from that part of the code which regulates business transactions:

59 If a man cut down a tree in a man's orchard, without the consent of the owner of the orchard, he shall pay one-half mana of silver.

60 If a man give a field to a gardener to plant as an orchard and the gardener plant the orchard and care for the orchard four years, in the fifth year the owner of the orchard and the gardener shall share equally; the owner of the orchard shall mark off his portion and take it.

61 If the gardener do not plant the whole field, but leave a space waste, they shall assign the waste space to his portion.

104 If a merchant give to an agent grain, wool, oil, or goods of any kind with which to trade, the agent shall write down the value and return (the money) to the merchant. The agent shall take a sealed receipt for the money which he gives to the merchant.

105 If the agent be careless and do not take a receipt for the money which he has given to the merchant, the money not receipted for shall not be placed to his account.

Various courts existed for the administration of justice and for carrying the provisions of the code into effect. In the past, judicial authority would appear to have been mainly in the hands of the priests, and trials would then be conducted in a portion of a temple set apart for this purpose. In Hammurabi's time, however, such priestly jurisdiction had well-nigh ceased, though the administration of the oath fittingly remained one of the duties of the ministers of religion. The documents of the period refer to "king's judges" and "city judges"; one of the regulations of the code lays down severe penalties against a judge who shall have reversed an earlier judgment, the implication being, of course, that he did so from corrupt motives:

> 5 If a judge pronounce a judgment, render a decision, deliver a verdict duly signed and sealed and afterward alter his judgment, they shall call that judge to account for the alteration of the judgment which he had pronounced, and he shall pay twelve-fold the penalty which was said in judgment; and, in the assembly, they shall expel him from his seat of judgment, and he shall not return, and with the judges in a case he shall not take his seat.

Severe penalties were also imposed on false witnesses. The litigant had the right of appealing directly to the monarch, if he considered that he had not been justly treated by the judges before whom he had appeared. The numerous letters of the period are largely concerned with litigation arising out of leases, sales, contracts, and so forth; there are some, too, which record the intervention or the decision of the king himself in cases which had been brought to his notice, either by way of appeal or in some other manner. Thus it is abundantly clear that, although there was as yet no sharp distinction between civil and criminal offenses, though the penal ordinances are crude, the Babylonians, like another branch of the Semitic race, the Hebrews, had a high respect for the sanctity of the law.

CHAPTER III

EGYPT TO THE CLOSE OF THE MIDDLE KINGDOM

> *Adore the king, Nematre, living for ever, in
> the midst of your bodies. Enthrone his majesty
> in your hearts. His two eyes, they search every
> body. He is the Sun, seeing with his rays. He
> illuminates the Two Lands more than the sun-disk.
> He makes the Two Lands green more than a great
> Nile. He hath filled the Two Lands with strength.*
> — From an Inscription of the XIIth Dynasty
> (J. H. Breasted, *Ancient Records of Egypt*,
> i, p. 327).

ANCIENT EGYPT, for all practical purposes, may be regarded
as synonymous with the valley of the Nile from Syene (Assouan),
just north of the twenty-fourth parallel, to the Mediterranean
Sea, a distance of rather more than five hundred miles. South of
this region, and geographically not a part of Egypt proper, lay
Nubia, the country of the Nile cataracts. It was, at least in
part, conquered and annexed to Egypt by the beginning of the
second millennium B.C. The long stretch from Memphis (near
the modern Cairo) to Syene, called Upper Egypt or the Upper
Kingdom, is a valley bordered by limestone hills and ridges. Its
width between Memphis and Thebes averages ten to twelve
miles; south of Thebes it becomes very narrow, not exceeding
an average of two miles across. Lower Egypt, or the Delta (so
called from its triangular shape, resembling the fourth letter of
the Greek alphabet), has a sea-front of about one hundred and
fifty miles, and a depth of about a hundred miles. On the west
of Egypt was desert relieved by occasional oases and inhabited
by Libyan tribes; westwards of the Delta was an approach to
Egypt by which on several occasions in their history the Egyptians were threatened by hostile invaders. To the east of the
Nile valley are rocky wastes through which one or two difficult
caravan routes led to the Red Sea. Eastwards of Lower Egypt

there was a causeway of immemorial antiquity to southern Syria. It followed the coast-line closely, but at certain times of the year it was liable to be flooded by sudden spring-tides. By another caravan route the traveller passed over desert and threaded his way past the northern spurs of Mt. Sinai, on his way to Palestine and beyond.

The isolation of Egypt and its inhabitants from other parts of the Ancient World has so often been stressed that a word of caution will not be out of place. The land of the Nile is not easy of access from either the west or the east; yet there were no insuperable obstacles in the way, even for large hostile armies or hordes of invaders. The Hyksos, the Assyrians, and the Persians, all attacked Egypt successfully from the east, while the onsets from the west were only less disastrous to her because less well-organized and attempted by smaller bodies of invaders. If, then, we seek an explanation for the fact that the Egyptians were never a colonizing people, and that their import and export trade was always relatively small, as compared with that of other ancient countries, we shall find it rather in the immense fertility of the Nile valley, which made Egypt self-sufficient and its inhabitants, as a whole, content to remain in the land of their birth. This fertility was entirely due to the river and its annual inundations of the adjacent valleys; for in Upper Egypt rain is a very rare occurrence, and even in the Delta rain-fall is slight and happens almost only in the winter months. Much depended on the right depth of the Nile floods. If the inundation was excessive, large tracts of country might be rendered unfit for cultivation; if it was insufficient, hardship and even famine were the result. When the river begins to fall, after the maximum inundation at the beginning of October, it leaves the land covered with mud deposits of remarkable fertilizing properties. The prosperity, then, of the people depended wholly on the satisfactory flooding of the arable soil.

In a previous chapter it has been noted that implements of the Old Stone Age show that the country was already inhabited at that early date. These objects are found in the sandstone and limestone hills which shut in the river valley; but they are not sufficient to enable us to form any clear picture of Palæo-lithic man in this region. Remains of Neolithic man, chiefly

graves and their contents, are however very abundant in Upper
Egypt, especially at Nakadeh. This site, after which some
Egyptologists have named the Neolithic civilization of Egypt, or
at least the later phases of it, the Nakadeh culture, is a little to
the north of Thebes and close to the point where the chief caravan route branches off from the Nile valley through the Wady
Hammamat to the Red Sea. We cannot doubt that Lower
Egypt, too, was already inhabited in the Late Stone Age; the
non-discovery of remains there is due to the more destructive
action of the river in the flat land of the Delta. Neolithic man
in Egypt was a remarkable craftsman. The pottery which he
made is well baked, and, though hand-made, is almost as accurate in form as if it had been turned on the wheel. Much of it
is decorated, and, besides this, is carefully polished, and toward
the end of the period, even glazed. Flint tools and weapons of
very fine workmanship abound; but the most remarkable fruits
of patience combined with skill are stone vases of various shapes.
Not only soft stones, like steatite, were used, but granite and
alabaster. These vessels are full of beauty and the craftsmanship displayed in the carefully carved spouts, handles, and ears
for suspension, is quite admirable. The Neolithic villages were
commonly surrounded by mud walls; the houses were constructed of mud and reeds, or else were built entirely of mud
brick. The most ambitious attempts at portraying human and
animal figures are found on slate slabs or palettes, which were
sculptured in low relief and belong to the end of the predynastic
period. Their primary purpose was to grind down green mal-
achite, which was manufactured into paint and used for personal adornment.

In the latest period of the Neolithic Age the two lands of
Upper and Lower Egypt seem respectively to have been unified
politically into two kingdoms. Details of this organization and
of the internal administration we possess none. But in later ages
the first historic dynasty that was recorded was one founded by
a man who succeeded in uniting Upper and Lower Egypt under
his sceptre. According to ancient tradition this was Menes or
Mena. On the other hand, the earliest kings recorded on extant
monuments are a king of Upper Egypt, whose royal name was
indicated by the sign of a scorpion; a king of Upper Egypt,

Narmer, who, as appears from a ceremonial palette representing his triumph over his neighbors in the Delta, made himself
master of Lower Egypt as well; and Aha, whose tomb has been
discovered at Nakadeh. In view of these historic names, Egyptologists disagree about the historical character of Menes, and
it has been suggested that Menes is really a legendary figure or
title, which to later ages embodied the earliest monarchs of the
first dynasty, under whom Lower and Upper Egypt were united
into a single kingdom. It is, however, more probable that Aha is
the divine or "Horus" name of Menes, and that he consolidated
the work of unifying the two kingdoms which had been begun
by his immediate predecessor, Narmer. Hence in later times
he, and not Narmer, was regarded as the founder of the first
dynasty.

Much uncertainty also still exists regarding the race or races
to which the Egyptians at the beginning of the dynastic period
belonged. It is at present impossible to form any final conclusions, for the ethnological theories put forward in recent years
by different experts, it must be admitted, largely contradict one
another. The earliest inhabitants were probably of a stock
closely akin to their neighbors in Libya and related also to the
earliest inhabitants of Crete and other eastern Mediterranean
islands. They were a short, dark, dolichocephalic type. That
they were somewhat more distantly related to the most western
branches of the Semites is also probable; but their original
home, like that of the Semites themselves, cannot be definitely
fixed. At the end of the predynastic period the Egyptians
first became acquainted with the use of copper, and this knowledge they probably owed to Asiatic immigrants who filtered
into Lower Egypt. Further discoveries, especially in southern
Mesopotamia, may well show that the debt owed by the earlier
Egyptians to the Mesopotamian peoples was far more considerable than has hitherto been supposed. That there was at this
early date also an admixture of peoples from northern Syria, or
even Asia Minor, whom some writers describe as "Armenoid," is
the most problematic hypothesis of all, and must for the present be discounted. It is unfortunate that, owing to the humid
character of the Delta, remains of the earliest period of Lower
Egyptian history are virtually non-existent.

The beginning of Dynasty I may be dated about 3200 B.C., and is therefore roughly contemporary with the earliest historic dynasty at Ur. The capital was at first at Thinis in Upper Egypt; but, some time during the IIId Dynasty, it was moved to Memphis, which, though in Lower Egypt, was close to the Upper Kingdom, and was therefore found to be a more satisfactory centre of government. The task of governing a country of such peculiar geographical structure must have been one of great difficulty. If we knew more about the latest years of the predynastic period, we should probably find that the work of the conquering kings was to weld together a number of tribes and principalities, whose chiefs subsequently became the king's vassals. Indeed, it is probable that the administrative units, or nomes (Greek *nomos*), into which Egypt was divided, were not merely artificial divisions, but largely based on the smaller tribal or political groups in the country during the Nakadeh period. The rulers of the earliest dynasties seem to have followed a policy of centralization of government in the capital, thus restricting as much as possible the influence and power of the nobility, who were in many cases descendants of once independent chiefs. The division into nomes was firmly established by the time of the IVth Dynasty (*c.* 2700–2550). Normally there were forty-two of these, twenty-two in Upper and twenty in Lower Egypt. Each was governed by an official nominated by, and solely and directly responsible to, the king.

The Egyptian monarchy was theocratic and, being theocratic, was absolute. The monarch combined within himself three functions. He was chief priest, he was commander-in-chief, and he was the judicial and administrative head of the state. The threefold character of the ruler as priest, general, and magistrate, is, of course, found in other early monarchies; but it was the special interpretation of the priestly functions of the king which gave to the Egyptian monarch a divine character not easy to parallel elsewhere. His claim to be the highest priest in his realm — the chosen intermediary between his people and the divine powers — was founded on the belief that he himself was the earthly incarnation of a god, who did not lose his divine nature during a transitory life on earth. He bore various titles which had reference to his divine character, of which the most important was that which described him as the son of Ra, the sun-god, or, at a later date when a syncretism of Ra and the god of Thebes, Amen, had taken place, of Amen Ra.[1] There is no indication that the Egyptians ever believed that, on the death of the king, the crown passed to his son or nearest male relative by divine right. The practice of some monarchs of the XIIth Dynasty of associating a son with themselves as co-ruler, must be regarded as purely a matter of political expediency, to insure the succession in the family. For, often enough, the succession on the death of a king passed to the strongest man, irrespective of his kinship to the deceased.

With the last king of the IIId Dynasty, Snefru, we enter a period about which it is possible to form a clearer picture than of the earliest dynastic era. It is the age of the great pyramids, an age, besides, about which for the first time we have a certain number of contemporary documents; these become more copious during the Vth and VIth Dynasties. To the period of the Vth Dynasty belong the oldest writings of a literary character that have so far been recovered. Finally, the Vth and, above all, the VIth Dynasties correspond to an age of marked political expansion beyond the frontiers of Egypt proper.

No remains of Ancient Egypt are more familiar than the pyramids, those vast tombs erected by Snefru near Sakkarah and at Gizeh by the greatest kings of the IVth Dynasty, Khufu (Cheops), Khafra, and Menkaura. They were erected by the respective monarchs during their lives, as the resting-places in which their bodies would be housed after death. They were surrounded by flat-topped tombs of much humbler proportions, which were the burial places of their chief courtiers. The largest of all the pyramids, that of Khufu, is four hundred and fifty feet in height. Its vastness bears witness both to the engineering skill of the early Egyptians and to the immense resources of the monarch; for over two million limestone blocks, each weighing on the average more than two tons, went into its construction. Yet it might well be asked whether any

---

[1] The importance of Ra in the Egyptian pantheon dates from the Vth Dynasty, as will be pointed out below. The older god of light, Horus, first in sanctity ever since predynastic times, then begins to occupy a position subordinate to Ra.

despot ever set his subjects to a more profitless and unproductive task than this. It has been well observed that the concentration of tombs of kings and their courtiers in the vicinity of the capital, Memphis, is emblematic of the political organization of the Old Kingdom.

The government was a personal autocracy exercised by the Pharaoh, and the nobles and officials who carried on the administration were closely dependent on him.[1] His chief minister, or vizier, was at this time usually a member of the royal family. The nomarchs, or governors of the nomes, besides being charged with the general control of their province, were responsible for the proper collection of taxes, and had limited judicial powers besides. The highest judicial court was in the capital and met under the presidency of the vizier. Office tended to become hereditary in certain families. A son who had at first filled a subordinate position, succeeds, on his father's death, to the higher office thus vacated, provided the king's good-will continues to be his. Even the highest officials seem to have been frequently moved from office to office, as we see from the biographical inscription of Methen, who flourished under Snefru. After holding many minor appointments he rises to the highest governorships, holding successively no less than twelve, partly in Upper, partly in Lower, Egypt.[2] The general character of the government remained the same under the rulers of the Vth Dynasty. Perhaps the most notable feature is the growing importance of the worship of the sun-god, Ra. While the kings continued to erect pyramids for their own use after death, they also sought visibly to glorify the god, whose "sons" they were, by setting up temples or monuments in his honor. Before the end of the dynasty the disadvantages inherent in a highly centralized government, if the ruler was weak, must have become very apparent; for, under the kings of the VIth Dynasty a radical change in the methods of administration can be observed.

But, above all, the VIth Dynasty was an age of foreign con-

---

[1] Cf. E. Meyer, *Geschichte des Altertums* (3d ed.) i, 2, p. 187. The word Pharaoh is a corruption of two Egyptian words meaning "royal house." By this circumlocution direct reference to the divine monarch was avoided.

[2] Translated in Breasted, *Ancient Records of Egypt*, i, pp. 76 ff.

quest and wars. Extant records inform us of travels undertaken by high officials and of military expeditions to the south and southeast of Egypt. Numerous graves excavated in Lower Nubia have proved that this region was, during the earliest period, inhabited by people who were racially the same as, or very closely akin to, the inhabitants of Upper Egypt. Already under the kings of the Ist Dynasty the political control of the Egyptian monarch reached as far as the first Nile cataract. Both under Pepi I and his son, Pepi II, the records seem to show that these rulers extended their sovereignty also over the region between the first and second cataracts, and generally overawed the negro tribes of Upper Nubia.[1] The earliest Egyptian reference to negroes belongs to this period, and there is no doubt that considerable numbers of them found their way northward as far as the district of the first cataract and settled there. Other expeditions are recorded against the desert tribes of the Sinai peninsula and southern Palestine. These important operations were trusted to one, Uni, who, from a subordinate position, rose under Pepi I to become first a judge and later the king's chosen general. Under the successor of Pepi I, Mernere, he became governor of the South. The long autobiographical inscription in his tomb at Abydos is the most important document extant for this period. The necessity for chastising troublesome neighbors was not the only reason for activity near Sinai; the desire to keep a firmer grip on the peninsula, in order more fully to exploit its mineral wealth, doubtless influenced the king greatly. His astonishing activity as a builder and restorer of temples led Pepi I to develop the red granite quarries near Syene. Expeditions by sea and land to Punt (Somali coast) were mainly commercial in their object. From there, as well as from Upper Nubia, the Egyptians procured gold, ivory, ebony, ostrich feathers, and incense. Such expeditions did not always pass off without accidents or loss of life. One of Pepi II's officials appears to have been assassinated by a desert tribe while making ready for a sea voyage to Punt.

[1] Dynasty VI lasted approximately from 2425 to 2240 B.C. Pepi I is said to have reigned over 50 years and Pepi II, who succeeded as a child of six and lived to be a centenarian, ruled 94 years.

The administrative changes which gradually came about during this dynasty were so drastic that the system in the end was the very antithesis of the centralized government characteristic of the three preceding dynasties. With some justice the VIth Dynasty has been described as a feudal monarchy. For, whereas the king's authority in religious and secular matters continued to be supreme, the power and independence of the provincial governors become very marked. They reside permanently in their respective nomes, only occasionally visiting the capital. Their official designations vary — city-governor, head of the nome, as well as different titles of nobility and rank — their offices tend to become hereditary, thus completing the change of Egypt from a country governed by an autocrat in his capital to one administered largely by a hereditary nobility, owing allegiance to the king, but all-powerful in their provinces. The process of change is the exact converse of that which we have already observed in the earlier period of Mesopotamian history. The danger obviously inherent in this new régime, if the king was a minor or else a weak ruler, did not fail to make its appearance in due course. The successors of Pepi II were short-lived nonentities, and the nobles took to war among themselves. The two hundred and fifty years (c. 2240–2000), from the end of Dynasty VI to the last rulers of Dynasty XI, are still extremely obscure. It was seemingly an age of civil war, during which one dynasty, centred for a time at Heracleopolis, maintained authority over a large part of Egypt, but was then challenged and finally overthrown by a rival dynasty at Thebes. Under Mentuhotep III, the last but one of the XIth Dynasty monarchs, the two Egypts were at last reunited under a single ruler.

With the XIIth Dynasty we at last reach a period of Egyptian history for which there is abundant documentary and other evidence. Incidentally, some of the inscriptions refer with gratitude to the fact that an era of anarchy and disunion has at length been succeeded by one of peace, prosperity, and good government. This copious evidence justifies the belief that in material welfare and in artistic achievement this age and the period of the XVIIIth and XIXth Dynasties form the two most brilliant epochs in the long history of Egypt down to Ptolemaic and Roman times. The XIIth Dynasty lasted for two-hundred and twelve years.[1] In the troubled years preceding it, Egyptian control over neighboring countries like Nubia must have relaxed or ceased entirely. The kings of the XIIth Dynasty had to do all over again the work of conquest accomplished by the rulers of the VIth. Operations in Nubia are thus heard of with some frequency, especially under Senusret I and Senusret III. The former set up a monument by the second cataract, commemorating his victories over the native tribes of this region. But the country was not thoroughly subdued till the time of Senusret III (Plate 3); he conducted no less than four expeditions into the cataract region. A little way to the south of the second cataract, at Semneh and Kummeh, two inscribed boundary stones were set up in the eighth and the sixteenth year of the king's reign. In addition, forts were built here on an island in the river and on the hills overlooking this point. Remains of four forts in Lower Nubia, that is to say, between the first and second cataracts, testify still further to the thoroughness of the Egyptian occupation. The inscribed boundary stones are of great interest. The one severely restricts the immigration of negroes from the South. They are forbidden to navigate the Nile below this point; only individual negroes, who are genuine traders, shall, for this purpose, be admitted north of the Egyptian frontier. The second inscription is a rather boastful notice, in general terms, of the king's achievements; but one paragraph, in which the conqueror exhorts his successors to maintain this frontier line, is worthy to be cited:

Now, as for every son of mine who shall maintain this boundary, which my majesty has made, he is my son, he is born to my majesty, the likeness of a son who is the champion of his father, who maintains the boundary of him who begat him. Now, as for him who shall relax it, and shall not fight for it, he is not my son, he is not born to me. — (Breasted, *Ancient Records*, i, p. 296.)

[1] The following are the rulers of the XIIth Dynasty with approximate dates:

Amenemhet I, 2000–1970	Senusret III, 1887–1849
Senusret I, 1980–1935	Amenemhet III, 1849–1801
Amenemhet II, 1938–1903	Amenemhet IV, 1801–1792
Senusret II, 1906–1887	Queen Sebeknefrure, 1792–1788

The overlapping of dates is due to the practice, followed by some of the kings, of associating their sons with themselves on the throne.

Save during the period of Hyksos domination, Nubia remained a part of the Egyptian kingdom. Its inhabitants came more and more under the influence of Egyptian civilization; but the rule of the Pharaohs over this dependency seems mostly to have been exceedingly harsh. Under an autocracy, which treated a large part of the population of Egypt little better than serfs, despotic misrule over an alien race is scarcely surprising. Contemporary documents also refer to several expeditions to Punt, and to the precious commodities brought back from that distant region. The northwest and northeast frontiers of Egypt were also exposed to attacks from time to time; we hear, for example, of a Libyan war under Amenemhet I. It is possible that these neighbors of Egypt gave trouble again during the later years of this dynasty. Exploitation of the Sinai peninsula was more intense than ever before. Doubtless military action was needed at times against the desert tribes; but the only definite notice of this kind known so far is one which records an expedition into southern Palestine in the reign of Senusret III. There can be little doubt that it was a mere punitive raid and not a serious attempt to bring that country under permanent Egyptian control. It is recorded on a stele set up by one of the king's officers, Sebek-khu, who had seen his first military service as a young man on one of the Nubian campaigns, and who at this time had been advanced to command the reserve troops. Of the general condition of Syria at this date we get a glimpse in the autobiographical inscription of a noble, Sinuhe, who had become a political exile and was finally restored to favor by Senusret I. During his long absence from Egypt, Sinuhe travelled extensively in Palestine; for some time he lived with a tribal chief, Emuienshi, who held him in great honor and whose daughter he married. He fought, too, under the standard of his father-in-law against hostile neighbors. For the rest, his was a simple pastoral and agricultural life, forming a marked contrast to the luxurious and artificial atmosphere of the Egyptian court.

In their administration the monarchs of the XIIth Dynasty were able to steer a middle course between the methods of the IVth and of the VIth Dynasties, mainly because they were strong rulers. The monarchy was in fact more powerful than it had ever been; at the same time the king could afford to entrust the vizier and other high officials with extensive powers, so that the local nobility and the nomarchs, whose positions continued to be largely hereditary, were effectively kept in check. While this system is a combination of a central government with a quasi-feudal régime, it is also a distinct step in the direction of the highly elaborate bureaucratic organization which was per- fected during the XVIIIth and XIXth Dynasties. Indeed, it is very probable that the power of the hereditary landed nobility was finally broken under the later rulers of the XIIth, especially under such princes as Senusret III and Amenemhet III. If, on the one hand, the governors of the nomes were closely controlled by the king, they, on the other hand, enjoyed very extensive authority in the provinces that they administered. Not only the agricultural population and rural districts, but also the towns, were under their general supervision; they were respon- sible for the collection of tribute and taxes within their nome, and for its punctual delivery to the royal treasury. We have no means of ascertaining the general character of their government; undoubtedly everything would depend on the individual gover- nor. That it was ever as perfect as Ameni claims that his ad- ministration under Senusret I was, may be doubted. But, if we make allowance for a certain amount of oriental hyperbole, which characterizes most of the sepulchral inscriptions, we may still believe that Ameni's government was equitable and clem- ent. He says of himself:

There was no citizen's daughter whom I misused, there was no widow whom I oppressed, there was no peasant whom I repulsed, there was no shepherd whom I repelled, there was no overseer of serf-laborers whose people I took for (unpaid) imposts, there was none wretched in my community, there was none hungry in my time. When years of famine came I plowed all the fields of the Oryx nome, as far as its southern and northern boundary, preserving its people alive and furnishing its food, so that there was none hungry therein. I gave to the widow as (to) her who had a husband; I did not exalt the great above the small in all that I gave. Then came great Niles, possessors of grain and all things, (but) I did not collect the arrears of the field. — (Breasted, *Ancient Records*, i, pp. 252–253.)

The judicial courts in the cities were in the hands of judges appointed by the king. Census lists, used both for taxation purposes and for the levying of troops, were kept in the capital and were under the general control of the vizier. The army at this time was composed partly of regular troops, partly of militia raised in the nomes as required, partly of non-Egyptian levies, especially Nubians. In this matter, too, the practice of the XIIth Dynasty is halfway between that of the Old Kingdom and of the XVIIIth and following dynasties.

With the end of Dynasty XII we enter on one of the most obscure, as it certainly was one of the most disastrous, periods of Egyptian history. In the scheme of Manetho there are five dynasties to fill up the two centuries, during which the land of the Nile fell first into internal anarchy and then became the prey of a foreign invader. The fragmentary list of kings, preserved in the famous Turin papyrus dating from the XIXth Dynasty, also contained many names of what must, for the most part, have been very ephemeral rulers. Briefly stated, it would seem that the early kings of Dynasty XIII failed to hold their kingdom together. First one and then another of the hereditary nobility rebelled and maintained a precarious independence. Thus, many of the kings whose names are recorded were, even for the brief period of their nominal kingship, not rulers of Egypt in fact. We cannot say whether the country was already quite in the grip of anarchy, when it was attacked by foreign assailants, or whether the invasion was in part responsible for the break-up of the kingdom. The later royal names in the list are largely those of foreign kings. Who these invaders were, whom the Egyptians of a later age referred to generally as "Shepherd kings," — the name Hyksos, now in general use, is a Grecized form, used by Josephus, of two Egyptian words — is still a moot point. In a general way there can be no doubt that the Hyksos invasion of Egypt was the ultimate outcome of a wide-spread clash of peoples, and of *Völkerwanderungen*, whose repercussions were felt throughout the Near and Middle East, as will appear in a subsequent chapter. It is not in the least necessary, or even likely, that the men who thus invaded Egypt towards the end of the eighteenth century B.C. were racially homogeneous. If the rank and file were in the main Semites from Syria, it is possible that their leaders, some of whom for a time sat on the throne of the Pharaohs, were of Aryan stock and akin

STATUE OF SENUSRET III

Plate 3

HEAD OF THUTMOSE III

Plate 4

to the princes of Hatti and Mitanni. To the Hyksos kings Manetho would assign two dynasties (XV and XVI); but, for reasons already indicated in the Introduction, it is not possible to trace either their conquest or their rule with any precision or in any detail. Lower Egypt suffered first and altogether more severely than the Upper Kingdom. Even if we allow for exaggeration on the part of later chronicles which refer to this era, the invaders proceeded ruthlessly. They maltreated the inhabitants, they burnt and pillaged the Delta in such a way that it did not fully recover its prosperity for over a century. The resistance of Upper Egypt was stouter, and the Hyksos only gradually extended their power southwards. Indeed, it is questionable whether they at any time exercised complete control in this part of the country. When the war of liberation began, that is to say, toward the end of the seventeenth century B.C., it was the men of Upper Egypt who took the lead in the revolt against the foreign despots, and bore the brunt of the fight for national independence.

The success of the Hyksos in overrunning so great a part of Egypt must have been partly due to the unsettled internal condition of the land on their approach. Partly their victories must be credited to their superior tactics, and especially to their superior armature. This is particularly true of their horses and war-chariots; for these formed a weapon of offense far more effective than any which the Egyptians could produce at that period. The Egyptians in time learnt the value of them; as pictures on monuments of the XVIIIth Dynasty show, the war-chariot had then become a regular and much valued part of the Egyptian military forces. The later Hyksos kings are to some extent known from monuments. The most notable seems to have been Khian, who dedicated statues of himself at Bubastis. Traces of him, moreover, have been found outside Egypt. The lid of an alabaster vase bearing his name was found by Sir Arthur Evans at Cnossus in Crete immediately under a Late Minoan I deposit; in Mesopotamia, near Baghdad, a small lion inscribed with Khian's royal name was recovered. These later monarchs became to a great extent Egyptianized; they adopted Egyptian manners and court etiquette, and even worshipped Egyptian gods. It has been pointed out that the Hyksos control over Upper Egypt was probably never complete; certainly, toward the end of their domination, an Egyptian dynasty (XVIIth) ruled at Thebes, though technically these princes were doubtless vassals of the Hyksos. But it was these rulers of Thebes who started the rebellion against the foreigners, a struggle which continued for about forty years with varying fortunes. The capture of Memphis by the Egyptians was the beginning of the end. The Hyksos were confined to the Delta, and at last they were driven out of Egypt altogether. The Egyptian prince under whose banner the Egyptians were liberated from alien rule, was also the founder of the XVIIIth Dynasty, Ahmose I. That he was a statesman and organizer as well as an able soldier was proved by the successful manner in which, after crushing two revolts in Egypt and recovering Nubia, he consolidated his position, and, after two centuries of anarchy and disruption, made the land of the Nile again a united kingdom under a single ruler.

CHAPTER IV

THE STRUGGLE FOR SYRIA

> *And even as I protect thee, so will I protect thy
> son; but thou, Duppi-Teshup, protect the king of
> the land of Hatti, the land of Hatti, my sons (and)
> my grandsons hereafter. And the tribute which was
> imposed on thy grandfather and thy father, — 300
> half-shekels of pure refined gold of first quality
> together with precious stones they sent to the land of
> Hatti — that do thou send likewise. And cast not
> thine eyes on another. Thy ancestors paid tribute
> to the land of Egypt, but do thou send it not. —*
> From a treaty between Murshilish II, King of
> Hatti and a Chief of Amurru. (J. Friedrich,
> *Hethitische Texte*, ii (1926), pp. 12–13.)

So far we have considered separately the earlier history of
Mesopotamia and of Egypt. By the middle of the second
millennium B.C. very great political changes had come over the
whole of the Near East, and for several centuries to come the
political history of Egypt is inseparably linked with that of
the Asiatic kingdoms. At the outset we must briefly touch
upon the early development of several of these states. In
every case our information about them — be it Assyria,
Mitanni, the Hittite kingdom, or the rulers of the Sea Country
who wrested southern Babylonia from the last kings of the
first Babylonian dynasty — is still woefully deficient.

It is probable that some Sumerians had found their way to
Assyria and had settled there by c. 3000 B.C. It may also
well be that a Semitic colony came there at an early date.
But we cannot tell how rapidly the progress of fusion of the
two races progressed, or the extent to which force was used
by the Semitic invaders. Ultimately the Sumerian stock here
was submerged as it was in the South. During the third
millennium Assyria was a small state, over which the more
powerful kings of the South — Sargon, Naram-sin, Dungi —

exercised a protectorate. It is more remarkable to find a Semitic colony making its way into Asia Minor and settling there soon after the beginning of the third millennium B.C. From Kara-Euyuk, near Kaisariyeh in Cappadocia, a number of cuneiform tablets, written in the Akkadian-Semitic tongue, are known, which prove the existence there of a flourishing community. Though its members worshipped the god Ashur, the view that they were Assyrian colonists seems untenable; at that early date Assyria was not in the position to send forth settlers to another land. Besides, the affinities between this settlement of Ganesh, or Kanes, and the Babylonian-Semitic culture are marked. Hence it is more likely that the founders of Ganesh were part of a Semitic body of colonists which left Mesopotamia early in the third millennium B.C.; of them one part found its way to Ashur, the other went farther afield into Asia Minor. There are reasons for supposing that the whole body started originally from Kish. We have referred in an earlier chapter to an expedition of Sargon of Akkad into Asia Minor. Its purpose was to help the citizens of Ganesh against a neighboring state which had caused them trouble. Sargon was only prevailed upon to undertake this enterprise after urgent representations had been made to him by the Cappadocian city. His timely aid saved Ganesh from destruction, and the place continued to be of considerable importance for centuries. Its interests appear to have been primarily commercial — at all events, the deputation which went to interview Sargon and implore his aid consisted of merchants. Also, the Kara-Euyuk tablets, which may be dated about 2000 B.C., deal almost wholly with business.

Already in the time of Hammurabi's son, Samsu-iluna, (c. 1904–1867 B.C.), the political troubles began. First, the most southerly part of the kingdom, corresponding roughly to the old land of Sumer, broke away and was ruled by an independent dynasty of sea-kings, about whom we know little more than some names, partly Sumerian, partly Semitic. Much about the same date a new people, the Cassites, dwelling in the hill country of Zagros, conducted their first raid into Mesopotamia. Nevertheless, the Babylonian dynasty survived for another century, although its last five monarchs ruled over a greatly reduced kingdom. The end came about 1750 B.C., but it was neither Cassites nor sea-kings who destroyed Babylon, deposing the last of the dynasty, Samsu-ditana. It was another people, the Hatti or Hittites, who swooped down on Mesopotamia from the interior of Asia Minor.

The origin of this people, whose kings from the fifteenth to the thirteenth centuries ruled over a realm embracing most of Asia Minor and disputed with the Pharaohs for control in Syria, is still unsolved. The inhabitants of the kingdom were certainly not all of the same ethnic stock. Whereas the bulk of the population was, as far as our records allow us to judge, autochthonous, with a strong Semitic admixture, as in the case of Ganesh, the ruling class, at the time when Hatti was politically powerful, was part of an Aryan or Indo-European body of invaders who, soon after 2000 B.C., began to push their way westward from central Asia. Another such wave of conquering immigrants settled about the same time in northern Mesopotamia on the east of the great semi-circular bend made by the Euphrates between latitudes 38° and 36°. The earlier dwellers in this region were probably racially akin to their neighbors in Asia Minor, and Mitannians are heard of before the end of the third millennium B.C. But the kings of Mitanni, as this district was called, who somewhat later made of it an important kingdom, were Aryans and worshipped Indian gods. Finally, the Cassites also were of Indo-European stock. Thus, in all three cases it is only the ruling caste, so far as we know at present, who represent the immigrant, Aryan element. We have no means of ascertaining whether these invaders acted at all in concert. In 1750 B.C. Babylon was destroyed by an invasion of Hatti, but the conquerors did not remain in the land. Shortly afterward (in 1749 or 1746?) the Cassite prince, Gandash, seized the Babylonian throne and founded a dynasty which ruled in Babylon for six centuries. Probably there was no concerted action between the two bodies of invaders; but the Cassites, who had troubled Babylonia before, simply seized their opportunity to make themselves master of a large portion of Mesopotamia, when the capital city had been laid waste by the Hatti. The kingdom now ruled over by Gandash and his successors was territorially much smaller than the realm of Hammurabi. The sea-kings in the South held out for about half a century before they finally succumbed to the new rulers of Babylon. In the North, Assyria for a brief space was a state of some importance under a king, Shamshi-Adad II (c. 1700–1680 B.C.), whose warlike ardor carried him beyond the boundaries of his kingdom into the Armenian highlands and into northern Syria. Yet it was a short-lived triumph. For the next three centuries Assyria became again a weak kingdom, dependent politically on one or other of its more powerful neighbors.

The political upheavals which have been briefly indicated had at the beginning reacted on Syria also, and ultimately on Egypt. For the Hyksos, whom in the main we must regard as Semitic (Canaanite and Amorite?) tribes, were either forced southward by pressure of a new people from the north, or else they may actually have been led to Egypt by some early Hittite chiefs, the records of whose prowess excavation has not yet recovered.

When, about 1500 B.C., the darkness surrounding the earlier history of the Hittites begins to be dispelled, we find a Hittite kingdom firmly established in central Asia Minor, with its capital at Hattushash on a hill overlooking the modern village of Boghaz-Keui. Architectural and sculptural remains were already to some extent known to exist on this site, which commands a point where several highways of immemorial antiquity meet, before the place was scientifically excavated by Hugo Winckler in 1906–07. The fortifications of the citadel were constructed of heavy polygonal blocks. A large palace or temple, whose ruins have been thoroughly uncovered, was built mainly of brick on lower courses of stone. A massive entrance gateway is flanked on either side by a great stone lion. Smaller fortifications were placed on several of the surroundings eminences; also, at a little distance from the citadel and town, there is a series of rock sculptures, which unhappily are so badly weathered that the interpretation of the subject represented is quite uncertain. A religious procession of persons, advancing from two sides and meeting in the middle, appears to be depicted. Among the figures we seem to recognize the great Mother goddess of Anatolia and her male consort, also the priest-king of Hatti and a number of Hittite warriors dressed in tunic and sleeved upper-garment, shoes with turned-up points, and high conical hat. They were armed with swords, bows, and spears. The character of these sculptures at Boghaz-Keui is closely similar to that of many monuments and rock sculptures known in other parts of Cappadocia and beyond. For this style of art can be traced in the West as far afield as Mt. Sipylus and the vicinity of Ephesus, and in the South as far as northern Syria. To the historical student, however, the most important discovery made by Winckler at Boghaz-Keui consisted of a large number of inscribed clay tablets. Some of these Hittite archives are written in Babylonian-Semitic and could be deciphered with comparative ease. But more are composed in Anatolian dialects, of which the latest investigators would distinguish not less than six. Although immense progress in elucidating these texts has been made by Hroszny, Forrer, and other scholars, so that their general content can be ascertained with fair certainty, much still remains to be done, both in deciphering tablets still unread and in improving the interpretation of the others in matters of detail. Nor has it been possible to classify these dialects with certainty; in the main they appear to be Indo-European, but they contain considerable foreign elements. All these archives, whether couched in Semitic or in the local dialects, were written in cuneiform script, which the Hittites had learnt from their Semitic neighbors. Besides this script, more primitive pictographic writing is known from Hittite monuments, but this still awaits decipherment.

Of eight early Hittite kings we at present know very little that is definite. The third in the list, Murshilish I, captured Aleppo and subsequently conquered Babylon, an achievement probably identical with the destruction of that city and the deposition of Samsu-ditana in 1750 B.C., to which reference has already been made. After the eighth monarch there is a gap in our information. When we come to the second series of Hittite kings, beginning with Dudkhaliash I (c. 1550?), we are on firmer ground. For it is under this dynasty that Hatti became a first-class power, and its kings sought to rival the Pharaohs of the XVIIIth and XIXth Dynasties as conquerors and rulers of empire. We cannot tell how extensive the earlier Hittite realm was, though the exploits of Murshilish I suggest that it may have extended to northern Syria and have included a good deal more than the Halys crescent. In any case, if such a greater Hittite kingdom existed for a while, it seems to have dropped to pieces again. For the earliest kings of the second series, Dudkhaliash I, Hattushilish II, Dudkhaliash II, conducted war with varying success against Aleppo, and had rivals for the control of southern Cappadocia and northern Syria in their neighbors, the Harri. The fourth king of the dynasty, Shupiluliuma, achieved such military success that he brought all Cappadocia and the region between the Halys and the upper Euphrates under his control, and advanced the frontiers of his realm to northern Syria and northern Mesopotamia. Since it is under him that the first serious clash between Hatti and Egypt occurred, we must now go back to consider the foreign policy of the Pharaohs of the XVIIIth Dynasty.

The founder of that dynasty, Ahmose I, did a great work in restoring peace and order in his disrupted kingdoms. It was left for his successors to undertake what, in the first instance, was a war of retaliation against Syria from whence the late oppressors had come. It is a moot point whether Amenhotep I invaded Syria, but it is certain that the third ruler of the dynasty, Thutmose I, did so. Though he might subsequently claim to have conquered all Syria to the Euphrates, his expedition was in truth no more than a raid on an extended scale. There was no single power in Syria and Palestine at that date to unify the country against an invader. Instead we find there a large number of tribes and small principalities, which were frequently at war one with the other. Northern Syria, except the region between the Lebanon range and the sea, seems to have been to some extent a protectorate of Mitanni. The territory, which in the Egyptian records is called Naharina, included the land between the Orontes and the Euphrates, as well as Mitanni proper on the east. For a half a century after Thutmose I's campaign no more is heard of Egyptian attacks on Syria. If the Egyptian monarchs declared a protectorate over Syria at this time, it can hardly have been very effective.

On the contrary, it seems clear that some effort was made by the Syrian communities to coöperate, in the event of renewed hostilities from Egypt. For, when finally Thutmose III in 1479 B.C. entered on his first Syrian expedition, he found a formidable coalition arrayed against him under the leadership of the prince of Kadesh.

If military prowess be the test of eminence, Thutmose III might deserve to be called the greatest of the Pharaohs (Plate 4). He conducted no less than seventeen campaigns into Syria; the history of his achievements, retold in considerable detail, survives in the form of annals inscribed on the walls of the temple of Amen at Karnak. In his first invasion Thutmose advanced as far as the undulating country to the south of Mt. Carmel, without encountering any serious opposition. But here, close to Megiddo, the historical original of Armageddon, he was confronted by an allied force of Syrian tribes. Thutmose's plan of battle differed, we are told, from that advocated by his general staff; nevertheless, on the morrow his strategic dispositions proved to be justified, for the Egyptian troops after a lengthy contest won a decisive victory. This was followed by the investiture and capture of Megiddo, and ample spoils were taken from the enemy. In successive years Thutmose followed up his first conquests systematically. Thus, step by step, he gained control of Phœnicia and the hinterland. His eighth campaign brought him to the Euphrates and to the borders of Mitanni. The king of Mitanni sent tribute, even as the king of Assyria had done some years before. His land campaigns Thutmose supported by naval operations off the coast, finally receiving the voluntary submission of Yantanai, which can be identified with fair certainty as the island of Cyprus. The record of Thutmose's exploits ends with the seventeenth campaign, in which he effectively quelled a general rising against Egyptian authority. Once more Kadesh played the part of leader. Though the Egyptian monarch reigned for another dozen years, he does not appear to have warred in Syria again.

During his lifetime the suzerainty of Egypt extended well-nigh to the Taurus. Neighboring states were overawed and paid tribute; besides those already mentioned, the Hittite king (Hattushilish II?) also found it politic to appease the great conqueror with gifts. Judged by later events the steps taken to keep an effective hold on the conquered territory were not very satisfactory. The Syrian chiefs were in the position of vassals to the Pharaoh. Younger members of their families were taken to the Egyptian court, there to be educated after the Egyptian manner. Occasionally the king sent his own officials on a tour of inspection through the dependencies; in addition, some garrisons were left behind to guard important strategic points. Yet, all this was not enough; for, ultimately, the loyalty-compelling force was the prestige and power of the Egyptian king alone, and Egyptian conquerors had the same experience as the Mesopotamian warrior kings of an earlier age. Almost immediately after the death of Thutmose III a serious rising against Egyptian authority was organized in the Lebanon district. The new king, Amenhotep II, who had been associated on the throne with his father for a few years, must needs inaugurate his independent reign by a punitive expedition into Syria. Besides achieving his immediate object, the king invaded Mitanni.

Subsequently more peaceful counsels prevailed. Mitanni became a subject ally of Egypt, and good relations between the two states were further cemented by a royal marriage. For Thutmose IV married a daughter of King Artatama of Mitanni. Of the purpose and results of an invasion conducted by Thutmose IV into Syria we know nothing. Yet the mere fact that it was needed is significant; it shows that the Egyptian hold over her Asiatic subjects was none too secure. Under the latest kings of Dynasty XVIII the bonds holding together the empire won by Thutmose III became weaker and weaker. Finally they broke altogether, and it became necessary for the early rulers of the XIXth Dynasty to attempt the subjugation of Syria afresh. However, the later years of the XVIIIth Dynasty, or more precisely the reigns of Amenhotep III and IV, are a period of quite exceptional interest to us, because of the ample, and in some ways unique, documentary material available for their study. It is on this age that light is especially shed by the Boghaz-Keui documents; but, above all, it is to it that the so-called Amarna archives belong. These, which come from the new capital founded by Amenhotep IV in Upper Egypt, consist of about 350 whole or partially preserved tablets, and, with the exception of a few lists of offerings, are all letters and despatches. They may be briefly grouped as follows:

1. Letters between Amenhotep III and Amenhotep IV and the Cassite rulers of Babylon.
2. Correspondence between Amenhotep IV and the king of Assyria.
3. Correspondence between Tushratta, king of Mitanni, and Amenhotep III and IV.
4. Two letters from the king of Hatti to Amenhotep IV.
5. A number of letters to the Egyptian kings from Abd-Ashirta, prince of Amurru.
6. Letters from his son, Aziru, to Egypt.
7. A very large collection of communications from the prince of Gubla (Byblos in Phoenicia), Rib-Addi, to the Egyptian kings.
8. Letters from Artahepa, governor of Jerusalem, and other Palestinian letters to Egypt.

Outwardly, during the greater part of Amenhotep III's reign, the imperial power of Egypt seemed still to rest on secure foundations. The rulers of Babylon and of Mitanni are in the one case friendly to Egypt, in the other case in close alliance. Assyria at this date still acknowledged the overlordship of Mitanni. The unknown quantity was the new Hittite monarch, Shupiluliuma, who ascended the throne shortly before 1400 B.C.; but the Egyptian king certainly did not recognize the danger to be apprehended from this quarter. However, there can be no doubt that Shupiluliuma was the chief instigator of the unrest and finally the rebellion against Egyptian authority which came to a head in Syria during the last years of Amenhotep III. The Amorite prince, Abd-Ashirta, and, after his death, his son, Aziru, very successfully played a double game. They attacked the coastal cities of Phœnicia, which held staunchly to Egypt, assuring the Egyptian government that they were helping to defend Phœnicia from the possible attacks of the Hittite king, who was raiding Naharina and Mitanni. In spite of constant despatches from the loyal prince of Byblos, Rib-Addi, who revealed the full treachery of the Amorite chiefs, the Egyptian kings were supine and unconvinced. When at last, shortly before the death of Amenhotep III, a punitive expedition was sent against Abd-Ashirta, it wrested from him Simyra, seized by him a year or two before, and momentarily checked Amorite intrigues. But, on the accession of a new Egyptian monarch,

Amenhotep IV, the situation in Syria rapidly grew worse. A more wide-spread revolt from Egypt culminated in the loss of both Simyra and Byblos, whose prince, Rib-Addi, was killed by Aziru. The last named, till then most adept in duplicity, so far overreached himself that, after he had made his peace with Egypt on terms favorable to himself, he was forced to become the vassal of Hatti. A portion of the treaty imposed on him by Shupiluliuma has actually been recovered among the Boghaz-Keui archives.

With the loss to Egypt of all northern Syria and of Phœnicia, her ally, Mitanni, was dangerously isolated. At a most critical moment King Tushratta was murdered by one of his own sons, Artatama; in the anarchy that followed the neighbors of Mitanni saw their opportunity. The Assyrian king proclaimed his independence and seized the eastern region of Mitanni, whose parricide ruler acquiesced in what the insecurity of his own position did not allow him to combat. After some years of great distress in Mitanni, Shupiluliuma, to whose court another son of Tushratta, Mattivaza, had fled for protection, interfered by force of arms. The Assyrian king was obliged to give up his ill-gotten gains, and Mattivaza was set up on the throne of Mitanni as the vassal of Shupiluliuma, whose daughter he also married. The chronology of these years is still very uncertain, but it is clear that a year or two before Amenhotep IV's death (1358 B.C.) all Syria had been lost to Egypt. Shortly before Shupiluliuma died he concluded a treaty with Egypt, which left northern Syria in Hittite hands, while the position of southern Syria and Palestine was left undefined.[1] It was for the Egyptians to recover those lands, if they could. It was a great empire that Shupiluliuma on his death

[1] It is uncertain which Egyptian king concluded the treaty with Shupiluliuma. If the latter died in 1359, it must have been Amenhotep IV. If, on the other hand, Shupiluliuma's dates are a little later, so that he did not die till *c.* 1349 B.C., the Egyptian king may have been Harmhab. In the *Cambridge Ancient History*, vol. ii, we find the treaty tentatively assigned to Harmhab in two places (pp. 134 and 318), yet in the second passage the dates of Shupiluliuma are given as 1411–1359. On p. 264 the treaty is assigned to Amenhotep III or his successor. The synchronistic tables (pp. 694 and 700) assign the treaty to Harmhab, the year of his accession being given as 1346 or 1350. Yet the death of Shupiluliuma is there placed in 1359.

(1359 B.C.?) left to his son Arnuandash. He reigned only a few years and was succeeded by his brother, Murshilish II. The Boghaz-Keui archives contain a number of treaties concluded by this prince with neighboring peoples. An agreement with the Amorite prince, Duppi-Teshup, was calculated to keep the Hittite protectorate over northern Syria secure.[1] Equally illuminating are the pacts made with the chiefs of Hapalla (Aleppo?) and of Mira and Kuwalija. From another Hittite

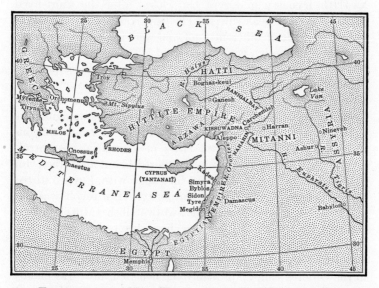

EGYPT AND THE NEAR EAST IN THE 14TH CENTURY B.C.

document we know that Murshilish, at the beginning of his reign, conducted campaigns for several years against Arzawa. It would seem that after a successful war these smaller states, which were in some sort of dependence on the king of Arzawa, became separate principalities under chiefs who were, like the ruler of Arzawa himself, vassals of Hatti. Though it has so far been impossible to fix precisely the geographical situation of these place names, there can be little doubt that Arzawa was the extended region in Asia Minor, which lay to the south and southwest of Hatti and was later called Cilicia, Pisidia, and

[1] Cf. the citation at the beginning of this chapter.

Lycia. In the Amarna letters a king of Arzawa corresponds as an independent prince with Amenhotep III; subsequently the kingdom had come under Hittite suzerainty before the wars of Murshilish, which were presumably necessitated by an attempt of the king of Arzawa to regain complete political liberty.

We have seen, then, that the Hittite empire reached its greatest extent under Murshilish II. In the meantime, the XVIIIth Dynasty in Egypt had closed after the short-lived reigns of several weak rulers. The early kings of the next dynasty were made of different stuff and were filled with ambition to restore the foreign empire of Egypt. The second of the line, Seti I, began by attempting the recovery of Palestine and Phœnicia. This region, which the Hittites had never tried to control, had seceded *en masse* from Egypt during the weak foreign government of Amenhotep IV. Seti I's campaigns were aimed at cowing the natives and especially at reasserting his sovereignty over the coastal cities of Phœnicia. Amurru's loyalty to Hatti seems to have wavered about this time; for Benteshina, prince of Amurru, in league with Egypt, stirred up a rebellion against Hittite authority. The revolt was put down by Murshilish's successor, Muwatallish (Mutallu), who deposed Benteshina. Later, we find this prince restored as ruler of Amurru by Hattushilish III, whose vassal he remained. Seti I in his fourth year met and defeated a "Hittite" army in the Orontes valley; probably the defeated force was mainly composed of local tribes who owed allegiance to Hatti. A treaty between Seti and Muwatallish, as far as the last named's interests are concerned, can merely have reasserted the *status quo;* for Hatti still controlled northern Syria.

A more serious threat to Hittite sovereignty in that region came in the time of Seti's successor, Ramses II. Nor was the Hittite king unmindful of the more serious attack which threatened his imperial interests south of the Taurus. For Muwatallish collected troops and raised levies in all parts of his dominions; these he led in person against the invader. In the valley of the Orontes, close to Kadesh, the two armies met in 1296 B.C. Though, at the end of a long day's fighting, in which Muwatallish showed superior strategy and Ramses's troops better discipline and superior powers of defense, the Egyptian monarch could claim to be master of the field, it was a Pyrrhic victory. Ramses had lost a whole division of his army and was no nearer to attaining his real objective. Subsequently, for about fifteen years, Ramses continued his campaigns in Syria. North of Phœnicia he failed to get any permanent hold on the country; nor does he seem appreciably to have weakened the authority of Hatti in that region. Eight years after Muwatallish's death his brother, Hattushilish III, negotiated a treaty with Ramses in 1280 B.C.[1] Of this important document we possess two incomplete copies of the Egyptian and considerable fragments of the Hittite version. There is a historical preamble, setting out the earlier relations between the two high contracting parties, and a reaffirmation of the treaties made by their predecessors. The two kings undertake to abstain from all aggressions on each other's spheres of influence and conclude a defensive alliance against mutual enemies, whether these be recalcitrant subjects or foreign states. There are also provisions for the extradition of political fugitives, who are to receive an amnesty in their respective countries, and against the permanent settlement of Egyptians in Hittite and of Hittites in Egyptian territory. It is beyond doubt that the Egyptian sphere of influence hereafter did not extend beyond the Phœnician coast, and that Amurru continued to be a Hittite protectorate. If we seek for a reason why Hattushilish took the initiative in coming to terms with his rival — and this seems to have been the case — we can probably find it in the marked growth of Assyrian power at this date. Shalmaneser I attacked Hittite dependencies, when he entered the old land of Mitanni and Hanigalbat which lay to the north of it. It was therefore to Hattushilish's interest to be at peace with his old enemy, Egypt, and to continue, as his predecessors had done, to foster good relations between Hatti and the Cassite rulers of Babylon. Under Hattushilish the Assyrian peril was averted, nor was it in fact that power which, half a century later, brought the Hittite empire to an end.

[1] Muwatallish died in 1288 and was succeeded by his young son, Urhiteshupash. In 1281 the latter was displaced by his uncle, Hattushilish III, the younger brother of Muwatallish.

The existing documents of Hattushilish are more numerous than those of any other Hittite monarch; one is of quite exceptional interest, being a long autobiographical account of the king up to the time when he was firmly established on the throne. Strongly religious in tone, — for Hattushilish piously attributes all his success and his preservation from many dangers to his patron goddess, Ishtar, — it is also full of romance. Hattushilish was the younger son of Murshilish II, and, being sickly in his youth, was made a priest of Ishtar. On the accession of his elder brother, Muwatallish, he was given an important province to administer, which aroused the jealousy of the previous governor, a man destined to be his life-long enemy. The latter's attempt to calumniate Hattushilish to the king failed. Hattushilish next saw much military service in different parts of Asia Minor; later still he was with his brother during the campaign against Ramses II. Then he had again to combat false accusations, brought against him by his old rival, who, in addition, seems to have caused him serious losses during his absence at the war. Having at last surmounted all these difficulties, he, on his brother's death, acted as regent for his nephew, who was apparently a minor when he became king. In time this youth tried to restrict his uncle's power, a circumstance which led to civil war and in the end to Hattushilish's occupation of the throne. This triumph Hattushilish owed mainly to his having previously won the prominent nobles to his side. His nephew and his old rival, who had supported the young king to the last, were both banished. Some little while before his accession Hattushilish had taken to wife the daughter of a priest of Ishtar. It is much to be regretted that this interesting record refers only in quite general terms to Hattushilish's own reign. In more or less stereotyped language the king states that he had received the homage of vassals, while princes of equal rank had sent him gifts. Of his former enemies some had now sought alliances, others had been utterly defeated by him.

It remains to chronicle one further episode in the relations between Hatti and Egypt. A dozen years or so after the treaty, Hattushilish paid a state visit to Egypt, and with him went his daughter. Her nuptials with the Egyptian monarch were doubtless celebrated with becoming pomp, while the fact that the two royal houses were now related by marriage helped to ensure future friendship between the two states.[1]

[1] The following are the kings of the XVIIIth and XIXth Dynasties with approximate dates:

XVIIIth Dynasty		*XIXth Dynasty*	
Ahmose I	1580–1558	Ramses I	1321
Amenhotep I	1558–1545	Seti I	1321–1300
Thutmose I	1545–1514	Ramses II	1300–1233
Thutmose II	1514–1501	Merenptah	1233–1223
Queen Hatshepsut	1501–1479	Amenmose	1223–1220
Thutmose III	1479–1447	Ramses–Siptah	1220–1214
Amenhotep II	1447–1420	Seti II	1214–1210
Thutmose IV	1420–1412		
Amenhotep III	1412–1376		
Amenhotep IV (Akhenaten)	1380–1362		
Smenkhkere	1362–1360		
Tutenkhamen	1360–1350		
Ai	1350–1346		
Harmhab	1346–1322		

CHAPTER V

EGYPTIAN CIVILIZATION

> *Egypt . . . has wonders more in number than any other land, and works too it has to show as much as any land, which are beyond expression great; for this reason, then, more shall be said concerning it.* — Herodotus ii, 35 (tr. Macaulay).

ALTHOUGH no caste system existed in Ancient Egypt, and no sharp cleavage between an upper and a lower class of free men, as it is found in Babylonia, the population in practice was made up of three or four groups, whose life and material prosperity differed greatly. We must, in fact, distinguish the official class, the town dwellers, the agricultural population, and the priests. In addition to these free men there was a very numerous slave class.

Since agriculture was the oldest as well as the most important occupation, the farming class might justly be regarded as the back bone of the nation. Yet, inasmuch as the landowners were the king himself, the priests, or the nobles, the average farmer is not likely to have eked out much more than a pittance for himself and his family. He was, in truth, little better than a serf; though he might suffer oppression and wrong, he might find it a long and difficult business to obtain redress.[1] In a year of poor harvest the rural population would of course be the first to suffer, and such years came from time to time, in spite of the care taken by some of the Egyptian monarchs to supplement nature and the Nile by canalization and by building reservoirs. Such was the purpose of Lake Moeris, constructed during the XIIth Dynasty by Amenemhet III; another artificial lake was built a little to the west of Thebes by some king of the XVIIIth or XIXth Dynasty. The system of canals

---

[1] Cf. the long story of the Eloquent Peasant, of which there is a good English version by A. H. Gardiner in *Journal of Egyptian Archæology*, ix (1923), pp. 5–25.

was intricate and old-standing; whether the proper maintenance of these was undertaken and defrayed by the state or
whether the farmers were, as in Babylonia, partly or wholly
responsible for the upkeep, we do not know. At all events,
from early times an official register was carefully kept of the
annual rise and fall of the river.

The crops chiefly cultivated were wheat, barley, and durra
(*sorghum vulgare*); the last-named, however, seems to have been
much less popular than it is in modern Egypt. Of great importance, too, was the growing of flax, since linen was the universally used material for clothing. No less ubiquitous was the
date-palm, while other fruits, as well as vegetables and flowers
in great variety, were grown extensively, either for ordinary use
or for the tables of the rich. The usual livestock — cattle,
sheep, goats, and pigs — was successfully reared. Oxen were
used in agricultural operations, while the ass was the commonest
draught animal. The horse, introduced from Syria or beyond
in the Hyksos period, was thereafter essential in the army. The
camel, though known, does not appear to have been employed
as a beast of transport save to a very limited extent.

The town dwellers were occupied in every variety of handi-
craft and in trade and commerce. From excavated town sites
we can see that the majority of houses were small and of simple
design, — a central courtyard on which a number of rooms
opened, — and that the streets were narrow. The new city,
built to be his capital by Amenhotep IV, was exceptional for its
more spacious roads and houses. The jewelry, furniture, and
the artistic productions generally, whether of the XIIth or the
XVIIIth and following Dynasties, reveal the astonishing skill
of the craftsman, as well as the luxury which surrounded the
king and the wealthy class. Much of the raw material was of
necessity imported from outside Egypt: from the Sinai peninsula, where the mines continued to be intensively exploited
after the repulse of the Hyksos; from Syria, and more especially
from Phœnicia and the Lebanon region; from Punt, whither the
queen Hatshepsut in the ninth year of her reign (*c.* 1493 B.C.)
sent five ships which returned laden with precious commodities of all kinds; and, lastly, from Nubia. This country during
the Hyksos period passed almost entirely out of Egyptian con-

trol. The kings of the XVIIIth Dynasty reasserted their
authority in Lower Nubia, and, under Thutmose III and
Amenhotep III, the frontier was advanced to the fourth Nile
cataract. Some of the royal expeditions extended even further
south than this, perhaps as far as the sixth cataract; but we
have no evidence that this remote region was permanently
an Egyptian protectorate.

The scribes formed an influential part of the city populations.
In their schools the Egyptian boy was taught to read and write;
then followed more specialized instruction in the proper method
of drawing up petitions and legal.documents, and of composing
official letters. The "school-texts" recovered in great quantity
from Egypt contain many model letters and petitions, which the
pupils probably memorized, as well as stories and lists of moral
saws calculated to improve the minds of the young. The scribes
were an important class because many administrative posts were
open only to those who had had the requisite training in letters.

The official class from the time of the XVIIIth Dynasty must
have been very numerous. The administration was now highly
centralized, and the work was carried on by a graded bureaucracy. The governor of Thebes, who acted as viceroy when the
king was absent on any foreign expedition, was, after the
monarch himself, the most important person in the realm.
From the time of Thutmose III a second viceroy was appointed
to act in Lower Egypt, his official residence being at Memphis.
In the tomb of one of the southern governors of the age of
Thutmose III, Rehkmire, there survives a long and famous
inscription, from which much can be learnt about the duties and
powers of that high office. Briefly, the governor was entrusted
with the direction of the entire administration, with one noteworthy exception. Although he was ultimately responsible
for the collection of taxes and inland revenue from the various
local authorities, he did not direct the finances of the country.
The treasury was in charge of another high official who was
responsible solely and directly to the king. Thus for his supplies
the governor must needs apply to the monarch himself; obviously this meant an important check on any over-ambitious
viceroy. The local officials, of course, differed greatly in status;
in places of strategic importance the control was purely military,

Plate 5

TEMPLE AT EDFU IN EGYPT

a

b

CNOSSUS: *a*. So-called Theatral Area; *b*. Grand Staircase

Plate 6

while elsewhere, though the descendants of local chiefs and landed aristocracy still ruled in name, the real power was vested in a sheriff appointed by the king.

Of the administration of law in Egypt during the Middle and New Kingdom we really know far less than in the case of Babylonia with its Sumerian and Semitic codes. That the law had been in some form or other codified before the XVIIIth Dynasty may be deduced from a statement that the vizier, who was head of the judiciary, shall have before him the forty rolls of the law when he is passing judgment. So far as Egyptian legal practice can be appraised, the civil ordinances regulating property, contracts, testamentary succession, and the family were worthy of a highly civilized people; the criminal law, with its use of torture for witnesses, whether free or slave, and its constant appeal to magic was still of a rather primitive and savage character. Besides courts at the two chief centres of Thebes and Heliopolis, we can safely postulate the existence of inferior courts in the more important cities of the two kingdoms. We do not hear that the priests, who by the XVIIIth Dynasty not only formed a class by themselves but began to become exceedingly powerful outside the religious sphere, possessed or could legally exercise jurisdiction. On the other hand, we may be sure that, as their power grew, they could exert their influence on any branch of the administration. The earlier monarchs of Dynasty XVIII, especially Thutmose III, had lavished gifts on Amen, to whose favor they attributed their success in war and their prosperity at home. The ministers of the god, the Amen priests, welcomed a royal generosity which promoted their own power. Under Amenhotep IV they received a rude check.

Much has been written concerning the religious reforms of this prince. Modern writers, struck by the emphasis laid upon the cult of a single divinity in a land which had been for centuries polytheistic, seem to have attributed to Amenhotep IV's monotheism a greater profundity and originality than is warranted. The cult of the sun-god was as old as Egyptian civilization. By the time of Amenhotep III, if not before, it had attained not only exceptional importance, but had taken a form unlike that of the earlier worship of Ra. Amenhotep III had regarded the sun's disc, called in Egyptian Aten, with peculiar reverence; it was left for his son and successor to exalt this cult to the exclusion of all others. Amenhotep IV came to the throne as a child; he was apparently still in his teens when, in the sixth year of his reign, he changed his name to Akhenaten, "pleasing to Aten," and tried to enforce this worship solely in his kingdom by abolishing all other cults and persecuting their adherents, especially the priests of Amen. He forsook the old capital at Thebes and on the site of the modern Amarna founded the city of Akhetaten. There, with his courtiers, he lived a devotee of the cult, which saw in the sun, whose disc alone the eye could see, the source of all life and growth. While the belief in a single deity as the life-giving and universal ruler of the world was a loftier conception than any known so far in Egypt or beyond, the surviving hymns to Aten are not remarkable for any great ethical content.[1]

Though outwardly his subjects might have to conform, Akhenaten's new religion did not obtain any great hold on the people. On the contrary, opposition to it, if latent at first, was strong, and within ten years of the king's death the new monotheism was rooted up and the worship of Amen was restored with greater pomp than before. The priests of Amen in the years that followed became continuously more powerful till, from the time of the XXth Dynasty, they dominated even the monarchs themselves. Both politically and economically the effects of Akhenaten's aberration were disastrous to Egypt. We have already seen how her Syrian empire dropped away; at home the people as a whole suffered from the exactions and tyranny of officials and tax-gatherers, as well as from the depredations of the soldiery. The administration became hopelessly corrupt because supervision by the central authorities had virtually ceased. Local authorities connived with the collectors of revenue in the nefarious task of fleecing the masses. The chief credit for restoring order in Egypt, and thereby enabling her people to recover their prosperity, seems to belong to Harmhab, whose surviving edicts are a historical source of great value. This man, who had filled important military and ad-

[1] For a translation of some of these Aten hymns see *Cambridge Ancient History*, ii (1924), pp. 117–119.

ministrative posts in Lower Egypt, was, thanks largely to the powerful support of the Amen priesthood, elevated to the throne some twelve years after Akhenaten's death. In that interval three short-lived rulers — the second of them was Tutenkhamen, the unearthing of whose tomb was one of the most sensational discoveries of recent years — were king in name more than in fact.

From early times the most characteristic expression of royal power and magnificence had been the erection of funerary or religious buildings. Such, for example, were the pyramids set up by the kings of the Old Kingdom. Pyramid building was to some extent revived by the monarchs of the XIIth Dynasty, but these later structures, the result of a conscious archaizing, are not comparable, either in size or workmanship, with the great tombs of Cheops and his successors. Rather, the most impressive buildings of the Middle Kingdom were temples like that set up at Heliopolis in honor of the sun by Senusret I, or the so-called labyrinth at Hawara built by Amenemhet III. This was an elaborate complex of halls and colonnades in the centre of which stood a pyramid, the last resting place of that monarch. Many of the nobles, too, built themselves fine tombs, the walls of which were covered with decoration in painting and relief. Long autobiographical inscriptions often accompanied the ornamentation, and much of the epigraphic material from which our knowledge of Egyptian history is derived is in this form.[1] During the Hyksos occupation many of the older buildings must have been destroyed or badly damaged. The rulers of the XVIIIth Dynasty vied with one another in restoring old structures and building new ones. Thus Queen Hatshepsut lavished great wealth on the construction of a temple at Deir el-Bahri. The building was dedicated to Amen and also commemorated the queen's father, Thutmose I. Thutmose III's activity as a builder was displayed in various parts of his kingdom, but even his prodigality seems to have been surpassed by Amenhotep III. The most ambitious monument set up by him has unhappily not survived. It was a mighty funerary temple at Thebes, standing on the western

---

[1] Cf. for instance the inscription of Ameni of which a part is cited above on p. 47.

bank of the Nile, and would appear to have been of unexampled magnificence. All that now remains are two colossal statues of the king, familiar to later ages as the statues of Memnon.[1] After Amenhotep III's time a marked decline in architecture set in. Later kings continued to build extensively; indeed, the extravagance of Ramses II went further than that of any of his predecessors. He restored, often with an utter absence of taste, and he set up a great variety of new monuments. But, to take but one instance, compared with earlier funerary temples, that which Ramses built for himself (the so-called Ramesseum at Thebes) is vulgar and pretentious. In place of the fine architectural proportions on which the artists of an earlier age had expended infinite care, the spectator viewing Ramses' temple finds nothing but immense and clumsy size. Under the successors of this king the decline in architecture, as in the other arts, was even more rapid.

Besides architecture, sculpture in the round and in relief, wall-painting in *tempera*, miniature carving, and the work of the jeweler and goldsmith were intensively and successfully cultivated at all periods. In portraiture two apparently contradictory tendencies can be noted. On the one hand, from early dynastic times strict artistic conventions were followed, the observance of which gives many Egyptian statues a stiff and lifeless appearance, however admirable the technical execution. On the other hand, as the amount of Egyptian sculptures has greatly increased, thanks to continuous excavation, it has become clear that at all times down to Dynasty XIX a love for more naturalistic or realistic presentation of the subject existed among some Egyptian artists. There were men, particularly during the fourth and the twelfth dynasties, who produced portrait statues of unsurpassed individuality. Even greater is the realism which we find in the representations of Akhenaten and his family, whether in sculpture or in painting. Ultimately formalism triumphed. There was much deliberate archaism as well, coupled with a vandalism displayed by later Pharaohs, which took the form of usurping the statues of older kings and

---

[1] There is a most interesting essay on these colossi and on stories connected with them in the late Lord Curzon's *Tales of Travel*, published in 1923.

putting their own names thereon. Occasionally bad taste went even further, and the face was worked over so as to resemble a little more nearly the features of the reigning prince.

Of remains of Egyptian literature the most characteristic, apart from the historical texts, are the religious texts. They include hymns to the gods, prescribed rituals for use in divine worship and at funeral obsequies, and an abundance of magic formulæ and spells, of which the most famous collection is the so-called *Book of the Dead*. Apart from the hymns there is a considerable amount of secular poetry, folk-songs, love-songs, even such doggerel verse as workmen sang at their daily task. The ancient Egyptian, like all orientals, had a passion for telling and listening to tales. The best surviving examples of such stories date from the XIIth Dynasty. In some cases the subject matter is purely imaginary, although even so it largely reflects the life and thought of the time; in others, especially in tales of the XVIIIth and XIXth Dynasties, the background of the narrative is historical. Among a very large variety of topics we miss the beast-fable, a type of story that, with other peoples and in other times, has enjoyed great popularity. Lastly we may mention the scientific literature. The mathematical *papyri* show that the Egyptians, contrary to a widely held belief, had only a limited knowledge of that science. That many of the Egyptians had keen powers of observation is suggested especially by the medical *papyri*. At the time of the Old and the Middle Kingdom the medical practitioners seem to have had marked skill in diagnosis; they had some knowledge of anatomy, they carried out simple surgical operations, and they used a pharmacopeia of considerable diversity. Later, under the New Kingdom, their scientific thought and experiments, whether in medicine or in astronomy, became dominated and warped by magic and superstitious practices.

CHAPTER VI

THE BRONZE AGE CIVILIZATION OF THE
MEDITERRANEAN AREA

> *According to oral tradition Minos was the earli-*
> *est prince to acquire a fleet. He conquered the*
> *greater part of what is now the Greek Sea, and he*
> *became master of the Cyclades and was the first*
> *coloniser of most of them, after driving out the*
> *Carians, and established his own sons there as*
> *governors.* — Thucydides, i, 4.

Nothing illustrates better the immense advance in our knowledge of early civilizations, brought about by archæological exploration during the past half century, than the discovery of a
great pre-Hellenic culture in the eastern Mediterranean. Just as
no one until the beginning of the present century dreamed of the
existence of a great Hittite empire in Asia Minor in the middle of
the second millennium B.C., so, too, it was not until the discoveries of Schliemann, from 1870 onwards, at Hissarlik, Tiryns,
and Mycenæ, and the no less sensational excavations of Sir
Arthur Evans at Cnossus from 1900, that it became evident
that the lands later occupied by the Greeks had been, for several
thousand years before, the home of a civilization no whit inferior to the contemporary cultures of Asia and Egypt. Brief
allusions in classical Greek authors, like Thucydides, to an
early pre-Greek maritime empire centring in Crete, which had
hitherto been treated as fables, were seen to be historically
justified;[1] while the examples of decorative art, described in
the Homeric poems and so long believed to be the outcome of
poetic fancy, are now known to reflect the memory of Minoan
and Mycenæan arts and crafts.

A regional survey of Bronze Age civilization in the Mediterranean must properly begin with the island of Crete, where
the oldest remains precede by sundry centuries those from other

[1] Cf. the quotation at the head of this chapter.

74

Aegean sites. The surprising discoveries of Evans at Cnossus in Crete naturally led to intensive exploration and excavation in other parts of the island, in which British, American, Italian, and Greek archæologists have all achieved important results. Thus, more than twenty town sites, varying in size and importance, — some are as yet only partially excavated, — six votive caves, and some two dozen miscellaneous sites are now known. All of these lie in the eastern two-thirds of the island; for it is a remarkable fact, not yet adequately explained, that the western portion of Crete (all that part lying west of an imaginary line drawn southwards from the modern village of Retimo) has so far no pre-Hellenic remains to show. Of all these Cretan sites Cnossus is easily first in importance, for two reasons: the discoveries from there are richer than those made in any other place, and it is only at Cnossus that excavation has yielded an unbroken series of objects from the Neolithic Age down to the dawn of the Hellenic period. With the help of undoubtedly Egyptian objects unearthed in Crete and others found in Egypt, which were a puzzle to Egyptologists until the discoveries in Crete showed that they were Cretan, Evans was able to formulate a chronological scheme for the pre-Hellenic culture in that island. He distinguished three main eras, each of which he subdivided into three shorter periods. To the newly revealed culture he gave the name, Minoan.[1] Though further discoveries have led to occasional modifications in the dating proposed by Evans, there is no doubt about its correctness in the main.

In a previous chapter (p. 4) it has been noted that deep Neolithic deposits at Cnossus show that the site had been inhabited continuously for centuries before the first appearance of metal. Copper first makes its appearance soon after the middle of the fourth millennium; but its use must at first have been very restricted, so that we have here an admirable instance of gradual transition, lasting several centuries, from the Later

[1] Evans' term, though not free from objections and attacked in some quarters, has come to stay. But the term Minoan must be confined to Crete. For the pre-Greek civilization of the eastern Mediterranean as a whole perhaps the best name is Aegean. Minoan will then = the Cretan phase of this culture. For the nine Minoan periods see the note at the end of this chapter.

Stone Age to the fully developed Bronze Age. With the beginning of the second Early Minoan period material progress became notably more rapid. The fullest evidence for Cretan civilization at that stage (the first half of the third millennium) comes not from Cnossus, but from the little island of Mochlos and the town site of Vasiliki. The construction of the houses was remarkably substantial. The lower courses of the walls were of stone, while above were placed layers of sun-dried brick, strengthened by cross-beams forming a framework for the whole. The inside of the walls was covered with lime-plaster colored red. Already the builders showed a taste for simple internal decoration; later this developed into the elaborate buon frescoes, which are among the most remarkable relics of Cretan art. Painted pottery occurs sparingly at first; but in the Early Minoan II and III periods it becomes much more abundant and its decorative design more ambitious. Above all, in the last stage of the Early Minoan Age the potter's wheel and the kiln have come into use, the result being a noteworthy advance in ceramic technique. Of great interest, and for chronological purposes of great value, are numerous stone vases found at Mochlos and elsewhere in Early Minoan deposits. Some of these are importations from Egypt, others are Cretan imitations of Egyptian work. This evidence for early contact between the two countries is very significant; as will be seen hereafter, relations between Crete and the Land of the Nile continued unbroken for fifteen hundred years. Small marble figurines from the Cyclades discovered on Early Minoan sites are similarly an indication of intercourse between Crete and some of the smaller islands of the Archipelago.

The great palaces at Cnossus and at Phæstus in the south of the island, which attained their greatest extent and magnificence at the beginning of the Late Minoan period, had been rebuilt and enlarged more than once; for their beginnings go back to the second half of the third millennium (Middle Minoan I–II). A certain irregularity in the plan of the palaces is therefore not surprising. Extensive traces of burning make it clear that some serious catastrophe took place toward the end of the Middle Minoan III period. Probably the damage was caused by an earthquake; at all events it did not interrupt

a

b

CNOSSUS: *a*. MAGAZINE OF STORAGE JARS; *b*. STONE DRAINS

Plate 7

a

b

a. HAGIA TRIADA WITH MT. IDA IN BACKGROUND; *b.* HAGIA TRIADA
Plate 8

the occupation of the sites, for the palaces were rebuilt without delay, and at the same time were enlarged. To the first half of the second millennium belong not only these two reconstructed palaces, but the smaller country-house at Hagia Triada near Phæstus, and also some of the best preserved Cretan town sites, for example, at Palaikastro, Zakro, Gournia, and Tylissos. The houses varied in size, while the usual building material is sun-dried brick. Dwellings with two stories were probably not unusual, at all events among the more prosperous citizens. The general plan of the Late Minoan palace at Cnossus deserves somewhat more detailed description; that at Phæstus, though on a smaller scale, was very similar in its general arrangement. The whole complex of buildings at Cnossus is grouped around an open rectangular court, measuring approximately 190 × 85 feet. There were entrances to the palace on the north, south, and west. What has been conveniently described as the official and religious part of the palace lay on the western side of the court. Behind this group of buildings a series of parallel store-chambers was situated. There the excavator found, still *in situ*, a great number of mighty jars once used for the storage of grain and other supplies (Plate 7*a*). This row of magazines opened out into a long gallery running north and south. In the official part of the palace lay the throne room containing still in position a throne of plastered and painted gypsum. The walls were once decorated with frescoes; two griffins flanked the doorway. The block of buildings on the east of the great court made up the residential part of the palace. On this side one of the most impressive sights of the palace confronted the spectator, a grand staircase of five flights, and a colonnaded hall on the ground floor (Plate 6*b*). There were probably four stories to the palace building. From the first, great care was taken to ensure an adequate water-supply and a good system of drainage (Plate 7*b*). For, in addition to the elaborate drains and piping of the Late Minoan I palace, we have the testimony of clay pipes of excellent workmanship, which date from the first Middle Minoan Age.

When we survey the material culture of Crete during a thousand years (*c.* 2400–1400 B.C.) as a whole, we are struck not only by the divers forms in which their artistry manifested it-

self, but by their astonishing technical skill. From the end of
the Early Minoan period the Cretan potters had favored two
styles of ceramic painting, light decoration on a dark, and dark
designs on a light background. While both methods of ornamentation went on side by side, the former style was most popular in the Middle Minoan, the latter in the Late Minoan era.
Again, though there was at all times great diversity in the
shapes, the Middle Minoan craftsman was most skillful in making small vases, whose fabric is often of astonishing thinness and
delicacy. The so-called Kamares ware was the finest achievement of the Middle Minoan potter. On a black or very dark
ground a polychrome design was painted in white, purple, and
red. In the Late Minoan period the finest vases are of larger
size, high jars and high-stemmed cups, with elaborate plant
and marine designs painted in dark colors on a cream or buff
background.

Specimens of the goldsmith's and metal-worker's art, though
naturally far rarer than pottery, are no less masterly in execution. Several of the finest examples of gold-work have not actually been found in Crete; but the two famous gold cups from
Vaphio in southern Greece (Plate 11) and the wonderful bowl
discovered quite recently by Swedish excavators at Dendra were
either Cretan importations, or, if made in Greece, their technique is so similar to Cretan work that they may be cited as
examples of Minoan art. Among the most beautiful objects
found at Hagia Triada are three vases of steatite, fashioned, as
their shapes suggest, in imitation of metal work and once covered with thin gold foil. Depicted on them in low relief are various scenes, for instance, a boxing match and a procession of
harvesters. Engraved gems and seal-stones, figurines carved in
ivory or modelled in ivory and gold, objects in bronze, and delicate inlay-work, as in a gaming-board of ivory, crystal, and
blue paste, all these illustrate the multiplicity of Cretan arts
and crafts.

Finally, we must note the frescoes. Inevitably these are all
in a very fragmentary condition, and the glory of their original
coloring has faded. Yet sufficient remains to show how varied
was the palette and how admirably naturalistic the drawing of
the Minoan painter, both in the Middle and the Late Minoan

periods. Apart from their interest as works of art, these wall-paintings are particularly valuable evidence for the appearance and dress, and, to some extent, the religion and amusements, of the pre-Hellenic Cretans. The dress of the men is very simple, consisting usually of nothing more than a loin-cloth and a short skirt or kilt over it (Plate 9). Cloaks, which are depicted here and there, would be used in bad weather or perhaps on ceremonial occasions. The women are dressed in close-fitting bodices and flounced, bell-shaped skirts. Both sexes alike are represented with remarkably narrow waists, and, by an artistic convention, the unclothed parts of the female figures are generally painted white, those of the men brown. Of the favorite sports and amusements in Minoan society we may single out dancing and bull-baiting.

Exploration, as well as the study of paintings, seal-stones, and so forth, has taught us much about the religious practices of this people. Characteristic sacred places, at least from the beginning of the Middle Minoan period, are rock sanctuaries and votive caves. Thus, in the extreme east of the island, at Petsofa, there is a sanctuary where the excavators found a number of human and animal figurines and also single limbs fashioned in clay. Clearly the divinity who was believed to haunt this sanctuary was worshipped for his or her healing powers. Close to Cnossus, on Mt. Iuktas, there stood another sanctuary, frequented, as the finds show, throughout the Middle Minoan Age. Again there existed several votive caves, near Kamares high up on Mt. Ida, close to Psychro below Mt. Dicte, and at Skoteino, about three hours from Cnossus in an easterly direction. The first two have been thoroughly explored, and from the objects found there it appears that, while the Kamares cave was much frequented in the Middle Minoan period, but abandoned at the beginning of Late Minoan I, the Psychro cave does not seem to have attracted worshippers till the very end of the Middle Minoan period but enjoyed much esteem in the centuries that followed. We have, at all events, continuous evidence for mountain and cave worship on the part of the Minoans. Their chief divinity was a mother goddess; associated with her in the cult was a young male divinity, a conjunction of deities which recalls similar cults in Anatolia. In her representations the mother goddess is reg-

ularly flanked or accompanied by beasts, especially wild creatures like lions, pards, snakes, and birds. The shrine of this
divinity in the palace at Cnossus contained a large variety of
remarkable cult objects, libation bowls and tables, cups and jugs
used in sacrifice, a marble cross, and charming faïence panels of
domestic animals. Trees and pillars, which we find both on
seal impressions, on paintings, and on a painted sarcophagus
from Hagia Triada, were important cult objects; so too was the
double axe. Such pillars may perhaps be regarded as aniconic
symbols of the deity.

Though the material civilization enjoyed by the pre-Hellenic
inhabitants of Crete has been revealed in all its profuse and
splendid variety, we are almost wholly in ignorance of their
political history and institutions. This is chiefly due to the fact
that we have no written records to guide us. For the epigraphic material, though fairly abundant, is still undeciphered.
There are several kinds of Minoan script; the earliest is pictographic and is known mainly from seal impressions. Its beginnings go back to the last part of the Early Minoan period.
While there is much truth in Evans' observation that these
pictographs, inasmuch as they represent various tools and objects in common use, animals, plants, and so on, are "an epitome
of Minoan civilization," their value, so long as they are unread,
is still only partial. From this, the earliest form of Cretan
writing, developed an earlier and a later linear script; that is to
say, the objects depicted in the picture writing became simplified into conventional signs. There are numerous clay-tablets
inscribed with such linear writing. Some are accounts, — Evans
has been able to identify some of the numeral signs, — others
may be letters or despatches, whose decipherment would without
doubt greatly advance our knowledge of topics which even
abundant archæological material cannot illuminate.

If, then, we are for the present ignorant of the character of
Minoan government, if we can only guess that the ruler of
Cnossus was also the overlord of lesser chiefs and cities in other
parts of the island, we can be a little more positive about the
foreign relations of Crete in the third and the second millennia
B.C. The archæological evidence is sufficient to warrant the
statement that commercial relations between Egypt and Crete

existed continuously.[1] A prehistoric road, running from Cnossus to Phæstus, can still be traced in places. It not only served to link Cnossus with the chief city in southern Crete, but by giving convenient access to the harbors on the south coast afforded a means of transit from the Cretan capital to the African coast which was quicker and safer than an all-sea journey. The relations between Crete and Cyprus, Asia Minor, and Syria, prior to the Late Minoan period, are still extremely obscure; but it is likely that further excavations in those regions may produce evidence showing the existence of such intercourse in the third millennium. It was, however, with some of the Cyclades and with southern Greece that the foreign relations of Crete were closest.

The Cyclades, owing to their smallness and their geographical position, must from very early times have been liable to be influenced by more powerful neighbors. The copious evidence furnished by the remains of three settlements of different dates at Phylakopi in the island of Melos is corroborated by the scantier finds from other islands, notably Paros and Thera. The earliest remains are contemporary with those of the Early Minoan period in Crete. Cretan influence, which seems to have begun not later than the beginning of the Middle Minoan epoch, had reached its maximum before the end of that age, and continued during the greater part of the sixteenth century B.C. It can scarcely be doubted that these islands had come directly under Cretan domination. Some intercourse with the

[1] In view of the assertion of some recent scholars that Egypt in her imperial days exercised sovereignty over Crete and other islands in the Aegean, it seems desirable to indicate the more noteworthy archæological data for Egypto–Cretan relations. They cannot be said to warrant such sweeping generalizations. (1) Egyptian stone vases in Early Minoan deposits. (2) Seal stones made in Crete but imitating Egyptian types of Dynasties VI–IX. (3) A Diorite monument of User (Dyn. XII) in a Middle Minoan II deposit at Cnossus. (4) Middle Minoan pottery found on several Egyptian sites (e.g. Abydos and Kahun) with objects of the XIIth Dynasty. (5) Vase-lid with cartouche of the Hyksos king, Khian, found at Cnossus. (6) Late Minoan objects found in Egypt contemporaneous with finds of the early XVIIIth Dynasty. (7) References in Egyptian inscriptions to the people of Keftiu; their general appearance on Egyptian paintings is very similar to the Cretans as known from the Cretan frescoes. (8) Association of Late Minoan III pottery with late XVIIIth Dynasty finds at Amarna.

mainland existed also. It became more intensive by the middle of the second millennium; and, when (*c.* 1400 B.C.) the power of the Cretan kings came to an abrupt end and the dominant influence in the eastern Aegean passed to Mycenæ, the islands were also affected by the changed political conditions. Cretan importations to the islands became scarce and finally ceased altogether, but mainland pottery found its way thither in abundance.

So far the finds of the earlier Bronze Age in southern Greece have not been very copious, and for the most part they come from a very restricted geographical area, the Argolid and the region about the Isthmus of Corinth. The dwellings inhabited by the people of this age were simple rectangular structures of sun-dried brick, often on stone foundations. While both plain and painted pottery has been unearthed in considerable quantities, metal objects are not abundant. Yet they suffice to show that men were no longer in the Neolithic Age. It is not till *c.* 1600 B.C., or shortly before, that Cretan influence on the Greek mainland becomes marked. Its outward manifestation is a very great advance in arts and crafts. The work of the native potter, though it does not disappear entirely, is for the time submerged by the popularity of foreign fabrics, which are promptly and successfully imitated. If Mycenæan art, though so close to Minoan, nevertheless developed something of a character of its own, we must attribute the fact to the survival, in some degree, of endemic styles of decoration. How the predominance of Cretan culture in Greece came about is an obscure problem. Did the kings of Crete introduce their Minoan culture in southern Greece by conquest, followed by some measure of colonization? Or should we rather postulate a more gradual process of peaceful infiltration? In the sixteenth century B.C. we find a dynasty ruling at Mycenæ and apparently exercising control over the whole Argolic peninsula. Contemporaneous with them, influential dynasties were established in Thebes and Orchomenus in central Greece. Were these Mycenæan princes a ruling caste, racially akin to the lords of Cnossus and governing a subject population in Greece of different stock? Or were they of the same race as their subjects, but successful in imposing on them the more advanced alien culture of Crete, the more so as they may for a time have been vassals of Cnossus? Much study and excavation are still needed before these questions, especially the ethnic problems involved, can be solved with even approximate certainty. The historian and the archæologist may well comfort themselves with the dictum of Edward Fitzgerald that the power of suspending judgment is an essential attribute of good scholarship.

At least there is no doubt about the power and prosperity of the sixteenth century rulers of Mycenæ. For the shaft graves in which they were buried were filled with examples of the potter's, the metal-worker's, and the jeweler's skill, rivalling the finest Minoan work. This is especially true of several bronze daggers on which hunting scenes were cunningly inlaid in gold (Plate 12), and of a series of gold masks which covered the faces of the deceased kings. About one hundred years later the kings of Mycenæ — presumably we have to reckon with a new dynasty, though it would be rash to assume also a marked racial difference — were interred not in shaft graves but in domed chambers, to which owing to their shape the name "beehive tombs" has been given. Examples of this type of funeral chamber have also been found, elsewhere than at Mycenæ, over a wide area; this circumstance, coupled with the fact that the same types of pottery and other objects have been discovered in different parts of the Peloponnese, Attica, Bœotia, and Eubœa, makes the assumption of a general hegemony exercised by Mycenæ over southern and central Greece, and by this time also over the Cyclades, extremely probable. The zenith of Mycenæan power was reached in the fourteenth and thirteenth centuries, that is to say, after the downfall of Cnossus and Phæstus. The citadel and palace of Mycenæ were enlarged, and similar building activity took place almost contemporaneously in the dependent stronghold of Tiryns.

The Mycenæan citadel was situated on the side of a hill from the summit of which the lords of Mycenæ could keep a look-out over a great part of the Argolid, northward to Corinth, southward to the Gulf of Nauplia. Massive, so-called Cyclopean, walls, constructed of great limestone blocks, enclosed the palace area, which could be entered by two gates. The chief, now dubbed the Lion Gate, was on the northwest side; it derives

its name from the triangular slab, carved in relief with two
rampant lions with a sacral pillar between them, which surmounted the lintel of the gate. The lintel itself is a huge block
of stone measuring 16 × 8 × 3 feet. The heraldic design of
the slab has its counterpart in Minoan and Mycenæan seal-
stones. There was a subsidiary entrance on the north, near the
eastern end of the fortification wall. The best preserved example from this age of fortification and palace construction on
the mainland is, however, at Tiryns; for, as a whole, the Mycenæan palace and walls are poorly preserved. The hill at
Tiryns contained an upper and a lower citadel. While the latter
seems to have been a place of refuge in case of need for the population of the plain, the upper citadel contained a palace. The
whole enceinte was strongly fortified. The thickness of the
walls varies between sixteen and fifty-seven feet. They are
strengthened with towers, while on two sides are galleries cut
in the rock into which a number of subterranean store-chambers
open out. The main entrance was on the east, and the road
led up an inclined plane through two pillared gateways into a
spacious courtyard. The chief hall of the palace, approached
through a vestibule, was of rectangular shape. In the centre
was the hearth; the floor was of concrete, while the roof was
supported by four wooden pillars. Though these have perished,
the stone bases into which they fitted still remain. Supplementary excavations have shown that the walls of the rooms in the
palace were extensively decorated with wall-paintings; their
character is very similar to that of the frescoes found in Crete.

Two other regions must be briefly noticed to complete our
survey of the eastern Mediterranean area. Northern Greece,
and the adjacent lands of Macedonia and Thrace, until late
were little or not at all affected by the Aegean culture. Exploration of Thessalian sites has proved the existence of a well-
developed Neolithic civilization there in the third millennium,
which lasted well on into the second. By the seventeenth
century B.C. this region had entered the Bronze Age. Its
cultural relations so far seem to have been mainly with the
North. There has been relatively so little systematic excavation
in this area, and scarcely any in Macedonia and Thrace, that
it is impossible to reach any adequate historical conclusions.

Plate 9

a

b

a. Cup-Bearer Fresco at Cnossus; b. Flying Fish Fresco from Melos

Courtesy of the Metropolitan Museum

a

b

BEE-HIVE TOMB AT ORCHOMENUS: *a.* Main Entrance
b. Entrance to Inner Chamber

Plate 10

The influence of Mycenæan culture seems by the fourteenth century to have extended into southern Thessaly, but it was not potent enough to drive out the more primitive local art and pot fabrics. The migrations of peoples, whose arrival coincides with the beginning of the Iron Age, wrought drastic changes which left no portion of Greece untouched.

Troy (Hissarlik), the first pre-Hellenic site to be investigated by Schliemann, stood a short distance inland, but overlooked the eastern entrance to the Hellespont (Dardanelles). Its geographical position laid its inhabitants open to foreign influences from at least two sides — from the uplands of Anatolia and from Europe. Of the remains of nine superimposed settlements at Hissarlik the last three do not concern us here because they belong to the Greek or Græco-Roman periods. The lowest settlement of all (c. 2500 B.C.?) belongs to the Chalcolithic, or to the very beginning of the Bronze Age. The second city was distinguished by a much more advanced culture. It was fortified with walls of sun-baked brick laid on massive stone foundations. Objects of gold, silver, and bronze show that its craftsmen were not greatly inferior to the artists of contemporary Crete. The pottery, too, is well made, but turned by hand. Apparently the potter's wheel was still unknown there towards the end of the third millennium. The third, fourth, and fifth settlements (c. 2100–1500 B.C.?) were very poor; their occupants cannot have exercised any political influence or power. At the same time archæological finds seem to show the existence of some trade connection between Troy, Thrace, and the Danubian basin. The sixth settlement, though small in size, was clearly occupied by a powerful dynasty. The palace that once stood there has gone; but the remains of the fortification walls, made of well-wrought stone and strengthened at intervals by turrets, show that the princes of Troy dwelt in a citadel as strong as were those of the rulers of Mycenæ and Tiryns.

When, after surveying the pre-Hellenic civilization of the Aegean as manifested to us in the archæological remains, we turn to the political history and development of this area in the third and second millennia B.C., we pass from concrete facts to the realm of highly speculative conjecture. In the third millennium the different regions within the Aegean area which have been described developed independently, though we must of course reckon with a certain degree of trade intercourse between them. By the beginning of the second millennium the more advanced culture of Crete was beginning to spread very rapidly beyond the limits of the island. It affected first the Cyclades and then the Greek mainland; so that, before the middle of the second millennium, the priest-kings of Cnossus exercised suzerainty over a considerable empire. In other words, not only the cultural but the political influence of Crete was paramount in the eastern Mediterranean until the catastrophe at the end of the Late Minoan II period (c. 1400 B.C.), to which reference has already been made. The nature of this disaster, in which not only the palaces at Cnossus and Phæstus were destroyed, but desolation came upon the many other Cretan towns which had enjoyed such signal prosperity in the preceding centuries, is obscure. But the completeness of the destruction caused makes the conclusion irresistible that foreign invaders were responsible. It is most likely that they came from the Greek mainland; for, though the great palaces in Crete were not properly rebuilt, their sites and the town sites also continued to be occupied. Minoan culture continued; the pottery and the artistic objects of the third Late Minoan Age are excellent, even though they lack the brilliance and costliness which distinguish the productions of previous centuries. In short, after c. 1400 B.C., if we know nothing of the political history of Crete, we can see clearly that the cultural history follows a course closely parallel to that of Greece or the islands. Here, as there, the expiring Bronze Age merges into the early Iron Age.

The truth is that the number of well-attested historical facts, or generalizations that are safe because founded on a sufficiency of archæological material, is regrettably small. Apart from the Cretan disaster the following data are of special importance:

1. The Egyptian records refer to two occasions on which invaders from over the sea joined in an attack on the Land of the Nile. In the assault at the time of Merenptah (cf. p. 95) the Libyans were reinforced by five different tribes. Of these the Ekwesh may perhaps be equated with the Achæans. Nearly

thirty years later Ramses III (cf. p. 96) was obliged to repel two more formidable invasions. The peoples of the sea formed an important contingent of this formidable horde of enemies.

2. Although, about the end of the twelfth century, the Mycenæan power was overthrown, and Mycenæ, Tiryns, and other sites were burnt, Mycenæan culture lingered on; it was not suddenly extinguished.

3. Greek tradition knew of a war between a Greek host and Troy. Several dates were assigned for that event; the most generally accepted placed the fall of Troy in 1183 B.C. Tradition further speaks of the Achæans as a dominant race or clan in Crete and Greece during the thirteenth century B.C.[1] The invasions of the Dorians into Greece is put fully a century later.

4. The beginning of the Iron Age in Greece can be dated approximately to 1000 B.C.; isolated iron objects are found earlier; in the interior of Anatolia this metal, it would now appear, was known at the beginning of the second millenium. It is, however, probable that the inhabitants of Greece owed their more extended knowledge of it to invaders from central Europe.

5. As far as the pottery is concerned — and there is little other material to work on for the period from 1100–900 B.C. — the two centuries after the downfall of Mycenæ seem to have been an age of great cultural depression. Before its conclusion a new style of pottery, called from the style of its decoration, Geometric, is found over a wide area. But we cannot associate this ware with any particular people or group of immigrants to Greece. It seems to be a development from the more debased form of Late Mycenæan art modified by some foreign influences. Two facts, moreover, are of great significance: although the decorative schemes on Geometric vases are crude and "primitive," on the technical side (well-levigated clay, good paint, etc.) they are excellent (Plate 13a). Secondly, while Mycenæan pottery varies little in character wherever it is found, the Geometric shows a great many variations. This fact is note-

[1] The thalassocracy of "Minos," mentioned by Thucydides, is generally interpreted as a maritime empire ruled by an Achæan dynasty in Crete in the thirteenth century. They would presumably be independent of, but on a friendly footing with, the Achæan rulers of Mycenæ.

worthy. It suggests that, after the overthrow of Mycenæ, Greece was broken up into small political and social groups, although their members may have been in many cases of the same stock. Such a condition of affairs would be promoted also by the peculiar geographical features of Greece, and was one which was actually in existence at the beginning of the "historic" period of Greece.

That considerable migrations from central Europe occurred in the second half of the second millennium is beyond dispute, but when and how often is quite uncertain. It has been argued that the Achæan rulers of Mycenæ, who dispossessed an earlier Mycenæan dynasty (that of the shaft-graves?) were in reality a central European body of conquerors. The view is by no means free from difficulties; but they are hardly as great as those encountered by scholars who, accepting later Greek tradition on this point at its face value, see in the Achæans only one of a number of tribes indigenous in Greece. Moreover, though later traditions represent migrations such as the Dorian as a single event, all historical analogies point to the fact that, when a considerable body of nomadic or semi-nomadic peoples are on the move, their infiltration into more distant region is a gradual process. It is thus possible that a further Achæan invasion occurred at a somewhat later date, and resulted in a wider distribution of Achæan political power in the thirteenth century. If that were so, it would not be surprising if the accounts written in a much later age combined into one what were really several migratory movements, prior to the latest with which the name of the Dorians is associated.

That the Greek legends of the Trojan war have within them a kernel of historic fact is very probable. That being admitted, one is tempted to regard the historic event — a war between a group of peoples from the Greek mainland, under the leadership of Mycenæ, and a coalition led by the lord of Troy — as an episode in the larger clash between East and West, which culminated in the overthrow of Hatti and the invasion of Syria.

The latest migratory wave into Greece, the so-called Dorian invasion, seems to have begun about, or soon after, 1100 B.C. The two to three centuries following this date are, in a certain sense, a formative period. For during that time new racial elements found their way into Greece, mainly from the Northwest, which in some cases dispossessed, in others coalesced with, the older population. Many of the mainlanders, deprived of their homes, were driven forth to found communities elsewhere. Thus Crete, the islands of the Archipelago, and the coast of Asia Minor all received their quota of new settlers. These earliest stages in the evolution of the city-states of historic Greece are entirely lost to our view. Whatever the significance of such names, the Greeks of a later time were accustomed to think that the whole body of Hellenes was made up of several large groups, differing one from the other to some extent in customs and speech. The Aeolian group was in occupation of Thessaly and Bœotia, and also of the most northern section of the west coast of Asia Minor, together with adjacent islands like Lesbos. The Ionians were in Attica, in most of the Cyclades, and along the central portion of the Asia Minor littoral, where they thus became the southern neighbors of the Aeolic communities. Finally, the Dorians occupied the greater part of the Peloponnese, Crete, Melos, Thera, and the islands near or off the southwest coast of Asia Minor, and some portion of the mainland lying opposite to these. The distribution of Greek dialects in historic times is in general accord with this grouping.

A review of the Bronze Age in the eastern Mediterranean may fittingly terminate with a brief account of Homeric society. This is not the place for even a short discussion of the numerous problems, archæological, linguistic, and literary, which together make up the "Homeric Question." Even granted that the *Iliad* and *Odyssey*, as they have come down to us, are substantially the work of a single genius, we can do no more than guess at the character of the earlier material utilized by the poet for his great epics. Bards or "Rhapsodes" must have exercised their art at the court of Mycenæan and Minoan chieftains, composing hymns in honor of gods or narrative poems recounting the exploit of a hero. Their choice of subject will often have been dictated by circumstances; that is to say, the most acceptable hero, whose deeds could be extolled in lays, would be the reputed ancestor of the chief whose guest or retainer the minstrel was. It was but a step — though admittedly a great one — to combine in a more intricate narrative a series of exploits of one hero, and to intertwine therewith the fortunes of lesser heroic figures. Thus the short lay developed into the longer epic. That the *Iliad* and *Odyssey* — the only complete heroic epics of Greece that have survived — were composed in the Iron Age is beyond dispute. The probability is that they are not later than *c.* 850 B.C., while their dialect proclaims the home of the poet to have been in Anatolian Ionia. But the society which they portray is in the main that of the late Bronze Age in the Aegean. Nevertheless, there are important features which belong to a later age than that. Such are the use of iron, the practice of disposing of the dead by cremation, not, as was the custom in the Minoan and Mycenæan civilizations, by inhumation, and, in general, the Homeric religion. To use the Homeric poems, as has often been done, in order to reconstruct a picture of early Greek society is only justifiable within certain limits. There was in archaic Greece a number of similarities to, or rather survivals from, the earlier epoch; for example, the likeness of the Spartan to the Homeric monarchy has often been pointed out. But, taken as a whole, these poems, in so far as they depict a uniform civilization, provide us with information which is complementary to the archæological evidence for the latest phase of Mycenæan prosperity and domination.

Homeric society is strongly aristocratic. It is only of the nobles that we get a detailed picture. To the rest of the free population references are sparingly made. They are taken for granted by the poet, as is the institution of slavery. Male and female slaves are found employed on the domains and in the palaces of the great. The title *basileus* (chief or king) is often applied to other nobles besides the king; for instance, in the land of the Phæacians described in the *Odyssey* there are twelve *basileis* in addition to King Alcinous. Thus, the monarch is merely the first among a number of leading chiefs, who are the immediate supporters of the throne and form the nucleus of an aristocratic council, which advises him and may even act as a check on the royal prerogative. Yet, with this limitation, the supremacy of the king is clearly defined. His office is hereditary, and he traces his descent from a divine or heroic ancestor, a fact which adds much to his authority. He combines within himself the function of commander-in-chief in war, judge, and priest. The prestige of Agamemnon in the *Iliad* is so great that even the venerable Nestor, when he gives advice in Agamemnon's council, is very submissive in tone. The economic basis of society is agriculture. The man without land of his own to till, who has to eke out a livelihood by working another's fields, is thought the most wretched of beings, little better than serf or slave. Of trades and crafts we hear little, as is to be expected in a society where the economy is still mainly that of the household. Most of what is needed even on a large domain is produced on the spot, and there is little specialization in callings. Nor are the nobles above doing manual work, if the need arises. Paris of Troy takes a hand in the building of his house, and the Greek Odysseus can make a raft, builds a part of his own palace, and knows how to mow and plow. Thus, when occasionally a specific occupation is named in the poems, it is either a craft which, owing to the exceptional technique required for its exercise, has already passed into the hands of specialists — *e.g.* the calling of the smith and worker in metal — or else it is one of a very limited number of professions, like that of the herald or the leech or the minstrel. The herald, since he acts as the messenger and general amanuensis of the monarch, is a person of some importance. Merchants are rarely mentioned and are most often foreigners, for example, Phœnician traders. So, too, the imported wares referred to here and there are chiefly luxury articles, like purple-dyed stuffs from Sidon. Commerce is carried on by barter, but metallic weights are in use. The two principal occupations of the nobility are hunting and war.

The social and moral ideas are those of a still rude and warlike people, of a society in which a man enjoys little safety outside his own group. Yet society is by no means wholly lawless. Blood-feuds can already be settled by payment of compensation to the relatives of the deceased. The community or its ruler does not interfere except on the demand of both parties to the feud. The sanctity of oaths is great; hospitality to the stranger who takes refuge at the hearth is a sacred duty. Strong, too, are the ties of family, as we should expect in a society that is strictly patriarchal. Homer's portraits of women — for instance, Helen and Andromache in the *Iliad*, Penelope and Nausicaa in the *Odyssey* — are not only masterly in themselves, but suggest that women in that age enjoyed a position of more dignity and somewhat more freedom than was generally the case in classical Greece. But there is also a less agreeable side to this picture of Homeric society. The stranger, except where he has sought and received the rights of hospitality in a particular house, carries his life in his hand among an alien community. Piracy is an honorable calling, and we may recall that Aristotle includes it among the occupations practised by men in a semi-nomadic state. The unhappy lot of the orphan boy is painted in a few poignant words by the poet. In this respect it is interesting to note a marked advance in humane ideas in the poet Hesiod (*c.* 700 B.C.); he decries injury done to orphans as one of the most serious offenses. Finally, there is here and there a primitive savagery in the Homeric poems. We may guess that there was more of it in the material utilized by Homer, but that he has softened most of the brutality present in earlier lays. We are still left, however, with one example of human sacrifice, Achilles' offering to the dead Patroclus. Shocking to Greek even more than to modern notions is the mutilation of Hector's corpse; and we may wince even at the stern punishment meted out by Odysseus, after the slaying of the suitors, to the unfaithful servants in his palace.

The gods and their worship in Homer seem to bear no resemblance to the divinities and cults, so far as we know them, of Minoan-Mycenæan days. Homeric men created the gods in their own image. The deities are, as it were, men and women of superhuman stature and beauty; immortal, all-powerful, and all-knowing; yet subject to the same pains and passions as mankind. Zeus, the "father of gods and men" presides in the assembly of the gods, envisaged by the poet to be situated on the summit of Mt. Olympus in Thessaly. Though the several deities have their several spheres of activity or avocations — Poseidon is god of the sea, Apollo the god of prophecy and patron of the arts, Ares the god of war — they are subordinate, though sometimes disobedient, to the will of Zeus. Thus the Pantheon of Homer is like a large superhuman family. Its

Plate 11

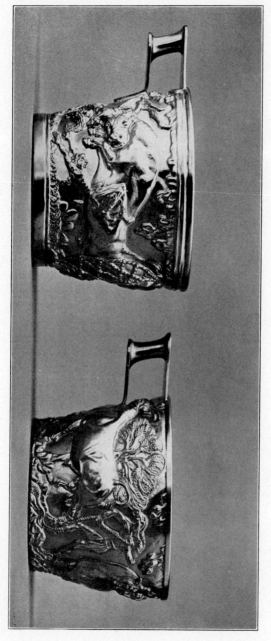

THE VAPHIO CUPS

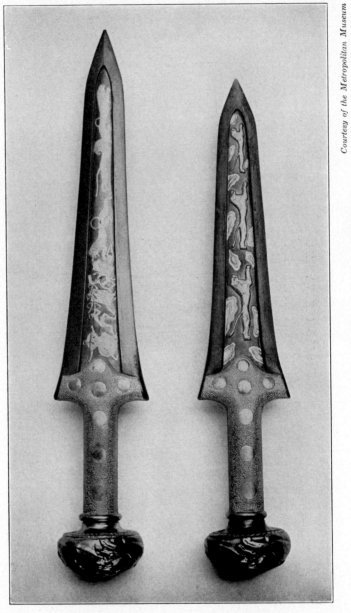

INLAID DAGGERS FROM MYCENÆ

Plate 12

members take some interest in human affairs; they reward the righteous and punish the evil-doer. Sometimes their interference is capricious; they harm those who do not deserve it, or support their favorites among mankind irrespective of their moral character. Some of the gods have temples erected to them by men, or they have sacred places set aside by men, which they prefer to all others — Zeus at Dodona in Epirus, Apollo in the Troad and at Delphi. The Homeric gods became the gods of Greece, those Olympian deities who were immortalized in the drama and in plastic works of art and were worshipped wherever Hellenes were gathered together. There were other elements in Greek religion, the cult of the dead and hero-worship, of which the former was certainly older than the Homeric poems. Of such worship and ritual there is scarcely a trace in the *Iliad* and *Odyssey*.[1]

[1] The following are the approximate dates of the Minoan periods. It should be noted that L.M. II is peculiar to Cnossus. On other Cretan sites L.M. I passes without break into L.M. III.

E.M. I	3400–3100	M.M. I	2400–2100
E.M. II	3100–2600	M.M. II	2100–1900
E.M. III	2600–2400	M.M. III	1900–1600

L.M. I	1600–1500
L.M. II	1500–1400
L.M. III	1400–1100

CHAPTER VII

SYRIA, PALESTINE, AND THEIR NEIGHBORS, 1200–900 B.C.

> *Now Israel went out against the Philistines to battle, and pitched beside Eben-ezer; and the Philistines pitched in Aphek. And the Philistines put themselves in array against Israel; and when they joined battle, Israel was smitten before the Philistines; and they slew of the army in the field about four thousand men.* — I Samuel, iv, 1–2.

THE second half of the thirteenth century B.C. was a very momentous period in the history of the Near East. The political power of Egypt and of Hatti was declining; new peoples, little heard of before, were emerging into greater influence in Palestine and Syria. In Babylonia, Cassite rulers continued to occupy their precarious throne, their chief anxiety being their northern neighbors of Assyria. The early attempts to advance to the middle Euphrates made by Assyrian kings had, as we have seen, been checked by Shupiluliuma and his successors. But the Assyrian kings of the thirteenth century, especially Shalmaneser I and Tukulti-ninurta, enlarged their kingdom by wars on the North and East; on several occasions they successfully attacked Babylon also. But though more than one Cassite monarch suffered defeat and even deposition at the hands of the hardy northerners, there was not yet any permanent control by Assyria over the Land of Two Rivers. Nevertheless, in spite of a temporary eclipse after the time of Tukulti-ninurta, the Assyrians stand out as the most vigorous of the Near-Eastern peoples at this time.

The most serious threat to Hittite power in the thirteenth century was in the West. Already in Hattushilish III's time a king of Akhkhiawa — the equation with Achæa, Achæans, is tempting but not certainly proven — is heard of as an enemy,

94

and aggression from this quarter apparently continued under Dudkhaliash III. When, about 1200 B.C., the Hittite empire in Asia Minor collapsed, it was before a combined assault of several peoples from the West who overran Asia Minor and flowed over into Syria and Palestine. We can only surmise that the military strength of Hatti had been seriously weakened before this time, and that this process had been accompanied by a certain degree of internal unrest and disintegration. The history of Asia Minor for several centuries after this catastrophe is still one of the unsolved problems. A portion of the Hittite people continued to survive to the eighth century in northern Syria. The capital of this late Hittite principality was at Carchemish on the Euphrates, a site which had for long been one of the southern outposts of Hittite power and civilization.

The western hordes who had destroyed one empire, by their proximity to Egypt threatened another. The Egyptian Pharaoh, Merenptah, who succeeded Ramses II, some twenty years earlier had had to defend his kingdom against foreign attack. The first assault came from his western neighbors of Libya. Infiltration, in some degree, of Libyans into Egypt had probably occurred for centuries past; occasionally Egyptian military intervention on and beyond the border had been necessary. But about 1220 B.C. the Libyans, reinforced by men from overseas — from Crete and perhaps the Greek mainland — attempted a regular invasion of the Land of the Nile. The attack was repulsed by Merenptah, but a possible renewal of the threat from this quarter must have caused him and his successors constant anxiety. In addition, after Merenptah's death (c. 1215 B.C.) several weak rulers occupied the Egyptian throne, and the last twenty years of the XIXth Dynasty seem to have been a period of anarchy at home. This disturbed internal condition offered a favorable opportunity for further assaults on Egypt from the West. These raids, though not so formidable as the invasion of 1220 B.C., nevertheless must have caused much damage to property and some loss of life. The second king of the XXth Dynasty, Ramses III, attempted to cope drastically with what had become a very serious problem. His energetic military reforms were carried out just in time. For now Libyans made common cause with the miscellaneous peoples who had destroyed Hatti and had swarmed into Syria. About 1194 B.C., and again two years later, formidable attacks by land and sea were launched against Egypt. By a supreme effort Ramses III and his people on both occasions defeated the enemy; the fact that Egyptian naval strength was greater and better organized than that of the invaders doubtless accounts to a great extent for the Egyptian success. Thus was the danger of another Hyksos occupation narrowly averted. But the days of Egypt as an imperial power were over. The remaining twenty years of Ramses's long reign were disturbed by occasional Libyan raids and by a domestic conspiracy. He was succeeded by a long line of undistinguished monarchs, all of whom bore the same name as he. The predominating influence in Near-Eastern affairs, which Egypt had exercised for so long, passed now to Asiatic powers; in the end Egypt became, and remained for centuries, the dependency of first one and then another Asiatic empire.

Of the peoples of Syria and Palestine, who now emerge into greater prominence, the most important are the Aramæans, the Hebrews, and the Philistines. The Aramæans were Semitic nomads who, on their first appearance in history, were in occupation of the desert lands bordering on the Middle Euphrates. From the sixteenth to the thirteenth centuries sections of these Bedouins filtered through into Syria, while others, crossing the Euphrates, moved on in the direction of the Tigris. In the twelfth century the Aramæans are again mainly concentrated in the Syrian desert. The check to their expansion northward and westward may have been due partly to the action of Assyria; still more it probably resulted from the general advance of foreign tribes from Asia Minor, which has already been noted. When, in the following century, the Aramæans become more prominent, they are firmly established at important points like Damascus, which gave them control of the great caravan routes from Syria into Mesopotamia.

The Hebrews, too, were originally nomads and racially not very different from the Aramæans. Before the middle of the second millennium they had entered Canaan from the North. At a time when western Palestine was still securely under Egyptian rule, these Semites must have eked out a bare existence in the hilly regions bordering on the River Jordan. Some of them, faced by the prospect of famine, eventually found their way to the frontiers of Egypt. Here the treatment accorded them was at first friendly; but later one of the Pharaohs compelled them to labor as serfs under the lash of Egyptian masters. Ultimately, after a prolonged period of captivity, they were enabled to leave Egypt. After passing a considerable time in the desert lands of the Sinai peninsula and the regions east of the Jordan, the wanderers entered the more fertile country of Palestine. Unfortunately there is still no kind of unanimity among scholars about the dates of, and the length of time consumed by, these movements, which in the Biblical narrative of a later date are familiar as the Going down into Egypt, the Bondage in Egypt, and the Exodus. The Jewish historian Josephus, writing in the first century A.D., brings the appearance of the Hebrews in Palestine into connection with the expulsion of the Hyksos. On this hypothesis their entry into Egypt must have occurred at some time between Dynasty XIII and XVII; the Exodus would have to be regarded as one episode in the expulsion of the "shepherd kings." There are, however, serious objections to so early a date for these migrations of Hebrew tribes, and it is safer to place the Egyptian sojourn under the later kings of the XVIIIth Dynasty and the Exodus during, or perhaps at the end of, the long reign of Ramses II. A well-known inscription of Merenptah informs us of a rebellion in southern Palestine at the beginning of that king's rule. Among the insurgents are the Isirail, whose name must clearly be equated with the Biblical Israel. From this notice it is obvious that, by the middle of the thirteenth century, Hebrew tribes had secured a definite foothold in the country west of the Jordan.

Originally nomadic and pastoral in their mode of life, they were gradually converted to an agricultural and stationary existence. A common interest united them, namely, to make common cause against the earlier inhabitants of the land, the Canaanites. Nevertheless, the geographical situation of the Canaanite cities, which separated the northern from the southern group of Hebrew tribes, made effective alliance difficult. The struggle must have lasted a good number of years and was carried on with varying success. In the process the invaders learnt not a little from their enemies; they became habituated to farming operations, to town life, and began to forget the life of the desert, and even paid honor to the gods of Canaan in addition to their own tribal god, Yahweh. At last a great Canaanite alliance was formed and opposed by six of the Hebrew tribes under the leadership of Barak, of the tribe Naphtali. The Song of Deborah (*Judges*, v) is a pæan of victory, commemorating the decisive defeat of the Canaanite army by the Hebrews. "The kings came and fought, then fought the kings of Canaan in Taanach by the waters of Megiddo. They took no gain of money. They fought from Heaven; the stars in their courses fought against Sisera. The river Kishon swept them away, that ancient river, the river Kishon."

Among the foreign peoples who entered Syria and Palestine and threatened Egypt after destroying the Hittite empire were the Philistines (Egypt. *Peleset*). Their appearance and settlement in southern Palestine thus occurred shortly after the time when the Hebrew tribes had finally broken the resistance of their neighbors in Canaan. Before the new and powerful immigrants the Hebrew tribes on the coast were compelled to retire into the hill country.

The racial origin and earlier home of the Philistines are still greatly disputed. The one certain fact about them is that they were a non-Semitic people. That they were Minoan Cretans, as has been suggested by some scholars, is impossible not only on chronological grounds but because the dress and armature of the two peoples were markedly different. On the other hand, local imitations of Mycenæan pottery — commonly called sub-Mycenæan — which have been unearthed in considerable quantities in Philistia, are very similar to wares found over an extended area of the eastern Aegean, namely in eastern Crete, Cyprus, and Caria. There is, moreover, a Hebrew tradition that the Philistines came from Caphtor. The equation Caphtor = Crete is now accepted by a majority of scholars. However, the balance of probability seems to lie with the view that the Philistines came originally from Caria, but that, before joining with other tribes in the attack on Egypt at the beginning of the twelfth century, they had found a temporary home in Crete. Their settlement in the coastal regions of Palestine then followed hard upon their repulse, together with the other attackers, by

Ramses III. In this new home, during the twelfth century, they consolidated their position by force of arms, and formed, in fact, a conquering aristocracy ruling over the earlier Semitic inhabitants of the land. Their success was due not so much to better arms and a more warlike temper as to a greater skill in political and military organization. Like the governing class of Spartans in a later age, the Philistines saw that their own security in the midst of a numerically superior subject population, whose race and customs alike differed from their own, could only be assured by imposing on themselves a strict military régime. The pentapolis of Philistine cities, — Ashdod, Gath, Ashkelon, Ekron, and Gaza, — formed a close political confederation of city-states, each ruled by a despot (*seren*). So long as their power remained unbroken these cities controlled the main highway from Egypt to Syria and beyond, while at Gaza there branched off the main route to the Dead Sea and to Arabia. Furthermore, at the time of their greatest political expansion, when their authority along the coast reached northward beyond Joppa, they were master of all the ports lying south of the Phœnician cities.

How long the Philistines were content to dwell in southwestern Palestine before embarking on a larger career of conquest, is by no means clear. It cannot have been less than fifty years, and was probably as much as a century. In this interval they seem to have become largely assimilated in speech and manners to the Canaanite peoples whom they had subjected on their entry into Philistia. During this period of Philistine consolidation the Israelites had suffered severely at the hands of the Bedouin tribes of Transjordania — Moabites, Ammonites, and Midianites. They were thus much weakened when the Philistines made a bold bid for supremacy over all Palestine. In a single engagement the latter crushed the military resistance of the Israelites, and further broke their spirit by capturing the Ark of the Lord and razing Shiloh. These events occurred in the first quarter of the eleventh century. Then, for about sixty years, Israel was held in subjection by the conquerors, who exacted tribute rigorously and minimized the danger of an Israelite rising by placing garrisons at various strategic points throughout the country.

When, about 1025 B.C., the first attempt to regain national
independence was made, it was begun in Transjordania, in the
land of Gilead, a region which seems not even to have been
a Philistine protectorate. The ringleaders in this struggle
were the prophet-priest Samuel and Saul, the Benjaminite
ruler of Gilead. Gradually Saul was able to rally many of
the Israelites to his standard. He fought with success against
the oppressors, until he was finally defeated and killed at the
battle of Mt. Gilboa, a little southeast of the historic site of
Megiddo. With this disaster ended the first attempt to throw
off the Philistine yoke. A second trial of strength was destined
to be more successful. For David of Judah, who had first
fought for Saul and then, after quarrelling with him, had fled to
and come to terms with the Philistines, became, after Saul's
death, ruler of Judah, with his capital at Hebron. For a while
the northern part of Saul's kingdom formed a separate state
under Saul's young son, Ishbaal. The Philistines do not seem
to have interfered with the arrangement, seeing rather in the
ensuing strife between the northern and southern groups of Israelites a safeguard against renewed aggression on themselves.
But, after the assassination of Ishbaal by two of his own officers,
David was able to establish an ascendancy over all the tribes
and was acclaimed king of all Israel. How long before this momentous event the Philistines may have begun to suspect the
loyalty of their vassal we cannot tell. But the unification of
Israel under David was followed by a Philistine invasion of
Judah. David was hardly prepared for so prompt an attack.
Since Hebron was not easily defensible, he retired to the hill
fortress of Adullam. From here he harassed the enemy by raids,
until such time as he had received reinforcements from the more
distant parts of his new kingdom. Then only he ventured on
open attack, and in two engagements defeated the Philistine
army decisively, forcing his opponents to retire back to Philistia.

The next step in the war of liberation was a sudden attack
on Jerusalem, held by the Jebusite allies of the Philistines.
Its capture was for several reasons of singular value to David.
It was the finest natural stronghold in the country; its strategic
position gave David an advantage such as his predecessor had

never enjoyed; and it was admirably suited to be the new capital of the united Hebrew kingdom, because it was, as it were, neutral territory. A capital in the old territory of the southern tribes might well have aroused the distrust or dislike of the northern group, who had but recently given their allegiance to the king. Strong in the possession of his new fortress-capital, David now began an offensive war against the Philistines. He invaded Philistia and captured one of its most powerful cities, Gath. These victories finally broke the political and military strength of the late oppressors of Israel. From henceforward the Philistines were confined to the narrow coastal strip of southern Palestine, which had been their first home when they entered the country two centuries before. The solemn installation in Jerusalem of the Ark of the Covenant, which had been recovered from the enemy in the late Philistine war, was now carried out by the king. It was an act of deep significance because it marked out the new political capital to be also the venerated centre of the Jewish faith.

David's career as a conqueror was no less remarkable than his work as the liberator of Israel. Though both the order and the details of the campaigns, which he conducted against his neighbors after the final defeat of the Philistines, are extremely obscure, it is clear that he fought with continuous success against the Moabites and the Ammonites to the east, the Aramæans to the northeast, and the Edomites to the south of his kingdom. Thus, in the end, he was lord of a realm which stretched from the head of the gulf of Akaba to the Lebanon, and which included all Transjordania south of Mount Hermon. The internal organization of this greater Israel was, it would appear, not at all fully carried out by David. Partly this may have resulted from the fact that his skill as an organizer was not equal to his eminence as a conqueror; partly it may have been due to lack of time, since consolidation of newly-won territories is necessarily a slower task than the conquests themselves. But the main reason was probably that the later years of David's reign were clouded by insurrections within his own kingdom and by quarrels within his own family. The former were, it is true, put down, and the disputes about the succession were, to all appearances, settled before the king's death. But when David

ended his days, Solomon, his son by Bathsheba and his successor, was faced by a renewal of the intrigues against him, which
were only ended by the execution of the principal plotters.

The long reign of Solomon (c. 975–935 B.C.) was not remarkable for further conquests; the wars which occurred in this
period were without exception defensive. Often, too, the king
secured by diplomacy what he could not or would not have
effected by force of arms. A raid by an Egyptian army is attested only in a late source, and it may well be doubted if it
ever happened. Solomon controlled the trade-routes between
Egypt and Phœnicia and Syria. A rising against Solomon's
authority in Edom failed; but the king found it politic to fortify
Thamar and leave a garrison there to guard the road to the
gulf of Akaba. Other cities in different parts of his realm, which
Solomon is credited with converting into fortified posts — e.g.
Hazor, Megiddo, and Beth-Horon — owed their importance
partly to their strategic position, partly to their situation relative to important highways of commerce. The Aramæans of
Damascus and the neighborhood, after their defeat by David,
seem to have been reduced to be tributary vassals of that
monarch. In Solomon's time Damascus, under the energetic
adventurer, Rezon, probably became again an independent
kingdom. With the Phœnician cities Solomon's relations, as
had been the case in his father's time, were friendly. To the
king of Tyre he conceded certain villages in the north of his
kingdom, probably in return for trade facilities; besides this,
the two princes concluded an alliance. Although, then, Solomon seems, in the main, to have kept intact the territories bequeathed to him by his predecessor, his internal policy was
such that it weakened the resources of his kingdom almost to
the point of exhaustion and antagonized a large proportion of
his subjects. Thus, on his death, civil war, which culminated
in the division of the realm of David and Solomon into the two
kingdoms of Israel and Judah, was soon followed by renewed
attacks on the part of their neighbors.

The fame of Solomon rests on his work as an administrator
and his magnificence as a potentate. It was due to him that
the kingdom was administratively organized in a way which
recalls the systems in force in Babylonia and in Egypt. The

country was partitioned, for purposes of taxation and local government, into twelve regions, corresponding roughly to the geographical divisions of the twelve tribes, but with the addition of the Canaanite cities which had been gradually absorbed into the realm. A royal official or governor was responsible for the administration in each of these provinces. Taxes were heavy; in addition, the king exacted compulsory labor from his subjects in order to carry out the vast building projects for which his reign was especially famous. Judah, being the home-land of the king, was partially exempted from the heavy burdens placed upon the rest of the population. The temple and the royal palace at Jerusalem took thirteen years to build. The whole complex of buildings was erected on the highest part of the hill of Jerusalem, and, being surrounded with a fortification wall, was completely cut off from the city itself, which stood on the lower slopes of the hill. The temple stood at the northern end, the very highest point; though sumptuously constructed of fine stone and cedar wood, its dimensions seem to have been relatively small.[1] It was divided into two unequal parts, of which the smaller inner chamber, the Holy of Holies, was the repository of the Ark of the Covenant. Thus the work, begun by David, of making Jerusalem the religious capital of the Jewish race was carried an important stage further. Jahweh, conceived by earlier generations to be a deity with no fixed abode, who might manifest himself to his people or their chosen leader in a storm-cloud or on a desert mountain-top, has become the god who, ever invisibly present in the temple at Jerusalem, presides over the fortunes of a nation.

To carry out these costly constructions, as well as to satisfy all the magnificent needs of an oriental court, the king was obliged to obtain much raw material and many commodities of great price from distant lands. Lebanon supplied the cedar wood, and it is probable that Phœnician workmen were also imported, to aid in the artistic decoration of temple and palace. Extensive trade was carried on with Syria, Egypt, and the land of Ophir (the Somali coast, the Egyptian Punt?). We are

[1] The dimensions of the actual temple building have been estimated at 124 × 55 × 52 feet. (*See* R. A. S. Macalister in *Cambridge Ancient History*, iii, p. 347.)

even told that one of Solomon's vessels joined with Egyptian trading-ships in making the journey to Tarshish (Tartessus) in southern Spain. Yet it must not be forgotten that this commerce was mainly, if not wholly, devoted to luxury articles.

Of external influences which helped to form the artistic productions of Solomon's age, as well as the elaborate court ceremonial enforced by the monarch, the strongest probably emanated from Egypt. This may even be true to some extent of the intellectual life of the period. For instance, though, as a whole, the Book of Proverbs is of later date, it is not unlikely that portions of it go back to Solomonic times. And in their general form those utterances irresistibly recall collections of moral maxims found in Egypt, like the sayings of Ptahhotep and Amenemhet. In the account of David's career (*II Samuel*, ix-xx) we possess a historical narrative which is contemporary or almost contemporary with the events that it narrates. That a very high place in the world's historical literature must be assigned to it has been admirably expressed by an eminent historian of the ancient world. "The account of David," he writes, "shows indubitably by its content that it dates from the time of the actual events, and that the narrator must have been very intimately informed about life at court and the characters and pursuits of the persons portrayed." Later the same writer observes: "It is astonishing that historical literature of this quality was possible in Israel at that date. It far surpasses any other known examples of historical composition in the Ancient Orient, the dry official annals of Babylonians, Assyrians, and Egyptians, as well as the stories, akin to fairy-tales, of Egyptian popular literature." [1]

But, though the era of Solomon was characterized by an immense advance in culture on the part of his subjects, though its splendor was such as to form the theme of countless legends in later times, the price paid was too heavy, and Solomon must bear the responsibility of bringing about the undoing of his father's work of political unification. For, on Solomon's death (*c.* 935 B.C.), the northern tribes petitioned his son and successor, Rehoboam, for alleviation of the heavy burdens imposed by the late king. Rehoboam, however, made no concessions.

[1] E. Meyer, *Die Israeliten und ihre Nachbarstämme*, pp. 485–486.

The North revolted under the leadership of Jeroboam, who had already in Solomon's time led an insurrection against the monarch's oppressive rule, but had on that occasion failed and been forced to go into exile.   Jeroboam on his return, was crowned king at Shechem. Hostilities between the two kingdoms of Judah and Israel (or Ephraim) lasted off and on for half a century. It was not till the time of Omri (c. 887 B.C.) that peace between the two monarchies was definitely established. The southern kingdom was now in a position of dependence on the northern. In the interval of civil war foreign attacks had added to the general confusion. An Egyptian raid in the time of Sheshenk (Shishak; c. 930 B.C.) extended as far as Jerusalem; while the northern kingdom had much to fear from the Aramaic kingdom of Damascus. Omri built himself a new capital at Samaria. The kingdom which he ruled included all northern Palestine, together with Moab and Ammon in Transjordania. In addition, he exercised suzerainty over the southern kingdom, while he and his son, Ahab, also fostered good relations with Phœnicia. In the later years of Ahab's kingship a far more formidable enemy than Aramæans or Egyptians first threatened the independence of all Syria and Palestine. From the middle of the ninth century the political history of the two kingdoms forms but an episode in the fortunes of the Assyrian empire.

CHAPTER VIII

THE ASSYRIAN EMPIRE

> *Over all Egypt I appointed kings, prefects,
> governors, grain-inspectors, mayors, and secre-
> taries. I instituted regular offerings to Ashur and
> the great gods, my lords, for all time. I placed on
> them the tribute and taxes of my lordship, regularly
> and without fail. A tablet, written in my name, I
> caused to be made, and the glory of the bravery of
> Ashur, my lord, the mighty deeds which I had
> accomplished, under the protection of Ashur, in
> my marches, and the victories, the booty of my hands,
> thereon I caused to be written, and for the astonished
> gaze of all my enemies I set up for future days.*
> — Inscription of Esarhaddon.

1. POLITICAL HISTORY TO THE FALL OF NINEVEH

WHILE paying the fullest tribute of admiration to the men
who, as related in the last chapter, built up a united and powerful kingdom in Palestine, southern Syria, and Transjordania, one
must admit that they could never have succeeded so well, if
during these centuries her greater neighbors had not been reduced to impotence. Egypt could never again hope to rule an
empire; the Hittite power was no more than a fast-dimming
memory of the past; Assyria, save for one brief spell, was a
small kingdom fighting for its existence against its neighbors,
none of whom had sufficient resources to cherish ambitions of
empire. Tiglath-Pileser I, who became king of Assyria *c.* 1115
and died *c.* 1102 B.C., conducted campaigns into southern
Armenia, Babylonia, and northern Syria as far as the shores of
the Mediterranean, which made his name feared, and momentarily compelled his conquered enemies to pay him tribute. But
on his death the short-lived Assyrian empire ceased to be.
There follow two centuries of Assyrian history that are all dark

in two senses: dark, because the glory of Assyria was utterly obscured; dark to us, because of the extreme paucity of the existing records. It is not till the early years of the ninth century and the reign of Ashurnasirpal (c. 884–859 B.C.) that fuller information is again available. From then down to the destruction of Nineveh in 612 B.C. there exists copious epigraphic material. It reveals the last and greatest period of Assyrian history as a long, and to the general reader somewhat wearisome, series of military campaigns.

In the late twelfth, and especially in the eleventh, century the Aramæan invasions of a large portion of the Fertile Crescent had recommenced with greater intensity than ever before. Their hold on northern Syria, where they were established in important centres like Aleppo and Damascus, was very strong. They were astride the great caravan routes leading from the Mediterranean and the Euphrates to Assyria and Babylonia. Southern Mesopotamia was invaded and thereafter largely peopled by Chaldæan tribes, who seem racially to have been closely related to the Aramæans. On the northern borders of Assyria a considerable kingdom became prominent politically from the end of the ninth century. This kingdom of Van, with its capital at Tuspas on the eastern shore of Lake Van, is referred to frequently in Assyrian records by the name of Urartu. At the period of its widest extent it embraced the greater part of modern Armenia. Though both the origin and the history of this Vannic people are still extremely obscure — their language is believed to belong to the Caucasian group — they played a part of considerable importance in the two centuries during which Assyria dominated the Near East.

Though he owed something to the work of his immediate predecessors, it was really Ashurnasirpal who began Assyria's days of imperial greatness. In his campaigns he advanced to the borders of Van; westwards he crossed the Euphrates and reached the Orontes, Lebanon, and ultimately the Mediterranean. His annals relate how the king captured numberless prisoners and vast quantities of booty, and how he slew in battle enemies without number. If but a tithe of the record be true, this monarch surpassed all oriental despots in ferocity and cruelty; flaying, impaling, and other barbarous methods

of execution were inflicted on his countless foes and captives.[1]
His successor, Shalmaneser III, though apparently less frightful in his methods, was equally tireless as a soldier. In thirty-
five years he is credited with no less than thirty-two expeditions.
Two of his achievements are of most general interest: his intervention in Mesopotamia had the result that Babylon became
for a time a vassal kingdom of Assyria. In northern Syria he
consolidated his father's conquests with some success, but his
first attack on central Syria had no permanent results. At
Karkar in the Orontes valley, a little northwest of Hamath, his
progress was barred by an allied force composed of contingents
from Phœnicia, from Syrian and Aramæan principalities, of
which the chief were Hamath and Damascus, and from the
kingdom of Israel under the leadership of Ahab. Although
Shalmaneser claimed a great victory, it cannot in reality have
been very decisive; otherwise he would hardly have abandoned
his advance southward. He repeated his attacks on several
later occasions; but, beyond exacting tribute from Phœnicia,
he effected nothing permanent. For even his fierce attacks on
Damascus in 842 and 839 B.C. failed in their object of crushing
the Aramæan power. Still, his hold on northern Syria and
eastern Cilicia was secure before his death; and this was an
acquisition of great value, since it gave him the control of the
passes over the Taurus into Asia Minor. As visible token of
his power the king rebuilt the old capital of his country, Ashur,
with great splendor.

Most troublesome were his northern neighbors of Van; for the
most that Shalmaneser was able to effect was to prevent their
incursion into Assyrian territory. A year or two before his
death the aging monarch saw a large part of his work undone.
A rebellion in which one of his sons was involved led to a partition of the empire, and only one-half remained faithful to him.
Another son had to fight for two years before he succeeded in
temporarily reuniting the empire under his sole sway. There
followed a period of internal unrest of more than half a century,

---

[1] Yet the philosophic historian might well ask whether these atrocities
were worse than, for example, the appalling cruelties inflicted on the Báb
and his followers in Persia in 1852. For this terrible persecution see E. G.
Browne, *A Traveller's Narrative Written to Illustrate the Episode of the Báb*
2 (1891), pp. 326 ff.

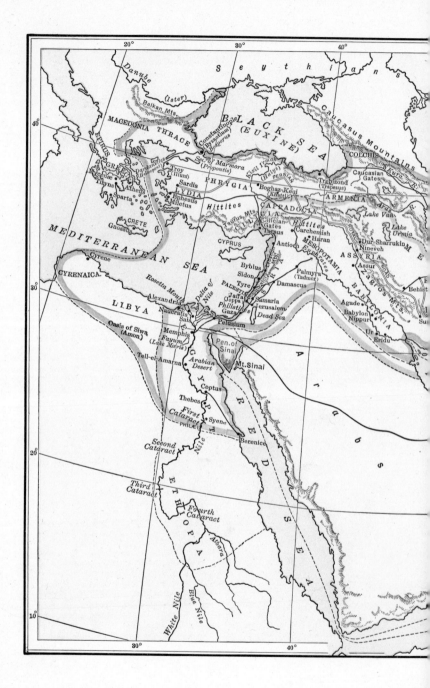

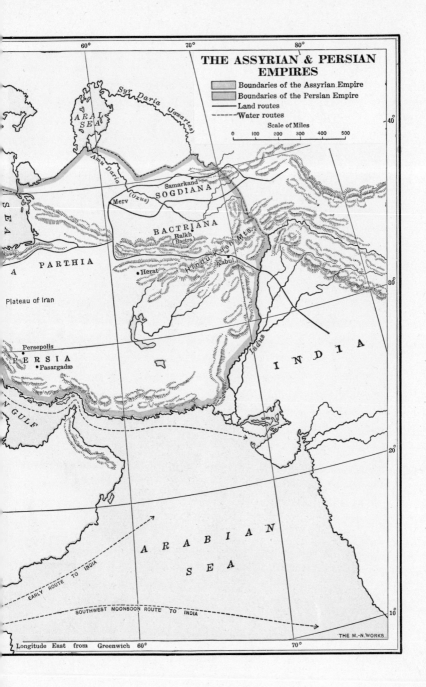

THE ASSYRIAN & PERSIAN EMPIRES

Boundaries of the Assyrian Empire
Boundaries of the Persian Empire
———— Land routes
- - - - Water routes

Scale of Miles

0   100   200   300   400   500

40°

Syr Daria (Jaxartes)

ARAL
SEA

Amu Daria

Samarkand
SOGDIANA

Merv
(Oxus)

BACTRIANA
Balkh
Bactra

30°

SEA

PARTHIA

HINDU KUSH MTS.

Kabul

Plateau of Iran

Herat

INDUS

Persepolis

PERSIA
Pasargadæ

INDIA

20°

GULF

ARABIAN

SEA

EARLY ROUTE TO INDIA

10°

SOUTHWEST MOONSOON ROUTE TO INDIA

Longitude East from Greenwich 60°

70°

THE M.-N.WORKS

during which several monarchs occupied the throne. When the Assyrian kingdom itself was disturbed by dynastic disputes, it was inevitable that there should be lack of authority in her dependencies, and the confusion was increased by raids from Urartu. The accession of Tiglath-Pileser III (c. 745 B.C.) brought to the fore a ruler who was able both to stabilize and to enlarge the empire. He gained complete control of Babylonia and reasserted Assyrian sovereignty in southern Syria. He invaded Urartu, and, though he failed to take its capital by storm, he put a stop to the activities of a hostile neighbor for a considerable time. He attacked Syria and Palestine with results more devastating to these countries than any previous Assyrian assaults. To some extent his task must have been facilitated by the practical exhaustion of Israel and its neighbors.

In the interval between Shalmaneser's western expeditions and those of Tiglath-Pileser III there had been little peace in Palestine or Syria. The prince of Damascus, Hazael, reinforced by other Syrian principalities, launched an attack against Israel and Judah soon after 840 B.C. First he conquered the whole of Transjordania; next he invaded the northern kingdom itself; and, finally, he ravaged Judah. It was only by the payment of heavy tribute that the rulers of both kingdoms were able to preserve at least a nominal independence. Under Hazael's successor the hostility of Assyria to her western neighbors was for once of benefit to Palestine, for an expedition of Adad-Nirari III against Damascus laid that kingdom low. The phenomenal recovery of the kingdom of Israel under Jeroboam II (c. 782–743 B.C.), and of Judah under Azariah, falls in the half century when the power of Damascus had been greatly reduced, and Assyria, as we saw, was involved in a turmoil of dynastic and civil dissension. But Jeroboam's work of reconstruction fell to pieces on his death. Faction and rebellion distracted the northern kingdom owing to the assassination of the rightful heir to the throne and to the attempts of several pretenders to seize the royal power for themselves. The most successful of these, Manahem, during his tenure of authority insured the non-interference of Tiglath-Pileser, with whose advent Assyria entered on the last, though most brilliant, stage of her imperial career, by the sending of tribute.

Manahem's son during the two years of his rule followed a
similar policy. But he was assassinated by Pekah, son of
Remaliah, who himself seized the crown and then adopted a
foreign policy which was to prove disastrous to him and to his
neighbors also. He formed an alliance with Damascus and
other principalities to withstand the aggressions of Tiglath-
Pileser, which might be expected when the tribute was no
longer forthcoming. The allies sought to draw Judah to their
side but without success. Thereupon they invaded the southern kingdom of Ahaz from the north, while the Edomites, who
had joined the alliance, entered Judah from the south. In his
extremity Ahaz, acting against the advice of the prophet Isaiah,
appealed to Assyria for intervention, and sent Tiglath-Pileser
gifts and swore fealty to him as his vassal.

Probably in 734 B.C. Assyrian troops appeared west of the
Euphrates. Damascus was captured and its population deported. Ahaz made his submission to Tiglath-Pileser in person
and was installed as vassal king of Judah. Israel was overrun and would have been completely laid waste, had not its
king been murdered by Hoshea, who at once submitted to the
Assyrian. As a vassal he was allowed to retain a greatly reduced kingdom, amounting to little more than the hill country
of Samaria. All Transjordania was annexed by Tiglath-Pileser,
while a large part of the population was deported by him. The
Assyrian monarch did not long survive these achievements.
Soon after his successor, Shalmaneser V, came to power, Hoshea refused payment of his tribute and submitted only on the
appearance of an Assyrian army in the West. When a similar
refusal occurred on a second occasion, a belated submission at
the eleventh hour was not enough. Israel was invaded by
Assyrian hosts and the capital city, Samaria, was besieged.
After a heroic defense, lasting three years, it fell. Shalmaneser
did not live to see these military operations completed, and it
was his successor, Sargon, who in 722 B.C. received the capitulation of the city. According to a Sargonid inscription nearly
thirty thousand inhabitants of the northern kingdom were deported by the king. Samaria now became the capital of a new
Assyrian province. To repopulate the country, drafts of persons from Syria and Mesopotamia were sent there by the king's

orders. Two years later Sargon decisively defeated a miscellaneous army of Syrians, Palestinians, and Egyptians at Raphia on the Egyptian border. The Egyptians, in order to prevent an invasion of their country, sent tribute; the resistance of Syria and Palestine was shattered; only Judah still remained intact, but, as before, a vassal or subject ally of Assyria.

Thanks to Sargon's other campaigns to the north, south, and east of his kingdom, the empire at his death was greater than any ruled so far by an Assyrian monarch. His successor, Sennacherib, was as active a warrior as the earlier Assyrian kings; at the same time his numerous campaigns were conducted not to enlarge the empire bequeathed to him by his father, but to quell risings, as in Syria and in Babylonia, and to consolidate his father's conquests. In 681 B.C. he was murdered by an elder son. His younger son, Esarhaddon, who had been governor of Babylon and marked out by his father for the succession, had to inaugurate his own reign by suppressing a rebellion within his kingdom. During his brief rule he kept up the warlike traditions of his line, his most spectacular undertaking being the invasion of Egypt.

Much of the recurrent unrest in Syria and Palestine, which necessitated numerous Assyrian expeditions to the west, was undoubtedly due to the machinations of Egypt. Not strong enough themselves to build up an imperial power, the Egyptian kings of the XXVth Dynasty nevertheless could intrigue with Assyrian vassals in Palestine, Phœnicia, and Syria, with the object of stirring up rebellion against Assyria, and in the somewhat forlorn hope of undermining the strength of the most powerful state in the Near East. Already in 700 B.C. Sennacherib had been forced to take energetic action in order to break up a coalition between Egypt, Tyre, Sidon, and Judah. The last-named kingdom was at this time ruled by the able and spirited Hezekiah. Through his rash diplomacy his kingdom suffered worse than any other state in the anti-Assyrian coalition. Judæan cities were captured by the enemy, and Jerusalem itself was invested; it would doubtless have succumbed to a siege, had not Hezekiah found it more politic at this point to tender his submission. A heavy payment of tribute was imposed on the rebellious vassal.

Esarhaddon early in his reign had to protect his northern borders against bands of invaders, called by the Greeks, Cimmerians, who, making their way from the Caucasus, overran central Asia Minor to the very frontiers of Assyria. An earlier but less formidable invasion, thirty years before, had been repelled by Sargon. When Esarhaddon by his victory over the Cimmerians had again made the northern part of his kingdom secure, he concentrated all his resources on preparations for an Egyptian expedition. At last in 671 B.C., after preliminary reconnaissances in previous years, he invaded the Land of the Nile. The vanquished Egyptians were compelled to pay tribute, and the ruler, Necho, was forced to become an Assyrian vassal. Two years after this Esarhaddon died. His successor, Ashurbanipal, ruled over Assyria for forty-three years. He continued the war against Egypt begun by his predecessor, with the result that for a few years Egypt became to all intents and purposes an Assyrian province. But in 651 B.C. either because the retention of Egypt within the empire was too costly or because the Assyrian needed all his military strength elsewhere, Psammetichus unhindered threw off his allegiance to Ashurbanipal. He had been accepted by the Egyptians of both Upper and Lower Egypt. Under him, the founder of the XXVIth Dynasty, the entire country was again governed by a single monarch, whereas in the centuries immediately preceding it had happened more than once that two rival monarchs governed in different parts of the country. For a little more than a century Egypt kept her independence, but she was annexed to the Persian empire by Cambyses in 525 B.C.

The wars in Ashurbanipal's time were very numerous. His generals were active in such widely distant areas as Cilicia, where a fresh Cimmerian force was repulsed, and in Elam which, having become a province half a century before, had revolted. This uprising against Assyrian authority was really part of a greater rebellion, stirred up by the brother of the king, who was governor of the Babylonian province. The rebel received support from various quarters of the empire. Hence the suppression of the revolt in Babylonia was necessarily followed by punitive expeditions against the more outlying insurgents. Thus, to cite but one example, Tyre and Akko in Phœnicia were

severely punished for the help which they had given the pretender. Glorious though the reign of Ashurbanipal might seem
to a contemporary, the empire in his day was really far less
secure than it had been in the days of Sargon and Sennacherib.
The number of enemies on the Assyrian borders was growing;
the continuous drain on her man-power was bound in the end
to bring about a collapse. It is significant that Ashurbanipal,
after his Elamite wars, enrolled in his own army large numbers
of the soldiers whom he had just conquered. And Sennacherib
had done the same after his campaigns in Syria. Though doubtless dictated by military necessity, to enroll a late enemy under
his standards was a hazardous experiment for the conqueror.
Only fourteen years after Ashurbanipal's death, Assyria fell
before the joint assault of her enemies from three sides, and her
vast empire was partitioned out between two of her conquerors,
the Medes and the Chaldæans.[1]

2. ASSYRIAN CIVILIZATION

That Assyrian society and culture were more or less slavishly
copied from Babylonia has long been a universally accepted
belief. But here, as in so many other fields of Ancient History,
explorations and study carried on during the last thirty years
have shown that belief to be at best a half-truth. It is still
very uncertain what were the chief influences which moulded
early Assyrian society; but we now know that in some very
noteworthy respects Assyria owed little or nothing to her
southern neighbor. Among recent finds, remains of legal enact-

---

[1] The following are the kings of Assyria from Ashurnasirpal to Ashurbanipal:

Ashurnasirpal	884–859	Tiglath–Pileser III	745–727
Shalmaneser III	859–824	Shalmaneser V	727–722
Shamshi-Adad V	824–811	Sargon	722–705
Adad-Nirari III	811–782	Sennacherib	705–681
Shalmaneser IV	782–772	Esarhaddon	681–669
Ashur-Dan	772–754	Ashurbanipal	669–626
Ashur-Nirari	754–745		

To this list may be added the Queen Regent, Sammu-ramat, who exercised
authority during the first three years of Adad-Nirari III, from 811 to
808 B.C. She is the historic prototype of the semi-mythical queen called in
Greek story Semiramis.

ments, of which the earliest copy belongs to the fourteenth or thirteenth century B.C., occupy a very important place. These juristic fragments are not part of a general body of legal ordinances, like the Semitic and Sumerian codes of Babylonia, but a series of enactments legislating on specific cases. While there is a certain proportion dealing with business contracts, sales, and the tenure of land, the more part is concerned with the position of women, marriage, and widowhood. Perhaps the most striking feature of Assyrian society which has become known through the discovery of this legislation is the levirate marriage. This institution, for whose existence in Babylonia there is so far little or no evidence, was observed also among the Hebrews. Further, these legal documents make it clear that Assyrian society was divided into three groups: a noble or upper class, a middle class including both craftsmen and what we should now call professional men, and a lower class. The organization of the members of the middle class into craft or professional guilds seems also to have been firmly established. Here, then, we have a definite parallel to earlier Babylonian practice. Yet we are not forced to postulate direct imitation on the part of the Assyrian.

The Assyrians were, above all, a warlike people. For their army the kings relied partly on a quasi-professional soldiery, who served for a definite period of time, and partly on a national or citizen militia. We have seen that in the latest period some kings even enrolled their late enemies under their standard. The standing or professional army was probably recruited in the main from the lower class of citizens. But it is not only the fact that the army is more prominent in Assyrian than in other ancient societies, which justifies the statement that Assyria was *par excellence* a military state. For the administration not only of Assyria proper, but of the empire as a whole, was essentially military in character. Yet, in the ruling of their vast territories, the Assyrian monarchs impress one as showing much greater knowledge of the art of government than the kings of Egypt or Babylonia. Unlike these, the later Assyrian kings did not rely wholly or mainly on the loyalty of local chiefs and princes after conquest. Instead, many of the conquered lands were organized as smaller administrative units, ruled by an Assyrian governor who was both civil and military head of the province. He was in constant touch with the king and the king's ministers, and, be it added, the viceroys were kept under close supervision by the ruler. One who was slack or inefficient had little chance of retaining his high office for long.

The towns appear to have enjoyed a certain degree of municipal autonomy; many received charters from the king conferring on the townsfolk privileges that were by no means negligible. Thus, although the town-governor was an imperial official, there was also a council of elders, who could lodge complaints against the governor directly to the sovereign; and, as is known from existing records, they sometimes did so quite successfully. Again, the townspeople were exempt from the *corvée* and, as a general rule, from military service. Thus, in tracing the slow evolution of imperial administration, we are justified in placing the Assyrian system halfway between the still crude methods of Egypt and Babylonia and the more closely knit imperial organization of the Persian empire, with its separation of civil and military authority, devised by the genius of Darius I.

The unfree class, whether agricultural serfs, who were tied to the soil which they cultivated for their masters, or slaves employed in urban centres, was large. Many of them, too, were enrolled in the military forces. Their condition, as in all slave-holding societies, varied immensely, and no generalization about the class as a whole is possible. Slaves in domestic service or employed by their owners in handicrafts — in the latter case they seem often to have worked at a trade independently, though obliged to pay an annual tribute to their owner — perhaps lived a life little different from the lower class of free men. On the other hand, the slaves employed in gangs on the building projects of the monarch and other heavy manual labor no doubt suffered as harsh treatment as did the slaves in the Athenian silver mines or the miserable inmates of the Roman *ergastula*.

Reference has already been made to the spread of the Aramæans during the earlier centuries of Assyrian history. From the ninth century their importance, economically, but not politically, throughout the empire steadily grew. Ashurnasirpal transplanted many of them to Assyria; Mesopotamia also contained large numbers. It is probable that much of the commerce in different parts of the empire eventually came into their hands. While the official language of business, as of diplomacy, continued to be Assyrian, from the eighth century notes and endorsements in the Aramaic language occur on documents, and these rapidly become more common. In the end, though this was not till the close of the fifth century B.C., Aramaic became the *lingua franca* in the Near and Middle East.

The Assyrian kings, with few exceptions, were like other oriental potentates, great builders. Temples, palaces, and sometimes new towns, erected at least in part from the vast spoil taken from the kings' enemies and the tribute wrung from them, were the outward manifestation of imperial power. Thus Sennacherib greatly enlarged the capital, Nineveh. His successor, Esarhaddon, rebuilt Babylon. But it was during the long rule of Ashurbanipal that Assyrian architecture and sculpture in relief reached its artistic zenith. This monarch's name is most famous for the vast library of cuneiform tablets which was collected and housed in Nineveh by the king's orders. In this enlightened work of bringing together and copying the records and literature of the past he was following the example of his predecessors. To cite but two examples, both Sargon and Sennacherib had on a smaller scale made similar collections. The library of Ashurbanipal contained many thousands of clay tablets inscribed with a great variety of subjects — historical annals, oracles and prophecies, mathematics, astronomy, medicine, lexicography and grammar; besides this there was a great quantity of correspondence and official archives. Most of the miscellaneous literature was borrowed from Babylonia. Babylonian poems and legends like the Epic of Gilgamesh (cf. p. 18), the Descent of Ishtar, and the Creation Epic, were copied and edited by Assyrian scholars, and much of this Babylonian literature would to-day be unknown but for the recovery of the Assyrian redactions.

Her science Assyria also derived from those same neighbors; but it is surely creditable to her kings that, immersed almost continuously in the practice of war, they nevertheless gave encouragement to some of their subjects to foster the arts of peace. The careful study of the heavenly bodies had been carried on in Babylonia for many centuries. Though the primary purpose of these observations was to further the pseudo-science of astrology, the foundations of a serious science of astronomy were thus laid also. The length of the solar and the lunar years had been ascertained at a very early date. By the seven so-called planets were meant the sun and moon as well as the five planets known at that date. Observations of the sun, moon, and Venus were recorded, and the twelve signs of the zodiac in the ecliptic were demarcated with approximate accuracy. Finally, much attention was paid to lunar and solar eclipses; again, though the purpose was mainly religious, valuable scientific observations also resulted therefrom.

CHAPTER IX

THE AGE OF GREEK COLONIZATION

A considerable time elapsed before Hellas became
finally settled; after a while, however, she recovered
tranquillity and began to send out colonies. —
Thucydides i, 12 (Jowett's translation).

In the opening chapters of his history Thucydides with a
masterly hand sketches in its main lines the development of
early Greek society. The general truth of his picture we are
not entitled to impugn. At first, we are told, there were constant migrations so that men's life and property were alike in-
secure. Trade and free intercourse were little known. From
the nomadic stage men passed into the pastoral; still later they
advanced to an agricultural mode of life. The change from an
unstable to a settled existence was momentous. Life became
more secure. Among men living a stationary life the ties of
family relationship are strong and form the basis of clan and
tribal organization. This in turn is at the root of the larger
political organisms, whose immediate origin may be attributed
to one of two circumstances. Either a dependent population
settled round a stronghold which afforded protection in time of
need, or a number of village communities amalgamated at a
common centre. In either case a rudimentary *polis* (state or
city-state) was created. In rapid review Thucydides refers to
the sea-empire of Minos, the power of Mycenæ, the Trojan wars,
and the ethnic movements which led to the formation of Greek
settlements in the islands and on the Anatolian coast. Finally
he points out how the geographical features of the country
promoted the breaking-up of larger groups of settlers in Greece
into much smaller units, which then proceeded to develop
independently.

It will be well at this point briefly to touch on the geography
of Greece. In proportion to the total area of the country

(approximately 45,000 square miles) its seaboard is exceptionally long. The coast-line on the south and east is indented by numerous inlets and bays affording either good, or at least adequate, anchorage for ancient maritime craft. On the west coast harbors are much scarcer, and, especially northward from the mouth of the Corinthian gulf, the coast is rocky and inhospitable save at a few points. The country as a whole is very mountainous, though the highest peaks — with the exception of Mt. Olympus, which rises to a height of 9794 feet — scarcely exceed 8000 feet. The lowland regions are mostly of small extent, being either narrow valleys between the uplands or else coastal strips like Achæa on the southern side of the Gulf of Corinth. The largest plain is that watered by the river Peneios in Thessaly; much smaller, though of considerable fertility, are the upper and lower Messenian plains, the valley of the Eurotas in Laconia, and portions of Bœotia. The regions where cultural advance was slowest — Arcadia and northwestern Greece — are precisely those where the intricacy of the mountain system is such as to make communication both within the area and with the world beyond unusually difficult. At the same time, the very limited resources of those areas retarded the growth of material prosperity. Thus it is only in the fourth century B.C. that the Arcadian cities emerge into some prominence politically, while the northwestern Greeks, especially the Aetolians, did not take a leading part in Greek affairs until the third and second centuries.

The rivers of Greece, though numerous, are, with few exceptions, small and unsuited for navigation. The largest was the Acheloos, which separated Acarnania from Aetolia. It, and some other streams, like the Peneios in Thessaly and the Alpheios and Pamisos in the Peloponnese, could be navigated in ancient times for a short distance from the mouth. But the majority of rivers, including some of the most familiar in Greek literature and story, like the Cephisos, Ilissos, or Eurotas, in the winter and spring, when they are fed by rains or mountain snows, have the character of mountain torrents; in the summer months they are shallow streams or even altogether dry. There is reason to believe that, what is true of the rivers and the climate generally at the present day, was substantially the same in ancient times. It was natural, therefore, that the sea should be the most important highway of communication; and, even from the fifth century B.C. on, when the number of main and subsidiary roads was considerable, the sea continued to be the chief avenue of travel and commerce.

A country in which the amount of land productive enough for self-support was as restricted as in Greece could only maintain a population which in proportion to the square-mileage was small. We shall find in this circumstance a leading cause for colonial expansion. The total number of independent communities in the Hellenic world was very great. Not only is this true of the mainland and western Anatolia, but some of the islands were divided between a number of city-states. Lesbos contained six independent cities and Rhodes three; even small islands, like Amorgos and Ceos, were the home of several autonomous communities. A few of these states, as early as the seventh century, were already politically more powerful, or economically more prosperous, than their neighbors. Such were Sparta, Argos, and Corinth in the Peloponnese; the island of Aegina, Chalcis and Eretria in Eubœa; islands in the Archipelago, like Naxos, Paros, Lesbos, Chios, and Samos; and cities like Miletus, Ephesus, and Phocæa on the coast of Asia Minor. The development of Athens was slower, and till the sixth century she was only a state of the second rank.

The growth of a state in which the political and social life was centred in a city was slow. The fact that the city-state was the ubiquitous form of Greek political community from the sixth century B.C. onwards must not make us forget that the city, which ended by being virtually synonymous with the state, was at first only a convenient centre for the transaction of affairs by groups of villages or clans. At the dawn of the Hellenic period government in the Hellenic states seems to have been uniformly monarchic; but the power of the king was already on the decline. The landed nobility, the heads of the influential families, formed the king's advisory council; in the end they became so powerful that they refused to leave the sole direction of government to a single head of the state who, whether his office was elective or hereditary, ruled for life. In some cases the change from monarchy to aristocracy — that is,

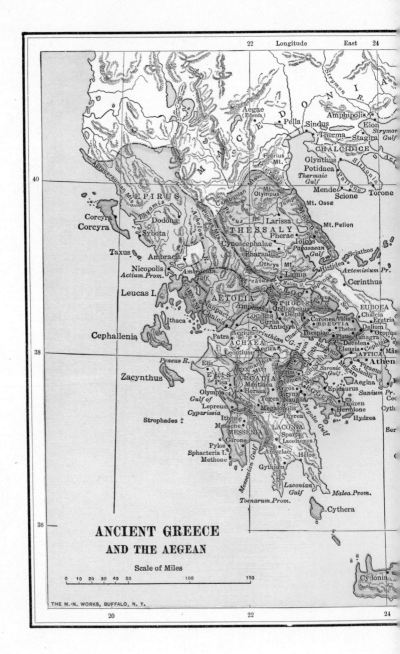

MACEDONIA

Aegae
(Edessa)
Pella
Sindus
Therma
CHALCIDICE
Amphipolis
Eion
Strymor
Strymor Gulf
Stagira
Pierius
Mt.
Olynthus
Potidaea
Thermaic
Gulf
Mende
Scione
Torone

Acti

Pallene
Sithonic

40

EPIRUS
Corcyra
Corcyra
Dodona
Sybota
Taxus
Ambracia
Nicopolis
Actium Prom.
Leucas I.
Ithaca
Cephallenia
Zacynthus

Mt.
Olympus
Tempe
Mt. Ossa
Larissa
THESSALY
Mt. Pelion
Pherae
Cynoscephalae
Pharsalus
Iolcos
Pagasaean
Gulf
Othrys Mt.
Histidea
Sciathos
Artemisium Pr.
Cerinthus

Ambracian
Gulf
AETOLIA
Amphissa
LOCRIS
Chalcis
Naupactus
Aegium
Patra
ACHAEA
Leontium
Aegira
Elis
Euboea
Orchomenus
Delphi
Corinthian G.
Antdyra
Cirrha
Thespia
EUBOEA
Chalcis
Eretria
Delium
BOEOTIA
Thebes
Plataea
Tanagra
Decelea
Eleusis
ATTICA
Athen

Peneus R.
ELIS
Pisa
Olympia
Gulf of
Lepreum
Cyparissia
Strophades

Erymanthus Mt.
ARCADIA
Mantinea
Heraea
Megalopolis
Ithome
Messene
MESSENIA
Corone
Pylos
Sphacteria I.
Methone

Argos
Tegea
Thyrea
LACONIA
Sparta
Lacedaemon
Amyclae
Gythium
Helos

Nemea
Tiryns
Nauplia
Argolic Gulf
Epidaurus
Troezen
Herthione
Hydrea
Aegina
Sunium Pr.
Ced
Cyth
Ser

Messenian Gulf
Laconian
Gulf
Taenarum Prom.
Malea Prom.
Cythera

38

36

ANCIENT GREECE
AND THE AEGEAN

Scale of Miles

0 10 20 30 40 50   100   150

THE M.-N. WORKS, BUFFALO, N. Y.

Cydonia

rule by the heads of the leading families — resulted abruptly from the deposition or murder of the king. In others a more gradual and peaceful evolution took its course. The king was forced to acquiesce in the limitation of his powers through the appointment from the nobility of one or more magistrates, who took over some of the duties hitherto carried out by the monarch. In such instances the name of king in the end survives only as the title of a magistrate. In some states the monarchy disappeared as early as the beginning of the eighth century B.C.; elsewhere it lingered on into the seventh or even the sixth century. In Sparta kingship, under a peculiar form and subjected to very definite limitations, survived as long as Sparta herself could claim to be an independent state.

The bulk of the population did not benefit by such constitutional change. On the contrary, whereas a single ruler, even if his first obligation and desire was to satisfy the nobles, would find it expedient to keep his subjects as a whole contented, and with this end in view to avoid unduly arbitrary acts, a ruling minority, whether they owed their authority to ancient lineage (aristocracy) or to a virtual monopoly of wealth (oligarchy), provided they were at one among themselves, could more readily govern in the interests of one class only, their own. Except in the case of Sparta and Athens, whose early history will be separately considered, information about the earlier constitutional development of the Greek *poleis* is very meagre in quantity and very poor in quality. It is a cause for bitter regret that of the one hundred and fifty-eight constitutions described by Aristotle, only one, his account of the Athenian constitution, is extant. But there was at all events one means of averting political revolution and relieving economic distress which among the more advanced communities of the Hellenic world was of almost universal application, namely colonization. It was a remedy for present ills which, though often fraught with peril for the colonizers, was productive of tremendous consequences for the Hellenic race.

Nowhere is the danger of reconstructing an important phase of Ancient History with a mind prepossessed by phenomena familiar in modern societies, and of attributing similar causes and a similar line of development to it, more apparent than in

most current accounts of Greek colonization. It cannot be too
strongly emphasized at the outset that only in a strictly limited
sense was the colonial expansion of the eighth, seventh, and
sixth centuries B.C. due to an economic cause. The early development of the Greek *polis* operated to the advantage of a minority of land-owners. The growth of the population as a whole,
coupled with the fact that the ruling aristocracies suffered more
heavily in time of war, and that their numbers steadily declined,
produced a condition of affairs in many communities which
might at any moment give rise to revolution. Territorially the
average city-state was exceedingly small; and, even if the ruling
class were thoroughly benevolent, it would be impossible for it
to provide land for all the citizens, once the population had increased beyond a certain limit. Thus relief was found when a
body of the poor and landless left their native place to found a
settlement elsewhere. In their newly chosen home the first and
most important business was the "dividing up of the land."
Those who till then had been landless and citizens in little more
than name, now became the land-owning burgesses of a new
polis.

Insofar as one can ascertain the forces leading to Greek
colonial enterprise, one may say that, inasmuch as colonization
was certainly encouraged by the ruling classes of the old Greek
cities, and successful new foundations, provided they remained,
as was generally the case, on good terms with the parent city,
added to her influence and prestige, the causes were political;
insofar as the land-hunger of the poorer classes was satisfied by
the sending out of a colony, economic reasons were operative.
But, to see in the desire for commercial expansion a primary
cause of colonization, to attribute to city-states like Miletus
and Corinth, which sent many of their citizens forth to found
new *poleis* elsewhere, a commercial or trade policy, is not only
to invert the true order of events, but to misread the ancient
evidence, and to interpret this aspect of the political and social
development of archaic Greece in the light of modern colonial
foundations. That the presence of many new city-states in the
more outlying parts of the Mediterranean or on the Black Sea
ultimately led to an increase of trade, and to a more intensive
interchange of commodities, no one would attempt to deny.

But this was purely a secondary development; and, moreover, the extent of the commercial intercourse existing in the Hellenic world of the sixth century B.C. has, without doubt, been much exaggerated.

There is a fundamental difference between a Greek and a modern colony. The latter always remains politically dependent on the mother-country, though the degree of dependence may vary; the Greek colony (*apoikia*), on the contrary, once it had been founded, became an independent city-state, whose members ceased to be citizens of the community which they had left. The subsequent relations between mother- and daughter-city were, in the majority of cases, friendly. Often agreements of various kinds existed between the two, which tended to make their relation closer than would have been the case between two states which had never been connected. The institutions adopted by the settlers in the newly founded community were, as was natural, most often modelled on those under which they had grown up in their former home. The same religious cults and festivals, the same calendar and month-names, with which they had been familiar since their childhood, were commonly transplanted by them to the colony. But however great the friendship for the mother-city, however close the moral and religious ties might be, the *apoikia* was a new and sovereign city-state, owing no political allegiance to the parent city.

It is instructive to note that the states which were most active in sending out bands of their citizens as colonists were situated in regions where the possibility of territorial expansion was very slight. In Miletus, Corinth, Megara, Chalcis, Eretria, and Phocæa, to mention only the more important, the geographical area of the *polis* was so limited that there was no solution other than emigration for a serious political and economic problem. For we must bear in mind that the Greek city-state was essentially an agricultural state, and that the ownership or occupancy of land, however restricted in amount, was almost inseparable from full citizenship. We shall have occasion to remark hereafter how, even much later than the age of colonization, commerce and trade, in Athens and elsewhere, were mainly in the hands of the non-citizen population.

The regions to which from the late eighth century groups of

settlers from the old city-states of Greece and the Asia Minor littoral chiefly found their way were in the West and the Northeast. Sicily and southern Italy, the Thracian coast, the shores of the Sea of Marmora and of the Black Sea, afforded land to the landless and ample opportunity for enjoying all the privileges of citizenship of which the colonists had been partially or wholly deprived at home. The colonists went out from the mother city under the guidance of an official founder (*oikistes*) to whom, in the first place, the task of organizing the new settlement was entrusted. We have no means of knowing of how large a body of persons an *apoikia* was generally composed. It must have varied greatly; for the number was not fixed, as was the case with the Roman and Latin colonies founded by Rome several centuries later. It is regrettable, too, that there are few data from which to judge of the relations normally existing between the colonists and the earlier inhabitants of the region occupied. Obviously no one generalization would be in place, bearing in mind the differences between the various natives with whom Greek colonists came into contact, and the circumstances under which a new foundation was made. It is probable, however, that in many cases the colonists were secured in their possession only after a good deal of fighting; probable, too, that disasters, like that which befell an Athenian colony sent to Ennea Hodoi c. 464 B.C., occurred from time to time in the earlier period of colonization.

Almost invariably the new Greek cities were on or close to the coast. Even if the immediate vicinity was soon made safe, there might be continued peril from the aborigines of the interior. Thracian tribes, like the Triballoi, appear to have been a constant menace to the Greek cities on the coast, raiding them with varying sucess at intervals. Similarly, the Lucanians in southern Italy from time to time attacked Greek settlements like Thurioi. Thucydides, in his sketch of early Sicilian history (vi, 2–3), makes it clear that many of the Greek colonists in that island had to fight and dispossess the natives before they could establish their cities. Save in the case of the colonies on the Black Sea, the remains of whose material culture seem to make it plain that the population by the fourth century B.C. was only half Hellenic, the new Greek cities kept their Greek charac-

ter for centuries. Intermarriage with natives, and the consequent fusion of races, was probably small in extent. The natives
rarely attained citizen status in the Greek communities; probably their position usually approximated that of resident
aliens in the older cities of Greece; for few colonies, so far
as we can tell, went as far as Heraclea Pontica, whose citizens
reduced a neighboring tribe to serfdom.

The Ionian city of Miletus surpassed all others in the number
of her colonies. From the very fragmentary information at
our disposal more than forty city-states can still be designated
as Milesian foundations. The total number may have been
nearly double that figure. With few exceptions, these colonies
were on the Black Sea; for example, Odessus, Olbia, Panti-
capæum, Theodosia, and, above all, Sinope, whose earliest
history as a Greek *polis* appears to go back to the middle of the
eighth century, while a subsidiary colony went there about a
hundred years later. Nearer home were such Milesian colonies
as Cyzicus, Proconnesus, and Scepsis. In these three settlements it is clear that Greek communities had already been
established for some time before they were strengthened by
these accessions of settlers from Miletus. Most of the Milesian
colonies were founded in the seventh century; but in very few
instances can we affix even an approximate date. Early in
the same century (c. 685 B.C.) the mainland state of Megara
sent out a body of colonists who settled at Chalcedon, at the
southern end of the Bosphorus and on the Asiatic side. Seventeen years afterward a second Megarian colony was established
opposite to Chalcedon on the European side. The site of Byzantium is unsurpassed in the Mediterranean for its natural
advantages. Yet the city in classical times was troubled occasionally by the Thracian tribes of the interior. Hence we
need not be surprised that its occupation took place only after
the Chalcedonians had for some years surveyed the scene from
the security of the Asiatic shore.

If Miletus acquired almost a monopoly of territory suitable
for occupation on the shores of the Euxine, the city of Chalcis
in Eubœa was no less active in Thrace during the seventh
century. The rivalry existing at home between Chalcis and
her neighbor, Eretria, extended also to their colonial founda-

tions. Thus, though Chalcidic cities on the Thracian coast were more numerous, several of the most flourishing *poleis* in this region at a later date were foundations of Eretria (Methone, Mende, Scione), or of other cities, like Paros (Thasos) or Corinth (Potidæa). The colonizing activities of Chalcis were, however, not confined to the northern Aegean. Almost a century earlier, that is to say, in the late eighth century, many of her superfluous citizens had begun to voyage to the West and found fresh homes at Cyme and Neapolis on the southwestern coast of Italy, and at Naxos in Sicily. For about a hundred years the periodic migration of Chalcidians westward continued, and many of the Greek settlements, which in the fifth and fourth centuries played an important part in the western Mediterranean, were daughter cities of the Euboic *polis;* to wit, Catana, Leontini, Himera in Sicily, and also Zancle, which, with Rhegium on the Italian side, guarded the straits between the island and the mainland.

Among the colonizing cities of the Greek mainland Corinth was easily first in achievement; indeed, in the extent and thoroughness of her colonial policy, she was surpassed by Miletus alone. The Corinthian colonies were to be found at various points along the route from the Gulf of Corinth to southern Italy and Sicily. Some eight are known to have stood on the northwest coast of Greece, from Oiniadæ to distant Epidamnus; chief, however, of these western Greek settlements was the island colony of Corcyra. In Sicily the Corinthians found that they had been largely forestalled by Chalcis. Yet, of the three or four Corinthian colonies in that island, one, Syracuse, was destined to become the premier Greek city in the western Mediterranean.

Though space forbids the enumeration of all the Greek cities responsible for the founding of colonies, there is one other which deserves special mention, Phocæa, the most northerly of the twelve Ionian cities. Information about its history is most scanty; yet there are sufficient indications that the Phocæans in the seventh and early sixth centuries were an extremely prosperous community. Herodotus (i, 163 ff.) tells us how Phocæan sailors had found their way westward as far as Tartessus in southern Spain, with whose king they

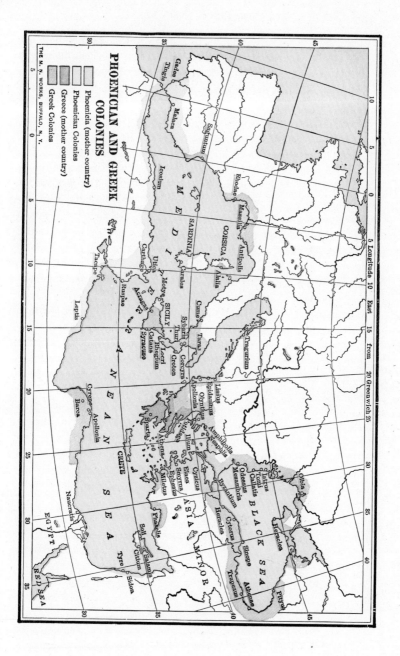

PHOENICIAN AND GREEK
COLONIES

Phoenicia (mother country)
Phoenician Colonies
Greece (mother country)
Greek Colonies

THE M. N. WORKS, BUFFALO, N. Y.

had then established friendly relations. The familiarity with the western Mediterranean thus acquired was in due course utilized for colonizing purposes. For, although the earliest Phocæan colony of which we have any record was at Lampsacus on the Sea of Marmora, — the traditional date of the foundation is 654 B.C., — the most famous *apoikia* sent out by the Ionian city was Massilia in distant Gaul (*c.* 600 B.C.). Half a century later when Phocæa herself was reduced by the Persians, a large part of her population, rather than live as subjects of an oriental power, emigrated to the West. Their efforts to secure a permanent foothold at Alalia in Corsica were frustrated by the hostility of the Etruscans. Ultimately they found a more permanent resting place at Elea in southern Italy. Closely connected with the foundation of Massilia was the gradual establishment of more than a dozen small city-states scattered along the coast to the east and west of Massilia herself. This group of Phocæo-Massiliot *poleis* maintained its independence and prosperity for many years, in spite of the hostility of the more powerful maritime states of Etruria and Carthage.

CHAPTER X

THE POLITICAL AND ECONOMIC DEVELOPMENT OF THE GREEK STATES TO *c.* 500 B.C.

> *For the real difference between democracy and oligarchy is poverty and wealth. Wherever men rule by reason of their wealth, whether they be few or many, that is an oligarchy, and where the poor rule, that is democracy. But as a fact the rich are few and the poor many; for few are well-to-do, whereas freedom is enjoyed by all, and wealth and freedom are the grounds on which the oligarchic and democratic parties respectively claim power in the state.* — Aristotle, *Politics*, iii, 8 (Jowett's translation).

1. SPARTA

ALTHOUGH such ancient testimony as we possess points to the fact that Dorian Argos was at the end of the ninth and the beginning of the eighth century the leading state in the Peloponnese, she did not retain that position long. The character of the ancient sources and the eventual issue of a long political struggle justify us in focussing our attention first on Sparta of all the Peloponnesian states. There is a certain epic interest in the tireless energy of her citizens, which made her before the end of the sixth century the premier military state in Hellas and the head of a powerful though loosely knit confederacy; something also to admire in the relentless logic, by which the entire social and economic life of a community was subordinated to what began by being a military necessity and ended by becoming a political ideal.

Only in recent years, especially since systematic excavations have been carried out at Sparta and in its vicinity, has the contrast become clear between early Sparta and the Sparta familiar from the pages of Herodotus, Thucydides, and Plutarch. In that earlier period — the eighth and seventh centuries —

Plate 13

a

Geometric Vase of Dipylon Style

b

Archaic Greek Vase
(So-called Melian Amphora)

THE ARCESILAS CUP

Showing King Arcesilas of Cyrene superintending the weighing of
silphium on shipboard

Plate 14

her general development was not markedly different from that of many other city-states. The phenomenon of a mixed population, consisting of a dependent or serf majority dominated by a ruling minority, who alone are in the enjoyment of civic rights, can be paralleled elsewhere, for example, in Crete and in Thessaly. The excavations at Sparta have shown that for fully a century and a half (from the end of the eighth century to *c.* 550 B.C.) the arts and crafts flourished as notably in Laconia as in any other part of the Hellenic world. Laconian pottery, both in technique and artistic design, can hold its own with the best contemporary products of Miletus, Samos, or Corinth. Architects and sculptors, who were active in this age at Sparta and at neighboring Amyclæ, even if they were foreigners not citizens, exercised their art at the invitation of Sparta's rulers. The designs of some of the artistic products of Laconia, notably certain ivory plaques representing the Spartan goddess Artemis Orthia, suggest Anatolian influences. This, coupled with the distribution of Laconian pottery (cf. Plate 14), and sporadic evidence from literary sources like Herodotus, prove that, whatever the extent and character of early Greek trade and commerce as a whole, Laconia at least performed its share. The "splendid isolation," which we associate with the Spartan state of the fifth century, was not yet.

In this earlier period, then, we must picture Sparta as one of the more powerful Peloponnesian states, gradually extending her territory and her influence, till either her aggressions or her growth in power brought her into conflict with formidable neighbors, especially Argos. The city of Sparta, formed, we are told, by the union of five adjacent villages, was the chief political unit in the valley of the Eurotas. Beginning with the conquest of the two promontories of Tænarum and Malea as well as the neighboring island of Cythera, the Spartans next turned their attention to the fertile regions lying west of Mt. Taygetus. The conquest of this region, Messenia, seems to have been completed by the end of the eighth century. The conquered populations of Laconia and Messenia were not uniformly treated. That part of them which was needed to cultivate the land occupied by the Spartan citizen body was reduced to serfdom. The others (*perioikoi*) were left personally free, but politically powerless. Thus in the enlarged Lacedæmonian state there were three elements of the population. The ruling class of citizens (Spartiatæ), who numerically did not comprise more than a tenth of the total inhabitants,[1] and the *perioikoi*, together compose the Lacedæmonians in the nomenclature used by the Greek historians. The *perioikoi* were numerous; they lived in communities of their own, occupying one hundred small unfortified towns. Some few of them were peasants; but the majority appear to have been engaged in industry and trade. Left largely to themselves, though under general Spartiate supervision, they owed as their one obligation to their overlords the performance of military service. Their general condition was very tolerable. They had a monopoly of trade and commerce, which was some compensation for the absence of political privileges. In this respect their position resembled in a general way that of the resident alien population of other Greek states, notably Athens. Only when Sparta was engaged in prolonged warfare — for instance during the last quarter of the fifth century — did the *perioikoi* suffer serious inconvenience or even hardship, owing to the prolonged interruption caused to their professional and commercial occupations.

Far different was the condition of the serfs (Helots). It was they who cultivated the land for their Spartiate masters. A certain number were assigned to each lot (*klaros*), which provided each citizen and his family with the necessities of life. The Helots and their families lived on these farmsteads. In the earlier period they were obliged to hand over one-half of all their produce to their master. From the sixth century onward they paid a fixed amount in kind annually; but we cannot tell whether, when averaged over a number of years, this was a more or a less severe exaction than the other. The power of the Spartiate master over his Helots was limited, since he could neither sell them, nor liberate them, nor put them to death. The ownership, and therefore the disposal, of the serf population were vested in the state, that is in the citizen body

---

[1] Later, *e.g.* in the fourth century, the proportion of Spartiatæ to the total population was even smaller. Though we have not the data from which to estimate the population of Lacedæmon at any given period, evidence for the steady decline of the citizen body is consistent and conclusive.

as a whole and its executive officers. The removal of Helots from one farm to another, or from agricultural work to perform military service, was likewise at the discretion of the government.

Since the primary purpose of the conquest of Messenia had been to acquire more land for the growing body of Spartiatæ, the greater part of her population after defeat was reduced to serfdom. Thus the Spartans acquired land for the landless citizens without having recourse to the all but universal remedy at this period for over-population, namely, colonization. For the solitary foundation of a Lacedæmonian colony at Taras in southern Italy (c. 705) was due to political causes — a domestic revolution whose genesis and progress are alike obscure. The oppressed Messenians did not acquiesce in their fate without a further struggle. About half a century after the Spartan conquest of Messenia (soon after 650 B.C.) the Messenians rose in revolt. It would appear that it took the Spartans many years before they finally broke the resistance of their neighbors. Nor could they have succeeded in this, had not the *perioikoi* remained loyal to them throughout. Even so the length and exhaustive nature of the late war, joined with the realization that a large serf population would always be a potential danger, unless exceptional measures for the security of the state were taken, led the Spartans to remodel their military and social organization.

The communistic military state, with its iron system of education for the young, and its regimentation of children and adults alike, suspicious of all foreigners, and indifferent or hostile to all that made up the amenities of life in other Greek states, that state which we think of as characteristically "Spartan," seems primarily to have been a product of the fifty years following the suppression of the Messenian revolt. Yet it is inconceivable that so well-organized a system could have been perfected in so short a time, had not its main features already been in existence before, and Sparta's social and political organization been in its general character essentially the same in earlier centuries, but much less rigidly enforced. The ancient evidence, though confused and sometimes contradictory, nevertheless bears out our contention; while the extreme divergence of opinion among modern scholars about such topics as the origin and date of the Spartan constitution, or the reforms attributed to a lawgiver, Lycurgus, whom some would accept as a historical person, and others elevate to the dignity of a hero or depress to the humbler status of a wolf-totem, illustrate the difficulty or even impossibility of separating what is early from what is late. The system now to be described was firmly established by the middle of the sixth century, and remained practically unchanged till the last half of the third.

Life in and for the community of citizens was the duty of the Spartiate, and from his birth he was trained under state supervision to become and to remain an efficient member of a military aristocracy. After birth children were inspected by the heads of the tribe, and, if sickly, were exposed in a ravine of Mt. Taygetus. Until they had completed their seventh year Spartan boys were reared at home; but after that the state took charge of their education. They were organized in troops according to age and were put under the supervision of the oldest and most efficient of the *eirenes*, youths between fourteen and twenty. The troops messed, slept, and trained together. Similar arrangements applied to the *eirenes* as a whole. The training, which gradually increased in severity as the boys grew older, was almost wholly physical; athletics, gymnastic and quasi-military exercises, hunting, coupled with strenuous and often harsh discipline, scanty clothing, and exposure to all weathers, were calculated to produce a well-developed and hardy young manhood. The supreme test of stoic fortitude was undergone by those youths who, as competitors for the honor of being acclaimed "altar-victor," submitted to the ceremonial flagellation carried out annually at the altar of Artemis Orthia. So severe was the ordeal that occasionally contestants died under it.[1] At twenty the Spartan youth began his proper military training. His life was passed in the barrack and in camp; and, although there were some few privileges enjoyed by men over thirty, the communal military life continued for all citizens up to the age of sixty. The men ate together in messes (*syssitia, phiditia*), fifteen to a mess, to

---

[1] The rite is commonly explained as a substitute for human sacrifice.

which each member was required to contribute a fixed amount of barley, oil, and so forth, derived from the lot assigned to him by the state and cultivated for him by Helots. Failure to make the fixed contribution brought with it partial loss of civic status and exclusion from the *syssition.* Spartan girls, though living in their homes, received a training analogous to that of the boys. The physical beauty of Spartan women, and the comparative independence which they enjoyed in contrast to woman's position in other Greek communities, are noted by the Greek writers.

Of intellectual training and pursuits among Sparta's citizens we hear very little. Memorization of parts of the Homeric poems or of the martial lyrics of Tyrtæus, learning and performance of Alcman's choral odes, — for early Sparta could boast of two lyric poets, — were scarcely sufficient mental exercise to counterbalance the incessant physical and military activity, and we are not surprised that even an admirer of many Spartan institutions, like Aristotle, condemns Spartan education as altogether too one-sided.

The constitution under which the Spartans lived had features which struck contemporary and later Greek observers as peculiar and archaic. Officially at the head of the government were two kings. The monarchy was hereditary in two royal families, the Agiadæ and Eurypontidæ, between whose representatives there commonly existed much rivalry. This, so far from being confined to their personal relations, at times reacted very decidedly on public affairs. Their functions and privileges in early times much resembled those of a Homeric *basileus.* They were supported in their duties by a council (*gerusia*) of twenty-eight elders. These were elected by the citizen body from those of their number who had completed their sixtieth year, and who offered themselves as candidates for the office. Once elected, the elders served in the *gerusia* for life. This council, besides collaborating with the kings and magistrates in the general business of government, owed a good deal of its power to the fact that it acted also in a judicial capacity. Before it were tried serious criminal offenses, condemnation for which rendered the accused liable to loss of civic rights, banishment, or even death. The assembly, composed of all citizens over thirty, was at Sparta named the *apella*, and was supposed to meet monthly at the time of the full moon. In early days it was summoned by the kings, who also presided at its regular meetings, and who could call extraordinary ones in case of any public emergency. The *apella* never developed into an influential deliberative body. Its members seem practically to have been restricted to listening to such measures as were laid before them by the *gerusia* or the magistrates, and to voting thereon. Questions of war and peace, treaties and alliances, disputes over the succession to the kingship, when such arose, and new laws, were submitted to the vote of the *apella*. But the strength of the magistracy and of the *gerusia* deprived this theoretical sovereignty of the people of most of its actual power. Nor did the *apella* act in a judicial capacity. In short, its most important function was that it elected in each year the magistrates, called ephors.

The origin of the ephorate, which, owing to the aforenamed method of election, Aristotle justifiably calls the democratic element in the Spartan constitution, is as obscure as that of the dual monarchy. The official list of ephors, we are told, went back to the middle of the eighth century (754–753 B.C.). That there were from the first five such officials is improbable. For that number is almost certainly connected with the redistribution into five tribes, in place of an earlier three, which did not take place till after the second Messenian war. One thing at least is clear, that the election by the citizens of magistrates holding office for one year, even though their duties and influence were at first very restricted, represents a very definite curtailment of the regal authority. The great development in the powers of this magisterial college dates from the middle of the sixth century; — Chilon, ephor in 556 B.C., is reputed to have been the first to raise the office to equal power with that of the kings. The powers of the monarch were gradually limited in every direction, though on occasion a strong man, like King Cleomenes I, might defy the ephoral college. The ephors superseded the kings as presiding officers in the *gerusia* and the *apella*; they decided all civil suits save two types, the decisions in which now constituted the sole remnant of what must once have been the extensive judicial powers of the kings. In the criminal cases brought before the *gerusia* the ephors initiated the prosecution;

in doing this they were but giving effect to one element in the general supervision or censorial power that they exercised over the entire citizen body. But it was not only in the internal government of the Lacedæmonian state that the ephors were supreme; they, too, guided the foreign policy of Sparta, negotiated with the representatives of other states, and even wielded considerable influence in the conduct of war. For, though the commandership-in-chief of the army was normally entrusted to one of the kings, it became customary for two members of the ephoral college to accompany the monarch on his campaigns. So, also, they issued instructions to military and naval commanders in charge of Spartan contingents, doing this on their own responsibility, or after consultation with the *gerusia*, and sometimes at least after ratification by the *apella*.

The Lacedæmonian army consisted of five Spartan regiments, corresponding to the five tribes, and of regiments of *perioikoi*. The Helots at first served only as soldier-servants to their masters in the field. But from the last third of the fifth century they were increasingly used as fighting troops. As a reward for this service they received their liberty; they then formed a separate class in the Spartan state, called *neodamodeis*, and a separate corps in the army.

The constitution and social organization of Sparta find their nearest parallel in the Dorian *poleis* of Crete; indeed it is hardly open to doubt that, when the Spartans at the beginning of the sixth century introduced sweeping reforms in their social system, they copied or adapted much from the practices of their traditional kinsmen in that island. Thus, agricultural work in Crete was carried on by a serf population resembling the Helots of Laconia and Messenia. The education of Cretan boys was very similar to the Spartan training, though perhaps not quite so rigorous. The Spartan *syssitia* have their parallel in the Cretan men's messes, called *andreia*. Considerable similarities also existed between the constitutions of Sparta and of the Cretan cities. But monarchy seems to have been abolished early in Crete, and the government was mainly in the hands of ten magistrates (*kosmoi*), who were elected annually from among a limited number of families. Thus the government of these *poleis* was more closely aristocratic than that of Sparta. In the Hellenic period these Cretan states, though they sometimes fought among themselves, seem to have played little part in the political history of the greater Hellenic world — a striking contrast to pre-Hellenic days, when the rulers of the island were for centuries the most powerful princes in the Mediterranean.

So far we have considered only the growth of the Lacedæmonian state and the characteristic institutions of Sparta as they were in the days of her greatness. But, in the process of advancing her political power in the seventh and sixth centuries, Sparta had been by no means wholly successful. Her earlier conflicts with Argos had generally ended in defeat. For Argos, after a temporary decline in the late eighth century, enjoyed another brief period as the leading state in the Peloponnese, or even in Greece, during the first half of the seventh. This appears to have been the time when she was ruled by King Pheidon, whose influence or authority extended beyond the Argolid to Corinth, Aegina, and Megara. The efforts of the Spartans at this time to expand westwards of Laconia were brought to nothing by their crushing defeat at the hands of the Argives in the battle of Hysiæ (c. 669 B.C.). It was more than a hundred years before the Spartans successfully retaliated on their old rivals, and, by defeating an Argive force, secured for themselves control over the district called Thyreatis (c. 546 B.C.). Long before this, however, Argive influence in Greece had waned. In particular she was outshone in prosperity by her neighbor, Corinth, and her territory no longer embraced the whole Argolic peninsula. Sparta, before her triumph over Argos in the middle of the sixth century, had attempted the military conquest of Arcadia on her northern frontier; but the venture did not succeed. The acquisition of Thyreatis was some compensation for her failure in the North. Moreover, we can dimly descry a marked change in Spartan policy after this date. What she failed to do by force of arms she at least in part effected by diplomacy. The process by which a league of Peloponnesian states under Spartan leadership was formed in the second half of the sixth century is as obscure as its inner organization and the obligations of its members. But, though this confederacy may have been a loosely knit aggregation of independent city-states, without even a rudimentary federal constitution, it was effectively held together, partly by the military prestige of Sparta, partly because the various Peloponnesian cities realized the advantages to be derived from such solidarity as was insured by membership in the league, unaccompanied as these benefits were by any loss of autonomy on the part of the members.

2. THE AGE OF TYRANTS

There is a general similarity in the political, constitutional, and economic evolution through which the many Greek *poleis*, other than Sparta and the cities of Crete, passed in the archaic period (*c.* 800–500 B.C.), because the conditions of life, in spite of local variations, were in a general way the same. We have already considered one of the most noteworthy, and in its effects most far-reaching, developments of this age, namely colonization. Internally both the older Greek cities and many of their daughter colonies progressed on similar lines. The ruling aristocracies governed only in the interests of their class. The mass of the people, though citizens in name, exercised no political influence. Yet a peasant population is long-suffering and even content, so long as it can earn or produce sufficient for its daily needs. Only when its livelihood is in danger, does it turn for help to the governing class; and, if no help is forthcoming, it will in the last resort rise against its rulers.

We cannot tell whether the majority of those who tilled the soil for the aristocratic land-owners were free tenant farmers, or were from the first in some degree dependents. Even if they were free, their difficulties in most parts of the Hellenic world were great. There was no soil there to compare for fertility with the rich acres of Mesopotamia or the Nile valley, and the margin of profit from the operation of a small farm can never have been ample. The tithes, too, which they must pay to the owners were heavy. For example, the Attic peasants before the Solonian reforms were paying the landed nobility one-sixth of their annual produce. Thus one bad season might be sufficient to put a man in debt. In his difficulty he would turn for help to his landlord, or, if he were a freehold farmer, to the owner of a large estate. In either case, by contracting a debt, even if he were free before, he came into the power of a member of the aristocracy. In the last instance the persons of the debtor and of his family were the security for loans. For it is probable that the enslavement for debt, which is definitely attested in early Athens and in early Rome, was in reality a general practice at this time. Moreover, in disputes there was no written law to which the debtor could appeal, if his treatment seemed unjust or harsh. Customary law there was; but it was handed down orally from generation to generation of the ruling class. There was little hope of bare equity, not to speak of forbearance for the debtor, while the governing families, to which his creditor belonged, were both the keepers and the interpreters of unwritten law. It is not surprising, then, that in many communities, when the people finally rebelled against their governors, their first constructive act was to choose some man, eminent for fair-dealing and common sense, as a lawgiver. Of such legislators Pittacus at Mitylene in Lesbos was one; apart from his work of codifying already existent customary law and framing new enactments to secure juster treatment for all the citizen body, he appears to have exercised a benevolent dictatorship for ten years (c. 585–575 B.C.). Among the Greeks of the West we hear of lawgivers like Zaleucus at Locri (c. 650 B.C.) and Charondas at Catana (c. 500 B.C.?).

The people's task of carrying through a successful revolution against aristocratic misrule was often facilitated by disunion among the rulers. The efforts of one or two aristocratic families to exert a dominating influence in the state might antagonize other members of the governing class. In that case the way lay open for an understanding between some less influential aristocrat and the people, whose cause he undertook to champion in return for their support in overthrowing what was now the common enemy of their interests. At Corinth in the early part of the seventh century Cypselus, with the support of the people (demos), drove out the ruling clan of the Bacchiadæ, and then governed the city as an irresponsible ruler. Almost contemporaneously the neighboring state of Sicyon passed under the control of Orthagoras who, unlike other such autocrats, was said to be of quite humble origin. Some twenty years later (*c.* 635 B.C.) we find Theagenes in power at Megara. In many of the Greek cities of Anatolia or of southern Italy and Sicily, such absolute rulers rose and fell, though often little more than their names have been transmitted to us. Hence it is impossible to distinguish the precise circumstances which in each case led up to the overthrow of aristocracy and the emergence of a despot. Nor did these changes all come about at precisely the same time; for, generally speaking, this stage in Greek constitutional development came later in the West than in Greece and Anatolia.

To this type of irresponsible monarchy the Greeks gave the name of *tyrannis.* The derivation of the word and of its fellow, *tyrannos,* that is, Tyrant, is uncertain; but the institution itself has certain clearly marked characteristics. The Tyrant was an irresponsible and absolute ruler; generally he owed his position to popular support or even election, and the first Tyrants in different cities often continued to rely for their position on the goodwill of their subjects.[1] Yet, in the last resort, the Tyrant's power rested on force, and very generally he had a body-guard of mercenaries. The first Tyrant was usually not the last, but the founder of a line. Cypselus of Corinth was succeeded by his son, Periander; Orthagoras of Sicyon is overshadowed by his magnificent grandson, Cleisthenes; the sceptre of Peisistratus passed to his two sons, Hipparchus and Hippias. The importance of the age of Tyrants in Greek history is beyond measure great. In the political sphere it marks the end of the oppressive rule exercised by the old aristocracies of birth. Now for the first time all classes of the population begin to be treated alike, and a majority can claim to be citizens in fact, not merely in name. In later pages we shall see how these despots furthered economic, artistic, and intellectual development in the Hellenic world.

[1] Many Tyrants were thoroughly benevolent rulers, *e.g.* Peisistratus. The evil connotation of the English word "tyrant" is absent from the Greek word, at all events in the earlier period. The essential notion underlying the word *tyrannos* is that of a monarch, absolute and irresponsible.

3. EARLY ATHENS

Though in the case of Athens references in later Greek writers to her earliest history are somewhat more abundant than to other Hellenic states, with the possible exception of Sparta; though, in addition, we are in the fortunate position of having in Aristotle's *Constitution of Athens* a single survivor from a large number of similar monographs compiled by him on other Greek constitutions, we can nevertheless discern only dimly that the early development of Athens was similar to that of the majority of *poleis*. That Attica had been occupied in Mycenæan times is proved by archæological finds from the Athenian Acropolis and half a dozen other Attic sites. According to later Athenian tradition the inhabitants of this little tract of Greece, with an area of approximately 1000 square miles, were *autochthones*, that is to say, indigenous. Thucydides maintains that the country was little affected in the period of the migrations. Compared with other parts of Greece Attica was probably little disturbed, and these generalizations may be accepted as in the main correct. There were at first a number of diminutive states in Attica, which were gradually amalgamated to form one state with Athens, whose geographical position near the sea and in possession of a natural stronghold, the Acropolis, must from the beginning have given her a superior position in Attica. This unification (*synoikismos*) continued to be commemorated at Athens in later centuries by an annual festival called the *synoikia*. The latest Attic community to be incorporated was Eleusis (*c.* 700 B.C.?). One result of this gradual process was that territorially the city-state of Athens, as distinct from the city itself, was conterminous with Attica, and therefore considerably larger than the majority of Greek states.

The government was at first monarchic; but step by step the nobles encroached upon or limited the royal power. This diminution in the regal authority was effected in two ways. On the one hand, the monarchy from being hereditary became elective; on the other hand, its tenure was limited first to ten years (*c.* middle of the eighth century?), and finally to one year (*c.* 683 B.C.?). The duties of the office too, were drastically curtailed, the conduct of military affairs being assigned to the polemarch (*polemarchos*) and the most important magisterial functions to the *archon eponymos*. Though the title king (*basileus*) continued to survive, the holder became merely an annually elected magistrate, whose duties were mainly concerned with religion. As elsewhere, so at Athens, the early kings without doubt were supported by an advisory council of clan-heads or nobles. But the oldest council of which we hear was the council of the Areopagus, composed of ex-magistrates. Since the last-named were chosen exclusively from the noble families, this council was at that time purely aristocratic. To the three senior magistrates — archon, basileus, and polemarch — there were added in the seventh century six thesmothetæ; somewhat later it became usual to refer to these nine officials as the nine archons. The duties of the thesmothetæ seem to have been from the first confined to judicial matters.

The civic population of Attica was divided into various groups of uncertain origin. We hear of a number of brotherhoods (*phratriai*), which in the religious sphere alone retained some importance in later historic times, of four tribes (*phylai*) each containing several *phratriai*, and of clans (*gene*). It would appear that the entire citizen body was included in the tribes and brotherhoods, but that membership in the clans was restricted to the nobility or, in other words, to the wealthier land-owners. It was this class which had gradually effected the abolition of the monarchy, and had arrogated all power in the state to itself, with the usual result that the rest of the population were citizens in name rather than in fact. The general economic distress toward the end of the seventh century was so great that a considerable part of the rural population seemed little better than serfs. "Thereafter it chanced," says Aristotle, "that there was civil strife between the nobles and the people. For in various other respects the constitution was all in favor of the few, and, in particular, the poor with their wives and families were in servitude to the rich. These poor were called *pelatai* and *hectemoroi* (sixth-part men). In accordance with this tithe (*i.e.* of one-sixth) they worked the lands of the rich. Moreover, the whole land was in the hands of the few. If the *hectemoroi* failed to pay this tithe, they and their children were liable to be sold into slavery. Furthermore, to the time of Solon, all loans were on the security of the debtor's person. Solon was the first champion of the people. For the mass of the people slavery was the hardest and most intolerable of the ordinances of the constitution. Not but what they chafed at other grievances; for, broadly speaking, they had no privileges."

Of an earlier lawgiver, Draco (*c.* 621 B.C.), we really know very little that is definite. He appears to have been the first legislator at Athens to formulate a written code of laws; but the only parts of his work that are to some extent known are those enactments which abolished the old blood-feuds and established a regular procedure for the trial of homicide. Though the Draconian reforms were doubtless of benefit in furthering order and security in Attica, they did nothing to remedy the serious economic evils to which Aristotle bears witness. Apparently in the seventh century it had been found expedient to classify the civic population according to the property which they owned. As was the case with the so-called Servian organization at Rome, so here the primary purpose of the classification was military. In both cases the individual was required to supply his own equipment. The *hippeis* (horsemen) belonged to the wealthiest or ruling class; the *zeugitai* (teamsmen?) were sufficiently well-to-do to serve as heavy-armed infantry in time of war; finally the *thetes* (workers for hire?) made up the poorest part of the civic body. Some of these last may have served as light-armed troops; but in general they were at this time exempt from military service, save perhaps in a great national emergency. Although this classification was in the nature of a concession by the ruling class to the populace, who from the mere fact that they bore arms were bound to exercise more influence in political affairs than before, the real power and the magistracies were still under the exclusive control of the richest class.

The first serious attempt to bring about a more equitable government, and particularly to arrest the gradual reduction to bondage of the small-farmer class, was made by Solon, who in 594 B.C. became *archon eponymos* and, to carry out the work of reform, was given extraordinary powers. It is curious that so little is known about the details of Solon's first and most drastic measure of reform, the *seisachtheia* or "shaking-off of burdens." As the name itself shows, it effected the cancellation of outstanding debts. So radical a step could only be justified by the exceptional conditions which needed to be remedied. Closely connected with this measure, and perhaps a part of it, was the absolute prohibition for all future time of enslavement for debt. Thus, whatever their earlier status may have been, the *hectemoroi* were converted by Solon into tenant farmers. They continued to pay, as before, one-sixth of what they produced to the owners, but, being included in the lowest of the census classes, benefited with the rest of the *thetes* by the constitutional reforms of Solon. For he amended the earlier three-fold division of the citizen body by separating the wealthiest men in the community from the rest of the *hippeis*. The minimum rating of each class was assessed in natural produce — grain, oil, and wine. To the first class belonged those whose returns amounted to not less than five hundred measures, its members being known henceforward as *pentakosiomedimnoi*. For the *hippeis* the minimum was three hundred measures, for the *zeugitai* one hundred and fifty, which was later changed to two hundred. The rest, whose income was less than this, made up the class of *thetes*.

Political privileges were graduated in an analogous way. The archons were elected from the first two classes, certain financial officials from the first alone. A number of minor magistracies could be held by *zeugitai*, and these were also eligible for the new council of four hundred (*bule*), instituted by Solon. The *thetes* were excluded from all these offices, but they were members of the citizen assembly (*ecclesia*). The *bule* — one hundred councillors were annually chosen from each tribe — being recruited from three out of the four census classes, had a much more democratic character than the old aristocratic Areopagus, which continued to be composed of ex-archons. We know little of the functions of the *bule* at this period beyond the fact that it helped the magistrates in a general advisory capacity. The powers of the *ecclesia*, too, which now elected the magistrates, were confined to certain matters affecting the community as a whole, for example, the ratification of declarations of peace and war, or the bestowal of the citizenship on foreigners, besides the elective functions already named.

The most striking innovation introduced by Solon was the institution of the *heliaia*. It was, as Aristotle remarked, the most essentially democratic part of the Solonian constitution. The *heliaia* was a court of justice in which the decisions rested with a jury, and adult male citizens over thirty years of age from all four classes were eligible to act as the jurors. It is probable that at first there was but one court, and that its duties were confined to hearing appeals from magisterial sentences. The increase in the number of courts, and the wide extension of their judicial powers, were a development of the following century. Nevertheless, by giving to the citizen body as a whole, whether acting in a political capacity (*ecclesia*) or in a judicial one (*heliaia*), the ultimate decision in certain cases, Solon fully merited the title, "first champion of the people." He had securely laid the foundations on which was built up the advanced democratic constitution of the fifth and fourth centuries.

An Athenian of the age of Pericles or Demosthenes might refer to Solon only with reverent admiration; to his contemporaries Solon's reforms were too essentially a compromise to bring about prolonged peace and harmony in Attica. The newly enfranchised part of the population resented the privileges which wealth and descent conferred on their more fortunate fellow-citizens; the old aristocracy of birth and the richest class were angry that they had been deprived of the exclusive control of the government. On the whole, the middle class benefited most by the reformer's work, and so they were the most contented. After his period of office Solon left Athens and was away for many years. When at last he came back to his home, he took no further part in Athenian political life. For more than a quarter of a century after Solon's archonship Attica was the scene of factional disputes, which threatened to undo all the good done by the reformer. We hear of three groups, "the men of the plain," "the men of the shore," and "the men of the uplands," whose feuds distracted the land with civil war. Yet we cannot be sure of the rival interests that these factions represented.[1]

To wide-spread unrest at home were added the further distress and burden of a foreign war. Athens may have been engaged in war with her neighbor, Megara, before Solon's time; she certainly fought with her shortly before 560 B.C. The main cause of hostilities was the possession of the island of Salamis, which had been in Megarian hands and was now acquired by Athens, after she had seized Megara's port of Nisæa, and thereby forced her rival to cede the island. The Athenian through whose energy and initiative these successes were won was Peisistratus, a young man of aristocratic birth. With the help of a body-guard, assigned to him by the vote of the people because of an attempt on his life by an assassin, and with the general support of the faction of the uplands, Peisistratus made himself master of Athens. But his position as Tyrant was not yet secure. After a brief period of rule he was forced to go into exile owing to the powerful coalition brought against him by the leaders of the two other factions, who sunk their own differences to unite in a common cause. Megacles, a member of the influential family of the Alcmæonidæ and leader of the "men of the sea-shore," was the most formidable of Peisistratus' opponents. The Tyrant's departure was the signal for a renewal of civil war, and was shortly followed by a fresh struggle with Megara, in which the Athenians lost their late conquests. In the distressful state of the country Peisistratus saw an opportunity for recovering the power he had lost. His wealth, derived largely from successful exploitation of silver mines in Thrace, he used to enlist a numerous body of mercenaries. With these he landed in Attica and was immediately joined by many of his old supporters. With this mixed force he defeated his political opponents utterly and again secured the Tyranny, exercising it till his death (*c.* 546–528 B.C.).[2]

[1] A facile generalization, now very popular, would equate the "men of the shore" with the great mercantile class whose interests clashed with those of the "men of the plain," who represent the landed proprietors. Unfortunately there is no justification for assuming the existence of mercantile magnates in Attica at this period; moreover, Aristotle expressly says of the "men of the shore" that they were agriculturists.

[2] For a different version, which tries to reconcile the contradictory and

When Aristotle characterized the rule of Peisistratus as more democratic than tyrannical, he meant that Peisistratus' arbitrary power was exercised for the good of the majority of his subjects, and that he did not abolish the existing constitution. His political opponents, members of the nobility of birth and wealth, were compelled to go into banishment. In some cases at least their property was confiscated; the land so acquired was parcelled out into small farmsteads. These the Tyrant allotted to the poorest class of citizens. The *hectemoroi* disappeared, and the small cultivators, new or old, became free-hold farmers. All had to pay to the ruler a tax of one-tenth, or, according to another account, one-twentieth; even if the larger sum be correct, the difference between one-tenth and the earlier tithe of one-sixth paid by the *hectemoroi* represented a considerable relief to the small cultivator. We are further told that Peisistratus advanced small capital sums to the new farmers, so as to give them a start and enable them to lay in the necessary stock. He made no attempt to change or abrogate the Solonian constitution; at the most he insured that the important magistracies were, as far as possible, held by his kinsmen or by reliable supporters of his régime. That, even so, his position rested directly on force could not be disguised; for the Acropolis was garrisoned by his mercenaries.

In his foreign policy Peisistratus aimed at cementing good relations with important foreign states, for example, with Sparta and the princes of Thessaly. Whether he won back Salamis from Megara, or whether the island only became permanently Athenian twenty years after his death, is a moot point. At all events the island had been recovered before the end of the sixth century. But that part of the Tyrant's policy which had the most far-reaching effect was his promotion of colonial enterprises. Sigeum on the Asiatic side of the Dardanelles was won by the Athenians, after a good deal of fighting with neighboring states, like Mytilene and Lampsacus, who feared that their own interests were being threatened. At the same time, Miltiades, member of an old Athenian family and once at least the political

---

in part fantastic stories about Peisistratus in the Greek writers and accepts the story that the Tyrant was twice exiled, cf. *Cambridge Ancient History*, iv, pp. 61 ff.

opponent of Peisistratus, led a colony to the Thracian Chersonese (Gallipoli). It has been suggested, not without some probability, that the islands of Lemnos and Imbros were first brought
under Athenian control at this time. Apart from the immediate
benefit accruing to the Athenian settlers in this region, the occupation of these geographically important sites was of great value
at a time when Athens was already looking to some extent to
foreign grain to feed her population. Indeed, an ordinance for-
bidding the export of Attic grain is attributed to Solon.

On Peisistratus' death his sons, Hippias and Hipparchus, seem
to have adhered closely to their father's policy for a number of
years. At last, however, a conspiracy, not due to general discontent but arising out of a private quarrel, was instigated by
two Athenians, Harmodius and Aristogeiton. Hipparchus was
killed, but his brother escaped the danger; while of the two ringleaders, Harmodius was slain outright and his companion was
subsequently executed (*c.* 514 B.C.). Hippias' government now
became more despotic, and his harshness, coupled perhaps
with a growing desire for political freedom on the part of his
subjects, brought about a general revolt against the Tyrant four
years later. But Hippias was clearly in a strong position, as is
proved by the fact that the Athenians only succeeded in ousting
him with the help of a Lacedæmonian contingent. The intervention of Sparta was due to the diplomacy of the exiled Athenian family of the Alcmæonidæ. They had won great influence
with the priests at Delphi, where they had rebuilt Apollo's temple, largely from their own resources. The vaticinations of a
grateful oracle were insistent in calling on Sparta, now the leading military state in Greece, to rid Athens of her Tyrant.
Hippias was allowed to leave Attica with his family, and retired
to Sigeum, which he held for a number of years as a vassal of
Persia. His departure was followed by a renewal of party strife
in Attica. After four years of civil unrest, Cleisthenes, son of
Megacles, the erstwhile opponent of Peisistratus, and now head
of the Alcmæonid family, with sufficient popular support overcame his political rivals led by Isagoras.

Instead of taking advantage of his strength, he introduced a
series of reforms and amended the Athenian constitution, so that
the Athenians after his day lived under a stable government for

nearly two centuries, and, save for two brief episodes, had no direct experience of the civil dissension (*stasis*), which sapped the strength and was the curse of many other Greek states. Cleisthenes' primary task was to devise means for abolishing the local interests and the power of the Eupatrid families, which had made possible the sixth-century factions of the shore, the plain, and the uplands, and in a different form had been responsible for the recent civil war. The old four tribes were abolished and the free population of Attica was redistributed on a territorial basis into ten tribes. Each *phyle* contained three *trittyes*, each of which was situated in a different part of Attica; each *trittys*, again, was made up of several smaller units — townships or rural districts — called demes (*demoi*). The total number of demes was originally one hundred; but it was gradually increased after Cleisthenes' time, so that, by the fourth century, there were not less than one hundred and fifty. Artificial as this rearrangement of Attica and her population seems in the too brief descriptions that have come down to us from ancient times, the work of the reformer endured, and was, as results showed, eminently practical. The long-standing family feuds and rivalries of clans ceased, because the new geographical distribution cut right across the old groups. Moreover, a new element was introduced into the citizen population by the enfranchisement of persons of only partial Athenian descent. Resident foreigners had lived in Attica since Solon's time at least, and their number had steadily increased, because their economic value to the state had been recognized by Peisistratus and his successors. Doubtless there had been intermarriage with Athenians, and it was the descendants of such unions whom Cleisthenes could now add to the civic body, when citizenship no longer depended on membership of phratries. Very possibly he enfranchised some resident aliens, with no Athenian blood in their veins, as well. It was, at all events, a far more liberal policy than that followed by the Athenian democracy fifty years later. The new tribes had approximately equal influence in the assembly (in which the town dwellers naturally had an advantage over the farmers who resided at a distance from the capital), because a deme in each tribe was situated in or near Athens. The new demotic division of the civic body formed the basis for military organization, taxation, and so forth. The lists of the demesmen that were compiled, and hereafter carefully kept up to date, furnished the material from which the census list of citizens was drawn up. The adjective derived from the name of the deme now formed part of the official name of every Athenian citizen.[1] Youths were admitted into their father's deme on the completion of their eighteenth year, after their legitimacy had been attested on oath by the parent. Admission to the deme was tantamount to attaining one's majority and full civic status.

Of no less importance were the constitutional changes introduced by Cleisthenes. The council of four hundred was enlarged to one of five hundred members to correspond more conveniently to the new tribal division. Fifty councillors were hereafter chosen by lot from each tribe. To facilitate the transaction of administrative business the *bule* was divided into ten committees or prytanies, each of which for a tenth part of the year shouldered the main burden of the council's work. While competent to decide minor questions on their own initiative, the prytanies had to refer all major questions to the decision of the whole council. The old magistracies were left untouched by Cleisthenes, and the archonship continued to be open only to members of the first and second census classes, with which likewise the reformer did not interfere. But the political power of the old magistracies rapidly declined and passed partly to the council, partly to a board of ten officials (*strategoi*) which, if not actually instituted by Cleisthenes, came into being very soon after his time. As their name, *strategoi* (generals), shows, these persons were originally appointed to command the military detachments raised from each of the ten tribes. They naturally very soon took over the general military and naval administration, sharing these duties for some years with the polemarch. The *strategoi* were annually elected, one from each tribe, and continued to be elected after other magistracies were regularly filled by lot. Within half a century they had become the chief executive magistrates in the Athenian state.[2]

---

[1] E.g. *Isokrates Theodoru Erchieus*, Isocrates, son of Theodorus, of the deme Erchia.

[2] The curious institution of ostracism, which some have attributed to

4. THE ECONOMIC DEVELOPMENT OF GREECE

The economic development of Greece in the earlier period is a topic fraught with difficulties. The literary evidence is of the scantiest, and the archæological is scattered and often not easy to interpret. The problem has been further complicated by a large number of modern writers who reconstruct the economic history of Greece during this and later ages in terms of nineteenth- and twentieth-century "big business." To do this they are obliged to read into the sporadic allusions found in Greek writers meanings which the text does not warrant, and to deduce from the archæological data conclusions which, at the best, are highly hypothetical, and which often are no more than wild conjectures. The result of this method can only be that the impressiveness of their admittedly fascinating picture of Greek trade and commerce is in inverse proportion to its historical veracity. We may begin with certain incontrovertible facts, which must never be forgotten in any discussion of the subject, and which show at the outset that deductions based on economic conditions existing in the modern world are in the highest degree fallacious.

Commerce in the Greek world was mainly carried on by sea. With the small sailing vessels of that day communications were necessarily very slow and the risks involved were infinitely greater than now. The rates of interest on loans, which now seem exorbitantly high, are eloquent proof of this contention.

Cleisthenes, may here be mentioned. Once a year the members of the *ecclesia*, after so deciding at a previous meeting, came together specially to record a vote against any citizen who might be regarded as dangerous to the state and whose banishment was therefore desirable. Not less than six thousand votes altogether must be cast for the proceedings to be valid. The person who received the largest number of votes — these were scribbled on pieces of potsherd (*ostraka*) from which the proceeding derives its name — was forced to go into honorable exile for ten years. His property was not confiscated, and he was reinstated in all his civic rights on his return. If the institution was really Cleisthenic, it was no doubt intended as a safeguard against any attempted renewal of Tyranny at Athens. But in the recorded instances of its use — the earliest was in 487 — it was the leaders of the political parties in the *ecclesia* who were liable to be sacrificed to party rivalry. So far from being generally beneficial in its effects, the institution sometimes resulted in the temporary loss to Athens of one of her ablest men.

Moreover, the winter months were, in general, a closed season, and maritime trade, like naval and military operations, was limited to seven, or at the most eight, months in the year (March to October). Even as late as the fourth century the methods of banking and transacting business were, as we can see clearly from the Private Orations of the Attic Orators, extremely primitive. It must be admitted that such conditions as are implied by these acknowledged facts were not favorable to the development of industry on a large scale, or to the creation of mercantile magnates. There is, in truth, a vast difference between the significance of the political and the economic life of the Greeks. The Greek *polis*, tiny though it was in comparison with the nation-state of more modern times, was in the fifth and fourth centuries a most highly developed organism. The political practice of Greek statesmen, and the political philosophy of Greek thinkers who, even when portraying an ideal Utopia, never forgot the reality of actual institutions familiar to them, convey a lesson of abiding value for all time. But their economic theory and practice, even on the most favorable estimate, was still in its infancy when the *polis* had passed its prime, and when its old age was cut short by the successful ambitions of Philip and Alexander of Macedon.

In the archaic period, with which we are here concerned, two facts stand out: Greek states were predominantly agricultural, and production was very largely governed by the economy of the household. Trade and commerce were universally carried on by barter to the beginning of the seventh century, and this method continued in many regions for very many years after the introduction of coinage. The comparative scarcity of gold and silver in the Aegean area would greatly retard the general adoption of an invaluable aid to commercial intercourse.[1] It is doubtful whether the Lydians or the Ionian Greeks deserve the credit of the momentous invention; for there is little ascertainable difference in date between the

---

[1] Siphnos was very prosperous in the sixth century owing to her gold and silver mines. Later the mines became exhausted and the prosperity of the island declined. Thasos and the coastal regions of Thrace lying opposite the island were rich in both metals. The mines at Laurium in Attica began to be worked in the sixth century, but were not more intensively exploited till the fifth.

earliest coins known from these two regions. Their example was followed by the people of Aegina, then by Corinth, Chalcis, Eretria, and thereafter, more slowly, by other mainland and island states. Before long the Greeks of the West also followed suit. Solon is credited with changing the weight standard of the Athenian currency from that used by Aegina to the lighter standard favored by Corinth and the cities of Eubœa. We can hardly doubt that the Athenians benefited by the change, which simplified trade relations with Corinth, their neighbors of Eubœa, and the Greek cities of the islands and Anatolia, where the lighter standard was also in use.[1] The same reformer, it may be mentioned in this connection, also prevailed on his countrymen to adopt a new system of weights and measures in place of the old Peloponnesian, so-called Pheidonian, standard which had hitherto been used in Attica.

The adoption of metallic currencies greatly facilitated and thereby also stimulated trade. On the other hand, where so many independent communities minted their own issues and these were not only not all on the same standard, but, what was more vital, differed in the purity of their metal, the full benefit of the new invention was not always achieved or maintained. At a later date the currency of Athens is specifically mentioned as one which, in contrast to the mintages of other cities, which hardly circulated — except at a loss — outside the particular localities in which they were issued, was readily accepted everywhere. The reason for this was simple. The Athenians did not allow their tetradrachms to deteriorate in quality and did not, as many Greek governments seem to have done from time to time, tamper with their coinage in order temporarily to improve their revenues. It was a piece of sharp practice which brought its own punishment. The earliest coins are of electrum, a natural alloy of gold and silver, and some of the Asiatic Greeks continued to strike electrum currency to the beginning of the fifth century. Broadly speaking, however, gold generally superseded the alloy in the

---

[1] The Aeginetan two-drachm piece (didrachm) weighed 193 grains (12.3 grams); the Euboic didrachm weighed only 135 grains (8.4 grams). This was the silver standard. The gold standard was universally 130–135 grains for the gold stater. The normal ratio of gold to silver was 1:13.

cities of Asia Minor and some of the islands, while silver was universally used in the mainland states and in the West.

The only industry of this age about which, thanks to excavation and the durable·character of the objects, we can form a fairly clear picture is the ceramic. The number of decorated wares of the archaic period is considerable; both in fabric and decoration they are of great merit. The place of manufacture is often doubtful, although the more notable and popular kinds have been assigned by archæologists with greater or less certainty to particular regions. One type of ware has thus been classed as Milesian, another as Samian; Corinthian ware, too, is found over a very wide area, as is another class of vases commonly called proto-Corinthian, though these are probably not a Corinthian fabric at all. We have seen that in Laconia also during the seventh and sixth centuries the potter's art flourished. In these and other centres there must have dwelt many craftsmen, each of whom made his wares in his own workshop, assisted by his sons and perhaps an apprentice and a slave or two. The political and social status of these men and of craftsmen engaged in the manufacture of other articles is difficult to determine. Many of them at this time seem to have belonged to the poorest class of citizens; but we have noted that in Laconia and Messenia such occupations were left to the *perioikoi*, while in sixth-century Athens Greeks from other cities began to settle permanently, and rapidly increased in number. Conditions similar to the Athenian are likely to have obtained in many other city-states where the prospects of trade and industry were for one reason or another promising. The excellence of Attic clay for pottery, the proximity of copper mines as in Eubœa, which furnished the raw material for the metal-worker, or the exceptionally favorable geographical situation of cities like Corinth or Byzantium, which made them important marts for the exchange of commodities, may serve as instances of natural advantages such as would attract workers from other parts of Greece. Where a particular variety of pottery is found over a wide area, it is not safe to assume that it all emanated from a single centre. There may have been many cases where the potter and not his wares emigrated to a new home in which he might hope more successfully to practise the craft than in the city of his birth from which excessive competition had driven him.

The use of slave labor, whether in the home or in the workshop, was probably very restricted in this age. The traffic in non-Hellenic slaves began to develop in the sixth century, and in the following century assumed much greater proportions. While, however, there is a danger of exaggerating the extent of this institution, especially in the earlier period, there can be no doubt that some slaves had been kept by the wealthier classes from earliest Greek times, just as was the case in the society portrayed in the Homeric poems. Apart from other evidence, the custom of enslaving insolvent debtors which has been noticed in an earlier chapter, offers clear proof of the prevalence of the institution.

The commerce between different regions in the Aegean, and from there to the Black Sea, Egypt, and the western Greeks was partly carried on in the interests of the food supply, — for with the growth of city-states many of them ceased to be wholly self-supporting, — partly in what may be broadly classed as luxury articles, such as decorated pottery, metalwork of various kinds, or the finer sorts of textiles. There must also have been a good deal of trade in raw materials, metal ores, timber for ship-building, perhaps also woollen yarn from those regions like Miletus in the East and southern Italy in the West, where sheep-rearing was practised greatly in excess of what was needed for local consumption. The governments of the states derived their profit from these enterprises indirectly. They imposed taxes on imports and exports, and often harbor dues as well. A city like Corinth, being a great centre of exchange, would secure a large revenue in this way. That her wealthy governing class engaged directly in commerce is not only not proven, but in the highest degree unlikely. These persons sold the excess of the produce of their estates and invested the capital which they accumulated from the land in loans to merchants or in carrying out contracts for their government.

It will be apparent from the foregoing remarks that we still know little that can be called certain about Greek economic life in the archaic period. Doubtless further excavations, especially along the Asia Minor littoral and in some of the more outlying parts of the Hellenic world will help to unravel some of the numerous outstanding problems and to fill in some of the worst gaps in our knowledge. But it is questionable whether it will ever be possible to trace the continuous growth of Greek commerce and industry in the earlier period as we can now, in spite of many obscurities, follow up the political and constitutional evolution of the Greek city-state.

CHAPTER XI

RELIGIOUS INSTITUTIONS, ART, AND LITERATURE IN THE ARCHAIC PERIOD

*For many and great are the reasons which
hinder us from doing this, even though we should
desire. . . . Then, secondly, there is the bond of
Hellenic race, by which we are of one blood and
of one speech, the common temples of the gods and
the common sacrifices, the manners of life which
are the same for all; to these it would not be well
that the Athenians should become traitors.* — Herodotus, viii, 144 (Macaulay's translation).

THE previous chapter, being mainly concerned with political history and institutions, necessarily stressed the absence of political unity in archaic Greece. There were independent city-states without number, and constant fighting between them. Nevertheless, if politically the Greeks were and remained incurably particularistic, they were also conscious of being all alike members of the Hellenic race, and this consciousness found its expression and its perpetuation in some of their most noteworthy religious institutions. The Greek word *barbaros*, should, down to the end of the fourth century B.C., be rendered in English by "non-Hellenic." For it was applied to all non-Greek races, — to the highly cultured peoples of Egypt or Persia as well as to the uncouth nomads of Scythia or the wild hillsmen of Thrace and the Anatolian uplands. Only from the Hellenistic period onward, when "Hellenic" signified community in culture rather than in race, can *barbaros* justifiably be translated "barbarian." The citation from Herodotus which heads this chapter is taken from the reply made by the Athenians to the Spartans when the latter were afraid that Athens might make a voluntary submission to Persia in 479 B.C. We are justified in thinking that the statement, put into the mouth of the Athenians by the historian, presents the general belief entertained by the Greeks in the fifth century. That the attendance at common sanctuaries of great

156

antiquity, and the periodic celebration of common religious festivals, were prime factors in insuring the essential homogeneity of the Hellenes is beyond dispute.

From very early times there existed in different regions of the Greek world leagues of cities, which were originally formed for a religious purpose. Representatives from a group of *poleis* met periodically at some sanctuary for the joint worship of a common protecting deity. Thus, there was a league of seven cities — four in the Argolid, Aegina, Athens, and Bœotian Orchomenus — whose meeting place was the shrine of Poseidon in the little island of Calaureia off the Argolic peninsula. At Cape Samikon in Triphylia a number of communities in that part of the Peloponnese joined together from time to time in the common worship of the same divinity. Similar religious confederations existed in Bœotia, at Delos, in Thessaly, and in Asia Minor.[1] The best known, and in every way the most important of all, was the Great Amphictiony of twelve tribes which met twice a year, in the spring in the shrine of Demeter at Anthela near Thermopylæ, and in the autumn in Apollo's sanctuary at Delphi. The fact that the members of this league were tribes, not city-states, shows the great antiquity of what was in origin a religious confederation, though, from the sixth century B.C. onward, it at different times exerted considerable political influence.[2] At the deliberations of the Amphictionic league each race or tribe had two votes, so that, in theory, even at a time when Sparta or Athens were the leading states in Greece, these two city-states were only a part of the Dorians and Ionians respectively. In practice, of course, the powerful states largely determined the voting of the tribes to which they belonged, and sometimes that of others as well.

Delphi, the autumn meeting-place of the Amphictiony, was a very ancient cult centre (Cf. Plate 15). It is mentioned in the

[1] The Pan-Ionian confederacy of twelve Ionian cities, whose meeting place was the sanctuary of Poseidon at Mycale, is held by some scholars to be political *in origin*.

[2] Such leagues existed partly for the mutual protection of the members and therefore served some political purpose from the first. This is shown by the wording of the Amphictionic oath, which even in the fourth century B.C. was still quaintly archaic. No member should destroy a city whose people were also members, or cut off their water supply in peace or war.

Homeric poems, being famed already for its riches, while its oracle is consulted by Agamemnon. Literary tradition points to the fact that the worship of the god Apollo was superimposed on an earlier cult of the Earth goddess. Delphi was the most famous oracular seat in the Greek world, and, in spite of occasional vicissitudes, continued to exist down to the later years of the fourth century A.D. Even older, it would seem, was the oracle at Dodona in Epirus, where the shrine was sacred to Zeus and Dione. It also, and "its priests with unwashed feet who couch on the ground" (*Iliad* 16,233), are named by Homer. These two mantic cult-centres surpassed all others in importance. For, though there were many other oracles — among the most notable was that of Apollo at Branchidæ near Miletus — the influence of these was, in general, only local. Dodona, and especially Delphi, were Panhellenic in their appeal and authority. Both oracles were extensively consulted by private persons on all manner of topics, and there can be no doubt that they exerted a weighty influence on human life, and that their advice was seriously regarded by the average Greek. The Delphic oracle, besides, at times wielded great political power. States sought the guidance of the god on matters of policy, and many tales were current about the oracular responses which often allowed of two interpretations. How deeply the oracle's counsel was valued in the earlier period is shown by the regular custom of seeking its advice before sending out a colony. It was not merely asked to approve the colonizing expedition projected by the mother-city, but often indicated the founder's name and the site on which the new settlement should be established.

The sanctuary, which attracted worshippers from every quarter of the Hellenic world, was gradually enriched by dedications and treasure given by pious devotees, by grateful recipients of Apollo's counsel, and by states who took a pride in embellishing this most national of all Hellenic holy places. Even foreign princes who, like Crœsus of Lydia, admired and were to a great extent imbued with Greek culture, lavished gifts on Delphi. Thus, in time, the temple and its precincts became a veritable museum of art, a show-place unrivalled save by Olympia, the hallowed spot on which were held the oldest and the most celebrated of the Greek athletic festivals (Cf. Plate 17).

The importance of the national Games as a unifying force, and their influence on Greek life and manners, were profound. The celebration at Olympia was traditionally two centuries older than the other three national festivals, held respectively at Delphi, the Isthmus of Corinth, and Nemea in the Argolid.[1] The Olympian and Pythian Games took place every four years, the Isthmian and Nemean every other year. The rules governing the athletic competitions, which, it must be remembered, were held in honor of a god — Zeus at Olympia and Nemea, Apollo at Delphi, Poseidon at the Isthmus — and were essentially sacred institutions, were extremely strict. Some further details about the Olympian festival will serve to illustrate this side of Greek civilization somewhat more fully. The competitors were required to be of pure Greek descent and of unblemished life. Those who, for one reason or another, were not in possession of the full civic rights of their state were ineligible. A long period of training (ten months) was also obligatory. There were separate athletic competitions for boys. Women, with the exception of the priestess of Demeter, were excluded from the celebration, but there was a separate festival for them, the Heræa, at Olympia. The Games took place at the time of the first full moon after the summer solstice, and during their celebration a sacred truce binding on all Hellenes was proclaimed. From the fifth century B.C., if not slightly earlier, the festival attained a far wider significance; it became an immense national Greek assembly, at which the various states vied with one another in providing magnificent equipment for their official delegates. The rewards of the victors at the Games were of the simplest kind, but states rewarded those of their citizens who were successful with high and substantial honors.[2] Thus, at Athens an Olympic victor on his return home was escorted, clad in purple and drawn by white steeds, into the city through a breach made in the city

[1] The traditional date of the first Olympian festival was 776 B.C. The dates recorded for the others were: Pythian festival at Delphi, 586; Isthmia, 582; Nemea, 573. It is probable that before these dates local celebrations had occurred from time to time at the respective sanctuaries.

[2] At Olympia the victor was crowned with a wreath of wild olive. At the Pythia the wreath was first of oak leaves, later of bay leaves. The Isthmian crown was made of wild celery in earlier years, later of pine; while the Nemean was of wild celery.

walls. He received the privilege of dining in the Prytaneum for life as the guest of the state, and a monetary gift as well. It would be quite erroneous to regard such treatment as a mere manifestation of the worship of athleticism. These demonstrations were inspired by strong religious feeling, by an implicit belief that the victor was a special favorite of the gods, and — on the principle of *mens sana in corpore sano* — qualified to perform the highest services for his country, in fact the nearest human approach to the perfect man. It was only from the end of the fifth century that undue specialization began to ruin the old spirit of the Games, and the athletes who competed tended to become more and more a special class, men of brawn with second-rate brains.

The athletic festivals, with their encouragement of the finest physical development of the human form, exerted a powerful and abiding influence on Greek art. They were also an inspiration to Greek literature, above all to the greatest of Greece's lyric poets, Pindar. Let us, in fine, hear the praise bestowed on the Olympian festival by one of the finest of the fourth-century writers. Even if we allow for some idealization, the claim he makes remains fundamentally true. "The men," says Isocrates (*Panegyricus*, 43), "who founded these festival assemblies deserve our praise. By them we are enabled to make truce with each other and interrupt existing enmities and then forgather together in one centre. Thereafter we join in common prayers and sacrifices and recall that we are all of the same kindred. In the future we are more kindly disposed to each other, and renew old guest friendships and form new ones, and that sojourn is of value to competitors and non-competitors alike."

It is probable that the despots of the sixth century did much to further the development and enlarge the scope of these national festivals. To Peisistratus belongs the credit of reconstituting several Attic festivals and religious celebrations in such a way that, within a century, they had ceased to be of merely local interest and were attended by visitors from all parts of the Greek world. The worship at Eleusis of the two goddesses, Demeter and her daughter, Kore (Persephone), with whom were associated several lesser male deities or heroes, was of great antiquity. The earliest literary reference to this cult is in the seventh-century Hymn to Demeter; its inclusion in the Athenian state religion is at least as old as Solon's time. The celebrations took place every year, but it was probably Peisistratus who instituted more elaborate ceremonies, to take place every four years. The chief religious offices in connection with the cult were hereditary in certain families. The general superintendence of the festival was entrusted to the archon basileus and four other officials. If we include all preliminaries, the entire celebration, which took place in the autumn, lasted eight or nine days. The culminating ceremonies, a solemn procession from Athens to Eleusis and the performance of the Mysteries, occurred on the last two days. The initiated were vowed to strict silence about what they had seen and done, and there is much uncertainty about the nature of the mystic rites on the last day. Apparently certain sacred objects were shown to the *mystai*, who also witnessed a religio-dramatic performance dealing with the grief of Demeter at the loss of her daughter and her joy when reunited with Kore. The uplifting effect on the worshippers is too well attested by the best classical writers to be doubted. Unlike the ordinary formal ceremonies of the state religion, the Mysteries satisfied man's emotional and spiritual craving and held out to him the hope of happiness after death. All Greeks, provided they were untainted by any religious pollution, might participate in the festival and, after the needful period of probation, become initiated. Thus the Eleusinian Mysteries became one of the important Panhellenic cults.

In the first month of the Attic year, corresponding to part of July and August, it had been the custom from early times to celebrate at Athens a festival in honor of the goddess Athena, Guardian of the City (Polias), which lasted from six to nine days. It was due to the initiative of Peisistratus that in the third year of every Olympiad the celebrations were conducted on a more magnificent scale. This four-yearly festival was known thereafter as the Greater Panathenæa. There were gymnastic and equestrian contests; the Pyrrhic war dance, supposed to have been introduced from Laconia in the time of Solon or Peisistratus, was performed by troops of armed men, the successful team being rewarded with the prize of an ox; the

"muster of men" was another team competition, in which the
best-looking and fittest men from each tribe paraded. From
Peisistratic days there was also a musical contest between
rhapsodists who recited portions of the Homeric poems; other
musical competitions were added in the following century.
The prize in the athletic events was a large amphora filled with
olive oil, and a garland of olive leaves. Innumerable specimens
of these Panathenaic amphoræ, varying in date from the sixth
century to the Hellenistic period, have survived and now
adorn the museums of Europe and America (Plate 16a). The
shape of the vases and the decoration are more or less constant.
One side was adorned with a figure of Athena in full armor, the
other with a picture of, or allusion to, the competition for which
the vase was won. The outstanding ceremony of the Greater
Panathenæa was a solemn procession from the city of Athens
to the Acropolis, in which both citizens and resident aliens
took part. A robe (peplos), spread sail fashion on a ship's
mast fixed on rollers, was conducted to the foot of the citadel
and then carried up to the temple of the goddess on the Acropolis, where it was solemnly dedicated to Athena. A great
sacrifice was also performed on an altar in front of the temple.
A regatta at Peiræus, in which crews from each tribe competed,
formed the after-celebration. The Panathenaic procession is
known not merely from literary sources, but is plastically
represented on the frieze which ran round the cella wall of the
Parthenon, the new temple to Athena on the Acropolis built
in the Periclean age.[1]

The worship of Dionysus, god of the vine, with its strongly
emotional and even orgiastic celebrations, was well established
among the rural population of Attica by the seventh century.
In the time of Peisistratus no less than three festivals in honor
of this deity took place each year, the Lenæa in January, the
Rural Dionysia in December, and the Greater Dionysia in
Athens itself during March. Of these three the last was either
newly instituted or else completely reorganized by the Tyrant.[2]

[1] See below page 326 and Plates 24, 25, and 26.

[2] The festival which at Athens became the Greater Dionysia is said to
have been transferred by Peisistratus from Eleutheræ to his capital.
This new celebration may, however, have been superimposed on an older
Dionysiac festival in Athens. This is not the place to enter into the numer-

By his action the worship of Dionysus became a part of the state religion of Athens.   More momentous, however, was the stimulus which the institution of this festival gave to the development of the Attic drama.   The singing of choral songs in honor of the god, accompanied by ritual dances, had long been customary.   A dramatic element was introduced into the performance only when the choirs were occasionally interrupted by a dialogue between the leader of the chorus and another, who at first may well have been the poet himself. Tradition makes Thespis the "father of tragedy" and the first victor in a dramatic contest held at Athens in 534-533 B.C. But for fifty years after that date nothing is known of the scope and character of the dramatic performances held at the Greater Dionysia.   Only from the time of the Persian wars can the history of Attic drama be clearly traced.

The Age of Tyrants corresponded to the century and a half which was the formative period of Greek art, the age when Greek lyric poetry all but reached its zenith, the age in which implicit belief in the old polytheistic religion and the mythologies and cosmogonies of earlier centuries was succeeded by scepticism and the spirit of inquiry on the part of a few bold speculators.   The patronage of absolute rulers and their desire to beautify their cities acted as a powerful stimulus to artistic achievement.   At Corinth and in other centres the despots erected temples and public buildings at great expense.   Poets and artists, whose creative work could shed lustre on, or help to give distinction to, the city in which they found a temporary or a permanent home, were welcomed by the Tyrants.   As usual, our information is fullest for Athens.   Peisistratus rebuilt the temple of Athena on the Acropolis and constructed the earliest initiation hall (*Telesterion*) at Eleusis over the site of an older sanctuary.   Both structures were fated to be destroyed by the Persians in 480-479 B.C.   He also began to build a temple at Athens in honor of Zeus Olympios; but it was not completed by him and his sons, and remained a fragment for many centuries.   The poets Anacreon and Simonides

---

ous problems connected with the origin of tragedy and comedy.   The reader interested in these questions is referred to the works enumerated in the Bibliography.

were honored guests at the court of Hippias and Hipparchus, while Peisistratus' zeal on behalf of religion has already been noted.

In the cultural evolution of the Hellenic race the Greeks of Asia Minor can justly claim to have been pioneers in every field. Early examples of Ionian art, moreover, like the ivories and other *objets d'art* found below the sixth-century temple of Artemis at Ephesus and belonging to the late eighth and early seventh centuries, show very plainly the study of non-Hellenic, that is to say, Eastern, prototypes by Ionian artists and craftsmen. Similar oriental influence can also be observed in mainland products, such as the ivory plaques from Sparta, or the decorative designs of Corinthian, and, to a less extent, of Laconian pottery. The earliest Greek sculptures in the round, however, and the earliest Doric architecture, seem to owe more to Egyptian models. Yet it was not long before the individuality of the Hellenic artist in either sphere asserted itself, and totally new art forms were evolved.

Though private dwelling-houses were at this time, and remained for centuries, of the simplest character, more stable and impressive edifices in honor of the gods were erected. Of the nature and appearance of other public buildings in this age we can, in the absence of remains, form no accurate estimate. The two styles of architecture known as Doric and Ionic developed contemporaneously. The former may be called Western, the latter Eastern, in this sense: In Sicily and Magna Græcia the Ionic order was rarely met with, while in Asia Minor the Doric was equally unpopular. In Greece both styles coexisted, but, judging by the extant remains, the Doric order was in much greater favor. The earliest shrines were small rectangular structures fronted with a vestibule, the entablature, roof, and pillars, where these were employed, being of wood. A great advance was reached when larger temples began to be set up and the rectangular building (cella) itself was surrounded by pillars, thus forming a continuous ambulatory (peristyle) round the outside of the cella. Wooden pillars were replaced by columns of limestone or marble, and finally the whole upper structure also was built of stone. In the remains of early Doric temples like the Heræum at Olympia (seventh century; *see* Plate 17*a*) and

a

b

DELPHI: *a*. Temple of Apollo; *b*. Colonnade of the Athenians with Polygonal Wall behind

Plate 15

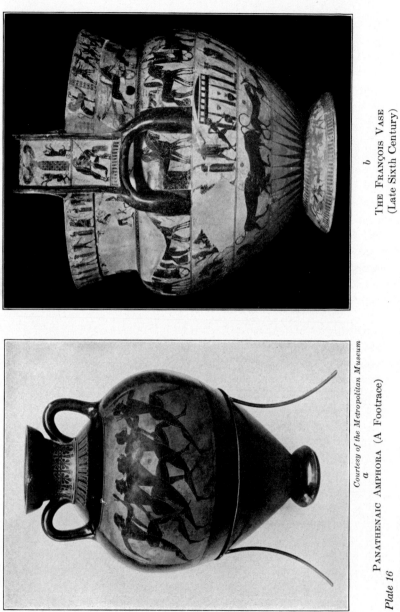

a

PANATHENAIC AMPHORA (A Footrace)

b

THE FRANÇOIS VASE
(Late Sixth Century)

Plate 16

the old temple at Corinth (sixth century) and some early examples in Sicily, the perfect symmetry of all the columns is still absent, and the individual columns are too short and heavy and generally of a clumsy appearance. The triangular gables formed by the ends of the roof at the short sides of the temple, *i.e.* at the east and west ends, were often decorated with sculptures. Fragments of such pedimental groups which once adorned temples on the Athenian Acropolis of the pre-Peisistratic and Peisistratic ages, though their execution is still crude, show considerable skill in their arrangement, so as to fit into a triangular space. The effect for the spectator, who would necessarily contemplate the pediments from some distance off, was heightened by a lavish use of color both on the sculpture and on the architectural details of the entablature. This custom of using coloration freely on statues and on buildings continued in the finest period of Greek art.

While the general plan of Ionic temples was very similar to that of the Doric, the columns rested on bases instead of directly on the stylobate, were of slenderer proportions, and were crowned with a volute capital in place of the plain Doric capital. The decoration of the entablature was also characterized by somewhat greater elaboration of detail, the architrave being surmounted by a continuous frieze instead of by a succession of separate plain or sculptured slabs (metopes) separated by triglyphs, as was the case in a Doric temple. The decoration of the lowest drums of columns, and of their bases, with sculptures in high relief, which is found in the sixth- and again in the fourth-century temple of Artemis at Ephesus, was an unusual addition to the plastic decoration of a temple. Such ornamentation was indeed in questionable taste and was not generally adopted.

Specimens of archaic sculpture in the round and in relief are much more numerous than examples of early architecture. There is a very great variety in the detail of the statues, and their number is so considerable that all stages in artistic development are represented, from the crudest figure, in which little more than the head and extremities are indicated, the torso being flat or round, but hardly suggesting the human form, to statues of the end of the sixth or the beginning of the fifth century, in which the artist has attained almost complete mastery in portraying free movement and life-like expression, and reproducing all with anatomical exactness. The two chief types are nude male and draped female figures, both represented in a standing attitude. Draped and seated figures are somewhat less common. The extant examples of early Greek sculpture are almost exclusively in stone. The earliest pedimental figures from the Athenian Acropolis are in soft poros; limestone was occasionally used, but in the great majority of cases the material is marble. Of this there were in the Aegean area a good many varieties, but the most popular were that from the island of Paros and that quarried on Mt. Pentelicus in Attica. The invention of hollow-casting in bronze made possible the creation of life-size statues in this substance. Though very few bronze figures — other than small statuettes — have survived from antiquity, there is abundant evidence to show that in the archaic period certain artists or schools of artists employed metal in preference to stone. The islands of Samos and Chios both produced noted artists in the sixth century. The art was handed on from father to son, and in the case of one Chiote family we have the names of artists belonging to four successive generations. This family of sculptors worked exclusively in marble; their contemporaries and, we may say, rivals in Samos specialized in bronze-casting. In the centuries that follow bronze was the favorite material for single statues in the round.

The rise and spread of Greek literature would hardly have been possible but for the invention of the alphabet. It is uncertain at what date the Greeks first became acquainted with the Phœnician alphabet; but, once they had been familiarized with the Semitic symbols, they rapidly adapted them to the needs of their own tongue. Some superfluous consonantal signs they used to express the vowels, which in Phœnician, as in other Semitic languages, were not written, and they also added four new letters to the alphabet. No extant Greek inscriptions are demonstrably older than the latter part of the seventh century, but the beginning of Greek writing is likely to be at least a century earlier. Moreover, the invention spread to all parts of the Hellenic world, and local differences in the forms, and sometimes in the value, of individual letters arose. The Ionians were once again in the van of progress. Their letters proved to be best adapted for all purposes, and, ultimately, the Ionic alphabet was universally employed, although uniformity was not finally achieved till the middle of the fourth century.

We have no means of knowing when the Homeric poems were first committed to writing; but, whether handed down orally or set down in the new script, they found many imitators. Save for a few fragments these lesser poems of the epic cycle have disappeared. But a group of shorter poems written in hexameter verse, the so-called *Homeric Hymns*, has survived. They are hymns in honor of certain gods, Apollo, Demeter, Hermes, and so on, but they are not all of the same date. The earliest may go back to the end of the eighth century, others do not antedate the sixth, showing how long the epic tradition lasted even after other and more popular forms of poetry had been created. The Greeks of the classical period were wont to associate with the name of Homer that of Hesiod. He lived at Ascra in Bœotia at the end of the eighth or the beginning of the seventh century. Of three works that have come down to us under his name, the *Works and Days* is certainly, the *Theogony* probably, a genuine work of the poet. The *Shield of Heracles* is a composition of later date and inferior merit. While the *Theogony* is a history of the creation of the world and of the gods, which the Greeks of later centuries regarded together with the Homeric poems as canonical, the *Works and Days* is a didactic epic, which is very loosely knit together and really falls into two unequal parts. The first and shorter section briefly traces the five ages of man, the longer portion depicts farm life in Bœotia, and provides many practical instructions for the farmer together with a goodly list of ill-omened actions which he should sedulously avoid. A short citation from the poem, which is written in hexameters, will help to illustrate its practical good sense and rustic tones:

But when the House Carrier (*i.e.* the snail) crawls up the plants from the ground, fleeing from the Pleiades, then is it no longer seasonable to dig about the vines, but rather to sharpen sickles and arouse the thralls, and to fly shady seats and sleep toward the dawn, in the season of harvest when the sun parcheth the skin. In that season must thou busy thee to lead the harvest home, rising up in the morning that thy livelihood may be secure. . . . But what time the artichoke bloometh and the chattering cicala sitting on a tree poureth his shrill song from beneath his wings incessantly in the season of weary summer, then are goats fattest and wine best, women most wanton and men most weak, since Sirios parcheth head and knee and the skin is dry for heat.[1]

Experiments in iambic and elegiac verse must have been made at a very early date, for by the seventh century both had been developed to a high degree of excellence. Little, if at all, later in date are various lyric metres. The poems composed in these were all intended to be sung to the accompaniment of the lyre. Thus a great quantity of poetry, much of it doubtless of first-rate quality, was put out in the two centuries preceding the Persian wars; but, save for a miserable remnant of citations preserved in later Greek writers, slightly augmented in recent years by the recovery of some additional fragments in Egyptian *papyri*, all this body of literature has been lost. Of the nature of the music which accompanied the lyric compositions we are entirely ignorant. Again the eastern Greeks were intellectually in advance of their mainland kinsmen. Archilochus of Paros (*c.* 650 B.C.) served as a mercenary soldier and spent some part of his life in Thasos before finally returning to his native island. He composed elegiac poetry in which he depicted episodes of his own life, and hymns to the gods which he wrote in the iambic, not the epic, metre. But he was most famous for his bitter lampoons and satire in iambics on some of his contemporaries, above all, on a well-to-do citizen of Paros, Lycambes, and his daughters, one of whom the poet had unsuccessfully wooed. In this last genre of poetry, satiric verse, Archilochus had his imitators and successors, notably Semonides of Amorgos and Hipponax of Clazomenæ, but none of them seems to have been his equal either in power or in diction. The contempt in which these poets, and for that matter Hesiod also, speak of the female sex suggests that under Ionian influence the position of women in some parts of the Greek world had changed considerably since Homeric days.

Elegiac poetry had many exponents: Callinus of Ephesus (*c.* 650 B.C.) and his contemporary, Tyrtæus of Sparta, Mimner-

---

[1] *Works and Days* (transl. by A. W. Mair), ll. 571 ff.

mus of Colophon in the next generation, and Solon the Athenian, and Theognis of Megara in the sixth century. Judging by the surviving fragments we can see that any of a large variety of subjects was regarded as suitable for treatment in this verse form. Thus Callinus and Tyrtæus called on their countrymen to perform deeds of prowess, Solon used the elegy to express his philosophy of life, Mimnermus and Theognis to sing of love and friendship, as well as to instil moral maxims and to convey their views on contemporary affairs.

Early lyric poetry is especially associated with the island of Lesbos. Here Terpander (c. 650 B.C.) is said to have founded a school of lyric bards. But it is in the first half of the next century that the two most famous singers of this island flourished, Alcæus and Sappho. The former was deeply implicated in the political disturbances in the island which led finally to the appointment of Pittacus as legislator and quasi-dictator for ten years. Alcæus, with other incalcitrant members of the Lesbian aristocracy, was compelled to go into exile. His contemporary, Sappho, also suffered banishment with her relatives for a space, but eventually a general amnesty enabled the political exiles to return to Mytilene. Alcæus' poems appear to have dealt with a great variety of themes — his political fortunes, his wanderings, the joys of the wine-cup, and love. Sappho's lyrics covered a more restricted field of subjects. She composed a number of wedding hymns (*epithalamia*) of which but a few lines have survived; but her most famous poems were inspired by personal passion for the girl pupils whom she instructed in song and dance. Of the writers of choral lyrics the best known was Alcman. Though not a Spartan by birth — he is said to have come from Lydia — Alcman spent most of his adult life in Laconia and wrote his poems in the Doric dialect. His hymns, of which only one substantial fragment remains, were composed to be sung antiphonally by two groups of girl singers at religious celebrations. Their content was partly mythological, partly in praise of the leaders of the choirs. We may conclude this brief sketch of early Greek poets with a reference to Stesichorus. Unlike the other poets already named he came from the far West, from Himera in northern Sicily. He was in every sense an innovator, who sought to use lyric poetry as a medium for long narratives dealing with heroic and mythological subjects. Although not enough of his verse has been preserved to permit a proper estimate of his poetic powers, and although he does not seem to have found any direct imitators, he probably exerted an indirect influence on lyric poets of the next generation, like Pindar and Bacchylides, in whose epinician odes stories from Greek mythology have a regular place.

Great as was the cultural progress of the Hellenes during the sixth century, as manifested in their art and poetic literature, those hundred years witnessed a yet greater achievement, revolutionary in character, — no less than the birth of science and philosophical speculation. Once more it was certainly Greeks of Ionia who first took the tremendous step — for such indeed it was — of setting aside the mythologies and crude cosmogonies of the poets and the more esoteric doctrines concerning the creation of the world, the gods, and mankind, held by the adherents of a mystery religion, like Orphism, and of setting man's reason in the place of faith.[1]

The first bold speculator whose name has been recorded as questioning the received explanations of the Universe was Thales of Miletus. Ancients and moderns alike have justly regarded him as the father of philosophy and science. We know little of his life beyond the fact that he was an influential statesman in his native city, and that he had become familiar with the astronomy of the Egyptians and Chaldæans. Whether he acquired his knowledge by travelling himself to these regions we do not know, nor is it necessary to assume that he did. For the settlement of Greeks at Naucratis, made in the seventh century with the good-will of the Egyptian monarch, had stimulated intercourse between the land of the Nile and the Aegean cities; while the lore of the Middle East could readily

---

[1] The adherents of the Orphic sect seem to have been found in all parts of the Hellenic world. They had a sacred literature of their own, chiefly of a prophetic character. Their cult was untrammelled by the limitations imposed on the official religion of the city-state. The central doctrine of their system was the belief in the immortality of the soul. The sufferings of earthly life are a punishment for transgressions committed in an earlier existence and the soul suffers many reincarnations. But the hope of final redemption was held out to those who lived an ascetic and morally pure life, and were strict observers of the ritual prescribed to the initiates.

reach the West through Lydia. Making the best use of what
he had learnt, Thales, we are informed, foretold a solar eclipse
which occurred in 585 B.C. Had he done nothing more than
make the mathematical and astronomical lore of the Orient
his own, his accomplishment would have been noteworthy
and doubtless influential in that age. But his real and epoch-
making achievement was that he was not content merely to
record observed phenomena of nature, but that he deduced
therefrom the general conclusion that all nature is subject to
fixed laws, and asked himself the question, "What is the world
made of?" In more philosophical terms, he was the first to
inquire into the material cause of the Universe. That his solution of the problem was crude, namely, that water was the
primordial substance, is of secondary importance. It was he
who began the process of rational inquiry, which subsequent
speculators carried many stages farther and to more scientific
conclusions. Thales does not seem to have committed anything
to writing, but he had at least one eminent disciple, Anaximander. He not only propounded a less simple but more profound explanation than his master of the growth of the physical
Universe, deriving all four "elements" from a primordial mist
or vapor, which he called "the Unlimited," but he interested
himself in geography and was reputed to have constructed
the first map of the world. Anaximenes, a younger contemporary of Anaximander, in one sense returned to the earlier
position of Thales, inasmuch as he found the original substance
in one of the "elements," air. In reality, however, his rational-
ism was more marked than that of either of his predecessors,
since he explained the genesis of the other three "elements,"
and of the heavenly bodies, from air by condensation and rare-
faction, such as he could observe in his actual experience.

In the meantime a new line of inquiry and explanation had
been begun by two Ionian Greeks, who, toward the end of the
sixth century, had found their way to the West. Pythagoras
of Samos left his native land in or soon after 530 B.C., perhaps
for political reasons — Samos being then ruled by the Tyrant
Polycrates — and emigrated to Croton in southern Italy.
Primarily he was a mathematician; but to the world at large
he was more familiar as an educator and the founder of a semi-

philosophical, semi-religious brotherhood, whose members were vowed to secrecy and to an ascetic life not unlike the followers of Orphism. Indeed, Pythagoras borrowed some of his religious teaching, including the doctrine of transmigration of souls, from this source. He has the distinction of being the first to propound that the earth is not flat but a sphere, and to evolve a doctrine which came very near to being the heliocentric theory of the Universe. The sun, moon, and planets, including the earth itself, are endowed with motion, he taught, and revolve around a central fire. This part of Pythagoras' teaching remained without influence, partly because so bold a generalization could not hold its own against the less lofty but more intelligible tenets of the Ionian school, mainly, however, because Pythagoras himself sought a solution for everything in mathematics, that is to say in numbers, to which he assigned a mystical significance. Even so, both his mathematical discoveries — e.g. the theory of progressions which he applied also successfully to acoustics, discovering that the length of a taut string stands in a fixed relation to the pitch of the tone emitted when the string is struck — and his philosophico-religious doctrines exerted a profound influence on later philosophers.

His contemporary, Xenophanes of Colophon, found a new home at Elea in southern Italy, though much of his life seems to have been spent in travel. He was not so much a philosopher as a poet and moralist, who in his verse criticized severely the anthropomorphic and anthropopathic religion of his countrymen, and preached a monotheistic belief in "one God, greater than any god or man, unlike man in form or thought, directing all things without labor by the thought of his mind, ever staying in the same place motionless."

Though Xenophanes is generally described as the founder of the Eleatic school of philosophy, its real founder was his pupil, Parmenides. He constructed an elaborate philosophical system in which he differentiated between Being, or a universal element of nature, which alone can be the object of knowledge, and an infinite plurality of modifications which can only be the object of opinion. His difficult but important metaphysical doctrines he expounded in a long hexameter poem of which

a

b

OLYMPIA: *a.* Temple of Hera; *b.* Temple of Zeus

Plate 17

some fragments alone survive. Finally we may mention Heracleitus of Ephesus who, though he probably did not die till *c.* 475 B.C., in a philosophical sense belongs essentially to the previous generation. He was a more thorough sceptic than any of the thinkers already named. In contrast to Pythagoras, or Parmenides, or, for that matter, to the Ionian physicists, he insisted that not Being but Becoming was the ultimate reality of the Universe. The world is constantly dying, he maintained, and constantly being reborn, and above all there is Reason (*logos*) which rules it, which "guides all things through all things"; he refers to this also as Fire, because that is the purest form in which this divine life is perceptible to human eyes or senses. Heracleitus' teaching, though for many years it did not perhaps win many adherents — his uncompromising and hostile attitude to other speculators and systems, and the obscurity of his own writings had much to do with this neglect — exercised a profound influence at the beginning of the third century B.C. on the early Stoics.

The thinkers whom we have considered, when they committed their tenets to writing at all, did so in verse. It was not until the latter part of the sixth century that prose compositions were attempted by the Anatolian and the mainland Greeks. The earliest prose writers were compilers of genealogies and chroniclers like Pherecydes of Athens (?) and Acusilaus of Argos. The most interesting of these authors was, however, Hecatæus of Miletus. His date is fixed by the fact that he advised his fellow Milesians against undertaking the Ionian revolt in 499 B.C. Hecatæus' scientific interest was in geography. He improved the map of Anaximander, and wrote a long explanatory work about it. Nor did he confine himself strictly to geographical data; for he occasionally added information about the customs and mode of life of peoples in different parts of the world. Hecatæus also composed a genealogical work in which he exercised more criticism than his predecessors in this field; but it was far less influential than the other compilation, which Herodotus half a century later did not disdain to use with some freedom for his history.

CHAPTER XII

THE NEAR AND MIDDLE EAST IN THE SIXTH CENTURY B.C.

> *Darius the King says: Under the protection of Ahura Mazda, these are the countries which do that which I place on them as commands; countries which muster here; Persia, Media, and other lands and other tongues; the mountains and the level country of this side of the sea and the other side of the sea, of this side of the desert land and of the other side of the desert land. All that I have done I have accomplished under the protection of Ahura Mazda. May Ahura Mazda, together with all the gods, protect me and my rule.* — Inscription of Darius at Persepolis.

THE downfall of Assyria resulted from a hostile coalition formed against her by her neighbors. To keep secure hold of Babylonia was a problem which many Assyrian kings had found difficult, not because its population was unruly, but because the ruler of Babylon, whether independent or a provincial governor appointed by the Assyrian monarch, was in a strong position, if he wished, to dispute Assyrian supremacy in the Land of the Two Rivers. Babylon had suffered cruelly more than once; most severe was her punishment when captured and sacked by Sennacherib. In Ashurbanipal's reign it was the disaffection of his brother, the governor of Babylon, which brought about the most serious threat to his authority that Ashurbanipal had to face. During the last quarter of the seventh century Babylonia was independent. Its one-time governor, Nabopolassar, had himself proclaimed independent king of Babylon in 625 B.C., and he seems to have been a man whose ability was not unworthy of his ambition. The Assyrian king was too harassed on his northern and eastern borders, and his kingdom too weakened by internal dissensions, to bring the disloyal governor to order.

174

Little is known of these eastern neighbors of Assyria, the Medes. They were an Indo-European people who had migrated apparently from Scythia (*i.e.* southern Russia) into Armenia. Finding the kingdom of Van too strong to be occupied or over-run, they had borne off to the southeast, to find a home on the western side of the Iranian plateau. The date of their settlement in that region can only be guessed. It probably occurred about 1000 B.C. At this time, and for many years to come, the Medes were a pastoral people. There were, we are told, six tribes, each containing a number of smaller groups or clans. While the régime of the family and clan was strictly patriarchal, there was evidently no more developed system of political organization. The clans seem to have lived more or less independently; sometimes, too, they warred among themselves. But, in the face of a foreign foe or invader, the Median tribes stood together to repel the common enemy of them all. In the Assyrian annals there are occasional references to this people and to the attacks of Assyrian kings. In a record of Shalmaneser III two peoples are named who may, with great probability, be identified as the Medes and their southern neighbors, the Persians. The last named were akin in race and speech to the Medes. They had probably migrated southward from northern Khorasan, ultimately to find a home in southern Iran (the region corresponding approximately to the modern Persian province of Fars). Separated from Assyria only by the Zagros mountains and, as it were, sitting astride the main highway from Mesopotamia into Iran and beyond, the Medes were naturally brought into contact with their Semitic neighbors earlier than were their kinsmen of the southern plateau. The Assyrian king, Shamshi-Adad IV, invaded Media and compelled its inhabitants to pay tribute. Further Assyrian expeditions into Media are mentioned in the Assyrian records during the eighth century, in the time of Adad-Nirari and Tiglath-Pileser III. The latter's task of subduing the Medes seems to have been facilitated by the disunion of the Median tribes among themselves, contrary to their usual solidarity. The conqueror claims to have brought back many prisoners and quantities of spoil in the shape of horses and cattle.

Yet another incursion is recorded in Esarhaddon's time, but

this does not seem to have seriously interrupted the process of unification, which was now going on in Media, and which was an essential prerequisite for future imperial greatness. According to the legendary account, this development dates from the time when one of the clan or tribal chiefs, Deioces, was unanimously accepted as head of all the Medes and assumed the royal name and style.[1] He reigned for fifty-three years (*c.* 708–655 B.C.) and made of the Medes a united people. He fixed his capital at Ecbatana (Hamadan) in the heart of the Zagros hills. It was a strong natural fortress, on the very summit of which stood the royal palace. In royal ceremonial and doubtless, too, in the more important task of government, the Median kings found their model in the Assyrian state. Deioces, by scrupulously punctual payments of the tribute, is said to have warded off possibly hostile attentions from his overlord. Thus he was left to carry out the work of building up the Median state undisturbed. His successor, Phraortes (*c.* 655–633), followed a similar policy toward Assyria, which was ruled at this time by its last great king, Ashurbanipal. Thus he met with no interference when he set out to conquer his southern neighbors, the Persians. When finally he was rash enough to try his strength against Assyria, he was killed in battle and his army was heavily defeated.

With the next Median king we are on firmer historical ground. Cyaxares, profiting, if the traditional account of his predecessor's death be correct, by that disastrous experience, strove to reform his military machine. The old system of the Medes, under which each clan chief furnished contingents to the king when called upon, did not produce a fighting force that was a match for a highly trained and largely professional army like the Assyrian. Cyaxares succeeded in reorganizing his military resources on the Assyrian model, and at the same time improved the armature of his men. Special care was taken to train the cavalry thoroughly, so that it became the strongest arm of the service.

The situation of Assyria was now becoming desperate, and even an alliance with king Psammetichus of Egypt only helped

---

[1] In accordance with the usual practice, the Greek forms of these names, for which Herodotus is our main authority, have been kept throughout.

to check for a time Nabopolassar's advance to the Middle Euphrates. Hordes of Scythians had in the meantime overrun eastern Asia Minor and increased the peril of the Assyrian kingdom. At first the Assyrian king was able to come to terms with the northern invaders, even to the point of receiving them as allies against his enemies. But, at the critical moment, the Scythians forsook him. For, in 614 B.C., Cyaxares entered Assyria, and, though his attack on Nineveh failed, he succeeded in taking Ashur and levelled it to the ground. Nabopolassar and he now formed a close alliance, a political and military union cemented by the marriage of Cyaxares' grand-daughter to the son of Nabopolassar. In 612 a grand assault on Nineveh was made. Enemies from three sides joined in the attack, for Cyaxares had won a diplomatic triumph by bringing the Scythians over to his side. Nineveh was taken and destroyed; the Assyrian empire was at an end. A remnant of the Assyrian troops escaped to Harran where, supported to some extent by Egypt, they held on for a few years. The Egyptian king for some little while had nursed the ambition of regaining control over Syria; for, since the last years of Ashurbanipal, Assyrian overlordship there had become quite ineffective. Nor would Assyria, allied now with Egypt against her numerous enemies, put any check on Egyptian ambitions. The efforts of Nabopolassar to recreate a Babylonian empire, on the other hand, would be a far more serious obstacle to Egyptian plans. Psammetichus of Egypt died c. 610 B.C.; the Babylonian forces were now commanded by Nebuchadrezzar, the son of the aged Nabopolassar, who succeeded his father as king in 605. The war in and about Harran seems to have dragged on till 605. In that year Nebuchadrezzar inflicted a crushing defeat on the Egyptian host at Carchemish on the Euphrates. Thus were the hopes of political aggrandizement, cherished by the Egyptian king, finally shattered. Syria was annexed to Babylonia, while the kingdom of Assyria was incorporated in the Median empire. The Medes, after their triumph at Nineveh, appear to have attacked their Scythian allies, and either put them to the sword or driven them from the country.

Although all Syria and Palestine were necessarily affected by these momentous happenings, the fate of the kingdom of Judah

was specially poignant. The king, Josiah, had reigned over that
land for many years. At first, like his predecessors, he was a
vassal of Assyria; but his religious reforms, completed by 622,
had also a political significance. For, by cleansing the temple of
Jerusalem and then other parts of his kingdom from Assyrian
and other foreign gods and rites, he was in effect throwing off his
allegiance to his overlord. The annexation of Samaria followed;
finally came the wholesale execution of the priests of Baal. For
a few years the kingdom remained unmolested. But when in
609 B.C. an Egyptian army moved to the aid of the hard-pressed
remnant of the Assyrian forces, Necho II found his way barred
at Megiddo by the army of Josiah. Whether Josiah took this
step because he had definitely allied himself to Nabopolassar, or
merely from hostility to Assyria and her ally, Egypt, is not clear.
In any case, without support from outside, he had undertaken a
hopeless task. In a brief engagement the Judæan army was
utterly beaten and the king himself was slain. His elder son
succeeded him, owing his position to the favor of Necho; but he
was an oppressive despot who tried to undo his father's religious
reforms. The result was that his subjects were split into two
religious factions, and the military strength of a small kingdom,
recently weakened by foreign attack, was still further exhausted
by intestinal strife. Soon after Necho's defeat at Carchemish
all Syria and Palestine were annexed by the Babylonian monarch.
Thus Jehoiakim of Judah, too, was forced to submit and pay tribute. After three years of vassalage, he, in 599, revolted against
Nebuchadrezzar; but death overtook him before the Babylonian
army appeared at the gates of Jerusalem. His young successor,
to save his capital from utter destruction, surrendered himself to
the invader. For many years he languished in prison, while of
his subjects some eight thousand with their families were deported to Babylon. The unhappy Jehoiachin's uncle, who
ruled under the name of Zedekiah, was installed by Nebuchadrezzar as his vassal. During the next ten years the situation
remained outwardly unchanged. But the influence of the na-
tionalists, egged on by priests and prophets, grew stronger, and,
what was more, it was now hoped that Egyptian support might
be won to counterbalance the might of Babylon. Thus, when
Judah once more rebelled, a terrible punishment came upon her.

Nebuchadrezzar defeated an Egyptian army, but he made no effort to attempt the annexation of that country. His bitterest anger was reserved for Judah. In 586 B.C. Jerusalem was stormed, its temple and its palace were levelled to the ground, its inhabitants slaughtered or deported, and the kingdom of Judah was no more. From that day Palestine was always controlled by a foreign power, and no independent Jewish state was able to establish or maintain itself there.

The destruction of Judah was but one episode in Nebuchadrezzar's victorious career. He had defeated the forces of Egypt more than once, and had dealt no less drastically with Egypt's Phœnician allies. At his death in 562 his empire, including, besides Babylonia proper down to the Persian Gulf, the Euphrates valley as far as the Taurus, Syria, and Palestine to the borders of Egypt, seemed built on stable foundations. In addition, during his lifetime, relations with Media continued uniformly good. That all his territory fell a prey to a new conqueror twenty-four years later was due to the feebleness of his successors and to dynastic disputes, and, consequently, to periodic revolutions in different parts of the realm.

It was not only the Babylonian king who had enlarged his empire after the downfall of Assyria. The Mede had during the early years of the sixth century advanced his authority northwestward until, by c. 590 B.C., the furthest frontier of his realm was the river Halys. Thereby he was brought into direct touch with the powerful kingdom of Lydia. The hostilities which ensued between the two states may have lasted some five years, for the last recorded engagement between the two occurred in 585 B.C. The war ended in a stalemate. Since it had been impossible to reach a decision by force of arms, Cyaxares of Media and Alyattes of Lydia came to terms. The Halys remained the boundary between the two kingdoms, and a marriage alliance between the two royal houses was the beginning of friendly relations which continued between the two states for the next thirty-five years. The political history of the interior of Asia Minor for several centuries after the destruction of Hatti is still almost unknown. No considerable power existed in Anatolia during the centuries in which its coast-line became dotted with Hellenic settlements, whose cultural progress and political development were more rapid than those of the states on the Greek mainland.

A Phrygian kingdom existed in Asia Minor in the ninth and eighth centuries, but such importance as it may have had declined in the seventh before the might of neighboring Lydia. The growth of Lydia into a first-class power was not unattended by set-backs. Invasions by Northerners, whom the Greeks called Cimmerians, devastated the country more than once and compelled the kings of Lydia to sue for help from Assyria. In return they were constrained to become the vassals of the Assyrian monarch.[1] Great uncertainty still surrounds the nature of the Lydian race and language. Archæological remains have shown that the Lydians had by the beginning of the sixth century attained to a high degree of civilization, and that their material culture had been considerably influenced by that of the Ionian Greeks. Whether they are rightly credited with the invention of coinage or not, their kings were certainly among the earliest rulers to issue a metallic currency. In the forty years following their war with the Medes the Lydians, secure on their eastern frontier by treaty, followed an aggressive policy in the West. The Greek cities of the coast were forced to submit to Lydian overlordship and to pay tribute to the Lydian king. The name of Crœsus, who was destined to be the last Lydian monarch, and who was far more Hellenized than any of his predecessors, became proverbial for magnificence and wealth.

During these years of Lydian power in the West, the Median empire was ruled by Astyages. The reputed splendor of his court and the despotism, not unmixed with harshness, of his rule, seem to stamp him as a typical Oriental potentate. His fate was not less characteristic of the East. On the appearance of a rival, many of Astyages' subjects revolted and went over to the former, and the Median king suffered defeat and deposition. His conqueror and successor was not a Mede but a Persian. Cyrus styled himself king of Anshan, a region corresponding to that part of Elam in which lay the ancient city of Susa. This was now Cyrus' capital, and became in time the capital and administrative centre of the Persian empire. After a successful war which lasted several years Cyrus had vanquished

[1] Cf. p. 112 above.

Astyages (c. 549 B.C.), and followed this by occupying the Median capital, Ecbatana. The inhabitants of the Medo-Persian empire seem to have been little affected by what appears essentially to have been a dynastic struggle, from which the Persian prince emerged victorious. It was not long before the new ruler showed that he was a man of boundless military ambition and ability. The friendly relations which had existed for nearly forty years between Media and Lydia did not satisfy him. Crœsus seems to have realized that a change of dynasty among his eastern neighbors might become a danger to his own kingdom. He went so far as to take the offensive by invading Cappadocia, and, after a siege, captured the fortress of Pteria. At the same time he concluded alliances with the rulers of Babylonia and Egypt, and entered into friendly relations with Sparta. But he underrated the genius and strategy of his opponent. Cyrus attacked Lydia before the normal campaigning season had begun, thus taking Crœsus by surprise and preventing him from receiving help from his allies. A battle fought close to Sardes was followed by the siege of that city and by its capitulation soon after. The fate of Crœsus is uncertain, but he ceased to rule and Lydia became a part of the Persian dominions.

The Greek cities — Miletus alone had previously come to terms with Cyrus — soon found that the end of Lydia did not mean the recovery of their political independence. In fact they merely received a new overlord, although a number of them only submitted after several years of fighting against the generals of Cyrus. Samos alone maintained her independence somewhat longer, and, under her Tyrant, Polycrates, became for a few years the foremost maritime state in the Aegean. But, when her ruler fell into Persian hands (c. 524 B.C.), she too was forced to pay tribute to the Great King.

While Cyrus's officers were thus advancing the authority of their master to the shores of the Mediterranean, he himself was engaged in campaigns of conquest, which seem to have taken him to the shores of the Caspian Sea, to the River Jaxartes in the Northeast, where he erected fortresses which were still in existence in the time of Alexander the Great, and to the frontiers of India. Of these warlike enterprises we know almost nothing.

The nearer neighbor of Persia, once the ally of Media, he did not attack for six years after the fall of Sardes. At last, in 540 B.C., he invaded the kingdom of Babylonia, his main objective being Babylon itself. The capture of the capital and the annexation of Mesopotamia cost the conqueror a comparatively small effort. For the people of the land were thoroughly dissatisfied with their ruler, Nabonidus, the last of the Chaldæan dynasty, and were ready to welcome the Persian king as their master. In 539 B.C. Cyrus was able to take Babylon; hereafter the Chaldæan empire, including Mesopotamia, Syria, Phœnicia, and Palestine, was incorporated in the Persian. Cyrus lived for another ten years, but of his acts and policy during that period we are ignorant, save in a few particulars. He was extremely tolerant, permitting his various subjects to practise their national religions without molestation. He allowed a colony of Jews, hitherto in captivity, to return to Jerusalem and rebuild their temple, and he at the same time gave back to them the gold and silver vessels which had been carried away from there by Nebuchadrezzar. The organization of the vast Persian empire into provinces, and the administrative system devised for their government, which shed glory on the reign and name of Darius I, may well have been projected and perhaps begun by Cyrus. He fell fighting in 529 B.C., but the ancient writers disagree about the enemy against whom this last and fatal campaign was directed.

His son, Cambyses, who succeeded him as ruler of a vast realm, seems to have been associated with his father on the throne during the last years of Cyrus' life. His cruelty and caprice were perhaps due to a diseased body, for he appears to have been an epileptic. The one outstanding event of his short reign (529–522 B.C.) was the subjugation of Egypt. The war was begun in 526 B.C. and successfully carried through in the next year. Thus the land of the Pharaohs enriched the Persian empire by another province of boundless resources. But during Cambyses' absence a serious rebellion against his authority was staged in Media. The king, after three years in Egypt, started to return to the centre of government, but on the way, for reasons that are unexplained, he committed suicide. The Median, Gaumata, who had begun the revolt against the late king, ruled for a few months and was then assassinated by a small band of Persian nobles led by Darius. He, though he was descended from another branch of the royal house, could claim to be the legitimate heir of Cambyses, since the latter had left no issue. The death of Gaumata was, however, followed by insurrections in various districts of the empire, and by the emergence of sundry pretenders to the throne. It took Darius several years before he had suppressed all opposition and his sole authority was acknowledged throughout the empire of Cyrus and Cambyses. If Cyrus justly ranks as one of the world's foremost conquerors, Darius is no less entitled to be regarded as one of the world's great administrators. The system of imperial administration and provincial government perfected by him marked an immense advance on earlier practice, whether in Egypt, Babylonia, or Assyria, and, in spite of imperfections, endured for nearly two hundred years, in fact, as long as the Persian empire itself.

The Medes and Persians had for centuries come under the cultural influence of their neighbors in Assyria and Babylonia. Their scribes in time had taken over the cuneiform script, and had adapted it to the needs of the Persian language. It is in this Persian cuneiform that the great inscriptions of the Persian kings were written, the most famous being at Persepolis (Behistun). Similarly, Persian architecture and sculpture, as illustrated, for example, by the remains at Pasargadæ, Susa, and Persepolis, are primarily indebted to Assyrian models. Thus, as we should expect, the Persian imperial administration is in the first instance copied from Assyrian practice. Darius, however, was able to achieve a unity in diversity within his empire, which went far beyond anything found in earlier empires. Many of his innovations were of first-rate importance. Civil and military authority in the provinces was to some extent divided. The central government, that is to say, the king, exercised a close supervision over his subordinates. This was made possible by the greatly improved communications between different regions of the far-flung empire. Of the good roads constructed by the king's orders the best known is the Royal Road described by Herodotus. It ran from Sardes and Ephesus in Asia Minor to Susa, a distance of nearly 1500 miles. Postingstations were placed at intervals of about fourteen miles (four parasangs), and an imperial post was maintained for the swift transmission of royal despatches and rescripts from the capital to the satrapies. The total number of provinces or satrapies was, according to Herodotus, twenty; in the Persian inscriptions the total is slightly larger. The difference must be due to the subdivision of several of the remotest and most extensive provinces, which the Greek writer regarded as single administrative units. The civil head of the province was the satrap or viceroy. In addition, there was in each satrapy a secretary, and a military commander who was in general charge of all the military garrisons in that province. These two personages were, to a great extent, independent of the viceroy, for they were directly responsible to the Great King himself. The duties of the secretary consisted in part in keeping watch on the satrap and reporting on his conduct to the king. Besides this there was a more general system of surveillance over the empire. The "Eyes and Ears of the King" were, in effect, travelling inspectors — usually they were members of the royal family — who each year, accompanied by military escorts, visited especially the more outlying satrapies, and then reported on their general condition to their master. Officials with somewhat analogous duties had been periodically sent into Syria by the rulers of the XVIIIth Dynasty in Egypt. If military operations in a satrapy were called for, the satrap also acted as the military head of the province. But, since the military commander, who must technically have been the satrap's subordinate, acted under the direct orders of the king, in practice the military authority of the viceroy was not unrestricted.

The inhabitants of the empire were treated with much toleration. Many were allowed a great measure of local self-government, and there was no interference with their religions, customs, and social institutions. Their one major obligation was punctual payment of the tribute, imposed on them partly in kind, partly in money. While the total amount payable by each province was assessed at Susa, its timely collection and transmission to the capital counted as one of the chief duties of the satrap. Persis, or Persia proper, being the king's own country, was exempt from regular taxation. The performance of military service, to which all subjects of the king were liable, rarely bore heavily on all parts of the empire at the same time. The finest part of the army was recruited from Persia and Media; and the detachments raised in time of war in other parts of the empire were usually commanded by officers of Persian or Median stock. The raising of the required levies in a given satrapy devolved upon the viceroy. The two chief weaknesses in this provincial system were the danger that the satraps might become too independent, and the occasional difficulty of obtaining coöperation between neighboring viceroys in face of a common foe. We shall have occasion later to note cases of satraps who went so far as to intrigue with their master's foes in order to bring about the discomfiture or even downfall of a rival governor.

Reference has been made to the general tolerance in matters of religion shown by Cyrus and Darius and their successors. Even in Media and Persia there was much variety in religious practice. The mass of the people there practised a nature worship in which the adoration of the four "elements," fire, earth, air, and water, played the most important part. The Median clan of the Magi observed a special ritual of their own which was of great antiquity but whose form at the time of the Achæmenid kings is unknown. For that part of the Persian sacred book, the *Avesta*, which deals with ritual, belongs to a much later date when there had in all probability been some fusion of the Magian religion with the teaching of Zoroaster. The date at which this teacher and prophet lived is much disputed; according to the most generally accepted view he flourished in the seventh century B.C. While his teaching was in the main ethical, he also preached a monotheistic belief in a supreme god, Ahura-Mazda. The worship of this divinity was older than the prophet, so that Zoroaster's doctrine was the exaltation of Ahura-Mazda to the exclusion of other deities. We have no means of knowing how wide-spread Zoroaster's influence was in the earlier period of Persian history. Darius in his inscriptions describes himself as standing under the protection of Ahura-Mazda, but later kings of the line associated other deities with the supreme god. Again, the general tolerance of the Persian rulers toward the gods of their subject races was

scarcely compatible with strict Zoroastrian belief.   The evidence
available seems to show that Zoroastrianism did not become the
dominant or state religion in Persia till many centuries after this
time.[1]

Darius' early military expeditions had as their purpose the
reëstablishment of his authority throughout the empire which he
had inherited. His first attempt at adding to his dominions was
an expedition into Scythia, that portion of Europe which lay
north of the Danube and abutted on the western and northwestern shores of the Black Sea. Although the traditional date
for this undertaking is 512 B.C., it may actually have taken place
a year or two before. Its purpose and the course it took are
shrouded in mystery. The fleet which accompanied and transported the large military force led by the king in person, was
drawn from the Greek cities of Asia Minor. Darius, having left
his naval detachment on the Danube, advanced with his army
into the unknown interior and seems to have been gone for a
good many months. He was finally forced to retreat back to the
Danube and suffered considerable losses on the way. The proposal of one of the Greek naval commanders to his fellow Greeks,
to sail away and leave Darius to his fate, was defeated by the
rest, notably by the Tyrant of Miletus, Histiæus. Although the
Scythian expedition was a complete failure, one of Darius'
best officers was detailed to effect the conquest of Thrace. As a
result of his operations all the coast from Byzantium to the
mouth of the River Strymon was forced to submit to Persia.
Another officer effected the conquest of Lemnos and Imbros.
The newly acquired territories together formed a new satrapy,
the twenty-first according to Herodotus' reckoning.

---

[1] Thus, in a very recent work, *La Perse antique et la civilisation iranienne*,
by the late Clément Huart (Paris, 1925), the discussion of Zoroaster and
his work is not introduced till the third section of the book where the
author deals with the Sassanian period of Persian history. This began in
224 A.D.

CHAPTER XIII

THE AGE OF THE PERSIAN WARS

Land of the East, thou mournest for the host,
Bereft of all thy sons, alas the day!
For them whom Xerxes led hath Xerxes lost —
Xerxes who wrecked the fleet, and flung our hopes
away!

How came it that Darius once controlled,
And without scathe, the army of the bow,
Loved by the folk of Susa, wise and bold?
Now is the land-force lost, the shipmen sunk below.

—Aeschylus, *Persæ*, 548–557 (Morshead's translation).

THE first quarter of the fifth century, judged by the political issues which were then decided, was one of three or four supremely critical epochs in the history of the world. Though it is generally as easy as it is misleading to speculate on what might have happened if a series of interdependent episodes had had an outcome different from the actual one, it is indisputable that a Persian victory over the European Greeks, followed, as it would have been, by a Persian suzerainty over Hellas, would have materially checked or altered the progress of Greek civilization to which all subsequent western civilizations owe so much.

Darius I, though his real greatness was as an administrator, was sufficiently like his predecessors to wish to essay the rôle of conqueror. It was only to the westward that he could satisfy his military ambition. His first European venture was, as we saw, a failure, although it was followed by the annexation of Thrace. How soon he would have tried to renew his operations in the ordinary course of events we cannot tell. Actually, the preliminary round in the struggle between East and West began in 499 with a revolt of the Greek subjects of the Great King in Asia Minor. Both the causes and the course of the Ionian Revolt, as it is called, are very obscure, because Herodotus, who is practically our only informant of this episode, has, partly owing to his own political prejudices, partly on account of the sources used by him, written a very unsatisfactory narrative of it. The restlessness of the Greek cities of Asia Minor, which ended in rebellion against their overlord, must have existed for a number of years before 499. Resentment at being tributaries of an oriental power, dissatisfaction at being — as most of the Ionian cities then were — ruled by Tyrants, elation at Darius' failure in Scythia, were some of the factors which influenced the minds of the Asiatic Greeks. The episodes cited by the Greek historian as the causes of the revolt merely precipitated the outbreak of hostilities.

It will be remembered that one of the Greek commanders who accompanied Darius on the Scythian expedition was Histiæus, Tyrant of Miletus. Some years later Histiæus was summoned to the Persian court at Susa for reasons that are not very clear. His place in Miletus was taken by his son-in-law, Aristagoras. The latter proposed to the Persian governor of the province of Lydia, Artaphernes, a military and naval expedition to the Cyclades, which, if successful, would bring Naxos and probably some other islands under his, and so, indirectly, under Persian, control. The Great King's permission for the undertaking was given, but the attempt to take Naxos failed. Thus Aristagoras was compelled to return to Asia Minor without achieving his object. His failure he judged — no doubt rightly — would bring upon him the anger of Artaphernes and punishment from Darius. Hence, on his return to Miletus, he worked to bring about a general revolt of the Greeks against Persia. As a proof of his genuine patriotism for Hellenic liberty he abdicated from his Tyranny. The readiness with which, besides Miletus, the other cities fell in with the proposal to rebel is sufficient proof that discontent had been steadily growing for some time. The Tyrants of the other *poleis* abdicated or were forcibly deposed.

Aristagoras, realizing how formidable was the undertaking to which all alike were now committed, went to Greece in the hope of winning substantial support from their kinsmen on the mainland. His application to Sparta for military assistance was refused. Athens promised and soon after sent twenty war vessels to help the insurgents, while the city of Eretria in Eubœa despatched five.   The material help which Aristagoras thus obtained in Greece was slight enough; we may guess that the moral effect on the Ionians of getting some outside support was considerably greater.   Once the revolt was an accomplished fact, the brunt of the fighting on the Persian side fell on the satrap of Lydia.   But Artaphernes seems to have had only a small detachment of troops at his disposal, and some weeks would elapse before the needed reinforcements from neighboring satrapies could arrive.   His intended objective was Miletus, the centre of the Greek rising, but his projected offensive was forestalled by the confederates, who began operations by boldly marching to Sardes (498 B.C.).   The citadel there held out, although the city itself fell into Greek hands; but the allies were deprived of the fruits of their success by a fire which broke out accidentally and spread so rapidly that they were forced to evacuate Sardes.   This was followed by their retirement to the coast, probably because they got wind of the near approach of Persian reinforcements.

The destruction of Sardes had important and immediate consequences.   The Eretrian and Athenian squadrons returned home, though whether from a genuine belief that their help would now no longer be required, or because of a change of policy toward Persia on the part of those two cities, is not clear.[1] Any depression which this retirement might ordinarily have caused among the allies was submerged in the exhilaration which they felt at the general rally to their cause on the part of the Thracian, Propontic, and Carian communities, and even Cyprus.   In spite of the vastly greater resources of the Persian empire, the allies, for the most part, held their own well in the first and second years of the war; and they might have effected much more, but for their lack of unity, which became more

---

[1] Much has been made of the fact that one Hipparchus, a member of the Peisistratid family, was elected senior archon at Athens for 496–495. This is supposed to denote that the influence of a pro-Persian party was in the ascendant.   This assumes, however, something of which we have no proof save Aristotle's vague statement (*Const. of Ath.* 22, 4) and the fact that Hipparchus was ostracized in 487, that the sympathies of this man on account of his descent were pro-Tyrannic, and therefore pro-Persian.

marked as the revolt progressed. Cyprus, it is true, was recovered by Persia in 497, but this success was counterbalanced by a severe defeat inflicted on a Persian army by the Carians. The disunion of the Greeks and their lack of a clear objective were especially palpable in 496–5. Nor was Histiæus, who had been sent to the West by Darius to act as mediator, able to help on a peaceful settlement. His interview with Artaphernes was so unsatisfactory that he went over openly to the allied cause and made his escape to Chios. His efforts to return to Miletus were equally futile, though his knowledge of Persian organization and tactics might have been of great service to the Greeks. In the end, with some ships obtained at Lesbos, he lived a semi-piratical life for two years. Ultimately he was caught and put to death by the satrap of Lydia. At last, in 494, the Persians began a new and serious offensive. A large fleet blockaded Miletus, while Artaphernes simultaneously despatched an army to invest that city from the land side. At this juncture the confederates mustered all their naval strength — according to Herodotus it amounted to 353 vessels. At the crisis, when the Persian fleet attacked, jealousy and treachery, which may have been the result of earlier Persian intrigues, did their work more effectively than the naval manœuvres of the enemy. Though the navy of Chios and other confederates more than held their own in the battle of Lade — a small island outside the harbor of Miletus — the fleets of Samos and Lesbos deserted at a critical moment. With the utter defeat of the Greeks ended all hopes of the ultimate success of the Greek cause. Miletus was captured a few months later, and then the remaining allies — including Caria and the cities of the Propontis and Thrace — were compelled to return to their Persian allegiance. The punishment of Miletus was severe; for a large part of her population was deported and much of the city utterly destroyed. Some of the other cities were similarly treated. After these rigorous measures the Great King reverted to his traditional policy of toleration. There seems to have been no appreciable increase in the tribute imposed on the Greeks, and, save in two instances, Tyrannies were finally abolished and democratic governments were set up in the Greek *poleis* by Darius' orders. It was a remarkable example of

a

b

a. Gortyn, Great Inscription Containing Law-code; *b*. Part of
the Plain of Marathon (Mt. Pentelicus in Background)

Plate 18

broad-mindedness on the part of an oriental despot who would be least in sympathy with any form of popular government.

Of the various operations which followed the battle of Lade and the fall of Miletus the latest was the recovery of Thrace by Mardonius in 492. Macedonia, too, acknowledged the authority of the Great King, and the Persian commander did his work thoroughly, though not without some mishaps. His army suffered losses at the hands of Thracian tribesmen, while a great part of his fleet was wrecked in a storm off the promontory of Athos. This last disaster necessitated extensive repairs to the fleet, and brought about a delay of eighteen months before the Great King sent out an expedition to chastise the two cities, Athens and Eretria, that had assisted his rebellious subjects.

Meanwhile, during the past fifteen years, the political situation in Greece had undergone some changes. Sparta (c. 494 B.C.) and her hereditary rival and enemy, Argos, had once more gone to war, and the Spartan king, Cleomenes, inflicted a crushing defeat on the Argives at Sepeia near Tiryns. Argos lost so many of her men that she was crippled for a generation or more, while Spartan military predominance in the Peloponnese and beyond was hereafter more marked than ever before. At Athens the democratic government ushered in by Cleisthenes' reforms functioned satisfactorily, though not without considerable rivalry between the leaders of the chief political parties. But, little as we know of the internal history of Athens at this date, it is at least clear that differences were settled constitutionally in the assembly, not by recourse to violence as in the preceding century. Truly Cleisthenes had done his work well! In 493–492 the senior archon was Themistocles, perhaps the greatest statesman ever produced by Athens. In his year of office he began those plans for the naval expansion of Athens which he was only able to complete a decade later, by beginning the fortification of Peiræus, five miles southwest of Athens. Thereby Athens acquired a first-rate harbor in place of the open bay of Phalerum which had mainly served her purpose in earlier years.[1]

[1] Early in 493 the historical drama, *The Capture of Miletus*, by the poet Phrynichus was produced at the Dionysiac festival. The audience was so overcome and contrite at having left their kinsmen in the lurch that Phrynichus was prosecuted and fined for reminding the Athenians of

The Persian operations in Thrace compelled the Athenian, Miltiades, Tyrant of the Thracian Chersonese and nephew of the elder man of the same name who led the first Athenian settlement to that district, to flee. He made his way to Athens in 493, and in the following years attained to great influence in his native city. This was partly due to his wealth, partly because he was a member of one of the old Athenian families; above all, however, his familiarity with Persian methods of warfare marked him out as the best leader that Athens could have at a time when she was expecting punitive reprisals from Darius. The preponderating influence of Miltiades in 491–490 for the time being forced Themistocles and his naval policy into the background. In the critical year 490, when the Persian fleet, commanded by Artaphernes the younger, son of the former Lydian satrap, and Datis, an experienced Median officer, sailed across the Aegean, Miltiades was one of the ten *strategoi* at Athens. The official commander-in-chief was at this date still the polemarch, who in 490 was Callimachus. Whatever the method by which it was effected — and the question is much disputed — it seems clear that the success of the Athenian military operations was due to Miltiades. Though they must have been generally aware of the impending danger, the Athenians were in doubt as to the precise plan of campaign which the Persians would adopt. Hence it was only when the latter had reached Eubœa that the proper measures for the defense of Attica could be decided and that an urgent message for help was sent to Sparta. That the Spartan government promised to send a military force as soon as the moon was full is the statement of Herodotus. Even if no religious scruples delayed their action, at least ten days would be needed for the necessary mobilization of the Peloponnesian troops and their march to Attica.

The Persian commanders, who were accompanied by the ex-Tyrant of Athens, Hippias, now a man of advanced years, after crossing the Aegean forced the submission of Carystus in south-

---

their misfortunes. The suggestion of J. Beloch (*Griechische Geschichte*, ii, 1, p. 16, note 3), which is further elaborated by E. M. Walker (*Cambridge Ancient History*, iv, p. 172), that the play was "political propaganda" for Themistocles' policy is ingenious but based on nothing but conjectures, some of which are very improbable.

ern Eubœa and then sailed up the straits to Eretria. The city
held out for six days, but was then betrayed to the enemy by
pro-Persian citizens and traitors. From Eretria the Persian
fleet sailed south along the Attic coast to the bay of Marathon,
guided thither by Hippias. Here a large part of the military
force was disembarked. In the meantime the Athenians had
passed a decree proposed by Miltiades authorizing the effective
military strength of Athens to march out and block the Persian advance, instead of remaining in the city and standing a
siege. So the Athenian army marched to Marathon, where they
were joined by a small band of men from Platæa, a little Bœotian
city which had been in alliance with Athens for some years. Together they encamped near the mouth of a narrow valley which
led out into the centre of the plain of Marathon (Plate 18).
The Persian troops who had landed were camped at the northern
end of the plain and may have numbered about 20,000. The
Greek force was not more than half that number strong. Datis
delayed for several days before ordering his men to march by the
coast road to Athens, while the fleet would sail round Cape
Sunium and so to the bay of Phalerum. From their position in
the valley of Vrana, Miltiades and Callimachus could narrowly
observe the movements of the enemy. Delay was of advantage
to them since each day brought the promised Peloponnesian
help nearer. At last the Persian general, probably because he
had learnt that the Spartans were approaching, gave the order
to advance. The Athenian commanders ordered an attack on
the enemy as they approached the mouth of the Vrana valley.
The Greek hoplites, when they had come within range of the
Persian archers, pressed forward at a quick march and tackled
the enemy at close quarters. The Athenian centre had a hard
time against the Persian troops opposed to it, but the right and
left wings carried all before them, and then, having routed the
Persian wings, came to their comrades' rescue and closed in on
the Persian centre, all but annihilating it. Nearly all the Persian vessels got safely away, but the military casualties were
heavy; for, not only had most of the centre been wiped out, but
a good many fleeing soldiers perished in the marsh at the
northern end of the plain. Herodotus tells us that 6,400 Persians lost their lives at Marathon, while only 192 Athenians

were killed on that day. In view of the character of the engagement the figures are not improbable.

Miltiades at once led his men back to Athens, realizing that the enemy had sailed for Phalerum and would try to surprise the capital. Also, though we cannot be sure how true the stories current in later times were, there are grounds for believing that Athens contained some disaffected citizens. If they succeeded in their treasonable designs, Athens might yet share the fate of Eretria. When Datis and Artaphernes reached the bay of Phalerum they found the Athenian army encamped by the city walls. Thereupon they abandoned the attempt at conquest and sailed back to Asia. Great as was the victory at Marathon and notable as were its results, its importance has sometimes been exaggerated. Even the victorious Athenians were fully aware that the Persian danger had been only temporarily averted, and that, after Marathon, Darius would more than ever plan to rehabilitate his military renown and impose his authority on European Greece. Nevertheless the recent campaign had weighty consequences at Athens. It ended for good any possibility that Tyranny would be restored there, and it gave the Athenians and indirectly other Greeks confidence, as they realized that Persians were not invincible, and that at close quarters the heavy-armed Greek foot-soldier could more than hold his own against even greatly superior numbers of oriental troops. Further, this achievement must have greatly enhanced the prestige of Athens in the eyes of other Greek states.

Three years later the Great King began preparations for a new and larger European expedition, but they were interrupted by a rebellion in Egypt. Toward the end of 486 Darius died, and five more years elapsed before his successor, Xerxes, steeled himself to carry out his father's plans. During this interval or respite the clash of political parties at Athens seems to have been very intense. Miltiades, the hero of 490, died in the next year under a cloud.[1] Recourse was had to ostracism almost every year, and several prominent citizens were in this way removed temporarily

[1] The expedition which Miltiades led to Paros, with the purpose of winning over that island which owed allegiance to Persia, was a fiasco. He was arraigned on his return to Athens and condemned to pay a heavy fine. But he died shortly afterwards from the effects of a wound contracted on the expedition. Cimon discharged his father's debt.

from the political arena. The two most influential men were Aristeides and Themistocles. The former, though a patriot of the finest type and universally respected for his personal integrity, was content to allow Athens to develop on traditional lines and was averse to the daring innovations urged by Themistocles. But the ascendancy of the latter was so great that in 483 Aristeides was ostracized. Four years before, an important change had been made in the Athenian constitution. The archonship ceased to be an elective office and was hereafter filled by lot. The polemarch at the same time was deprived of his military functions, and his duties were confined to judicial decisions in certain classes of civil litigation. The result was that the importance of the archons rapidly declined, and the board of *strategoi* became the chief executive of Athens. Moreover, the presiding *strategos* was elected from the whole body of the Athenian citizens, the others being chosen from the tribes. In practice, if not in theory, his authority seems to have been greater than that of his colleagues. Reëlection at the end of the year of office was permitted and could be repeated indefinitely.

In 488 B.C. Athens had become involved in a war with her neighbor, Aegina, — a war which from the nature of the case was purely naval. The mismanagement of it strengthened the hands of Themistocles, who was not at that time in office. But several years elapsed before he finally prevailed on his countrymen to embark on a program of naval building which was far in excess of what was needed to worst the Aeginetans and was intended to make Athens the first maritime state in Greece, putting her at the same time in a far stronger position when the Persian attack on Greece should be renewed. At last, in 482, Themistocles succeeded in carrying a decree which authorized the building of two hundred war vessels. The Athenian treasury had at that time a large surplus, which was now used for naval purposes, because the silver mines at Laurium had become unusually productive owing to the recent discovery of very rich veins of ore. Thus Themistocles with his pertinacity and farsightedness persuaded the Athenians to make a tremendous effort in the two years before Xerxes' attack, and to begin a career of maritime expansion which made Athens mistress of the eastern Mediterranean for more than half a century.

The new Persian king does not appear to have been over anxious to carry out his father's plans for the conquest of Hellas, but the influence of the queen mother, Atossa, and of his counsellors, among whom was Mardonius, carried the day. By 482 the expedition had been planned, and the following year was taken up with preparations on a vast scale. It was proposed to enter Greece by Thrace and Macedonia, the fleet meanwhile sailing along the coast and keeping in close touch with the army. A bridge of boats moored together was built across the Hellespont, a canal was cut through the end of the Athos promontory — it was nearly a mile and a half long — so as to avoid the dangerous circumnavigation, stores of supplies were set up at various points along the land route, and orders were despatched to all the satrapies to furnish contingents of troops for the undertaking. Thus, by the winter of 481, a large host had assembled in Asia Minor. The army which actually set out for Europe early in the following spring may have numbered 100,000 to 150,000 men; the total naval force perhaps amounted to upward of 500 vessels.[1]

These vast preparations could not in any case remain unknown in Greece, but the Persian king made known his intentions before by sending, in the winter of 481, envoys to various Greek city-states demanding their submission. A congress of representatives from the Greek states had already been held in the autumn at the Isthmus of Corinth. A Hellenic league was formed under Spartan leadership; differences, like the quarrel between Aegina and Athens, were sunk in face of the common danger; reprisals were voted in advance against any Greeks who "medized," that is to say, voluntarily submitted to Persia; and defense measures were discussed. In spite of all, Argos and some other communities remained neutral, and the loyalty to the Greek cause of many parts of northern and central Greece was not above suspicion. Though we have no certain information about the strength of the confederate

---

[1] No one accepts the impossible figures given by Herodotus, two and a half million fighting men and 1207 ships. The conjectures of the moderns are multitudinous, but anything like certainty is impossible. For discussions of the problem and different estimates cf. J. Beloch, *Griechische Geschichte*, ii, 2, pp. 61–81, and *Cambridge Ancient History*, iv, pp. 271–276.

forces by land and sea, they cannot have been much more than half those of the enemy, perhaps 60,000 to 70,000 men in the army and a fleet of a little over 300 ships. Strategy therefore demanded that the Greeks should remain on the defensive, until they could engage by land or sea in a position where natural advantages would to some extent counterbalance numerical inferiority. The three main defensive positions against an army from the northeast were the vale of Tempe in Thessaly, the pass of Thermopylæ, and the Isthmus of Corinth, the last and strongest line of defense. But to concentrate on this from the beginning meant abandoning all northern and central Greece, and might mean the defection of Athens with her powerful navy. Thessaly could not be held save by a combined Greek force, most of whose members would have been fighting far from their own homes. Tempe, though the natural gateway into Greece from the northeast, was not the only pass which an army of invaders could use. Thus, though a military detachment was sent to Thessaly early in 480, its commanders found that the Thessalians as a whole were unwilling to fight. The expeditionary force therefore made its way back to the Isthmus, and the Thessalians on the Great King's approach submitted. The Persian host had left Sardes in the spring, and reached Therma in Macedonia toward the end of July. By the middle of August the army had passed through Thessaly and come to the western end of Thermopylæ, while the fleet, after encountering a severe storm off Cape Sepias, which wrecked or drove on shore a large number of vessels, finally anchored at the mouth of the Gulf of Pagasæ.

Meanwhile the Greek fleet, over 300 strong, had proceeded to the northern end of Eubœa, where it moored off Cape Artemisium in order to bar the progress of the enemy's navy. On land it had been decided to defend the pass of Thermopylæ. A small Peloponnesian army was reinforced by contingents from Phocis, Locris, and Bœotia; the whole force, which may have numbered 10,000 men and was commanded by the Spartan king, Leonidas, occupied the pass with the purpose of delaying the advance of the Persian host until the Greek fleet had fought a decisive action by sea. In short, the land operations were subordinated to the naval, and there can be little doubt that the master mind on the Greek side was Themistocles, although the supreme command on both elements was in Spartan hands. Xerxes, whose original plan was a combined attack by land and sea on the pass, found his calculations upset by the storm which damaged and temporarily disorganized his fleet, and by the strength of the Greek naval preparations. After some days, he decided to force the pass with his army alone, but his direct attacks were beaten off for two days. In the evening of the second day a Persian detachment, guided by a renegade Greek, was despatched by a mountain pass to attack the Greeks in the rear. Even this manœuvre might have been defeated by the Greeks if the Phocian contingent, which had been detailed to guard against this very danger, had not allowed itself to be surprised, and then fled in panic. When the Greek army in the pass found the Persians in possession of the surrounding hills they were seized with dismay, and some tried to escape before it was too late. The Spartan king and 300 Spartiates fell fighting in the pass to a man. The total Greek losses in the three days' fighting and the pursuit on the third day are said to have been as high as 4,000 men. Leonidas and his Spartans on that day won undying glory for the heroism of their death; but it is probable that the disaster might have been avoided, if the Spartan king had been a really able commander as well as a brave soldier.

The allied fleet had in the meantime, after some preliminary skirmishes, been engaged in a naval battle with the enemy. But, although the Greeks held their own, they were unable to force a decision, and both sides suffered severe casualties. When the news reached them that the enemy had seized the pass, the Greek naval commanders at once decided to retire to the Saronic Gulf and the Straits of Salamis, whence they could defend the approach to the Isthmus of Corinth, and at the same time afford protection to the non-combatant population of Attica, if and when they evacuated the country. For Xerxes' success at Thermopylæ meant that all Greece north of the Isthmus of Corinth lay open to him. Hence Themistocles prevailed upon the Athenians to put their whole trust in their navy. The women and children and those too old to fight, together with such personal property as could be moved, were transported to Salamis, Aegina, and the Argolid. In the three weeks following the action at Thermopylæ the Persian army passed through Phocis and Bœotia into Attica, which was thoroughly laid waste, and the buildings on the Athenian Acropolis were burnt in revenge for the destruction of Sardes. The Persian fleet had sailed along the Attic coast and took up its position in the Bay of Phalerum. The confederate Greeks were now divided in their counsels. One part urged the retirement of the fleet to the Isthmus, where they would be in close touch with the army. The Athenians, Aeginetans, and Megarians demanded the defense of the Salaminian straits. Themistocles, as commander-in-chief of the Athenian squadron, in addition urged the strategic advantages of this position, and his advice prevailed. The narrow waters between the island and the mainland would give an advantage to the Greek vessels, which were numerically inferior, and Xerxes would not wish to risk a naval engagement save in more open waters. An early decision was, nevertheless, imperative, because the season was getting late and the commissariat problem with so large an armada must have been extremely difficult. One night (September 22, 480 B.C.?), therefore, the Great King ordered his fleet to move, with the object of taking the enemy by surprise at dawn on the next morning. The move was successful, and early next day the Persian ships, having entered the straits and ranged themselves parallel to the Attic coast, bore down upon the enemy. The battle was begun by the Phœnician fleet, which formed the right wing of the Persian navy, and was opposed to the Athenians, who were on the Greek left. The latter succeeded in forcing back their opponents, whose fresh manœuvres, as they were carried toward the Persian centre, not only threw their own line into disarray but the central squadron as well. The Greeks pressed home their advantage, bearing down on the disorganized Persian lines to drive them out of the straits. In the confusion that ensued many Persian ships collided among themselves; others that escaped for the moment were subsequently caught and rammed by the Aeginetans on the Greek right. At the end of the day the sea was strewn with wrecks and dead. Thus does the Persian messenger describe the crucial fight in the play of Aeschylus, who himself was serving with the Athenian forces: [1]

                                        . . . And first
    One Grecian bark plunged straight, and sheared away
    Bowsprit and stem of a Phœnician ship.
    And then each galley on some other's prow
    Came crashing in. Awhile our stream of ships
    Held onward, till within the narrowing creek
    Our jostling vessels were together driven,
    And none could aid another; each on each
    Drave hard their brazen beaks, or brake away
    The oar-banks of each other, stem to stern,
    While the Greek galleys, with no lack of skill,
    Hemmed them and battered in their sides, and soon
    The hulls rolled over, and the sea was hid,
    Crowded with wrecks and butchery of men.

The Persian vessels that escaped retired to Phalerum. What percentage of the whole fleet was destroyed we cannot tell, but probably not more than a third. Xerxes, however, decided to attempt no further operations that year, and after a few days gave orders for a general retirement. The damaged fleet was sent back to Asia, while the army retired the way it had come. In Thessaly the king left a strong army of occupation in command of Mardonius, whereas he himself returned to Asia Minor with the rest. The rigor of the Thracian climate in the late autumn caused his men much hardship and was responsible for many deaths.

Early in the following spring military operations began afresh. The Greek leaders, who were now more confident, were prepared to abandon their defensive position at the Isthmus and to risk an open engagement with Mardonius. A confederate Greek fleet, a little over 100 strong, was sent off to the Cyclades to guard the islands and keep watch for any Persian fleet that might try to sail across the Aegean. Mardonius, on the other hand, tried to detach the Athenians from the Greek alliance by generous promises, but without success. Knowing that he could not force the Greek defense at the Isthmus with-

---

[1] Aeschylus, *Persians*, ll. 409 ff. (E. D. A. Morshead's translation).

out naval collaboration, he nevertheless marched into Bœotia, in the hope of drawing out the Greek army to give him battle, and of overawing the Athenians by his proximity to Attica. Unable to defend their country without assistance, — and the Peloponnesian mobilization was not yet complete, — the Athenians once more evacuated Attica, refusing Mardonius' second offer of terms as they had refused the first. And so their country was ravaged again within twelve months. Mardonius' movements had been rapid and had taken the confederate army unawares. The Spartan king and commander-in-chief, Pausanias, however, sent an advance detachment to Megara with all speed to reinforce the town garrison. The help arrived just in time. Mardonius, rather than waste time over a siege which was not essential to his plans, or risk an open engagement in Attica, which in any case was too desolate to afford food for his army, retired to Bœotia. There he encamped near Platæa on a site best adapted for his tactical plans when the enemy should appear. The central Greek states, Bœotians, Phocians, and Locrians, had submitted voluntarily to him, and their military contingents were enrolled on his side.

The Peloponnesian army now moved from the Isthmus, being joined on its way to Bœotia by Megarian and Athenian detachments. The total strength of the Greeks was perhaps 60,000 men; Mardonius' army, including his compulsory allies from northern and central Greece, was only slightly more numerous. Tactical moves and counter-moves on the part of the two hosts, and occasional skirmishes between small groups, went on for nearly a fortnight before Mardonius, thinking to take advantage of the Greek divisions, when in changing their position early one morning they had been thrown into some disorder, gave the signal for a general attack. The battle raged for many hours, but in the end the heavy-armed Greek infantry carried the day as it had done eleven years before at Marathon; and, when Mardonius himself was killed, the Persian centre finally broke and ran. The Persian second-in-command, Artabazus, under cover of the cavalry managed to rally a good part of his army and to effect an orderly retreat into Thessaly, and so back to Asia. But the Persian camp was stormed by the Greeks, and immense quantities of booty were taken by them. An attack on Thebes followed; after three weeks' siege the city was compelled to capitulate. The leaders of the pro-Persian party were subsequently executed and the league of Bœotian cities, which had existed under the head-ship of Thebes since the middle of the sixth century, was disbanded.

The allied fleet, whose headquarters were at Delos, had in the interval seen no sign of the Persian navy. During the summer the admiral-in-charge received an urgent invitation from the islanders of Chios and Samos to cross to Asia Minor, since on his appearance the Asiatic Greeks would rise in general revolt against their overlord. The chances of a notable success seemed good, and the Greek fleet sailed from Delos to Asia Minor. On news of its approach a Persian naval squadron lying off Samos retired to the neighboring mainland coast at Mycale. Here the Persians landed, beached their ships, and formed an entrenched camp; and here, in the last days of August or the first days of September, 479 B.C., they were at-tacked and defeated by the Greeks. The Persian ships were burnt, probably by the Persians themselves, when they saw that their position was hopeless. After this stirring success the victors proceeded to the Hellespont and invested Sestos, which commanded the straits and was held by a strong Persian garrison. The siege was prolonged into the late autumn. The Peloponnesian part of the allied force returned home before the end, leaving the Athenians, supported by their newly liber-ated Ionian allies, to carry on. At last the place capitu-lated, and with the capture of this important strategic point the Greek operations of 479 came to an end. Truly it had been a memorable year. For had not the oriental invader been driven out of Greece, while a second victory, that at Mycale, had brought about the liberation of the Asiatic Greeks after they had been subjects of a foreign power for nearly a century?

Simultaneously with the epic conflict between Persians and Greeks in Hellas and Asia Minor there occurred events in the western Mediterranean which no less decisively insured the freedom from foreign control of the Sicilian and Italian Greeks. Of the political history, during the seventh and sixth centuries, of the numerous Greek cities founded during the age of coloni-

zation very little is known. Their general constitutional development, their social and economic conditions, seem to have
been very similar to what is already familiar from Greece and
Anatolia. Till the second half of the sixth century the Greek
poleis in Sicily generally lived at peace with one another,
although certain cities were more powerful than the rest.
Thus, Acragas under her brutal Tyrant, Phalaris, enjoyed a
brief period during which her political influence in the island
surpassed that of any other city (*c.* 570–555 B.C.). It was fortunate for the western Greeks that they warred so little among
themselves at this period, since they had strong neighbors to
whom the growing prosperity of the Hellenic communities
seemed a challenge and a menace. In Italy the chief power
was the Etruscan kingdom; [1] but we have no evidence that
the Etruscans tried at any time to interfere with the Greeks
of Magna Græcia, though at the height of their power they
controlled Campania and a good part of the western coast
southward from their own territory.

Very different was the attitude of Carthage. This city had
originally been founded by Phœnicians from Tyre (*c.* 800 B.C.).
Before this Phœnician emigrants and traders had occupied a
number of sites on the northern coast of Africa and in southern
Spain, but none of them attained to the importance of Carthage.
Before the middle of the sixth century she was undisputed
mistress in all this region, having extended her control over
all Phœnician settlements in the western Mediterranean and
secured three towns or trading stations in northwestern Sicily,
— Motya, Solus, and Panormus. That, in these circumstances,
the Carthaginians would sooner or later try to restrict the
growth of the western Greeks, who might become political and
commercial rivals, was obvious. From the scanty sources
available it would appear that Greek cities were at war with
Carthaginians on two or three occasions during the sixth
century. More fully attested is the naval battle in 535 B.C., at
which the Phocæans of Alalia in Corsica fought against the
allied navies of Carthage and Etruria. Alalia was subsequently
abandoned by the Greek settlers and passed under Etruscan
domination. The Carthaginians a few years later conquered

---

[1] For the Etruscans see further below, Chapter XX.

all the coast-lands of Sardinia, though they failed, or perhaps did not seriously attempt, to subdue the natives in the interior. The most serious check to Carthage was a naval defeat inflicted on her by the Greeks of Massilia (*c.* 530 B.C.?). The two states thereafter concluded a treaty delimiting the regions in which each was to exercise political control without interference from the other.

The last years of the sixth century and the early years of the fifth were a time when numerous Tyrants attained to power in Sicily and southern Italy. The kind of conditions which brought about these changes can to some extent be illustrated from the case of Syracuse. Here, until the end of the sixth century, the landed proprietors (*gamoroi*), who were the descendants of the original colonists, exercised a narrow and oppressive oligarchic rule. Their land was tilled for them by a serf population composed mainly of Sicilian aborigines (Sicels). The free citizen population (*damos*) was made up of small proprietary farmers, craftsmen, and traders. But, since magistrates and officials were exclusively chosen from among the *gamoroi*, and a citizen assembly, if it existed, had no powers, the members of the *damos* had few if any political rights. Doubtless similar conditions were to be found elsewhere in Sicily and Italy, and in due course brought about revolution and Tyranny.

In the early years of the fifth century the most powerful of these despots were Anaxilas of Rhegium, Hippocrates of Gela, and Theron of Acragas. The ablest of these was Hippocrates, who extended his sway over at least four cities besides his own. On his death (*c.* 485 B.C.) he was succeeded by Gelon, who had served with distinction in the late Tyrant's army. At the invitation of some of Syracuse's oppressed population who were in revolt against their masters, Gelon interfered in the affairs of that city by armed force, and having occupied it made himself Tyrant there, leaving his brother Hiero to govern Gela. Gelon next greatly enlarged Syracuse, strengthened it with new fortifications, and built great docks in the harbor to accommodate his nascent navy. By marrying the daughter of Theron, Tyrant of Acragas, who was also master of Himera in northern Sicily, he brought about close and friendly relations with the despot who, next to Gelon himself, was the most powerful ruler in the island. That other Greek cities viewed this situation with alarm is not surprising, and it is probable that Carthage also foresaw the possible loss of her Sicilian dependencies. Hence a clash between her and Gelon was only a matter of time. That it came already in 480 was due to an appeal from Himera to Carthage to interfere on her behalf in Sicilian affairs. Anaxilas also entered into friendly relations with the Semitic power.

In the summer of 480 therefore a large Carthaginian expedition sailed for northern Sicily and invested Himera, which was strongly fortified and held by Theron himself. He, on the approach of the Punic forces, sent an urgent message for support to the Tyrant of Syracuse. Gelon with a large army — it is said to have amounted to 55,000 men all told — marched to the relief of his father-in-law, and outside the walls of Himera engaged the Carthaginian forces (September ? 480 B.C.). He inflicted a crushing defeat on the invaders, and then dictated terms to them by which they were obliged to pay a heavy indemnity, but were left in possession of their cities in the northwest of the island. That Gelon's great victory coincided in point of time with the Greek victory over Xerxes at Salamis led later Greek writers to assume that Carthage had attacked the western Greeks at the suggestion or request of the Persian monarch. But in Herodotus there is no hint of such a Perso-Punic understanding, and Carthaginian interests in Sicily, coupled with the invitation extended by Himera, are quite sufficient to account for the Punic invasion. That it was actually undertaken in 480, and that the fight at Himera occurred about the same time as the battle of Salamis, was a coincidence.

Gelon's prestige in Sicily and beyond, and his popularity in Syracuse, were immensely enhanced by his victorious campaign. But within two years he died and was succeeded by his brother Hiero, since his own son was an infant. The twelve years of Hiero's reign (478–466 B.C.) were notable for their magnificence and for the prosperity of Syracuse. The city was adorned with fine public buildings, paid for out of the spoils of Himera. The despot attracted to his court the most distinguished poets of the day, among others, Simonides, Aeschylus, and Pindar. The last-named celebrated Hiero's victories in the chariot races at Olympia and Delphi in more than one fine epinician ode. It is in one of these that he refers to Gelon's victory at Himera:

From Salamis shall I essay to win for my reward the favour of the Athenians, but at Sparta I shall tell of the battle before Cithæron, those battles twain in which the Medes with curved bows suffered sorely; but, by the well-watered bank of the river Himeras, (I shall win reward) by paying my tribute of song to the sons of Deinomenes, — the song of praise, which they won by their valour, while their foemen were fore-spent.[1]

Politically Hiero's greatest triumph was a naval victory which he won in 476 over the Etruscans off Cumæ. Thereby he saved Cumæ — reputed to be the oldest Greek settlement in the West — from foreign domination.

Truly it may be said that by the end of the first quarter of the fifth century Hellenism had emerged triumphant throughout the whole Mediterranean area.

[1] Pindar, *Pythian Odes*, 1, 75–80 (J. E. Sandys' translation). Of the extant odes of Pindar the first Olympian and the first three Pythian were written for Hiero. The second Pythian, however, celebrates a victory not at the Pythian games but at the Iolæa at Thebes.

CHAPTER XIV

THE RISE AND DECLINE OF THE ATHENIAN EMPIRE

*To maintain our rights against equals, to be
politic with superiors, and to be moderate with
inferiors, is the path of safety.* — Thucydides
v, 111 (Jowett's translation).

1. FROM 478 TO 431 B.C.

WITH the repulse of Xerxes and Mardonius the relations
between Hellenes and Persians entered on a new phase. The
Greeks of Asia Minor and the adjacent islands had for the
moment recovered their political independence; to keep it they
needed more strength than their own unaided resources could
give them. The interest of Sparta and the other Peloponnesian
states in the cause of the Anatolian *poleis* was at best lukewarm;
but in 478 a small confederate fleet under the command of
Pausanias did cruise in the Aegean, and, after bringing about
the defection from Persia of several islands lying off the Carian
coast, and of a part of Cyprus, expelled the Persian garrison
from Byzantium. Pausanias' arrogant conduct, however, gave
offense to the allies serving under his command and the Spartan
government was obliged to recall him. The Asiatic Greeks, who
in 478 had joined Pausanias' squadron, now turned to Athens
and invited her to put herself at the head of a maritime confederacy which should serve a twofold purpose. It would insure
that the cities lately under Persian suzerainty would not relapse
into their former position of subjects to an oriental despot, and
it would make possible offensive operations against Xerxes, with
the object of freeing all those Hellenic communities which were
still under his domination.

The general organization of the league, the conclusion of
agreements between Athens and her new allies, the definition or
assessment of the military, naval, or financial obligations to be

undertaken by the constituent members, were by common consent entrusted to Aristeides, who in 478 was in charge of the Athenian detachment serving under Pausanias. Delos, Apollo's sacred island and the seat of an old religious confederation, was chosen as the meeting place of the new league; the temple of the god was designated as the treasury in which the confederate funds should be stored. Each member undertook to make a certain contribution annually, its amount and character being fixed by Aristeides and graduated according to the resources of the particular city. From the first there were two classes of members. Some states — for instance, Chios, Lesbos, Samos, Naxos, and Thasos — had substantial navies of their own. These, or a part of them, they bound themselves to put at the disposal of the league as required. But the greater number of *poleis* were much smaller, owning no naval forces to speak of, and they met their liabilities to the confederacy by paying an annual tribute (*phoros*) in money into the federal chest. The funds thus accumulated would be used partly to defray the cost of upkeep of the allied navy, partly to finance the expeditions undertaken by the league. How far these smaller cities were required to furnish contingents of men to act as rowers or fighters is quite uncertain. Each city was free and independent, and through its representatives voted at the federal congress in Delos, the principle followed being apparently one city one vote, irrespective of its importance or power. The executive was from the beginning left to Athens, that is to say, the chief command was exercised by Athenian admirals, and the financial business, collection of the tribute, and so forth, was under the control of ten *Hellenotamiai*, who were Athenians elected by the Athenian *ecclesia*. The total sum which was annually collected from the allies according to Aristeides' assessment was, so Thucydides states (i, 96), 460 talents ($552,000 = £110,500). Epigraphic evidence, however, shows that this amount was not exceeded thirty-five or forty years later, when the membership roll of the league was far larger than in the first ten years of its existence. Hence it is likely that the amount collected in the early period was considerably less, and that Thucydides' figure is only appropriate to the years after *c.* 454 B.C.

Themistocles' statesmanship for fifteen years had so moulded the destinies of Athens that this maritime league under Athenian leadership may be called the direct outcome of his policy. It was he also who, in the years immediately following the war with Xerxes, persuaded the Athenians to rebuild the fortifications of Athens in spite of the protests of the Spartan government. For the head of the Peloponnesian league was to some extent suspicious of Athens' growth in power, and loath to see Athenians turn their city into a fortress of the first rank. This accomplished, Themistocles carried through the work first begun in 493–492 B.C., — the fortification of Peiræus and of the two smaller harbors of Zea and Munychia, adjacent to it. The total length of these walls was approximately seven and a half miles. Each of the harbors was protected on the sea side by strong moles. Athens now possessed a port and naval base worthy of the head of a great maritime confederacy, and before long Peiræus became the foremost commercial mart in the eastern Mediterranean. Twenty years later, in 457, the Athenians took a further and very necessary step. Hitherto, had an invader attacked Athens, he could have cut off the capital completely from its port. To prevent any such possibility in time of war the Athenians constructed two "Long Walls," one connecting Athens with Peiræus, the other with Phalerum.[1] The fortification of the two cities was the last important public service performed by Themistocles for his country. In the next few years his influence steadily declined, as that of Cimon, son of Miltiades, mainly through his military successes, grew. One leading feature of Cimon's foreign policy was the maintenance of good relations with Sparta and the Peloponnesian league, whereas Themistocles, after his diplomatic duel with the Spartan government in 478 concerning the fortification of Athens, was consistently hostile to that state. At last, in 471 or 470, recourse was had to ostracism, and Themistocles was forced to go into exile. After some years of residence at Argos, where he seems to have been actively engaged in anti-Spartan propaganda, he was compromised by revelations

---

[1] In 445 a second Peiræus wall, parallel to the first, was built and the wall from Athens to Phalerum was allowed to fall into disuse. Between the two Peiræus walls, the "North Wall" and the "Middle Wall," ran a high road connecting the city with its port.

made by Pausanias before his death. The latter had been
actively intriguing with Persia, and Themistocles seems to
have been aware of some at least of Pausanias' designs. The
Athenian was summoned to his native city to stand his trial
for high treason; but, whatever the degree of his guilt or innocence may have been, he took no risks. He left Argos,
and, after several years of moving from place to place in
Greece, he finally made his way to Asia Minor. From there
he went as a political refugee to the Persian capital and was
well received by the new king, Artaxerxes I, who had succeeded Xerxes in 464. He was established regent of Magnesia-
on-the-Mæander, and lived there till his death about a dozen
years later. With regard to the later years of Themistocles'
career the ancient evidence is too conflicting to justify us in
passing judgment on it. The sentimentalist may shed a tear
that the victor of Salamis ended his days as a dependent of
Persia; the dispassionate student of history will remember
Themistocles' inestimable services to Athens and to Greece,
and will be content to accept the éloge of Thucydides:

For Themistocles was a man whose natural force was unmistake-
able; this was the quality for which he was distinguished above all
other men; from his own native acuteness, and without any study
either before or at the time, he was the ablest judge of the course to be
pursued in a sudden emergency, and could best divine what was likely
to happen in the remotest future. Whatever he had in hand he had
the power of explaining to others, and even where he had no experience
he was quite competent to form a sufficient judgment; no one could
foresee with equal clearness the good and evil event which was hidden
in the future. In a word, Themistocles by natural power of mind and
with the least preparation was of all men the best able to extemporize
the right thing to be done.[1]

The development of the maritime confederacy, so auspiciously
initiated in 478–477 B.C., and the imperial position thereafter won
by Athens, were, above all, the work of Cimon, who in 476 had
become head of the naval forces of Athens and thereby admiral-
in-chief of the allied fleet, a position which he retained for fifteen years. His first success was the capture of Eion at the
mouth of the Strymon river. The place owed its importance
to its proximity to the mines of Mt. Pangæus and was still

[1] Thucydides i, 138 (Jowett's translation).

held by a Persian garrison. In the next few years Scyros was seized, its inhabitants were expelled, and the island was colonized by Athenian settlers. Carystus in southern Eubœa was compelled to become a member of the confederacy (c. 470 B.C.). A year or two later the Athenians did not hesitate to use coercion against Naxos. The islanders desired to sever their connection with the league, which, so far as we can tell, they were entitled to do under the original terms of the alliance. But the retirement of so strong a member from the confederacy might easily have been followed by other secessions, and the maritime empire which Athens and Cimon were building up step by step would very soon have collapsed. Hence the Athenians chose to interpret the action of Naxos as a revolt, and laid siege to the island (469 or 467 B.C.). When they capitulated, the Naxians ceased to be wholly autonomous: their fleet was impounded by Athens, and they became her tribute-paying subject allies. Whether Athens, on the basis of the original treaty by which Naxos had joined the league, was able to put forward any legal justification for her use of compulsion or not, is not known, nor is it of any material importance. What mattered was that her action at Naxos, and the coercion she had used to make Carystus a league-member, made it clear to all the world that she was not content to be head of a voluntary confederacy, but was aiming at its conversion into an Athenian empire. In 465 the Thasians, undeterred by the fate of Naxos, indicated their intention to retire from the league. It was the prospect of an Athenian colony coming to settle at the "Nine Ways" (the site of the later Amphipolis), a few miles inland from Eion, in order to exploit the natural wealth of the district, — lumber and mines, — which, we may suppose, was the main cause of the quarrel between the island and Athens. The colony of 10,000 actually set out and reached its destination in 464; but, shortly after, the settlers were attacked and all but wiped out by Thracian tribes of the interior. Thasos meanwhile had been blockaded by the Athenians, and after two years the islanders, having applied in vain to Sparta for help, surrendered. Thasos, like Naxos, became a subject ally; her fortifications were razed and her navy confiscated; in addition, she was forced to give up certain dependencies on the mainland opposite to Thasos and all interest that she had hitherto held in the Pangæus mines.

While the relations between Athens and her allies were thus undergoing a gradual change, the original purpose of the league was not forgotten. There were still substantial districts within the Aegean area which owed allegiance to Persia. To deprive the Great King of these subjects, and to include them in the maritime confederacy, were the objects of a strong expedition, composed of two hundred Athenian and allied vessels, that set sail under Cimon's command in the spring of 468. Caria and Lycia were the objective; systematically the communities there were won over, many of them joining the Greek alliance readily as soon as Cimon appeared. Others were held by Persian garrisons and had to be reduced by force. The most formidable resistance might have been shown by Dorian Phaselis. Her interests were largely commercial, and much of her trade was with Syria and other regions subject to Persia. But friendly relations had also existed for some time between her and Chios, and it was owing to the intermediation of the Chians that Phaselis agreed to surrender to Cimon. Meanwhile the Persian government sent military and naval forces to Pamphylia to protect or recover the towns threatened by the allies. Before the end of the summer Cimon had inflicted a double defeat on the enemy by the River Eurymedon, and then captured an additional squadron of eighty vessels which was on its way to reinforce the Persian main fleet. This campaign was Cimon's greatest achievement; its effect was to leave the navy of Athens and her allies in undisputed control of all the Aegean as far as Cyprus, and to confine the Persian navy to the narrow waters between that island and the Syrian coast.

While the Delian confederacy was thus carrying out its aims, and was at the same time passing more and more under Athenian control, the Spartan government was faced with a succession of problems. Important members of the Peloponnesian league were showing signs of discontent with Spartan leadership. One of the Arcadian cities, Tegea, allied herself with Argos, and Sparta was forced to undertake a campaign against these allies. A little later a more general rising of all the Arcadian cities, except Mantinea, against Spartan authority again necessitated military action. In both these wars the efficiency and discipline of the Spartan troops carried the day. Yet, that Sparta's position as head of the league was after this more unchallenged than ever before was partly due to the half-hearted attitude of Argos, and to the fact that at Athens, thanks to the strength of the Cimonian party, a philo-Laconian policy was the order of the day. In 464 a disaster befell Sparta, which, if her authority in the league had not been firmly re-established a few years before, might have led to her political extinction. A violent earthquake shook Laconia, causing great destruction and loss of life. The oppressed and discontented Helot population of Messenia saw an opportunity for turning on their masters. They revolted *en masse* and were even joined by some Periœcic communities. An attack on the city of Sparta failed, and the Helots were decisively defeated in the field. They now took refuge on Mount Ithome, which already in the seventh century had served as a rallying point for the Messenians. The siege of this stronghold was long and difficult; besides, as Thucydides tells us, the Spartans were not adept at operations of this kind. They accordingly summoned the help of their allies, including Athens, which, it must be remembered, was still a member of the Hellenic confederation formed in 481 B.C. When this request for aid came before the Athenian assembly, a heated debate seems to have ensued. Cimon, true to the view that he had consistently advocated, that Sparta and Athens should stand shoulder to shoulder as the leaders of Greece, urged that an expeditionary force be sent to Laconia without delay. The anti-Laconian party at Athens was also that party which desired to bring about a more complete democratic régime at home, and abroad to enforce more ruthlessly the authority of Athens in the Delian league. What may thus be called the democratic party was also the imperialist party, whose program could only be opposed to a policy of alliance and friendship with Sparta. Its leader at this time was Ephialtes, a man of whose career we know practically nothing, but whose great ability is not open to doubt. On this occasion, however, he and his party were not yet strong enough to defeat the supporters of Cimon. The relief expedition to Sparta was approved and started out forth-with, with Cimon himself in charge. It proved to be the only time that Cimon's military genius failed him; for what reason we do not know. Even he could not bring the Messenians to capitulate, and, eventually, the Spartan government took the drastic step of curtly dismissing the Athenian force. This action, if it was a serious error of judgment on the part of the Spartan ephors, also reacted very strongly on the political situation at Athens, and on Cimon's own career. Ephialtes' party gained the upper hand, and, within a year of his return from Ithome, Cimon was ostracized, the alliance between Athens and Sparta was regarded as at an end, and the Athe-nians, by way of direct challenge to the head of the Peloponnesian league, contracted alliances with Argos and with Thessaly. A few months later, that is, before the end of 461, Ephialtes was murdered, probably by a member of one of the oligarchic clubs whose methods of political warfare were as crude as their in-fluence on affairs at this time was small.

His successor as head of the democratic party was Pericles, who in the next few years carried through to the end the sweeping constitutional reforms begun by Ephialtes.[1] Athens' most famous statesman was the son of Xanthippus, the ad-miral of the Athenian squadron which fought at Mycale; on his mother's side he was a member of the Alcmæonid clan, being in fact the great nephew of Cleisthenes. The finest speaker of his age, he was in temper and bearing an aristocrat rather than a popular leader. Withal he was reserved in manner, frugal in his private life, the friend of artists and philoso-phers. Though, from time to time, called upon in the perfor-mance of his office as *strategos* to take charge of military or naval expeditions, his ability in that character was little more than mediocre. The foreign and domestic policy of Athens for the next thirty years was, with one brief exception, the policy of Pericles; for more than half that period his authority was often challenged. For twelve years preceding the out-break of the great Peloponnesian war he was in effect the benevo-lent autocrat of Athens.

The unfortunate disagreement with Sparta in 461 made hos-

[1] See p. 294 below.

BUST OF PERICLES

Plate 19

tilities between Athens and some of the Peloponnesian states inevitable. The Spartan government, it is true, was not anxious to force the issue; but Athens, by cutting herself off from the Hellenic confederation, gave a handle to Corinth and Aegina, both of whom were jealous of her growth as a maritime power. In 460 Athens concluded an alliance with her neighbor, Megara, then involved in a quarrel with Corinth; this agreement meant war between Athens and the Isthmus city. The so-called first Peloponnesian war continued at intervals from 459 to 445. An Athenian victory over the Corinthian and Aeginetan navies in 458 was followed by the siege of Aegina, which capitulated in 457. The city-state that had so long been the proud rival of Athens was then enrolled as a tributary subject in the confederacy; with her independence she lost her navy. The successes of Athens brought the Peloponnesian league as a whole into the field against her. In 457 a Peloponnesian army was despatched to Bœotia to restore the Bœotian league with Thebes at its head, and thus create a more formidable and potentially hostile neighbor to Athens on her northern frontier. The Athenians replied by sending an army across Cithæron, which engaged the enemy at Tanagra but suffered defeat. The Peloponnesians, instead of following up their victory, and especially securing the position of Thebes, returned home. Before the end of the campaigning season the Athenians entered Bœotia a second time, defeated a Bœotian army decisively at Oenophyta, and compelled the Bœotian cities to join the Athenian alliance. Their neighbors of Phocis had already done so voluntarily, and, under pressure, the Locrians followed suit.

Thus, in 456, Athens was mistress of central Greece as far as the pass of Thermopylæ. By concluding treaties with most of the cities of Achæa her influence extended also into the Peloponnese, and, by 455, she controlled a valuable naval base on the northern shore of the Corinthian Gulf. For in 455 the revolted Messenian Helots had at last surrendered to the Spartans, on condition that they be allowed to emigrate from the country. With the help of Athens the exiles were settled at Naupactus which had lately been wrested from the Locrians. The value of this place to a power like Athens was obvious, as it commanded the entrance to the Gulf of Corinth, and that at a time when, through her close alliance with Megara, Athens also controlled the Megarian port of Pagæ, as well as Nisæa on the Saronic Gulf. In 454 Athens seemed to emphasize her imperial position by transferring the treasury of the league from Delos to Athens. That the Delian confederacy was in reality a league no longer, but had become an Athenian empire must have been clear to many as far back as 461. But the removal of the treasury, and the dedication thereafter of one-sixtieth of the annual tribute to Athena, the patron goddess of Athens, was interpreted by enemies as an act of imperial arrogance, and may have caused heartburning to some of her allies as well. It is not improbable that there was a more practical and immediate reason why the change was made in 454.

Five years before this the Athenians had equipped a large naval expedition, and sent it to Cyprus to free the whole of that island from Persian control. When the two hundred Athenian and allied vessels had already set out, a request for active support reached the Athenians from Inaros, a Libyan prince, who was the ring leader of an Egyptian insurrection against Persia. To damage Persian interests by helping to bring about the loss of one of her richest provinces seemed a dazzling prospect to the Athenians. A part of the Cypriote fleet was detached and ordered to proceed to Egypt to coöperate with the insurgents. For several years all went well, but the arrival of large reinforcements from Persia altered the situation. The rebellion was crushed, and the Athenian expedition, together with a relief force of fifty vessels sent out in 454, was wiped out almost to a man.[1] The loss of ninety or a hundred vessels with all their crews and fighting men was a serious blow to Athens; it also caused a temporary weakening of her naval control in the Aegean, and the removal of the Delian treasury may have been due to the fear that Persia might follow up her late success by sending a naval squadron to raid the Cyclades.

After 455 the war in Greece languished for some years. The

[1] That only a portion of the Cypriote fleet — forty or fifty vessels — was despatched to Egypt in 459, and that the Athenian expedition to Egypt was not as great a disaster as suggested by Thucydides, has been demonstrated convincingly by M. Cary in *Classical Quarterly*, vii (1913), 198, and by F. E. Adcock in the *Proceedings of the Cambridge Philological Society* for 1926. Their conclusions have here been adopted.

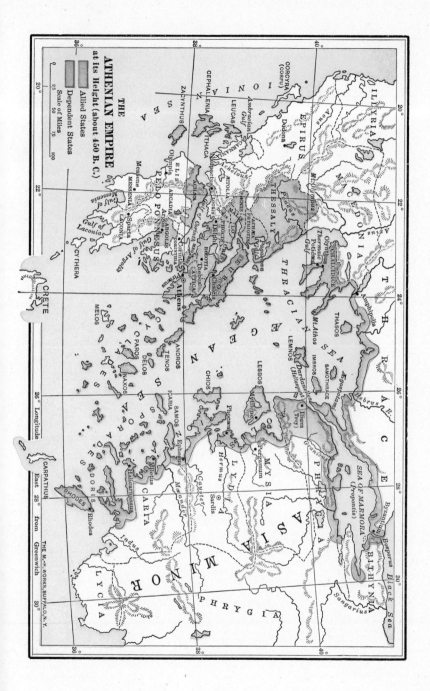

THE
ATHENIAN EMPIRE
at its Height (about 450 B.C.)

Allied States

Dependent States

Scale of Miles
0 25 50 75 100

THE M.-N. WORKS, BUFFALO, N.Y.

failure of the Egyptian enterprise made the Athenians anxious, when they had had time to make good their losses, to retaliate on Persia. But a fresh expedition on a larger scale could only be undertaken if Athens were free from the danger of being attacked at home. In other words, if the war against Persia was to be continued, Athens must come to an accommodation with Sparta. In 451 Cimon's period of exile came to an end and he returned to Athens. The political situation there was such as to restore him at once to a position of authority; and for two years — the only occasion in his long career — Pericles, in modern parlance, led an opposition minority. Through Cimon's efforts a five years' truce was concluded between Sparta and Athens, the latter abandoning her alliance with Argos. The Argives for their part signed a thirty years' treaty with Sparta. In the following spring (450) the second part of Cimon's program was carried out. A fleet of two hundred Athenian and allied vessels under his command sailed for Cyprus. After capturing some minor places he laid siege to Citium; but in 449 the great commander died, the victim of an epidemic which also attacked many of his troops. The siege was abandoned, but before leaving these eastern waters the Athenian fleet attacked the Persian off Cypriote Salamis and won a striking victory. No less than one hundred enemy ships were taken, and the disaster of 454 was amply avenged.

With Cimon's death Pericles' ascendancy in the Athenian *ecclesia* was quickly reëstablished. One of his first acts was to send an embassy to Susa to come to terms with the Great King. An agreement was reached after both sides had made substantial concessions. Athens undertook to interfere no more in Egypt or Cyprus, both countries being acknowledged as Persian dependencies. The Persian king bound himself to send no warships into the Aegean and to abstain from attack on the Greek cities of Asia Minor. While not formally renouncing his authority over those who had once been his subjects, he acquiesced in the situation that had existed in Ionia and Aeolis since 478, and in Caria since the Eurymedon campaign. The friendly, or at least peaceful, relations between the two powers endured for nearly forty years.

In Greece, on the other hand, the truce concluded in the

winter of 451–450 was not fated to last for the whole period. Pericles, it is true, was at first pacific. In 448 he invited all the states of Greece and the Greeks of the islands and Asia Minor to attend a Hellenic congress at Athens, to discuss various matters of interest to all, primarily the restoration of buildings and temples destroyed during the Persian wars. The magnificent project failed because of the opposition of the Peloponnesian states, and especially of Sparta. Nor can the last named state be blamed for her refusal; acceptance would have been equivalent to acknowledging herself second in importance to Athens among Greek states. A dispute about the control of Delphi in the next year led to a renewal of hostilities and a general movement against the Athenian land-empire. The Bœotian cities, led by oligarchic exiles, became actively hostile, and at Coronea their army inflicted a decisive defeat on an Athenian contingent sent to repress what the Athenians, apparently against Pericles' advice, were pleased to believe was only a slight revolt against their authority. It proved a costly and disastrous error; for many Athenians had been captured by the enemy, and, in order to ransom them, Athens was obliged to renounce all control over Bœotia. The loss of Bœotia was followed by the defection of Phocis and Locris, in which again the Athenians could only acquiesce. The Bœotian league from this time became more formidable than ever before, and Thebes once more became its acknowledged head. The constitutions of the cities that made up the league appear to have been oligarchic without exception.

In the summer of 446 Athens was hit in a more vital quarter. Eubœa revolted, and Pericles himself took charge of the operations needed to reduce the islanders to obedience. But now a strong Peloponnesian army passed the Isthmus, Megara rebelled against Athens, its citizens massacred the Athenian garrison in their city, and in a few weeks a hostile army was encamped on Attic soil. At this critical moment Pericles needed all his diplomatic skill to avert disaster. He opened negotiations with the Spartan king, Pleistoanax, who was in command of the Peloponnesian army, and, being prepared to make heavy concessions, prevailed on the king and his advisor, Cleandridas, to withdraw from Attica. The provisional agreement reached by the generals in the field was in the winter following ratified by their respective governments. By the terms of the treaty, which was made for thirty years, Athens acknowledged the independence of Megara, withdrew from the Megarian harbors of Pagæ and Nisæa, abandoned her alliances with Achæa, in fact, gave up all that she had won in Greece during the past fifteen years, save only Naupactus and Aegina. The last-named was to recover her full autonomy, while remaining a member of the Athenian empire; but this provision of the treaty was subsequently ignored by Athens, and the position of the Aeginetans remained unchanged. Sparta and her allies, on their part, formally acknowledged the maritime empire of Athens. Disputes arising between members of the two leagues, the Athenian and the Peloponnesian, were to be submitted hereafter to arbitration. When this danger to Athens was over Pericles returned to Eubœa — the threat to Attica in the previous year had obliged him temporarily to give up the recovery of the island — and quickly reëstablished Athenian authority there. A part of the population of Chalcis was expelled; the inhabitants of Histiæa were altogether evicted, and their town, under the name of Oreus, became a settlement of Athenian cleruchs; other communities were punished by a partial loss of their territories.

Pericles' policy of making Athens a great land power, as well as maintaining herself as the first naval power of Greece, had ended in failure. Her position in 445 was, territorially speaking, no better than in 461 (if we except the cases of Aegina and Naupactus); she had, however, expended large sums and lost many men in what proved to be very ephemeral successes. It is due to Pericles to observe that he showed his statesmanship in rectifying his mistake before it was too late, and in effecting a settlement in 445 which, though in one way a humiliation to Athenian pride, left her naval empire intact and recognized by the rest of Greece.

In this empire there were now only three states — Lesbos, Chios, and Samos — which were completely sovereign, with their own navies. The rest were all dependent on Athens to a greater or less extent, and all paid tribute. From 443 the empire, to facilitate the collection of *phoros*, was divided into five tribute areas, — Thrace, Hellespont, the islands, Ionia, and Caria. Five years later (438), as the size of the Carian region had been reduced by the defection of some communities there, and the Athenians did not think it worth while to attempt their recovery by coercion, the remaining part of Caria was united with Ionia to form one district. The allies, apart from the three independent states, whatever form their government had previously taken, had been compelled by Athens to adopt democratic constitutions. All alike were in numerous cases subject to the jurisdiction of the Athenian law-courts, which tried serious criminal offenses in which members of an allied state were involved, as well as certain types of civil cases, especially commercial litigation. There are no adequate grounds for believing that the treatment received by citizens of allied states was not as a rule equitable. For the statement of the soured oligarchic writer, who in the last quarter of the fifth century composed a treatise on the Athenian constitution, need not be taken too seriously, when he observes that the citizen of an allied state "must needs behave as suppliant in the court of law, and clasp the hands of the jurors as they enter. Hence the allies feel more and more that their relation to the Athenians is that of slaves to masters." Still, it must be admitted that, inasmuch as this subordination to the Athenian *dicasteria* was a concrete and palpable proof of partial loss of independence, it was a cause of discontent among the allies. Another of their grievances was that Pericles and the Athenians after 454 did not hesitate to use part of the tribute money purely in their own interest, for example, for the beautification of Athens by temples and public buildings. Such resentment is perfectly intelligible, although Pericles could fairly reply that it was due to Athenian energy and initiative that the eastern Mediterranean had been made safe for all who dwelt on its shores — neither Persians nor pirates any longer threatened the peaceful Greek merchant vessel; and that the security thus enjoyed by all members of the empire had resulted in a great increase in their material prosperity.

That the assessment of tribute was, with very few exceptions, carried out by Athens was another cause of complaint; yet, as the executive had been from the first in Athenian hands, and by

general consent the original assessment had been entrusted to
an Athenian, Aristeides, Athens in her imperial days could not
be expected to relinquish a prerogative that she had exercised
when only head of a league. And the complaint would only
have been justified, if she had greatly and arbitrarily increased
the amounts which each member was liable to pay. But we
know that no appreciable increase in the *phoros* was imposed
before 425. The most serious, and the most justified, grievance
of the allies is to be found in the establishment of the Athenian
cleruchies. The cleruchy (*kleruchia*) was a body of settlers,
sent to some district outside Attica but subject to Athens, who
retained all the rights and privileges of their Athenian citizenship. While following their ordinary vocations they also formed,
in effect, an Athenian garrison in dependent territory; the fact
that they continued to be Athenian citizens marked them out as
a privileged group in those communities where they were settled
side by side with the earlier inhabitants. Settlements of this
kind were essentially different in character from Greek colonies,
which, once they had been founded, became independent political organisms, and their citizens ceased to enjoy the civic
rights of the city-state from which they had emigrated. The
earliest Athenian cleruchy was sent out before the end of the
sixth century; fifty years later such bodies of Athenians were
established in Lemnos, Imbros, Scyros, Chalcis, and some other
places. The cleruchy could, in the economic sphere, serve the
same purpose as a colony, though differing from it in character.
In other words, it was a means of providing for poor citizens of
an over-populated city-state.

The second period of Pericles' government in Athens was
noteworthy for extensive "colonial" activity. Between 450
and 437 numerous cleruchies were sent out, for instance, to
Eubœa (Oreus), Andros, Naxos, and the Thracian Chersonese.
A body of Athenians, in about 443, proceeded to Brea in Thrace.
This settlement, the site of which is unknown, was a colony, not
a cleruchy. But for the chance discovery of an inscription
recording certain regulations for this *apoikia*, we should not
know of its existence. Another colony, destined to play a more
prominent part in Greek affairs, was that founded at the "Nine
Ways" in 437. The earlier attempt to colonize this site had, as

we have seen, ended in disaster; but now, under the name of Amphipolis, the new city flourished greatly and soon overshadowed most of the other Greek communities in Thrace. The Hellenic colony which was planted at Thurii in southern Italy was made up of citizens from various *poleis*, a goodly quota being Athenians.

In 440 an event occurred which, but for the energetic action of Pericles, might have seriously disturbed the stability of the empire. Samos and Miletus became involved in a dispute, in which Athens sided with Miletus. After some preliminaries, including an attempt of the Athenians to replace an oligarchic by a democratic constitution in Samos, the island openly seceded from Athens; her example was followed by Byzantium. After a siege lasting eight months, starvation in Samos did the work which the Athenian siege engines were unable to do, and the Samians capitulated. They were treated as the Naxians and Thasians had been a quarter of a century before. Byzantium, doubtless realizing the hopelessness of a single-handed conflict, hastened to return to her allegiance. It may have been partly to settle outstanding questions in this vitally important spot, commanding the entrance to the Black Sea, but it was especially to promote Athenian interests in a more general way, that Pericles, probably in 437, sailed with a large fleet to the Propontis and the Euxine. Athenian settlers were established in several districts bordering on one or other of those seas; but perhaps the most valuable result of this voyage was a friendly agreement signed between Athens and Spartocus, ruler of the Cimmerian Bosporus (Crimea). This prince and his successors granted Athens certain commercial privileges affecting the export of grain, which were of inestimable value to a city-state now importing more than half the wheat necessary for feeding her population.

Thus Pericles did his utmost to strengthen the Athenian empire and to widen the field of Athenian influence. In this direction his achievement, in contrast to his disastrous efforts to create and maintain a land empire, were not only eminently successful and beneficial at the time, but of lasting effect.

2. THE PELOPONNESIAN WAR, 431–404 B.C.

In spite of all, it was not many years after the agreement had been signed between the Peloponnesian states and Athens before ominous signs began to appear that the peace would be broken long before the expiration of the treaty. It is not easy to apportion blame to, or to determine the responsibility of, either side for the prolonged struggle known as the great Peloponnesian war. It is probably true to say that Pericles was mainly responsible for bringing about an open rupture in the particular year 432–431; it would be grossly unjust to attribute the war simply to his imperial ambitions. He foresaw that Athens would inevitably be involved very soon in a great fight with her Peloponnesian neighbors. Being convinced of what was bound to occur in any case within a very few years, he may have forced the issue at the last because, if Athens had to go to war, he wished her to do so at a time and under circumstances that were favorable to her, and above all, while he himself was still alive and able to guide her destinies. In the *History* of Thucydides we have a full and masterly account of the struggle from 431 to 411, and the historian, who analyzes the preliminaries to the war with a great wealth of detail, is careful to distinguish those events which immediately preceded the rupture, and were thus the immediate reasons for the war, from the real, though less tangible, causes that lay deep down in the character of Greek city-states and of the two groups of combatants.

However great the advantages derived by the subjects of Athens from their membership in her maritime empire, neither they nor the rest of Greece could forget that they had lost that possession which was dearest to the Greek heart, political autonomy. Nor, when the Spartans, in going to war, claimed that they did so in order to liberate the Greeks from enslavement by Athens, were they conscious hypocrites. That they failed thirty years later to be true to their earlier professions, and were then far worse oppressors of Hellenic liberty than ever the Athenians had been, proves only that their leaders when power was in their grasp did not know how to use it. In 432 Sparta hesitated to go to war; it was other members of the Peloponnesian league who had to use all their influence with the head of the league to take the final step. Corinth especially was bitterly hostile to Athens, partly because she was filled with jealousy of the state whose naval power had far outstripped her own, partly through exasperation at the events of 435–432 in which her interests suffered seriously.[1] There were, in fact, two incidents which had ended in open conflict between Corinthians and Athenian troops, though both were in outlying parts of the Hellenic world. Corinth in 435 was involved in a quarrel with the powerful island-state of Corcyra, which had originally been a Corinthian colony. The latter, after some initial successes, found herself in a position of dangerous isolation; in her difficulty she appealed to Athens for alliance and help. After a lengthy debate the Athenian *ecclesia* acceded to the Corcyræan request. Before the end of the summer of 433 the presence of Athenian vessels in Corcyræan waters had deprived Corinth of a victory over her daughter-city. The Corinthian government was naturally annoyed; a few months later their annoyance was increased to exasperation. The city of Potidæa in Chalcidice was also a Corinthian colony, and her relations with the mother-city were closer than usual, since her chief magistrates came to her annually from Corinth. But Potidæa had been a member of the Athenian empire for some time, and had recently had her tribute considerably increased. Relying on the support of Corinth and of the Macedonian king, Perdiccas, who looked with disfavor on Athenian expansion in Thrace, and was himself scheming to bring about a general revolt among the Athenian allies in Thrace, the Potidæans prepared to revolt. The Athenians, learning what was in the wind, delivered an ultimatum. When their demands were not met, an Athenian squadron was sent off to bring the recalcitrant ally to order. Corinth despatched an officer with a body of irregulars to help her daughter-city in her need, and this force succeeded in reaching Potidæa before the Athenian blockade had become fully effective. The Corinthians now

---

[1] Yet, when Samos in 440 appealed to the Peloponnesian league for help against Athens, it was Corinth who urged non-intervention. This was of course only five years after the conclusion of the thirty years' peace; also the Corinthians may well have felt that it was undesirable, as it certainly was against the terms of the peace, to interfere in what was a domestic quarrel within the large Athenian family.

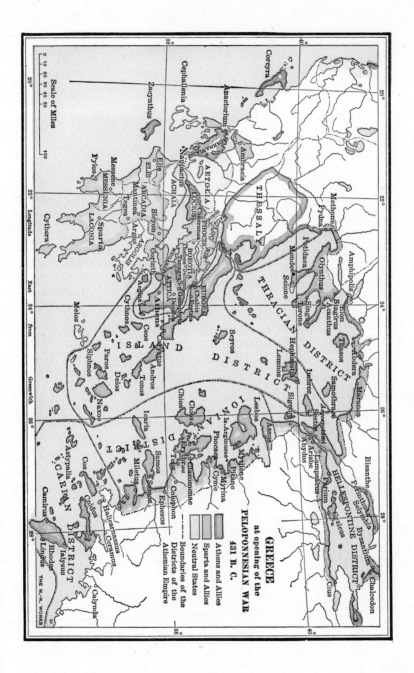

GREECE
at opening of the
PELOPONNESIAN WAR
431 B. C.

Athens and Allies
Sparta and Allies
Neutral States
----- Boundaries of the
Districts of the
Athenian Empire

Scale of Miles
0 10 20 30 40 50   100

THE M.-N. WORKS

exerted themselves to make Sparta and the Peloponnesian league proclaim war on Athens.

Some months before the representatives of the league had convened at Sparta, Pericles had prevailed upon the Athenians to take a step which would either hasten on a war which he already regarded as inevitable, or else would so intimidate the enemies of Athens that they would fail to rally to the support of Corinth. In the summer of 432 the Athenian assembly passed a decree excluding the Megarians from all the markets and harbors of the Athenian empire. It is true that the Athenians at this date had several legitimate grievances against their neighbor; nor had they forgotten the defection of Megara in 446 and the slaughter of the Athenian garrison. Nevertheless, the decree, which meant the economic ruin and the semi-starvation of Megara, was far more than a punitive measure inflicted by Athens on an offending neighbor; it was a challenge to the enemies of Athens as a whole, a demonstration of what Athenian control of the eastern Aegean could do.

At the Peloponnesian congress, held in the autumn of 432, the Spartan government was won over by the war party in its own city and in the league. A majority of the league voted for war, but the winter months were still spent in diplomatic exchanges. Had Athens been prepared to make some concessions, it is doubtful whether Sparta would have finally broken off negotiations. Though the first fighting occurred in the early spring of 431 with a surprise attack by the Bœotians on Athens' ally, Platæa, general hostilities did not open till the end of May. Virtually all Greeks save those of the far West were involved in the struggle that now began. The enemies of Athens comprised all the Peloponnesian states, except Argos, and most of the Achæan cities, which remained neutral; Megara, Bœotia, Phocis, and Locris in central Greece; and, in the Northwest, Leucas, Anactorium, and Ambracia, all of which were in close and friendly relations with Corinth. Athens, in addition to her subjects and her two independent allies, Lesbos and Chios, had on her side Corcyra, Zacynthus, most of Acarnania, Naupactus, and Platæa. As regards the "sinews of war" she was in an infinitely stronger position than her enemies. A reserve of 6000 talents lay on the Athenian Acropolis, and there was a large and regular income each year from the tribute of her subjects. The opponents of Athens commanded no such resources; and, though the suggestion was put forward by Corinth that the treasures of Olympia and Delphi be used by them to finance the war, the religious sentiments of a majority of her allies were evidently opposed to such sacrilege, since the suggestion was never adopted. Nor did they succeed in their efforts to enlist the active support of Persia in the fight against Athens.

Pericles' plan of campaign was, briefly, to evacuate Attica and bring all the population inside the walls of Athens and Peiræus, leaving the enemy to do such material damage in the country as they could. For the Athenian food-supply was safe as long as the Athenians controlled the sea. Her naval strength Athens must use to harry the coasts of the enemy, and, so far as possible, to carry out an economic blockade of the Peloponnese. At all costs a military engagement must be avoided; for the Peloponnesian army outnumbered the Athenian field-force by more than two to one. It is a proof of Pericles' tremendous hold on his countrymen that he prevailed on them to abandon farms and homes, and crowd into the city, and that, later, when they knew the foe was ravaging and burning crops, vineyards, and oliveyards, he was able to restrain them from rushing out to fight. The invasions of Attica by a Peloponnesian army were at first almost annual occurrences. The Athenians attacked the Megarid and Argolid more than once, but these expeditions were subordinate to the naval operations undertaken over a wider area.

The first serious blow suffered by the Athenians was not inflicted by the enemy. In the early summer of 430, when the Peloponnesian army for the second time had invaded Attica, an epidemic which had already ravaged many parts of the Persian empire reached Peiræus and Athens. In spite of the careful and detailed description of the symptoms and progress of this plague, which Thucydides, who was himself a victim, has left us, it has not been possible for medical experts to identify it with any disease now known. But there is no doubt about its deadly character, especially when, through overcrowding, indifferent housing, and bad sanitation, the conditions were so favorable to the spread of contagion. The death rate was very high, the situation in the city being made worse by the fact that many of the dead had to be left unburied. The worst phase of the pestilence was in 430–429, but there was a recurrence in 427, and cases continued to occur for a further two years before the disease had entirely spent its force. The total death-roll in these years is said to have been no less than a third of the population; for in 430 the infection had been carried to the besieging force at Potidæa by a supplementary detachment of troops sent from Athens to expedite operations against the rebellious communities of Chalcidice. The physical illness of the citizens was not the worst part of the visitation. The misery all around them, the uncertainty of existence caused by the knowledge that though they were alive one day they might be dead the next, slackened the moral fibre of the Athenians and brought out their worst passions and a readiness to commit any excess. "Knowing not what would become of them, they disregarded all the ordinances of gods and men."[1] Seeking for a scapegoat, they found him in the statesman who had been responsible for massing them in the city and had prevented them from going out against the enemy.

In 430 Pericles was indicted for misappropriation of public funds. He was found guilty, — no doubt quite unjustly — fined, and deposed from his high office. Yet in a few months, in the early spring of 429, the Athenians had repented of their action, and Pericles was reëlected to the office of *strategos*. Before the end of that year the great statesman died, and there was no one to replace him. Thucydides, in his appraisal of Pericles' character and abilities (ii, 65), expressly stresses the unrivalled authority which, by his personality and force of character, his personal integrity, and his knowledge of mass psychology, he had been able to exercise over the Athenians. Although the general policy which he had laid down for them at the beginning of the war was to a great extent followed for the next eight years, there was no single man to guide the ship of state. Party warfare succeeded the Periclean autocracy, and for a space the two outstanding politicians at Athens were Nicias and Cleon. The former was a rich land-owner; he had

[1] Thucydides, ii, 52.

the backing of the wealthy class, on whom a great part of the expenses of the war devolved, and of the farming population. The peace party or moderates, whichever we call them, though no less patriotic than their political opponents, on the one hand proceeded, as far as possible, along Periclean lines, on the other they counselled moderation toward the allies; and, if a suitable opportunity for making peace should present itself, they were prepared to make concessions to save the prolongation of the war. Cleon was a man of very different type and antecedents. Whether the "tanner" had actually practised his craft himself or merely owned some slaves, from the profit of whose leather work he derived an income, we do not know; at all events he sprang from the proletariat, and to it he looked for support when his native ability brought him to the front as a politician. His regular supporters were those on whom the burden of war lay least heavily, and who either immediately or in the near future could derive some profit from it.

For several years after Pericles' death neither group of combatants could boast of any striking successes. Had her enemies possessed a commander of genius, Athens, weakened as she was by the plague, might have been forced to come to terms within the first five years of the war. Potidæa at last surrendered in the late autumn of 430; the operations had cost Athens dearly both in men and money. So, for the present at least, she abandoned the attempt to recover completely her grip on Chalcidice. On the other hand, the Peloponnesian efforts to detach the Athenian allies in northwestern Greece, and to deprive Athens of her base on the Corinthian Gulf at Naupactus, failed miserably, partly owing to the incompetence of the Peloponnesian commanders, partly through the skill of the Athenian, Phormio, who won two notable naval victories in the Corinthian Gulf against greatly superior forces. Athens' little ally, Platæa, was assaulted by a Peloponnesian army in 429 — the year in which the plague made an attack on Attica unsafe for any invader — but without success; the active siege was, however, changed to a blockade. At last in 427, after a part of the garrison had managed to escape to Athens, the rest of the Platæans were forced to surrender, and, after a trial which was a mockery of justice, were put to death. The help which Athens had promised her ally had never come, but there were, from the Athenian point of view, extenuating circumstances. She probably had not the men available to risk a battle in the open with the Peloponnesian army, and only a clear victory could have saved her besieged friends. For, before the end of 428, Mitylene, the chief city in Lesbos, had revolted, and all the lesser cities in the island, except Methymna, followed suit. The Athenians needed all their resources to punish a defection which, if neglected, might easily have become the signal for a general rising of her allies against her. In the summer of the next year, shortly before the fall of Platæa, Mitylene capitulated. Cleon persuaded the Athenians to visit their utmost fury on the unhappy city, and to put to death all the adult males and enslave the women and children. Fortunately more moderate counsels prevailed on the day after this decision had been made by the assembly, and the order for this mass execution was countermanded in time. Even so a thousand of the chief men of Lesbos were executed. The land of the Lesbians was confiscated and handed over to 3000 Athenian settlers, to whom the former owners who continued to cultivate the land were obliged to pay a heavy tithe. Costly as the operations had been — and in order to meet her immediate needs Athens for the first recorded time levied a property tax on the wealthier citizens and denizens — they seem to have had a generally salutary effect on the members of the Athenian empire. Before the end of 427 the Athenians for the first time cast their eyes to the far West. In the autumn of that year, and again in 425, they sent small squadrons to Sicily to help their allies there against the growing and aggressive power of Syracuse.

The period of Tyrant-rule, through which all Sicily had passed in the early part of the century, had come to an end c. 465. Everywhere despots were deposed and a period of civil war followed. The older Sicel population for a brief spell was organized by one, Ducetius, and made its influence strongly felt; but its power collapsed as quickly as it had arisen. By c. 445 general peace at last reigned again in the island, and the leading position among the Sicilian cities was by common consent accorded to Syracuse. In the early part of the Peloponnesian war Syracusan statesmen were showing a disposition to change that leadership into a more definite sovereignty, the result being a renewal of warfare in the island.

There were at least three communities in the far West which had had treaty relations with Athens for some time. Segesta had concluded an alliance with Athens in 453, Leontini and Rhegium had done the same somewhat later, and their treaties had been renewed in 433–432. Although the Athenian operations of 427–424 in Sicily did not lead to any substantial results, they did make the Athenians more familiar with that country. The venture had been urged on by Cleon and the war party, whose aims were frankly imperialistic in the worst sense. It may have prevented coöperation between the Dorian cities of the island, like Syracuse, and the Peloponnesian league. By 424 the Sicilians had settled their differences among themselves after a pan-Sicilian congress at Gela. The Athenian commanders, in face of this development, could do nothing but withdraw from the island. A disappointed Athenian assembly, on their return to Athens, fined one and exiled the other.

Meantime neither side in the main theatre of war had been able to win any substantial advantage. The most noteworthy operation was the Athenian capture of Pylos on the west coast of Messenia, which gave them a serviceable base from which to harry Spartan territory. A further blow was dealt to Sparta by the Athenian seizure and occupation of the island of Cythera. The capture of Pylos, moreover, had other than military results. The Athenians had taken 292 Lacedæmonian prisoners, of whom 120 were full Spartan citizens. The fact that these were in Athenian hands prevented the Peloponnesians from continuing their annual invasions of Attica, since an exasperated Athenian assembly might have retaliated by putting the prisoners to death. Again, Cleon had won all the credit, which more properly belonged to the Athenian commander, Demosthenes, for the successful conclusion of the Pylos campaign, and for the moment his ascendancy in Athens was so great that he carried through a measure for the drastic reassessment of the tribute payable by the subjects of Athens. The actual sum now assessed against them was nearly 1000 talents. That the action of the Athenians was unpopular in the empire we cannot doubt; on the other hand, there was some justification for raising the *phoros*, because most of the cities had greatly advanced in wealth and prosperity during the past half century. In some instances, where the resources of a city had not increased, no additional tribute was imposed, or the amount previously fixed was actually reduced.

In the next three years, 424–422, the tide began to turn against Athens. An attempted surprise attack on Bœotia failed through the incompetence of the Athenian generals, and the Athenians suffered a severe defeat at Delium. The Spartan commander, Brasidas, who had already performed some notable acts in the war, at the head of a small contingent made his way with much secrecy to Thrace. There, with great diplomatic skill, he sowed disaffection among the subjects of Athens. He made himself master of Amphipolis, and the loss of this city, quickly followed as it was by the secession of other Chalcidic communities, was one of the severest blows that Athens had suffered so far. The Athenian efforts to oust Brasidas and, above all, to recover Amphipolis failed; finally, in an engagement fought near that city in 422, Brasidas and Cleon, who was in charge of the Athenian operations, were both killed. The death of Cleon was a blessing for Athens. It removed the one dominant man of the war party at Athens, and the moderates, led by Nicias, were able to convince their war-weary countrymen of the need of coming to terms with the enemy. The Spartan government, too, at this time was disappointed that the Peloponnesians had been unable to make any permanent impression on the strength of Athens, and so was pacifically inclined. In the spring of 421, after preliminary negotiations during the winter, a peace was concluded between the chief combatants.

For Sparta to conclude peace with the Athenians was one thing; to ensure that the terms of the agreement would be accepted by all her allies was another, and proved to be impossible. So for three or four years Greece witnessed a tangle of diplomatic moves and counter-moves, agreements and counter-agreements, at the end of which Sparta had reasserted her authority in the Peloponnesian league, while Athens was in a more isolated position in Greece than before. The events of 421–416 can here be only very briefly touched upon. Inability on the part of Sparta to persuade the Bœotians, Corinth, and some other states to agree to the peace of Nicias for a moment led to the break-up of the Peloponnesian league. To counterbalance its loss of influence with some of the most powerful allies, the Spartan government made approaches to Athens and contracted a defensive alliance with the late enemy. But a change in the Spartan ephorate and in the political leadership at Athens made this understanding inoperative almost at once. On the expiry of the thirty years' truce, concluded between Sparta and Argos in 451, the Athenians allied themselves to Argos. Sparta settled her differences with the Bœotian league and Corinth, but the alliance between Athens and Argos was enlarged to include two Peloponnesian states, Elis and Mantinea, each of whom had a quarrel of her own with Sparta. It was not till 418 that the general peace was again broken in Greece. An attack by Argos on Epidaurus, a member of the Peloponnesian league, led to Spartan intervention. In the summer of that year a Lacedæmonian army, reinforced by contingents from Tegea and other Arcadian cities who were loyal to Sparta, decisively defeated an allied force of Argives, Mantineans, and Athenians close to the city of Mantinea. The result of this Spartan victory was to restore to its former solidarity the Peloponnesian league, and to reëstablish completely the hegemony of Sparta. Argos was compelled to form a new alliance with her victor, and the Athenians found themselves deserted by their recently found friends in the Peloponnese. The calculations of the Spartans respecting Argos were, however, upset by a revolution in that city in 417, as the result of which a democratic government took the place of the former oligarchy. The several efforts of the Spartans to get the Argive oligarchs restored to power were unsuccessful but meant that the two states were intermittently at war for several years. The Athenian-Argive alliance, on the other hand, had been renewed for a period of fifty years in 417.

At Athens the interval between the peace of Nicias and the sailing of the expedition to Sicily in 415 had served to bring to the political front a young rival to Nicias for the control of the assembly and of Athenian policy. Alcibiades, the nephew and ward of Pericles, having completed his thirtieth year, was in 420 elected to the office of *strategos*. For the remainder of the war he was to be the evil genius of Athens. Handsome, endowed with a great personal fascination and exceptional intellectual gifts, he was indulgently forgiven by the Athenians for the vagaries and occasional ostentation of his private life, while the war party saw in him the makings of a brilliant leader working for their advantage. Yet his whole career shows that he lacked stability and character, that personal ambition, not the interest of his country, was the motive power of his political conduct. First and last he was a self-seeking politician; to put him, as some modern writers have been inclined to do, in the same class as a Pericles or a Themistocles is an insult to the memory of those men and to the critical faculty of the modern student of Athenian history. It was Alcibiades who was responsible for the various *rapprochements* with Argos and the break-down of the more friendly relations between Sparta and Athens. His policy did not go unchallenged, for the influence of Nicias was still very strong; and, just as he had brought about the peace of 421, so he continued to desire peace with Sparta. Finally in 417 recourse was had to the obsolescent expedient of ostracism. The result was farcical, inasmuch as the adverse vote of the assembly pronounced the decree of exile against Hyperbolus, a politician of the stamp of Cleon, but without his ability, who had been prominent in the counsels of the war party for some years. It is not unlikely that this outcome was the result of an understanding between Alcibiades and Nicias, brought about by the persuasive tongue of the younger man because he had cause to fear for his own position.[1]

In 416, at Alcibiades' instigation, the Athenians committed a shocking act of injustice. The island of Melos, a reputed Dorian colony, was, though one of the Cyclades, not a tribute-paying member of the Athenian empire. The Athenians had made earlier but unavailing efforts to press the Melians into alliance with themselves. Now they delivered an ultimatum,

---

[1] After the case of Hyperbolus ostracism seems to have been entirely abandoned at Athens. In 417 it had proved quite useless for the purpose for which it was originally intended.

and, when their demands were opposed, besieged the island.
On its capture they killed off the adult males and sold the women
and children as slaves. Then they sent a body of Athenian
settlers to the island. Such harsh treatment, however deplor-
able, was by the usage of the time condoned by public opinion
in the case of revolted allies or even active combatants in the
war. So to act toward a small neutral state nothing but the
most brutal cynicism could justify.

With the war virtually at a standstill in Greece the minds
of the Athenians were once more filled with ambitions of conquest in Sicily. The arrival, in the late autumn of 416, of an
embassy from their old ally, Segesta, provided an excuse, if
one was needed, for despatching an Athenian expedition to
the West. The peaceful settlement of Sicily reached by the
congress at Gela in 424 had lasted very few years. Syracuse
had attacked and destroyed Leontini, and then, at the request
of Selinus, she had intervened in a quarrel between that city
and Segesta. The Segestan envoys at Athens promised that
their city would provide the Athenians with funds to carry on
operations in Sicily on their behalf. The Athenian assembly,
with surprising caution, did not commit itself at once, but
sent representatives to the West to investigate on the spot the
financial strength of their ally. When they returned to Athens
a few months later they brought with them a substantial sum
in cash and a promise of more to come. The renewed deliberations of the *ecclesia* showed that there was a great majority
in favor of the enterprise. The spokesman of this majority
was Alcibiades, who saw in an expedition, which he hoped to
lead himself, a magnificent opportunity of furthering his own
ambitions and satisfying his lust for power. Thus the timely
and urgent counsel of Nicias against the proposed undertaking
was set aside; when, at a second meeting of the assembly,
he tried to deflect the Athenians from their purpose by representing that the force which they intended to send was quite inadequate, they were so far from being deterred that they
voted a much larger armament. The command was entrusted
to Alcibiades, Lamachus — an experienced soldier but without
political experience or influence — and Nicias. The appointment of so ill-matched a trio to act jointly in the conduct of

a difficult war was the first of several vital errors committed by the Athenians. Preparations were now pushed on with speed and with the determination that men, ships, and equipment should all be of the best. Almost the entire population was carried away with a boundless enthusiasm which Plutarch describes graphically when he writes, "that the young men in the wrestling schools and the older men sitting in their workshops or in the lounges of the gymnasia drew outline maps of Sicily and the details of the sea surrounding the island and the harbors and places on the side of the island facing Africa." [1] The total force of Athenians, strengthened by some of their allies, amounted to 134 ships of war, 130 smaller vessels for taking supplies, 5100 heavy and 1300 light-armed troops, and 30 cavalry. Since the normal complement of a trireme was 200, the total personnel of the expedition was more than 27,000 men.

An act of sacrilege cast a certain gloom over Athens shortly before the fleet was due to sail. In one night almost all the busts of Hermes, which adorned numerous shrines and also the vestibules of dwelling-houses in the city, were hacked and mutilated by impious hands. A wanton act of this kind aroused all the latent superstitions of the masses. An oligarchic revolution was feared by many, and the almost hysterical condition of the people gave ample scope for informers and occasion for numerous investigations and prosecutions. The political enemies of Alcibiades exploited the situation for their own ends. Information was laid about other sacrilegious acts which had taken place in the past, especially a mock celebration in a private house of the Eleusinian Mysteries, in which Alcibiades was supposed to have taken part. The latter wanted an immediate trial, but his enemies managed to get it deferred, so that it could take place when the soldiers and sailors with whom he was a favorite were no longer in Athens. To postpone the sailing of the expedition was impossible, and Alcibiades was therefore forced to depart for Sicily with a prosecution on what might well be a capital charge hanging over him. The armada left Athens before the end of June, 415; after a review at Corcyra it proceeded in three divisions to Italian

[1] Plutarch, *Nicias*, 12.

and Sicilian waters. At Rhegium three scout vessels, which
had been sent on in advance to Segesta, rejoined the main
fleet, bringing with them the unwelcome news that the Segestans
had deceived the Athenians when they promised ample financial aid, and that only thirty talents were available. The council of war that was now held by the three commanders showed
that a radical difference existed between them regarding the
best plan of campaign. Nicias wished to confine the operations
to assisting Athens' ally, by moving at once against Selinus;
Lamachus urged an immediate attack against the real enemy,
Syracuse; Alcibiades, whose proposal carried the day, argued
that they should, before beginning active operations, try to
win as many allies in the island as possible. Thus precious
time was lost at the outset. When the Athenians arrived
at Catana they were met by the state trireme *Salaminia*
which had been sent to bring Alcibiades home to stand his
trial. Allowed to return in his own ship, Alcibiades escaped
from his escort, made his way to the Peloponnese, and finally
reached Sparta, quite ready to play traitor to his country.
The responsibility for the mutilation of the Hermæ was supposedly brought home to members of the oligarchic clubs.

Nicias, after this, ill-advisedly continued to follow Alcibiades'
plan of action, with the result that a serious attack on Syracuse
was not made till the spring of 414. In consequence the Syracusans had ample time to make preparations against the danger
that threatened them, and, above all, they were able to com-
municate with their mother-city, Corinth. Through her good
offices the Spartan government was persuaded to send a
Lacedæmonian officer, Gylippus, to take charge of the small
relief expedition equipped by Corinth, and of the general defense of Syracuse when he reached Sicily.

The Athenian operations against Syracuse started auspiciously; for, owing to the enemy's negligence, the Athenians
were able to get control of the hill, Euryalus, and the high plateau, Epipolæ, which overlooked and commanded the city. The
object of the Athenians was now to cut off Syracuse entirely
from the land side, by constructing a wall running approximately
north and south across the peninsula on which the city was
built. Their opponents sought to prevent this by building

counter-walls at right angles to the Athenian works and so to hinder them from completing their plan. Twice the Syracusans were defeated, and their constructions captured and demolished. On the second occasion the Athenians suffered a severe loss in the death of their best officer, Lamachus. Before the northern end of the Athenian wall had been carried to the sea, and thereby completed, Gylippus, who had landed in northern Sicily by this time and had there collected a considerable body of auxiliaries from Himera and other cities, had managed to elude the vigilance of the Athenians and had made his way into Syracuse. The unaccountable negligence of Nicias in failing adequately to guard the ascent to Euryalus, thus allowing Gylippus to slip through and past the Athenian lines, cost the Athenians dear. Nicias had, it is true, reason for believing that the Syracusans were on the point of surrendering to him on conditions; yet this was no excuse for relaxing the siege operations or for gross military negligence.

The arrival of Gylippus, which occurred in the nick of time, marks the turning point of the Syracusan fortunes. The citizens were heartened by his presence, by the realization that they were not forgotten by their friends in Greece, and by the arrival of much needed reinforcements. Gylippus, for his part, took infinite pains to improve the discipline and efficiency of the Syracusan army. The third counter-wall was now successfully built after they had driven back the attacking Athenians, who were thus prevented from completing the blockade of the city. By the autumn of 414 the Athenians were strictly on the defensive and thoroughly disheartened besides. Their losses from fighting and sickness had been considerable, and Nicias, who was himself suffering from an organic disease, was desirous of abandoning the whole enterprise. Fearing to do this on his own responsibility, he sent an urgent despatch to Athens in which he put two alternatives to the council and the assembly: either to allow the withdrawal of his troops or to send a large body of reinforcements. In case the second course should be adopted he asked to be relieved of his command. But the assembly were not yet convinced that the situation in Sicily could not be retrieved. A fresh armament was voted, which, before it reached Syracuse, totalled 73

triremes, 5000 hoplites, and 3000 miscellaneous light-armed
troops. The command was intrusted to Demosthenes and
Eurymedon; yet Nicias was not superseded, but instructed
to coöperate with his new colleagues. A small advance rein-
forcement was sent off under Eurymedon as soon as possible;
the second expedition did not sail till the spring and reached
Syracuse in July, 413.

The winter months had been a period of military inactivity
in Sicily; but, when the campaigning season of 413 began,
it became more than ever clear how invaluable to the Syracusans
the presence of Gylippus was. At his instigation they reorganized their naval forces and equipment with the hope of successfully attacking the Athenian fleet in the harbor when
opportunity offered. Without the destruction of their navy
the Athenians could not be completely crushed, and a means
of escape remained open to them. Both by land and sea
the advantage, in spite of some set-backs, rested with the Syracusans, and, when at last the second Athenian expedition
arrived, it was not a moment too soon. On the previous day
the enemy had won a notable victory in the harbor, and the
position of Nicias and his men was well-nigh desperate. Demosthenes urged on his colleague the necessity of an immediate
offensive, with the object of destroying or capturing the
Syracusan counter-wall. This done, it would be possible
to shut in the city completely. But for a direct assault by
day conditions were unfavorable; the enemy were too strong
and too well disciplined. Hence a night attack was planned
by way of Euryalus. All went well at first on the critical
evening; but, once well on the plateau, when the alarm had
been given and the fighting had become general, the advance
Athenian force pressed on too far, and, being met by a fresh
detachment of the enemy, was pushed back in disorder, and
the main body of their men was thrown into confusion. The
Syracusans drove home their advantage and the whole Athenian
army was thrown back with very heavy loss — perhaps as
much as 2000 men. The sequel to this disastrous failure
Demosthenes foresaw would be a new and energetic offensive
by the Syracusans; he therefore urged immediate departure
on his colleagues. Once more Nicias could not steel himself

to take decisive action; also, he still appears to have entertained hopes that the philo-Athenian party in Syracuse — how large it was we do not know — might play into his hands. For three weeks the Athenians remained on the watch, yet inactive, during which time Gylippus had secured additional help in Sicily, and some overdue reinforcements from Greece also arrived at last. In view of this even Nicias could hesitate no longer. On August 27th, 413, the retirement from Syracuse was to be undertaken; in the evening, however, when all was ready, a total eclipse of the moon occurred. The soothsayers protested that nothing could be done until twenty-seven days had elapsed. Was the advice mere folly, or were there traitors among the Athenian interpreters of celestial phenomena? We do not know; but Nicias, religious or superstitious, whichever we choose to call him, obeyed their advice.

Gylippus had quickly learnt of the intended retirement of the enemy and of the consequences of the eclipse. He thus laid his plans for cutting off the Athenian retirement by land, at the same time staking his hopes on the successful issue of a grand assault on the Athenian fleet. In their first naval engagement the Syracusans drove the Athenian vessels on shore; though they had suffered severe casualties themselves, they were once more masters of their own harbor. They at once closed its entrance with warships and other craft securely anchored together, anticipating that their opponents, as soon as they had effected the most necessary repairs to their vessels, would try to escape by sea. In this they calculated correctly. When the Athenians tried to make good their escape they were defeated and driven back to shore with heavy loss. Their commanders wished to make a second attempt to break through with their remaining sixty triremes; but now the crews refused to embark, and there was nothing left but to retreat by land. For six days they retired, dogged by the enemy. At last the two divisions in which the army was marching got separated. Demosthenes' was the first to be surrounded and forced to surrender on the seventh day, to the number of 6000. On the eighth day the army of Nicias was overwhelmed as it was desperately trying to fight its way across the Assinarus river. The official captives on this occasion numbered 1000, but many Athenians had been privately taken prisoner by Syracusans. To the survivors the Syracusans were merciless. Nicias and Demosthenes were executed, an ignominy spared to Eurymedon, who had fallen in an engagement before the final retreat. The other captives were imprisoned in stone quarries near Syracuse where most of them perished after many weeks of untold suffering. Truly, the people of Melos had been heavily avenged!

The catastrophe in Sicily, a disaster to a Greek state of hitherto unparalleled magnitude, her enemies believed would be followed by the immediate collapse of Athens. In holding out instead for another eight years against a most formidable coalition of opponents, the Athenians showed indomitable courage and resourcefulness; but this would have availed them little if they had not been helped by the crass incompetence of their enemies' higher command. In Greece, active hostilities between Athens and Sparta had been reopened by the spring of 413. King Agis with a Peloponnesian army invaded Attica; he seized and fortified Decelea, and having sent part of his troops back remained in occupation there with the rest. Decelea on the slopes of Mt. Parnes was situated about a dozen miles from Athens and a like distance from the Attic-Bœotian frontier; it was a position from which the whole of northern Attica, and especially the land route from Athens to Oropus and Eubœa, could be controlled. Moreover, as Thucydides observes (vii, 27), the Athenians had in the past suffered only from temporary invasions of Attica; now they were for the rest of the war to have an enemy force permanently within their frontiers. Raids in different parts of Attica became frequent, cattle and flocks were destroyed, more than 20,000 slaves deserted; later on it became impossible properly to work the silver mines at Laurium. In fact, the population of Attica was compelled to reside continuously in the capital, which became like an armed camp in a perpetual state of siege. Yet, while she had command of the sea, Athens could not be starved into submission. After the disaster in Sicily the possibility or need of crushing Athens on her own element was borne in upon her foes, and during the winter months, 413–412, they engaged in great naval preparations. That same interval of six months' virtual suspension of fighting was the salvation of the Athenians. It enabled them to take stock of their resources and to effect such changes and reforms in administration as seemed called for by the exigencies of their situation. The first need was money, since the treasury was exhausted. To increase the tribute would have been too dangerous a measure when the subjects of the empire were already restive and disposed to revolt. The *phoros* was therefore abolished and the Athenians calculated that they would get a safer as well as a larger income by imposing a 5% tax on all imports and exports throughout the empire. It is regrettable that we are ignorant of the details of this financial experiment; nor do we know the total sum forthcoming in any year. The fact that the Athenians were able to carry on the war so long is sufficient proof that their calculations in 413 were approximately correct.

The war party at Athens was deemed responsible for the Sicilian catastrophe, and suffered eclipse. To put the executive in more responsible hands the assembly voted the appointment of ten commissioners (*probuloi*), who took over many of the most important functions of the Council of Five Hundred, for example, the direction of finance and the superintendence of naval construction. At the elections for the *strategia* held early in 412 several of the newly elected officers were men of marked oligarchic sympathies, another sign that the disasters suffered by the Athenians, when the government was in the hands of advanced democrats, were producing a strong reaction against the extremer forms of democracy.

Meanwhile, the anti-Athenian coalition was steadily growing. The Syracusans sent a naval squadron to join the Peloponnesian navy. Many of the Athenian subjects or allies in Ionia were intriguing with the enemy, and in 412 many of them openly revolted. Of these the chief was Chios; the secession of this powerful state was a very severe blow to the Athenians, who now used the reserve fund of 1000 talents, which had been set aside for a naval emergency at the beginning of the war, in order to increase their ship-building. One consequence of the revolt of Ionia and the coöperation of the Peloponnesian fleet with Athens' late subjects was that the main theatre of the war was transferred to the eastern Aegean. An additional reason for this is to be found in the intervention of Persia in Greek affairs at this date. The occasion for reasserting his authority over the

Anatolian Greeks seemed to Darius II to have come, and his two
satraps in western Asia Minor were given a free hand to assist
the enemies of Athens.   Unfortunately for the interests of the
Great King, Tissaphernes and Pharnabazus, under the influence
of personal jealousy or ambition, did not collaborate; but each
worked only to recover the Greek cities in the vicinity of his own
satrapy.   It was with Tissaphernes that the Spartans first came
to an understanding; from him they now secured funds, without
which they could hardly have carried on the war over so wide an
area.

The operations in the Aegean during 412 and 411 were indecisive in character.   Though Athens failed to recover any
appreciable part of what she had lost, she inflicted much loss
on her opponents and prevented them from carrying out any
combined movements against her.   This achievement was the
more noteworthy because the year 411 saw an oligarchic revolution in Athens itself.   By the beginning of that year the
Athenians had lost all Ionia save only the island of Samos,
which remained staunchly loyal to them and now became the
headquarters for Athenian operations in the Aegean.   Many
of the leading men in the Athenian fleet were disposed to favor
a constitutional change at Athens.   In communication with
the influential members of the oligarchic clubs at Athens —
the most prominent was Antiphon, by profession a writer
of law-court speeches and a man who combined great legal
knowledge with a remarkable gift for organization and intrigue — the Athenian oligarchs at Samos had also got in
touch with Alcibiades.   Undoubtedly some of the energetic
measures taken by the Spartans in 413 and 412 had been due
to his astute advice.   But a quarrel with King Agis made
it advisable for Alcibiades to leave Sparta, which he did by
joining the Peloponnesian fleet destined to help the revolted
Chians.   His real aim was to bring about his own recall to his
native country; to pave the way for this, he now made his
way to the satrap Tissaphernes and began to intrigue against
Sparta, as he had previously intrigued against Athens.   To
the Athenian oligarchs at Samos he sent communications
promising Persian support for Athens, provided an oligarchy
were set up there.   When the point of negotiating with the

satrap himself was reached, the oligarchs found that Alcibiades had promised more than he could perform, and almost immediately afterward Tissaphernes made a fresh agreement with Sparta. But the oligarchs at Samos had no intention of dropping their plans for a revolution at Athens, and, indeed, matters there had gone too far.

There were many responsible and moderate-minded citizens who wished to see a considerable modification of the democratic régime which had prevailed in recent years. Hence the actual revolution, though it was preceded by some assassinations and terrorization, for which the extreme section of the oligarchs was responsible, was effected with comparative ease and little disturbance. A council of Four Hundred was elected, ostensibly as a provisional government, until such time as a proper constitution could be drawn up, in which full citizen rights would be limited to 5000 persons, able to perform civic and military duties at their own expense, in other words, the wealthy and middle classes. The Four Hundred, or at least the extreme part of that body, once in power, aimed to keep it, by ignoring or postponing the nomination of the 5000. But there were reasons why their régime was doomed to failure almost from the beginning, quite apart from the exasperation caused by their excesses when in power. In the first place, there was no unanimity among the Four Hundred themselves, but they were divided into two factions. One of these was composed of extremists, led by Antiphon, and two men who had once been democrats, Peisander and Phrynichus; the other, whose leading spirit was Theramenes, was genuinely desirous of establishing the "limited democracy" of the 5000.

Secondly, the oligarchs had gravely miscalculated the sentiments of the Athenian military and naval forces stationed at Samos. Knowing that the leading officers were sympathetic, they anticipated that the rank and file would accept without demur the constitutional changes effected at home. Herein they were utterly mistaken; for the troops deposed their oligarchic commanders and elected others in their place, chief among them being Thrasybulus and Thrasyllus. They followed up this decided and practical expression of their views by what was, in the circumstances, an astute move. They recalled

Alcibiades and appointed him their chief *strategos*. Although his fresh attempts to bring about a rupture between Tissaphernes and Sparta failed, it was his influence which, for the time being, reconciled the Athenians at Samos to the proposed moderate democracy of Theramenes. This knowledge strengthened Theramenes' hands, and he and his adherents succeeded in deposing the Four Hundred after four months' misrule at home and failure abroad. For their peace overtures to Sparta had been rejected and their inefficient government had encouraged Euboea to revolt. The direction of affairs now passed into the hands of approximately nine thousand citizens, all, in fact, who belonged to the first, second, and third Solonian classes. This limited democracy remained in power for seven months. Of the extreme members of the Four Hundred some escaped, others, among them Antiphon, paid for their short-lived tenure of authority with their life.

In the spring of 410 the Athenian fleet commanded by Alcibiades annihilated the Peloponnesian fleet off Cyzicus. This striking success produced a strong political reaction at home. The old democratic constitution by which every citizen was a member of the sovereign *ecclesia* was restored. It was unfortunate that the leading position in that assembly was grasped by the demagogue Cleophon. For, whereas he appears to have been a man of great ability, his war policy was similar to that of Cleon, allowing for the altered circumstances of Athens. Like Cleon he was an able financier, but resolved to prosecute the war at all costs. Thus, through his influence, the Athenians more than once — for instance, after the battle of Cyzicus — rejected offers of peace made by their opponents. The operations which culminated in the Athenian naval victory in 410 had followed hard upon the successful efforts of their enemies to bring the Athenian subjects in the Propontis and the Hellespontine region to revolt. In spite of great efforts on the part of Alcibiades, who was still in command of the Athenian forces, few of these places were recovered during the next two years. His greatest success was the recovery of Byzantium before the end of 408. Early in the following spring, after eight years' absence from his native city, he returned to Athens, where he was received with enthusiasm and elected chief *strategos* for the ensuing year. His triumph, this time through no fault of his own, was to be short-lived. The Great King, dissatisfied with the dilatory conduct of his satraps, decided on stronger measures to recover his hold on the coast lands of Asia Minor. He sent his younger son, Cyrus, to the West to take complete charge of Persian operations and to coöperate closely with Sparta. At Athens the unfortunate experiences of 411 had embittered the people, once they were again in full control of the government, and made them suspicious of all who had, or were believed to have, sympathy for oligarchy or indeed anything short of extreme democracy. In consequence there were many unjust prosecutions before the popular jury courts, and much corruption; the class of professional informers, who had long been an unsavory element in Athenian society, did a thriving business; worst of all, the Athenian people on more than one occasion during the last years of the war showed a lamentable lack of confidence in, and even injustice to, their leaders. Of this popular caprice Alcibiades was a conspicuous victim. In the late summer he proceeded to the Aegean in charge of the Athenian forces, in order to continue the task of winning back as many as possible of the revolted subjects of Athens.

The arrival of Cyrus in the West coincided with the appointment to the Spartan chief command of Lysander. This man's earlier history is quite obscure, but he was probably the ablest person whom Sparta produced during the whole course of the war. Though as a commander he may not have been quite the equal of Brasidas or Gylippus, he was, what in a Spartan was a singularly rare gift, an adept diplomat and the very person to succeed in his relations with an oriental prince. Helped by Persian gold, Lysander quickly established an ascendancy over the cities of Ionia and enlarged his fleet of seventy vessels to ninety, their headquarters being at Ephesus. Here, in the early spring of 406, he defeated the Athenian fleet which was stationed at Notium and under the command of Antiochus during the temporary absence of Alcibiades. The latter had warned his subordinate to avoid an open engagement, but his orders were disobeyed. Though the defeat was not especially heavy, Antiochus had lost fifteen triremes, while the responsibility for the reverse fell on Alcibiades. At the elections held at Athens shortly afterward for next year's *strategia*, popular resentment against Alcibiades was so intense that he was not reappointed. He did not risk a return to Athens but withdrew to Thrace, where, realizing some time before that he might one day need a place of refuge, he had acquired two castles.

It was a Spartan rule that the office of admiral-in-chief could not be held for more than one year. Hence in 406 Lysander was succeeded by another officer, Callicratidas. The change was unwelcome to Cyrus and probably prolonged the war by a year. In the early autumn of 406 was fought a naval battle between the Peloponnesians and the Athenians in which the numbers engaged — 150 Athenian against 120 Peloponnesian ships — were greater than in any sea-fight so far known between Greeks. To make the effort of equipping so large a number of triremes and manning them, the Athenians had been forced to melt down the silver plate in their temples and to press into service on ship-board every available man, including denizens and even slaves. The engagement near the Arginusæ islands, between Lesbos and the mainland, ended in a striking Athenian victory, and the Peloponnesians lost more than half their fleet with the crews. The Athenian losses in the battle were only twenty-five ships. Twelve of these were still afloat, but badly disabled. After the fight the sea became rough and the Athenian commanders — eight out of the ten *strategoi* of the year — failed or were unable to rescue the crews struggling in the water. Something like 2000 sailors perished in this way after the battle. When news reached Athens about the battle, jubilation at the victory was mingled with rage at what was regarded as the criminal negligence of the admirals. All eight were impeached, but only six actually stood their trial, the other two deeming it wiser to go into voluntary exile. The proceedings at the trial were in the highest degree irregular, and the unhappy men were condemned to death on a single vote, in direct violation of constitutional law. This flagrant piece of injustice the Athenian people followed up by a no less flagrant piece of folly. Overwhelmed by the disaster at Arginusæ, the Spartan government once more made peace proposals; but the Athenians rejected the enemy's overtures, being swayed by Cleophon, "who appeared in the assembly drunk and wearing his breastplate, and prevented peace being made, declaring that he would never accept peace unless the Lacedæmonians abandoned their claims on all the cities allied with them." [1]

The urgent representations of Cyrus and of many of the Ionian Greeks now led the Spartans to reappoint Lysander, technically in a subordinate office, actually in charge of operations. The reconstruction of the Peloponnesian fleet after the catastrophe of the previous year, and even with generous financial aid from Persia, took time. The summer was therefore well advanced before Lysander began operations in the Aegean. With the object of striking Athens in her most vulnerable point, the Hellespont and approach to the Black Sea, whence she derived her food supply, he attacked and captured Lampsacus. The Athenians who had been renewing their offensive against Chios, at once followed the enemy and took up their position in the straits at Aegospotami on the European side, opposite to Lampsacus.[2] For several days they tried to draw out Lysander to give battle, but in vain. Then they became less vigilant, and on the fifth day most of the crews went on land for foraging and other purposes. Suddenly Lysander swooped down upon the Athenians before they could get their ships into battle array, or even before many of the crews had had time to get on board. Of the 180 Athenian vessels only twenty made good their escape. Of the crews of the others many got away to Sestos and the Chersonese, but, even so, several thousand were taken prisoner. Those who were Athenians were subsequently put to death.

It was the end for Athens. She had neither men, money, nor fleet with which to continue the struggle. The very few cities which she still retained of her once mighty empire went over to, or were taken by, the enemy. Samos alone remained

---

[1] Aristotle, *Constitution of Athens*, 34 (Kenyon's translation).

[2] Alcibiades on this occasion came from his castles in Thrace and advised the Athenians to take up safer anchorage at Sestos. His well-meant and well-founded counsel was ignored. In 404, when Sparta was rounding up Athenian exiles everywhere, Alcibiades fled to Pharnabazus. The satrap, on the demand of Lysander, executed him.

faithful to the end, and, in gratitude, the Athenians conferred their franchise on all the islanders. When the news of the disaster in the Hellespont reached Athens, horror and desperation seized the citizens. We cannot do better than transcribe the famous passage in Xenophon who lived through those awful days. Though he did not write his *Hellenic History* till many years later, the memory of Athens' agony after Aegospotami must still have been vividly present to his mind.

It was night when the *Paralus* reached Athens with her evil tidings, on receipt of which a bitter wail of woe broke forth. From Peiræus, following the line of the Long Walls up to the heart of the city it swept and swelled, as each man to his neighbor passed on the news. On that night no man slept. There was mourning and sorrow for those that were lost, but lamentation for the dead was merged in even deeper sorrow for themselves, as they pictured the evils they were about to suffer, the like of which they had themselves inflicted on the men of Melos, who were colonists of the Lacedæmonians, when they mastered them by siege; or on the men of Histiæa; on Scione and Torone; on the Aeginetans, and many another Hellenic city.[1]

The energy of desperation seized the Athenians. Every preparation for standing a siege was made, and with many there still lingered a faint hope that the enemy might grant peace on terms. Soon a Peloponnesian army entered Attica under the command of King Pausanias and joined forces with King Agis and his garrison from Decelea. Shortly after Lysander sailed into the Saronic Gulf, and Athens and Peiræus were thus completely invested by land and sea. During the winter months only the fleet continued the blockade, since the Spartans had no intention of attempting a difficult and costly assault when in a few months famine would do its work. Efforts were made by the Athenians, through Theramenes, to persuade Lysander not to proceed to extremes, but the Spartan rejected any proposal short of unconditional surrender. When a congress of Peloponnesian states and their allies met in the spring there were some who urged the complete destruction of Athens. The chief advocates of this ferocity were the Corinthians and Bœotians, but to such a course Sparta would not assent. The terms imposed on Athens were as severe as they could be, consistently with

---

[1] Xenophon, *Hellenica* II, ii, 3 (Dakyns' translation).

leaving her an autonomous state. Starved into surrender, the Athenians had needs to accept the destruction of their Long Walls and the fortifications of Peiræus, the loss of their fleet, save only twelve vessels, the loss of the few remaining dependencies left to them outside Attica, including Lemnos, Imbros, and Scyros, and the recall of their political exiles. Lysander, having received the formal surrender of Athens, sailed to Samos and, after two to three months' siege, compelled the islanders to capitulate. Then he intervened once more in Athenian affairs. Bitter struggles had begun at Athens, since Theramenes and other oligarchs deemed the time ripe for instituting an oligarchic régime in the city. With the support of Lysander, who threatened dire penalties if the government at Athens were not reconstituted on the lines proposed by Theramenes, — which he could do with an appearance of legality because the Athenians had not completed the demolition of their walls and had therefore broken the terms of the peace, — the democratic constitution was abolished and the direction of affairs put into the hands of thirty persons, all of whom were oligarchs, though, as the sequel showed, of very different views and aims.

CHAPTER XV

THE POLITICAL HISTORY OF GREECE TO THE DEATH OF PHILIP II

> *Yet all the faults committed by the Spartans in those thirty years, and by our ancestors in the seventy, are less than the wrongs which, in thirteen incomplete years that Philip has been uppermost, he has inflicted on the Greeks; nay they are scarcely a fraction of these, as may be easily shown in a few words.* — Demosthenes, *Third Philippic*, 25 (Kennedy's translation).

1. The Empires of Sparta and Thebes

It is regrettable that the few contemporary sources which we possess for the early years of the fourth century are, where Sparta is concerned, not free from bias. Xenophon, the admirer of her polity and institutions, is frankly enthusiastic for Sparta and her king, Agesilaus.[1] Isocrates, on the other hand, who does not hesitate to criticize his fellow Athenians, under the influence partly of the memories of his youth and earlier manhood, partly of his political theories, is always inclined to depict Spartan policy and conduct in the most sombre colors. Hence, while we sorely miss some dispassionate and profound delineator of the short-lived Spartan and Theban hegemonies, who might rank with the historian of the Athenian empire, Thucydides, we must seek for a mean between the extremes of partisanship and enmity. Even thus, the verdict will be against Sparta. Granted the shortcomings and misuse of power, of which Athens as an imperial state was guilty in the fifth century, were frequent, granted too that many of the complaints made against her by her allies were justified, it still remains true that the Athenian empire was a work of constructive statesmanship,

---

[1] It is only in the last section of his *Hellenic History* that Xenophon gives the impression of having to some extent lost faith in Sparta, and even allows himself to make adverse criticisms (*e.g.* V, iii, 27 — V, iv, 1).

and an effort to bring at least a part of the Hellenic world into closer coöperation. Even if it was of most benefit to Athens herself, it also promoted the prosperity of all the other cities, great and small. In 404 Sparta had a great opportunity of shouldering the burden of empire fairly, and of promoting political harmony and union among the Hellenic states on a wider basis than ever Athens had succeeded in doing; but her failure, and the political decline which followed it, were far more complete than the Athenians'. In truth, Sparta's traditions and narrow military régime fitted her neither to inaugurate a true federal organization, like the leagues which arose elsewhere in Greece in the third century, nor yet to lead and knit together into a looser confederacy a multitude of scattered maritime communities. Finally, the statesman who had brought the Peloponnesian war to a successful conclusion, was of the stuff of which Tyrants were made, and was influenced solely by motives of personal ambition. In the communities that had lately belonged to the Athenian empire oligarchies were uniformly established by the action of Lysander, in many cases only after brutal scenes of violence and bloodshed. Had the Spartans in 404 adhered to the professions made by Spartan leaders at the beginning of the Peloponnesian war, they would have tried to adapt and enlarge the Peloponnesian League to include the late empire of their beaten foe. Actually Lysander's methods were those of unqualified tyranny and terrorization through the small oligarchic Boards of Ten (*decarchies*) which he set up in the different Aegean communities. Their system of government, or rather misgovernment, was similar to that of the Thirty at Athens, and often they were, like the Thirty, supported and abetted in their misrule by Spartan garrisons commanded by a Spartan commander (*harmostes*).

Another important factor in the general political situation, which developed in the decade after Aegospotami, is to be found in the attitude of Sparta to her allies. We have already seen how, when she had concluded a truce with Athens in 421, she took little cognizance of her allies' interests. In 405–404, when she had emerged triumphant from the war, her treatment of her confederates, without whose help she could not have beaten Athens, was even more cavalier. In general, the Peloponnesian states were still too overawed by her military prestige to turn against her. A few years later some of them were emboldened to take up arms against the head of the league when involved in renewed warfare with Persia. The Bœotians were more daring. The unsatisfactory peace of 405–404 quickly reacted on the state of political parties in Bœotia, and anti-Spartan leaders seem to have predominated in the Bœotian league. At all events, in spite of a Spartan prohibition, the Bœotians gave a friendly welcome to Thrasybulus and a number of other political exiles, who had fled from Athens at the installation of the Thirty. The misrule of this oligarchy, which endured for eight months, was far more noxious than that of the Four Hundred had been in 411. Theramenes again represented the moderate element, but now he had no outside support, and a majority of his colleagues sided with the extremist, Critias. For the first few weeks of their government they sought to give an appearance of legality to all their acts; but soon, on a specious pretext, they applied to Sparta for a harmost and garrison. Once these were established in the Acropolis the extremists began a systematic persecution of wealthy citizens and resident aliens, in order, after killing them off, to seize their property. The roll of citizens was restricted to 3000 only, instead of to all able to serve as hoplites. The others were disfranchised, and could be put to death without trial. These high-handed measures were strongly opposed by Theramenes, but he was overruled. Then Critias, fearing his continued influence and opposition, struck his name off the civic list and had him executed.

The friendly disposition of Thebes to the Athenian refugees was providential. With her help Thrasybulus and some seventy companions entered Attica and in the late autumn of 404 seized the fortress of Phyle (Plate 20a) on the slopes of Mt. Parnes. The efforts of the Thirty to dislodge them failed, as did an attack by the Spartan garrison in Athens. Gradually more and more men flocked to the standard of the liberator. At last, when his force numbered about 1000, Thrasybulus one night led them to Peiræus and occupied the hill of Munychia. Here he was welcomed by the inhabitants, many of whom joined him. With this augmented army he defeated an attack by the Thirty and their supporters. Critias was killed fighting, and

a

b

a. Fortress of Phyle; *b.* Fourth-century Fortification Wall
near Peiræus

Plate 20

his removal greatly weakened the authority of the Thirty. The assembly of the 3000 deposed them and appointed a board of Ten to take their place. One or two of the Thirty were reëlected, but the rest fled to Eleusis. Although the executive at Athens was thus changed, an agreement with the democrats at Peiræus was not reached. The latter, though unable to occupy the city, reduced the oligarchs to such straits by the summer of 403 that these appealed to Sparta to intervene. For the moment Lysander's influence there predominated, and military and naval forces were despatched to crush the democratic faction in Peiræus. But there was not wanting a large number of persons at Sparta who had been viewing Lysander's career, his inordinate ambition, and his utterly ruthless methods, with alarm and disapproval. These opponents of Lysander now gained the upper hand. He was superseded, and the settlement of Athenian affairs was intrusted to King Pausanias. Through him and a board of fifteen commissioners, who were sent from Sparta for this express purpose, a peaceful agreement was arranged. A general amnesty was proclaimed from which only the surviving members of the Thirty and Ten, and a few of their immediate subordinates in Athens and Peiræus were excluded. Eleusis was to form a separate city-state, to which any Athenians — that is to say, those with oligarchic sympathies — could withdraw within a specified time-limit. With the constitution now to be set up at Athens the Spartan commission did not interfere. Hence the full democracy, in which all citizens had political rights, was restored. Two years later Eleusis was reincorporated in the Athenian state without any opposition from Sparta.

Meantime the Lysandrean régime had broken down generally in the Aegean area. The decarchies were abolished and the cities allowed to restore their "ancestral constitutions." But the most difficult problem confronting the Spartan government was the nature of its future relations with Persia. In return for the aid which the Great King had given in the last years of the Peloponnesian war he expected the formal cession of all the Asiatic Greek cities. In reality, after 405, Sparta had made peace with Athens without consulting Persia, and still retained her hold on the Hellespontine region, though Ionia had been ceded to Cyrus. In the same year Darius II died and was succeeded by his eldest son, who ruled under the name of Artaxerxes II. The queen mother, Parysatis, however, had intrigued to secure the succession for her younger son, Cyrus. Foiled in his attempt to obtain the throne on his father's death, Cyrus now plotted to attain his goal by force. In 401 his preparations were completed, and he set out from Asia Minor at the head of a large army, composed partly of Greek mercenaries, partly of oriental troops. In the summer Cyrus' host, numbering nearly 13,000 Greeks, about as many orientals, and 2600 cavalry, engaged the considerably greater army of Artaxerxes at Cunaxa, about eighty miles north of Babylon. Though Cyrus' soldiers won the day, Cyrus himself was killed, so that the Greek portion of his army was left without a leader or a purpose. At first they were granted a truce to leave the country, and were escorted up the Tigris as far as the Greater Zab by Tissaphernes. The Persian satrap stood high in the confidence of his master and had been a bitter enemy of Cyrus and Parysatis. He now treacherously seized the Greek officers in command of Cyrus' mercenaries and had them put to death. The troops, however, elected other commanders from among themselves. Under these leaders they pushed on, trusting ultimately to get back to Greece and to their homes. Encountering tremendous hardships, caused partly by the severity of the climate, in part by the attacks of the wild hill tribes through whose territory they passed, they made their way through the heart of the Armenian highlands and ultimately reached Trapezus on the Black Sea. Among the Greek officers who led the retreat was the Athenian Xenophon, whose *Anabasis* gives a graphic account of Cyrus' expedition and the subsequent adventures of the Greek mercenaries.

By 400 relations between Sparta and Persia had become very strained. Though giving no official support to Cyrus, the Spartan government had facilitated his recruitment of Greek mercenaries; it had also failed to carry out all the terms of the agreement between the two states. Moreover, some of the Greek cities which had reverted under Persian, that is to say, under Cyrus', control in 405, had regained their independence when that prince set out for the Middle East. Above all, in 400 Tissaphernes was once again installed as satrap of both Caria and Lydia; his relations with Sparta had never been very harmonious. When he proceeded to attempt the recovery of some of the lately revolted Greek communities in his satrapy, these appealed to Sparta for aid. Rather than abandon the Asiatic Greeks entirely to a foreign power, the Spartans sent an expeditionary force to Asia Minor, primarily to the relief of Cyme, which was being attacked by the satrap. By this action Sparta actively renewed hostilities with Persia, and, with some intervals, the two states were at war for the next fourteen years.

Sparta's most substantial successes were won by her King Agesilaus in 396 and 395; but his military career in Asia Minor was cut short by political developments in Greece, which forced his government to recall him. The anti-Spartan coalition between Corinth, Argos, Thebes, and Athens, which had come into being by 395, was in the first place the result of the genuine discontent of Sparta's allies with the treatment they had received at the end of the Peloponnesian war. It was strengthened by Persian diplomacy and Persian gold distributed by a Greek agent of the satrap Pharnabazus. The influence of this Persian governor had steadily increased as that of Tissaphernes declined, — the latter was deposed in 395 and subsequently executed, thanks to the implacable hostility of the queen mother, — and he had been largely instrumental in procuring an admiral's commission in the Persian fleet for the exiled Athenian commander, Conon. The earlier operations of the Persian navy in the Aegean (396–395) were not greatly successful, although a democratic revolution at Rhodes, followed by the island's secession from Sparta, was a symptom of the waning loyalty of Sparta's allies, which the presence of a powerful rival might, as in this case, change into open defection. In the summer of 394, however, the Persian fleet completely crushed the Peloponnesian naval force commanded by Agesilaus' brother, Peisander, in an engagement off Cnidus. This victory, which in effect ended Sparta's hegemony in the Aegean and left the Persian navy mistress of that sea, was due partly to the skill of Conon and the large number of Greeks who were included in the crews of the Persian vessels, partly to the doubtful loyalty, and, at the crucial moment, the defection of that part of Peisander's force which had been recruited from the maritime allies of Sparta. It was Sparta's punishment for a decade of misgovernment and oppression.

In 393, after a general cruise in Aegean waters, which completed the break-up of Sparta's maritime empire, the Persian fleet returned home. But, with Pharnabazus' permission, Conon with a naval detachment sailed to Athens, from which he had been a voluntary exile since 405, and where he was now rapturously received. The Athenians, emboldened by their new alliance with Corinth, Argos, and Thebes, had begun to reconstruct their fortifications. Conon now used his men and the funds he had received from Pharnabazus to complete the building of the Long Walls. In the next three or four years Athens began in a small way to rehabilitate herself as a naval power. She recovered Lemnos, Imbros, and Sycros, and she concluded alliances with a number of island states and cities in Asia Minor. These efforts turned out to be premature; for Sparta, after an abortive attempt to make peace with Persia, which was followed by renewed hostilities, at last effected a more permanent settlement. It ended the war with Persia and also the so-called Corinthian war on the Greek mainland, which Sparta and the anti-Spartan coalition had been carrying on during the past eight years without decisive results on either side. But, although it was Sparta who through her envoy, Antalcidas, initiated the peace, it was Artaxerxes II who dictated the terms. In the winter of 387 the satrap of Lydia, Tiribazus, called a congress of Greek representatives at Sardes. To them the behests of the Great King were solemnly read. Early in 386 the King's Peace, or Peace of Antalcidas, was subscribed to by all the Hellenic states. By its terms the Greeks of Asia Minor and Cyprus reverted under Persian suzerainty; the other Greek states were to be independent, and alliances like those recently contracted by Athens, or even the Bœotian League in which Theban authority predominated, were to be given up.

The King's Peace, and Sparta's rôle in bringing it about, have been severely censured by ancient and modern observers

alike. And, undoubtedly, in one sense it was a calamitous con-
fession of failure in the larger problems of political organization that, just a century after the Persian wars, the Asiatic
Greeks should be allowed to revert once more under the Persian
yoke. If much of the blame for the ignominious peace of 386
rests with Sparta, some of it also must be assigned to the opponents of Lacedæmon on the mainland, who had not hesitated
to attack her when all her resources were needed in Asia Minor,
and to accept Persian gold. The Asiatic Greeks themselves
we cannot justly censure. They had had severe burdens placed
upon them by Athens when she was mistress of the seas; they
had suffered heavier exactions from Sparta, and more ruthless
interference with their autonomy and systems of government.
Small wonder if they at last concluded that materially they
would be no worse off — perhaps better — when their main
obligation was to pay an annual tribute to the Great King. And,
though it was a hardship to be required to supply troops from
time to time to an overlord, it was assuredly no novelty for
them to be bound by such military liabilities.

The adverse effects of the Peace were more patent in Greece
itself and in the Aegean area outside the Great King's jurisdiction. If, before 387, Sparta had, under the blighting influence
of Lysander, grossly misused her authority in the Aegean,
she now, under the guidance of her king, Agesilaus, and with
the pretext of strictly enforcing the terms of the Peace, interfered in the most high-handed manner with the liberties of
autonomous states. Thus in the Peloponnese she dealt harshly
with the cities of Mantinea (385) and Phlius (379); in Thrace
she intervened with a military force, at the request of one or
two cities which were unwilling to join the league of Greek
city-states — the so-called Chalcidic league that had grown
up since the last half of the fifth century under the leadership
of Olynthus. This intervention was not restricted to safe-
guarding the autonomy of two insignificant poleis in Chalcidice.
The ascendancy of Olynthus in the league was as marked as
that of Thebes in the Bœotian confederacy before 387 or after
371, and this circumstance gave the Spartans a pretext for
using force to break up the confederation as being contrary to
the terms of the King's Peace (379). But the most flagrant act

of violence, committed by a Spartan officer, Phœbidas, and subsequently condoned by the Spartan government on the advice of Agesilaus, occurred in 382. Phœbidas, who was in charge of a detachment destined for Chalcidice, when passing through Bœotia was approached by members of the oligarchic faction in Thebes. Although Sparta and Thebes were at peace, he fell in with the treacherous plan laid before him and seized the citadel of Thebes, the Cadmeia. This act, the failure of the Spartan government to punish Phœbidas and give redress to Thebes, followed by the cynical retention of the Cadmeia, damaged Sparta's prestige immensely and outraged the sense of right even of her admirers.[1] For the moment her authority throughout Greece was greater than it had ever been. There is a certain poetic justice in the fact that the state which Sparta had most deeply wronged, within little more than a decade destroyed Sparta's predominant position in Hellas.

It was fortunate for Thebes that at this crisis in her history she produced two men of markedly different character, but both of sterling ability and devotion to their country. The one, Pelopidas, with a number of Theban exiles who had found a temporary home in Athens, carried through a successful plot in the winter of 379. The pro-Spartan oligarchs in Thebes were overthrown, the Spartan garrison driven out, and Thebes regained her liberty. The other Theban, Epaminondas, though not involved in this conspiracy, became, in the anxious years that followed, the chief guide of Thebes' policy and the builder of her short-lived empire. In 378 her position was very precarious. Her action produced open war between herself and Sparta, and Sparta's position in central Greece was strong because she had placed garrisons in several of the Bœotian cities. In their rather isolated condition the Thebans sought an Athenian alliance. At Athens there was an influential party opposed to a rupture with Sparta; but their hesitation was changed to indignation when a Spartan officer, Sphodrias, who was in command of the Lacedæmonian garrison at Thespiæ, in the early spring of 378 and, apparently on his own responsibility, made a raid into Attica by night with a view to seizing Peiræus. His attempt failed as it deserved to do; its immediate

---

[1] Cf. the note on page 250 above.

political consequence was a Theban-Athenian alliance concluded in the summer of the same year.

In 378 and 377 Peloponnesian armies invaded Bœotia and ravaged the territory of Thebes. But, as the Thebans remained within their walls, Agesilaus was unable to make any impression on the enemy beyond the material damage done to fields and crops. Another projected invasion in 376, commanded by the other Spartan king, Cleombrotus, for reasons that are obscure, was abandoned before the Lacedæmonians had reached their objective. In the next five years the Thebans, partly by military action, partly by diplomacy, won over nearly all the Bœotian cities and reconstituted the Bœotian confederacy, securing for themselves predominant representation in the counsels of the league and reserving to Thebes alone the right to issue a federal coinage.

Another factor during these years greatly strengthened the anti-Spartan movement in Greece. The King's Peace, which had for the moment compelled the Athenians to abandon their few maritime alliances, was not strictly observed by them for long. Before 380 Athens had made new treaties with Chios, Byzantium, Rhodes, and Mitylene. In 377, when hostile feelings for Sparta were strongest at Athens, the Athenians issued a more general invitation to Hellenic, and even non-Hellenic, states — the Greek subjects of the Great King were specifically excluded, as any attempt to bring them in would have ruined the chances of success — to join a maritime league under Athenian leadership. Great pains were taken in formulating the constitution of this, the so-called Second Athenian Confederacy, to avoid all those features which had been obnoxious in the Confederacy of Delos and might lead potential members to fear a renewal of Athenian imperialism. Each member was completely autonomous; the allied states sent representatives to a congress (*synedrion*), which met at Athens periodically, but from which Athens herself was excluded. The decisions of the league and the determination of its policy rested jointly with the congress of allies and the Athenian council and assembly. Though the executive was from the first in Athenian hands, no regular tribute was to be collected, as had been the case in the Delian League. The allies paid contributions to defray the expenses of the confederacy's operations, but not, so far as we know, at any stated intervals; we are also quite ignorant how the amounts were determined or collected. The financial organization cannot have been left entirely at haphazard; yet there is no trace of any carefully thought out scheme similar to that of Aristeides a hundred years before. It was significant that the Athenians specifically bound themselves to refrain from sending settlers to allied territory, or even from owning land there. For had not the cleruchies been one of the chief grievances of Athens' allies and subjects in the fifth century? It would be interesting to know how differences of opinion between the congress of allies and the Athenian *ecclesia* were composed. The history of the league suggests that, after a few years, the Athenians became less scrupulous in observing the rights of the allies, and we may suspect that the will of the Athenian assembly generally prevailed. The number of members was at first small. Besides the four Athenian allies mentioned above and Methymna, Thebes joined in the first year of the league, also the Eubœan communities except Oreus, and a few islands and cities in the northern Aegean.

The avowed purpose of the league was to check the further aggressions of Sparta in the Hellenic world, but this did not preclude offensive operations against the Lacedæmonian state and the Peloponnesian league. The Spartan reply to the naval activity of Athens was to send a Peloponnesian fleet to interfere with the Athenian grain trade; but in 376 it suffered defeat at the hands of the Athenian admiral, Chabrias, off the island of Naxos. The consequences of this victory in the second year of the Athenian Confederacy were striking. By this single success Athens recovered her maritime supremacy in the eastern Aegean, and a great number of new members were enrolled in the league. While Chabrias was active among the Cyclades and in Thrace and the Hellespont, Timotheus, the son of Conon, won adherents in northwestern Greek waters. Among these accessions were most of the Cyclades, the cities of the Chalcidic league which had come into being again a few years after Sparta's intervention, additional cities and islands in the northern Aegean, Corcyra, Acarnania, Cephallenia, and King Alcetas of Epirus.

While the Bœotian Confederacy and Athens' new maritime league were each gaining strength, a short-lived hegemony was established in Thessaly by the genius of one man. Jason, the ruler of Pheræ, had by 374 united all the cities of Thessaly save Pharsalus under his sway, and, by the following year, Pharsalus too was forced to surrender to him. The military strength of this federal realm, as we may describe it, was very considerable, numbering 10,000 hoplites, 6000 cavalry, and abundant light armed troops besides. Exceptionally gifted both as a commander and as an organizer, Jason aimed at widening his political influence beyond the borders of Thessaly. He made friendly alliances with Macedonia and with the Bœotian League; but the efforts of Athens to secure this powerful ally were unsuccessful. This and other circumstances brought about a distinct change in the foreign policy of the leading Athenian statesman, Callistratus, who at no time seems to have been very friendly to Thebes. The financial straits of Athens were very acute; her maritime allies were unwilling or unable to furnish regular subsidies, and measures of coercion, though used by some of the Athenian commanders, were both contrary to the terms and dangerous to the stability of the Confederacy. Thebes, too, though an ally, seems to have given little or no financial help. In addition, the growth of the Theban power aroused the suspicions and fears of a large section of the Athenian people. Thus already in 374 the Athenians made overtures of peace to Sparta, and an agreement was actually reached. Hardly had this been done, when Timotheus was guilty of a technical violation of the treaty. Hostilities were begun afresh, and the war dragged on in a desultory way till 371. By that year the position of Thebes in central Greece was stronger than ever, while Jason of Pheræ was, rightly or wrongly, believed to be planning a naval program that would have been a direct menace to the Second Athenian Confederacy. The Athenians were all the more ready to come to terms with Sparta, when that state took the lead in calling together a congress in the spring of 371, which was attended by all the Greek states and also by a representative of the Great King.

The peace treaty of 371 was a reaffirmation of the King's Peace of 386, but the Athenian Confederacy was recognized as

not contravening the provisions for the autonomy of each city-
state.   Besides this, the Spartan government undertook to
withdraw its garrisons from the few places which remained to
her of her short-lived empire.   These terms were accepted not
only by Sparta and Athens, which were chiefly responsible for
bringing about the settlement, but by all the lesser *poleis*.   But
Epaminondas, in his character of Theban representative,
claimed the right to sign for the whole Bœotian League.   This
was peremptorily refused by the president of the congress, the
Spartan king, Agesilaus, who went so far as to strike Thebes from
the list of signatories, thereby excluding her from the provisions
of the peace.   This arbitrary action, for which Agesilaus must
bear the whole blame, was followed up by an immediate order
to the Spartan king, Cleombrotus, who was stationed in Phocis
with an army of Peloponnesian troops said to have been 10,000
strong, to invade Bœotia and to attack the Thebans unless they
took immediate steps to abandon their control over the Bœotian League.   Cleombrotus, following instructions, invaded
Bœotia, and, by Leuctra, near the western end of the Theban
plain, found himself opposed by a Bœotian army decidedly
smaller than his own, perhaps 6000 hoplites and 1000 horse.
The decisive victory won by Epaminondas and his Bœotians
over a larger force of what had hitherto been regarded as the
finest heavy-armed soldiers in the Hellenic world, was due
partly to his skillful combination of infantry and cavalry attack,
partly to the massed assault by his choicest troops in a column
fifty deep, which he directed against the strongest part of the
Peloponnesian army, namely, the Lacedæmonian division.   No
less than four hundred Spartiates, including Cleombrotus himself, were killed; the beaten army, however, retreated in orderly
fashion and evacuated Bœotia.

The results of the Bœotian success were of the most far-reaching kind.   Thebes was for a decade the most powerful state in
Greece, but the period of her military hegemony, though
auspiciously begun, only accelerated the general political disintegration of Hellas.   The immediate sequel to Leuctra was
the enlargement of the Bœotian League by the accession of
Eubœa, whose cities seceded from Athens, and of the Acarna-
nians.   Orchomenus, the last Bœotian city to remain outside

the league, was now compelled to join. Alliances were concluded with the Phocians, Locrians, and some lesser peoples in central Greece.

In the following year Jason of Pheræ was assassinated, and the Thebans, though they had been on friendly terms with him, can hardly have seriously regretted the passing of so powerful a despot, whose ambitions might in time have threatened their own position in Greece. Meanwhile the Peloponnese was the scene of what was nothing less than a political upheaval. After the heavy losses incurred at Leuctra the number of full Spartan citizens was reduced to 1000 or little more. It was the penalty for the narrowness of the Spartan view in not permitting any modification of the "Lycurgean" institutions and jealously refusing to admit any of the other inhabitants of Laconia or Messenia to the privileges of Spartan citizenship. Nor was it only in her own territory that Sparta was threatened with disruption. Some of her Peloponnesian allies, especially the Arcadians, who had long chafed under Sparta's military demands but had been overawed by her supposedly invincible troops, now openly seceded. Mantinea, destroyed as a city by Sparta in 385, was rebuilt and strongly fortified; then its citizens, with most of the other Arcadian cities, formed a federation of their own. In 370, backed at first by the support of Epaminondas and a Bœotian army, the Arcadians coerced those communities in the country that had so far refused to join them. In 369 they founded a new city, Megalepolis, which was to be the federal capital, and at the same time formed one of the constituent members of the federation.

Epaminondas in 370 invaded Laconia, thereby preventing Sparta's attempts to stop the formation of the Arcadian League. Besides ravaging Sparta's home-land he entered Messenia, freed the Helot and Periœcic population, and helped them to form a new and independent state of Messenia. Only a few communities in the extreme south of that district remained faithful to Sparta. On Mt. Ithome, with its unhappy memories of the past, a capital was built. Extensive remains of its town walls and fortified towers are among the finest examples of military architecture in Greece. In 370 Sparta had repelled the attack of the invader on her own city and had maintained

her independence; but she was powerless to arrest the formation of two substantial states on her northern and western
frontiers. In her need she received some assistance from Dionysius I of Syracuse, with whom she had been in alliance since the
beginning of his Tyranny. Various efforts to bring about a
peace settlement were made between 369 and 366, and the
support of the Persian king was sought by the different groups
of belligerents. But, though Thebes, through her representative Pelopidas, secured a Persian rescript in her favor, she was
unable to secure its acceptance by Sparta and Athens.

Nowhere did the Thebans succeed in deriving any lasting
benefit from their many ephemeral successes. After Jason's
death they had been led to intervene more than once in Thessalian affairs, and for a brief space Thessaly was under Theban
control. In 366 Epaminondas secured the adherence of Achæa
to the Bœotian alliance, but the Theban government followed
up this diplomatic success by sending military garrisons there
and using force to set up democratic rulers in the Achæan
cities. Oligarchic counter-revolutions were the immediate result, and the Achæans, from being allies of Thebes, concluded a
treaty with Sparta. Anti-Theban feeling in Greece grew apace.
The Arcadian League was trying, not very successfully, to enlarge its territory by warring against several lesser neighbors,
but without regard for its late ally and helper. Athens in 366
formed an alliance with the League, while from 366 to 364, after
successful operations by Timotheus, her maritime confederacy
was enlarged by the accession of Samos, Sestos, and a number
of Thracian cities. The Theban reply to this diplomatic and
naval activity on the part of Athens was, on Epaminondas'
advice, to equip a Bœotian fleet, 100 vessels strong. With it he
scored a temporary success by bringing about the defection
from the Athenian Confederacy of Byzantium and one or two
other states. Nevertheless the Thebans had neither the spare
men nor the money to maintain themselves as a naval power in
addition to holding on to their military hegemony; therefore
after this one year (364) no more is heard of their undertakings
on the sea.

War-weary as many or most of the Greeks must have been,
no general agreement was possible amid the clash of contending

interests and rivalries of party, each advocating a different foreign policy within the cities themselves. The most serious rupture came about in the Arcadian League. Here a strong anti-Theban group was gaining a predominating influence in the councils of the League; in 363 the disagreement had become so acute that the unity of the federation was destroyed. The Mantineans and northern Arcadians contracted alliances with Sparta and the Achæans; they were in friendly relations also with Elis and Athens, from both of which they were to receive military assistance. Tegea and Megalopolis, on the other hand, remained staunch to Thebes and fought on her side when a strong Bœotian army in 362 entered the Peloponnese under command of Epaminondas, with the immediate object of enforcing Theban authority in the recalcitrant cities of Arcadia. The battle fought in the plain to the south of Mantinea would have been a sweeping Theban victory had not Epaminondas been mortally wounded at a critical point in the engagement. Thus the plan of attack which he had evolved was never carried to a finish, and the military results of this encounter were indecisive. Following the counsel given by the dying Epaminondas, the Theban government now convened a congress, and peace was concluded on the basis of the *status quo*. Thereby the Arcadian League was split into two federated groups; Messenian independence was confirmed, though for this reason Sparta held aloof from the agreement; the Bœotian League and the Second Athenian Confederacy remained as before, and the autonomy of each signatory to the peace was guaranteed.

In its political effects the battle of Mantinea was equivalent to a Theban defeat. The loss of Epaminondas was irreparable, though it may well be doubted whether he could ever have succeeded in building up a stable Theban empire. The eminence of his achievement as a military commander and as a tactician, whose innovations introduced important changes into the methods of land warfare, must not blind us to the fact that his only acts of constructive statesmanship were the liberation of Messenia and the part he played in furthering the Arcadian League. While it would be unfair to assign all the blame to him for the complete failure to establish a successful and lasting hegemony over a great part of Greece, we must admit that not only the Thebans but Epaminondas himself lacked both the vision and the experience necessary to emulate a Pericles or even a Lysander. Even had this brief empire been more securely established than it was, it is questionable whether the Thebans would have had the resources to maintain it. The death of Epaminondas not only meant the collapse of Thebes as the leading state in Hellas, but was also disastrous to the Bœotian League, which rapidly declined in military efficiency and political influence, and to Thebes' own position in the League.

If it is difficult to expend much sympathy on the Spartans themselves for their reduction to the status of a third-rate power, it is true nevertheless that their decline and the break-up of the Peloponnesian League was a disaster for the whole of Greece. For the passing of that loose but effective organization signified the destruction of what had been for nearly two centuries the one stable political group in the Hellenic world. Thus, unwittingly, Thebes prepared the way for the relatively easy subjugation of Greece by the ruler of a kingdom which, though its fortunes had for long been partly interwoven with those of the northern Greeks, was yet regarded as standing outside the aggregation of Hellenic polities.

2. THE RISE OF MACEDON

The Macedonians had for centuries been little affected by the culture and institutions of their Greek neighbors. They lived in scattered villages, and there were few fortified places and no towns of considerable size. The population was in the main made up of a powerful landed aristocracy and free peasants. Monarchic government had continued there without interruption, though with many vicissitudes to the rulers, and the king's position and authority were not unlike those of the Homeric chiefs. An absolute ruler in some respects, the Macedonian monarch was, nevertheless, subject to certain restrictions imposed by custom, and was not independent of the good-will of his nobles. Not till the end of the fifth century did a Macedonian sovereign attempt to infuse some measure of Hellenic culture into his subjects and generally to consolidate his loosely knit kingdom. Archelaus (413–399) improved the organization of his army, built forts and roads, and instituted a festival after the model of the Hellenic games, which was held at Dium at the foot of the northeastern slopes of Mt. Olympus. To his court he attracted a number of distinguished artists and poets, the musician and lyric poet, Timotheus, the tragic poets, Euripides and Agathon, and Zeuxis, the most eminent painter of his day.

For forty years after Archelaus' death Macedonia was in so disturbed a condition that most of his work must have been undone. While dynastic quarrels and conspiracies led to frequent changes of kings — one of them, Amyntas III, however, managed to keep his throne for twenty-one years — the Illyrians overran Macedonia, and for a number of years the Macedonian rulers were obliged to buy off these unruly neighbors with an annual tribute. In 359 a desperate crisis ensued. King Perdiccas, with the aim of ending these ignominious payments, attacked the Illyrians; but his army was heavily defeated and he himself was slain. His death was followed by the appearance of several pretenders to the throne, and a large part of the kingdom fell into the hands of the enemy. The legitimate heir to the throne was a child; so his uncle assumed the regency. Philip II, as we may at once call him, although he probably did not set his nephew aside and himself assume the kingly title for several years, was aged twenty-three. As a youth he had spent three years as a Macedonian hostage in Thebes, where he had been well treated, had acquired familiarity with Greek institutions and culture, and, above all, had become thoroughly acquainted with the excellent Theban military organization and tactics, and their chief creator, Epaminondas. On his return home he had held a responsible governorship in Macedonia, so that in 359, in spite of his youth, he had valuable and varied experience. Partly by timely gifts, partly by military action, Philip restored order out of anarchy in his kingdom and inflicted defeat on his Illyrian neighbors. Then he set himself to secure the most essential prerequisites for the creation of the greater Macedonia which he aspired to rule — a substantial source of revenue and a first-class army. Macedonia was still at this time a loose collection of clans and tribes. By forming what was virtually a new army Philip also went far toward creating a Macedonian nation. Earlier kings had in war-time relied primarily on their cavalry recruited from the landed aristocracy. The foot-soldiers had been of quite secondary importance and had lacked both cohesion and training for war, though in themselves hardy and brave fighters. Philip's aim was to make his infantry as effective a military weapon as his horse, and, by assiduous practice of both, to attain the best tactical combination of the two. Thus he enrolled his subjects according to their tribes and clans, and, as far as possible, kept them together to form territorial divisions or regiments. All the heavy infantrymen were armed alike, their chief offensive weapon being a pike or lance (*sarissa*). The characteristic Macedonian tactical infantry formation, the phalanx, varied in depth from eight to sixteen men, and was therefore much shallower than the Theban massed formation favored by Pelopidas and Epaminondas. The men, too, were drawn up in more open order, whereby more room was ensured for the skillful use of their pikes, and less reliance was placed on mere shock tactics and weight of numbers. By an elaborate system of rewards and promotions in all branches of the military service Philip encouraged healthy ambition and rivalry among his men; while by constant practising, whether in actual warfare or in manœuvres, he turned them into the finest standing army that the world had yet seen — proud of their regiments, loyally devoted to their king, and proud of their name, without distinction of clan or tribe, of Macedonians.

The needs of his treasury rather than the desire for conquest dictated Philip's first military operations outside Macedonia. By the autumn of 357 he had captured Amphipolis, and followed this up by making himself master of the mining districts of Mt. Pangæus. There, on the site of an earlier settlement, Crenides, a larger town soon arose, named Philippi, while the intensive working of the gold deposits soon produced a copious and steady flow of bullion into the king's chest. The revenue from this source was estimated at not less than 1000 talents a year. The Athenians, who protested against Philip's activities in Thrace, where they had dependencies, he put off with specious promises which he had no intention of fulfilling. The Athenians for the next three years had too many commitments nearer home to oppose Philip's successful progress in Chalcidice and the Gulf of Therma. Technically, however, they were at war with Macedonia from 357 onwards. Their success in that year in recovering Euboea from Thebes was more than offset by a revolt of three of their strongest allies in the Confederacy — Chios, Rhodes, and Byzantium. These states were soon after joined by Cos, and, as their operations against Athens progressed favorably, by many other members of the maritime league. The cause of these defections is none too clear. In the main, however, the Athenians seem to have had only themselves to blame. During the previous decade they had more than once interfered with the autonomy of this or that ally; forgetful of the original terms of the Confederacy, they were once more striving to substitute imperial domination for the alliance of equals. After three years they were obliged to make peace on terms which reduced the Confederacy to a shadow. Nothing was left of it after 355 save Euboea, a part of the Cyclades, a few communities in Thrace, and the adjacent islands in the northern Aegean. Financially Athens was thoroughly exhausted, since the late war had cost fully 1000 talents, and her income hereafter was greatly shrunken.

During these years Philip had been very active in Thrace and by 353 controlled the whole of Chalcidice directly or, in the case of the Olynthian Confederacy, by alliance. He had also been drawn into the political affairs of Thessaly and central Greece. Simultaneously with the decline of the Boeotian League, their neighbors of Phocis had a brief period of striking military success. The so-called Sacred War originated in the refusal of the Phocians to pay a heavy fine imposed upon them, for an alleged act of sacrilege, by the Council of the Amphictionic League, acting under Theban influence. Rather than submit to the coercion of their neighbors, they decided to resist by force; they were fortunate in being led for several years by military commanders of unusual ability. Carrying on at first as best they could themselves, supported by some mercenaries, they soon found themselves in grave need of funds. They then seized Delphi and did not scruple to use its stored-up treasure to finance the war. They inflicted losses on Boeotia, contracted alliances with Sparta and Athens, though they derived little support from either, and eventually widened their sphere of action by entering Thessaly, whose inhabitants were traditional enemies of Phocis. But they had reckoned without Philip. He, too, had intervened in Thessalian affairs at the request of certain cities, while others, fearing to pass under Macedonian rule, turned to the Phocians for help. The Phocian leader, Onomarchus, had the distinction of beating Philip's troops twice in 353; but in the next year Philip had an ample revenge. For he won a battle against the Phocians, in which not less than 6000 of them were slain, among them Onomarchus. In the summer of that year, after having secured some important bases in Thessaly, Philip advanced toward Thermopylæ. The Athenians, mindful of their alliance with Phocis and seeing an opportunity to checkmate the Macedonian enemy, whose greatness few of them as yet realized, sent a military force to occupy the pass. To force it would have cost Philip more loss and effort than it was worth; so he retired northward again, willing to bide his time.

The energetic intervention of Athens on behalf of her allies was surprising in view of the state of political parties there at this date. The leaders of the war party, who had been largely to blame for the war of 357–355 that had ended so unsatisfactorily, had for that reason lost influence. From 354 the Athenian statesman who gained a remarkable ascendancy over his countrymen was Eubulus. Entrusted with the administration of the Theoric Fund for four years, and very possibly for eight, he exercised a general control over all finances at Athens and was during that period the guiding spirit of Athenian policy.[1] The results of his careful régime were soon evident. State debts were discharged, the fleet was overhauled, defenses and docks

---

[1] As the ancient authorities are not at one, it is a moot point whether the *Theorica* were already paid to a restricted extent in the Periclean Age, or whether they were not introduced till the fourth century. Originally a small payment was made to the poorest citizens to enable them to attend the Greater Dionysia. Then the practice was extended to other festivals, the amount of the payment — originally one drachma — was increased, and the number of recipients was enlarged. From Eubulus' time, at least, the superintendence of the Theoric Fund, in which all surplus revenues were deposited, carried with it a general control over all the state finances. In his time the departments of state were not stinted; yet it was disastrous that all income in excess of what was needed for regular expenditure was diverted to popular amusement thinly disguised as religious observance.

that had fallen into disrepair were reconditioned. Over and above this, there was always a sufficient surplus to pay for the pleasure of the people, and from this time revenue that was left over after the year's budget had been balanced was earmarked for this purpose. Thus the material recovery of Athens from the continuous wars of the fourth century, and especially the war with the allies, was marked. But, on the other hand, Eubulus was loath to engage in any new military or naval undertakings, even when the political situation would have made this the wisest course for Athens. By determined action in 352–351 she could have checkmated or seriously retarded the successes of the Macedonian king. It was, moreover, one of the most notable developments of the fourth century that, to a steadily increasing degree, fighting was left to mercenaries. These professional soldiers were drawn from the young men in various Greek cities; to them a life of adventure and the prospect of good pay or ample booty were more attractive than a more settled existence in their native towns. Many, too, were drawn to mercenary service by impoverishment, such as was general in Greece after the Peloponnesian war. The most profitable opportunities were generally open to those who entered the service of the Persian king and his satraps, and the demand from that quarter for Greek professional soldiery was constant. The days when the able-bodied manhood of a Greek *polis* in time of need formed its defense, or when its army and navy in offensive wars were mainly recruited from the citizen body, were passing rapidly away. In a democratic state, like Athens, a further difference between the fifth and the fourth century is noticeable. Whereas in the fifth the business of government and of military command was commonly combined in the same person — we may instance Cimon, Pericles, Alcibiades, and Cleon — in the fourth century the two functions were not united in a single individual. The politicians of fourth-century Athens were not soldiers; her military and naval commanders, as a rule, exercised little or no political influence. In the small city-state of antiquity this division into two classes of professional politicians and professional captains was disastrous. Each played for his own hand; the call of patriotism and the good of the community were too easily forgotten.

To no one were these evils more apparent than to the Athenian politician who, from 351, was the most prominent opponent of Eubulus and the peace party, and the most open denouncer of Macedonia and its king. Demosthenes, who was born in 384, on attaining to manhood was obliged to turn to professional speech-writing to earn a living, since he had been deprived of most of his patrimony by dishonest guardians. Overcoming by assiduous practice certain physical disabilities, he ended by being the greatest orator of his day and of antiquity. Although several of his extant speeches, which were delivered before 351, deal directly or indirectly with political issues, it was not till that year that, in his so-called *First Philippic Oration*, he first clearly enunciated the anti-Macedonian policy which, save for one brief interval, he consistently advocated throughout his life. Philip, after his set-back at Thermopylæ, was once more active in Thrace; his operations in the eastern part of that region, where Athens still had allies or dependencies, and the fact that his warships damaged Athenian interests in the Aegean, caused the Athenians serious alarm. Demosthenes with fine eloquence bade his countrymen keep a fleet of fifty vessels ready at all times to protect the Athenian possessions in the Hellespont and Thracian Chersonese. At the same time he demanded of them, or a portion of them, personal service in army or fleet, and urged them to have done with exclusive reliance on professional soldiery. But the advice of a still young and untried man was not followed. In 349 he repeated his proposals even more pressingly in his three *Olynthiac Speeches*, but the Athenians only acted upon them, and then very imperfectly, when it was too late. A rupture between Philip and the Chalcidic League, of which Olynthus was the head, led this city to appeal for aid to Athens. But, while the Athenians were deliberating, and, after they had made a formal alliance with Olynthus, were failing to send prompt and sufficient help, Philip acted with decision. By the summer of 348 he had, after reducing the lesser Chalcidic cities one by one, finally forced Olynthus itself to capitulate. His treatment of these cities — most of them were razed to the ground and their populations enslaved — was unusually ruthless. As revolted allies the Olynthians, in case of defeat, had, according to Greek usage, to expect harsh punishment; but, in view of the clemency shown by Philip on other occasions — for example in 338 — it is regrettable that we are ignorant of the reasons for his savagery in 348.

Against Athens Philip had scored another success at this time by actively supporting the Eubœan cities in their revolt from Athens; the whole island, with the exception of Carystus, thus passed out of the Athenian Confederacy. By the winter of 347–346 even Demosthenes and the other leaders of the war party saw the imperative need of coming to terms with the Macedonian monarch. Ten envoys were therefore despatched to treat with him. An agreement was reached and, after a good many delays, was signed by both parties by the summer of 346. Each retained such possessions as it held at the time. Hence the peace was all in favor of Philip, while the Phocian allies of Athens had been expressly excluded from the settlement. Their power had been waning for some years, and now Thebes and the Amphictionic League urged Philip to proceed against them. Deserted by all their allies, their main army surrendered to Philip at Thermopylæ, and then their cities submitted one by one. Their punishment was severe, but much less harsh than that accorded to the Chalcidic communities. They ceased to exist as a corporate state; they were disarmed and scattered in villages; they were compelled to repay, in the form of a heavy annual tribute, what they had taken from the Treasure of Delphi. Their votes in the Amphictionic League were taken over by Philip, who thus gained formal admission into what was a Panhellenic institution. In the same year he presided at the Pythian festival held at Delphi. There can be no doubt that this recognition of his Hellenic status was, in spite of the sneers of his enemies at Athens and elsewhere, greatly valued by and valuable to the Macedonian king.

Technically the peace between Philip and Athens lasted for six years. But the former was indefatigable in strengthening his hold on Greece by diplomatic means, and at the same time he now began to plan a war against the hereditary enemy of the Greeks, Persia, in which he would be commander-in-chief of a Panhellenic army. That his attitude to Athens, now the most considerable of the Greek states politically, as well as the

artistic and intellectual leader of Greece, was conciliatory was
due to the need he felt of either gaining her active support in
these ambitious projects or at least of making sure of her friendly
neutrality.   But the Athenians, ashamed of the peace of 346
and the abandonment of Phocis to Philip, were now far more
ready to listen to Demosthenes and his younger supporters, like
Hypereides and Lycurgus.   In other words, the anti-Macedonian party was gaining the ascendancy in the Athenian
ecclesia.   Thus, when Philip began to intrigue diplomatically
in the Peloponnese, the Athenians, at Demosthenes' instigation,
sent envoys to warn the Peloponnesian states against Philip's
blandishments.   By 342 the king had found that the influence
of his inveterate enemies in Athens was too strong, and, in the
realization that a renewed clash with that city was bound to
come, he recommenced operations in eastern Thrace, so as to
secure firmly all the region between the Hellespont and the
Black Sea.   The threat to the Thracian Chersonese was a vital
blow at Athens; for the Athenians had been in occupation of
this region for many years, and its loss might mean the strangu-
lation of their grain trade with the cities on the Euxine and
might even bring them near starvation.   The interests at
stake, and the need for a supreme effort, were urged upon them
by Demosthenes in what, apart from the long *Oration on the
Crown*, are his two finest political orations — *On the Affairs of
the Chersonese* and the *Third Philippic*.   Nor was his success
limited to an oratorical triumph.   Philip, having unsuccessfully
tried to persuade Byzantium and Perinthus to make war on
Athens, treated their refusal as a *casus belli*, and in 340 laid
siege to Perinthus.   But Byzantium, Athens, and the Persian
satraps of Asia Minor all sent timely aid; after some months
Philip abandoned this enterprise and attempted to take Byzantium by surprise.   Here too he was foiled.   Thus Athens
and he were again openly at war, and the Athenians, in winning the first round, had scored a decided success.   For Demosthenes it was a great personal triumph.   At last he was
able to prevail on his countrymen to take a step which he had
advocated for a decade, to devote to war purposes the surplus
revenue which hitherto had been paid into the Theoric Fund.

A new Sacred War, arising out of a trivial incident, led the

Council of the Amphictionic League to invite Philip's intervention once again. It was just such an opportunity as he desired. Passing Thermopylæ, he occupied Elatea in Phocis which controlled the roads to Thebes and Athens. His envoys to Thebes demanded that she should support him in an attack on Athens, or at least remain neutral and permit the passage of his army through Bœotia. But Demosthenes, as soon as the occupation of Elatea became known at Athens, persuaded the Athenians to send to Thebes and offer an alliance, backed by the promise of immediate military support. The Thebans, to their credit, accepted the Athenian proposals, and both states made efforts to win additional help, especially from the Peloponnese. Most of the states there elected to remain neutral, — awe of Philip and his earlier diplomatic intrigues combined to bring this about, — so that the only reinforcements that Athens and Thebes received were from a few smaller states whom Athens had won over to an anti-Macedonian alliance a year or two before. Philip did not strike till the summer of 338. After some initial successes which forced the allies to abandon the passes from Phocis into Bœotia, he met them in the plain of Chæronea. Numerically the two armies were fairly equally matched, each being about 30,000 strong; but Philip's superiority as a general, and the better training and greater mobility of the Macedonian divisions, combined to bring about a crushing defeat of the allies, though the Thebans especially fought bravely and desperately to the last.

With this victory Macedonian hegemony over Greece was assured. The Peloponnesian states, apart from Sparta, acknowledged Philip's supremacy. Against Thebes he was most embittered, because her policy toward him had been equivocal for some time. Some of her chief anti-Macedonian leaders were executed, the government of the city was intrusted to a pro-Macedonian oligarchy, and a Macedonian garrison was established in the Cadmeia. Soon after, Philip also placed troops in Chalcis and Corinth. Against Athens he adopted no punitive measures. She lost the Chersonese; she was obliged to disband her Confederacy and to ally herself with Philip; but she was permitted to retain a few extra-Attic possessions, — Lemnos, Imbros, and Scyros, also Samos and Delos.

Before the end of 338 Philip summoned a congress of Hellenic states at Corinth, attended by delegates from all the states of central and southern Greece, except Sparta, and of the Aegean islands. The autonomy and independence of all were proclaimed, and there was formed a federation of *poleis*, whose disputes were hereafter to be referred to a Common Council of the Greeks meeting at Corinth. Internally the several communities were to be governed according to the constitutions existing at the time of the congress. The federated Greeks formed a defensive and offensive alliance with Macedonia, whose king in case of war would be commander-in-chief by land and sea. In that case each member of the League was required to furnish a certain contingent of ships and troops. Severe penalties were fixed against those citizens of any *polis* in the federation who should attempt to subvert its government, or who conspired with, or entered the service of, any foreign power (*e.g.* Persia). Some of these provisions make it clear that Philip, over and above the statesmanly desire of uniting all Greece in harmony, and of substituting arbitration for suicidal conflicts between cities and groups of cities, was also perfecting his plans for an attack on Persia. Whether he aimed merely at the liberation of the Anatolian Greeks, or harbored more ambitious designs of conquest, we do not know. But his intention to lead an expedition into Asia Minor became generally known when, in 337 B.C., he summoned a second Hellenic congress to Corinth. Here the war on Persia was formally determined, and the needful preliminaries arranged. An advance force under Philip's trusted general, Parmenio, set out across the Hellespont in the following spring. It was the king's intention to join him with the main army before the end of 336. But in the summer, shortly before the date fixed for his departure, he was murdered by one of his own officers in the midst of the ceremonies attendant upon his daughter's wedding to Alexander of Epirus.[1]

Philip's premature death occurred at a very critical moment.

---

[1] The assassination was reported to be an act of vengeance for a private wrong. But it is not improbable that there were political motives behind it, and that the wronged and banished wife of Philip, Olympias, was the real instigator.

His work of unifying Hellas had only just been accomplished,
and the change from the normal political life of the Greek
poleis was so fundamental that years were required before all
would readily welcome what to many now was as distasteful
as it was inevitable.   In the world's history, where one man
has steadily built up such a political structure as had been
raised by Philip, and then almost at once has passed from the
scene, his creation has rarely survived his death for long.   It
was the singular and fortunate experience of Macedonia that,
on the death of the greatest ruler whom she had yet experienced,
the throne was filled by his still greater son.   And though, as
we shall see, Alexander was snatched away before his task was
finished, he had carried the work begun by Philip many stages
farther, and his achievements changed the political, economic,
and social aspect of the ancient world.

As for the outcome of the struggle between Greece and Philip,
which culminated in the battle of Chæronea and the Congress
of Corinth, it is idle and unjustified to brand the Greeks of the
fourth century as the degenerate descendants of the victors at
Marathon and Salamis, or of the contemporaries of Pericles.
Their genius, expressed in material culture, literature, and art,
was not inferior to that of their ancestors in the previous century.   But their political institutions had proved unadaptable
to changed conditions.   It was not only political theorists, like
Isocrates, who saw the necessity of coöperation and alliance
between city-states and strove for Panhellenic unity.   The
many examples in the fourth century of the formation of
federations and leagues are sufficient proof that men of affairs
were experimenting in the creation of larger and more composite
political organisms than the *polis*.   But, interesting and significant as these experiments were, they were only partially successful.   Local rivalries and jealousies, which often had their roots
in the more than half forgotten past, triumphed over all other
considerations.   When we remember that from 431 to 338 there
was scarcely a year when all the Greeks were at peace, and very
few during which whole groups of *poleis* were not engaged in
hostilities, we can see how impossible it was for unity to be
imposed on Greece from within.   Hence, though we may not
approve all the methods and acts of Philip and his son, we can-

not deprive the former of the credit of having partially solved a difficult political problem, and the latter of the glory of giving a new meaning and mission to Hellenism.

3. THE WESTERN GREEKS DURING THE FOURTH CENTURY

This survey of the political history of the fourth century must conclude with a brief account of the western Greek world. After their triumph against Athens in 413 the Syracusans had sent a squadron to Greece, which for a few years coöperated with the Peloponnesian forces. At home a more extreme form of democratic government became the order of the day; nor was it long before the peace of Sicily was disturbed by the familiar bickering of rival cities. A far greater danger to western Hellenism, however, was the revived lust of conquest and revenge that now filled the Punic state. Not without reason the Carthaginians calculated that Syracuse and the rest of Sicily would be exhausted by their recent struggles against Athens; and, when an appeal from Segesta for help against her old foe, Selinus, reached them, they had an excuse, if one were needed, to intervene in the affairs of the island. A great naval and military expedition was equipped and sailed for Sicily in 409. Selinus was taken after a short siege and destroyed; then Himera in northern Sicily suffered similar treatment. In both cities the Punic armies massacred the inhabitants with indescribable ferocity. In the case of Himera this brutality was the barbarous satisfaction for an old grudge, since it was here that a Carthaginian host had suffered ignominious disaster seventy-one years before. Providentially for the Greeks the Punic commander desisted from further conquests and returned home. Three years later another attack was launched; but in the interval some preparations were made in Syracuse to offer a more effective resistance to the next Carthaginian invasion. In 406 the offensive was renewed; before the end of the year the Carthaginians had taken Acragas. The help given to that city by Syracuse, reinforced by troops from other cities in Sicily and even from southern Italy, was ineffective, apparently owing to the ineptitude of the higher command. It was even whispered that treason had been at work. At all events a new board of *strategoi* was elected, among the new officials being a young and as yet little known citizen, Dionysius. More drastic changes, partly under the influence of the Carthaginian danger, followed quickly. Successful intrigues enabled Dionysius to get his new colleagues deposed and to secure his own appointment as sole *strategos*. It needed only a story, to the effect that his life had been threatened, to persuade his countrymen to assign him a body-guard of 600 men. Thus, within a few months, Dionysius had become a Tyrant in fact, though not in name, since the established constitution was not abrogated. His rise to power had many general points of similarity to that of the sixth-century despots of Greece.

The difficulties which confronted him were tremendous; for, in addition to the precariousness of his own position, there was added the anxiety of the Punic peril. He did not hesitate to sacrifice Sicily, at least temporarily, in order to make sure of his throne. He gave up the defense of two Sicilian cities, which he at first aided against the common enemy, and then came to terms with the Carthaginian general. The Tyrant obtained official recognition by Carthage of his authority; but most of the island, save for Syracuse and a few lesser communities in the East, passed under Punic control.

For the next seven years Dionysius worked unceasingly with two objects in view, to make his own despotism unassailable and to develop Syracuse into a great naval and military state. He converted the acropolis of the city (Ortygia, or the Island) into an impregnable castle, in which he himself resided, guarded by foreign mercenaries and surrounded by friends and supporters on whom he could rely absolutely. Next, he greatly strengthened and augmented the defenses of Syracuse, built new harbor-works, and enlarged the Syracusan navy until, we are told, it numbered not less than 300 vessels. Every branch of the military service was carefully reorganized, and professional soldiery was at all times employed in great numbers. Above all, with the aid of skillful engineers he devised new engines of war for use in siege operations, of which the most famous was a catapult capable of hurling big stones a distance of several hundred yards.

He now set himself to bring all eastern Sicily under his

domination. This he effected in the course of three or four years, though on one occasion he came very near to disaster. By 398 he was ready for the task which had been present to his mind from the first, a war of revenge on Carthage, to be attended by the complete expulsion of Phœnicians and Carthaginians from Sicily. Whether his army really numbered 80,000 infantry and 3000 cavalry, as is said, may well be doubted; in any case he was the master of a military and naval strength greater than that controlled by any Greek state up to that time. His first war against Carthage was carried on in 398 and 397, and resumed in 392. The earlier successes of Dionysius were followed by severe set-backs, till finally Syracuse itself was besieged by the enemy on land and sea. It was now that the value of Dionysius' elaborate defenses was fully demonstrated. The strength of the Syracusan walls was proof against all assaults, till at last the enemy, weakened by a plague which decimated their ranks, were completely repulsed. The renewed war in 392 was indecisive, and at the end a treaty was signed between the two combatants, which left Dionysius master of the greater part of Sicily, while the Carthaginian strongholds in the northwestern corner of the island remained intact.

Dionysius next embarked on a policy of conquest in Italy. At the end of six or seven years he had gained control over the greater portion of Magna Græcia, and had established settlements as far afield as Ancona and Hadria on the western, and Pharos and Issa on the eastern, shore of the Adriatic. The two additional wars which he fought with Carthage (in 383–378 and in 368) led to some loss of territory in Sicily, and he suffered more than one naval and military reverse. Yet it was still a wide dominion which passed to his son when Dionysius died in 367.

Dionysius I was indubitably one of the most remarkable figures of antiquity. Two facts make it difficult to form a full and fair judgment of him. Almost our only source for his reign is the compilation of Diodorus (first century B.C.), who drew on fourth and third century historians but was thoroughly uncritical in his method. Secondly, the Tyranny of Dionysius was unpopular among his contemporaries and execrated by succeeding generations of Greeks, so that the real eminence of the man soon becamed obscured, and he was thought of merely as a type of unconstitutional and ruthless despot. Yet, harsh as some of his actions seem to have been, he was not capriciously cruel; for, first and last, he was a statesman who managed to maintain his authority and a great dominion for nearly forty years. As a general his only equal in Greek history was Philip II, his only superior was Alexander the Great. As a diplomat, as in matters of religion, he had no conscience; and it is perhaps the severest criticism that can be levelled against him that he was prepared to truckle to Carthage for a time and sacrifice Hellenic interests in order to secure his own despotism. He had disregarded Greek conventions by living with two wives at the same time. The eldest son of one of these unions, Dionysius II, succeeded to the throne in 367. But as he had been jealously excluded by his father from any share in the government and was by nature a rather feeble character, it was not surprising that the Syracusan court became the scene for intrigue. At first, the young ruler's kinsman, Dion, exerted a wholesome influence; but after a time Dion's enemies, led by the historian Philistus, gained the upper hand and compassed Dion's downfall and banishment. The latter's attempts to overthrow the Tyranny plunged Syracuse into years of unrest and civil war. Dionysius was expelled for a time, but still matters in Syracuse went from bad to worse, especially after Dion's assassination (354).

The other cities, which had formed part of the realm of Dionysius I, fell into the hands of different petty despots, and the prosperity of the whole country was grievously undermined. Dionysius II returned to Syracuse, and even after the Syracusans in desperation had chosen Hicetas as their general to restore order and defend the city against a new Carthaginian attack, managed to hold the castle of Ortygia. The Syracusans also sent an urgent appeal for help to Corinth, who listened sympathetically to the prayers of her daughter-city in 344 as she had done in 414. Timoleon was despatched with a small body of volunteers and mercenaries to make common cause with the Syracusan patriots. He soon showed that he was endowed with unusual ability as a general and a statesman. Hicetas had played false and allied himself with

Carthage, because his real aim was to become Tyrant of Syracuse himself. But Timoleon overcame all obstacles. He stormed Syracuse and received the Island from Dionysius II, who surrendered to him. In Syracuse and in the other Greek cities, after their despots had been expelled, moderate democratic governments were set up under Timoleon's supervision. A large number of Greeks from the mother country (60,000?) emigrated to the West to help in repopulating the Sicilian *poleis*. Above all, Timoleon inflicted a crushing defeat on a great Punic army in an engagement fought near the River Crimisus in the early summer of 341. Two years later a treaty between Carthage and Syracuse was signed, which reëstablished the boundary between the Greek and Punic spheres in the island that had been fixed after Dionysius I's second Carthaginian war. In 338 Timoleon retired universally honored into private life. Two years later he died; his work was not destined long to survive him.

STATUETTE OF SOCRATES

Plate 21

CHAPTER XVI

GREEK CIVILIZATION IN THE FIFTH AND FOURTH CENTURIES

One would be justified in the view that Athens is situated in the centre of Hellas and of all the inhabited world. . . . Although Athens is not surrounded by the sea, yet, being accessible to all winds like an island, it imports what it needs and exports what it wishes; for Athens is near the sea. By land, too, it receives much by way of commerce, being in fact a mainland city. — Xenophon, *Ways and Means*, i, 1.

1. ECONOMIC DEVELOPMENT

IT was noted in an earlier chapter how it is impossible to form anything more than a very sketchy picture of the economic life of the Greeks in the archaic period. From the time of the Persian wars the information to be gleaned from various sources becomes more copious, but mainly for one state only, Athens. In the case of other communities it is as scanty, — sometimes scantier, — for the fifth and fourth centuries as for the seventh and sixth. Even so basic a question as the size of the population of the Hellenic world, or of any part of it, at this period must remain unanswered. In the case of Athens alone some tentative figures may be hazarded. The adult male population of the Athenian state at the outbreak of the Peloponnesian war seems to have been approximately 50,000 to 55,000. Following the normal calculation, which makes these one-third of the whole citizen body, we arrive at a total figure of 150,000 to 165,000 men, women, and children of civic status. The resident aliens had steadily increased ever since the sixth century and, as will be seen, were a most vital factor in the economic life of Athens. In 431 there were probably not less than 40,000 to 45,000 of these, one-third of this number being again reckoned as adult males. The slave population used to be

283

greatly exaggerated, mainly on the basis of an ill-informed
statement by a late writer. But, even at the most conservative
estimate, there cannot have been less than 80,000 to 90,000 of
them in Attica, and they may have been slightly more numerous.[1] While the total population of the Hellenic world
probably did not alter appreciably during the fourth century,
the proportion of citizen to non-citizen population in particular
city-states did undergo very definite change. An extreme example is furnished by Sparta. Her system was so rigidly exclusive that the normal wastage of citizens was never made
good; at the same time not a few not killed in war got into
arrears with the contributions that they were expected to make
from their allotments, and in consequence forfeited these,
and with them their full civic status.[2] In Athens the plague
and the Peloponnesian war, especially the Sicilian expedition,
had heavily reduced the adult citizen population. To some
extent she recovered from these losses; but the proportion
of free aliens to citizens steadily rose during the fourth century,
until it was as much as 1:2. The slave population also was
greatly augmented in that age.

The importance of the resident foreigners for Athenian trade
and commerce was immense. The Athenian state granted these
metoikoi or denizens little beyond freedom to pursue their calling; on the other hand, it enforced a number of rules with which
they had to comply. They were required to pay a small head-
tax and to register formally as resident aliens, after they had
found an Athenian citizen willing to stand sponsor (*prostates*)
for them. Hence in each deme, besides the list of citizens of that
deme, there was kept one of resident metics. In most cases of
litigation the denizens could only plead indirectly through their
sponsor. Non-compliance with these regulations might lead to
legal prosecution of the offending metic, and the maximum penalty fixed for the guilty was to be sold into slavery. Furthermore, the denizen was debarred from owning landed property;
he was liable to military service, and, provided his wealth was

[1] Thucydides (vii, 27) relates that in 414–413 over 20,000 Attic slaves
deserted, and he adds that the majority were craftsmen.

[2] Cf. Chapter XVIII for the decline of the Spartan citizens in the third
century.

sufficient, he was obliged to bear the same financial burdens as the richer classes of citizens. The grant of citizenship was a privilege or reward only rarely conferred on resident aliens. Somewhat commoner was the bestowal, on those who had deserved well of the state, of what was known as *isoteleia*. The metic so rewarded was exempt from poll-tax, could litigate without the intervention of a *prostates*, and, in the matter of financial and military liabilities, was on a footing of complete equality with the citizens. The greatest privilege of all, which was commonly associated with *isoteleia*, but which is always separately specified on the inscriptions that are our main source of information, was the right of owning landed property. The number of such privileged denizens was not inconsiderable from the end of the fifth century onwards.[1] They formed a class intermediate between the civic body and the ordinary metics.

The majority of denizens were humbler folk engaged in a great variety of occupations. Nor must it be forgotten that many artists, writers, and philosophers, who made Athens their home permanently or for a prolonged period, and whom one consequently tends to think of as Athenians, belonged in fact to the metic class. Such were the speech writer Lysias, the sculptor and engraver Mys, the architect and friend of Pericles, Hippodamus of Miletus, and the philosopher Aristotle. On an inscription recording the names of those employed in 408–407 on the building of the Erechtheum at Athens fifty per cent are those of metics.[2] The numerous persons employed in trade or engaged in commerce, whose litigations are recorded in the *Private Orations* of the Attic Orators, are without exception denizens.[3] These facts are very significant. While no one would suggest that free Athenian citizens did not, both in the fifth and the fourth centuries, to some extent engage in trade and industry, it

---

[1] One of the best known examples of an *isoteles* was the wealthy Cephalus, the father of the orator Lysias. Cephalus has been immortalized by being introduced as one of the speakers at the beginning of Plato's *Republic*.

[2] To be precise, thirty-five metics out of a total personnel of seventy-one. Twenty names are those of citizens and sixteen those of slaves.

[3] That some of the speeches attributed, for example, to Demosthenes and included in the corpus of Demosthenic orations may not actually be his does not affect the present question. They are genuine and contemporary law-court speeches whoever their author.

seems clear that they formed a minority of the producing class. To the outbreak of the Peloponnesian war agriculture was still the main occupation of the citizens. From the time of Pericles, moreover, the state offered more and more paid employments to its citizens. Though the remuneration was small, little in the way of additional income was needed by the Athenian to eke out an existence. Nor can it be doubted that, had Athens been really a commercial state, in the sense that a majority of her citizens was directly engaged in trade and mercantile pursuits, she would have restricted competing foreigners and even expelled them beyond her borders, instead of encouraging their residence in Athens or Peiræus.

The existence of metics can be proved for more than three score Greek *poleis*, but it is only in the case of Athens that fuller details about their status and activities are available. To deduce, as has been done, that, because the number of denizens was exceptionally great at Athens, their general treatment there must have been better than in other cities is fallacious. The Greeks from other centres who migrated to Athens in preference to Corinth, for example, did so because, from the time of Pericles to the rise of Alexandria, enterprise in trade and commerce at Athens was more profitable than elsewhere.

The distribution of slaves in Greece was geographically very uneven. In Laconia and Messenia, in Crete, and in Thessaly, the large serf population performed the agricultural work for their masters; and, though technically they must be classed as serfs over whom the individual master had only limited control, in fact they were state-owned slaves. Their treatment and the conditions under which they lived were often harder than those of slaves elsewhere, over whom the individual owner had power of life and death. At Sparta it was the deliberate policy of the government from time to time to authorize a secret police of Spartan young men to put to death summarily Helots suspected of insubordination or disloyalty, and thereby to keep this vast subject population in a condition of constant fear. In other regions, where the communities were mainly agricultural or pastoral, for instance in Bœotia or in Arcadia, few slaves seem to have been employed even as late as the second half of the fifth century. In an important city like Thebes, however, their numbers would be greater and tended to increase. Thus we learn that the Thebans, in their last extremity, when dire punishment threatened their city and themselves from Alexander the Great in 336, emancipated many slaves so that these might loyally aid in the defense of the city. The slave class was most numerous in states like Athens, where there was much mercantile and industrial activity, and where, it may be added, this human merchandise was most easily come by. For the great majority of slaves were acquired by purchase and were of non-Hellenic race. Those whose only asset was physical strength and endurance were employed in the silver mines at Laurium. That they worked there under appalling conditions, and that their treatment was brutal, is unhappily beyond dispute. Much better was the lot of slaves employed in domestic service, and in arts and crafts. If and when a slave was skilled in any occupation, simple self-interest would make the master treat him reasonably well. Nor are we justified in doubting that the average Athenian was decently humane to his servile dependents. On the other hand, the frequent use of the lash, to which there are so many semi-humorous references in the comedies of Aristophanes, and the practice at criminal trials of taking slave-evidence only under torture, illustrate the darker side of the institution. If an Athenian master put his slave to death, he was liable to be tried not for murder but for manslaughter. This is an interesting compromise between putting the slave absolutely in his master's power and setting him on an equality with free men. A slave who suffered persistent ill-usage could seek sanctuary and demand to be sold to another master. In ordinary life there was little to distinguish slave from free man in outward habit, and he was allowed access to most religious celebrations and festivals. Manumission was a not infrequent reward for faithful service. Sometimes the master freed a slave during his own life-time; frequently his last will provided for the manumission of his slaves after his death. If freed while his master lived, the slave's status was analogous to that of a metic. He was required to take his late master as a patron or sponsor. There were many cases, too, where servile craftsmen were set up in business by their owners, to whom they then paid a certain percentage of their earnings.

Agriculture had always been, and continued to be, regarded as an honorable occupation, worthy of a citizen. It was one, however, which in the majority of city-states became necessarily more and more difficult to practise profitably. The constant warfare hit the farmers more directly than other members of the community, so that, in Attica for example, it was the rural population who suffered most severely during the Peloponnesian war. Again, the methods followed in raising field crops continued to be primitive. In the fifth century it was still the usual procedure for crops to be grown on a particular piece of land only in alternate years, the land lying fallow in the intermediate periods. Even in the fourth century the cultivation of alternating crops seems to have been the exception rather than the rule. The absence of machinery — even the plow was of the simplest pattern — made farming a slow and laborious process. In many parts of Greece, too, the climatic conditions were not favorable to intensive cultivation of wheat and other cereals. Thus in Attica it was found that the raising of vines and olive trees was more profitable and more suited to existing conditions. Hence the amount of wheat and barley grown there was only a small part of what was needed to feed the large population of Attica, while wine and oil were her two chief articles of export. Many other city-states were similarly dependent on the import of foreign cereals. Bœotia and Thessaly, on the other hand, and much of the Peloponnese, were, under normal conditions, self-sufficient. In the Peloponnese it was only maritime cities with restricted territory and a large population, like Corinth, which were compelled to import foreign grain.

By far the most important grain-raising region was south Russia; Egypt, Cyprus, and Sicily also grew more cereals than they needed for home consumption. Both in the days of her imperial greatness and in the fourth century it was mainly from the Pontic regions that the Athenians obtained their grain. For this reason the control of the Dardanelles and of Byzantium — or, failing this, friendly relations with the last-named city — formed an essential part of Athenian policy. From the last quarter of the fifth century through the greater part of the fourth the Athenians had a commercial agreement with the princes of the Cimmerian Bosporus, by which they were exempted from the payment of export duties at Black Sea ports. Not all the grain thus brought to Peiræus was needed to feed the inhabitants of Attica. A portion — the limit fixed by law in the fourth century was one-third — was reshipped from Peiraeus to other cities. Yet the government, though it gave constant attention to the safety of the food supply and appointed special officials to regulate the import and export at Peiræus, left the important carrying trade entirely to private enterprise. What is more, if the grain-dealers in Lysias' twenty-second speech are, as we have reason to believe, typical, the merchants engaged in this commerce were predominantly non-Athenians, that is to say, denizens. The cereals grown in the western Greek world and exported to Greece mainly supplied Peloponnesian states like Corinth.

Although industry and commerce flourished in many Hellenic centres, and the states derived profit therefrom through the customs and harbor dues which they exacted, their scope and character, and the general methods of business in both the fifth and the fourth centuries have often been misunderstood. No Greek government, so far as we know, ever legislated for the advantage of, much less subsidized with a view to some important commercial undertaking, its mercantile class. Commercial treaties, of which a number are known from inscriptions, were unlike what is now meant by such. Their object was not to help and extend the trade of the community but solely to facilitate the importation of necessaries, like grain and material for ship-building. Capitalists were forbidden by law to invest capital for the benefit of foreign states. Undertakings for which the government was directly responsible were nevertheless left to private contractors to fulfil. Thus the Athenian treasury derived a five per cent royalty from the silver mines at Laurium; but the actual exploitation was left to private lessees, who purchased mining concessions and worked them with slave labor. Similarly, public works were entrusted to private enterprise.

The production of manufactured articles was in the fifth century carried on by free, metic, and slave craftsmen in their own workshops, with the help of a few subordinates, servile or free. From the end of that century production on a somewhat larger scale, and with a more extensive use of servile labor, became more common, and in the fourth century probably drove many a master craftsman out of business. Men of means invested capital in small factories in which thirty or forty slaves might be employed under a slave or freeman overseer.[1] To the Greeks of the period this might seem "mass-production"; to the modern it appears as only a slight extension of the older system, coupled with a greater reliance on servile labor.

Master craftsmen owning their own workshops sold their wares in part directly to buyers, partly through middlemen or petty traders. The merchant engaged in maritime traffic regularly accompanied his merchandise, and disposed of it in person at such centres as he chose to visit. Occasionally we hear of several men working in conjunction or partnership. Owners of vessels in like manner used them to carry their own cargoes, though they might also take another merchant and his commodities with them on their journeys. But we do not find shippers who made their money exclusively by the transport of other men's freight. Both the shipmaster-merchant and the merchant travelling in another's boat were, in other words, middlemen operating on borrowed capital. Nothing, in fact, is more noteworthy in the business life of Greece than this divorce of the capitalist from the merchant and trader. The latter regularly borrowed money to purchase the wares in which he traded; he was not himself the owner of capital. Loans on bottomry are frequently mentioned in the Attic Orators. These were a favorite form of investment, for they might turn out to be extremely profitable. But the risks were great also; hence the rate of interest exacted was usually very high.

[1] It is commonly stated that Cephalus, or his son, Lysias, who inherited the property, employed 120 slaves in a shield factory. This example is cited as the largest Greek factory of which we have any record. Yet even for this one case the evidence for so large a number of hands is far from conclusive. For the statement of Lysias (xii, 8 and 19) does not warrant the conclusion that the slaves confiscated in 404 by the Thirty were all factory employés. The list of objects seized embraces all Lysias' effects, so that some of the 120 slaves are likely to have been those employed on domestic duties in what had been a large and wealthy household.

Plate 22

SEER FROM EAST PEDIMENT OF THE TEMPLE OF ZEUS AT OLYMPIA

APOLLO FROM WEST PEDIMENT OF THE TEMPLE OF
ZEUS AT OLYMPIA

Plate 23

By the fourth century the business of banking had to some extent developed. The more successful money-lenders now also received money on deposit and operated on a larger scale with other men's capital, as well as with their own. While, on the one hand, we find prominent bankers, like Pasion and Phormion, engaging in a variety of monetary transactions necessitating, for example, an elaborate system of book-keeping, we observe on the contrary that the ordinary merchant transacted his business on the simplest, not to say on a primitive, plan. Written receipts for loans are nowhere mentioned; sums are deposited or paid in the presence of witnesses. When we find a speaker in one of Demosthenes' speeches putting the question, "Who would be so unwise as willingly to pay money to a person making a written application?" we realize how far removed from anything like a developed banking system the Greeks still were. In truth, no proper credit system was yet in operation. The transference of sums of money was carried out literally, by the transport of bullion or coin from one place to another. In short, industry and commerce, though intensive judged by ancient standards, were carried on in the simplest way and differed not only in volume but in kind from what is now commonly understood by those terms.

When we turn to consider the finances of the Greek states, we have once more to admit that only in the case of Athens is it possible to speak with any precision about the financial organization of the state, that is, of income and expenditure, and of the distribution of financial burdens among the inhabitants of the country. In fifth-century Athens the chief sources of revenue were the tribute from the subjects and allies, royalties from the Laurium mines, rents from state-owned property, market dues and harbor dues on all imports and exports, court-fees, fines, and confiscations. In the following century the most important of those sources, the tribute, existed no longer. We are almost totally ignorant about the finances of the Second Athenian Confederacy; but, even if the Athenian government in time controlled the contributions of the League members, the amount was paltry compared to the *phoros* of the fifth century, and defrayed only a small part of Athens' heavy expenditure.

There was no regular direct taxation — apart from the head-tax paid by the denizens — but the state was relieved of a considerable portion of the burden which its treasury would otherwise have had to bear by the costly public services known as liturgies. These were undertaken by the wealthier citizens and, save in one case, metics. They were of two kinds, the so-called recurrent liturgies and the trierarchy. The latter, to which citizens only were liable, entailed the cost of equipping and keeping a trireme or ship of war in good condition for one year. The state provided the hull and some tackle, and paid a small sum to the crew; for the rest the trierarch was responsible, and very often he also augmented the sailors' pay. During the fifth century there appears to have been no difficulty in finding the necessary trierarchs to undertake this heavy responsibility singly. But toward the end of the Peloponnesian war it became necessary to divide the cost of a trierarchy between two persons. In the fourth century further modifications were introduced at different times, the general purpose being to distribute the expense among groups of citizens, and at the same time to graduate their contributions according to their several means. Of recurrent liturgies there were a number, most of them being connected with religious celebrations and athletic festivals. Thus, to cite but two examples, the *choregia* entailed the equipping and training of a chorus for the dramatic performances held at the Greater Dionysia or Lenæa; the *gymnasiarchia* similarly took care of athletes in training for the public games. In this way, it will readily be seen, the treasury was quit of a great part of the outlay coincident with the numerous religious celebrations. The performance of these services, at all events in the fifth century, was regarded as a patriotic duty, and the rich citizen commonly made it a point of honor to spend more than the minimum required of him. In the succeeding era this frequent drain on their resources was often felt as a burden by those on whom the costly duty fell.

The one direct tax on citizens and resident aliens of means was the *eisphora*. Other states besides Athens occasionally had recourse to this extraordinary tax on property but it is of the Athenian levy that most is known. It was only sparingly used in the fifth century, the earliest certain instance occurring in 428–427. In the last years of the Peloponnesian war the same means of temporarily easing the urgent financial straits of the treasury were again employed. In the fourth century its use became more and more frequent. By 378–377 a system of collection by companies (symmories) had been introduced, which, owing to abuses and unfair distribution of the required payment among the members of each symmory, had to be revised on more than one occasion. The denizens in all likelihood paid somewhat more heavily than the citizens; for it was one of the privileges sometimes conferred on deserving metics to be classed with Athenians in the payment of this tax. This implies that, without such a concession, a metic of wealth was worse off than a citizen.

The financial difficulties of the Athenian government were almost constant during the first half of the fourth century. The retrenchment and careful supervision of the public income instituted by Eubulus for a time restored an all but bankrupt state to solvency. No less efficient was Lycurgus' administration after 338. When we see how much could be effected by careful management in the days of Athens' political decline, we are forced to assume, even where we have no direct evidence for it, a great deal of wasteful expenditure and inefficient handling of the public purse during earlier decades.

2. THE PROGRESS OF DEMOCRATIC GOVERNMENT AT ATHENS

The system of government inaugurated by Cleisthenes remained substantially unaltered for nearly fifty years. In this period, although the sovereignty of the Athenian *ecclesia* was in a sense already accepted as an axiom of the constitution, there was one institution which might be said to be irreconcilable with the principle that the will of the people must prevail. The ancient Council of the Areopagus still exercised some control. It was described as the guardian of the laws; and, though we are ignorant of its powers, and to what extent it used them, the ancient authorities are agreed that the reduction of the Council to a mere court of justice for trying cases of homicide was a landmark in the history of Athenian democratic government. This change was effected by Ephialtes and the Progressives in 462–461. Henceforward there was no one to interfere even indirectly with the will of the people, least of all a rather narrowly oligarchic body of ex-magistrates taken from the wealthy class and continuing their membership of the Council for life. For such, in spite of its venerable antiquity backed by religious sanctions, the Areopagus must have seemed to all except the most conservative element in the commonwealth.

Five years later the reforming party introduced another innovation, of a sufficiently drastic nature. Hitherto only the members of the first and second Solonian classes had been eligible for the archonship. By a law passed in 457–456 the privilege of being a candidate for this office was extended to the third class, the *zeugitai*.[1] Though these posts were politically of quite secondary importance, since election by lot had been introduced, and the *strategia* had become the chief executive magistracy, they were still held to confer much distinction, if little influence, on the holder.

However democratic the constitution might be in theory, in practice the possession of some wealth made for greater opportunity to take part in public affairs, so long as magistracies and other services to the state were unpaid. Thus the introduction of payment to the jurors in the *Heliaia*, to the members of the Council of Five Hundred, and to all magistrates other than the *strategoi*, must count as the most radical of the Periclean reforms. Not content with providing this remuneration for performing civic duties, Pericles also introduced a small payment to soldiers and sailors on active service. It remained only to reward the members of the assembly for their attendance at its meetings. But fully half a century passed before this practice, the logical conclusion to Periclean precedents, was adopted. It was introduced by Agyrrhius during the first decade of the fourth century.

The sovereignty of the *ecclesia* was ensured in every sphere and by a variety of devices. The responsibility of even the

---

[1] The fourth class or *Thetes* remained ineligible by the constitution, but the law was tacitly ignored, at all events in the fourth century.

highest magistrates to it was secured by requiring them at the end of their year of office to undergo an official scrutiny (*euthyne*) of their administrative acts. Attempts to subvert the constitution by introducing legislation contrary to the existing laws rendered the proposer liable to be arraigned on a charge of "unconstitutional action." So important was this means of protecting the Athenian democracy that the person indicted was tried not in the ordinary courts of law but by the *ecclesia*, which for this purpose acted in a judicial capacity. All business to come before the assembly was first considered by the Council, and resolutions intended for the *ecclesia* were drawn up by the Council in the form of a preliminary decree (*probuleuma*). In practice the Council was bound in much of the public business that came before it to act on its own responsibility, in consultation with the Board of *strategoi*. Yet be it remembered that the councillors, like all the magistrates, were subject to the *euthyne* when they went out of office.

In an ancient democracy, where each adult male citizen took a direct part in the government, it was bound to follow that in practice the control of affairs should devolve mainly on the urban population. The farmers of Attica, especially those who lived at some distance from the capital, could not attend every meeting of the *ecclesia*, whereas the inhabitants of Peiræus and Athens suffered from no such disability. It was inevitable that Athenian policy should most commonly be determined in the interests of the town-dwellers, instead of the civic body as a whole. It was the former who, in all probability, were most jealous of their citizenship, and whose wishes Pericles gratified in 451–450, when he passed an act which we may label reactionary, if we will, but which must be recognized as eminently characteristic of the ancient Greek *polis* and its inhabitants. By limiting the citizen body to those of Athenian descent on both sides, Pericles abrogated one of the most enlightened measures of Cleisthenes.[1] Had that ordinance existed in the earlier part of the century, some of the most prominent men at Athens — for example, Themistocles — would have been debarred not merely from office but from civic rights. It has already been noted that after Pericles' death a very marked change came over the Athe-

[1] See above pp. 148–149.

nian democracy. Not only was the rivalry of party, which had been quiescent for fifteen years, revived, but the *ecclesia* was often swayed by men whose policy was framed solely in the interests of party or class (Cleon), or even of personal aggrandizement (Alcibiades).[1] The ascendancy of men like Cleon and Cleophon also exhibits the preponderating influence of the voters in Peiræus and Athens. The leading men in Athenian affairs were no longer exclusively or mainly recruited from the landed-property owners, but came from the urban population and from the humbler strata of society. That the Athenian of property and more aristocratic connexions could, however, still command the respect and even affection of the *ecclesia* is shown by the case of Nicias.

With all its weaknesses — and they were not negligible — her democratic constitution provided Athens with a stable government, such as was sadly lacking in many other Greek states, whether oligarchic or democratic. The spectre of *stasis*, revolution resulting from extreme party rivalry, which haunted so many Hellenic *poleis* — the ancient writers have left us fearful pictures of the lengths to which class bitterness could go in Corcyra, Argos, and Syracuse [2] — descended on Athens for two brief periods only, in 411 and 404. The loss of life and the hatred engendered on those occasions, though grievous in themselves, were small compared with what occurred elsewhere.

The weakness of the Athenian democracy in the next century was the result largely of economic conditions. While the income of Athens was less, her expenditure was not correspondingly reduced. In fact the payments for attending the assembly and the lavish distribution of festival money (cf. p. 270 n.) were a tremendous drain on the treasury. Many of the wealthier fam-

---

[1] The unofficial character of these "demagogues" has often been stressed (cf., for example, E. M. Walker in *Cambridge Ancient History*, v, p. 108), but the example commonly cited, namely Cleon, does not support this view adequately. For during most of the period of his ascendancy Cleon held office, though not always the highest. He was a councillor in 428–427, Hellenotamias in the year following, and *strategos* probably every year from 425 to his death. This leadership of the people by persons not in office is characteristic rather of the fourth century.

[2] For the most famous example of *stasis*, that at Corcyra, see Thucydides, iii, 70 ff., together with his reflections on the causes of political unrest (iii, 82–83).

ilies had been hard hit by the Peloponnesian war; yet, though their circumstances and those of their descendants remained reduced, the financial burdens placed on them by the state continued and even grew heavier. But the most serious indictment that can be brought against the ordinary citizen was his growing disinclination to shoulder the responsibilities inherent in citizenship of an ancient city-state. We have noted Demosthenes' denunciations of his fellow citizens for leaving it to mercenary troops to do their fighting for them. The development of professional soldiering was indeed inevitable as the science of warfare became more complicated; but in the intervening times of peace these soldiers of fortune were a menace to peaceful communities. It was not, however, only in military but also in political affairs that a certain apathy filled the citizen. As it has been put, though in somewhat extreme terms, "the one mortal disease, whose workings can be traced in manifold ways, was the severance of the individual from the state; everywhere private needs were superseding public claims." [1] Although the leading politicians at Athens, who frequently did not actually hold office, were predominantly of the middle class, the voters on whom they depended, and whose good-will and support they had to secure at all costs, were chiefly members of the poorest class living in or near the city. It was thus difficult even for the best of the Athenian statesmen — Callistratus in the first half, Demosthenes in the second half of the fourth century — to persuade the assembly to follow a consistent foreign policy; while in home affairs caprice and indiscriminate legislation too often took the place of constructive statesmanship. More often than not those who held the highest offices, like the *strategia*, exercised little control over the assembly, and had correspondingly little say in the formation of policy. Only occasionally do we find the same man — for instance, Eubulus or Lycurgus — occupying an important official position and at the same time exerting a predominating influence on the conduct of affairs.

We know too little of the internal affairs of other Greek states at this period to compare their governments with the Athenian. Yet we have every ground for believing that no

[1] S. H. Butcher, *Demosthenes*, p. 5.

considerable *polis* enjoyed a better government than Athens. Thus it was not only disagreement among the various city-states, such as has been described in a previous chapter, but the weakness of their internal government, which led to the eclipse of the Greek *poleis,* and hastened on the era of the great monarchies.

CHAPTER XVII

GREEK CIVILIZATION IN THE FIFTH AND FOURTH CENTURIES — PHILOSOPHY, LITERATURE, AND ART

> *To sum up: I say that Athens is the school of Hellas, and that the individual Athenian in his own person seems to have the power of adapting himself to the most varied forms of action with the utmost versatility and grace. This is no passing and idle word, but truth and fact; and the assertion is verified by the position to which these qualities have raised the state.* — From the funeral oration of Pericles in Thucydides, ii, 41 (Jowett's translation).

WHATEVER may be the modern student's final judgment on the political history of Greece, the efficiency and shortcomings of Hellenic constitutions, and the character of the economic life from the Persian wars to the age of Alexander, it is beyond dispute that the intellectual and artistic achievement of Hellas in that era was unique in the history of the world.

In the sixth century by far the most intense intellectual activity had been manifested by the Greeks of Ionia, whether in their own home-land or abroad. The fifth century continued to produce some thinkers who, starting from the philosophical position occupied by the Ionian physicists, speculated on the origin and nature of matter, or who, like Empedocles of Acragas (died *c.* 436 B.C.), evolved a theory in which an effort was made to reconcile the views of Heracleitus with those of the Eleatic school. More radical and of far wider, though not immediate, influence were the speculations of Leucippus (*floruit c.* 450 B.C.) and his disciple, Democritus. Not content with theories which derived all matter or Being from four "elements," Leucippus postulated an indeterminate number of small particles or atoms moving through gravitation in space. With this hypothesis he proceeded to explain the creation of the material Universe, and he also applied it to the mental processes. The system was elaborated by Democritus, and, half a century after his death, it was adopted with some modifications by Epicurus and his followers. The philosopher Anaxagoras, who for a time resided at Athens, where he enjoyed the friendship of Pericles, was in some respects more conservative than the atomists in his explanation of the nature of Being; but in teaching that the Universe was ordered and directed by an all-knowing Mind or Intelligence (Nūs) he was going greatly beyond anything propounded by previous philosophers; at the same time he rejected a purely mechanical explanation of the Universe such as was taught by Leucippus and his pupil. Anaxagoras' metaphysical doctrine exerted a profound influence on thinkers of the next generation or two, notably on Plato.

The larger Hellenic public seems to have been little interested or affected by these speculators; though popular prejudice, probably combined with the political intrigues of Pericles' opponents, brought about Anaxagoras' trial and condemnation for impiety about the year 450. The philosopher avoided the fatal consequences of an adverse verdict by hasty flight, and lived in peace for another two decades at Lampsacus on the Propontis.

Of far more immediate consequence were the activities of a number of men who, though ironically enough many of them had been disciples of the philosophers, led what was really a direct intellectual revolt against their teachers. With the advent of the Sophists, as they were called, the movement for higher education in the Hellenic world begin. Their influence, moreover, extended far beyond the boundaries of educational theory and practice; it left a deep mark on political thought, and on literature, especially prose writings, of every kind. The elementary education provided in Greek city-states in the two centuries under consideration was of a simple character. Its purpose was to teach reading and writing to boys from seven to thirteen or fourteen years of age, and to impart to them some acquaintance with earlier Greek literature. Homer, some portions of Hesiod, and such selections from the Lyric and Gnomic poets as might, besides their literary value, help to impress the chief civic and private virtues on the young mind, made up the sum of the authors studied. In this process memorization played a very important part. To this we may add some instruction in the simplest arithmetical calculations, and in singing and playing on the seven-stringed lyre. Provision was also made for the physical training of the boys in wrestling-schools set apart for their use. The schools were, so far as our information goes, uniformly conducted by private persons; consequently their quality varied greatly. It is very possible, though not certain, that the state in general so far concerned itself with the education of the young as to insist that parents should provide their boys with some schooling.[1]

Girls ordinarily were instructed in domestic duties and accomplishments by their mothers in the home. There is no clear evidence before the Hellenistic epoch that they received any school tuition. A woman with any literary training was exceptional, and the majority of Athenian women and girls probably could not read or write. With the completion of elementary schooling the boys of the poorer citizens or metics would be apprenticed to a trade, or go to work on their fathers' farms. For it is essential to bear in mind that the higher or secondary education imparted by the Sophists entailed far more expense for the parent, and in consequence was only within reach of the well-to-do minority.

A clear understanding of the general aim of the Sophists will also make clear the chief reason for their rise in the middle of the fifth century. The purpose which they had in view, and which they professed to attain, though not all on precisely the same lines, was to teach the adolescent youth of their day "political excellence"; in other words, to train them so that they might properly fulfil all the duties of citizenship, and take part in public affairs adequately equipped for the task. It was thus the emancipation of a large portion of the Hellenic world after the Persian wars, and the more active political life of a majority of the civic population, especially in democratic states, which created a demand for mental training of a more advanced kind than the schools could provide, together with technical

---

[1] The Spartan and Cretan systems of training youth had a special character of their own and have been briefly described above, p. 132.

instruction in some subjects with which the public man of the future must needs be familiar. Above all, as will be seen, the scientific study of speech and the right use of words, that is to say the art of rhetoric, would be indispensable alike in political assemblies and in courts of law. The aims of the Sophists being essentially practical, it is natural that they should have disregarded or rejected abstract speculation about the Universe, and should have concentrated on the study of Man. This scepticism toward abstract thought and inquiry into the ultimate reality of things was expressed by several of the Sophists in pregnant sayings, of which the most famous is Protagoras' dictum, "Man is the measure of all things, of those that are that they are, and those that are not that they are not." [1]

Their attention to political theory was noteworthy. The city-state was regarded as the result of a conscious intelligence, being created by Law, not existing by Nature. The antithesis between Nature and Law, on which Protagoras especially insisted, was far-reaching in its effects. It might easily be interpreted as subversive of traditional religion, and, according to one account, Protagoras, the champion of Law — that is, of traditional morality and organized society — was actually arraigned for impiety while at Athens. Again, in discussing different forms of polity, the Sophists were led to pay attention also to non-Hellenic peoples. They contrasted their customs and institutions with those of their own race. By transcending the particularistic views of states and governments held by the average Greek, including most men of affairs, the Sophists became the first exponents of Panhellenic ideas.

These teachers did not establish schools of higher learning in any given place; they were essentially itinerant professors, who visited the numerous cities of the Greek world for short periods. They lectured on various topics to general audiences, and at the same time attached to themselves regular pupils,

---

[1] That is to say, what seems to be true to A is true to A, what seems to be true to B is true to B. Any inquiry must be either for what we know or for what we do not know. To search after the former is absurd, and after the latter is impossible. Since in the second alternative we should not know for what to look; and, even if we found it, how could we recognize that it was the object of our search?

a

b

THE PARTHENON: *a*. West Front; *b*. East Front

Plate 24

a

b

a. Parthenon, South Side; *b.* Temple of Nike

Plate 25

from whose parents they received fees for the instruction that they imparted. Most famous among these Sophists were Protagoras of Abdera, Gorgias of Leontini, Prodicus of Ceos, and Hippias of Elis. Gorgias, who visited Athens in 427 B.C. in the character of envoy from his native city, specialized in the study of rhetoric, and may be regarded as the real founder of artistic Greek prose. Protagoras, in addition to his interest in political science, adapted the antithesis between Nature and Law to educational theory. To get the best results the educator must see that natural gifts in a pupil are guided and brought to fullest flower by training and practice. This threefold division — natural ability, training, and practice — which Protagoras was the first to enunciate, was adopted and developed by all the great educators of the fourth century. Protagoras and Prodicus, again, can claim to be the founders of scientific grammar, which was indeed a necessary preliminary to rhetorical study. Hippias, finally, appears to have been a scintillating personality, who prided himself on the universality of his knowledge and accomplishments. Though brilliant, such a man was necessarily also more shallow; and it is significant that he exerted little influence after his time, whereas Protagoras and Gorgias, each in his sphere, left their mark on the thought and writings of the next generation.

Reckoned by many of his contemporaries as a Sophist, Socrates, son of Sophroniscus, nevertheless differed from those teachers radically in several important respects. He was born in 470–469, but the known facts of his life are few. His father was a stonemason, and he himself for a time appears to have practised the craft. He took part as a hoplite in the siege of Potidæa, and later fought at Delium and Amphipolis. Late in life, in 406–405, he served as a member of the Council of Five Hundred, and alone stood out against the illegalities at the trial of the generals after Arginusæ. His great bodily endurance, simplicity of life, and the fits of abstraction into which he fell from time to time, were as familiar to his contemporaries as his pronouncedly plain features (Plate 21). It is probable that he was for a time a pupil of one of the less known physicist philosophers, Archelaus; and it is in the character of one speculating about the material structure of the Universe that he is burlesqued in Aristophanes' comedy, the *Clouds*, first performed at Athens in 423. Finally, in 399, Socrates was arraigned for impiety and for "corrupting the youth" of Athens, and condemned to drink the hemlock. It is now generally recognized that the trial and the verdict were the result of the strong political, that is to say democratic, reaction against the oligarchs at Athens, some of whom had been intimate, though unworthy, disciples of Socrates. It is also clear that, had Socrates taken any steps to conciliate the jurors, he could have saved his life. It was the last twenty-five years of his career that he devoted to what he regarded as nothing less than a religious mission in the highest sense. His teaching was primarily concerned with human conduct. Convinced that the ethical conceptions and the actions proceeding therefrom of the majority of his fellow-men were erroneous, he set himself the twofold task of eradicating false opinions, and then suggesting a more correct and upright habit of thought. He was no formal teacher. His class-room was the world at large, the market-place, the wrestling-school, the shop, the houses of friends. There he engaged all and sundry in conversation, and by skillful use of question and answer — the dialectic method — strove to convince them of their false thinking and ignorance, and then by the same method to lead them on to ethically right concepts. His personality, perhaps even more than his conversation, must have made a tremendous impression on all with whom he came into contact. He had many disciples, though there was no formal relation of teacher to pupil and no remuneration by the one to the other, as in the case of the Sophists. Socrates' unique position in Greek history is in the first place due to his consistently noble and upright life, and to the fact that he was willing to pay the highest price, his life, rather than recede one iota from his inmost convictions. But scarcely less important than the man himself is the circumstance that, although not strictly a philosopher — in the sense that he elaborated no metaphysical or ethical system — he was the fountain head of some six different philosophical schools. These were founded by disciples, each of whom took over some part of Socrates' teaching, and on that based a systematic philosophy.

By far the greatest of these pupils was Plato. He was born

Plate 26

b

a

PARTHENON FRIEZE

a

b   *c*

THE ERECHTHEUM: *a.* EAST END; *b.* NORTH PORCH; *c.* SOUTH
PORCH

Plate 27

in 427 B.C. After Socrates' death he abandoned his intention of devoting himself to public affairs. For about twelve years after 399 he lived partly in Athens, partly abroad, visiting both Egypt and Sicily. In, or soon after, 387 he started a school of higher education in his own residence.[1] The rest of a long life — he died in 347 — he devoted to teaching and to the composition of many writings in which he set forth his doctrines for the benefit of a larger public. The method of presenting a theory or, conversely, of demolishing false arguments by question and answer, which had been used with such effect by his master, Plato adopted and perfected as a literary form. All his works are composed as dialogues between several speakers, Socrates being generally the principal character.[2] In his earliest dialogues Plato analyzes various moral qualities — for instance, courage, piety, self-control — in order to set out more clearly the principle which was at the root of Socrates' ethical teaching, the equation of virtue with knowledge. It was only about the time that he set up as a teacher in Athens that in the *Phaedo,* and then in the *Republic,* he put forward the doctrine which forms the foundation of his philosophical thought throughout his life, though it underwent sundry modifications and extensions in his later works. In constructing the Theory of Forms or Ideas, Plato contrasted the objects of sense, which are in themselves transitory and unreal, with the general Forms or Ideas from which they derive their name. These alone partake of reality and alone are existent, to be apprehended by the mind alone. They are "the eternal archetype of which the sensible objects are the copies." All learning consists in recollection; for the soul, before it begins its career in the human body, has known the archetype and can be reminded of it when it perceives its imperfect copies in the world of sense. The highest Idea, which is the fountain of all existence and of all knowledge, is the

---

[1] The name given to it, the Academy, was really the name of a public garden situated nearby, to the northwest of the city, three-quarters of a mile from the Dipylon gate.

[2] Even Plato's latest and longest work, the *Laws,* which he did not live to revise, makes some attempt to keep the dialogue form. But there are lengthy passages where a detailed exposition is entrusted to a single speaker, so that the reader for a time forgets that there are other interlocutors.

Idea of the Good, which is identified with God or the Demiurge, who created the Universe by imprinting the Forms on the formless matter of chaos. In a later treatise, the *Timaeus*, Plato sketched this cosmic creation-process, though he admits that his picture is no more than an approximation, the absolute truth of the Demiurge's work being unattainable. Though even a brief examination of Platonic philosophy is beyond the scope of this volume, some account of his greatest work may here be given.

The *Republic* begins with a discussion of the nature of justice. Various current theories are propounded, but all of them are found inadequate by Socrates, who is finally called upon to forsake the rôle of destructive critic and be constructive. In order to find justice at work — and thereby be better able to define it — in the human soul and in the political community, there follows an analysis of human society and the building up of an ideal state. Plato's psychological tenets are closely interwoven with his political and educational theories. The human soul is a living thing, in which there are three elements striving for the mastery, the appetitive, spirited, and rational. The first is at the root of purely physical needs and desires, some of which are necessary (*e.g.* the desire for food in order to sustain life), some unnecessary. Spirit is the mainspring of such qualities as courage or righteous indignation, and, provided it be subordinated to the rational part, is its natural ally. Excess of spirit will however produce bad developments; for example, courage will degenerate into pugnacity or cruelty. The rational or highest part of the soul is the fountain head of intelligence, and of those emotions which make men susceptible to the beauty of literature or art. For the soul to function in the best possible manner it is needful for its three constituents to be adjusted in perfect harmony, the first and second being in subjection to the rational part. So, too, in the state there are three classes of work necessary for its good, and consequently three classes of persons who are needed to perform it. Lowest in the body politic, and analogous, as it were, to the appetitive part of the soul, are the producers of material commodities necessary for physical existence, the craftsmen, tradesmen, and so forth. Here Plato advocates a high degree of specialization in craft and industry; but the producing class is not part of the citizen body, although individual members, in case of special ability, may rise to one of the two higher classes who alone are citizens of the commonwealth.[1] These two, the Auxiliaries and the Guardians, are respectively the younger men, whose task it is to protect the state from its internal and external enemies, and the older men, to whom is assigned the work of legislation and of governing the state. Here, again, the analogy to the spirited and the rational parts of the soul is evident. The main problem of education is the right adjustment of the three parts of the soul in the individual, and Plato devotes his almost exclusive attention to moral training, to the method of developing character, and to the type of character to be developed. The training of the intellect is only undertaken as a primary aim in the case of those who are selected, on attaining to manhood, as fitted to become the future rulers of the state. Their higher education lasts from twenty to thirty years of age, and consists in the main of higher mathematics, that being in Plato's view the most suitable of those studies "which are of universal application." The ablest of the young men so trained will then be chosen to continue their studies for another five years, from thirty to thirty-five, which will be devoted to dialectics and metaphysics. These will in time become the wisest and most responsible of the Guardian class. In order to pursue their education and fulfil their functions in the state without the distraction of material cares or responsibilities, both the Auxiliaries and the Guardians live under a completely communistic régime. There is to be community in property and in women. The last-named are according to their several abilities to be trained in the same manner as the male Auxiliaries and Guardians. Strict eugenic regulations are laid down governing marriages, and the children born of these unions will be reared in state institutions. Toward the end of his great work Plato, who has described his ideal government of the state, proceeds to an examination of various kinds of constitution, and the human characters which correspond to them, these being progressive degenerations of the ideal. His political theories he was to revise and formulate

[1] Cf. on this last point the "myth" or allegory in *Republic*, iii, 414-415.

afresh in two later works, the *Statesman* and the *Laws*. In this last work, realizing that he had portrayed an unattainable ideal in the *Republic*, he has depicted a second-best state. Though this book falls short of the grandeur of conception which permeates the *Republic*, and, owing to its diffuseness and occasional obscurity, has often been neglected, it contains, among much else that is of deep interest, criticisms of existing political systems in Greece, and also Plato's maturest reflections on education, put forward after well-nigh forty years of practical experience as an educator.[1]

We know very little of the inner organization, the curriculum and methods of teaching, the research, carried on in the Platonic Academy; but it can be safely assumed that its working was, as it were, the sublunary counterpart of the education of the Guardians in the *Republic*. In the *Laws* Plato has outlined a scheme by which all instruction and training from earliest youth would be supervised by the state. Suitable buildings and staff would be provided and the various studies from stage to stage, from elementary schooling to what we should call advanced university work, would be graded and brought into proper relation with one another. The radical nature of such proposals will be clear, if it be remembered that all education in Greece had so far been left to private initiative, and that consequently there had been little necessary coördination. If the educational system of the *Republic* found its practical expression in the Academy, the principles advocated by Plato in his last work, that the state or the community should take charge of the education of its citizens, supervise the appointment of teachers, provide proper accommodation, and so forth, were to a great extent realized in the Hellenistic Age, although the character of much of the instruction imparted would not have won the approval of "the god among philosophers."[2]

Aristotle, the greatest of Plato's disciples, was a native of

---

[1] It is not the least fault of most current text-books on the History of Education that Plato's *Laws* are either very summarily dismissed or else passed over. It would be presumptuous, though not difficult, to hazard an explanation for this neglect.

[2] *Deus philosophorum*, as Cicero calls Plato in his treatise, *On the Nature of the Gods*, ii, 32.

Stageirus in Thrace, a Greek town in a "barbarian" region. The early environment in which he thus grew up is not without significance to any one who reads his penetrating analysis of the characteristic attributes of Hellenic and non-Hellenic peoples (*Politics*, iv (7), 7). His father was for a time physician at the Macedonian court, a circumstance to which Aristotle may have owed, at least in part, Philip II's invitation to become the tutor of young Alexander. On attaining manhood Aristotle emigrated to Athens, and was for twenty years a member of the Platonic Academy, first as a pupil, later as a teacher. After Plato's death he was in Asia Minor for a space, and then, in 343, he was summoned to Macedonia. In 335 or 334 he returned to Athens and there set up a philosophical school of his own.[1] When, in 323, Alexander's premature end was the signal for an outburst of anti-Macedonian feeling at Athens, which was extended to any one who had been associated with the late king, Aristotle was forced to retire to Eubœa. There he died early in the following year.

Steeped in Platonic doctrines in his earlier life, he had the scientific rather than the creative mind, which led him to modify or reject not a little of his master's teaching. Concerned especially with observing all the processes of nature, he evolved a great philosophical system embracing alike the material world and the world of the mind. We owe a double debt to Aristotle as a mapper out of the sciences and as the inventor of a scientific method. Rigorously applied this process was made up of three stages: first, it was necessary to collect and test current opinions; second, to reach a hypothesis or general law, involving the collection of particulars; third, by deduction, to apply hypotheses to particular instances. The fact that he only partially succeeded in the titanic task which he set himself was inevitable because scientific experimentation was still in its infancy. Though Aristotle himself did much to promote this, and his successors — for instance, Theophrastus — carried on in particular fields of scientific research, his collected evi-

---

[1] The school was subsequently known as the Lyceum, since he taught in the gymnasium of that name. The alternative appellation, Peripatetics, Peripatetic School, is derived from a Greek word signifying "to walk around," that being the practice of Aristotle while discoursing to his hearers.

dence was at times insufficient for safe generalization. Yet
even so, few men have achieved so much in a life-time. Not
only did he knit together into his system all the knowledge
that the Greeks up to that time had obtained, but he made
his own contributions to science, which were of much importance, and greatly in advance of previous investigations. His
work on zoölogy was the first systematic attempt at classifying
the various animals into genera and species; and the descriptions of the habits and character of many of his subjects be-
tray both first-rate powers of observation and keen powers
of reasoning. It is of great significance that Aristotle enun-
ciates an evolutionary doctrine of progress from the lower to
the higher forms of life; he is still sufficient of a Platonist,
however, to explain this process as due to the design and act
of creative Nature. His philosophical system, following his
own division, may be classified under groups: Speculative
Philosophy aiming at truth, Practical Philosophy aiming at
happiness, and Poetic (*i.e.* Creative) Philosophy aiming at an
artistic product.[1] Each of these groups can be subdivided,
so that the first includes metaphysics, physics (*i.e.* the natural
sciences), and mathematics; the second, ethics, economics,
and politics; the third, painting, sculpture, and literature. The
extant writings of Aristotle, which, with the exception of the
treatise on the Athenian Constitution, are the lecture notes
of the master, or in some cases perhaps of pupils, can be
similarly grouped, the *Metaphysics* and scientific treatises dealing with parts of group 1, the *Ethics* and *Politics* with those of
group 2, the *Poetics* and *Rhetoric* with those of part 3. Of the
extant writings of Aristotle the two which are now of the most
universal interest, and which also show the philosopher's wisdom and analytical power at their best, are the *Ethics* and
the *Politics*. The latter is the profoundest contribution to
political science made by any ancient writer.

We have already seen the valuable function performed in
the fifth century by the Sophists as professors of higher education, and how the study of rhetoric occupied a leading place in

---

[1] Logic is not so much a part of the system as the indispensable prerequisite to it. Its proper comprehension must precede inquiry into any
of the three branches of philosophy.

their curriculum. It cannot be gainsaid that there was a dangerous side to this tuition. The scientific study of language and prose composition might be perverted to serve unworthy ends; nor can we doubt that this was sometimes the case. Hence the serious criticisms of the Sophists made by Plato, not only in his earlier works like the *Gorgias*, but in his latest treatise (*Laws*, x, 889e), and the more ebullient attacks of Aristophanes in the *Clouds*, against teachers who merely ruin youth by instructing them how to make the worse argument appear the better. Thus, besides the study of rhetoric proper, two things at least were essential, if the Sophistic education was to fulfil its avowed purpose, to train men to be good and efficient citizens. First, a good knowledge of subjects like history, literature, and jurisprudence was indispensable; for, without that, speeches would perhaps be brilliant or ingenious, but they would be devoid of substantial argument. Secondly, and most important of all, the Sophist must inculcate in his disciples sound ethical principles, the acquisition of which would make it impossible for rhetoric to be used for ignoble purposes.

It is precisely these needs that are stressed by the greatest Sophist of the fourth century, and which he set himself conscientiously and methodically to fulfil in the school of which he was the head for well-nigh half a century. Isocrates, who was born in 436 B.C. in Attica, received as good an education as was then procurable, since his father was a citizen of comfortable means. He studied for a time with Gorgias, but physical disabilities debarred him from a public career; in addition, he lost his patrimony in the political disturbances at the end of the Peloponnesian war. Hence he was obliged for a few years to eke out a subsistence as a professional writer of law-court speeches. At last, about 387, he set up as a teacher of higher education, continuing at the head of his institution until his death at the advanced age of ninety-eight (338). The normal period of training in his school was three to four years. In the course of his long career he had many hundreds of pupils; a large percentage of them subsequently became noted men in the most divers walks of life. Isocrates' influence as an educator, and as the second founder of rhetoric, was profound and lasted for centuries, affecting not only higher education in the Greek world of the Hellenistic Age, but, in time, Roman writers on the theory of education and rhetoric, notably Cicero.

His service as a teacher was, however, only a part of Isocrates' life-work. He was also a political essayist whose aims have frequently been misunderstood, just as the influence of his political doctrines has been underrated. From the publication in 380 B.C. of his greatest work, the *Panegyricus*, to his last long work, the *Panathenaicus*, which appeared a year before his death, he was a consistent advocate of Panhellenic unity, first under Athenian leadership, later, when he saw that the leader must come from outside the bickering congeries of Hellenic polities, under that of Philip of Macedon. To label Isocrates an "arm-chair" politician is to overlook that his *Panegyricus* certainly contributed to the successful formation of the Second Athenian Confederacy; that his discourse, *On the Peace*, helped to promote the peace policy of Eubulus; and that the influence of his thought on Athenian politicians in the anxious decade from 350 to 340 can still be demonstrated clearly in at least one case, that of Aeschines. Had we the utterances of other members of the philo-Macedonian party at Athens, we should doubtless find many more traces of the Isocratean political program. It is perfectly arguable that Isocrates was wrong and Demosthenes was right in the question of what was Athens' best policy at this juncture; it is indefensible to treat the views on public affairs expressed by the great educator as of no account.

In the seventh and sixth centuries the poetic genius of the Greeks had manifested itself in lyric, elegiac, and iambic poetry. In contrast to this the greatest poetic artists of the fifth century were, with one exception, dramatists; and the four playwrights whose poetic achievement we can still fully appraise from their extant works were all Athenians. With their passing, this form of poetic composition waned also, and the fourth century is preëminently the age of the great prose writers of the Greek world. Again Athens had all but a monopoly of the talents.

The one outstanding lyric poet was Pindar. He was born in the last quarter of the sixth century, but his artistic life belongs to the first half of the fifth. His fame rests on the *Epinician*

Plate 28

TEMPLE OF POSEIDON AT PAESTUM (Southern Italy)

STATUE OF HERMES HOLDING THE INFANT DIONYSUS
(By Praxiteles)

Plate 29

Odes, songs commemorating the athletic victories won at the four great festivals of Greece by competitors from all parts of the Greek world. For the remains of other Pindaric poetry found during recent years in papyri from Egypt, though of great interest to the literary historian, have added nothing to Pindar's poetic reputation. But, though he was the contemporary of Aeschylus, and lived in the days when the Greeks repelled the Asiatic invader and during the momentous decades which saw political and social changes of unparalleled significance, he appears little affected thereby in his poetry. In spirit he belongs to the sixth century; he is full of aristocratic pride, and his ideal manhood is a nobility such as in his time must have all but passed away. He upholds the old traditional religion; at the same time he seeks in many places to rationalize it, and particularly to gloss over those episodes in Greek mythology, which were not only repellent to the people of an enlightened age, but might be deemed unworthy of divine beings. The unexampled richness and variety of Pindar's diction, coupled with his vivid imagination that pours forth the most varied and unforgettable imagery of language, render his poetry deserving of being called sublime. Yet, although his poems abound in moral saws, these too are of the traditional sort. And, just as there are moments when we are tempted to call Pindar a monotheist, only to be confronted a few lines later with echoes of the old polytheism; so, if we are not wholly borne away by the purely poetic beauties of his odes, we are obliged to confess that he is lacking in that deeper insight into religion and into men's hearts which characterizes, though in different ways, all of the Attic dramatists.

Next to nothing is known of the drama before the fifth century. It is only when the eldest of the three Attic tragic poets, Aeschylus (524–456 B.C.) had begun his poetic career that the drama as a literary form was fashioned. Seven of his plays are still extant.[1] The earliest of these, the *Suppliants*, cannot be precisely dated, but probably was composed soon after 499, the year in which Aeschylus is said to have begun exhibiting plays at the Dionysiac festival. Tradition attributes to him the intro-

---

[1] He wrote ninety plays in all, winning the first prize at the dramatic festival at Athens on thirteen occasions.

duction of a second actor, an innovation which made possible a proper dramatic dialogue; whereas, before, the lyrics of the Dionysiac chorus had been separated at intervals by dialogues between a single actor and the leader of the chorus. Aeschylus' earlier plays can be performed with only two actors; but when, about 468, a third actor was added — and this remained the fixed number for tragedy — he availed himself of the innovation. Hence a further great advance in dramatic technique became possible. The dramatist's powers are seen at their highest in the great trilogy, *Agamemnon*, *Libation Bearers*, *Eumenides*, which was produced at Athens two years before his death. The subject matter of Aeschylus' tragedies and that of his successors was taken from mythology and heroic legends, familiar to his hearers from youth up, from Homer and the poems of the epic cycle. Historical subjects were rarely portrayed, though not wholly unknown. For such was the *Capture of Miletus* by Phrynichus, produced in 493, which so upset the Athenian audience that they fined the poet. Such also is the extant *Persians* by Aeschylus (472). Its setting is in Persia; the persons represented — the queen mother, Atossa, the king's messenger, the chorus of Persian elders, and finally Xerxes himself — are all Persian. But it is first and foremost a noble panegyric on Athens' achievements at Salamis. That, however, is not all. The early part of the play contains more than a hint of the attendant horrors of war, the uncertainty of the issue, the anguish felt by the relatives of those who have gone to fight. Over all is the contrast between human endeavor and human pride, and Fate or the Will of God, which can bring one to nought and humble the other. It is a theme recurrent in Aeschylus' plays. He is not a fatalist as the term is ordinarily understood; but he believes that there exists a nexus of events which leads up naturally or inevitably to any great human misfortune. He is, too, the upholder of Law, Order, and Justice against tyranny and injustice; it was a dominant theme in the trilogy of which only the *Prometheus Bound* has survived, and it is brought impressively before us in the final play of the *Oresteia* and its concluding scenes. Of Aeschylus' purely poetic qualities the grandeur of his language and the matchless metaphors, especially in his choral odes, strike every reader at once.

As a dramatist his power of psychological analysis is profound. Clytemnestra and Cassandra in the *Agamemnon* are among the unsurpassed figures of tragedy for all time.

Sophocles (496–406 B.C.) was the son of a well-to-do Athenian citizen. He himself at different times held important offices in the Athenian state — he was *strategos* in 440 and one of the ten *probuloi* appointed in 412–411 — and he was, judged by the number of times that he won the first prize at the dramatic festivals, easily the most successful of the three tragic poets. His earliest victory occurred in 468; but of the seven extant plays the earliest, *Antigone*, was produced in 442 or 441, the latest, *Oedipus at Colonus*, was not performed till some years after the dramatist's death.[1] Sophocles abandoned the practice of writing three plays on a single continuous theme; instead, although at the festivals it was necessary to offer a trilogy in competition, each of his dramas treated of a separate subject. In his plays Sophocles takes the heroic legends in their accepted form. His characters act and speak in strict consistence with their situation; they do not become, as often in Euripides, the mouthpieces of the poet's own views. The action in Sophocles' dramas, too, is steadily directed to one tragic climax, although the poet shows great diversity in the means which he employs to his end. Thus, *Oedipus the King* is in the matter of plot a masterpiece of intricate construction. From the point of view of dramatic structure it is the greatest of all Greek tragedies; while in the grandeur of its conception it is surpassed alone by Aeschylus' *Agamemnon*. Yet in the *Philoctetes* there is scarcely any plot. The entire interest of the play centres in the psychological analysis of the leading characters, the contrast between them, and the reaction of one upon the other. As a literary artist Sophocles made the Attic Greek language a subtle vehicle of every mood and thought, in a way that was rarely equalled and never surpassed. He is typical of his age and country, Periclean Athens, both in his restraint and detachment, which some critics, contrasting his strictly objective treatment of his characters with the personal note struck here and there by his two rivals, have wrongly interpreted as due

---

[1] To the seven complete tragedies we may add the considerable fragments of an eighth play, a satyric drama, found on an Egyptian papyrus.

to lack of sympathy and understanding, and in his attitude to moral law and to religion. For he strives to bring venerable tradition into harmony with the higher conceptions of morality and beliefs, which were characteristic of the best thought of the age.

Of Euripides (480–406 B.C.) eighteen genuine plays have survived, the *Rhesus*, though included among his works, being of disputed authorship. Of these the earliest is probably the *Alcestis* (438), the latest the *Bacchae* (406), which was not produced till after the poet's death. In more ways than one Euripides was an innovator. His choral odes commonly are mere interludes in the play, and have little connexion with its plot or action. Again, he increased the length and importance of the opening prologue. The result is often somewhat undramatic; but the convention gave the poet greater freedom in the treatment of his actual play, by enabling him to explain fully to his hearers the precise situation at the opening of the dramatic action. It is, however, not merely on the technical side, and in the matter of experiments with metres, that Euripides broke with tradition. While both Aeschylus and Sophocles were, each after his manner, idealists, Euripides is an uncompromising realist in the handling of his themes. His characters often utter views which, but slightly disguised, are the poet's own sentiments on social, ethical, and even political questions. Deeply affected by the Sophistic movement, Euripides frankly questioned the truth of many accepted opinions on religion and morality. His characters are not cast in the heroic mould, but in their good and bad qualities are essentially human. Whether the dictum attributed to Sophocles, "I draw men as they ought to be drawn; Euripides draws them as they are," is a genuine utterance of the older poet or not, it expresses one leading characteristic of Euripides' art. It is noteworthy that his greatest characters are almost without exception women, Medea in the play of that name, Phaedra in the *Hippolytus*, Alcestis, Hecuba, Electra, Iphigeneia. In the depth of his understanding and in his sympathy for women he surpassed both his predecessors; yet it was one of the commonest taunts against him in his day that he was a woman-hater. Euripides in this and in other respects was but partially understood in his own time, and, judged by contemporary standards, he was by far the least successful of the three tragic poets. But his innovations, the romantic quality and the "love-interest" in his plays, and the fact that his dramas were in general not typically Athenian, made him the favorite dramatist of later ages.[1]

In the next century tragedies continued to be written, but they were inferior to the works of the three great masters. Plays were written to be read rather than performed; while in the theatres, as Aristotle observes (*Rhetoric*, iii, 1403b), "the actors are now of greater moment than the poets." It became customary to revive one or more of the old masterpieces at the dramatic festivals, in addition to producing new plays, which are lost to us, and which in all likelihood did not survive for any great time in antiquity.

Attic comedy developed more slowly than tragedy. Of the three leading writers of comedy Cratinus seems to have begun his literary career about 450 B.C. Eupolis and Aristophanes (*c.* 448–388) were approximately contemporaries. It is, however, of Aristophanes alone that we can properly judge, since eleven of his plays have come down to us, while those of his rivals have not survived. The earliest comedy that we possess, the *Acharnians*, was produced in 425, and appears to have been the third play written by the youthful poet. His latest play was the *Plutus* (388). The feature which perhaps strikes the modern reader of Aristophanes' plays first is their outspokenness. Contemporary personages and institutions were fearlessly attacked or burlesqued. Public opinion approved this license, since the efforts made once or twice in the fifth century to restrict this extreme liberty of speech were unsuccessful. But Aristophanes was far more than a humorist with a knack of composing telling plots and easily flowing dialogue, that is generally witty and occasionally gross. In his choral songs as a whole, and throughout his greatest extant play, he shows himself an imaginative poet of the first rank. That he was a literary critic of a high order is clear to every attentive student

---

[1] Thus, it is significant that the Roman writers of tragedy, both those of the Republican age and Seneca, in borrowing from Greek models, were indebted almost wholly to Euripides. Aeschylus was too archaic and heroic, Sophocles too typical of Periclean Athens to be satisfactorily transplanted.

of the *Frogs* (405), with its evaluation of the Attic tragedians, as well as from the intensely clever parodies of Euripides' plays introduced into the *Peace* and the *Women at the Thesmophoria*. Three of his comedies are, in effect, pleas for the Peace party, the *Acharnians*, the *Peace* (421), and the *Lysistrata* (411). In the *Clouds* he satirizes certain intellectual movements of the age, Socrates being taken, somewhat unfairly, as typical of a class. In the *Wasps* he makes fun of his fellow countrymen's love for litigation and the law-courts. The *Birds* (414), now generally and rightly conceded to be his masterpiece, is more a play of the imagination, a fantasy full of exquisite poetry mixed with rollicking fun. It depicts the founding of a bird-commonwealth by two Athenians who have grown weary of the life and bustle of their city. Incidentally the play contains much amusing parody of conditions in contemporary Athens.

If the needful allowance be made for exaggeration and burlesque, the Aristophanic comedies are invaluable for the light that they throw on the manners and life of the Athenians of the day. Aristophanes represents for us the older generation who, then, as in all ages, contrast unfavorably the behavior of the young folk with their own in their more decorous youth. He shows us, in the person of Philocleon in the *Wasps*, the varying moods and influences to which the average Athenian, acting as juror in the *Heliaia*, was subject. He depicts, too, the joys of country life, pillories the fashionable way of behaving in the streets or at dinner parties, and in his minor characters brings before us a whole gallery of types familiar to every Athenian in his daily life — tradesmen of all sorts, the informer, the down-at-heels poet, a councillor, an oracle-monger, or one of the Scythian archers who formed the police force of Athens.

Of fourth-century comedy it is difficult to form an adequate judgment, since nothing but the titles of plays and some few fragments have survived. It is clear, however, that the poets of that age had not the same license of speech as their predecessors. Political plays were no longer written, and occasional ridicule of well-known persons was directed not against public men but, for example, against prominent philosophers. The names and characters were fictitious; the poets dealt with types of character and professions. Parodies of literature, philosophy, and even mythology were very popular; the old badinage and invective was replaced by innuendo (Cf. Aristotle, *Ethics*, iv, 8). Love intrigue began to be a favorite topic for the plot, and in this respect especially the comedy of the fourth century prepared the way for the comedy of intrigue that flourished in the early Hellenistic Age.

We saw how the spirit of inquiry, which had pervaded the Hellenic world in the sixth century, had among other effects produced the first attempts at a rational presentation of geographical and historical data. The first author to produce a history in a literary form was Herodotus (*c.* 484–425 B.C.), a native of Halicarnassus, whose manhood was spent partly in Samos and Athens, partly in extensive travels, partly, since he joined the colony to Thurii, in the West. This is not the place to enter upon the vexed question of how his history was composed, and whether his primary interest was in geography, while his historical inquiries resulted from a later and secondary phase in his intellectual life. In the *History* as it has come down to us — the division into nine books is a later arrangement — the second half (Books vi to ix) narrates the Persian wars of 490 and 480–479. The earlier half of the work is devoted to a review of the manners, institutions, and history of various oriental peoples included in the vast Persian empire. Herodotus derived his information from oral tradition and local beliefs, from predecessors, especially Hecatæus of Miletus, and, above all, from personal observation on his travels and conversations held with natives of the lands he visited. Hence inevitably the treatment of the various regions is unequal. While, for example, his section on Egypt, which he had himself visited, in addition to having Hecatæus' work, is long and detailed, his observations on Lydia or the Scythians are proportionately a good deal briefer. A similar disparity is observable also in his accounts of earlier Greek history, introduced into different parts of his book. As a story-teller Herodotus is inimitable, and he is a literary artist of the first rank, so that his history has enjoyed a deserved popularity throughout the ages. Of his merits as a historian opinions both in ancient and modern times have varied. His weaknesses are undeniable. He has little understanding of military affairs; his natural piety leads him to respect oracles and supposed supernatural phenomena which a more sophisticated writer would have rejected or sought to rationalize; at times — and this is specially noticeable in the Greek portions of his book — he is swayed by political likes and dislikes, so that, for instance, he is partial to Athens and to the Alcmæonid clan, and grossly unfair to Themistocles. Yet we cannot dispute the justice of the title, "the father of history," bestowed on him by Cicero. Herodotus is eminently broad-minded; he has a deep admiration for eastern civilizations, especially Egypt, and he is capable of doing justice even to the strange customs of uncivilized peoples like the Scythians. Where his statements are the result of personal observation he is highly trustworthy, a fact which modern exploration and research have borne out again and again. Where he depends on others he is naturally at the mercy of his informants; but it would be an error to regard him as quite uncritical. His criticism takes the form of suppressing traditions and statements which he sees cause to reject; or, wherever he himself is in doubt, of giving several traditions of a particular event, leaving the decision to his reader's judgment. Thus, within certain limits, he exercised the function of criticism; he applied it to single questions and details, but he had not yet learnt to apply it to the larger problems of history. He ascertained the truth to the best of his ability, and set down in connected form the traditions and accounts of historical occurrences. Thus, in truth, he fully merits the name bestowed upon him by the Roman writer.

The tremendous intellectual activity, and its rapid progress, during the latter half of the fifth century cannot be illustrated better than by this bald statement of fact, that scarcely more than a quarter of a century separates the *History* of Herodotus from the historical work of Thucydides, son of Olorus. He was born about 471; the known facts of his life are few. He was a victim of the plague in 430–429, and held the office of *strategos* in 425–424, being subsequently banished for his failure to effect the relief of Amphipolis. Exiled for fully twenty years from his native city, he spent the time partly on his ancestral prop-

DEMETER
(Original of the Fourth Century)

Plate 30

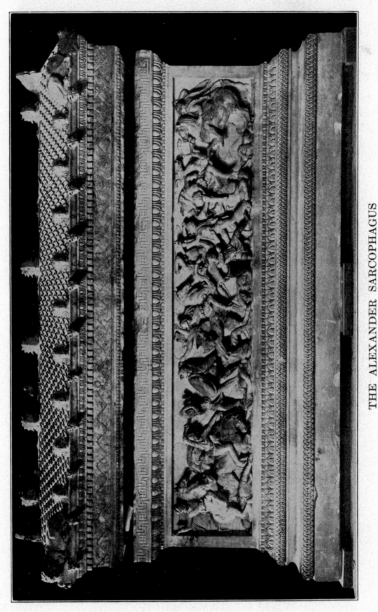

THE ALEXANDER SARCOPHAGUS

Plate 31

erty in Thrace, partly in travel to collect material for his *History*. He returned to Athens in 403, and seems to have died not many years later, leaving his work incomplete. It was of the war, in which so large a part of the Hellenic world was engaged for nearly thirty years, that he set himself to compose a critical narrative. Actually his extant work covers the period from 431 to 411, the first book being in the nature of an introduction, in which he gives a valuable sketch of the earlier development of Hellas, and a summary of Athenian history from 478 to 445, in addition to a detailed examination of the diplomatic and other preliminaries to the Peloponnesian war.

His historical method he has himself very fully explained (i, 21–22); the chapters are worthy of the most careful study, though here only a brief citation can be given.

Of the events of the war I have not ventured to speak from any information, nor according to any notion of my own; I have described nothing but what I either saw myself or learned from others of whom I made the most careful and particular inquiry. The task was a laborious one, because eye-witnesses of the same occurrences gave different accounts of them, as they remembered or were interested in the actions of one side or the other (i, 22).

It is difficult for a modern student to realize how remarkable, indeed how revolutionary, Thucydides' enunciation of what historical writing is, and what it should aim at, must have seemed in the historian's own day. The points he emphasizes are: (1) the difficulty of getting reliable information about the earlier history of Greece; (2) an equal difficulty, though due to different causes, of obtaining exact information about the events of the war itself; (3) his purpose and method in introducing speeches into his narrative; (4) the care he took to obtain accurate data himself. With regard to the first of these claims, Thucydides, instead of accepting the current legends and myths, has drawn a picture which, as we now know, corresponds in all essentials to reality. He knows of a period of migratory movements, when there were not yet settled political communities in Greece, and of a thalassocracy in the eastern Mediterranean, which he associates with the name of Minos. If he accepts the Trojan war as a historical occurrence, his contention is largely borne out by modern archæological discoveries. He goes on to trace the gradual evolution of more settled communities, and sketches the main features of Archaic Greece. A writer who could thus throw overboard popular beliefs and legends, and construct a rational account of early Greek history, in which the main factors are accurately appraised, including the importance of sea-power, commercial expansion, and the accumulation of wealth, would fill us with complete confidence in his veracity when he came to deal with contemporary events, even if we had not other means of checking his unflinching truthfulness. No part of his work has been so criticized and so misunderstood as the speeches which he puts in the mouth of the principal actors in the war or of the spokesmen of particular states. If we are convinced of his eminent love of truth, we cannot do other than accept his own statement concerning the speeches: [1]

> As for the speeches uttered by the several parties, either when about to make war, or when already in it, I was at a hard pass for the proper recollection of their words in simple exactness, whether heard by myself or by sundry others who recounted them to me; they are here expressed according as I supposed each person would have spoken what was most requisite for treating the actual matters before him; and I have adhered as closely as I could to the general purport of what was really said.

At the same time it is worth remembering that, though Thucydides did not allow literary art to get the better of his conception of historic truth, he was nevertheless profoundly influenced by the Sophistic movement of his day. To show his scrupulous care in narrating events, describing topography and so forth, in short, to demonstrate that he lived up to his own very high standards, it is enough to mention his account of the Plague, which is a model of what such an account should be; his description of Syracuse, which those who have gone over the ground acclaim a work of detailed precision; or the caution that he uses in dealing with figures. When he tells us (v, 68) how and why it is impossible to give the numbers engaged at the battle of Mantinea, we may regret the absence of the information,

---

[1] Thucydides, i, 22; the translation of these passages is from *Clio Enthroned* by W. R. M. Lamb.

a

b

ATHENS: *a.* Dionysiac Theatre; *b.* Temple of Olympian Zeus

Plate 32

a

b

ATHENS: *a.* MONUMENT OF LYSICRATES; *b.* HOROLOGIUM OF ANDRONICUS (So-called
Tower of the Winds)

Plate 33

but we are filled with respect, both for the reasons adduced by the historian for his silence, and for the critical faculty which would have nothing to do with vague guesses or partisan estimates.

Above all, Thucydides was the first to enunciate a philosophy of history. He set himself to determine the causes underlying the political actions of city-states, and of the men who directed their affairs. The motives and characters of the main actors in the war — Pericles, Cleon, Alcibiades, Nicias, Hermocrates of Syracuse — are made clear to us with a masterly hand and a masterly economy of words. So objective is Thucydides' treatment that he gives comments of his own only on the rarest occasions. The facts which he sets out, whether in the narrative or in the speeches uttered by these men, are sufficient clue to the understanding of their psychology. With their personal lives, and the trivialities dear to the biographer, he had no truck; it was their mental attitude, and the actions that sprang from it, which were his concern.

Much of the most modern criticism levelled against Thucydides is futile, and proceeds from the mistaken practice of importing the ideas of the nineteenth and twentieth centuries into the study of the ancients and their works. He is blamed, for example, for neglecting the social and economic history and conditions of his time, or for giving a one-sided account of the origins of the war. His achievement can properly be judged only in the light of the times and circumstances in which he lived. Estimated in this way he is easily the greatest of the ancient historians. Judged by the standards of our own time, his mental attitude and his methods, within the limits of his subject, still stand as a model for the true historical student who would conscientiously combine accurate inquiry with searching and unbiased criticism.

With the passing of Thucydides there was a marked decline in historical writing. What was intended as a continuation of Thucydides' book was given to the world by Xenophon in his *Hellenic History*. It, and his account of the March of the Ten Thousand (cf. p. 254), together record the history of Greece from 411 to 362. There are, however, a number of important omissions, of which one of the most striking is the early history of the Second Athenian Confederacy. From the literary point

of view these works, like his minor writings, are agreeable and
fluent. The *Anabasis*, moreover, has the vivid charm which
only an eye-witness, imbued with the spirit of adventure as
well as gifted with an easy pen, could attain. As a historical
writer Xenophon is honest, and strives to the best of his power
to be accurate; but he lacks the understanding, the philosophic
detachment, and the analytical power of his great predecessor.
Hence he fails as a whole to give a coherent picture of the period
with which he is dealing, and he is often at a loss to interpret
the political motives of the chief persons and governments at
that time.

Other fourth-century historians are known to us directly
from fragments, indirectly through their works being used by
compilers of a later age. The chief were Theopompus and
Ephorus, both pupils of Isocrates. Both were greatly influenced
by the political theories and the Panhellenic outlook of their
teacher; but the profounder influence was exerted on their
minds by the rhetorical training that they had received.
Theopompus composed a continuation of Thucydides, covering
the years from 410 to 394, but his greatest work was a history
of Philip II of Macedon, which was also in effect a history of
the Hellenic world during the middle of the fourth century.
Ephorus' work was in one sense more ambitious; it was a
general history of the Greeks from the earliest times down to
340 B.C. Both authors were extensively used by later writers,
a circumstance at least partly due to the fact that they were
attractive and easy to read. The writing of history had now,
under the influence of rhetoric, become a literary art; form and
expression were the prime consideration, to which historical
accuracy, criticism of sources, and unbiased judgment were
subordinated. The amusement of the reader, anxiety that he
should not be wearied by continuous application to the essential
subject of the work, which led to the introduction of amusing
or sensational anecdotes, or passages of fine writing empty of
content, impaired the dignity and true worth of historical
composition, a phenomenon not unfamiliar in our own day. In
addition there was often the aim of making historical works
serve a didactic purpose, the writer himself being influenced
by the teaching of this or that philosophic school. Thus there

was every reason why, from time to time in later centuries, a truly critical mind should group together the trio, Herodotus, Thucydides, and Xenophon, as the three outstanding historical writers of Greece.

The great development in prose writing in the fourth century was the direct outcome of the Sophistic movement. The Alexandrian critics of the following age, in their work of preserving and editing the texts of the great orators, established a canon of ten whom they regarded as of outstanding merit; among them we may mention Lysias, Demosthenes, and Isocrates. The century which, as we saw, was singularly poor in poetic output, produced a series of prose authors as eminent in their art as were the Attic dramatists in theirs. The writings of Plato and Demosthenes remained each in their kind unapproached and unapproachable by the Greeks of later centuries. In the field of oratory, one Latin writer alone, Cicero, deserves to be set side by side with Demosthenes.

The development of sculpture and architecture from the time of the Persian wars was no less rapid and striking than the progress of literature and thought. It is unfortunate that for our knowledge of the works and styles of the greatest artists we depend, apart from literary notices, almost entirely on later copies, which are of very unequal merit. On the other hand, for the fifth century, the sculptural remains of three temples provide a very fair index of artistic progress. The pedimental sculptures from the temple of Aphaia in Aegina belong to the first quarter of that century. They represent scenes from the Trojan war. The problem of adapting a group of figures to a triangular space has been successfully solved. The individual figures, though not altogether free from archaic stiffness, are immeasurably in advance of what sculptors of an earlier age had achieved in the lifelike presentation of motion. Every variety of pose is found there — figures at rest, archers kneeling and on the point of discharging their missiles, wounded warriors in the act of falling backwards or already stretched upon the ground in dying agony. Yet by the still somewhat conventional treatment of the faces we are reminded that we are viewing artistic products in the transition stage from lingering archaism to full mastery of an art.

Shortly before 450 B.C. the fine temple of Zeus at Olympia was completed. Of the building itself little remains beyond the ground-plan and the lowest drums of some columns (Plate 17b). It was a Doric temple of normal type, with six columns on the short and thirteen on the long sides. The sculptural decoration consisted of twelve metopes, six at the east and six at the west end, depicting the labors of Heracles. They are fine examples of relief sculpture, in which, however, the spirited presentation of the hero's sundry tasks is to some extent offset by stiffness in the treatment of detail. The author was probably a Peloponnesian artist, but he was certainly not the same who made the pedimental groups. These — their authorship, too, must remain uncertain — are notably greater in conception and execution, and must be ranked with the finest examples of ancient art. The scene represented on the eastern pediment was the chariot race between Pelops and Oenomaus; that on the western, the fight between the Lapiths and the Centaurs. The magnificent figure of a seer comes from the former, while the central figure of the west pediment is Apollo, an impressive portrayal of the nude male figure (Plates 22 and 23). When its poise and anatomical accuracy are contrasted with the nude male statues of the previous age, the immense advance, both artistically and technically, is at once apparent. The second half of the fifth century was marked at Athens by great building activity. With the construction of a new temple in honor of Athena on the Acropolis are linked the names of two of Athens' most distinguished artists, the architect Ictinus, and the sculptor Pheidias.

This temple, the Parthenon, was more or less completed by 438, having been begun nine years before. It was a Doric structure, with eight columns on the short and seventeen on the long sides (Plates 24 and 25). The continuous frieze above the walls of the cella was a non-Doric feature. The ornamentation of this noblest of Greek temples comprised forty-six metopes, forming part of the normal entablature of a Doric temple, and depicting scenes from various mythological episodes; the pedimental groups; and, finally, the frieze portraying the Panathenaic procession, to which reference was made in an earlier chapter (Plate 26). The mythological subjects of the east and west pediments were both specially appropriate to Athens and her patron goddess, Athena. On the east, the birth of Athena in the presence of the Olympian deities, on the west, the contest between Poseidon and Athena for the lordship over Attica, were plastically presented. Even in their present much damaged condition the surviving figures show the complete mastery which the artist had attained in every detail of his art. We may instance the superb modelling of the nude male figures, as in the recumbent figure of "Theseus" or the torso of Poseidon, and the elaborate drapery of the seated female figures. Though Pheidias may not have executed any part of the Parthenon sculptures himself, it is usually conceded that the general design is his, the execution being left to other artists working under his direction. Pheidias was famous above all for his portrayal of divinities, his two masterpieces being the gold and ivory statue of colossal size of Athena Parthenos, placed in the newly built temple on the Acropolis, and the statue of Zeus Olympios at Olympia. It is impossible to form any adequate conception of either of these works from late and small copies, or from coin representations.

If Pheidias was acclaimed the greatest sculptor of the fifth century — or according to some the greatest of all Greek sculptors — there were other artists of eminence second only to him. We may single out Myron the Athenian and Polycleitus the Argive. The former flourished in the first half of the fifth century, the latter was the somewhat younger contemporary of Pheidias. Both specialized particularly in athletic subjects and the portrayal of the nude male form. Polycleitus was noted also for his gold and ivory statue of Hera at Argos.

Another famous work of the architect Ictinus was the enlarged Telesterion at Eleusis. The great initiation-hall measured 170 feet square and was supported by six rows of seven Doric columns. Contemporary with the building of the Parthenon was the construction of the great entrance gateway to the Acropolis, the so-called Propylæa, the work of Mnesicles, begun in 437 and finished five years later. During the earlier part of the Peloponnesian war there was little further beautification of Athens; but toward the end of the century came the erection of the exquisite little temple to Athena Nike on the southwest

corner of the Acropolis and of the joint temple to Athena and
the hero Erechtheus, called the Erechtheum. In both these
buildings the Ionic order was used (Plates 25b and 27). A bold departure from convention was made by Ictinus in the third of his
great works, the temple of Apollo near Phigaleia in Arcadia.
The architect combined the Doric with the Ionic order by
introducing Ionic half-columns in the interior of the cella.
Between the last two — there were six on a side — was placed
a single Corinthian pillar. Though the effect was impressive,
the innovation was not generally copied. The artist Scopas,
however, in the next century combined all three orders in the
temple of Athena Alea in Arcadia.

Among the Greeks of Asia Minor the Ionic order remained the
favorite. Although the fifth century seems to have been a
period of artistic depression there, the fourth was marked by a
great revival of art. Two of the most famous temples of antiquity were the temple of Apollo at Didyma near Miletus and
the new temple, replacing the sixth-century structure, of Artemis
at Ephesus. A remarkable building in the Ionic style was the
tomb of Mausolus, native prince of Caria, who died in 352.
This lofty edifice was composed of a substructure 42 feet in
height, a cella surrounded by an Ionic colonnade and resting
on the substructure, and a stepped pyramid forming the roof
and crowning the whole. Many sculptures adorned this building, in the construction and decoration of which several of the
leading artists of Greece were said to have been employed.

The fourth century, like the fifth, produced many sculptors
of merit; but three, Praxiteles, Scopas, and Lysippus, surpassed
all the others. The first and second were approximately contemporaries, and their artistic activity belongs to the first half
of the century. From the hand of Praxiteles we possess one
undoubted original in the marble statue of Hermes holding the
infant Dionysus, which was found by the excavators at Olympia. Though reckoned a minor work in antiquity, the statue has
a unique interest and value for us in being an original. Contrasted with the athletic statues of Polycleitus, which, it is true,
are known only from copies, we note in the Hermes more grace-
ful proportions of the human figure together with a more
delicate treatment of the muscles and texture of the flesh. The

head is highly idealized, the perfection of Greek male beauty (Plate 29). Praxiteles' versatility was notorious in antiquity. He worked both in bronze and in marble, though more in the latter material, and the range of subjects depicted by him was unusually diversified. He made many statues of divinities, the most famous of all being his Aphrodite at Cnidus. It was an innovation to represent the nude female figure, above all in a goddess, who in this work is portrayed as preparing for the bath. Although the work is known to us only from copies, we can still admire the beauty of the head — a worthy peer of the Hermes — and the grace of the pose, the modelling of the flesh, and the skillful treatment of the drapery which the goddess is allowing to glide down on to the hydria at her side. A fine example, by an unknown artist, of a draped female figure of the fourth century is provided by the statue of Demeter now in the British Museum (Plate 30).

Of Scopas, besides his work on the temple at Alea, far fewer works are recorded than in the case of his contemporary. Among the most successful of his creations was a Bacchant portrayed in a state of Dionysiac frenzy. The ancient writers stress Scopas' skill in depicting passion and emotional depth in his figures. He seems thus to have been, in a sense, the ancestor of the greater realism in art, sometimes transcending what can safely be attempted in sculpture without grotesqueness, which characterized many of the productions of the Hellenistic Age.

Lysippus was the contemporary of Alexander the Great, of whom he made many portraits in bronze; extant busts of the great conqueror are probably all to some extent reminiscent of Lysippean originals (Plate 34). The artist, who is the best representative of the Peloponnesian art of the fourth century — Praxiteles was an Athenian, Scopas a native of Paros — was extremely prolific. His statue of Poseidon became, as it were, the canonical representation of that deity, even as Pheidias had made the ideal types of Athena and Zeus, and Polycleitus of Hera. Besides his portraits and his statues of divinities, Lysippus was also the creator of many athletic figures.

The authorship of the so-called Alexander sarcophagus (Plate 31) is not known. It was found at Sidon in 1887 and is a glorious specimen of fourth-century work. On the two long sides are represented a battle between Alexander and the Persians, and a lion hunt. The short sides are adorned with hunting scenes; in the gables of the lid were other scenes from war. The whole was elaborately colored, a practice followed by the Greeks, as we saw, from early times, both for their marble statues and on certain parts of temples.

It is a remarkable fact that the age which saw a great decline in dramatic composition was characterized by more luxurious theatre-building. In the fifth century the masterpieces of the great poets were performed in temporary structures, built mostly of wood. The fine stone theatres, of which a number are still to be seen in Greek lands, belong to the fourth century or to the Hellenistic Age. One of the earliest, and in point of preservation the finest of all, is that at Epidaurus, the work of Polycleitus the younger. The stone theatre at Athens belongs to the second half of the century, although parts of what can still be seen — for instance the tessellated floor of the orchestra — are of much later, that is of Græco-Roman, date (Plate 32a). Other fourth-century examples are the large theatre at Megalepolis and the smaller structure at Thoricus in Attica. Those at Priene in Asia Minor and at Delos are Hellenistic.

Of the great painters in these centuries — Polygnotus in the first half, Zeuxis and Parrhasius in the second half of the fifth century, Apelles in the age of Alexander — we know too little to permit of any definite judgment on their art. The humbler art of the Attic vase-painters, however, can still be studied in all its detail by the specialist. It reached its zenith in the fifth century. The so-called red-figure vases show extreme beauty and great variety in their shapes. The designs were now commonly carried out by a different artist, and are distinguished by marvellous skill in the portrayal of muscles, draperies, and every kind of pose and action. There is, too, an all but infinite diversity of subjects depicted: mythological episodes in endless profusion; scenes from daily life; for example, the school, the palæstra, the banquet, Dionysiac revels, and other kinds of religious celebration. The popularity of the works of the Attic potters and vase-painters was maintained throughout the fifth and into the fourth century, but the later specimens, though they exhibit no less skill, in addition to innovations in treatment, brighter coloration by the use of subsidiary colors, and more abundant ornamentation, lack the freshness and naturalism of the best fifth-century works. Then, in the fourth century, the Athenian ceramic industry declined. The most productive and successful centres of manufacture in that century and the next were to be found in the West, in the Greek cities of southern Italy.

CHAPTER XVIII

THE GREEK WORLD UNDER ALEXANDER AND HIS SUCCESSORS

The Stoic state is directed to this one all-embracing principle, that we should not order our lives by cities and by parishes, and our outlook should not be determined by our several private interests, but we should regard all men as fellow citizens and fellow townsmen, and there should be one single life and world, as it were, one gregarious flock reared in common by a common Law. This is the ideal laid down by Zeno, imagined by him as a dream or image of a philosophic good order and state: but Alexander added the deed to the word.
— Plutarch, *On the excellence of Alexander* i, 6.

WHEN he succeeded to the throne, Alexander, then only twenty years of age, was faced almost at once with a situation which would have tested to the utmost the resources of a mature man. But over and above his own transcendent natural gifts, he had had the ideal education of a prince and had shouldered responsibility at an exceptionally early age. From the time that he was thirteen he had had Aristotle as his tutor. Thus, besides his training in physical and military exercises and in hunting, in all of which he excelled from early youth, his intellectual education was directed by the profoundest thinker of the age. Already at sixteen Alexander had been entrusted with a position of authority, while at Chæronea he had fought with conspicuous bravery and success. Philip's death was the signal for general unrest in Greece; it needed only the appearance of Alexander at the head of a military force to suppress for the time being the anti-Macedonian feelings there. He was formally elected as his father's successor in the Amphictionic League, and also as commander-in-chief of the League of Corinth. Early in 335 B.C. he conducted difficult campaigns in the interior of Thrace, which took him as far as the Danube,

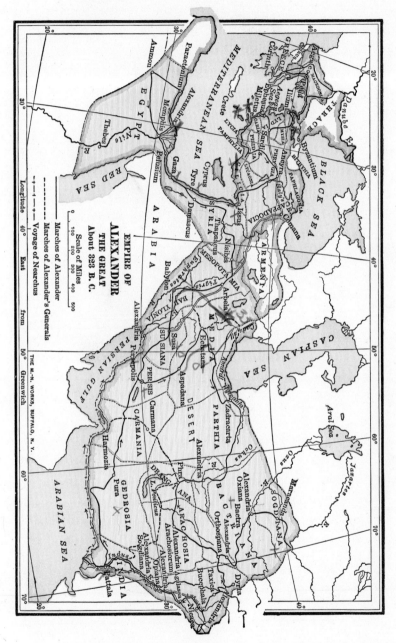

EMPIRE OF
ALEXANDER
THE GREAT
About 323 B. C.

Scale of Miles
0 100 200 300 400 500

———————— Marches of Alexander
-------------- Marches of Alexander's Generals
—+—+—+— Voyage of Nearchus

Longitude   40°   East   from   50°   Greenwich
                30°   50°

THE M.-N. WORKS, BUFFALO, N. Y.

and he also suppressed an Illyrian rising. A false rumor of his death reaching Greece was at once followed by the revolt of Thebes. Alexander's swift descent on that city stopped the progress of the Greek insurrection. The disloyal city was captured and razed to the ground; its people were sold as slaves.

The young ruler now prepared to carry out his father's plans for a war against Persia and for the conquest of Asia Minor. In the spring of 334 he crossed the Hellespont with an army of not less than 30,000 infantry and 5000 cavalry, drawn from Macedonia, the Greek cities of the League, and from some other regions. On the River Granicus he won his first victory against a decidedly smaller Persian army, commanded by the Great King's ablest officer, Memnon. Many of the Greek cities in Asia Minor readily went over to Alexander. In general his approval of democratic governments brought about the downfall of the Tyrants or oligarchies who had ruled under Persian suzerainty. But the conquest of Asia Minor — or the greater portion of it — did not pass off without much fighting. Miletus and Halicarnassus were both captured only after a siege. His fleet, recruited from the allied Greeks, Alexander now dismissed, leaving the Persian navy at large in the Aegean. But his calculation that it would effect little damage to his interests or his lines of communication, and, especially, that Persian attempts to draw the Greek states of the islands and the mainland on to a general anti-Macedonian rebellion would prove futile, was correct. In 333, after conquering Cilicia, he descended into northern Syria, where he found his progress barred by a Persian host, commanded by Darius III in person. The size of the forces engaged in this great battle near Issus was greatly exaggerated in antiquity, and cannot be determined with any certainty. Alexander's army must have been slightly smaller than that which fought at the River Granicus. For, though he had received reinforcements, he had also been obliged to leave some garrison troops in Asia Minor. Hence it can hardly have numbered much over 25,000 men all told. The army of Darius, composed partly of orientals, partly of Greek mercenaries, was perhaps 30,000–35,000 strong. Although the Great King had won a tactical advantage in choosing the site

where he compelled the Macedonians to fight, neither he nor
his staff were Alexander's equals as strategists in the actual
battle. The Persian guard and the Greek mercenaries put up
a good fight, but the flight of Darius was followed by a general
break-up and pell-mell retreat of his army. It was a great
victory for Alexander, and its political consequences were far-
reaching. The disaffection, which was still latent in Greece and
which might well have burst forth into a general revolt against
Macedonian overlordship, such as Alexander's regent, Antipater, would have found it difficult to suppress from Macedonia
with the limited troops at his disposal, was succeeded by wiser
counsels when the news of Alexander's triumph at Issus became
known. The Syrian and Egyptian provinces of the Persian
empire, for their part, were far from being genuinely loyal to
Darius. The realization of this fact must have weighed heavily
with Alexander, who, as is probable, now and now only envisaged as a possibility the conquest of the Persian empire.

Save for two places, Syria passed into his hands without
resistance. But Tyre and Gaza stood out and had to be reduced
by force. The siege of Tyre, which lasted for seven months,
was one of Alexander's greatest achievements. The defenders,
whose city stood on an island, expended all their skill and
ingenuity in beating off the Macedonian attack; but each new
defensive measure Alexander countered by fresh devices.
Finally, after the Tyrian fleet had been destroyed or captured,
a grand assault was made and part of the wall breached. As
the men of Tyre had slain some Macedonian prisoners they
could expect no mercy at the hands of the victorious enemy.
After the slaughter of the fighting men and the sale of the non-
combatants into slavery, Tyre was occupied by a Macedonian
garrison. Later in the year Gaza also fell after a spirited resistance. Egypt passed into Alexander's power without a struggle;
for the Persian governor, knowing that the people were disaffected
to Persia, took no risks and surrendered at once to the conqueror.
The most momentous event of his visit to Egypt was the foundation of the city of Alexandria on the Egyptian coast, close
to the Canopic mouth of the Nile. It was the first, and proved
to be the greatest, of the numerous settlements established by,
and in this, as in many other cases, named after Alexander.

BUST OF ALEXANDER THE GREAT

Plate 34

If, in the first place, the new city was intended to replace Tyre as the great harbor and exchange mart between East and West, it is not unlikely that the founder to some extent foresaw that its admirable situation would quickly make it the foremost port in the whole Mediterranean.   Alexander's visit to the desert and oasis, where was situated the oracle of Amen, who was identified with Zeus by the Greeks and whose prophecies were regarded with peculiar veneration, was a romantic episode rather than a profound act of policy.   Yet the Egyptian priests, seeing in him the successor of the Pharaohs, acknowledged him as the son of Amen-Ra, in other words as a god and the son of a god.

Meanwhile the terms which had been proposed by Darius III had been rejected by Alexander; and in the spring of 331 he returned to Syria. From there he advanced to Mesopotamia, crossing the Euphrates and then the Tigris without encountering serious opposition. The Great King, instead of trying to bar his progress at the Euphrates, had mustered an army considerably greater than that which fought at Issus in a level plain between the Tigris and a tributary. The third of the engagements between Alexander and the Persians was fought on October 1, 331, and derives its name from the small village of Gaugamela close to the battle-field, or, alternatively, from the more considerable town of Arbela, some miles to the southeast. The battle was stubbornly contested; but, as in the previous year, with the flight of Darius himself, once it became known, the Persian lines gave way and a general pursuit by the victors followed. While the defeated monarch fled into Media, the conqueror marched on Babylon, which opened its gates to him. From there he undertook the invasion of Persis, and, after defeating the satrap Ariobarzanes, captured Persepolis and Pasargadæ. In these royal residences, as in the capital at Susa, which had already submitted, he secured immense quantities of silver and other spoil. In the spring of 330 he entered Media; having received the submission of Ecbatana, he hastened on in pursuit of Darius, who was now the virtual prisoner of Bessus, satrap of Bactria. Soon after, the Persian king was killed by his companions before Alexander could seize his person. The assassins escaped.

From 330 to 328 Alexander was fully occupied with the difficult task of conquering the northeastern provinces of the empire. By the victory at Gaugamela, followed by the death of Darius, he had been accepted as the successor of the Persian kings; but in the more outlying regions there was still much resistance to be overcome. His campaigns in these years took him as far east as Bactria and Sogdiana, that is to say, to Afghanistan and Turkestan. His chief opponents were Bessus, who had assumed the kingly title after Darius' death, and Spitamenes of Sogdiana, whose military skill gave Alexander more trouble than that of any other opponent. By the end of 328 both had been reduced. Alexander's progress through these distant regions was marked by the foundation of many new settlements and colonies, whose importance for the subsequent spread of Hellenism was incalculable.

In 327 his restless ambition led him to invade northern India. Of the many princes in this country some allied themselves with him, others opposed his passage. Of the latter the most notable was King Porus who confronted him with a large host on the Hydaspes (Jhelum) river. He was defeated; but, after surrendering, he was reinstated in his kingdom and became Alexander's ally. Soon after the further progress of the Macedonian conqueror was brought to an abrupt end by the action of his troops. Wearied by the strain of continuous campaigns in exceptionally difficult country, and exhausted also by the severity of an unfamiliar climate, they refused to march on into unknown regions. Alexander could not but yield, and so he made his way to Patala near the mouth of the Indus. On the way he fought a campaign against the Malli, in the course of which he contracted a wound which was nearly fatal. From Patala Alexander led his army through the Gedrosian desert (Baluchistan), while his admiral Nearchus was sent in charge of the fleet, which had been built on the Jhelum at the beginning of the Indian campaign, to explore the sea-route to the head of the Persian gulf and the mouths of the Tigris and Euphrates. The record of observations, which the admiral took along the whole coast as he skirted it, were of great practical value, as Alexander had intended them to be. For his purpose was to develop for commerce a direct sea-route between the estuary of the Indus and the Euphrates. The return of the army was attended by terrible casualties, since, owing to the heat and lack of water, many of his men dropped on the road and failed to rise again. It was but a remnant of his army which at last reached the region of Carmania safely.

During the year 324, which Alexander passed partly at Susa, partly at Opis on the Tigris, and at Ecbatana, he was busy mainly with problems of imperial organization, and under the necessity of rectifying abuses which had crept into the administration during his prolonged absence in the Far East. Early in 323 he moved to Babylon and now elaborated plans for an Arabian expedition. But in June he contracted a fever from which, worn out as he was by his tremendous exertions, not by the intemperance which later detractors with insufficient proof have attributed to him, he never recovered. After nearly a fortnight's illness he died in the thirty-third year of his age.

In all the ancient accounts of Alexander his military achievements are narrated with more or less detail, and, according to the sources used, with very varying degrees of accuracy. Concerning his eminence as a general ancients and moderns are agreed. As one scholar has recently observed, "that he was a great general is certain; Napoleon's verdict suffices." [1] We may cite, too, the verdict of a great nineteenth-century historian of Greece: [2]

We trace in all his operations the most careful dispositions taken beforehand, vigilant precaution in guarding against possible reverse, and abundant resource in adapting himself to new contingencies. Amidst constant success, these precautionary combinations were never discontinued. His achievements are the earliest recorded evidence of scientific military organization on a large scale and of its overwhelming effects.

Of what Alexander actually accomplished in the way of organizing his huge empire, and of his further plans to weld it together, we hear but little. Even the work of conquest was incomplete at the time of his death; for example, northern Asia

[1] W. W. Tarn in *Cambridge Ancient History*, vi, p. 425. His chapters are now easily the best account in English of Alexander's career.
[2] G. Grote, *History of Greece*, xii, chap. 94.

Minor as far as the Caspian Sea, together with Armenia, all territory which had formed part of the Persian empire, had been left untouched by him. Nor had there been time for the conqueror to devise any permanent system of imperial government. The absence of this, coupled with the withdrawal of Alexander's unique personality, which alone had held a vast empire together, after his death resulted in the immediate partition of these dominions. Nor can it be said that his temporary measures for ruling the former Persian empire were greatly successful. As in Persian days, the territories were divided into provinces or satrapies, and at first some positions of high authority were entrusted to Persians as well as to Macedonians. But this plan did not work out well, and the king was obliged to replace oriental by western governors. But even the Macedonian officials, whom he left in charge in western Asia and in Mesopotamia during his progress to central Asia and India, proved in many cases unworthy of this trust, having been guilty of peculation and worse forms of misrule. The most notorious offender was Harpalus, who had been left in charge of the royal treasury at Babylon. After a riotous career there, Harpalus, having embezzled a vast sum, retired to Tarsus, and, finally, with the remnants of his spoil fled to Greece. Thus, when Alexander returned from India, he found it necessary to make many changes in his administrative personnel.

In the course of his advance eastward he had founded many new cities, most of them being half Graeco-Macedonian, half oriental in population. These, of which there are said to have been no less than seventy, were important for insuring the security of the empire; still more, however, Alexander wished their function to be the dissemination of Hellenic culture in the Orient. His efforts to fuse the inhabitants of East and West more completely by promoting the intermarriage of Macedonians or Greeks with Iranians, and by creating corps of oriental troops carefully trained on the Macedonian model, had little permanent effect. Such drastic measures were doomed to failure, whereas the gradual spread of Greek ideas and customs and, in many of the cities, of Greek law, continued undisturbed in the centuries that followed. Of immense value for promoting commercial intercourse between different parts of the empire were his monetary reforms. He introduced a uniform silver currency throughout his vast realm, adopting the Attic standard for the purpose, and abolishing the gold standard of Persia. His silver coins were issued from a large number of mints in different parts of the empire; in a few cases he appears to have permitted older local issues to continue for a space.

There was one aspect of Alexander's policy which gave serious offense to some of his Macedonian subjects, and which at the same time had important developments in the Hellenistic Age. The heroization of dead persons was a very ancient form of religious practice in Greece; isolated instances are recorded, at all events in the fourth century, of divine or semi-divine honors being paid to a living personage, for example, to Lysander by the people of Samos. But the deification of the reigning monarch, which Alexander demanded of the Greek cities in 324, when he asked them to honor him as a divine being, was to introduce into Hellas what was essentially an eastern conception and usage. The theocracy of the Egyptian kings has already been noted; in Persia, though the ruler was not deified, Darius and his successors described themselves as under the protection of Ahura-Mazda.[1] Moreover, the servile adoration which they demanded and received from their subjects would be construed by westerners as a mark of divinity. The earlier stages in Alexander's progress towards this un-Hellenic claim to divine kingship, which should be regarded as a matter of considered policy and not the result of vanity, still less of religious exaltation, were the adoption of oriental dress, of Persian court etiquette, and, finally, of the Persian custom of prostration, to which even his Macedonian staff-officers were expected to conform.

In 330 a conspiracy was detected, and Philotas, who commanded the pick of the Macedonian cavalry, was implicated; after a summary trial he was put to death. While some excuse can be brought forward for this action of the king, his subsequent order for the execution of Philotas' father, Parmenion, was a crime. For, not only was Parmenion one of the oldest and most trusted of Macedonian commanders, — he had been one of Philip's chief supporters, — but there was no evidence to con-

[1] Cf. the citation at the beginning of Chapter XII above.

nect him with the attempted treason. The murder, in a fit of passion, of Cleitus, a trusted officer who had once saved Alexander's life, and the execution of Aristotle's nephew, Callisthenes, who was the court historian, for supposed cognizance of a later conspiracy, were other episodes which have marred the fair fame of the conqueror. These abuses of royal power were due to personal rather than political motives; in the case of Philotas it is likely that reasons of state determined Alexander's action.

Many writers have speculated on what might have happened, had Alexander's life been prolonged, and it has often been argued that his eastern conquests would have been followed by the reduction of Carthage and of Italy, where Rome was by that time the leading state. Not only are such speculations futile in themselves, but they presuppose something for which the evidence is lacking. For we have no grounds for believing that, even as late as 323, Alexander had ever conceived the notion of becoming a world conqueror. His projected Arabian expedition is thoroughly attested; but, had it taken place, it would only have rounded off his Asiatic conquests. Of any further plans we know nothing.

The unity of the empire ceased abruptly on his death. Nominally the crown passed to the late ruler's feeble-minded brother, Philip Arrhidæus; a little later the son of Alexander and Roxane was born, and was associated with his uncle as joint monarch. In reality, political power rested with the chief military commanders and provincial governors, the men who had been Alexander's most trusted helpers. Of these the most notable were Antipater, who had been left behind as regent of Macedonia and Greece; Antigonus, governor of Phrygia; and the army commanders at Babylon, — Perdiccas, Ptolemy, Lysimachus, Eumenes, and Craterus. For the moment Perdiccas secured the regency. But there were too many claimants for the chief authority to make a peaceful division of the empire possible, still less to preserve its unity under a single ruler. From the first we can distinguish certain groups which stood together; thus, Antigonus, Ptolemy, and Craterus were in agreement with Antipater, while Eumenes supported Perdiccas. Before the end of 321 fighting had begun.

Craterus was slain in battle, and Perdiccas was murdered by his own troops. A partition of provinces and a division of responsibility followed, but it was of short duration. For, two years later, Antipater died at an advanced age, and the struggle was renewed with more intensity than before. It will suffice to indicate very briefly the main stages in the prolonged warfare between the successors of Alexander from 319 to 281.

During the first twenty years of this period the outstanding personality was Antigonus, who gradually built up for himself a position of exceptional strength. Controlling after a few years Asia Minor, Syria, and Mesopotamia, and master of the royal treasury, he was well on the way toward uniting under his single command the greater part of Alexander's empire. But his successes produced a coalition of rival aspirants for power, who might otherwise have played only for their own hands. Chief of these were Cassander, Antipater's son and now ruler of Macedonia; Lysimachus, governor of Thrace and the Propontis; Ptolemy Lagus, viceroy of Egypt; and Seleucus, who in 321 had obtained the satrapy of Babylon, had subsequently been expelled by Antigonus, and who now joined his enemies. In 312 Seleucus recovered Babylon, and, though he did not yet assume the royal title, the dynasty of which he became the founder dated its origin back to that year.[1]

Supported by his son Demetrius, Antigonus carried on against his rivals with varying fortunes to the year 301. His army, commanded by Demetrius, suffered a severe defeat at Gaza in 312, fighting against the forces of Ptolemy. Six years later Demetrius had his revenge; for he beat an Egyptian fleet off Cypriote Salamis, and followed up this success by occupying the whole island. In the same year, and to commemorate this victory, Antigonus assumed the royal title. His rivals followed suit. Finally, in 301, the armies of Seleucus and Lysimachus won a striking victory over Antigonus' hosts at Ipsus in Phrygia. The defeated monarch, rather than live to endure a diminution of his fortunes, took his own life on the field of battle. The five monarchies into which Alexander's empire had thus been broken up were now reduced to four. Of Anti-

---

[1] For the so-called Seleucid Era see above, p. 8.

gonus' realm one part, Asia Minor, fell to Lysimachus' share, while Syria was annexed by Seleucus. Demetrius, legitimate heir of Antigonus, remained without a kingdom, but the powerful fleet which he still commanded made him master of the Mediterranean, and enabled him to control the islands and some important sea-port towns. Thus there was little chance that the death of Antigonus would be followed by a cessation of war. Actually the struggles were prolonged for twenty years after Ipsus. With the defeat and death of Lysimachus at the battle of Curupedium (Lydia) in 281 Seleucus became master of Asia Minor. Though he himself was assassinated shortly after, his son Antiochus now ruled over what territorially was the greatest of the three remaining Hellenistic kingdoms.

During this half century after Alexander's death the fortunes of the Greeks, both in Hellas and in the West, had been varied and troubled. The mainland states for the most part were now but pawns in the ruthless game played by their more powerful royal neighbors. The discontent of the Greek city-states had been smouldering ever since Philip II's death. We saw how Thebes had received short shrift, and how the success of Alexander at Issus had damped the spirits of even the most ardent anti-Macedonian patriots. An attempted insurrection by Sparta about the same time was a complete failure. At Athens the years following Chæronea were marked by considerable prosperity, mainly owing to the careful financial administration of Demosthenes' younger contemporary, Lycurgus. The prosecution of a certain Ctesiphon for illegality, in proposing that Demosthenes be rewarded with a gold crown for his patriotism in the struggle against Macedonia, was the *cause célèbre* of 330. Demosthenes undertook the defense, while his old antagonist, Aeschines, acted as prosecutor, and his attack was really aimed at Demosthenes, rather than at Ctesiphon. The trial is only of interest now because the speeches of the two rivals have survived, and because Demosthenes' oration, *On the Crown*, which is in reality a defense of his whole political career, is perhaps the finest of all his utterances. Aeschines lost his case, and retiring from Athens, soon after died.

Of a very different character was the scandal which arose at

Athens in 324.   Harpalus, Alexander's dishonest treasurer, on reaching Greece, tried to foment an anti-Macedonian rebellion. The Athenians detained Harpalus and deposited what was left of his treasure, amounting to a very considerable sum, in the Parthenon.   Within a short time Harpalus escaped, and it was further discovered that half of the bullion had disappeared.   Several prominent persons, among them Demosthenes, were arraigned before the court of the Areopagus for accepting bribes.   Demosthenes, with two other leading men, was found guilty and heavily fined, but, being unable to comply, he went into banishment at Aegina.   The circumstances surrounding this trial are very obscure, and the guilt or innocence of the great Athenian patriot cannot now be established with any certainty.   If he did accept money, we can at least feel sure that he did so from political purposes, not for his personal enrichment.   His exile was of short duration.   For, when the news of Alexander's death reached Athens and Greece, a general insurrection broke out through the country, in which the Athenians and the Aetolians took the lead.   For his patriotic exertions on behalf of the allied Hellenic cause Demosthenes was recalled to his native city.   It devolved on Antipater to stamp out this rebellion; but against so large a muster of opponents his forces were inadequate.   He suffered a defeat in the field, and was then driven back on Lamia in southern Thessaly, where he was besieged through the winter of 323–322. But the Greeks failed to make the best of their opportunities. Reinforcements for the Macedonian viceroy arrived from Asia, and within a few months the tables had been turned.   The Athenian navy suffered two defeats, and in the summer of 322 the allies were heavily beaten at Crannon in Thessaly.   For Athens the terms that she was now compelled to accept were bitter.   A Macedonian garrison was sent to occupy Munychia; the democratic constitution was abrogated and replaced by a moderate oligarchy, in which only some 9000 of her propertied citizens had full civic rights.   Finally, she was obliged to surrender the most prominent of her anti-Macedonian leaders, among them Demosthenes.   But he anticipated capture and certain condemnation to death by committing suicide.

The mainland states, being naturally regarded by the rulers

of Macedon as dependents of that kingdom, were now constantly involved in the greater disputes of the successors of Alexander. For the enemies of Cassander found one means of undermining his power in trying to foster an anti-Macedonian coalition in Hellas.   After Cassander's death the Macedonian crown passed to several princes in rapid succession, and in these wars, too, at least a part of the Greeks were more than neutral spectators.   The political life of Athens was especially stormy during these years.   Not long after Antipater's settlement civil disturbances there led to changes of government, until in 317 the city passed under the able administration of Demetrius of Phalerum. He owed his position, and the maintenance of it for ten years, to the close support of Cassander and the continued presence of a Macedonian garrison in Munychia. Though he was regarded by many as a Tyrant under another name, the decade of his administration was one of peace and prosperity for the Athenians. But in 307 the city was taken by Demetrius, nicknamed "the besieger of cities" (Poliorketes), the son of Antigonus. He was hailed by the Athenians as a liberator because he permitted them to restore their democratic régime.   The city now became one of the chief prizes in the contest between Demetrius Poliorketes and Cassander for the control of Greece, and its history was correspondingly troubled. In 303, when Demetrius' power was at its height, he revived under the presidency of his father and himself the Hellenic League of Corinth created by Philip II thirty-five years before. The disaster at Ipsus in 301 reacted strongly on the political situation in Greece, and the League rapidly went to pieces. For thirty-eight more years the Athenians, amid varying fortunes, maintained a partial political independence; finally they succumbed before a new Macedonian ruler in the so-called Chremonidean war, — it was named after a leading Athenian politician, Chremonides, — and from 263 their city became virtually a Macedonian outpost in Greece.

Of the greater Hellenistic kingdoms Egypt was the most secure, and its kings, the Ptolemies, though they suffered occasional reverses at the hands of their rivals, were safe in the possession of the country, sheltered by a powerful fleet. For a time they were masters also of southern Syria and overlords over a number of communities in the Aegean. Internally, Egypt, as will subsequently appear, in the third century enjoyed a period of astonishing prosperity, while the capital, Alexandria, besides its commercial preëminence became a centre of scientific and intellectual activity. The great empire of Seleucus and his son Antiochus was too far-flung to endure in its entirety. In Asia Minor several independent states came into being under local princes, although their political fortunes were inevitably linked to some extent with those of their more powerful neighbors. Such minor kingdoms or principalities were Armenia, Pontus, Bithynia, and Cappadocia.

There is a certain element of romance in the meteoric rise to power of Pergamum in northwestern Asia Minor and of its rulers. This strongly fortified city had for a space been held by Lysimachus; but its governor, Philetærus, had gone over to Seleucus in 281, subsequently becoming the acknowledged ruler of the city and a vassal of Syria. Moreover, the Syrian king left him in possession of the abundant treasure stored in the city by Lysimachus. During the eighteen years of his rule Philetærus continued on good terms with Syria; at the same time he used his wealth to cement good relations with his Greek neighbors on the coast and to build up a strong military force composed of mercenaries. His successor, Eumenes, after defeating a Syrian army in the field, attained complete political independence. Under him and later rulers the territory of Pergamum was steadily enlarged, and Pergamum became the strongest, as well as the richest, of the lesser kingdoms of the Near East. It was the shrewd policy of its rulers to watch with care the political moves of the three greater monarchies, Egypt, Syria, and Macedon, and, by their adherence to one side or another, to exert a decisive influence on the course of international affairs.[1]

The far-eastern or central Asiatic portions of the old Persian empire also became separate states by the middle of the third century. Most noteworthy were the kingdom of Bactria, and especially the realm formed out of the old territories of Persis and Media by the Parthians, a half-civilized Iranian people of

[1] Attalus I, the successor of Eumenes, was the first Pergamene ruler to assume the title of king.

whom little is heard before this date. This Parthian kingdom was, however, destined to develop into a great empire, the rival of Rome for the control of the Near and Middle East.

As if the confusion on both sides of the Aegean caused by the warring ambitions of rival monarchs were not enough, a new and unexpected complication in the political situation was produced by the invasions of the Celts or Gauls — the Greeks called them Galatæ — in 279 and the following years. While one horde overran Macedonia in 279, and northern central Greece as far as Delphi in 278, other tribes invaded Thrace and Asia Minor. In Greece the chief credit for defeating and then expelling the enemy belonged to the Aetolians. In Asia Minor the Gaulish marauders tarried longer, and finally settled in northern Phrygia, or, as it now came to be called, Galatia. In Thrace Antigonus Gonatas, son of Demetrius Poliorketes, defeated the Celts in 277. Till then he had only some possessions which his father had held in Greece. But, after his striking victory, he entered Macedonia and secured the throne, which his father had held before him for a brief period, in 276. The founder of a new Macedonian dynasty had to fight hard for a dozen years to maintain his position. At first he was attacked and all but expelled by Pyrrhus of Epirus, a region which, after being a Macedonian dependency for many years, had under the rule of this able prince become a formidable and independent military power.[1] Pyrrhus was killed fighting in Greece in 272; but not long afterward Antigonus' resources were strained to the utmost by a war against Egypt and a coalition of Hellenic states, of which Athens was the chief (266–262), the Chremonidean war to which reference has already been made. Although the later years of his reign — he died in 239 — were seldom free from war, Antigonus made of Macedonia a great and united kingdom, such as it had not been since the days of Philip and Alexander. His suzerainty over a great portion of Greece, secured after the Chremonidean war, did not remain unshaken.

The most formidable obstacle to a united Greek confederation under Macedonian overlordship were two leagues, whose growth in the third century was one of the most interesting

[1] For the Greeks of the West after the time of Timoleon and for Pyrrhus' operations in Italy and Sicily see below, p. 382.

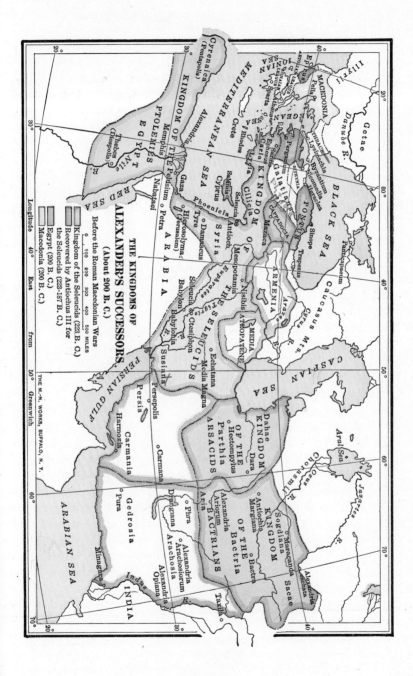

THE KINGDOMS OF
ALEXANDER'S SUCCESSORS
(About 200 B. C.)

Before the Roman Macedonian Wars

0   100   200   300   400   500 MILES

Kingdom of the Seleucids (223 B. C.)
Recovered by Antiochus III for
the Seleucids (223-187 B. C.)
Egypt (200 B. C.)
Macedonia (200 B. C.)

Longitude 40°   East   from   50° Greenwich

THE M.-N. WORKS, BUFFALO, N. Y.

political developments in Greek history. Allusion has been made to the Aetolian League, and its services to Greece at the time of the Gaulish invasions. Aetolia, which during the fifth and most of the fourth century was culturally and politically one of the most backward parts of Greece, had even at the time of Alexander's death no considerable towns. The league of its inhabitants, formed originally for military defense, was thus at first composed of a number of cantons or rural districts. Gradually larger towns began to grow up out of the villages, so that when the Aetolian League was at its height, from c. 279 onwards, it had to a great extent been converted into a federal union of cities. By the second half of the third century the League controlled either directly, by enlarging its federal membership, or indirectly, by various forms of alliance, all central Greece from the Maliac gulf to the Gulf of Corinth and the mouth of the Achelous, southern Thessaly, and at various times a number of cities lying outside that area.

The Achæan League began in a small way as a federation of a few cities. Of these there were ten in 272; but another quarter of a century elapsed before this federal union began to have much more than local importance. In 251 the city of Sicyon, which had been ruled for some time by a Tyrant, was liberated from despotic misrule through the energy of one of her exiled citizens, Aratus. Sicyon now joined the Achæan League, and her example was followed by other cities outside the geographical area known as Achæa, namely by Megara, Troizen, Epidaurus, and Corinth. Moreover, Aratus became the leading spirit of the enlarged League and remained so for over twenty years, being reëlected every other year to the chief executive magistracy, with which was combined the commandership-in-chief in war.

These two Leagues, and especially the Achæan, about which we are somewhat more fully informed, have deservedly aroused the interest and sympathy of students of history and political science, since they were true examples of federal union, and, as such, can claim to be the most elaborate political organisms known in the ancient world. In the Aetolian League all citizens of the constituent cities or districts were members of the federal assembly, which elected the federal magistrates and officials.

Of these the chief was called *strategos;* he was both the civil and the military head of the League, held office for one year, but could be reëlected after an interval. The assembly was the sovereign power of the League, and remained so throughout, to the extent of performing its electoral functions and deciding questions of peace and war. But for other purposes, as the size of the organization grew, it became impracticable to leave business to a large body which met only twice a year. Hence a small group of persons, called *apokletoi*, collaborated permanently with the *strategos* and the other magistrates. There was also a council, whose members were chosen by the assembly to represent the constituent cities proportionately to their military strength. This council does not appear to have exercised much authority; the *apokletoi*, however, were chosen from among its members.

The Achæan League, too, may originally have had both an assembly and a council. But in the period of its greatest prosperity the two important bodies which decided its affairs were the *synodos* and the *synkletos*. The former seems to have been composed of delegates from all the constituent states, appointed by the respective cities in proportion to their size and importance. Whereas the general policy and business of the League were decided by this meeting of delegates, certain questions involving relations with other states, and decisions about peace and war, were left to the *synkletos*, which was in effect an assembly of all citizens over thirty years of age. The executive was in the hands of the *strategos*, who could be reëlected every other year, but not annually, and some other magistrates, together with ten *demiourgoi*, whose duties must have approximated to those of the Aetolian *apokletoi*. In both Leagues, finally, the constituent communities were independent states with their own constitutions and law-courts. In the Achæan League we even find individual cities issuing their own currency, though there was also a federal coinage.

Unfortunately there were several factors which militated against the efficiency of these two organizations, and prevented them from being politically as influential, and in military affairs as potent, as they should have been. During a great part of their history the two Leagues were hostile to one another;

and, while the Aetolians were for a number of years the allies of Macedon, it was the policy of Aratus, at least for a time, to seek the friendship and support of Egypt. Too much was left to the constituent cities, since there was no adequate administrative machinery for federal business. Thus, the fact that it was left to each city in time of war to levy and maintain its own contingent of troops impaired the League's military efficiency, and added greatly to the difficulties of the *strategos*. In the Achæan League, since peace and war were voted by the *synkletos*, the soldier under thirty had no voice in deciding questions in which he was, nevertheless, vitally concerned. Nor can we praise — though the history of Greek Tyranny makes us understand the reason for the prohibition — a system of electing the chief executive for one year only, and of prohibiting his immediate reëlection, however eminent his abilities.

The personality of Aratus to a great extent surmounted this difficulty; for he seems to have been strong enough to insure the continuity of his policy during the alternate years when he was out of office. Lastly, though our information on this matter is scanty, the lack of a proper federal organization of finance was bound, in time of war, to involve both Leagues in frequent difficulties.

The Achæan League steadily grew, especially after the death of Antigonus Gonatas. For his successor, Demetrius II, almost at once found himself at war with both the Aetolian and the Achæan Leagues. Though he inflicted some loss on the former, the latter, thanks in the first place to the energy of Aratus, was steadily enlarged by the adherence of more and more Peloponnesian city-states. It was his ambition ultimately to marshal the whole of the Peloponnese to form a solid anti-Macedonian federation; that it was frustrated was mainly due to Sparta. Filled with a stubborn pride, which compels our admiration even if we cannot approve its wisdom, the Spartans had refused to bow to the will of Philip II and Alexander, and had been punished by some loss of territory. Little is heard of Sparta from the time of her abortive attempt to shake off Macedonian authority in southern Greece in 331 (cf. p. 342) until 272, when Pyrrhus of Epirus, in the course of a war against Antigonus Gonatas, invaded Greece. Many of the Hellenic communities received him readily, but Sparta elected to throw in her lot with the Macedonian king. She evidently believed that a temporary friendship with a power to which she was otherwise consistently hostile would serve her interests better than alliance with the brilliant but unstable Epirot. Supported by a Macedonian force sent from Corinth, she repulsed Pyrrhus' attack on Laconia; the same year saw his death at Argos. Under her king, Areus, Sparta now enjoyed a few years of extended political influence in Greek affairs, and concluded alliances with Elis and some of the cities of Arcadia and Achæa. There followed occasional petty wars with her neighbors for the next quarter of a century.

When the Achæan League, inspired by Aratus, was rapidly becoming the most formidable power in Hellas, Sparta concluded an alliance with it. Her internal condition at this time was, however, marked by acute economic distress. The rigid conservatism of her citizens, the evil results of which in the fourth century have already been noted (cf. p. 284), had not relaxed in the third. Thus, about 245, the total number of Spartiatæ had been reduced to 700, and even of these, in whose hands the landed property was concentrated, many were overloaded with debt. The young king Agis, who came of age in 244, supported and tutored by his uncle Agesilaus, now projected a radical scheme of reform. Affecting to base his drastic innovations on the venerable ordinances of Lycurgus, he proposed a cancellation of debts and a redistribution of the land, so that those Spartans who had forfeited their full citizenship and lost their allotments could be reinstated. Furthermore, he aimed to increase the citizen body by the enfranchisement of 4500 *perioikoi*. These proposals were productive of a violent struggle, leading to the expulsion of the king's opponents. At this critical juncture Agis was compelled to fulfil Sparta's obligations as an ally of the Achæan League by leading a Spartan contingent to coöperate with Aratus against the Aetolian League, which was now threatening an attack. On his return from the campaign in 241 Agis found his political enemies in control at home. He was arraigned for treason and executed. Once more had the forces of reaction triumphed at Sparta. The Spartan king, Cleomenes III, who came to the throne six years later, was more successful. In 226 with a mercenary army at his back, he carried out a *coup d'état* at Sparta. The ephorate and *gerusia* were abolished, and a new council was instituted to take the place of those venerable bodies. The franchise was extended to several thousand *perioikoi*, and a redistribution of the land was effected. Reforms were introduced in the army, and the famous Spartan training of the young, which had fallen into desuetude, was revived.

But Cleomenes was not content to play the rôle of economic and constitutional reformer. He set himself, by force or by diplomacy, to enlarge the political influence of Sparta. The program which he aimed to carry through could have but one outcome in the Peloponnese, a rupture between Sparta and the Achæan League. By 227 hostilities had begun; and both in that year and in 226 Cleomenes inflicted decisive defeats on the forces of the League. Peace negotiations followed, and now the Spartan king demanded to be instated as commander-in-chief of the League in time of war. To Aratus the acceptance of this condition meant not only that his own authority would be reduced to comparative insignificance, but that the Achæan League, and the Peloponnese as a whole, would pass once again under the general direction of Lacedæmon and its ambitious ruler. The alternative he saw was to bring about a foreign intervention. Since the relations between Sparta and Egýpt were extremely friendly, there remained only the ancestral enemy of the League, Macedonia, to which to appeal. Yet, since Aratus had spent all his life in trying to create a strong anti-Macedonian power in the Peloponnese, the step he now contemplated, if taken, would be tantamount to the destruction of his life-work. Harsh judgments were passed on him in antiquity, and have been since. The action of the League under his guidance once more illustrates the bitterness of Greek to Greek, which, throughout Hellenic history, made any permanent national unity impossible — the unattainable dream of a few idealist statesmen and political thinkers. That a contrary decision, that is to say the acceptance of Cleomenes' demands, would have made any appreciable difference to the course of Greece's history in the next fifty years is in the highest degree improbable.

Cleomenes' reply to the Achæan refusal of recognition was a renewal of hostilities. Heavily subsidized by Egyptian gold, he was able to augment his mercenaries, and his military successes brought about the defection from the Achæan League of many Peloponnesian cities. Others he took by force. By the spring of 224 the agreement between Aratus and the Macedonian king, Antigonus Doson, who had succeeded Demetrius II in 229, had been signed, and Antigonus at once marched to the Peloponnese, occupied Corinth and Argos, and compelled Cleomenes to retire to Arcadia. During the winter, when campaigning was at a standstill, the Macedonian reconstituted the Hellenic League from which, apart from the common enemy, Sparta, only the Aetolians kept aloof. Cities which had recently gone over to Cleomenes now as quickly fell away from him; yet for nearly two years he carried on against a stronger foe, until in the spring of 222 he was completely defeated by Antigonus at the battle of Sellasia in Laconia. Cleomenes himself made his escape to the coast, and thence to Egypt. His attempt, two years later, to return with some supporters to Laconia failed, and he committed suicide. His enemy and rival, Aratus, lived till 213, still influential in the counsels of the League, but the dependent of Macedonia. It was said that he was poisoned at the instance of the young Macedonian king, Philip V, who had succeeded Antigonus Doson in 221. The change of ruler in Macedonia at that date seemed to the Aetolians an opportunity for increasing their own power, and they attacked the Achæan League. From this act of aggression there developed a general war between them and Philip with his Hellenic allies, which lasted for three years. Peace was concluded in 217. The Aetolians, who had suffered severe losses, were glad to accept the mild terms imposed by the Macedonian monarch. He, on his side, was anxious for peace in Hellas, so as to have a free hand to undertake a war in which success promised a rich reward. Few men — and certainly Philip was not one of them — at that date realized the strength and endurance of the western power of Rome, which in 217–216 was passing through one of the greatest crises in its history, and among whose active enemies Philip was now to be numbered.

CHAPTER XIX

THE HELLENISTIC AGE

> *The Museum forms a part of the palaces. It has a promenade, a lounge, and a large hall, in which the learned scholars who belong to the Museum dine in common. This community also owns property in common. A priest, who in former times was appointed by the King but now by Caesar, is president of the Museum.* — Strabo, xvii, i, 8.

THE Hellenistic Age, that is to say, the period of about two centuries between the death of Alexander and the time when Roman control was firmly established in the eastern Mediterranean, was long regarded as a period of decadence and material decline. Fuller knowledge, the result of extensive excavations, has demonstrated this conception of the Hellenic world after Alexander to be erroneous. At the same time it is now possible to see more clearly the striking differences between this and the preceding age.

The political developments which were sketched in the last chapter caused something little short of revolutionary changes, even though the process of change was gradual, not sudden. Of the innumerable Greek cities, which had for centuries been for the most part autonomous states, the greater number were now dependent on, or actually incorporated in, one or other of the leading monarchies. The old constitutional forms are kept, magistrates are elected, assemblies and councils meet, but they have sunk to the status of municipal officials and town councils. Of the highly developed urban life in the period we have abundant evidence from the inscriptions; the life and conditions in the country districts are less heard of now than before. In spite of the continuous warfare in the period, there is, especially among the smaller cities, a marked disposition to settle disagreements not by the sword but by arbitration. Another method, extensively adopted to restrict the operations of war, was found in declaring many sanctuaries and the lands attached to them inviolable. Gradually the principle was also extended to whole cities and their territories, and to individual members of communities — and these were numerous — which had entered into specific treaty relations with one another. A greater humanity in the relations of man to man was not merely an ideal preached by the adherents of philosophic schools — for example, the Stoics — but found its practical expression in several ways. The treatment of slaves, if we except the wretched inmates of the mines, tended to become gentler, and manumissions were common. Greeks taken prisoner by Greeks were regularly ransomed. The usages of war — again there were some brutal exceptions — were somewhat less harsh than in an earlier age. Such changes arose from a multiplicity of causes, which it is hard to analyze with precision, just as it is often difficult to separate cause and effect. The great increase in intercourse resulting from the altered political conditions, the break-down of the old system of isolated and mutually jealous city-states, and the development of greater facilities for commerce and travel, together with the realization that, whatever local political differences might exist, all Hellenes were the inheritors of a common culture, notably changed the aspect of Greek society.

But there were other and less admirable features. Though there is not sufficient material on which to base even the most tentative statistics, it is clear that the population of Greece, at all events toward the end of the period, was not even stationary but sensibly declining. The epigraphic remains seem to leave no room for doubt that smaller families were the rule in the second century, and that the practice of infanticide, especially of female children, was far from uncommon. The land could support only a limited number of persons, while the development of industry and commerce was not of such a kind as to benefit the majority of the population. The difference between the wealthy few and the impoverished many became much more sharply accentuated than it was in the days of Greek freedom. The social revolution at Sparta, though the best known, is far from being the only instance of civil disturbance

arising from the abject poverty of the masses and the demand
for better conditions, especially a redistribution of the land.
And there are on record cases where such struggles were sufficiently severe to necessitate the intervention of this or that
suzerain power.

It is the wealthy who appear most often in the inscriptions.
They formed the ruling class in the cities; from among them
were chosen officials and councillors; and, in justice to them, we
may add that many of them were lavish with their wealth for
the benefit of the community. Many are the inscriptions commemorating public benefactions of divers kinds. For much of
the cost of beautifying towns with public buildings, of celebrating public festivals, great and small, of providing for the education of the young and for their proper supervision, was defrayed
by private donors. At times, too, wealthy princes spent large
sums on Greek cities with which they were on friendly footing.
No better instance of this can be cited than the munificent
patronage extended to Athens by several of the Attalids of
Pergamum.[1]

In their extensive empire Seleucus and his successors exerted
themselves to promote the process of Hellenization. To that
end they were most active in fostering the growth of many new
cities. These Seleucid foundations thrived in all parts of the
realm, as it was at its greatest extent, in the central Asiatic
provinces and Mesopotamia, as well as in Syria itself and in Asia
Minor. The capital city, Syrian Antioch, Tarsus in Cilicia, and
Seleuceia on the Tigris were all destined to play an important
part, culturally and economically, for centuries to come. Seleuceia was primarily a Greek city, but contained also a large native population. It became in time one of the largest cities in
the world, with well over half a million inhabitants. Even in
those urban communities, whose inmates were mainly Asiatics,
Greek forms of government and administration were often
imitated or directly adopted. In sharp contrast to the semi-
independent status of the city-dwellers was that of the rural

---

[1] Thus, Attalus I presented a number of sculptures commemorating
his victories over the Gauls. Attalus II was the donor of a colonnade on
the eastern side of the Athenian agora. Another colonnade was presented
by Eumenes II.

population. The agricultural workers were serfs, a condition which was of course far older than the Seleucid era, and irrespective of whether the land that they tilled was owned by the monarch or private persons. The only exception was to be found on the farm-lands belonging to Greek cities, where the tillers in general had the status of free peasants.

Ptolemaic Egypt presents a strong contrast to the Seleucid kingdom. There no such Hellenizing process would have been possible; and the early princes of the royal house, though Græco-Macedonian, made no attempt to imitate their Syrian neighbor. Apart from Alexandria and Ptolemais, a new foundation in Upper Egypt, there were no Hellenic centres in Egypt; and Alexandria became in time a composite city of various nationalities. At first the Greek element predominated and remained more or less pure; but gradually, by intermarriage, a more homogeneous Græco-Egyptian population developed to take the place of the earlier and separate ethnic groups. The Jewish colony there, which grew very rapidly, was granted substantial privileges by different Ptolemies; within a century there were many smaller Jewish settlements in different parts of Egypt. They remained distinct, however, from both the Greek and the native population. The Ptolemies, unlike any of their contemporaries, developed a most complicated yet efficient system of state-control in the industrial and commercial life of their country. All important productions and manufactures were royal monopolies. As it has been put, "the king was the first industrial and commercial magnate in the land." To carry out this control by the government, that is to say, by the monarch, over industry and commerce as well as over agriculture, elaborate census statistics were periodically collected, and a vast bureaucracy, grading down from the highest ministers of the king to the humble village headman, was needed to ensure efficient working. The lot of the mass of the workers was unenviable. Their income rarely rose much above, and sometimes fell below, the bare margin of subsistence. Riots and strikes were no infrequent occurrence, but could be promptly suppressed, or else appeased by slight concessions. While it is beyond dispute that the result of this intensive system was a tremendous development of all the natural resources of the country — for centuries Egypt became the chief granary of the Mediterranean world — and filled the royal treasuries with untold wealth, it meant an exploitation by the Ptolemies of the mass of their subjects, without any adequate return to them, which it would be difficult either to parallel or to defend.

Under the energetic rule of the earlier Ptolemies and Seleucids a remarkable expansion of trade, especially between the Mediterranean world and the East, was seen. The records taken by men like Alexander's general, Nearchus, which taught the Greeks much about the Persian Gulf and Indian Ocean, were of great value to the merchants of the next generations. The chief avenue of trade from India to the Seleucid kingdom led by sea to the head of the Persian Gulf; thence it passed up the Tigris to Seleuceia, and thence by one or other of the caravan routes across the desert to Antioch, Tyre, or Damascus. Two overland routes from central Asia and India, a southern one through Susa and a more northern one through Media, both led to Seleuceia, which thus became a mart of exceptional importance. The kings of Egypt promoted exploration of the Red Sea, the Somali coast, and southern Arabia. A voluminous trade between those regions and Alexandria developed rapidly, and in time was even extended to southern India. In the Mediterranean area also there was much commercial activity. Merchant boats of larger tonnage were constructed, and many maritime cities, even those of quite secondary importance, made a considerable outlay on improving their harbors. While Alexandria's exports and imports far surpassed those of any other centre, Rhodes, Corinth, Delos, Ephesus, and Cyzicus all prospered exceedingly. Sporadic evidence suggests, moreover, that many smaller communities, proportionately to their size and resources, did no less well. Some advance in business methods is another noticeable feature of the age. Letters of credit were now by no means uncommon, and in Ptolemaic Egypt at all events a banking system of considerable intricacy, which was closely connected with the royal control of industry and trade, was developed.

No better proof of the universality of Hellenism in this epoch can be found than the following circumstance: Attic Greek, which already in the fourth century had with insignificant

exceptions become the regular literary language, now became
the universal language of polite intercourse, of diplomacy, and
of business. Thus we find it used not merely by the Ptolemies
and their officials but by Egyptian peasants — though often
incorrectly enough — in appeals and litigation. It was employed by the Roman government when it intervened in the
affairs of the Near East; and the study of Greek in Rome and
Italy then progressed rapidly, so that by the beginning of the
first century B.C. a good working knowledge of that tongue was
a necessary part of the equipment of every educated man.
Above all, be it noted that for the benefit of the Jews of the
Dispersion — that is, the numerous Jewish colonies outside
Judæa — their sacred scriptures were translated into Greek.
The Pentateuch had been so rendered before the end of the
third century; gradually all the books of the Old Testament
became available in the common language of intercourse.[1]
For long the Greek version was freely used by even the learned
Jews and enjoyed high authority, so that the erudite Philo
quoted it, and regarded it as of equal value with the original
Hebrew text. The existence of this translation and others of
a later date also enabled non-Jews to become familiar with
Hebrew writings, a fact which was to become of supreme importance to the early Christian communities.

A very notable development of the Hellenistic Age is the
spread of education, and the realization by the city governments
that this was a matter which should not be left entirely to private initiative and enterprise. There was a general tendency for
municipal or town authorities to exercise some control. At the
same time much of the money needed for such purposes was
provided, not by the treasury, but by grants or bequests of
public-spirited citizens. Copious epigraphical material shows
that these varied greatly both in size and purpose. In 200–
199 B.C. a citizen of Miletus gave no less than ten talents of
silver, from the interest of which four school and four gymnastic teachers were to be paid; in addition, a certain proportion

---

[1] To the modern Old Testament scholar this version, called the *Septuagint*, is of superlative importance, because it preserves in translation a
text which is about a thousand years older than any extant Hebrew manuscript.

of the annual income was earmarked for religious processions and sacrifices, in which the city youth were to take part. At Teos a somewhat similar gift was made by a generous citizen. In 159 the people of Delphi successfully appealed for financial aid to King Attalus II "on behalf of the teaching of their children." The people of Priene and Halicarnassus were less fortunate when they applied to princes for funds. Promises were forthcoming, but apparently nothing further. Smaller bequests in different towns were intended to support a single teacher or some educational official; to provide for the regular purchase of oil for use in the wrestling-schools; to help to defray the cost of gymnastic competitions; to subsidize new, or pay for the repair of old, school-buildings or equipment; to provide for baths; and, quaintest of all, to pay for a good supply of sponges, as well as for some one to guard the clothes of the bathers!

If we may now suppose that all boys in the towns, and a good many from the rural districts, received some elementary schooling, and we also have evidence that more attention was paid to teaching the same rudiments to girls, more advanced tuition continued to be, as before, only within the reach of the upper class. The word, *ephebeia*, or training of the *ephebi* (young men from eighteen to twenty years of age), which had in the fourth century signified their compulsory military training, in the Hellenistic period acquired a somewhat wider meaning. The institution ceased to be compulsory; it was limited to one year's duration; and, from being military, the training became athletic and intellectual. The teachers appointed by the community to instruct the *ephebi* were all instructors in physical training and athletics. But attendance at the schools of rhetoric and philosophy was a compulsory part of the young men's curriculum during their ephebic year. The life which the students lived was largely communal in character, and its organization was left mainly to the youths themselves. They elected from among themselves a number of the ablest and most popular *ephebi*, who performed various duties and had varying privileges. By analogy with the institutions of the municipality, they were designated by the titles, archon, polemarch, thesmothetes, and so forth. This system, which was of great benefit to

the sons of the wealthy, prevailed, as the inscriptions attest, in
every larger Hellenic community, not only in Greece but in Asia
Minor and Syria, in Alexandria, and as far west as Massilia.
The general organization was probably the same everywhere,
though in matters of detail there were naturally variations.
Thus, the age of admission in Egypt, where boys reached
maturity more quickly than in Greece, was appreciably lower.
Though every city would have its rhetors, there were a few
centres which became particularly famous for their teachers
of this subject or of philosophy. Such, for example, were
Athens, Pergamum, Rhodes, and, particularly at a later date,
Antioch. Cities like these in time attracted students from all
quarters of the Hellenic world.

The most influential philosophic schools in the period were not
the Academy and the Lyceum, nor yet the minor sects founded
by members of the Socratic circle, though all continued to
flourish fitfully, but the Stoics and Epicureans. By the older
philosophers the community were considered to be of primary
importance; to it the individual and his claims are essentially
subordinate. Even to Aristotle, therefore, "Politics" takes
precedence over "Ethics." After his time this attitude is
entirely reversed.

The Stoic school was founded by Zeno of Citium in Cyprus
about 306 B.C. For many years he taught in the Painted Stoa
at Athens, and though at first he seems to have had few hearers,
he ended by being universally respected and admired. About
the same time Epicurus, a Samian of Athenian descent, founded
a philosophic school at Athens that was destined to rival the
Stoic for centuries. It was the Stoics who first adopted the
threefold division of philosophy into physics or natural philosophy, ethics, and logic or dialectics. Their conception and system
of the Universe was extremely materialistic, being also borrowed
very largely from earlier thinkers, for example, Heracleitus,
Aristotle, and the Cynics. Their ethical system, on the other
hand, was highly idealistic. Indeed, as formulated by the
founder and his immediate successors, it was so exacting and
austere that later teachers of the school found it necessary to
modify some of Zeno's precepts. In the application of their
moral science there are important characteristics which had a

far-reaching influence. For they claimed to have found a substitute for the two main supports which had hitherto upheld men in their daily conduct, the law of the state and the old religion of Greece. In the ideal state of the Stoics all differences of nationality have been merged in the common brotherhood of man. The earlier Stoics, recognizing that such a world-state was an ideal impossible of attainment but one toward which men should strive, believed and taught that men must not neglect either the political life or the life of the family. Only by association with his fellows can a man approach even approximately to the higher ideal. It was only in a later age, in the days of imperial Rome, that prominent Stoic teachers, influenced by existing political conditions — for the Roman empire was far removed from the Stoic world-state — sometimes betrayed an aversion to the family and the state. If their doctrines exerted no substantial influence on the rulers of the world, they contributed profoundly toward raising moral standards and promoting a greater and wider humanity.

The Epicureans were out-and-out individualists. The founder of the sect held quite frankly that the state was made for man, and not man for the state. Such a belief, openly expressed in an earlier age, might well have involved him in a prosecution for impiety or treason. He had no interest in science and natural philosophy for its own sake, but studied it only in order to further his ethical teaching. Sensation he regarded as the only criterion of truth; everything must depend on natural causes. When men were cognizant of that, they would be able to follow a right conduct, untrammelled by fear of the gods and superstitious beliefs. Epicurus borrowed his explanation of the material Universe wholesale from Democritus; that is to say, he took over the atomic theory of the earlier thinker, but introduced some modifications into it. Everything is matter; even the soul is composed of atoms, though they are of much greater fineness or rarity than those of the body. He differs from Democritus in asserting the freedom of the human will, a doctrine at variance with the Democritean theory of necessity. Epicurus denied that any superhuman power interferes with human affairs, laying down that all things in the world must be referred to mechanical causes. The existence of the gods — who are composed of atoms finer than human beings — is not denied. They dwell apart, unconcerned with the working of the Universe or with the affairs of men. In his ethical system pleasure, in the negative aspect of freedom from pain and all that is unpleasant or disturbing, is the highest good. It is important to remember that Epicurus was not a hedonist; his "pleasure" is mainly mental, and it has virtue, that is to say, moral excellence, as its indispensable concomitant.

Athens remained the headquarters of the philosophic schools and never lost her premier position in this respect, even when distinguished philosophers, belonging to this or that sect, for a while attracted numerous disciples in some other city. Apart from philosophical studies, however, she ceased to be the intellectual centre of the Hellenic world. Literature, linguistic and scientific research, flourished in various places; among them the position of Alexandria was long preëminent and unique. The credit for this belongs to Ptolemy I, and even more to Ptolemy II. The so-called Museum (*i.e.* temple of the Muses) at Alexandria was founded as a religious guild. Its buildings included a spacious mansion in which the members dined in common. They were nominated by the king, and, besides their subsistence, received salaries and enjoyed certain privileges. Some gave occasional lectures in public; but this was not obligatory. For the Museum was not an educational establishment but an institute for research. Great and successful efforts were made by the king to attract the most eminent persons in literature and science to Alexandria. A great library, which by the middle of the third century seems to have boasted of not less than half a million manuscripts, was another of the glories of the city. And, in both that century and the next, a number of exceptionally able and learned men presided as librarians of this magnificent collection. Ptolemy II seems to have been something more than a patron of science and the arts. He had the most varied interests. He took part in philological discussions, he was a good connoisseur of painting, and he spent much money and labor in forming a collection of rare animals from the interior of Africa.

It is in one way difficult to evaluate the worth of Hellenistic literature because the bulk of it has perished. At the same time its very non-survival cannot be wholly the result of an accident. We shall indeed not err in believing that, in the main, its attraction was more ephemeral than, and lacked the enduring worth of, the earlier literature of Greece. It has already been pointed out how poetry and the drama declined during the fourth century, and how its great productions were the philosophical writings of Plato and the speeches of the orators. The popularity of rhetoric in the Hellenistic, and subsequently in the Græco-Roman, Age continued unabated. If there was no longer any room for the political oratory of a Demosthenes, there was still ample use for panegyric and forensic oratory. Rhetoric, using the word in its widest sense,[1] was the most practical of studies, because it fitted a man for the varied activities of public life.

The so-called New Comedy had many exponents, of whom the chief were Diphilus, Menander (died in 291?), and Philemon (died in 262). It was rooted in Athens, and after the passing of its writers in the third century it languished entirely; nor was it successfully imitated elsewhere. The recent recovery of papyri, containing considerable fragments of several plays by Menander, has somewhat amplified our knowledge of compositions which previously could only be judged from the Latin adaptations of Plautus and Terence.[2] Menander's comedies had all the elements which ensure popularity: they were well constructed; they portrayed the life of a certain section of the well-to-do citizens, especially the amorous and often not too nice adventures of young men about town; they were composed in the most limpid Attic Greek; and they abounded in witty phrases and epigrammatic, quasi-proverbial sayings. But they lacked entirely the vigor, the wholesome if occasionally daring or coarse satire, and the poetic fire of Aristophanes' immortal works.

The idyll and the epigram were two popular literary forms perfected in the Alexandrine period. Both, and especially the epigram, were adapted to treat a great variety of themes; and the epigram remained a favorite verse form for many centuries. Both, too, were studied and imitated by the poets of Rome. The age also saw the production of sundry didactic and literary

---

[1] See above, p. 302.   [2] See below, p. 436.

epics. To the former class belongs a long astronomical poem by Aratus of Soli in Cilicia, which enjoyed a great vogue, and later was more than once translated into Latin, for example, by Cicero. Of literary or romantic epics we may mention the *Argonautica* of Apollonius. It is a lengthy and uneven work in which passages of singular beauty and passion are mingled with long and somewhat arid and pedantic, pseudo-Homeric, descriptions and narrative. This work does not appear to have enjoyed much popularity; but, more than two centuries later, it was read by Vergil, who derived some inspiration from it, and did not disdain to imitate some of its episodes in his own far greater epic.

Theocritus (flourished *c.* 270), although a Syracusan by birth, spent a good part of his life in Alexandria. His bucolic poems or idylls have often been imitated — for instance, by Vergil in his earliest work, the *Eclogues* — but never equalled. They depict with charming naturalness the life of the country folk and shepherds of Sicily, and its rustic scenery.

If the Hellenistic era does not rank very high as an age of creative literature, the world owes an incalculable debt to the critics and philologists of Alexandria. Zenodotus (*c.* 280), Eratosthenes (*c.* 234), Aristophanes (*c.* 195), and Aristarchus (*c.* 170), all of whom in their turn were keepers of the great library at Alexandria, carried on linguistic researches, and textual criticism and exegesis of the writers of early and classical Greece. Copies were made of those precious works, spurious writings were distinguished from genuine, careful recensions of the Homeric poems were prepared, in which supposed interpolations of a later date were marked, learned commentaries were compiled on most of the important classical authors, and, in each branch of literature, certain writers and their works were selected and classed as canonical.[1] Granted that these scholars were occasionally arbitrary in their criticisms and in their handling of the ancient texts, they in the main did their work wisely and well. But for their indefatigable "cult of the past" many of the masterpieces of Greek literature might never have

---

[1] The best known is the Canon of the Ten Attic Orators, namely Antiphon, Andocides, Lysias, Isocrates, Isæus, Aeschines, Demosthenes, Lycurgus, Hypereides, and Deinarchus.

survived to delight and instruct later generations down to our own time.

Research in the natural sciences had been late in developing in the Hellenic world, and it was Aristotle who more than any other man, by his teaching and by his own investigations in biology, gave an immense stimulus to further inquiries into that vast field of human knowledge. His successor at the Lyceum, Theophrastus, made invaluable contributions to botanical studies. Mathematics engaged the attention of Eucleides (Euclid); while Eratosthenes, whose literary labors and duties as librarian formed only a small part of his activities, deserves to be regarded as the greatest scholar of his age for his diversified work in mathematics, astronomy, scientific geography, and chronology. The greatest mathematician of the ancient world was Archimedes, the Syracusan (died 212 B.C.). In astronomy the outstanding names are those of Aristarchus of Samos (c. 310–230) and Hipparchus (flourished c. 140). The former has the distinction of propounding a heliocentric theory of the Universe, making all the planets move in circles about the sun, which he discovered to be many times larger than the earth. Later scientists, mainly perhaps because, in the absence of adequate instruments, they were unable to make their practical observations of the heavens tally with Aristarchus' theory, rejected it. Thus the truth remained obscured till the discoveries of Copernicus eighteen centuries later. Hipparchus, although he reverted to the geocentric theory, was a scholar of great eminence. He may be regarded as the founder of trigonometry, he discovered the precession of the equinoxes, and he was responsible for several important astronomical calculations.

The researches in physiology and anatomy made by Herophilus and Erasistratus in the first half of the third century were noteworthy. The former stressed the importance of pulsation, and, by his researches on the more important organs of the body and the dissection of animal and human corpses, greatly advanced knowledge of anatomy. While the credit of discovering the nerves also belongs to him, and their connection with the brain, which he regarded as the seat of intelligence, it was probably Erasistratus, not Herophilus, who went a step further and distinguished the motor from the sensory nervous

system. The anatomical researches of these two men of science
also made them daring and successful surgeons in their day.
But their momentous contributions to knowledge had less effect than might have been expected, since they were, as it would
seem, too advanced for their contemporaries. Greek medical
science produced only one more man of the first rank, Galen,
who flourished at the end of the second century of our era.

The intensity and general prosperity of urban life found its
outward expression in carefully planned and well-built towns.
The excavation of sites like Delos, Priene, Magnesia, or Miletus, enables one to obtain a far clearer notion of a Hellenistic
city than any that can be formed of one in the age of Pericles
or of Demosthenes. These numerous Greek and Græco-
Oriental towns one and all had certain common features; in
all there were temples, an *agora* or market-place, a townhall,
a theatre, a gymnasium, and public baths. Otherwise the
plan of different cities varied, being in fact mainly determined
by the nature of the territory occupied. Paved streets were
still the exception; and, though care was taken to ensure an
adequate and wholesome water-supply, open drainage was
the general rule. Subterranean sewers are mostly an improvement of Roman date. The private houses were adequately
comfortable without being at all elaborate. In Delos the
dwellings are built around a single court which usually has a
colonnade. The chief room of the house is at the farther end
of the court, the smaller apartments opening on the sides.
Some, at least, of the Delian houses had an upper story. In
Priene the colonnades are absent. A long passage regularly
leads from the street to the courtyard, on three sides of which
are various rooms; at the far end of it is a pillared vestibule
giving access to the main reception room. Temple architecture
shows no marked change from that of the previous century,
save perhaps that the ornate Corinthian order rapidly gains
in popularity.

Two great and costly structures deserve special mention.
The harbor of Alexandria, as befitted so important a centre,
was the finest in the world. On Pharos island, guarding its
entrance, a great lighthouse, reputed to have stood almost 400
feet high, was built by the architect-engineer Sostratus. This

impressive as well as useful building deserved to be reckoned, as indeed it was, one of the wonders of the world. At Pergamum the great altar of Zeus was a splendid monument set up by the Attalids. Upon a lofty base stood an Ionic colonnade, which surrounded on three sides a great court. In the middle of this the actual altar was situate. The base in question was decorated with a great frieze, whose total length was fully 400 feet. The subject represented was the battle of the Gods and Titans. The figures were in high relief and of more than human size. In the treatment of this relief, which can still be studied in the Berlin Museum, as in much of the sculpture of the earlier Hellenistic period, the influence of Scopas is still discernible.

In portraiture, similarly, which was a very popular form of art, the influence of Lysippus and his school must have lasted for a considerable time. The general characteristics of Hellenistic sculpture are a love of novelty, both in seeking new subjects and in treating old themes in a new way; a constant and even excessive desire for depicting movement; and a realism which is in strong contrast with the art of the classical period, and in time often degenerated into grotesqueness or veritable anatomical studies. This last tendency we see exemplified both in the famous Laocoön group and in the Heracles of the Villa Farnese. Among the finest surviving examples of Hellenistic sculpture in the round are the Aphrodite of Melos (2d century?) and the Winged Victory from Samothrace (c. 250?). The total output of plastic art in the third and second centuries must have been enormous, and the copious remains are but a tithe of the total. Much of what has survived shows great excellence; but we miss in this epoch outstanding masters of the art who could be set side by side with a Pheidias or a Praxiteles. In painting much the same happened. The art in general, and especially mural paintings, were exceedingly popular. What little has survived, though interesting in several ways, is from the artistic standpoint third-rate. In any case we hear in literature of no Hellenistic peers of an Apelles or a Zeuxis.

CHAPTER XX

ROME TO THE BEGINNING OF THE THIRD CENTURY B.C.

Unless, however, I am misled by affection for my undertaking, there has never existed any commonwealth greater in power, with a purer morality, or more fertile in good examples; or any state in which avarice and luxury have been so late in making their inroads, or poverty and frugality so highly and continuously honoured, showing so clearly that the less wealth men possessed the less they coveted. — Livy, Preface to the *History* (Roberts' translation).

1. THE BEGINNINGS

ITALY, if the term be used in its geographical sense, comprises two regions differing both in extent and in physical character. The northern section is bounded on the north by the long chain of the Alps, on the south by the Apennines, and is watered by the largest river in the country, the Po (Padus), and a number of lesser streams. This area forms an exceptionally fertile plain. The southern portion is the Italian peninsula, bisected through its whole length by the Apennines. Though long — the distance is about 650 miles — this country is narrow, since the distance from sea to sea nowhere exceeds 150 miles. The Apennines for fully two-thirds of their length approach more nearly to the eastern side of the peninsula; it is on this side also that they attain their greatest height. Except in the South (Apulia) there are no fertile tracts of considerable size, and there is, too, an almost complete absence of harbors on the east coast. On the western side, where the mountains do not approach so nearly to the sea, there are many valleys and fertile plains watered by streams, none of which even in antiquity were navigable for more than a few miles from the estuary. The west coast also offered more shelter for sea-going vessels, in

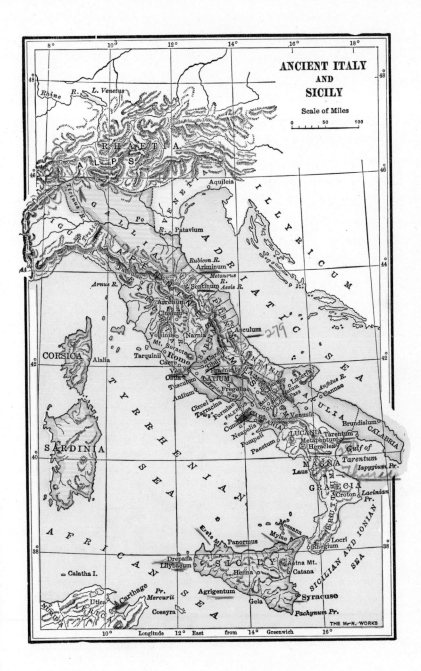

ANCIENT ITALY
AND
SICILY

Scale of Miles

0   50   100

the form of a goodly number of small ports. As the size of
the ships and the volume of maritime trade increased, only a
few of these were found adequate; so that in the later Republican and imperial days of Rome, two or three ports on the
west coast absorbed most of the sea traffic. This country, which
was not specially adapted for commercial expansion, and which
was poor in mineral resources, was compensated by the richness
of her soil, and for centuries her inhabitants were predominantly
agriculturists.

Although the Alps have often been described as a great natural barrier, the truth is that, in spite of their altitude and extent,
they at no time protected the regions lying to the south from
invasion. Traces of Palæolithic man have been discovered in
various parts of Italy, while the remains of the Late Stone Age
are abundant. The Bronze Age was preceded by an intermediate period, in which copper had become known and copper implements were used side by side with those of flint or stone. The
first invasion into Italy for which we have any clear evidence
corresponds with the beginning of the Bronze Age. The newcomers came from central Europe and the Danube valley,
bringing with them the use of bronze; they are also distinguished from the earlier inhabitants of Italy by their burial
customs. For, whereas the latter uniformly interred their dead,
the former practised cremation. So far as we can tell, successive
waves of immigrants moved southwards over the Alps into
northern Italy during the second millennium B.C.; so that,
before the beginning of the Iron Age (c. 1100–1000), they were
in occupation of the entire Padus valley. South of the Apennines they appear to have gained little hold, as few of their
settlements have been unearthed in central or southern Italy.
The inhabitants of these regions, however, under the influence
of the peoples from the north developed their own Bronze Age
civilization. New ethnic movements and groupings resulted at
the beginning of the Iron Age, caused by fresh immigrations,
especially from the Danubian area. The newcomers, like their
predecessors of the Bronze Age, cremated their dead. Nevertheless there were considerable regions where the older inhumation continued to be practised. Though it is not possible here
to enter into the intricate questions of ethnology connected

with the various types of prehistoric remains — Neolithic, Bronze Age, and Iron Age — the foregoing remarks will have made it clear that the population of Italy at the dawn of the historic period was ethnically very mixed.

About 800 B.C. we find a new and racially quite distinct people in possession of the western half of central Italy north of the Tiber. The Etruscans present one of the great problems of history. For fully four centuries they were the most powerful state in Italy. Extant wall-paintings, vases, and metal-work show them to have been the possessors of a material civilization of an advanced kind. For these remains, if heavily indebted to Greek models, and hence rather lacking in originality, are nevertheless of high technical excellence. Their architectural and engineering skill was most remarkable; it later exerted a deep influence on Roman architecture and methods of construction. Great attention was paid to funeral rites and the proper disposal of the dead, as we can see from extant sarcophagi, and impressive tombs carved in the rock and decorated with mural frescoes. Yet the origin and race of this people are quite uncertain. Although many Etruscan inscriptions are extant, written in the Greek alphabet which they had taken over and adapted, these are still unread.[1] The most likely hypothesis is still that the earlier home of the Etruscans was on the eastern shores of the Mediterranean, whence they emigrated in the troubled years after the so-called Dorian invasion and the migrations resulting therefrom. There are features in their culture, especially in their religious practices — for example, divination from the entrails of animals — which accord best with the hypothesis that they were an oriental people; and perhaps the excessive luxuriousness and addiction to licentious habits, with which they are charged by the Greek historian Theopompus, afford additional evidence to the same effect. In the seventh century their political influence was gradually extended beyond the limits of Etruria, northward into the Padus valley, southward across the Tiber into Latium and into Campania. Two cities in the last-

---

[1] Some advance toward the solution of this difficult problem appears, however, to have been made by A. Trombetti in his recent work, *La lingua etrusca* (Florence, 1928). Cf. the review of it by A. H. Sayce in *Antiquity* ii, (1928), pp. 378–380.

named region — the most fertile in all Italy — which grew to be very important communities, were apparently Etruscan foundations. These were Capua and Nola. To the Etruscan alliance with Carthage in order to keep the colonizing activities of certain Greek states in check, reference was made in an earlier chapter (pp. 127; 203). In the fifth century their power rapidly declined; while the invasion of Etruria by the Gauls early in the fourth century inflicted a blow on the Etruscans from which they never recovered. With the Greek settlements on the coast of Italy and Sicily, which were founded during the seventh and sixth centuries, they seem in general to have remained on friendly terms. It is through them that the Etruscans imported painted Greek pottery and other luxury articles; also the strongest outside influence on Etruscan art, and to some extent religion, was Greek. Only in the fifth century hostile gave place to friendly relations, in their war with Cumæ and, a quarter of a century later, with Syracuse (p. 206).

The political organization of Etruria would seem to have been lacking in solidarity; in the long run this conduced to the disruption of their kingdom. The Etruscans themselves were a conquering minority, who had subjected the native races of the regions where they settled, treating them as serfs or as a dependent population. Their several cities were ruled by a warlike aristocracy, generally under leadership of a single prince. It is not clear, however, what degree of coöperation existed between these cities at any given date. Nor, under the conditions existing, could it be expected that rulers and ruled should gradually coalesce to form a contented and united people. Thus, the moral degeneration of the later Etruscans, resulting in a loss of warlike efficiency, and a decline in their numbers, may also have been contributing causes to their political collapse.

Latium, to which we have already referred, was the name given to the lowland district lying south of the Tiber, and bordered on the east by the Apennines. At the time when the Etruscan power was in the ascendant, the inhabitants of Latium, a simple farming population, were settled in a large number of small towns or villages. Though in face of common danger they might act in concert, we have no clear indication of an effective political union among them.   They celebrated each year a religious festival in common in honor of their god, Jupiter Latiaris, a cult of great antiquity.   But of the Latin League we get no definite information — and even then it is little enough — until the fifth century, when the military leadership had passed to a city-state that was not strictly one of the Latin communities, though a large part of its population was ethnically of Latin stock.

The origins of Rome are very obscure.   Later Roman tradition fixed the city's foundation in the middle of the eighth century (753 B.C.).   There are no means of determining the precise significance of this date; but such archæological evidence as exists makes it clear that settlements on the site existed during several previous centuries.   As a site Rome had several advantages over the Latin settlements.   It was built on hills which were easily defensible; being situated at some distance from the sea, it was protected from possible raids by corsairs.   At the same time communication with the sea was feasible, since the Tiber was navigable from its estuary as far as Rome, a distance of fifteen miles.   Finally, at the point where Rome stood there was in the river an island, and an easy crossing from the southern to the northern bank.   The settlement grew very gradually from small beginnings; and, though the stages of progress cannot be determined with any precision, and the time occupied in the process is quite uncertain, traditions which were current at a much later date cannot be ignored.   The earliest city proper was later designated by the name of *Roma quadrata;* it was here that centuries after, when Rome was an imperial state, the oldest cult objects were still to be seen.   The festival of the *Septimontium* (seven regions) was of great antiquity, and probably began by being a common religious celebration of a number of adjacent communities, which subsequently joined together to form one body politic and one city.   When a later enlargement of the city took place it was divided into four regions, which included the Palatine hill and the four ridges called Cælian, Esquiline, Viminal, and Quirinal, and fortified.   In addition there stood within the city walls its citadel, the Capitoline hill.   The seventh hill of Rome, as we know it in later times was the Aventine; its inclusion inside the fortified area of the city was probably not effected till some time after the Regal period.

That the population of Rome was racially not uniform is certain. While the Latin element was the strongest, there was also a considerable admixture of hill-peoples, like the Sabines; and later an Etruscan element was superimposed, when Etruscan princes occupied the city and other parts of Latium and held them in subjection. The government at Rome in early days was monarchic, the latest kings being apparently Etruscan conquerors. The accounts of later Roman historians, like Livy, doubtless preserve some general traditions of the dim past which are correct; but they are too overladen with myth and legend to be accepted as they stand. There are, besides, many survivals in Roman religion, which point indubitably to a mixture of races, and to a fusion of peoples of different stock at an early date in Rome's history.

The basis of Roman society is the *familia*, a term of wider significance than our word "family," since it included, besides the father, mother, and their issue, the slaves and dependents of the household and its property and estate (*res familiaris*). The *familiae*, and not the individuals, were the units, by the aggregation of which the larger political and social groups were evolved, — the clan, the tribe, and the body politic itself. Roman society was strongly patriarchal, and kinship was taken into account only in the male line. The children of a man's son and brother were regarded as in direct relation to himself (*agnati*). The children of his daughter or sister are only "sharers of birth" (*cognati*). Of course very soon, after a few generations, the evidence for agnate relationship must have become blurred; nevertheless, the families recognized a common authorship, a fact indicated in their common name. A group of *familiae* formed a clan or *gens;* the members of it held common religious observances, which formed a most vital part of Roman religion, though naturally less is known about them than of the ceremonies conducted by the state and its official representatives. No woman could be head of a family; she was always in the power (*manus*) of a male relative or, after marriage, of her husband.

The Roman kingship presents both similarities to, and differences from, other early monarchies. The king (*rex*) is at the head of the community in the threefold capacity of leader in war, judge in matters affecting the community as a whole, and intermediary between his human subjects and the supernatural powers. In his capacity as religious head he is supported by technical advisers on the proper performance of all religious ceremonies. The king — and later on the chief magistrates — performed the rites of the state religion, even as the head of the family carried out the religious celebrations of the household. The college of priests (*pontifices*) and the priests of individual gods, like the *flamen* of Jupiter, and the augurs, charged with the duty of divination by observing the flight of birds, were, so to say, specialists in the various ritual practices; they were not the official intermediaries between the gods and the community. The authority vested in the king was expressed by the Romans by the single word, *imperium*, a term that cannot be precisely rendered in English; but the nearest equivalent is "sovereign power." By virtue of his *imperium* the monarch exercised his various functions, and had — at least in time of war — the power of life and death over his subjects. The checks on the king were very real, even if they were laid down in no written laws. Though he held office for life, he attained it by election, not by hereditary right and succession. Custom (*mos*), moreover, demanded that he consult the heads of families and clans, who formed an aristocratic council of "elders" (*senatus*), on important measures and questions. Continued violation of *mos* would have brought with it its own punishment. The Roman people (*populus Romanus*) as a body had little influence. If any matter was laid before them in their assembly, they could approve it or reject it, and no more. This assembly was called *comitia curiata*, or assembly of wards, of which there were thirty, each composed of a number of *gentes*. The voting in the assembly was by groups, not by heads, that is to say, each *curia* had one vote. This system of group-voting continued in Republican times and was adopted for the later assemblies. This is a fact of great importance, and the practice is in strong contrast to that of democratic Greek states, like Athens, where, at least from the time of Solon, each citizen exercised his individual franchise in the *ecclesia*.

In respect to its origin one of the most puzzling features of early Roman society is the existence of two classes, the Patricians (*patricii*) and the Plebeians (called collectively *plebs*). Whether or not the sharp distinction between the two, between a privileged and an unprivileged class, was, at least in part, due to an original racial difference is a matter of dispute. It is at all events clear that the *populus Romanus* was made up of these two separate groups, and that in both political influence and social and economic status the Plebeians were in a position of marked inferiority. The Patricians formed an aristocracy which owned most of the land; they had dependent upon them a goodly number of *clientes*. These owed their Patrician patrons the duty of military service under their standards, and probably other obligations which are no longer known. The clients or vassals in turn received protection from the Patricians in whose service they stood. The Plebeians were made up of the miscellaneous mass of the free population, comprising small farmers, day laborers, and artisans; their only political right consisted in membership of the curiate assembly. The end of the monarchy came traditionally in 509 B.C. Whatever the precise truth underlying Livy's picturesque narrative of the expulsion of the tyrannical Tarquinius Superbus, it appears to have been a joint rising of Patricians and Plebeians against a foreign, that is to say, an Etruscan, despot. The free commonwealth (*libera res publica*) succeeded this event, and the powers hitherto exercised for life by the monarch were now entrusted to two Patrician magistrates (consuls) holding office for one year. Although the Plebeians, it is presumed, had taken their part in the work of liberation, the Patricians now arrogated all power to themselves. In fact, it seems likely that the position of the plebs was now worse than in monarchic days, when the king relied to some extent on popular support to counter any attempt of the nobility to wrest too much authority to themselves, and, conversely, might be expected to shield the ordinary citizen on occasion against an oppressive noble.

The *imperium* was now vested in the senior magistrates whose authority was absolutely equal. One could veto the acts of the other; yet, in general practice, however useful such a safeguard might be, it is obvious that some working arrangement and division of duties must have been followed. What it was we do not precisely know. On the other hand, there are not wanting instances of a disagreement, or even deadlock between the senior magistrates, leading to a dislocation of all public business. At the beginning of the Republican period we find a new assembly of the people in existence. The *comitia centuriata* (assembly of centuries) was the outcome of reforms ascribed traditionally to the sixth king of Rome, Servius Tullius. The primary purpose of the so-called Servian organization was military. The whole citizen community was divided into five classes according to their wealth. Each class was subdivided into a certain number of centuries, half of which were made up of the older men (from 46 to 60), half of the younger (from 19 to 45). Each class had its special military equipment, the citizen having to provide his own and doing so according to his means. Thus the wealthier citizens in time of war formed the cavalry and heavy-armed infantry, while the poorer persons in the lower Servian classes were more simply equipped, and were in fact the light-armed troops. Lower than any of the five classes stood five centuries of the humblest folk, who had no means to provide their fighting gear, and who served as artisans. In all there were 193 centuries, and the assembly which now met and voted by centuries superseded the older *comitia curiata* in all matters, save a few connected with religion and inheritance. The preponderant influence of the richer citizens in the centuriate assembly was ensured by the system of group-voting. For the number of centuries in the first class (80) was far larger than that in any other class (20 centuries in classes 2, 3, and 4; 30 in class 5); so that it is obvious that the first class, together with the 18 centuries of cavalry — who were also recruited from the wealthiest persons — could command a majority of votes alone. The *comitia centuriata* now elected magistrates and sanctioned legislation. It also had an important judicial function to perform. The enactment, which Romans of a later age regarded with peculiar veneration, since it safeguarded the liberties of the subject, was traditionally passed in the very year in which the last king was expelled from Rome. This Valerian law of appeal (*Lex Valeria de provocatione*) gave the citizen the right of appeal to the centuriate assembly from the sentence of a magistrate. For the consular *imperium* had a twofold character: the *imperium* exercised in the field in time of war was absolute, that is to say, there was no appeal from any sentence passed by the commander on active service. But the *imperium* exercised at home was the constitutional power of the magistrate. From it, by virtue of the Valerian law, the citizen could appeal to the centuriate assembly.

The senate was wholly, or almost wholly, a Patrician council at this time; for, if a few wealthier Plebeians were admitted, they exercised no influence there. The political inferiority of the Plebeians was only overcome, the economic and social disabilities under which they lived were only righted, after a long and at times bitter struggle. That these changes were so slowly effected was due in part to the power which the Patricians derived from being great landed proprietors, in part to a marked conservatism and respect for law and authority inherent in the Roman character. But the most important single reason why the so-called Struggle between the Orders lasted for more than two centuries is to be found in the external history of Rome during that period. The political expansion of Rome in Italy entailed numerous wars, some of which, like the Second Samnite War, lasted for many years. Whether these struggles were defensive or aggressive is immaterial; they at all events necessitated such frequent mobilization of the Roman citizenry that internal reforms were bound to be retarded. It will be convenient first to trace the growth of Roman power in Italy, and then to revert to her internal development.

2. THE EXPANSION OF ROME IN ITALY

Rome's wars in the fifth century were conducted partly against her Etruscan neighbors, partly against various hill-tribes which at different times raided or threatened the independence of the communities in Latium. Of these tribes the most frequently named were the Aequi on the east and the Volsci on the south. The fall of the monarchy seems to have been followed by years during which the Romans were hard pressed to hold their own against Etruria. A distinct improvement in their situation came when they reached a formal agreement with the Latin League (traditional date, 493 B.C.). It was a free and equal alliance, in which Rome counted for no more than any other city. Its aim was the mutual protection of all against Etruria, and against their neighbors in central Italy. The constant warfare between the League and the hill-peoples went on for years with fluctuating fortunes. But gradually the resistance of both Aequi and Volsci was broken. This result, we may guess, was largely due to the greater power of co-operation possessed by the League; Rome also derived some advantage from an alliance concluded by her with the Hernici, whose territory was situated between that of her two chief enemies.

The political fortunes of the Etruscans were, as we saw, already on the wane during this period. Nevertheless the city of Veii in southern Etruria was the near neighbor and inveterate enemy of Rome. Frequent hostilities between the two states led to no decisive results, until at last, c. 396 B.C., a war, which according to Roman tradition had endured for ten years, ended in the complete triumph of the Romans. The land of the conquered city was annexed and much of it distributed to the poor Plebeians of Rome; a part of the inhabitants was enslaved, but many seem to have been received into the Roman state, since the population of Veii had been mixed and contained a strong Latin element. It is natural to inquire why the other cities of Etruria had not given active support to Veii. The reasons are probably two: it has already been noted that there was a lack of political solidarity among the Etruscan cities. Secondly, a formidable danger threatened Etruria from the North. During the fifth century northern Italy had been overrun by a new horde of invaders, the Gauls. They had settled in the Padus valley, expelling the Etruscans from that region, which, owing to its Gaulish population, became known as "Gaul on this side of the Alps" (*Gallia Cisalpina*). Rome had scarcely recovered from her duel with Veii, when Gaulish tribes swarmed through Etruria and advanced to within a few miles of Rome. By the river Allia a Roman army barred their progress on the Tiber city, but the attack of the Gauls was irresistible. The Roman army was shattered, and the capture and sack of Rome followed, the citadel of the Capitoline hill alone proving im-

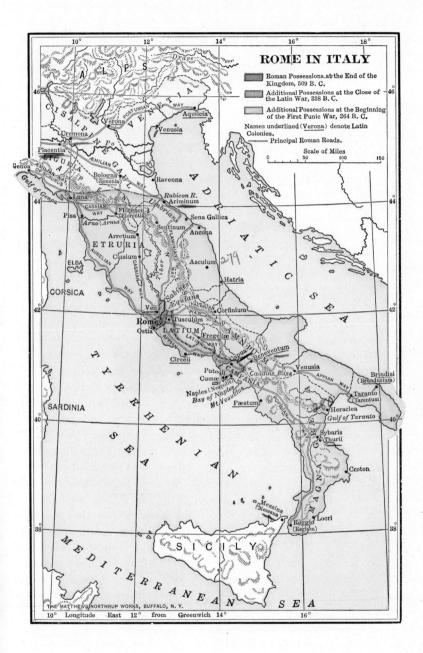

ROME IN ITALY

Roman Possessions at the End of the
Kingdom, 509 B. C.

Additional Possessions at the Close of
the Latin War, 338 B. C.

Additional Possessions at the Beginning
of the First Punic War, 264 B. C.

Names underlined (Verona) denote Latin
Colonies.

——— Principal Roman Roads.

Scale of Miles

0   50   100   150

THE MATTHEWS-NORTHRUP WORKS, BUFFALO, N.Y.

10° Longitude East 12° from Greenwich 14° 16°

pregnable to the attackers. The Gauls, content to receive an indemnity, and, according to the historian Polybius, apprized of an attack on their new homesteads in Cisalpine Gaul by the tribe of the Veneti, retired from Rome after six months' stay in central Italy. Though they had destroyed a great part of the city, they had not broken the spirit or solidarity of Rome and her allies, and the recovery of the former was rapid. Rome was rebuilt, and fresh and improved fortifications, remnants of which can still be seen, were constructed. Although the fourth century witnessed some further raids into Italy by the Gauls, these were more effectively repelled; and their results were trifling compared with the attack of 387 B.C., which the Romans of later generations always regarded as one of the direst episodes in their history.

The general success, in spite of occasional setbacks, of the Romans in their wars reacted also upon the Latin League. Rome, from being merely the leader of a number of equal states, had gradually gained a distinct ascendancy. The threat to their independence made the Latin cities as a whole restive, and caused individual attempts at secession. Such attempted defections were uniformly treated by Rome as hostile acts, justifying an appeal to arms. The only result of the ensuing wars was further to strengthen Rome's hold on Latium, since she regularly bested her opponents. Of the conquered territories of the Volsci and Aequi, moreover, she had annexed a portion and had settled colonies of her citizens there. That the Latins did not benefit territorially in the same way from wars in which they had borne their share of the fighting was a fruitful source of discontent.

South of Latium lay the fertile land of Campania, whose prosperous communities suffered severely from time to time from the raids of tribes inhabiting the hill regions to the east and northeast. With these, the powerful Samnites, Rome seems to have concluded a general treaty of amity about the middle of the fourth century. A little later, however, certain Campanian cities appealed successfully to Rome for support against the Samnites.[1] The result was the First Samnite War (343–1 B.C.)

---

[1] Capua, once an Etruscan settlement, had been populated by Samnites when these expelled the Etruscans from all Campania. By the

which ended indecisively; Rome concluded a fresh treaty with her late enemies. One result of this Roman intervention appears to have been a close alliance between Capua and Rome, an agreement which alarmed other communities in Campania. Hence, when in 338 the long-standing discontent of the Latins came to a head, and her allies declared war on Rome, some parts of Campania joined in with them. Within two years the Romans succeeded in breaking the resistance of their foes. The Latin League came to an end as a political federation, although the religious association of the Latins with its annual festival to Jupiter Latiaris survived for centuries. Two cities, Præneste and Tibur, alone remained independent, and were permitted to renew their treaties with Rome; the others were merged into the enlarged Roman commonwealth. Agreements were also concluded by the Campanian towns with Rome, so that Roman influence now extended as far south as the Volturnus river. A few years of peace were followed by a more prolonged Samnite war (327?–304 B.C.), which originated in a dispute over a recent member of the Roman alliance. But, indeed, greater issues were at stake; for the outcome of the struggle between Samnium and Rome would determine whose should be the leading political power in Italy. The Samnites won some striking successes, especially in the early years of the war. Later on they found allies in the Etruscans. But Rome, from her command of Latium and the old territory of Volsci and Aequi, had a great advantage in being mistress of a compact territory, and able to prevent the junction of two sets of enemies. The drain caused by the war on the resources of both groups of combatants must have been very heavy. Yet, when finally peace was concluded, the resistance of the Samnites themselves was far from being broken, and within less than a decade a Third Samnite War began. Nevertheless, Rome had derived some political advantage from a twenty years' struggle. A number of smaller hill-peoples, till lately numbered among the enemies of Rome, were now enrolled as her allies. Fresh Roman colonies were planted at strategic points commanding

---

middle of the fourth century the citizens of this wealthy city, like the other Campanian towns, were the envy of their kinsmen in the hills, and they naturally sought for support elsewhere.

the recently disturbed areas. For their last attempt at over-throwing the threatened supremacy of Rome in Italy the Samnites sought for outside help. Their own resources were not equal to the task, more especially after the defection of some of their former allies to Rome. They therefore tried to bring about a coalition between themselves, Etruria, Umbria, and Cisalpine Gaul. We can only guess that Rome, faced with a situation more critical than any that she had yet encountered, owed her triumph mainly to her success in dividing the enemy. One great victory, however, she won against heavy odds over a joint Samnite and Gaulish host at Sentinum (295). It took a number of years before the Samnites were reduced, and sporadic fighting with Gauls and Etruscans also put off the day of peace for a good many years. But the threat to Rome's authority had been averted; and, when in 280 she was drawn into a war with a foreign invader, her political control extended from the Arno and Aesis rivers to Apulia and the borders of Lucania. Again new colonies had been established in the years immediately preceding, for example, at Hatria in the northeast (289), and at Venusia, centuries later to become famous as the birthplace of the poet Horace, in the south (291). In the extreme south of the peninsula the Lucanians, for a time the allies of Rome, and the Bruttians were still independent; so, too, were the numerous Greek cities on or near the coast, chief of which was Tarentum. It is probable that the advance of Rome southward in Italy had alarmed the powerful Greek city for some time. To the smaller Hellenic *poleis* with less resources a more immediate, indeed a constant, danger was their Lucanian neighbors. Thurii invoked the aid of Rome in 282, and with her help the Lucanians were defeated. This action was unwelcome to the Tarentines, who regarded Thurii as a possible rival to themselves for Greek supremacy in Magna Græcia.

Hostilities between the South Italian hillsmen and the Hellenic cities were no new thing. In the past the latter had on many occasions obtained outside support, but from kinsmen in other parts. In 342 Sparta sent her Italian colony a force of mercenaries; in 333 Alexander, king of Epirus, came to the aid of Tarentum; but his ambition to make himself the master of all southern Italy led his allies to turn against him. His career was cut short by the dagger of an assassin from among his own troops (331). Nearly thirty years later Sparta once again sent help across the sea, while shortly afterward the ruler of Syracuse intervened in southern Italian affairs. In Sicily the settlement effected by Timoleon (see p. 281) does not appear to have endured for long. Factional disputes broke out afresh in Syracuse, and before long Carthage recommenced her aggressions on the Sicilian Greeks. Once again it was a despot who to some extent retrieved the situation. Agathocles made himself tyrant of Syracuse in 316. He succeeded in uniting the Greek communities under his sway and in keeping Carthage in check. After some years of warfare he concluded a treaty, by which approximately half the island remained Carthaginian. The other half now formed the kingdom of Agathocles. About 300 he crossed over to southern Italy, assisted the Greek cities there against the Lucanians, and enlarged his own dominions by acquiring a small strip of Italian territory. Eleven years later (289) his ambitious plans for the renewal of the war against Carthage, and the expulsion of the Carthaginians from Sicily, were cut short by his death.

The Roman intervention on behalf of Thurii very soon led to a rupture with the Tarentines. The appearance of a small squadron of Roman vessels in Tarentine waters was treated as a hostile act; for, by an earlier treaty, Rome had undertaken to send no ships north of the Lacinian cape. The Roman naval detachment was attacked, while a land force from Tarentum was sent against Thurii and sacked the city after expelling the Roman garrison. Rome's diplomatic protests were treated with contempt, making a declaration of war the swift and inevitable sequel. The Tarentines were probably emboldened to act as they did by the hopes which they entertained of winning a powerful ally to their side. For it seems likely that they had already got into communication with Epirus, now ruled by that able, if erratic, prince, Pyrrhus (Cf. pp. 346; 349). In 280 Pyrrhus landed in Italy with a force of between 20,000 and 25,000 men, together with a number of elephants. These beasts had been employed with some success at the battle of Ipsus and on other occasions in the wars of Alexander's successors. In Pyrrhus' first two engagements with the Romans — at Heraclea in 280 and at Ausculum in 279 — they contributed not a little to his decisive victories. Negotiations between the Epirot prince and Rome after the second battle came to nothing, the reason being the action taken by Carthage and by Syracuse. Carthage, fearful that Pyrrhus' ambitions would lead him to Sicily and threaten Punic interests in the island, proposed to Rome an alliance which was accepted. The diplomatic relations between the two states, which were soon to become bitter rivals for more than half a century, appear to go back to the earliest days of the Republic. Several earlier treaties between Carthage and Rome existed, but these had only defined the respective spheres of influence of each, as well as certain privileges conceded to Roman citizens when in Punic territory. The Syracusans and Sicilians, on the other hand, disunited since the days of Agathocles and in fear of both Carthage and a body of Agathocles' former mercenaries, who had occupied Messana and converted it into a "free-state of robbers" that was a constant menace to the Greek communities, appealed to Pyrrhus to intervene in Sicilian affairs. The Epirot crossed to Sicily and for four years (278–275) waged war against Carthage in the island. He won some striking successes, but the Sicilians after a time became lukewarm in their support, and ultimately came to terms with Carthage independently. They were unwilling to bear indefinitely the heavy demands of men and supplies which he laid upon them, as they realized that his only aim was his personal aggrandizement. Disheartened, Pyrrhus returned to Italy in 275; in the same year a part of his army was heavily defeated at Beneventum by a Roman force. He now abandoned his Italian adventure entirely and withdrew to Epirus, leaving only a garrison behind in Tarentum. That city held out against Rome for some time longer, but in the end was forced to come to terms like the rest of Rome's opponents in southern Italy. The Greek cities were now enrolled as Roman allies and were granted separate treaties with their conqueror. The citadel at Tarentum was converted into a Roman fortress. By 265 Roman authority was supreme throughout the Italian peninsula.

The precise reasons for Rome's success in the earlier centuries of the Republic down to the beginning of the third are often no longer discernible; yet there were certain characteristics of Roman policy and political conduct which account for it in a more general way. The practice of planting colonies in recently vanquished territories was steadily followed, with the result that, in the end, a network of such communities stretched over a great part of the peninsula. Toward the end of the fourth century, when the radius of Roman activity and political intervention had been extended over a much wider area, she began the practice of constructing roads connecting the more important points within her sphere of influence. The earliest of these was the Appian Way, from Rome to Capua, built during the later stages of the Second Samnite War. We have already seen how her geographical position, and that of her oldest allies, enabled her in war-time to control the inner lines of communication, and effectively to bar systematic and sustained coöperation between enemies not adjacent to one another. In her dealings with defeated foes and with allies her policy was to bind them to herself by separate agreements, at the same time fostering any rivalries and disagreements among the communities themselves. Here the Italians not infrequently played into the hands of the Roman government.

Rome's policy has sometimes been denounced as selfish and her methods as unscrupulous. Such accusations are easily made; but they are of little significance, when we consider that they can be and have been levelled against any state which has been in the position of striving for political expansion. It is of more importance to see the effect of Rome's unification of Italy under her hegemony; and indubitably the communities of Italy benefited by being united under her leadership. As a rule she did not arbitrarily interfere in the internal affairs of the towns; and these in turn prospered, because they were no longer distracted by petty strife among themselves. About one-third of the territory south of the Arno and the Aesis rivers was actually Roman; the rest was held by communities in alliance with Rome. Here, however, there was great diversity, which must be briefly elucidated.

The Romans had established two kinds of colonies, and distinguished two kinds of citizenship. There was, first, a group of settlements of Roman burgesses — generally there were 300 in each such colony — who retained their full Roman citizenship and formed the ruling class in the communities in question. The older inhabitants in general received the partial Roman citizenship or, in other words, private rights without the public rights; that is to say, they could not vote or hold a Roman office. These colonies of Roman citizens were all on, or close to, the sea. Next, there was a considerable number of *municipia*, towns composed of those who had the private rights alone. In the main this meant the right of intermarriage (*connubium*) and of unhindered trade (*commercium*) with Roman citizens and with the members of other *municipia*. This group steadily increased to the beginning of the third century, but it was not uniform. Most of the old Latin settlements were now *municipia*, but there were a good many such outside that area. Some were independent in their local government, others received annually a magistrate sent from Rome.

The second class of colonies were the Latin colonies or "allies of the Latin name"; they form a vitally important group and have been described as "offshoots of Rome herself." They had been sent out from Rome from time to time, and ultimately there were thirty-five in all, the last to be founded being Aquileia in 183–181. The number of colonists sent to form these settlements was relatively large. The smallest number recorded is 2500, the largest (Venusia) 20,000. They were independent communities in close alliance with Rome, and they possessed the rights of *connubium* and *commercium* with Rome and with each other.[1] Those communities which did not belong to one or other of these three categories — Roman burgess colony, Latin colony, town of citizens with private rights only — formed the very numerous body of the Italian allies. Each of these allies had a separate treaty with Rome; each was autonomous, save that in its relations with other states it bound itself not to act

---

[1] The inhabitant of a Latin colony could gain or recover his Roman citizenship in several ways: *a*) by holding a magistracy in his town, after which he was a full *civis Romanus; b*) by accusing or procuring the conviction of a Roman magistrate for financial malpractices; *c*) by prolonged residence in Rome, provided that he had left an adult son behind in the Latin colony. The recovery of full citizenship above referred to applies of course only to the original settlers, who lost it when they went out to found the colony.

except through Rome and with Rome's sanction. Also the Italian allies were by their several pacts required to furnish troops, or, in the case of the maritime Greek states, naval contingents, to Rome. The extent to which they enjoyed *connubium* or *commercium* with Rome or with one another is uncertain and a much disputed problem. While many, if not all, probably did have these privileges with Rome, it is unlikely that in general they had them with each other. For one effect of such close relationship would have been a tendency to knit the Italian communities together, which was precisely the result which the Roman government at this time was anxious to prevent. In one matter Rome was unrelenting, since any laxity or concession might in the end have led to the collapse of the political federation that she had so laboriously and so efficiently built up. Any attempt at secession was treated as a *casus belli*, and the treatment meted out to a community that had seceded, and was then made to submit by force of arms, was always rigorous. We shall see how during, and at the end of, the Second Punic War Rome treated certain of her former allies with exemplary severity.

3. The Struggle between the Orders and the Development of the Roman Constitution

It was not many years after the beginning of the Republic that the first successful efforts were made by the Plebeians to obtain some protection of their interests and their class. Their main grievances were that the Patricians granted to them no allotments of state land (*ager publicus*), which increased in quantity as Rome expanded politically; and, secondly, that the laws of debt permitted the personal enslavement of debtors by their creditors. To obtain redress through the medium of the centuriate assembly was hopeless, since, as we have seen, that body was controlled by the wealthy Patricians. Hence it was necessary for the Plebeians to organize themselves effectively, and to find means of exercising their vote to some purpose. Traditionally as the direct outcome of a revolt and a secession from Rome, they won the right of choosing two representatives of their own, called tribunes of the plebs (*tribuni plebis*), whose powers, though very limited at first, were adequate to afford some protection to their class, and also gave that class official leaders (*c.* 494?). Somewhat later their number was raised to five and ultimately to ten (*c.* 457?). Moreover, the Plebeians, in consequence of the Publilian law (471), acquired the right of holding formal meetings of their own body, which elected the tribunes annually, and at other times were competent to pass resolutions binding on the plebs as a whole. The voting was by tribes, the origin of which is very obscure. But it is clear, at least, that the *tribus* were local divisions, there being at first 4 within the city walls. To these additional tribes were added, as the territory occupied by the Romans was enlarged, so that, by the early years of the fourth century, there were 25. By 241 this number had been increased to 35 and was never exceeded afterward. Through these tribes also — and perhaps that was their original purpose — the *tributum*, a tax on property, was assessed and collected. It had originally been a war-levy raised when need arose; but when the cost of military upkeep increased — and at the end of the fifth century the practice came in of paying the common people in the army a small sum by way of wage — the *tributum* was annually imposed. It was not finally abolished until 167.

A third improvement achieved through Plebeian agitation in the earliest period was the codification of existing law. Where the government was in the hands of the aristocracy, and customary law was handed down orally within the privileged families, equitable treatment of the rest of the community could not be insured. We have already observed similar conditions, and similar demands that the law be written down, in the early Greek states.[1] In 451 a board of ten Patricians was charged with the task of codifying the law; a second board continued the work in the following year. But its members abused the wide powers with which they had been entrusted, and were suspected of tyrannical designs. A revolution and secession of the plebs was the immediate sequel, but a compromise was soon effected between the two orders. The board of ten resigned, while the code of the Twelve Tables was published. Only fragments of this early Roman law have survived; they deal

[1] Cf. p. 138.

for the most part with civil law. The regulations concerning debt and such criminal legislation as is known were still very harsh. At the same time the right of appeal from magisterial sentences to the *comitia centuriata* was reaffirmed. The effect of having the law in writing must have been to give all the citizens a greater feeling of security, whether against arbitrary action by Patrician magistrates or against irregularities of tribunes, supported by the Plebeian assembly. One other measure which greatly increased the importance of the last-named body was passed at this time. It was now enacted that resolutions voted by it (*plebiscita*) could become binding on the people, provided they received the formal approval of the senate. This meeting of the plebs (*concilium plebis*), as is clear from its name and origin, was open only to Plebeians. But the tribal organization had during the fifth century also been utilized for a new assembly (*comitia tributa*), of which all the citizens were members. It was presided over by a magistrate, whereas the *concilium plebis* was summoned and directed by the tribunes. The earlier history of the tribal assembly is very uncertain. It seems soon to have acquired legislative power, its voting procedure being less unwieldy than that of the centuriate assembly. But in the earlier period its resolutions had probably to come before the *comitia centuriata* and be ratified by it.[1]

Hitherto intermarriage between Patricians and Plebeians had been prohibited; but in 445 this embargo was lifted by the Canuleian law. The importance of this enactment was very great, for it broke the jealous exclusiveness of the aristocracy very effectively. The children of a Patrician father and a Plebeian mother would now acquire the same status as their father — they would count as Patricians. It is obvious, how-

---

[1] The *concilium plebis* and *comitia tributa* have been the subject of endless controversy owing to the intricate and sometimes contradictory nature of the evidence. Some modern scholars would eliminate the *concilium* entirely, asserting that there were never more than three assemblies at Rome, the *comitia curiata*, *comitia centuriata*, and *comitia tributa*. This would certainly simplify the problem, but to the present writer seems unpermissible. Difficult as the ancient evidence is, it does seem to leave no doubt that there was a distinction between the *concilium plebis* and the *comitia tributa*, and that both continued to exist and function side by side to the end of the Republic.

ever, that though the Plebeians had very sensibly improved
their position in the commonwealth, anything like complete
political equality was unattainable so long as they were shut
out from the magistracies. The efforts of Canuleius to render
Plebeians eligible for the consulship failed. But the Patricians
were driven to introduce an innovation, by which they really
surrendered some part of their prerogative. It was enacted
that in any year in which circumstances seemed to make it
desirable, the consulship could be suspended, and the place of
the two senior magistrates taken by a board of military tribunes
with consular power. To this office Plebeians were to be eligible. The military tribunes were appointed on many occasions
between 444 and 367, although it was not till 404 that a
Plebeian was actually elected as a member of the board. The
number of these officials varied at different times, the largest
number recorded being nine, the smallest three. In 421 the
junior magistracy known as the quæstorship was thrown open
to the Plebeians, the number of quæstors being at the same time
increased from two to four. While two of them continued to
act as assistants to the consuls, two were put in charge of the
treasury (*aerarium*), though subject to the control of the senate
and the senior magistrates. They themselves now ranked as
independent, if junior, magistrates. For a while the struggle
between the Orders seemed to be quiescent. There were several
occasions when Plebeians tried to get their economic grievances
righted by securing for their class allotments of land; but the
measures put forward never became law. There are, too, not
wanting signs of a certain divergence of interests amongst the
Plebeians themselves; for there had grown up a class of wealthy
Plebeians, whose ambitions were not necessarily in line with the
desires of their less fortunate fellows. Later the Patrician government for its part seems to have made some concessions, since
several land allotments for the benefit of the plebs are recorded
for the early years of the fourth century. Also a number of
Latin colonies founded at this time helped to ease economic and
social distress.

Yet there still remained much cause for complaint, especially
in respect of the harsh treatment of debtors and the unhappy
condition of many small farmers, whose livelihood had been

jeopardized during their absence on military service, and who on their return to their homesteads had been forced to borrow, thereby sinking more and more deeply into debt. The difficulties of the small agriculturist were increased by the losses and destruction resulting from the Gallic invasion, so that we are not surprised to find an intensive renewal of the struggle against the Patrician government only a few years after the disaster at the Allia. This Plebeian agitation, led by two tribunes, C. Licinius Stolo and L. Sextius Lateranus, is said to have lasted ten years. At last, in 367 B.C., the so-called Licinio-Sextian Rogations were passed and could be counted a triumph of the Plebeian cause. The office of military tribune with consular power was abolished, and the consulship was restored as an annual magistracy. Moreover, Plebeians were now eligible for it; indeed, within a few years their position was further strengthened by the proviso that one consul each year must be a Plebeian. It is true that the Patricians still succeeded in winning something in the nature of a compromise. The new office of prætor was instituted, and to him was entrusted the civil jurisdiction in Rome hitherto exercised by the consuls. Like them the prætor was invested with the *imperium*. This new office was for a time restricted to Patricians; so, too, was another freshly created magistracy, the curule ædileship. These ædiles were charged with the superintendence of public works. Other reforms of Licinius and Sextius, besides that affecting the consulship, were economic and not political in their aim. The condition of debtors was ameliorated by a grant of considerable relief. Interest already paid by a debtor was deducted from the principal; the remaining debt was to be paid off by installments in three years. Thirdly, the two tribunes passed legislation to prevent monopoly of occupation of state-lands by the wealthy. The amount of *ager publicus* which any person could now legally occupy, paying a nominal rent to the government, was limited to 500 *jugera* (*c.* 330 acres). No fresh allotments were provided for by this piece of legislation; but the restriction would in the future, so it was hoped, leave more public lands available for distribution.

The offices that were open only to Patricians — the newly created prætorship and curule ædileship, and the censorship

instituted *c.* 443 — were during the course of the next half-
century thrown open one by one to the Plebeians. Even the
priesthoods, with one or two exceptions, could after 300 be
filled by them. There remained one final triumph for the so
long inferior Order. In 287, after an embittered struggle, the
Hortensian law was passed, which established the *concilium
plebis* as an independent legislative body. *Plebiscita* passed by
it attained the force of law and were binding on the whole
community, irrespective of senatorial sanction. The *comitia
tributa*, too, by this time was a sovereign law-making assembly,
in fact it now became the chief legislative body in the Roman
commonwealth. There was now really no reason for these
two to continue separately; all distinction between Patricians
and Plebeians having been obliterated, a meeting restricted to
Plebeians might seem superfluous. Roman conservatism, together with the memory of what the *concilium plebis* had accomplished in the struggle for liberty and equality, may account
for its survival to the end of the Republic.

The tribunes, who in earlier years had been mere representatives of the plebs, from the end of the fourth century became
recognized as regular magistrates of the Roman people; for
some time they had been admitted like the curule magistrates
to the senate, though at first the part they played in that body
was mainly passive. As one might say, they held a "watching
brief" there for their Order. It might have been supposed that
with all magistracies open to members of either class at Rome,
with the electoral and legislative authority of the people as a
whole expressed respectively in the *comitia centuriata* and the
comitia tributa — at all events from the second half of the third
century, when the centuriate assembly was so reorganized that
the first class could no longer dominate the vote — the sovereignty of the people in the commonwealth would be assured,
and would exist not only in theory but manifest itself in practice.
Actually, however, it was the senate which in the third and
second centuries gained almost complete control of the government. As a result of the admission of Plebeians to all magistracies a new nobility grew up, distinct from the old Patriciate,
and composed of those who had held curule offices and were
members of the senate. These office-holders, it is true, owed

their position to popular election by the centuriate assembly; yet the advantages of wealth were never more apparent than in their case. The wealthy Plebeians attained to office and to the senate; the poor members of the Order were rarely successful. After a generation or two it was further seen to be an advantage to be a member of a family whose members had already attained to office. The old predominance of Patricians had disappeared; in place of it there grew up a new Order, part Patrician, part Plebeian, and from it the senate was now constituted. The *nobiles*, as we find them from the third century on, are synonymous with the senatorial class.

CHAPTER XXI

ROME AND CARTHAGE, 264-201 B.C.

> *No states, no nations ever met in arms greater in*
> *strength or richer in resources; these Powers them-*
> *selves had never before been in so high a state*
> *of efficiency or better prepared to stand the strain*
> *of a long war; they were no stranger to each others'*
> *tactics after their experience in the first Punic*
> *war; and so variable were the fortunes and so*
> *doubtful the issue of the war, that those who were*
> *ultimately victorious were in the earlier stages*
> *brought nearest to ruin. —* Livy, xxi, 1 (Roberts'
> translation).

1. ROME AND CARTHAGE, 264-219 B.C.

WITH the extension of Rome's control over all southern Italy,
which might easily be followed by an early intervention in
Sicily, it must have been borne in upon Carthage that this
state, with which in the past she had concluded treaties favorable to herself and her maritime supremacy in the western
Mediterranean, would soon have to be enrolled among her
enemies. Carthaginian power had not been wholly exempt from
vicissitudes. There had been times when her possessions in
Sicily had been limited to the three strongholds in its northwest
corner. But recently she had come well out of the war with
Agathocles, and *c.* 270 B.C. she controlled more than half the
island. Apart from this, her empire embraced the north coast
of Africa from approximately longitude E. 15 (from Greenwich)
to the straits of Gibraltar, some territory in southern Spain,
part of Sardinia, the Balearic islands, and Malta. A portion of
the native population of northern Africa was tributary to her,
and from it she levied detachments of troops, especially cavalry.
To maintain the integrity of this empire, and to protect the
commerce from which her wealth was mainly derived, a powerful navy was the first requisite. Yet past events — *e.g.* the
war against Massilia *c.* 500 B.C. — and still more those of the

first war between her and Rome, suggest that the great reputation of the Punic navy was not wholly deserved. Citizen
army she had none to speak of at this time. For her land fighting she relied mainly on mercenaries, whom her vast wealth
allowed her to engage in great numbers when the need arose.
Her subjects also furnished her with valuable troops; for example, the Numidian cavalry already noted, and the famous
slingers from the Balearic islands.

Her constitution and government are but imperfectly known,
but seem to have been sufficiently unlike what was usual among
oriental peoples, and sufficiently like the government of some
Greek states, to attract the attention of Aristotle. Yet the
mixed constitution of Carthage which he analyzes, at least during the period of the Punic Wars, did not always work harmoni-
ously. Two senior magistrates (*suffetes*), annually elected by
the citizen assembly, were nominally at the head of the government. Since, however, the chief power rested with a senate of
300 and a smaller council (of 30?), the rule was predominantly
oligarchic, the senators and councillors being members of the
richest families. Their wealth was derived in some cases from
commerce, in others from the possession of landed estates
profitably run by serf or slave labor. The assembly, however,
elected the chief military officers in the state, and herein lay a
possible source of friction or disunion within the body politic.
In the third century the most prominent Carthaginian family,
the Barcidæ, relied on the support of the assembly, and to a
great extent determined the foreign policy of Carthage. The
jealousy of the Punic oligarchy nevertheless might lead to
intrigue and dissension at home, and abroad to insufficient
support being given to the eminent military leaders who were
members of the Barca family. It was this situation which, as
will be seen, contributed largely to the ultimate failure of
Carthage in the second war with Rome.

In Syracuse, after the departure of Pyrrhus, faction was again
rife. The distress caused by intestinal warfare was aggravated
by the raids of the Mamertines in Messana. In Syracuse's hour
of need the direction of affairs was entrusted to the *strategos*,
Hiero. He inflicted a severe defeat on the Mamertines, and was
then accepted by the Syracusans as their king, ruling under the

name of Hiero II. He followed up his first military success by an attack on Messana, thereby becoming the unwitting cause of a prolonged struggle between the two leading powers in the western Mediterranean. For, when Hiero blockaded the city, divided counsels prevailed among its inhabitants. One faction sought help from Carthage, another appealed to Rome. The Roman senate, according to Polybius' narrative, hesitated to commit itself to an intervention which could only lead to war with Carthage; it might perhaps even be interpreted as a violation of earlier agreements between the two states. Abstention, on the other hand, would put Carthage in possession of Messana, and might lead to her winning all Sicily. In that case Carthage's proximity to the new allies of Rome in southern Italy might be a danger to them and to Roman supremacy in the peninsula. The decision was laid by the senate before the centuriate assembly, whose vote was for intervention.

With the help of one faction in Messana a Roman expeditionary force was admitted into the city, after eluding the Punic fleet by night, and after the Carthaginian garrison had by a plausible deception been induced to withdraw from the city. Carthage and Rome were now at open war, and the former concluded an alliance with her ancient foe, Syracuse. The twenty-three years' war which thus began falls into several clearly marked stages. From 264–261 the scene of operations was wholly in Sicily. A Roman army besieged Syracuse, and, though the city was not taken, Hiero was sufficiently impressed to throw over his Semitic allies and join Rome. For the rest of his long reign — he died in 215 B.C., being then more than ninety years of age — he remained her faithful ally. The Romans next attacked and reduced Agrigentum, in spite of the large mercenary force sent by Carthage for its defense. The sack of the town, and the enslavement of the population by the Roman commander, was an inexcusable act of barbarity, which had the effect of alienating other Sicilian communities from Rome. The Romans now purposed to force the enemy to evacuate the whole island; but this was a project which could only be realized by a power having an adequate fleet at its disposal.

The second stage of the war is characterized by great naval activity. In the building and equipment of a large fleet the

Romans doubtless derived much assistance from their Greek allies in Italy. But the tactics which they proposed to adopt were such as to place the brunt of the attack on their land-troops serving as marines on ship-board. A large grappling contrivance called the "raven" (*corvus*) was fashioned for each warship, with which the enemy vessel could be held, preliminary to being boarded by the Roman troops. This method of converting a naval action as far as possible into a land fight was no new thing; it was indeed the older type of naval fighting in Greece, which in some instances survived well into the fifth century. In 260 a Roman fleet of 120 vessels, reinforced by some allied ships, decisively defeated the Carthaginian fleet off Mylæ in northeastern Sicily. In spite of this success the Romans found it impossible to dislodge the enemy from his Sicilian strongholds. Operations dragged on for several years. An indecisive naval action fought off Tyndaris in 257 was followed in 256 by a second decisive Roman victory off Ecnomus on the south coast of the island. Foiled in its plan of winning all Sicily, the Roman senate had by this time decided to carry the war into the enemy's own country, and this naval victory facilitated the task of transporting an expeditionary force to Africa. What the strength of this Roman army was must remain doubtful, but it was no doubt adequate to compel the Carthaginians to sue for peace, provided it remained undivided.[1] The senate, however, made a fatal mistake. Overconfident owing to the satisfactory issue of the first fighting on African soil, they recalled a great part of the army, leaving a mere 15,000 men under M. Atilius Regulus to "finish the war." The Carthaginians, helped by a body of Greek mercenaries, and especially by the military skill of one of their number, a Spartan called Xanthippus, annihilated Regulus' army, taking him and some other officers prisoners. Thus the Roman attack on Africa had failed utterly. The same year (255) saw a Roman naval disaster; for the fleet, which had rescued a few survivors of the African catastrophe, was totally wrecked on its return voyage off the southern coast of Sicily.

[1] The figures given in the ancient writers are impossibly high, viz., 330 ships and 140,000 men all told on the Roman side, 350 vessels and 150,000 men on the Carthaginian.

The third period of the war (255–249) is mainly a record of Roman naval mishaps, of which the worst was their defeat at the battle of Drepana in 249. These disasters were to some extent offset by their capture of Panormus; this deprived the enemy of one of its three Sicilian bases. However, all the efforts to take Lilybæum by assault failed, and the siege was finally converted into a blockade. By this time both combatants were suffering from war weariness. The Roman government, besides, was in serious financial difficulties. The fleet could not be rebuilt, and the Romans relied on carrying on the war with their land forces alone. It was perhaps the best opportunity for a decisive blow by sea, and for cutting off Sicily from Italy, that presented itself to Carthage during the war, but she failed to take it. Instead, only some futile raids were made on the Italian coast; then, in 247, a new commander took charge of operations in Sicily, namely, Hamilcar Barca. For five years he conducted a most damaging guerilla war on the Romans, first from Eircte, overlooking Panormus, then from Eryx lying above Drepana. Skillful as were his manœuvres and costly for the enemy, they could not bring the struggle to a decisive issue. The exhaustion of both sides had led to a stalemate, when the Roman senate, the treasury being empty, appealed to the patriotism of its citizens. The money needed to rebuild the fleet was raised by private subscription, and in the summer of 242 two hundred Roman vessels of the most up-to-date design put to sea. A decision was not long in coming. The objective of the Romans was now to hasten the reduction of Lilybæum and Drepana. The consul, C. Lutatius Catulus, was in supreme ✳ command, and near the Aegates islands, off the northeastern corner of Sicily, he intercepted and decisively defeated a relief expedition and navy hastily sent across from Africa to the island. Negotiations initiated by Carthage were not long delayed; by the peace signed in 241 she undertook to pay a heavy indemnity of 3200 talents over a period of ten years, to evacuate Sicily, to abstain from any attack on Rome's ally, Syracuse, and to surrender Roman prisoners without ransom.

The first bout between the two west Mediterranean powers had been fought, and Rome had won on points. Weary and exhausted as both combatants were, neither had been per-

✳ Cat′-u-lus – not Cat-tul-us, the poet

manently incapacitated, and a small but far-seeing minority in
either state must have realized that a renewal of the struggle
for supremacy was only a matter of time. Actually almost a
quarter of a century passed before the second clash came. This
interval was used to good purpose by both belligerents. Carthage sought, under the inspired leadership of the Barcidæ, to
recoup herself for the loss of Sicily by conquest elsewhere;
Rome consolidated her position in Italy. In addition both
states had domestic troubles to face, though of very different
character. The Carthaginian government was confronted immediately after the war with a mutiny of its mercenary troops,
who were supported by some of its native subjects in Africa.
Unable or unwilling to pay their hired fighters what they demanded, the Carthaginians had to strain every nerve for three
years before the mutineers were crushed. The Romans did
not hesitate to take advantage of their late enemy's domestic
difficulties. In 238 they occupied Sardinia at the invitation of
a body of Punic mutineers there; the protests of Carthage were
met by a declaration of war. Unable to fight, Carthage was
forced to surrender all claims to Sardinia and Corsica, and to
pay an indemnity of 1200 talents. Rome by questionable
means thus acquired two fresh extra-Italian territories; she
also won the undying hatred of Carthage.

Foremost among the Punic enemies of Rome was Hamilcar
Barca, who had done such good service in Sicily, and who more
recently had been responsible for crushing the mutineers in
Africa. His political program was for some years strongly opposed by the Carthaginian oligarchy. Hamilcar's immediate
proposal was that the Carthaginians should undertake the conquest of the Spanish peninsula, thereby compensating themselves for the loss of the three islands near Italy. Two years
after the ignominious capitulation to Roman demands, that is
to say, in 236 Hamilcar having carried his point, crossed to
Spain. Until his death in 229 he, partly by diplomacy, partly
by fighting, was busy in building up a considerable empire in
Spain. His son-in-law, Hasdrubal, who succeeded him in the
Spanish command, continued Hamilcar's policy and was responsible for the foundation of New Carthage (*Nova Carthago*),
which now became the capital of the Punic dependencies in

Spain. In 226 the Roman senate sent representatives to nego-
tiate with Hasdrubal, with a view to placing a limit to Carthaginian expansion in the peninsula. A treaty was concluded
by which the Ebro (*Iberus*) marked the point beyond which
no Punic soldiery was to pass. This agreement does not appear
to have been acknowledged or ratified by the Carthaginian
government; but for the moment it served its purpose as far as
both Rome and Hasdrubal were concerned. The reason for the
action of the Roman senate is not too clear. Probably the Romans
were uneasy at the rapid expansion of their rival in Spain;
though, as they made no effort to secure northern Spain for themselves, they could hardly imagine that an agreement, such as
they had made, would do more than effect a temporary postpone-
ment of a second war, which they probably regarded as inevitable. The Greek city of Massilia, which had long been in friendly
alliance with Rome may have precipitated the action of Rome in
226. For the foundation of New Carthage and the progress of
Hasdrubal in Spain might threaten the maritime interests of
the Massiliots, and the independence of some Græco-Iberian
towns on the east coast of Spain which were in alliance with
them.

The treaty did not prevent Rome a year or two later from
making an alliance with Saguntum, an independent city-state
situated some distance south of the partition line. Since her
action does not seem to have been challenged by Hasdrubal, it
was clearly not regarded as a violation of the agreement of 226.
In 221 Hasdrubal was murdered by a personal enemy, and
Hannibal, son of Hamilcar, though only twenty-six years of
age, became commander-in-chief in Spain. Meanwhile some
noteworthy changes had occurred in Italy. The Gaulish tribes
in the Po valley, reinforced by new bands of their kinsmen from
across the Alps, became very restive. In 236 they threatened
Ariminum, but advanced no further, as they fell to quarrelling
among themselves. Eleven years later a more dangerous invasion of Italy was attempted; but the Gauls, after doing some
damage, were driven back and heavily defeated at Telamon
(225). The Romans followed up their victory by three campaigns in *Gallia Cisalpina*, by the end of which they had compelled the Gauls to acknowledge their authority. Two Latin

colonies and fortress towns were established in the Po valley, at Cremona and Placentia.

Rome's responsibilities were growing. Her allies on the coast of southern Italy suffered severely from the piratical attacks of Illyrians. This semi-barbarous people, whose capital was at Scodra, was in 229 ruled by Queen Teuta as guardian of her son, who was a minor. Their chief occupation and means of livelihood was piracy and occasional coastal raids on peaceful districts in northwestern Greece. The Roman government intervened on behalf of its allies; but, so far from giving redress, the Illyrian queen caused one of the Roman ambassadors to be murdered. In the first Illyrian war (229–228) Teuta was forced to submit, and Rome concluded alliances with several Greek states on the eastern shores of the Adriatic. A second military intervention became necessary in 219. The most important result of these two operations was that Rome was brought into friendly relations, but without any formal treaties or commitments, with the two leading states in Greece, the Aetolian and the Achæan Leagues. But she also incurred the suspicions of the Macedonian king, Philip V, who had come to the throne in 221, and who, before many years had passed, allied himself with Rome's bitterest enemy, the Carthaginian Hannibal.

2. THE SECOND WAR WITH CARTHAGE

The fact that the Roman government had its hands very full in 219–218 with the remnants of the Illyrian war, the settlement of Cisalpine Gaul, and the foundation of the Latin colonies already named, must be held to account for its apparently dilatory attitude to the crisis which had now developed in Spain. By 219 Hannibal's plans for a war of revenge on Rome were ripe. But, though his hold on Spain to the south of the Ebro was secure, and his military forces were in prime condition, he was doubtful of the support of his home government. For the influence of the Barcidæ had waned, and the Carthaginian oligarchy was disinclined to renew the struggle with Rome. Hannibal staked his hopes on provoking a Roman declaration of war, and in those circumstances receiving the support, even if reluctant, of his government. In 219 an opportunity offered for precipitating a rupture. On the pretext that the Saguntines had acted in a hostile manner toward a Spanish tribe owing allegiance to Carthage, Hannibal attacked Saguntum, and, after an eight months' siege, took it. The city had at once appealed to Rome; but the senate acted circumspectly, because to Rome a fresh war with Carthage at this point was anything but opportune. A diplomatic protest was lodged at Carthage, demanding Hannibal's surrender and satisfaction for the wrong done. Hannibal had judged rightly when he assumed that in a crisis such as this the Punic oligarchy would not leave him in the lurch. Rome's demands were refused, whereupon she declared war.

Once hostilities had become inevitable, the Romans prepared immediately to take the offensive. Of the two consular armies one was detailed for Spain, the other was despatched in the first place to Sicily, whence an invasion of Africa was to be carried out. Given an opponent such as Carthage had been in the first war, these plans were perfectly feasible. For Carthage had not recovered her naval supremacy since 241, and was therefore not in a position to stop either the main expedition to Africa or the subsidiary one to Spain. The Romans were, however, to learn that their enemy was not so much Carthage as Hannibal, a military genius with a highly trained Punic-Spanish army. They could not foresee the bold offensive that he had planned. Having perfected his preparations during the previous winter, he set out in the spring of 218 to invade Italy by land. After crossing the Ebro he advanced rapidly through northeastern Spain, though not without meeting with some resistance from the natives. Without mishap he traversed the Pyrenees by one of the most easterly passes. Part of his military force was left behind in Spain in charge of his brother Hasdrubal. He himself, when he entered Gaul, had an army of about 50,000 infantry, 9000 cavalry, and 40 elephants. It was only when he reached the Rhone and prepared to cross it — probably just above Arles — that he met with serious opposition from a Gaulish tribe on the east bank. His further progress was one of continuous danger and hardship. He had indeed eluded the Roman consul, P. Cornelius Scipio, who had reached Massilia when Hannibal was preparing to cross the Rhone. But the hostility of the tribes from the river to the Alps, and the late season when he finally traversed that last barrier into Italy, played havoc with his army. To the intense misery caused by snow and ice was added the suffering caused by scarcity of provisions. Thus, when Hannibal descended into the kindlier plains of Cisalpine Gaul, he found that his army had been reduced to less than half the number which had set out from the Pyrenees.[1]

The rapidity and unexpectedness of the Punic invasion had forced the Roman senate and consuls to revise their war plans drastically. T. Sempronius Longus was recalled from Sicily, while Scipio at Massilia, finding that Hannibal had escaped, sent on the bulk of his army to Spain under his brother Gnæus, whereas he himself with a small detachment returned in haste to Italy by sea. In spite of the lateness of the season he crossed the Apennines and advanced in Gallia Cisalpina with such troops as he could master. The attempt to prevent Hannibal from crossing the Padus was frustrated; for the Romans had the worst of a cavalry skirmish by the River Ticinus. When Sempronius with his consular army had joined his colleague, the two commanders decided on an immediate offensive. Near the River Trebia the first pitched battle of the war was fought, and ended in a heavy defeat of the Romans. The political results were as disastrous as the destruction of three-quarters of the Roman army — only 10,000 out of 40,000 were able to make an orderly retreat to Placentia — for now the tribes of Cisalpine Gaul as a whole declared for the invader. It was Hannibal's hope and expectation that the Italian and Latin allies of Rome would do the same when he appeared in the Italian peninsula; but herein he was mistaken.

After spending the rest of the winter in northern Italy, he, in the early spring of 217, marched across the Apennines as far westward as possible, again evading the Roman troops. Four new legions had been sent to reinforce the survivors of the Trebia; together they were massed at Arretium and Ariminum, preparatory to invading the Po valley at the beginning of the campaigning season. The consul, C. Flaminius, at once took

[1] Hannibal probably used the pass leading over the Col Clapier or Little Mt. Cenis.

up the pursuit of the elusive Hannibal. But, when his army 35,000 strong was marching through a narrow defile on the northern shore of Lake Trasimene in Etruria, it found itself trapped and surrounded by the enemy. Flaminius died fighting; of his army not more than 10,000 escaped to Rome, the rest being either slain in battle or subsequently cut down. Both here and on the Trebia not a little of Hannibal's success had been due to the excellence of his Numidian cavalry.

In Rome, in spite of popular clamor, the senate kept its head and, in view of the national emergency, appointed Q. Fabius to the dictatorship. Probably there was a general expectation that Hannibal would march on Rome; it is certain that he had neither the men nor the siege apparatus requisite for such a task. Indeed, it is more than doubtful whether he harbored any such intention at any time. His aim seems rather to have been to break the power of Rome in Italy by causing her allies to break away from her *en masse*. But the wholesale defections did not take place. Fabius, for his part, followed the wise, if unpopular because unspectacular, plan of avoiding any open engagement, and, by following at the enemy's heels, keeping him constantly on the alert. Thus, too, he caused Hannibal the maximum difficulty in maintaining the Punic commissariat. Nevertheless, Hannibal could not be prevented from doing much damage by laying waste the country. He overran Samnium and part of Campania, where, as yet, he failed to win over Capua, and also Apulia. Here he passed the winter.

It was not till late in the spring of 216 that another decisive action was fought. In Rome the winter months had been used to raise additional troops, and generally to make good, so far as possible, the disasters and loss of the two previous years. Fabius' dictatorship had expired, and in 216 the government returned to its normal form. The two consuls were C. Terentius Varro and L. Aemilius Paullus. The season opened with a repetition of the previous year's "playing for position." By June Hannibal had taken up his position at Cannæ in Apulia, where the level plain would enable him to use his horse to the best advantage. Of the two Roman commanders, Paullus was cautious, Varro precipitate, and unfortunately, by the practice then existing, the two were in supreme command on alternate days. It was not long before Varro offered battle to the enemy. The result was a veritable massacre of Romans. For the simple massing of troops against Hannibal's centre was too puerile a method of fighting against a superb tactician like Hannibal. He allowed his centre to retire before the Roman onslaught, and then gave his light horse the signal to harry the exposed flanks of the enemy, while the heavy cavalry attacked in the rear. Thus, step by step, Varro's army was completely surrounded and all but cut to pieces. It is likely that Rome lost not less than 50,000 men on that day, while another 10,000 were taken prisoner. Paullus was among the slain; Varro escaped and subsequently rallied the Roman survivors, not more than 15,000 out of a total army numbering nearly 80,000 men.

The Roman fortunes were now at their lowest. It was not only her loss in man-power, but the political consequences of this defeat, which seemed to make her plight well-nigh desperate. A good many of her southern Italian allies, among them Capua, declared for the invader. Early in 215 old King Hiero of Syracuse died, and, under the influence of pro-Carthaginian counsellors, his young successor, Hieronymus, declared for Carthage. In the same year Philip of Macedon allied himself to Hannibal and intimated that he would invade Italy, a promise which he was never able to fulfill. Rome was saved by two things, the indomitable spirit of her citizens, which was never greater than when the outlook was darkest, and the solidarity of the majority of her allies. For all the Latin, and most of the central Italian, allies continued to stand by her; so, too, did the Greek cities in the south. During the next few years the Romans were engaged on five or six different fronts; against Hannibal himself in central and southern Italy, against Capua, which they besieged in 212, against Syracuse, invested in 213, in Spain, and, finally, in Epirus against the Macedonian.

At Rome in 216 four fresh legions were levied, though, to do this, it was necessary to call on youths under the normal military age. The faithful allies of Rome, too, raised new contingents. Moreover, the bitter experience of the past three years was not without its beneficial effect on the government; for, during the remainder of the war, we find that competent and experienced men alone were appointed to the higher military commands. Hannibal, hampered by the fortress towns of the enemy and watched by consular and prætorian armies, was slowly but surely reduced to remaining on the defensive. He won over and captured several Greek cities in the south, notably Tarentum, whose citadel he failed to take; but, though he thus obtained access to the sea, he derived little advantage from this. For the hoped-for reinforcements from Africa did not come. By 212 the Romans were in a sufficiently strong position to besiege Capua, and all Hannibal's efforts to relieve the city were in vain. He even executed a forced march by night through Latium to the outskirts of Rome, hoping by this threat to force the enemy to withdraw a part of their army outside the Campanian city. But Rome was not to be taken by surprise, and Hannibal was obliged to retire without effecting his purpose. In 211 Capua capitulated; its people were treated with exemplary severity. The ruling oligarchs were put to death, and the rest of the citizens enslaved. The entire territory of the city was made Roman state-lands, which were subsequently farmed out to numerous lessees. "It was settled," writes the Roman historian, "that Capua should be simply a lodgment and a shelter, a city merely in name; there was to be no corporate life, no senate, no council of the plebs, no magistrates."[1]

In the previous year Syracuse, after enduring a siege for more than twelve months, was reduced by M. Marcellus, one of the ablest commanders on the Roman side during the long war. While the situation of the Romans in Italy and Sicily was thus steadily improving, the danger from Macedon had also been averted. A Roman fleet patrolled the Adriatic, and Rome allied herself with a coalition of Greek states — the Aetolian League and King Attalus of Pergamum were the most prominent — which was carrying on a war against Philip. This so-called First Macedonian War dragged on with varying success to the chief combatants until 205. Rome herself was able to leave most of the active fighting to her new allies; but the joint action of all debarred Philip from maturing his plans for a western expedition.

Finally there was the Spanish theatre of war. Here striking successes had been followed by disaster. The two brothers,

[1] Livy xxvi, 16 (Forster's translation).

Gnæus and Publius Scipio, from 217 to 213 carried on operations
with very satisfactory results. They not only prevented Hasdrubal from sending reinforcements to his brother, but they
gradually extended the Roman protectorate over a great part
of the peninsula. In 214 they were able to occupy Saguntum;
in the next year they formed an alliance with the Moorish
prince, Syphax, who had begun hostilities against Carthage in
northern Africa. But in 212–211 the tide turned. Hasdrubal
crossed over to Africa and gave Syphax a sound beating. The
alarming situation in Spain, moreover, stimulated the lethargy
of the Carthaginian government. A substantial body of reinforcements was equipped and despatched to the Spanish seat of
war. In 212 both Roman commanders suffered defeat and were
killed within a month of one another; all the territory that they
had won south of the Ebro was lost again. The drain of the war
in Italy and Sicily at that time prevented the senate from sending fresh troops to Spain until 211. Nevertheless Carthage had
lost a great opportunity. A more far-sighted statesmanship
would have sought to strike effectively at Rome in Italy; to
do this, the expeditionary force should have been sent to Italy
to help Hannibal. With such timely assistance in 213 he might
still have brought Rome to her knees. As it was, after the fall
of Capua, he was compelled more and more to remain strictly
on the defensive in southern Italy. Once more his hopes of much
needed aid were to be raised, only to be frustrated in the eleventh hour.

In 211 the senate was at last able to send a picked force of
12,000 men to Spain. Its commander appears to have been
undistinguished; so in the next year a most unprecedented
appointment was made. The conduct of the Spanish war was
entrusted to P. Cornelius Scipio, son of the Publius who had
fallen in 212, although he was only in his twenty-fourth year,
and not yet qualified under normal conditions to hold a senior
magistracy or command. He owed his election, we are told, to
popular agitation and the vote of the centuriate assembly. It
is likely that the influence of his family and clan — the *gens
Cornelia* was one of the oldest and most influential at Rome —
contributed not a little to his appointment. However that may
be, he set out for Spain in 210 with an additional legion. Spend-

ing the winter at Tarraco, he began operations in 209. They opened with a striking success. The Carthaginian forces being engaged elsewhere in fighting Spanish tribes, New Carthage had been left with only a small garrison of 1,000 men. Scipio was able to surprise the city and to capture it with little difficulty. Great quantities of stores thus fell into his hands at a critical time. Moreover, the political results of his success and of his studied moderation toward his Spanish prisoners, whom he permitted to return to their respective homes, were soon apparent. Many native tribes went over from Carthage to Rome. In 208 Scipio advanced into southern Spain, and there, at Bæcula, he defeated Hasdrubal. Nevertheless, the Carthaginian was able to carry out an orderly retreat. Then, with about 10,000 men, he set out rapidly to join his brother in Italy. Crossing the Pyrenees by one of the western passes, he eluded Roman vigilance. During the winter he enlisted large numbers of Gauls in his service, and, in the spring of 207, he crossed the Alps without mishap or serious casualties. It is impossible to determine how much, if any blame, attached to Scipio for letting the enemy escape from Spain. If the Roman commander was seriously at fault, the fact had long been forgotten when he returned to Rome triumphantly in 206.

The chief event of 207, and the anxiety of the Roman people prior to and during the crisis, have been depicted by Livy in some of the finest chapters of his *History*. Yet it can scarcely be doubted that, for the sake of dramatic effect, the danger threatening Rome at this point has been not a little exaggerated. Even if Hasdrubal had succeeded in joining his brother, it is impossible to believe that their combined armies would have forced the Romans, who had held their own against greater odds for almost a decade, to capitulate. However, we cannot fail to believe in the anxiety of the senate, or the popular excitement when Hasdrubal appeared in Cisalpine Gaul. The Romans were not taken by surprise as they had been in 218; for Hasdrubal's presence in Transalpine Gaul through the winter months was of course known to them, and their preparations were laid accordingly. The two main armies in 207 were entrusted to the consuls C. Claudius Nero and M. Livius Salinator. The former was sent to southern Italy to hold

Hannibal in check, while Livius' base was at Ariminum.   Two
circumstances weighed the scales against Hasdrubal, — an error
of judgment and a piece of bad luck. He arrived in Italy sooner
than he was expected; but, instead of utilizing this advantage
to the utmost, he committed the mistake of laying siege to
Placentia.   He failed to take the place through lack of siege
engines, and precious days were lost. The ill-luck that befell
him was that his despatch, wherein he gave information to his
brother, which would enable Hannibal to meet him at a given
place and date, was intercepted by the Romans in southern
Italy.   Nero was thus fully apprised of what the enemy intended.   Leaving a part of his army to watch Hannibal, he
hastened by forced marches with 8000 men to join his colleague
in the north.   On the Metaurus River the combined Roman
armies, about 50,000 strong, gave battle to Hasdrubal, whose
forces, with the allies that he had enlisted on his route, were
numerically about the same strength.   But the Gaulish troops,
on whom he had so largely to rely, were much inferior in discipline and armature to the Roman legionaries and auxiliaries.
The invading army was annihilated; Hasdrubal himself was
killed, fighting bravely to the last.   With this disaster went
Hannibal's last hope of success.   For four more years he maintained himself in southwestern Italy among the Bruttii.

Meantime Carthage had sent some further reinforcements to
Spain; but even an augmented Punic army there could not prevail against Scipio.   By the summer of 206 the peninsula was
wholly in Roman hands, and the victor returned to Italy in the
autumn of that year.   Admiration for his achievement, and an
immense popularity which he owed largely also to his personal
qualities, received their expression at the consular elections.
He was chosen by the unanimous vote of all the centuries.   His
ambition now was to carry the war into Africa; but a great
proportion of the senators were opposed to this plan.   Their
motives may have been various — hesitant conservatism dis-
trusting another foreign expedition, jealousy of a young and
brilliant commander, recollection of what their fathers related
of Regulus' disastrous fate in 255.   A compromise was reached;
Scipio was given a free hand, but only the fleet and troops in
Sicily were assigned to him.   For the rest he had to raise such

volunteers as he could. His popularity saved him. The allies
of Rome vied with one another in helping him by putting men
and material at his disposal. In 204 Scipio landed in Africa;
it is uncertain how large a force he had been able to muster.
He achieved little in the first season's campaign; but in 203 he
won over the Numidians to his side, which so weakened Carthage's resources in fighting men that she instituted negotiations
for peace. The Roman commander granted an armistice while
Carthaginian envoys were sent to Rome; at the same time the
Punic government recalled Hannibal from Italy. The most
probable account — that of Polybius — states that the Carthaginians violated the armistice. Hence the peace terms agreed
to at Rome were abortive. The final engagement of the war was
fought in 202 hard by Zama. The Romans during the long
years of the war had learnt much from the enemy; nowhere
was this more clearly seen than in this battle, in which the
Roman and Italian cavalry showed a notable superiority over
the enemy's horse. In addition to this their Numidian allies
did yeoman service. Even so Hannibal might have averted
disaster had his troops been reliable. But his mercenaries gave
way at a crucial point in the fight. The complete defeat of their
army now compelled the Carthaginians to accept the peace
terms dictated by Rome. They retained their own territory,
but Numidia was to become an independent kingdom, and was
henceforward an ally of Rome. They had perforce to give up
all their ships of war save ten, and to hand over all prisoners of
war. They were required to pay an indemnity of 10,000 talents
within fifty years. Worst of all, the Carthaginian government
had to bind itself to carry on no wars outside Africa, nor any in
Africa without Rome's permission. Thus, in effect, Carthage
ceased to be a wholly autonomous state.

Rome had finally emerged triumphant from a long and desperate duel. It left her undisputed mistress of the western
Mediterranean, and, as the next fifty years were to prove, the
most formidable power in the Ancient World. Some of the
reasons for her success, and for Hannibal's failure, will have
become apparent in the preceding narrative: the solidarity
and loyalty of her allies even at the most crucial moments;
her unquestioned control of the sea, which Carthage made no

effort to challenge; the lack of support given to Hannibal, and the inability of Philip V to assist his Punic ally. In fairness to the Carthaginians we may say that the fault was ultimately with her political and social system. We have seen how Carthage relied on mercenaries, native subjects, and allies, to fight her battles. The drain of prolonged warfare must have so strained her resources that she found it increasingly hard to pay for the upkeep of her army. Shortage and arrears of pay quickly render professional soldiery, feeling no deeper allegiance — which is the outcome of citizenship — to the state they serve, half-hearted, if not actually mutinous. The Moorish allies and subjects of Carthage similarly tended to turn against her in the hour of adversity. For had she not done little save exploit them in the past? Thus the unsettled condition of her African dependencies in the later stages of the war diverted much of her attention and her resources from the main theatres of the war. In contrast to this, her opponent's armies were composed of free citizens of Rome, and of Latin and Italian communities. If, especially in the earlier years of the war, they were inferior, man for man, to Hannibal's highly trained troops, the experience of successive campaigns made that disparity disappear; while the *morale* of a citizen army was a more powerful guarantee for ultimate victory than even the deep personal loyalty inspired by Hannibal in many of his men.

Yet the cost for the victor had been heavy. Rome's treasury was all but empty. Southern Italy after a dozen years of continuous fighting there was desolate, and those regions never properly recovered their prosperity. The toll in lives had been fearful. The number of Roman citizens liable to military service at the end of the first decade of the war was reduced by nearly a sixth. It is probable that the allies had suffered even heavier losses. Nor were the effects on the social and economic conditions of Italy, and on the Roman constitution, negligible, as will subsequently be shown. Lastly, the Roman government was now called upon to shoulder imperial responsibilities, and to tackle the thorny problem of provincial administration.

CHAPTER XXII

ROME AND THE NEAR EAST

> *The surprising nature of the events which I have undertaken to relate is in itself sufficient to challenge and stimulate the attention of every one, old or young, to the study of my work. Can any one be so indifferent or idle as not to care to know by what means, and under what kind of polity, almost the whole inhabited world was conquered and brought under the dominion of the single city of Rome, and that too within a period of not quite fifty-three years?* — Polybius, i, 1 (Shuckburgh's translation).

THE ink was scarcely dry on the peace protocol of Carthage and Rome, when the victor intervened in the intricate political affairs of the eastern Mediterranean states. The motives and aims of the Roman government at this juncture have been very variously interpreted. Of the three Hellenistic monarchies, Egypt was at the end of the third century the weakest in a military sense. Her relations with Rome before 202 B.C. appear to have been slight. Friendly embassies of the two states had exchanged visits in 273, but there is no evidence that any formal alliance was concluded between them. During the Second Punic War Egypt had supplied Rome with grain — at profiteering rates, as it would seem — at a time when there was considerable danger of famine in Italy. In 203 King Ptolemy IV died, and the throne passed to his infant son. The king of Syria, Antiochus III, had recently recovered some of the eastern territories that had been lost during the reigns of his predecessors. To these he now aimed to add southern Syria, a dependency of the Ptolemies. Philip of Macedon, too, after the very mediocre successes of his recent war against the Greek states, was greedy for further conquests. These two monarchs, seeing Egypt nominally ruled by a child, actually by his corrupt and unwarlike ministers, concluded a pact to deprive Egypt of

411

all her foreign possessions and to divide the spoil. Antiochus took the offensive against her at once in southern Syria; but Philip's task of wresting Egyptian dependencies in the Aegean area was less simple. It aroused at once the enmity of those smaller states, whose interests had not been threatened by the fact that some regions of Thrace and Asia Minor acknowledged Egyptian suzerainty, but who could see only a grave danger to their own political independence in the aggressive tactics of the Macedonian, especially when allied to the Syrian monarch. Rhodes and Pergamum both appealed to Rome to intervene on their behalf. Egypt, too, turned to the western power for support against Antiochus. An Athenian embassy swelled the list of petitioners at Rome; for a quarrel between some of the Greek allies of Philip and Athens had led to an attack on that city.

The Roman senate was in favor of declaring war on Philip; popular feeling as expressed in a meeting of the *comitia* was adverse. For, after more than sixty years of all but continuous fighting, the Roman people needed and desired peace. The senate, however, carried its point, mainly by the argument that Philip, if not checked, would try to invade Italy; partly also by playing on the superstitious fears of the masses. How, then, are we to interpret senatorial action in 200 B.C. which made peremptory demands on Philip and, when he rejected them, declared war on him? We are not justified in attributing to the Roman government at this time an aggressive policy of expansion in the eastern Mediterranean. Until the Illyrian wars, and then Philip's alliance with Hannibal, Rome had not concerned herself with affairs in the Near East; and even on those occasions she did no more than safeguard her own interests in Italy and Italian waters. That her government was influenced by sentimental reasons in espousing the Greek cause is an amiable assumption not borne out by the facts, which point to the circumstance that her Philhellene politicians and soldiers were in a decided minority. While we may allow for a certain measure of resentment against the Macedonian king for joining the ranks of Rome's enemies in 216, the real fear of the senate was not Philip alone, but what might develop from a coalition between him and Antiochus. The abrupt realization of this by a senate, which so far had little knowledge of the Hellenistic monarchies, determined its action. We shall see that it was not till thirty years later that Roman policy in the Aegean can justly be described as aggressive.

In the so-called Second Macedonian War Rome was from the first supported by the Aetolian League, and by the navies of Pergamum and Rhodes. The other Greek states of any moment were for the present neutral. For nearly two years the war was barren of results; in 198, however, the consul, T. Quinctius Flamininus, took over the command of the Roman armies, and in this year and the next carried out a brilliant offensive. Philip, after a severe defeat on the borders of Epirus and Thessaly, was driven back to the Macedonian-Thessalian frontier. The Achæan League now joined the active enemies of Philip, and that monarch was in sufficient straits to institute negotiations for peace (winter, 198). The terms laid down by Rome were too peremptory for his acceptance; it needed another campaign to compel his submission. In 197 a decisive action was fought in Thessaly at Cynoscephalæ. A stubborn contest in which about 25,000 men were involved on either side, ended in a complete Roman victory. To the student of ancient military history the battle is of special interest because the superiority of the legionary organization over the Macedonian phalanx was here clearly demonstrated.

Forced now to accept the peace terms imposed by Rome, Philip lost all his possessions outside Macedonia, and undertook to enter into no foreign alliances or wars without Roman sanction. His army was reduced in size, and he was called upon to pay a war indemnity of 1000 talents. There was an interesting sequel to the war. The Roman commander-in-chief, Flamininus, attended the Isthmian festival in 196, and there formally proclaimed the independence of the Greek states. That he was a friend and admirer of Greece is clear; it is no less clear that he could not have acted as he did without the approval of the senate. In the general action of the Roman government at this period — the terms dictated to Philip were far less severe than its allies of the Aetolian League desired — we have clear proof of its unwillingness to derive any territorial advantage from the war, or to be drawn any further into Eastern affairs.

That a well-known Philhellene carried out the instructions of the Roman senate does not prove that philhellenism was the motive which determined its decision. The complicated problems arising out of the peace settlement and declaration of Greek autonomy detained Flamininus another two years in Greece. Then, in 194, the Roman garrisons were withdrawn from there.

Meanwhile Antiochus had prosecuted his attack on Egypt with much success. A victory at Mt. Panium in 198 made him master of southern Syria; then he proceeded to annex Greek cities in Asia Minor that had hitherto been Egyptian dependencies. The Rhodians, who declared war on Antiochus and with their fleet prevented him from capturing important bases like Samos, at the same time made urgent representations to the Roman government. But, so long as the Syrian king's activities were confined to Asia Minor, the senate was unwilling to intervene. Even when the king crossed the Hellespont and began to acquire strategic points like Sestos, and to rebuild Lysimacheia, Rome contented herself with diplomatic protests, insisting that Antiochus should abstain from occupying any European territory. Had the issue been a simple one between Rome and Syria, it is possible that hostilities would have been avoided. But certain other factors, or rather persons, intervened to complicate the Near Eastern situation and make war unavoidable. Shortly before 193 Antiochus was visited by a distinguished exile from Carthage, no less a person than Hannibal. We may surmise that his counsels were not in favor of a peaceful acquiescence in Rome's demands. At the same time, when war had begun, his military genius, as well as his knowledge of Roman tactics, might have been invaluable to his host, had the latter been disposed to accept his advice. The final complication, however, was the action of the Aetolian League in inviting Antiochus to Greece, promising him widespread support there as soon as he appeared. The Aetolians, even if the unfavorable estimate of them in Polybius, who, like his father, played a prominent part in the affairs of the Achæan League, be in some degree discounted, were never remarkable for political stability. We have seen that they were dissatisfied with Rome's settlement of 196. With the help of Antiochus they now hoped to become the dominant power in Greece.

In 192 Antiochus sailed to Greece with a very moderate force of 10,000, trusting in the Aetolian promises and grossly underestimating the resources of Rome.

A reluctant senate was compelled to go to war, unless it was prepared to stultify its previous action toward the Greeks. A single campaign, and a single Roman victory on the historic site of Thermopylæ, sufficed to drive the Asiatic invader out of Greece (191). But the Romans, having gone so far, and mindful at last of the interests of friendly states like Rhodes and Pergamum, decided to restrict Antiochus' power in Asia. A Roman and Greek allied fleet twice defeated the Syrian navy in the Aegean, and thus prepared the way for the Roman expeditionary force that landed in Asia Minor in the summer of 190. Again the immeasurable superiority of Rome's disciplined legionaries over the numerous but motley host of Antiochus was shown. The king was routed in an engagement fought hard by Magnesia near Mt. Sipylus, and then was driven to make peace on Rome's terms. His possessions in Asia Minor he was forced to give up, the boundaries of his much reduced kingdom being hereafter the Taurus mountains and the Halys River. He undertook not to attack any friends or allies of Rome, and he was required to pay a heavy indemnity within a stipulated time. The allies of Rome, Rhodes, and Pergamum, received considerable additions to their respective territories; other communities were enrolled as free and independent allies of Rome. Small kingdoms and principalities in the interior — for example, Bithynia — similarly became client kingdoms of the conqueror. The Aetolians came off more lightly than might have been expected. They had to pay an indemnity, and ceded Cephallenia to Rome. For the rest they, too, were formally enlisted among the free and autonomous allies of Rome, but with the special obligation of furnishing troops when required. It is noteworthy that the Roman government still abstained from making territorial annexations on the Greek mainland.

There was one feature of the Roman settlement which was productive of endless disputes and finally led to drastic action on Rome's part. The Achæan League had been enlarged so as to include most of the communities of the Peloponnese, Sparta not excepted. The adherence of these new members was for the most part forced, not voluntary. Frequent disagreements, and no less frequent appeals to Rome by both parties in a dispute, were the result. A further complication was caused by the divided policies in the states themselves. Generally speaking, the oligarchic or aristocratic party courted the favor of Rome, while the democratic party worked for absolute independence of Roman arbitration in Greek affairs. The senate, whose attitude to Near Eastern questions was beginning to undergo a marked change, while not intervening directly, now followed the plan of giving the weight of its support to the aristocratic factions in the Hellenic cities.

It was not, however, in Greece only that trouble was brewing. Philip V, in accordance with his treaty obligations, had assisted Rome in her war against Antiochus. So far from being rewarded for his services, as he had hoped, by an extension of territory or a greater degree of autonomy, he received nothing. In 185 he appears to have violated his treaty by invading districts outside Macedonia. Rome peremptorily ordered him to withdraw, a command which he could not but obey. But the last six years of his life were devoted to restoring, as far as possible, the prosperity of his kingdom, with the ultimate aim of trying conclusions with Rome once more when his resources were sufficient. His bitterness against Rome was inherited by his son, Perseus, who came to the throne in 179. The early years of his reign Perseus spent in strengthening his position by fostering good relations with his neighbors. He formed an alliance with a Thracian prince, Cotys, and came to a secret understanding with King Genthius of Illyria, who was a nominal ally of Rome. Bitter jealousy of Pergamum, which with Roman support had grown great at the expense of Macedonia and Syria, animated Perseus as it had his father. King Eumenes of Pergamum for his part reported the activities of the Macedonian monarch to Rome; finally, in 172 he visited Rome in person to lay before the senate a long list of complaints against Perseus. That body, which had been watching the progress of Perseus for some time, found in the accusations of Eumenes a final justification or pretext for ordering the Macedonian's unconditional submission to Roman demands. When he refused, the Romans declared war (171).

The first three years of the Third Macedonian War were remarkable only for the incompetence of the Roman commanders sent to Greece, and the fecklessness of their opponent. By energetic action at the beginning Perseus could probably have brought over a great part of Greece to his side, the Roman force in Epirus at that time being small. As it was, the appearance of additional legions, and the activity of Roman envoys in Greece, deprived him of almost all help from that quarter. Nor did Asiatic states like Bithynia and Syria, with which he had previously entered into friendly relations, now attempt to help him. In 168 the appointment of an able commander-in-chief, Aemilius Paullus, completely changed the military situation. Advancing through Thessaly he gave battle to Perseus close to Pydna in southern Macedonia. Perseus' troops fought bravely; but in the end they were defeated with very heavy loss; for 20,000 are said to have fallen and 11,000 taken prisoners. The king himself escaped, but was subsequently captured and sent to Rome, where he died a few years later.

Even now the Roman government was unwilling to annex the conquered kingdom. Instead, an experiment was tried which cannot be said to have justified itself by results. Macedonia was broken up into four republics, of which only the most northern, in view of its savage Thracian neighbors, was permitted to have an army. The land-tax formerly paid to the king was reduced by half, and this sum was collected for the benefit of the Roman treasury. Estates and mines, which had been royal property, were confiscated by Rome. To isolate each of these small states as far as possible, intermarriage and commercial relations between them were prohibited, Rome applying the principle that she had already followed in Italy. During the next two decades internal dissension in the respective governments, and petty disputes between the republics, proved the unwisdom of the Roman experiment. Then, in 149–146, a pretender appeared, by name Andriscus, who claimed to be a son of Perseus. His appearance aroused great popular enthusiasm, and he enjoyed some ephemeral successes before the rebellion was suppressed by Rome. The four republics were now dissolved, and Macedonia was converted into a Roman province governed by a Roman viceroy.

The changed attitude of the senate to the Eastern question at the conclusion of the Third Macedonian War showed itself not only in its actions in Greece, but in its high-handed treatment of Rome's old-standing allies, Rhodes and Pergamum. The island state had been guilty of no hostile act, but had unwisely attempted to mediate in the recent dispute between Perseus and Rome. After the war the terms of her treaty with Rome were revised to her disadvantage, so that, from being autonomous, the Rhodians became dependent allies. At the same time they were deprived of their possessions on the mainland of southwestern Asia Minor. Worst of all, in view of the fact that Rhodes was a maritime state, Delos was made a free port by Roman action, and from this time for fully a century became the leading mart in the Aegean area. According to a very trustworthy source, the people of Rhodes within a few years could complain that their receipts from customs dues had sunk from 1,000,000 to 150,000 drachmæ.[1]

Even less justifiable was the manner in which Rome sought for a pretext to reduce the power of Pergamum. This state had been valuable to her while Macedonia and Syria were of account. When this was no longer the case, the senate was anxious to humble this Roman ally. Eumenes was accused of hostile designs, and, when he came to Italy to defend himself, was met at Brundisium and sent back to his country. He lost Pamphylia and Galatia, which now became independent principalities, but he was allowed to retain his throne. To complete his chagrin he saw the Roman government showing marked favor to his neighbor, the king of Bithynia. Eumenes' successors, Attalus II and Attalus III, also resigned themselves to the inevitable. On the death of Attalus III Pergamum became a Roman province (133 B.C.). During and after the Third Macedonian War Rome also intervened in the affairs of Syria and Egypt, so that her position as arbiter in the whole Mediterranean was clear to all.

Lastly we must note her policy in Greece after 168. Among the state papers of Perseus, which had been captured by the Romans, were many that incriminated prominent persons with anti-Roman sympathies in Greek states. A number of these the Roman authorities brought to trial and executed.

[1] Polybius xxxi, 7, 12.

Besides this, numerous hostages were taken from the various cities and sent to Italy. The Achæan League suffered worst of all. One thousand of its prominent men were thus transported into exile. Harsh as was this treatment, historical literature at least benefited by Rome's action. For, among the Achæan exiles in Rome was the historian Polybius, whose residence in that city, and the happy circumstance that he obtained the acquaintance and then the friendship of many distinguished Romans, produced in him a deep admiration for the new world-power, and inspired him to write the history of its growth. This work in its final form covered the period from 221 to 144 B.C., with a briefer introductory section which sketched events from 264 to 221. Only Books I to V have survived entire; of the other thirty-five there remains a considerable collection of extracts and fragments. The purpose of his work was didactic. It was not intended for the general public, but for politicians and men of affairs, who would be helped by a study of the past in handling the problems of the present and future. Though not free from political bias, Polybius was extremely conscientious in verifying all his data and carefully sifting the evidence that he accumulated. He had had personal experience both as a soldier and a statesman in the Achæan League. As a critical historian he ranks next to Thucydides among ancient writers. He is his equal in the technique of historical writing, but he lacks both the philosophical detachment and the deep insight into the affairs of men and states which characterize the Athenian.

The settlement of Greece in 167 did not pass off without excesses which it is impossible to condone. Civil war in Aetolia was attended by the massacre of several hundred members of the anti-Roman faction, a deed to which the Roman government was privy, if not directly bearing responsibility for it. The punishment of the Epirots for aiding Perseus was not less brutal. Numerous towns in Epirus were destroyed, the widespread ruin of the settlements being accompanied by a wholesale enslavement of the inhabitants. The Roman protectorate over Greece endured for two decades. Then, in 148, a renewed dispute between Sparta and the Achæan League occurred, and the matter was referred to Rome. But before the Roman commission of inquiry appeared on the scene, the Achæan League had taken up arms against their neighbor. The commissioners summoned a congress at Corinth and notified the League that certain members of it would be detached to form independent communities. By 147 the anti-Roman factions in the cities had quite gained the upper hand. They were joined by the communities of Bœotia, Phocis, Locris, and Eubœa, and war was declared on Sparta.

The reply of the Roman government was prompt. While the Roman commander in Macedonia invaded central Greece and suppressed the rising there, L. Mummius was despatched with a naval and military force to southern Greece. The allies were defeated in an engagement near Corinth, and then that city was forced to surrender. It was sacked and burnt; its people were enslaved, and the numerous art treasures, for which this ancient Greek *polis* had long been famous, were deported to Rome. The Greek leagues were now dissolved and the individual cities compelled to enter directly into alliance with Rome. The character of each treaty depended on the past action of the particular city. Those which, like Athens, Sparta, and Argos, had stood consistently on the side of Rome remained autonomous allies. The others became tribute-paying subjects. The governor of Macedonia exercised a general supervision and control in Greece, which was not formally converted into a province until the last quarter of the first century B.C., for the Greek communities were allowed their own jurisdiction and administration, a privilege not granted to regular provinces, or only to isolated cities in them. At the same time Rome saw to it that the local governments were aristocratic. Thus for more than a century after 146 the fiction of an independent Greece was upheld. The place of Corinth as leading city was taken by Argos, which became the headquarters of Roman and Italian business affairs in Greece.

Macedonia was not the only protected state which in the middle of the second century was changed into a province. The year of the destruction of Corinth is also the year which saw the end of Carthage. Though shorn of political power, the Carthaginians appear in the fifty years following the end of the Second Punic War to have made a remarkable recovery economically. Peace, and a government that was careful not to offend Rome, enabled the Punic merchants to build up a material prosperity, which the long struggle with Rome had brought to the verge of ruin. The greatest thorn in their flesh was their neighbor, Numidia, which had not only been set up as a strong kingdom by Roman action, but which continued to enjoy the favor of the senate. Knowing this, its ruler, Massinissa, more than once made encroachments on, or laid claim to, Carthaginian territory. Carthage appealed to Rome to arbitrate, and commissions of inquiry were appointed to inquire into the matters under dispute, in 161 B.C. and again four years later. The findings of the commissioners supported the claims of the Numidian king. It was becoming clear that a majority in the senate were in favor of the complete suppression of their old rival. In Carthage the natural reaction was the emergence into political prominence, and ultimately into control, of a patriotic party. A crisis did not, however, arise until 151. In that year the Carthaginians and Massinissa's troops actually came to blows. The Roman government promptly declared war on Carthage, basing its action on the peace terms of 201, which forbade Carthage from making war without Roman consent. Even the Punic patriots quailed and were anxious to submit to Rome. But a Roman army followed the ultimatum at once, and the Carthaginians were required to disarm and to evacuate their city, being permitted to settle elsewhere where they would, provided the site was not less than ten miles from the sea. Compliance spelt Carthage's commercial ruin.

Rome's demands had the result of uniting all the Carthaginians in a last desperate struggle for their liberties. Preparations were made day and night to put the city in condition to stand a siege, and the incomprehensible slackness of the Roman commanders helped them in their feverish task. For, instead of enforcing instant compliance, a month of inactivity followed the Roman proclamation. When at last they did take steps to occupy the city, they found that it had been put into a strong state of defense and was ready to offer prolonged resistance. The operations of the besieging army dragged on. After a number of months the Roman soldiery began to be decimated by disease caused by the marshy territory all about their camp. Exasperation at Rome for the delay in reducing Carthage led to an unusual appointment. In 147 the son of Aemilius Paullus and grandson by adoption of the victor of Zama, P. Cornelius Scipio Aemilianus, though not yet of legal age, was appointed to the consulship and to the African command. Having restored discipline in the Roman camps, he carried on the siege with energy, among other measures taken being the prevention of a leakage of supplies into Carthage provided by a friendly native chieftain. Early in 146 starvation had done its work. The city was captured, and after another week of desperate resistance the citadel also fell. Reluctantly, but in obedience to the orders of the senate, Scipio carried out the complete destruction of Carthage, which is said to have burnt for seventeen days. Such of its population as had survived famine and siege was sold into slavery. The territory of Carthage was now organized as a Roman province, named Africa, the seat of government and centre of business being at Utica. Numidia continued, as before, to be an autonomous native state in alliance with Rome.

It is not easy to understand, and it is difficult to justify, the motives of the senate in willing the destruction of Carthage. Though there were many prominent men who were opposed all through to the policy of humiliating and finally of destroying the Punic state, a senatorial majority, whose chief spokesman was M. Porcius Cato, by the middle of the second century favored extreme measures. Cato had been a member of the Roman commission to Africa in 157. Already inclined to regard Carthage with dislike and suspicion, he seems after his visit to have been convinced that her recovered prosperity would in time lead to her political resurrection. From then to his death in 149 B.C. he urged the destruction of Carthage on every occasion in the senate. Though his fears may have been chimerical, he and many other Romans of influence had become intolerant of any state which might at any time be a hindrance to Rome's undisputed authority in the Mediterranean. We have already observed the growth of this uncompromising imperialist doctrine in the case of Rome's intervention in Macedonia, Greece, and Asia Minor.

CHAPTER XXIII

ROMAN GOVERNMENT AND CIVILIZATION DURING THE THIRD AND SECOND CENTURIES B.C.

> *Consequently, if one were staying at Rome, when the consuls were not in town, one would imagine the constitution to be a complete aristocracy; and this has been the idea entertained by many Greeks, and by many kings as well, from the fact that nearly all the business they had with Rome was settled by the senate.* — Polybius, vi, 13 (Shuckburgh's translation).

1. Government at Home and in the Provinces

It will have been observed how, in the two preceding chapters, the phrases "Roman government" and "Roman senate" have been used almost synonymously. After the final triumph of the Plebeians in 287 the Roman constitution theoretically might be described as democratic. Not only were all regular magistracies open to members of both Orders, but the Roman people made the laws and was responsible for electing the magistrates. Nevertheless this sovereignty of the *populus Romanus* during the century and a half of Rome's foreign wars and overseas expansion was not in actual practice maintained. There were many reasons why in these years of stress the reins of government should be controlled by the senate. The machinery by which the popular assemblies were set in motion was cumbersome. Neither the *comitia centuriata*, nor the *comitia tributa*, nor yet the *concilium plebis*, could meet unless convened by a magistrate, since no fixed dates for meetings were set, as was the case, for instance, with the *ecclesia* in fifth- and fourth-century Athens. Had the senior magistrates, the consuls and prætors elected in the centuriate assembly, kept their authority so that the senate would have been virtually restricted to acting as an advisory council, with limited administrative functions, the sovereignty of the people might have been upheld. But in fact the magistrates became more and more dependent on the

423

senate. The encroachment of senatorial authority was gradual.
Consular power had suffered some diminution through the creation of other magistracies, notably the prætorship. The senate
also instituted the practice of fixing the division of duties between the consuls in their year of office, a matter previously
determined by the two senior magistrates between themselves.
Of the lesser offices the tribunate was in the most peculiar position. The conception of the tribunes as champions of an
oppressed plebs was now an anachronism. The senate, however,
saw in the tribunate a very serviceable tool for building up its
own supremacy. The tribunes were used by it to keep in
check, by the timely use of their veto, senior magistrates
who threatened to act independently of the senate. Again,
during the anxious period of the great wars rapid decisions
and rapid legislation were constantly called for. The process
of convening the assemblies was, as was pointed out, troublesome. It was also necessarily tedious, because many voters
lived at a distance from Rome. Nor would the *comitia* have
been so competent to take decisions in war-time as a body of
men with some administrative and magisterial experience
like the senate.

It was not, then, by any deliberate amendment or suspension
of constitutional procedure, but through a gradual process
called for by the political and especially the foreign affairs of
Rome, that the senate reached its position of almost unchallenged supremacy. Recorded occasions on which popular demands overrode or forced the hands of the senate are extremely
rare. Equally scarce are the cases where a magistrate defied
senatorial authority.[1] Lastly we may note that it became a
thing tacitly understood that no legislation be proposed by
a magistrate in the assembly, or passed by that body, without
the consent of the senate. Thus the senate's control was
exercised on every hand. The treasury and the direction of
finance were its concern. The two quæstors in charge of the
aerarium could, save in one instance,[2] make no disbursements

---

[1] An example is afforded by C. Flaminius, for whose agrarian bill see
page 430.

[2] The exception was the two consuls while in Rome. They could draw
on the treasury without application to the senate.

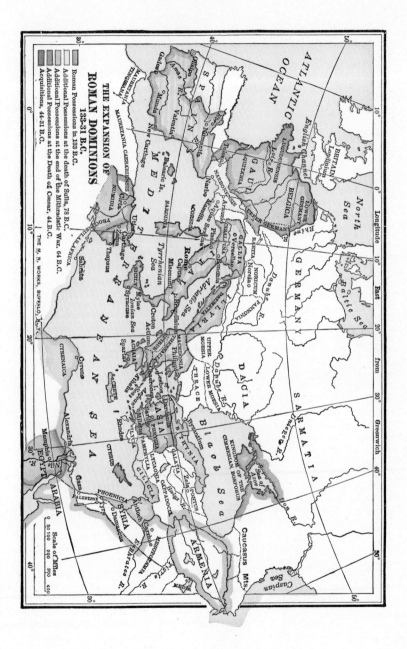

THE EXPANSION OF
ROMAN DOMINIONS
133-31 B.C.

Roman Possessions in 133 B.C.
Additional Possessions at the death of Sulla, 78 B.C.
Additional Possessions at the end of the Mithradatic War, 64 B.C.
Additional Possessions at the Death of Caesar, 44 B.C.
Acquisitions, 44-31 B.C.

Scale of Miles
0 50 100 200 300 400

THE M. N. WORKS, BUFFALO, N. Y.

without its authorization. New taxation, though it became law by
the action of the *comitia*, was first approved by the senate, and its
form and scope embodied in a senatorial decree. Declarations of
war and peace, subject to ratification by the centuriate assembly,
were made, and all diplomatic relations with other states were
carried on, by the senate. Even a consul in the field could conclude no more than a truce for a limited period. Treaties and
terms of permanent settlement must be referred to the home
government; and there are not wanting instances where the
senate repudiated agreements made by Roman commanders.

One of the greatest problems which had confronted the Romans ever since 241 B.C., and to a greatly increased degree from
the beginning of the second century, was how best to administer
extra-Italian territories acquired in successive wars. After 146
the Roman provinces were Sicily, Sardinia and Corsica, the
two Spanish provinces of Hither and Further Spain organized
in 197, Macedonia, and Africa. To these was added in 129 the
province of Asia, which was formed out of the kingdom of
Pergamum bequeathed to Rome by Attalus III on his death in
133. Eight years later southeastern Gaul was annexed and
converted into the province of Narbonese Gaul. To each of
these large districts Rome sent a governor who had previously
filled the consulship or prætorship at Rome. The need of more
senior magistrates for this purpose led to a gradual increase in
the number of prætors annually appointed. The judicial duties
of the *praetor urbanus*, or city prætor, had so grown by the middle
of the third century, that it was found necessary to appoint a second prætor to act as president in all cases of litigation between
Roman citizens and aliens (*praetor peregrinus*). By 197 four additional prætors were elected each year, a number which was not
increased for more than a century. The normal length of a
provincial command was a year, but the period could be prolonged. The appointment of ex-magistrates to govern provinces
as proconsuls and proprætors, and the extension of their office,
were matters which the senate kept within its control.[1] It also

[1] The forms proconsul, proprætor in Latin are comparatively late.
They are derived from the earlier and more logical expression that such
and such a man governed *pro consule* or *pro praetore*, *i.e.*, " for " or "in
place of a consul" or "prætor."

largely determined the size of the military establishments in the provinces. For, while consuls or governors of consular rank could, on their own initiative and by virtue of their consular *imperium*, levy troops to the number of two legions, any forces in excess of this amount had to be sanctioned by the senate. Prætors and proprætors, unless they were invested with consular authority, as was commonly the case with the governors of the Spanish provinces, were entirely dependent on the home government in the matter of the army put at their disposal.

From the first the Romans decided not to follow in their extra-Italian dependencies the procedure which they had adopted, and which had worked so well, in Italy. The provincials were definitely on a footing inferior to the Italian allies of Rome. They were disarmed, they paid tribute, and they were subject to the jurisdiction of the Roman governor, from whom there was no appeal. In every province, however, there were some favored communities which were tax-free, and which, by virtue of a special treaty with Rome, enjoyed a certain amount of autonomy, so that, for example, they lived under their own laws. Rome was chary of disturbing local institutions and divisions — tribal or otherwise — if these did not conflict with her own political sovereignty or endanger the peace of the province. Existing institutions, which could be adapted to her scheme, were taken over with little or no modification. Thus, when Sicily became a province, the judicial and administrative regulations that had been in force in Hiero's kingdom of Syracuse remained in use; similarly in Greece, and later in Rome's Græco-Asiatic provinces, the municipal organization of the numerous cities continued more or less undisturbed. But in provinces like the two Spains, where the inhabitants were politically and socially backward, the problem of the conqueror was more complicated.

It was perhaps unfortunate that, at the time when Rome acquired the Spanish peninsula, her main attention was focussed on the East, not on the West. On the whole Rome's treatment of the two Spains during the second century forms one of the most disagreeable episodes in her history. With few exceptions — among these we may honorably name Cato and Ti. Sempronius Gracchus, father of the better-known tribunes of 133 and

123 B.C. — the Roman army commanders and governors in Spain were men of inferior ability, while many of them were guilty of serious excesses. Many of the numerous tribes in the peninsula in any case looked askance at the permanent occupation of their country by a foreign state; and the work of pacification and settlement would thus have taken some time even under the most favorable conditions and the most conscientious direction. As it was, the peninsula was constantly disturbed by wars and native risings, some of which seem to have been actually provoked by Roman officers anxious to win military honors by dishonorable means. From 154 to 133 B.C. — if we disregard earlier and more sporadic outbreaks — warfare and rebellion in Spain were continuous. A great national revolt in the south led by Viriathus was only crushed in 139 after eight years of fighting. In Hither Spain the rising lasted even longer, and was only finally ended by the siege and capture of Numantia by Scipio Aemilianus in 133. After Scipio's settlement, Spain, with the exception of the northwestern corner of the peninsula, which was not finally pacified till the time of Augustus, gave no further trouble; it was not, however, unaffected by Rome's civil wars in the first century. The progress of Roman civilization in the interior was slow, the main centres of Roman influence being in the south and near the coast. There two Latin colonies had been settled in 206 and 171. Furthermore, many time-expired soldiers, whose service had been in Spain, and who intermarried with native women, made that country their permanent home. But it was long before Rome realized the full value of the Spanish provinces, which were both fertile and rich in mineral deposits. The great age of Hispano-Roman prosperity and culture did not come till the first and second centuries A.D.

The main features of Roman provincial government were the same everywhere. The senate laid down certain general principles to be followed when a new province was acquired. The details were worked out by a small senatorial committee appointed for the purpose, and its recommendations, when formally ratified, formed the content of a *lex provinciae*. If these provisions had always been scrupulously observed, provincials would rarely have had cause for complaint. The defects of the Roman system in Republican days were to be found elsewhere. The governor normally held his appointment for only one year.[1] Although he had had some administrative, judicial, and military experience, he had, more often than not, no special acquaintance with the country or people whom he was to rule. The quæstor, who accompanied him and whose chief duty was to act as financial secretary, and three legates of senatorial rank, formed his official staff. But their experience was generally as limited as his own.[2] If he misgoverned or oppressed the natives, it was extremely difficult for them to get redress. For appeals to the government at Rome, or action to get the governor impeached, were very costly matters, and in the end redress was by no means certain. The many recorded instances of Roman provincial governors in the second and first centuries B.C., who spent their year of rule merely to enrich themselves, and in so doing were guilty of gross malpractices, might tempt one to condemn the system utterly. To do so would be unfair, since with a Verres or a Catiline we can contrast a Julius Cæsar or a Cicero. Nevertheless, though conscientious, fair, and efficient proconsuls and proprætors must have been many, we have one clear proof that already in the middle of the second century abuses had become very common. By the *Lex Calpurnia* of 149 B.C. a permanent court of justice was set up, before which officials accused of extortion and provincial maladministration could be arraigned. Cases were tried under the presidency of a prætor before a jury of fifty senators. The institution of this, the first standing criminal court at Rome, shows plainly that the evil it was intended to combat was very rife. In practice the existence of this court did not prove a satisfactory remedy. The fact that the jurors, being senators, were trying one of their own Order, and that, too, they often regarded profit-making at the expense of the provincials as a legitimate though not a legal proceeding, coupled

[1] In Spain, at all events in the second century B.C., a two-year tenure was quite regular.

[2] The practice of sending young men of senatorial families in the suite of a provincial governor, so that they might get some preparatory insight into provincial administration and public affairs, is not likely in most cases to have had more than a general educative value. They were designated the companions (*comites*) of the governor, but had, of course, no official status.

with the difficulty and expense for provincial complainants attendant on conducting a prosecution, very greatly limited the effectiveness and utility of the new court.

In Italy the Roman government instituted few changes beyond punishing allies, who, like the Capuans, had sided with the enemy. But it was noticeable in the second century that the Romans were becoming laxer in the observance of the treaties between themselves and the Italian and Latin communities. Interference in local government, reduction in the amount of war-booty assigned to the allies, and heavier military exactions imposed on them by Rome — all these matters helped to change what had so long been loyal feelings of friendship into a sense of grievance, discontentment, and ultimately smouldering anger, which burst into conflagration in the early years of the first century B.C.

The greater security of northern Italy was a matter which received the earnest attention of the government in the second century. During its early years the authority of Rome in Cisalpine Gaul was reëstablished after several campaigns. Between 189 and 181 B.C. four new colonies were established at Bononia, Parma, Mutina, and Aquileia; also, excellent military roads were completed, leading from Rome to the Padus valley both by the eastern and the western coast routes. This work of reconstruction was followed by campaigns in Liguria, whose tribes had in the past not at all or very imperfectly recognized the sovereign power of Rome. They were now forced to submit, and thus the way was paved for the further advance of Rome into Narbonese Gaul during the last quarter of the century.

2. Economic and Intellectual Life

During the third century agriculture continued to be the main occupation of the Roman people, and the chief source of wealth to rich and poor alike. The small farmer worked his land himself, assisted by his family and a few slaves, who at this time were mostly Italians enslaved in war. In these circumstances the economic effects of the great wars were bound to be especially unfavorable. Hannibal's devastations, and the all but constant military service required of the yeomen-citizens of

Rome during the third and second centuries, began the ruin of Italian agriculture. The government was not blind to the serious situation existing in the last years of the Hannibalic war, and did what it could to resettle refugees on the land. The senate, we learn from the Roman historian, advised the consuls to see to the reinstatement of Plebeians on their holdings. "The people found it, however, anything but an easy matter. The small-holders had been carried off by the war, there was hardly any servile labor available, the cattle had been driven off as plunder, and the homesteads had been either stripped or burnt."[1] Yet at other times the senate considered rather the interests of its class. In 233–232 C. Flaminius, as tribune, in spite of strong senatorial opposition, carried an agrarian bill, the purpose of which was to insure the distribution in small allotments to poor citizens of the so-called *ager Gallicus* in northern Picenum.

Had the Second Punic War been followed by a period of peace, the damage and dislocation caused in the preceding half century might have been righted. Instead, the wars in Spain and in the eastern Mediterranean continued to be a drain on the man-power of Rome and Italy. The position of the small farmer came to be more and more difficult. Called away for years on military service, he at last returned to find his farm dilapidated or mortgaged, and in the end he was forced to give up. Then he drifted to the city, to eke out such a living as he could and swell the unproductive proletariat of the capital. There were, too, other factors which exerted a powerful influence on the agricultural situation. In the last years of the Hannibalic war, when the Roman treasury was nearly empty, the senate acquired loans from wealthy private citizens, in return for which these were allowed to occupy considerable tracts of *ager publicus*. We do not hear that the senate subsequently liquidated its debts and reasserted the state ownership of this land. Rather the tendency was toward the growth of more and more large estates, owned by members of the senatorial class, and the steady disappearance of the small farmer. Before the end of the third century the importation of grain from Sicily to feed the Roman population was found to be cheaper than to grow it at home. Consequently the culture of olive and

---

[1] Livy, xxviii, 11 (Forster's translation).

vine, together with cattle and sheep-farming, were replacing the raising of field crops. Cattle raising, however, demanded wide pasture-lands, and, to be profitable, must be carried on on a large scale with a heavy outlay of capital. Hence the altered character of farming in Italy also promoted the increase of the *latifundia*, as these large estates were called. Finally, the cheapest way of running such estates was by an intensive use of slave labor. Slaves, which in the earlier period had been relatively few and of Italian stock, became very abundant in the second century, when many thousands were imported from Greece and the Near East. It is probable that the system of working the land with large slave-gangs was to a great extent copied by the Roman land-owners from the Carthaginians. It is certain that they did so less successfully than the Punic aristocracy. The main reason for this seems to have been that the average Roman landlord troubled himself little about the working of his estate. His bailiff was, like the laborers, a slave, and was expected to furnish satisfactory returns year by year. It was clearly to the slave-overseer's interest to make ample allowance for accidents, and not to allow the owner to expect too much. Under conditions such as these the farming of many estates ceased to be a really profitable undertaking.

A man like the elder Cato must be regarded as an exception to a general rule. Frequently as he was employed in the service of the state, and constant as he was in his attendance in the senate, he nevertheless found time to supervise personally his moderate-sized farm in the Sabine hills. A practical farmer himself, he was also the author of the earliest of several extant Latin treatises on agriculture. His work is mainly a practical manual of farming, and he does not profess to offer any solution of existing economic problems. He is, however, aware of the existence of some of them. While he does not expect the owner to live permanently on his estate, he lays the greatest emphasis on the need for personal supervision, and warns against the practice of leaving everything to the bailiff. Cato's overseer was a slave, and there is nowhere in the manual any suggestion that the farm-manager should be a free man. All the regular labor employed on the farm is servile. It is on special occasions only, when more hands were temporarily required, that hired workmen are to be employed. These may have been either free or slave. Nor, although he would be the first to maintain that the farmer class are the backbone of the community, does Cato advocate that large estates, instead of being run by slave labor, should, at least in part, be cultivated by a number of free tenants. This was a solution which was only tried at a much later date; and when the practice had become more extended and the slave-gang system began to disappear, the decline of Italian agriculture had already gone too far to be arrested.

Industry and commerce developed slowly at first. In the second century B.C., however, progress became more rapid, a fact largely due to the abundance of slaves — many of them were skilled craftsmen — then introduced into Italy. The Romans themselves held aloof from these occupations. The average Roman household was all but self-sufficient. On Cato's farm, however, we find that most of the tools and equipment needed have to be provided either by skilled labor, imported temporarily for the purpose, or else by purchase from the nearest town. Among the regions which at that time were industrially most efficient and most forward, Etruria and Campania were the chief. In both all kinds of metal work — to cite but one industry — had been successfully made for centuries. An interesting passage in Livy (xxviii, 45) shows how important was the contribution made by the Etruscan cities in 206–205 to the war materials needed by Scipio for his African expedition.

Commerce, again, was mainly in the hands of the coast-dwellers of southwestern and southern Italy. Puteoli on the Bay of Naples, which had an excellent natural harbor, became the chief commercial port in the peninsula. In 194 B.C. a small band of Roman colonists was sent there; but they formed a ruling aristocracy, and commercial enterprise remained in Greek and Græco-Italian hands. It is not possible to quote any act or legislation of the Roman government which was aimed at improving or extending Roman trade. On the contrary, the senate and the financial class affected to despise the calling of the craftsman or merchant. Even in the matter of coinage Rome was slow to act. Although large lumps or bars of copper or bronze had been used as an exchange medium from very early times. while large copper coins were cast from about the middle of the fourth century, it was not until a year or two before the First Punic War that a Roman silver currency was issued. The silver *denarius* at this time was equivalent to ten of the old copper coins (*as*), the smallest silver piece being the *sestertius* (two and a half asses). In 217 an important and lasting alteration was made: the value of the as was reduced, and hereafter the *denarius* was worth sixteen asses. From now the usual method of reckoning amounts was in sesterces, each of which was equal to four of the new asses. Gold coinage, save for a year or two during the Hannibalic War, was not issued. The sovereign position of Rome in Italy now made itself apparent in the matter of currencies. The various communities allied to Rome, who had been minting their own silver, were gradually deprived of this prerogative, though they continued in many cases to strike their own copper or bronze pieces. These, too, became less and less in the second century; finally, in 89 B.C., they were prohibited altogether, and only Roman issues of silver and bronze circulated.

The wealth of the senatorial class was derived from land, and senators by a law of 218 B.C. were debarred from engaging in commerce. There was, however, another class whose importance steadily grew during the second century. The Roman government regularly entrusted the carrying out of state contracts to private persons. In the earlier period of Rome's history these would be relatively few. But in the second century, when much wealth had accumulated in the treasury, the number of contracts for public buildings, highways, and other public works, was greatly augmented. Moreover, the state now owned valuable mines in the provinces, the working of which was, on the same principle, leased out to private persons. The contractors, and those who financed all these undertakings, from being an insignificant group, became a very powerful class. From the later part of the second century they became regularly known as the *ordo equester* or equestrian class. The name was an extension or derivative of a name used officially in the Servian organization. The *equites* had once been those citizens whose wealth had been sufficient to enable them to serve as cavalry in time of war, when they provided their own horse and equipment. The name later attained a wider significance, being applied to all those whose property qualification was equivalent to what would have been requisite to allow them to act in that military capacity. This was at a time when Rome relied almost exclusively on her allies to furnish the necessary contingents of horse for military undertakings. The sharp, though unofficial, division of the civic population into the senatorial and equestrian classes and the mass of the people was a development fraught with most serious possibilities. It was unfortunate, too, that when the people began to challenge the authority of the senate, the assemblies at Rome were for the most part ruled by the urban proletariat (*plebs urbana*), the rural voters exercising a marked influence only on rare occasions.

The second century, which in so many other ways, was a momentous epoch in Roman history, was of peculiar importance for Rome's cultural development. Greek influences had filtered through to Rome from very early times. This can be illustrated from the case of Roman religion. The primitive Roman and Italian deities, who were somewhat shadowy and impersonal beings, and whose favor must be sought and anger appeased by periodical ceremonies performed by the king or the senior magistrates, in time received many of the characteristics of their more frankly anthropomorphic Greek counterparts. In the age of the Punic wars the twelve major deities of the Roman state religion had become equated with the twelve leading divinities in the Greek pantheon. From Etruria the Romans had taken over the practice of divination by the flight of birds or the inspection of animal entrails; from the Greek city of Cumæ they had derived — traditionally toward the end of the regal period — a collection of Greek oracles, the so-called Sibylline books, whose care was thereafter entrusted to special keepers. On many critical occasions, moreover, these oracles were officially consulted by the government, which then acted on their advice. Livy names several such occasions during the anxious years of the Second Punic War. Thus the Sibylline books were questioned in 217 and 205 B.C. In another year the advice of the Delphic oracle was sought. At other times steps were taken to suppress itinerant and unauthorized soothsayers, — we may suspect that they were

mostly foreigners, — who played upon the superstitious fears
of the masses. Perhaps the most remarkable step taken by the
senate was, acting on the instructions of the Sibylline oracles,
to introduce in 205 B.C. the worship of the Mother goddess of
Asia Minor, the Great Mother of Ida (*Magna Mater Idaea*),
into Rome. With the consent of King Attalus the sacred black
stone of the goddess was transferred to Rome from Pessinus in
Phrygia. Once the war was over the senate became alarmed at
the orgiastic ritual of the cult, and prohibited Roman citizens
from taking part in it. Hence the worship of the Great Mother
was for many years restricted to the alien and slave population.
The worship of Dionysus was a recently introduced cult, when
in 186 B.C. it was found that the celebrations of its rites in
Italy, and even in Rome, were attended by serious abuses and
much moral laxity. The senate therefore prohibited religious
guilds in honor of the god, and restricted the number of
celebrants of the cult at any given time or place to five.

The general penetration of Greek culture into Rome began
about the middle of the third century and became very intense
in the second. Latin literature begins with translations and
adaptations of Greek works. For, though there may have
existed a native Roman or Italian popular poetry before this
time, all trace of it has vanished. The earliest name in Latin
literature is that of Livius Andronicus, who translated the
Odyssey into the so-called Saturnian metre, and also brought
out renderings of Greek plays. His younger contemporary,
Cn. Nævius — both poets flourished in the second half of the
third century — showed somewhat more originality. He wrote
plays on Greek models; but some of them had plots taken
from Roman life. He was also the composer of the earliest
Latin epic, a poem in Saturnian verse on the First Punic War. A
very great advance was made by Ennius (*c.* 200–180 B.C.) and
Plautus (*c.* 180 B.C.). The former's most famous work was a
long national epic, called *Annales*, and written in hexameter
verse. It narrated the fortunes of Rome from its reputed
foundation by Aeneas to the poet's own age. Only fragments
of it remain, but even from these we can gain some notion of
Ennius' vigor and remarkable poetic imagination. From this
epic even Rome's greatest poet, Vergil, did not disdain to bor-

row and derive inspiration. Ennius' other writings — he was a prolific author — included tragedies, comedies, and *saturae*, miscellaneous compositions of verse and prose dealing with a variety of topics. Of Plautus it is possible to form a clearer judgment; for of his many plays twenty have survived. They were adaptations of Greek plays of the New Comedy; but, in spite of the Greek setting of the plots, they contain much that is characteristically Latin or Roman. The plots are well, sometimes even intricately, constructed and abound in comic situations. There is an astonishing variety in the metres, and great force and a most copious vocabulary distinguish the dialogue. The delineation of character, within the limits necessarily imposed by a comedy of intrigue, in which the chief persons are stock characters, is admirable. We may add that the comedies are a source of considerable value to the social historian of Republican Rome. Both comedy and tragedy continued to be written through the second century. The former after Plautus had its most notable exponent in Terence (*c.* 166 B.C.), six of whose plays have come down to us; the latter in Pacuvius and Accius, whose works are lost.

Latin prose developed somewhat more slowly. The earliest prose annalists of Rome, like Q. Fabius Pictor (*c.* 210 B.C.) wrote in Greek. Fabius' work covered the period from the beginning of Rome to the third century. It was not a mere catalogue of briefly stated facts but had some pretensions to style. Besides early Roman traditions, records kept by the priestly colleges, archives of prominent families, state documents like treaties, Fabius used some Greek sources (*e.g.* Timæus), at all events for the later portions of his book. Other and lesser annalists continued to use the Greek language. Hence the "father of Latin prose" is an honorable title that belongs to Cato. In addition to his multifarious public activities and his life-long interest in farming, he found time to compose important writings. Besides his treatise on agriculture, which is the only one of his works to survive, he wrote a large work, partly historical, partly antiquarian in content. This, called *Origines*, was extensively used by later antiquarians like Varro, and also by some historians. The first three books dealt with the origins of Rome and the Italian communities, and contained much information about early customs, institutions, and religious practices. Books IV to VI seem to have been more purely historical. The latest sections, in which he narrated contemporary events, were strongly personal in tone, as was not unnatural from one who had taken so prominent a part in his country's affairs. Some of his speeches he introduced into the *Origines;* but he also appears to have published a large number separately. Cato was known to his contemporaries as the bitterest opponent of the Hellenic culture which was permeating the educated classes of Rome in the second century. Yet even he was constrained to learn Greek late in life; and, what is more, it is probable that he was somewhat more indebted to Greek historical models when he wrote the *Origines* than he would have cared to admit. His style was straightforward, idiomatic without much ornamentation, yet abounding in pithy phrases and telling illustrations taken from daily life.

It was in the second century, too, that Greek philosophy, literature, and rhetoric became more familiar to the upper class at Rome. In 168 B.C. Crates of Mallus, a noted Greek grammarian, gave public lectures in Rome. In 155 B.C. three Greek philosophers, Carneades the Academic, Critolaus the Peripatetic, and Diogenes the Stoic, came from Athens to Rome as ambassadors of their city. In the intervals between their official duties they gave public discourses and did much to stimulate interest in Greek literature and philosophy. Nor must we forget Polybius, who began by being the tutor of the sons of Aemilius Paullus and ended by being the intimate friend of the members of the Scipionic circle. To this intellectual group also came for a time the leading Stoic philosopher of the day, Panætius of Rhodes.

It was a natural consequence that the educated Roman should strive to master the Greek tongue and see that his sons had the opportunity to do the same. Greek teachers, slave or free, became regular inmates in the establishments of wealthy Romans. Greek rhetoric was expounded and studied at Rome; and, though the senate in 161 B.C. passed an edict expelling Greek teachers of philosophy and rhetoric from the city, it is more than doubtful whether this ordinance had more than a very transitory effect. By the beginning of the next century

Latin rhetoricians were teaching the scientific use of that language, basing their scheme of rhetorical study on Hellenic models. Truly "captive Greece had led the conqueror captive," and there was no branch of intellectual activity fostered at Rome which was not heavily indebted to Greek prototypes. Finally we may note that the tremendous increase in wealth resulting from Rome's eastern wars produced a new standard of living among the well-to-do classes. The simplicity which had distinguished the homes of even the greatest of Rome's citizens in the past began to disappear, and large and luxurious establishments took their place. Thus was accentuated the difference between the ruling and wealthy classes on the one hand, and the poor urban and rustic population on the other. The government was not blind to some of the dangers which it believed would arise from this growth of luxury, and several sumptuary laws were passed during the second century. Legislation of this type, however, is rarely if ever effective, and Rome was no exception to the rule.

CHAPTER XXIV

THE POLITICAL HISTORY OF ROME, 133–78 B.C.

Those who hated the Gracchi and endeavored the most to disparage them, never durst deny, that of all the Romans of their time, nature had disposed them most happily to virtue, or that this disposition was cultivated by the most excellent education. — Plutarch, *Comparison of Agis and Cleomenes with the Gracchi* (Langhorne's translation).

THE position of unchallenged supremacy held for so long by the senate began sensibly to wane after the Third Macedonian War. There were indications that the legality of the wide powers, which it exercised without the sanction of any law or constitutional enactment, would be called in question, once the pressure of foreign wars had been relaxed. The profound social and economic changes in Rome and Italy at this date, which accentuated disparity in wealth between the governing and the governed class of citizens, and resulted in a constant increase of the urban proletariat, were likely to hasten on a movement for reform and the reaffirmation of popular sovereignty. There was a number of prominent senators — chief amongst them were Scipio Aemilianus, C. Lælius, P. Licinius Crassus, and Appius Claudius — of liberal views, who formed a small but influential group of moderates in politics, and stood between the senatorial oligarchy, which was not prepared to yield any particle of its power, and the popular leaders, who now set themselves to reëstablish the authority of the assemblies and remedy existing economic evils. The Calpurnian Law of 149, and another enactment which was passed in 141 and which instituted the ballot at elections, were measures sponsored by these moderates. But these enactments were only slight palliatives, aiming at the reform of single abuses without perceptibly weakening the senatorial position. It was not till 133 that it was directly attacked. One of the tribunes of that year was Ti. Sempronius Gracchus, elder son of the man who had been twice consul and also governor in Spain, and of Cornelia, who was a daughter of Scipio Africanus and, by common consent, a woman of exceptional culture and force of character. Gracchus had so far followed the usual career of a young man of senatorial family. He had seen military service in Spain and served as a quæstor in the same country. Among his supporters at first, it should be noted, were many prominent persons in the state, especially the moderates led by Scipio.

To Gracchus the most urgent problem seemed to be how to revive agriculture in Italy, and especially to rehabilitate the small farmer and wrest from the senatorial land-owners the large tracts of public land in Italy which they had annexed to their use, often with little or no legal right. He therefore introduced an agrarian bill, which in the first place revived the provisions of the Licinio-Sextian Rogations. The state was to reassert its ownership of all *ager publicus* in excess of a certain maximum, which each present occupier was to be allowed to retain. This maximum was 500 *jugera* (about 330 acres), to which Gracchus added an additional 250 *jugera* for each of two, but not more than two, sons. The state domains, of which the state would now recover effective control, were to be parcelled out into small allotments of 30 *jugera* (20 acres) and assigned to the poor and landless citizens. These farms were to be inalienable, and their holders would be required to pay a small rental to the government. A commission of three was to be appointed to carry out all the provisions of the bill, once it had become law. Tiberius' proposal met with intense opposition from the senate, which naturally supported those who were in occupation of the state lands. One of Tiberius' colleagues in the tribunate vetoed the bill when it came before the assembly. When he resolutely refused to withdraw his interdict, Gracchus prevailed on the people to vote Octavius' deposition from office. The bill was then passed, and a commission, consisting of Tiberius, his younger brother Gaius, and Appius Claudius, was elected. Other measures were now projected by the radical tribune, chief among which was one to utilize the treasure of the lately deceased king of Pergamum, Attalus III, whose kingdom had been bequeathed to Rome, for helping to set up the new allotment-holders by purchase of stock and implements. This bill could be interpreted by the senate as a direct attempt to interfere with its authority in a matter which had always been entirely under its control. Tiberius, moreover, had himself nominated as a candidate for the tribunate in 132. Such re-election, if not positively illegal, seems to have been unprecedented. The tribunician elections for 132 were held before the new measure of Gracchus had been passed. They were attended by serious rioting, in the course of which he, with some 300 supporters, was killed by a body of irresponsible senators and their retainers. The agrarian bill, however, remained in force after its author's murder, and the commissioners carried on their task till 129. In that year, mainly it would seem because of the resentment of the Latin and Italian allies of Rome, who were in danger of losing some of the land which they had been allowed to occupy and whose poor citizens were not going to benefit by the new allotments, the senate, largely at the instigation of Scipio Aemilianus, took steps to suspend the commission. Scipio paid with his life for his well-meaning attempt to effect a compromise. He was found dead one morning in his house; and, though the circumstances surrounding his death were never cleared up, it was the general belief that some extreme supporters of Gracchus were responsible for the deed.

For several years the authority of the senate remained unshaken, if not wholly unchallenged. The only success achieved by the Popular party, as we may now call it, in the interval between 133 and 123, was an enactment which made reëlection to the tribunate legal. At the tribunician elections held in 124 Tiberius' brother Gaius, recently returned from a quæstorship in Sardinia, was a successful candidate. It was not only a genuine wish for reform, but a passionate desire to avenge his brother, which spurred on Gaius to essay a most difficult task. The domination of the senate must be broken and the sovereignty of the popular assemblies reasserted in unequivocal fashion. Profiting by the recently passed law, he was able to stand for reëlection for 122. The precise chronological order of his numerous bills, introduced during his two-year period of office, cannot always be established. Among the first, however, was one which reaffirmed the right of appeal of every citizen to the centuriate assembly in case of a capital sentence. In effect this deprived the senate of the right of appointing commissions with judicial powers, such as that which had prosecuted the adherents of Tiberius in 132; it also challenged the validity of the senate's passing a "final" or "emergency" resolution (*senatus consultum ultimum*), which had the effect of authorizing the consuls to take all steps they thought necessary to insure public security, and suspended all the ordinary processes of law. The senate was indeed the target at which Gaius aimed several other telling shafts. The duty of acting as jurors in the permanent court which tried cases of provincial extortion was by his judiciary law transferred from the senate to the equestrian class. Yet another measure compelled the senate to designate the provinces to be governed in any given year by the two consuls before the election to the consulship of the magistrates in question. In the past the assignment had been done after the elections, so that the senate had been able to keep any consul whom it regarded as potentially dangerous to its interests out of the most important posts. The effect of Gracchus' law was to decrease senatorial authority, by making it impossible to exclude from the leading provincial commands consuls who sympathized with the Popular party, or at least were not purely subservient to senatorial policy.

Among Gaius' earlier bills was one which revived his brother's commission, suspended in 129, and a frumentary law authorizing the monthly distribution of grain to the Roman proletariat at a reduced price — one-half the market price — the deficit to be made good by the treasury. With regard to the commission, if the commissioners were to have any further land to distribute, they would have to confiscate *ager publicus* occupied by the Latin and Italian allies. This could be done with safety, only if the allies received the right kind of compensation. Gracchus let it be understood that he was preparing a measure for their whole or partial enfranchisement. The method of taxing the recently formed province of Asia was drastically changed by another Gracchan enactment. In place of a fixed sum annually rendered to Rome by the province, where it had been collected by and among the provincials themselves, the exaction of tithes was left to Roman contractors (*publicani*), who paid a stipulated amount into the treasury at the beginning, and then made what profit they could during the process of gathering in the dues in the province. This measure not only placed the provincials at the mercy of the *publicani*, but greatly strengthened the financial class, the *ordo equester*, which backed the financial operations and the tax-farmers.

Apart from the agrarian and grain laws, the Gracchan bill which was most calculated to be advantageous to the Roman populace was one providing for the foundation of several colonies in Italy and one on the site of Carthage, to be called thereafter Junonia. This proposal was not put forward till 122, and the senate, through Gaius' colleague in the tribunician college, Livius Drusus, tried to outbid the reformer. So far Gracchus' position had been unassailable. It was only when he took steps to carry out his promises to Rome's allies that he lost ground rapidly with his erstwhile supporters. The Roman voters — however equitable the scheme might seem to any fair-minded man — were not ready to see the Italians and Latin communities put on a footing of political equality with themselves in the Roman state. Thus, when Gracchus proposed that the Latin allies should receive the full, and the Italians the private, rights of Roman citizenship, many of his followers wavered. The opportunity was not missed by Drusus. He interposed his veto, and then introduced several vote-catching measures, of which the chief was one to establish a number of Italian colonies. Gaius' hold on the voters was irremediably shaken, and he failed to be reëlected for a third year of office. Soon after his second term had expired, his political opponents took steps to rescind his colonial law, though the colonization of Carthage had already begun. Riots ensued when Gracchus appeared to defend his measure. Many of his still faithful supporters were killed; he himself, seeing the hopelessness of his position, committed suicide.

How is the work of these two brothers to be appraised? Both had paid for their ideals with their lives; both had failed, at least in part, in the task that they set themselves. In the case of Tiberius, his unconstitutional conduct in bringing about the deposition of Octavius, and still more his unprecedented action in seeking office for a second time, brought the full force of senatorial opposition upon him. Then, while the more judicial Fathers deliberated, the extreme section of the senate took the law into its own hands. The real cause of Gaius' undoing was his espousal of the allies' grievances. Of his many enactments the one dealing with colonization lapsed at once; the agrarian bill, since there was no more land to assign without encroaching on the territories occupied by the allies, became a dead letter. Many of the other laws remained in force for the present, but produced evil results which Gaius could hardly have foreseen, and would doubtless have essayed to remedy, had his career as a statesman been prolonged. The equestrian jurors, for example, were too often corrupt, because their financial interests in the provinces led them to condone rather than to condemn the malpractices of provincial governors. The system of taxation in Asia all but ruined that province in the next fifty years, and its subsequent recovery was very slow. Finally, the policy of selling grain below cost price, which Gaius may have intended merely as a temporary measure to relieve existing distress, set a precedent on which every succeeding Popular leader, anxious for the support of the *plebs urbana*, tried to improve. The great historical importance of the Gracchi, however, lies not in any or all of their specific legislative acts, but in the fact that they permanently undermined the sovereignty of the senate and successfully asserted the sovereign power of the people. In so doing they exalted the tribunate to a position of supreme importance in the constitution. They began a political conflict between the wealthy and official oligarchy and the Popular party, which only ceased with the end of the Republic, for which it was indeed largely responsible.

For the moment, however, the mortal wound inflicted by Gaius Gracchus on the prevailing system of government was not apparent. The Popular party had no leader of weight during the next decade; when at last it won a striking success at the polls, it was due to the general indignation felt at recent and flagrant examples of senatorial misrule and corruption. In 118 the king of Numidia, Micipsa, died. His country was now for some years the scene of civil war and intrigue. The adopted nephew of the late king, Jugurtha, after causing both of Micipsa's sons to be assassinated, made himself master of the kingdom. `It was the duty of the senate to intervene from the first; instead, the gold of Jugurtha persuaded senatorial commissions of inquiry to decide in his favor, or at least to maintain a non-committal attitude. Thus it was not till 111 that the senate, compelled by the popular outcry in Rome, reluctantly declared war. Jugurtha, nevertheless, still succeeded in neutralizing the effect of Roman military intervention in Africa by bribery. At last an incorruptible Roman commander, Cæcilius Metellus, was appointed to take charge of the war. Though methodical, his operations did not bring a speedy decision. The combined influence of the equestrian class and the Popular party brought about the election of C. Marius to the consulship for 107, and his appointment to succeed Metellus, whose adjutant he had been, to take over the African command. Marius, born in 155, was of humble origin. He had seen much military service, and by dogged determination had attained to the tribunate in 119, and four years later to the prætorship. In 114 he had been proprætor in Spain. From 107 to 105 he wore down the resistance of the Numidian usurper till, with his capture, the war was brought to an end. Numidia, now divided between several chiefs, remained in clientage to Rome as before.

Meanwhile a most threatening situation had developed on Rome's northern and northwestern frontiers. From 125 Roman armies had operated against several tribes of Transalpine Gaul, and in 121 southeastern Gaul, with the exception of the territory of Rome's ally, Massilia, was formally annexed as a province. A strong military camp was established at Arausio (Orange), while in 118 a colony of Roman citizens settled at Narbo. The main purpose of the Roman government at this date was to obtain secure control of the land communication between Italy and Spain. It happened that the occupation took place not long before important tribal movements in north-central Europe threatened the peace of both Gaul and Italy. German tribes moved southward from the shores of the Baltic, chief among them being the Cimbri. Overrunning the territory of Celtic tribes in their gradual progress, they directed their first threat to Italy from across the eastern end of the Alps near the colony of Aquileia. Although they defeated a Roman army in the vicinity (113), they did not advance farther. By 109 they had moved slowly westward and appeared in Gaul, where, in conjunction with the Teutones, another migrant tribe, they again beat a Roman army in the field. Their efforts to get land on which to settle in northern Gaul or in the Roman province were fruitless. In 107 their attack was renewed, and they were reinforced by several other tribes. They now overran southern Gaul as far as the Atlantic ocean, and once more defeated a Roman consular army. Worst disaster of all, in 105 two Roman forces combined were utterly annihilated by them at Arausio. An immediate invasion of Italy seemed certain. Popular excitement, and anger at the failure of the senate and senatorial generals to cope with the barbarians, led to the election of Marius as consul for 104, even before he had returned from Africa. Fortune was kind to Rome and Marius at this juncture; for the Germanic tribes, instead of following up their successes by an immediate attack on Italy, broke up into two main groups. The Cimbri crossed the Pyrenees and made a marauding expedition into Spain, while the Teutones and other tribes remained in Gaul. Thus two years passed, which Marius, reëlected year by year to the consulship — a violation of constitutional practice which, though justified by the exceptional political situation, set a most dangerous precedent — utilized to carry out a reform of the Roman army that was both necessary and far-reaching in its consequences. Actually he seems to have begun his changes in the last years of the Jugurthine War, by calling for volunteers to the army on a far more extensive scale than had ever been done before.

Since the earliest days of Rome citizens, provided they had a certain property qualification, had been obliged to perform military service. The minimum amount of property bringing this obligation with it had, however, been lowered more than once, as the difficulty of finding sufficient men increased, and the wealthier Romans especially were often allowed to evade service. At first the tactical unit in the Roman army had been the phalanx, made up of members of the first, second, and third Servian classes; their armature, which they provided themselves, was not uniform. The fourth and fifth classes formed the light-armed troops. Some time before the First Punic War considerable changes were introduced. The legion, made up of thirty maniples or companies, each 120 strong, replaced the phalanx. Though a lowered property qualification was still retained, the division of the legionaries was now determined by their experience rather than by the equipment which they were able to provide. And in this last matter the government now subsidized its poorer citizens.

Marius' reform was a twofold one: on the one hand his army was made up mainly of volunteers, who enlisted for a long period of years (16), and who, since the property qualification was now abolished, were chiefly taken from the proletariat. He thus created an army of professional soldiers, who came to regard themselves as the servants of the general under whom they enlisted rather than of the state whose citizens they were. In the second place, he introduced noteworthy changes in the tactical organization and the armature. The size of the legion was increased, and the smaller unit within the larger was henceforward the cohort. Ten of these made a legion.[1] The legionaries were equipped alike with defensive armor, and for offense with a lance (*pilum*) and a short sword (*gladius*). Immense pains were spent on the training of the cohorts, so that they became tactical units of deadly precision and great mobility. With this reconstituted army Marius triumphed where half a dozen other commanders had grievously failed. In 102 he utterly routed the Teuton host at Aquæ Sextiæ in Gallia Narbonensis, and in the following year, in conjunction with Q. Catulus, he no less decisively defeated a great army of Cimbri at Vercellæ in the Cisalpine province. Small wonder that the savior of Italy and Rome should have been reëlected for a sixth time to the consulship (100).

Obscure *novus homo* that he was, he had first been elected as the people's choice; the military skill, amounting to genius, that he had displayed, proved that that choice had been right. The Popular party, languishing since the days of C. Gracchus, now

---

[1] In theory the cohort at full strength was 600 men, and the legion similarly 6000. In practice there was a good deal of variation and the numbers generally somewhat lower. Especially would this be the case with legions operating in a distant theatre of war. Some of J. Cæsar's legions at the beginning of the civil war contained only half that number.

hoped to find him as successful in politics as he had been in the field. Failing that, they at least trusted to carrying through an anti-optimate program with his support, the more so as he could always rely on a strong military backing. C. Servilius Glaucia and L. Appuleius Saturninus, the one prætor, the other tribune in 100, were the most prominent of the Popular leaders. Already at the elections for this year methods of terrorization were used; and, when Saturninus during the course of the year brought forward a series of demagogic measures, the manner of their passing by the *comitia* was little better. When the next elections came on and Glaucia was a candidate illegally for the consulship, the Popular leaders were responsible for the murder of Glaucia's fellow candidate and rival. The senate passed a *senatus consultum ultimum* and required Marius to restore order in the capital. Saturninus and Glaucia had by their outrageous behavior alienated a majority of even their immediate supporters. They and some others were forced to capitulate to the consul; but he was unable to prevent their assassination by their infuriated opponents. Marius himself left Italy at the end of the year, as unpopular as ever with the senate, and, in addition, distrusted and discredited with the Popular party, whose leaders he had been unable to save or to protect.

For a few years the senate and the *equites* formed an informal coalition, the direct result of the excesses committed by the *populares* in 100. Many prominent men among the last named were subsequently prosecuted, while the laws of Saturninus were repealed. However, the conduct of the *equites* as jurors in the courts of law soon brought this temporary *rapprochement* to an end. Their corruption, and the resultant miscarriage of justice, were notorious, and can be illustrated from two trials during this time. M'. Aquillius, whose guilt as provincial governor is undoubted, was acquitted because he happened to be on good terms with the capitalist class. Rutilius Rufus, whose conduct both as a man and as an administrator was exemplary, was found guilty on a false charge and forced to go into exile. This unhappy condition of affairs it was the primary aim of M. Livius Drusus, son of C. Gracchus' opponent, to mend, when he became one of the tribunes for 91. His judiciary bill was a compromise — to recruit the jurors from both the senatorial and equestrian classes. But it satisfied neither party, and Drusus had to make sure of adequate support to get it passed. Hence he introduced an agrarian law to provide for colonies in Italy and Sicily, and a bill lowering the price of grain for the purchaser in Rome. His agrarian measure he intended to make effective by enfranchising the allies of Rome. Thus he took up afresh the grievances of those allies, which had been ignored since the days of C. Gracchus. This enfranchisement, besides its inherent justice as a reward for many years of loyal service, would enable the state to recover the *ager publicus* that they occupied, and thereby give effect to Drusus' colonizing projects. But the disinclination of all sections of the Roman community — senators, *equites*, and proletariat — to admit all the inhabitants of Italy to political equality with themselves was as strong as it had ever been. Drusus' well-meant efforts failed, and he himself was murdered. His death, and the fact that they were once more to be deprived of the franchise which he had promised them — it is, however, more than doubtful whether Drusus could have secured the passage of his bill had he lived — ended the patience of the Italians and drove them to arms.

The rising against Roman authority began in Picenum, but rapidly involved the greater part of the peninsula. A federal union was formed by the communities with a capital at Corfinium, whose name was changed to Italia. The chief executive was vested in two consuls, supported by twelve prætors and by a council or senate of delegates. A federal currency was also issued, and it is clear that the aim of the Italians was not simply to extort fair treatment from Rome by an appeal to force, but to oust her from her proud and sovereign position in Italy. In 90 the allies won striking successes in the field. It was a fortunate circumstance for the Romans that Etruria and Umbria, where their wealthy aristocracy predominated, and the Latin colonies remained faithful. Yet the pressure of the enemy before the end of the year was such that the government deemed it wise to make timely concessions, which were in truth equivalent to the complete abandonment of its earlier intransigent policy. A law (*Lex Julia*) was passed conferring the Roman franchise on all loyal communities; while in 89 the Papirian law assured the same for any citizen of any allied community who should apply for it within a specified time. The inhabitants of *Gallia Cisalpina*, south of the Po, received the full, those to the north of the river the partial, franchise by the Pompeian law passed in the same year. These measures had the effect of preventing a further spread of the war. In 89 and 88 the Roman higher command was superior to that of the enemy, and the disasters of 90 were retrieved. The federal capital, too, though situated in the middle of Italy, could not compare with Rome as a strategic centre.

Of the Roman generals who gradually broke the resistance of the allies the most outstanding were Cn. Pompeius Strabo (consul in 89) and L. Cornelius Sulla. The latter had served as a junior under Marius in Africa; since then he had filled the usual offices up to the prætorship, and had acted as governor in one of the near-eastern provinces. It was in Asia Minor that a most serious danger to the eastern provinces and protectorates of Rome arose, before the Italian war had come to an end. Sulla, elected consul for 88, had been designated to take charge of the Roman operations overseas, a task for which not only his high office but his previous experience marked him out. This appointment was, however, illegally challenged by Marius, who, after living in retirement for some years, had taken a not very successful part in the recent war against the allies. In 88 he prevailed on one of the tribunes, P. Sulpicius Rufus, to introduce a bill, which was carried by terrorizing the voters, and which transferred the Asiatic command from Sulla to Marius. The latter, engaged in reducing Nola, one of the last strongholds occupied by the Italians, marched with his army on Rome, and, after taking possession of the city, procured a decree of outlawry against Marius, Sulpicius, and some other Popular leaders. He then caused the Sulpician laws to be repealed, and strengthened the authority of the senate by an enactment which made senatorial sanction to any bill brought before the *comitia* necessary before the bill could become law. Thus, what had by custom and in practice been almost invariably the case before the days of Ti. Gracchus, was now enforced by law. Of the two chief outlaws, Sulpicius was killed, but Marius made good his escape to Africa. In the beginning of 87 Sulla embarked for Greece with five legions.

Since the days when Rome annexed Macedonia, extended a protectorate over Greece, and took over the former kingdom of Pergamum, Egypt and Syria, once so great, had rapidly declined. The Roman government had nothing further to fear from either, which perhaps lulled it into a false sense of security. For, while the old powers were waning, new ones were growing, which in time might threaten Roman authority and interests in the Near East. The small kingdom of Pontus, stretching along the southern shore of the Black Sea, under its king, Mithradates VI Eupator, had, during the last years of the second and the early years of the first century, developed into something very different from the other petty principalities of Asia Minor. Mithradates had begun by extending his protectorate over the Greek communities on the south coast of the Euxine; then he successfully assumed overlordship over the cities along its eastern and northern shores, of which those grouped about and on the Crimea were the most important. Of Iranian stock, this monarch was at the same time familiar with Hellenic culture and institutions. His naval and military forces were organized on Greek lines, and, while the higher commands were exclusively entrusted to Greeks, a large part of the rank and file were also recruited from his Greek subjects and allies. It was the king's ambition to extend his dominions westward and southward in Asia Minor, and he looked with covetous eye on Bithynia and Cappadocia. Apart from the fact that the king of Bithynia was a client ally of Rome, any advance in these regions would disturb the Roman settlement of Asia and bring a powerful and ambitious prince to the very frontiers of the Roman province. Several attempts at encroachment on Cappadocian territory were frustrated by Roman intervention, and Mithradates was content to bide his time. As the years passed, he had increasing hopes of general support from the Greeks of Asia Minor and European Greece, whose discontent at Roman suzerainty became steadily more intense.

At last, when the sovereignty of Rome in Italy was challenged by her allies, the Pontic king struck. He occupied Cappadocia, overran Bithynia, and then advanced into the Roman province of Asia, where he was received with enthusiasm by the inhabitants. A great massacre of Romans and Italians was per-

petrated at his instigation, after the weak Roman garrisons
had been overpowered (88). On the lowest ancient estimate
80,000 perished on this occasion. Greece now joined in the
rising against Rome, and in 88 Mithradates despatched military
forces across the Aegean. But he had waited just a little too
long before launching his offensive against Rome. For, by
the time that his troops reached Greece, Rome had all but
ended the war in Italy. Early in the next year (87) Sulla
appeared in Greece. Hereupon the Peloponnesian states made
haste to disown their promises to Mithradates. Athens and
Peiræus, occupied by a Pontic force, were Sulla's first objective;
after a siege lasting nearly twelve months the city capitulated.
Then, during the course of 86 Sulla defeated Mithradates'
main army twice, at Chæronea, and again at Orchomenus in
Bœotia, thereby forcing the enemy to evacuate Greece. After
wintering in Thessaly, he crossed to Asia Minor in 85. Meanwhile the action of a hostile senate at home had turned out to
his advantage. L. Valerius Flaccus, consul in 86, had been
sent out to supersede him; but he was slain by one of his own
officers, Fimbria, in Asia Minor. The assassin assumed command of Flaccus' army and with it reduced Mithradates to
severe straits. The king, who had already had communications
with Sulla after the defeat at Orchomenus, was now even
readier to come to terms. Sulla, anxious to return to Italy,
and not without fear that Fimbria would get the main credit
for Mithradates' reduction, was very willing to make what he
probably realized would only be a temporary peace between
Rome and the Pontic king. Mithradates abandoned all claims
to Cappadocia and Bithynia, whose former rulers were restored,
and retired to Pontus. He also undertook to pay a substantial
war indemnity to Rome. Fimbria took his own life, when his
soldiers deserted him for Sulla on the latter's appearance in
Asia Minor. The treatment meted out to the Greek communities for siding with Mithradates and carrying out the massacre
of 88 was exceedingly severe. Intelligible as a measure of
vengeance, it was quite devoid of sound statesmanship. For,
by compelling the provincials to pay a huge indemnity (20,000
talents) over and above five years' arrears of taxation, liabilities
which they could meet only by borrowing from Roman capital-

ists, Sulla ruined for years to come what was potentially one of the most prosperous of the Roman provinces. An additional hardship was that the troops which had lately served under Fimbria were left in the province, and were billeted on the inhabitants.

While Sulla had thus been fully occupied in the Near East, anarchy prevailed in Rome and unrest in Italy. After the war with the allies had been all but stamped out, their position was not as favorable as they had hoped or might reasonably expect. The Roman government, having been forced to make wide concessions, tried to limit their effect by restricting the new voters to eight out of the thirty-five tribes. Since the effective vote was by tribes and not by individuals (cf. p. 374), the new voters would exercise very little influence. The tribune Sulpicius in 88 introduced a bill which was equitable, — nor are we justified in doubting that his intentions were honest, — to distribute the recently made citizens through all the thirty-five tribes. With the abrogation of the Sulpician laws by Sulla the Italians saw themselves once again robbed of their rights, and some continued or resumed their resistance to Rome. Of the consuls for 87 one, C. Octavius, was a supporter of the senate, the other, L. Cornelius Cinna, was an extreme member of the Popular party. The latter now revived the Sulpician enactment respecting the new voters. Rome became the scene of civil conflict, from which Cinna, supported by Marius who had returned from Africa with a body of Numidian troops, emerged triumphant. A reign of terror followed, in which many of Marius' political opponents and former enemies were done to death or proscribed, their property being confiscated. The election of Marius to a seventh consulship, for the year 86, was carried through, but he lived to hold the office for only a few weeks. His death can have been regretted by no one; his life, after the military triumphs of his middle years, had been a tragedy.

Now, in 86, was the first time, since Ti. Gracchus first challenged senatorial authority, that the Popular party was in control of the government. Violence and oppression prevailed. Save for carrying through the enrolment of the Italian voters into all the tribes, we do not hear of a single measure of constructive statesmanship. Even ordinary constitutional forms were disregarded. Cinna kept the consulship from year to year, until he was murdered in 84 by mutinous soldiery. Cn. Papirius Carbo, his associate, was consul in 85, 84, and again in 82; in this last year C. Marius the younger, son of Sulla's rival, was also elected to that office, although he was in no wise qualified and only twenty years of age. The only able and honest man among the leading *populares* was Q. Sertorius who, owing to these very qualities never played a leading part in their counsels. He was prætor in 83, and in the next year proceeded as governor to Spain, a momentous circumstance both for the province and for the senatorial party at Rome. Sulla, who in his absence was proclaimed a public enemy, returned to Italy in the early part of 83, prepared to fight for his own position and for the restitution of senatorial authority. For eighteen months Italy was again the scene of civil war. In a series of engagements Sulla crushed his political opponents and their armies, and those Italians who, like the Samnites, had taken their side. Then he had himself proclaimed dictator in the last weeks of 82. His first act was a ruthless proscription of political opponents — between four and five thousand names appeared on the lists — followed by the confiscation of their property. Many of the communities in Italy, which had resisted the dictator, now found themselves deprived of part of their land, which Sulla settled with his disbanded veterans. He resigned the dictatorship at the end of 81 but held the consulship in 80. Then he retired into private life; but, within little more than a year, he died at the age of sixty.

Sulla's reform of the Roman constitution, carried through by a series of enactments in 81 and 80, did not even survive for a decade after his death. Its primary aim was not merely to reëstablish the authority of the senate, as it had been prior to 133, but to strengthen that authority with legal sanction that it had never had before. Thus, the tribunate was reduced to complete impotence, and the holder of that office was debarred from seeking any higher magistracy. The *comitia tributa* ceased to have any importance save to elect the tribunes and plebeian ædiles. Legislation was entrusted to the centuriate assembly, and, in any case, was subject to senatorial approval. The judiciary law of Gracchus was rescinded, and the panels of jurors for the courts of justice were once again chosen annually from the senatorial class. None of these measures endured; nor did they deserve to, since they revived and extended a system of government which had already been proved to be no longer adequate for an imperial state. Some other measures were more enduring because they were equitable, or else were aimed at procuring a more efficient administration. Thus Sulla, carrying further the principles of the *Lex Villia annalis* of 180, fixed by law the regular order of the magistracies, — quæstorship, prætorship, consulship, — as well as the lowest legal age at which any of these offices could be held.[1] An interval of ten years between two tenures of the consulship was also enacted. The number of lesser magistracies was increased, especially to meet the needs of provincial administration, so that from now twenty quæstors and eight prætors were chosen each year. The regular procedure, frequently operative in the past, was now for the consuls and prætors of any given year to take over a provincial command in the year immediately succeeding their magistracy. The quæstorship, moreover, by a new arrangement, carried with it automatically membership of the senate, a body which was increased by the dictator to six hundred. Finally, the number of permanent courts of justice for the trial of criminal offenses (*quaestiones perpetuae*) was raised to six or seven, and their procedure was regularized.

Though he did not seek permanently to exercise a personal autocracy, but restored oligarchic government at Rome, Sulla had set an example by his action in 88, and again in 83–82, which other military leaders in the next half century were not slow to copy. Senatorial government was not only full of shortcomings, but it was powerless to check the ambitions of men who could enforce their demands because they had an army at their back. And so the army reforms of Marius, owing to the circumstances of the time, brought with them political consequences of which he had never dreamed.

---

[1] It was Cicero's proud boast that he held all the offices *anno suo*, that is, at the earliest legal date. Thus he was quæstor in 75 — he was born in 106 — prætor in 66, and consul in 63.

CHAPTER XXV

THE POLITICAL HISTORY OF ROME, 78–29 B.C.

But you, Fathers of the senate, how long will you keep the Republic in insecurity by your delays, and meet arms only with words? Forces are levied against you; money is raised, publicly and privately, by extortion; troops are led out, and placed in garrisons; the laws are under arbitrary and capricious management; and yet you, meanwhile, think only of sending deputies and preparing resolutions. — Sallust, *Histories* i, fragment 77.

SULLA imagined that he had inaugurated a new era of Roman power with the senate in a position of undisputed supremacy. The year of his death does indeed mark the beginning of a fresh epoch, but in a sense very different from what he intended. The years from 78 to 70 witnessed a keen struggle between the senate and the Popular party; they also furnished proof that in the future the army commanders were to be the real masters of the Roman world. Finally, it was a period of grave dangers in Italy and beyond.

Of the consuls in 78 Q. Lutatius Catulus was a universally respected member of the senatorial party, and M. Aemilius Lepidus posed as the champion of popular rights, but his promises to rescind the more obnoxious of Sulla's enactments were probably no more than a blind. When in 77 he took over the command of Cisalpine Gaul and had an army to use, he marched on Rome, intent on a revolution which should secure his own absolute position. He was defeated by Catulus and fled to Sardinia, where he soon died. In itself the attempt at violence was perhaps not very serious; but it showed where the danger to peace chiefly lay, and it had indirect consequences of greater moment.

Among the younger men who had rallied to Sulla's standards on his return from the East were M. Licinius Crassus and

456

Cn. Pompeius, son of the consul of 89. Crassus, born about 115, had very nearly suffered the fate of his father and elder brother, both of whom perished at the time of the Marian proscriptions. He managed to escape from Italy, however, and, after some years spent in Spain and Africa, he joined Sulla in Italy in 83, and became one of the dictator's ablest lieutenants. Rewarded with grants of confiscated property, and by the timely purchase of depreciated lands, Crassus in those years laid the foundations of that immense wealth to which he subsequently owed his prominent position in public affairs. Pompey, born in 106, had seen his first military service under his father in the Italian war. In 83 he raised volunteers in Picenum, where his family estates lay, and with these joined Sulla. His military ability was such that, in spite of his youth, he was entrusted with the task of crushing the Marian factions in Sicily and Africa. In 78–77 he was put in command of troops by the senate, and helped to suppress the rising of Lepidus. The sequel was, however, unexpected and inconvenient to the government. The only province which had not submitted to Sulla was Spain, where Q. Sertorius had by tact and personality gained a remarkable ascendancy over the natives. A senatorial governor and general, Q. Cæcilius Metellus, was sent out against him in 79, but was unable to make headway against the military genius of his opponent. Moreover, Sertorius received welcome reinforcements in the shape of the survivors of Lepidus' army commanded by M. Perperna. In that same year (77) young Pompey, instead of disbanding his troops, once the insurrection in Italy was over, kept them in the vicinity of the capital and demanded of the senate that he be sent to Spain against Sertorius. The Fathers reluctantly acquiesced; and so Pompey, who was not yet thirty and had held no curule office, went forth invested with the proconsular *imperium* and in charge of a proconsular army. Yet for several years Sertorius was more than a match for his two opponents; and, though by 72 his resources had been heavily reduced, he would in all likelihood have carried on a guerilla warfare indefinitely, had he not been treacherously murdered by Perperna. With the passing of Sertorius the resistance to the senatorial commanders quickly collapsed; so that in 71 Pompey was able to return to Italy with an enhanced military reputation, which his operations in Spain by no means justified.

Much had happened in his absence. The Popular party had struggled hard to get the tribunate restored to its former dignity; but, beyond securing by the Aurelian law of 75 the removal of the provision in Sulla's law which debarred tribunes for seeking higher office, it had not achieved its aim. At the beginning of 74 a most threatening situation developed in the Near East on the death of the king of Bithynia, Nicomedes III. Following the example of Attalus III of Pergamum, the late monarch left his kingdom by will to Rome. But Mithradates, whom eight years of peace had restored to all or more than all his former prosperity, and who was allied by marriage to Tigranes, king of Armenia, thought the time had come for renewed aggressions on Rome. Anxious to mass as many enemies against Rome as possible, he allied himself with the numerous and well-organized pirates of the Mediterranean — their chief strongholds were in Crete and in Cilicia — and even entered into communication with Sertorius in Spain. Both the consuls of 74 were sent out to quench this most dangerous conflagration in Anatolia. While M. Aurelius Cotta was less than competent, L. Lucullus was not merely a general of outstanding ability, but had had the inestimable advantage of serving under Sulla in the former war against the Pontic king.

In 73 a slave rising started in Campania, which rapidly spread over the greater part of Italy. It was not the first occasion on which the Romans had been brought face to face with the peril inherent in the presence of a large servile population in their territories. But in the past such disturbances had been confined to the provinces. Serious slave insurrections had broken out in Sicily in 136 and again in 104; in both instances several years of military intervention were needed to restore complete order there. In 73 a small band of gladiators, led by a Thracian ex-brigand, Spartacus, escaped from the training school near Capua, and lived by pillaging the surrounding country. Efforts by the authorities to suppress these men were quite fruitless, and their number rapidly grew. Slave herdsmen, runaways from estates, robbers, and miscellaneous riff-raff, swelled the ranks of the insurgents, so that we are told that there were 70,000 of them by the end of the year, and that they controlled most of southern Italy. When the government took more stringent measures and sent out consular armies to suppress the outlaws, who were devastating the country and terrorizing and maltreating the population wherever they went, they defeated these as they had previously beaten the smaller forces sent out against them. At last, in 71, M. Crassus, who had had extensive military experience with Sulla, and who was prætor in that year, was put in charge of ten legions. With these he gradually wore down Spartacus and his men, and finally inflicted a crushing defeat on them. The senate had meantime associated Pompey with him in the command; he, on his return from Spain, wiped out in Cisalpine Gaul a force of 5000, who had escaped from the general rout in southern Italy. A frightful example was made of the 6000 slaves who were captured; for they were crucified along the Appian Way, to deter other slaves from doing as they had done.

There were now two army commanders in Italy, each with a large military force at his back. Though their feelings to one another were neither now, nor at any time, very cordial, both Crassus and Pompey saw that it was to their own interest to coöperate for their mutual advancement; for neither could have attained to absolute power without fighting the other. The senate, even had it wished, was powerless to prevent their plans, and the two were elected consuls for the year 70, although it was only in the previous year that Crassus was prætor, while Pompey was under age and had held none of the lower magistracies. So soon were Sulla's elaborate regulations set aside! Pompey, too, was immensely popular with the masses, who were dazzled by his brilliant military career. Naturally, then, the *populares* were eager to win him over to their side. Crassus, by reason of his great wealth, not only could exert considerable influence in the senate, but was closely in touch with the equestrian class and their financial speculations. The year 70 saw the end of the Sullan constitution. The tribunate, and with it the *comitia tributa*, recovered all their earlier importance as the result of a law sponsored by Pompey. A struggle over the constitution of the jury-courts lasted for the greater part of the year, until in November the bill of L. Aurelius Cotta, which had all the characteristics of a compromise, was passed. Henceforward the jurors for the criminal courts were annually chosen in equal numbers from the senate, the *equites*, and a third group of citizens (*tribuni aerarii*), who were men of moderate means falling short, nevertheless, of the equestrian census. It is probable that the revelations made at a famous trial in the summer of 70 helped to secure the necessary votes for Cotta's bill. The ex-governor of Sicily, C. Verres, was arraigned for extortion in his province.

In the trial M. Tullius Cicero acted as prosecuting counsel. Born in 106, Cicero came of an equestrian family settled at Arpinum. He saw brief military service during the Italian war, and then, in the troubled years from 88 to 82, he devoted himself to the study of literature, philosophy, and, above all, oratory. In 80 he defended a certain Sextus Roscius, brought to trial on a charge of parricide. The speech, *For Roscius of Ameria*, is extant, and is of great interest; first, because, in spite of imperfections, it clearly presages the future unrivalled eminence of Cicero as an orator and advocate; secondly, because it draws a vivid picture of the awful conditions prevailing in the years immediately before, and especially Sulla's proscriptions. It required courage, too, to attack, as Cicero did, an influential freedman of the dictator. Unfortunately it is uncertain whether Cicero won his case. From 79 to 77 he was absent in Greece, continuing his oratorical and philosophical studies. In 75 he began his official career as quæstor in Sicily. During his stay there he became familiar with conditions in the island, and his fair and upright conduct brought him many friends among the provincials. It was but natural that they should turn to him to help them to obtain justice in 70.

The Roman procedure in trials of this kind was elaborate. At a preliminary hearing the prosecution and the defense stated their cases at length, only little evidence being normally taken from witnesses at this stage. Then, after an interval, the main trial came on. Cicero, realizing that Verres' powerful friends would exert themselves to the utmost on his behalf in the interval between the first and second trials, and would not hesitate to suborn the jurors, adopted an unusual course at the opening session. Contenting himself with a brief address, he brought forward his most important witnesses. The evidence given was so overwhelmingly damaging that Verres went into voluntary exile at once, and did not stay for the second trial. The five extant speeches of Cicero for the second trial were not delivered in court, but were published by him subsequently. Even if some allowance be made for the fact that they are the utterances of an advocate, they afford a fearful picture of the avarice, cruelty, rapacity, and utter disregard of the legal rights of the provincials, of which a Roman governor could be capable. Moreover, but for Cicero's skillful, if unorthodox, handling of the opening proceedings, it is more than likely that Verres would have got off. Cicero's reward was that he was elected to the curule ædileship for 69 at the head of the poll; two years later he was returned as one of the prætors for 66.

At the end of their year of office neither Crassus nor Pompey took over a provincial command. Pompey was content for the moment to retire into private life; for he was biding his time until he could obtain the command of the Roman forces in the eastern Mediterranean. The Mithradatic war had now been in progress for five years. Though Cotta in 74 had made several bad blunders, Lucullus retrieved the situation. The Pontic king was compelled to abandon the siege of Rome's ally, the city-state of Cyzicus. His fleet was forced to retire into the Black Sea, and his armies to withdraw to Pontus, where Lucullus inflicted a heavy defeat on them near Cabira in 72. Mithradates deserted his troops and fled to Tigranes of Armenia. The submission, voluntary or after siege operations, of various cities, especially the Greek maritime towns in Mithradates' southern kingdom, was systematically procured by Lucullus and his lieutenants in this and the following two years. In 70 Lucullus introduced reforms in the Roman province of Asia, which were as welcome to the provincials as they were detestable to the financial magnates at Rome. He gave considerable relief to debtors; he prohibited any higher rate of interest than 12 per cent; and, in general, he so ordered the taxation and finances of the province, that the inhabitants were out of debt at the end of four years, and a new era of prosperity in Asia could begin. But Lucullus had made the equestrian class and the *publicani* his implacable enemies. To their intrigues he owed his lack of support in the next three years, and his ultimate recall.

Armenia had formed part of the Seleucid empire; but after the defeat by Rome of Antiochus of Syria, it had become an independent kingdom, and, in spite of the growing power of its neighbor, Parthia, had remained so. Tigranes I, who came to the throne in 95, was an able and ambitious prince, bent on enlarging his territory when opportunity offered. About 83, when Parthia was distracted by invaders from Scythia, Tigranes annexed northern Syria and some Parthian dependencies in northern Mesopotamia. At the same time he founded a new capital in the south of his realm, called after himself, Tigranocerta. In 70 Lucullus demanded from the Armenian king the extradition of Mithradates. It was refused; whereupon Lucullus, who was at Sinope, leaving a portion of his army behind to guard the territory recently won from Mithradates, with the rest hastened south, crossed the Euphrates, and marched straight on Tigranocerta. His swift approach took the enemy somewhat unawares. He laid siege to the city, and when Tigranes approached with a relieving host, and, against Mithradates' advice, provoked an open engagement, the Roman legionaries, though greatly outnumbered, routed the Armenian army.[1]

The city capitulated shortly afterward (69). But now Lucullus' troubles began. Having reason to believe that Parthia, with whose monarch he had previously been in friendly communication, was playing a double game, he proposed to march against her, but his troops mutinied. He now decided to advance on the old capital of Armenia, Artaxata. Although he inflicted a second defeat on the enemy, the severity of the climate compelled him to retire southward before he had forced the surrender of the city. To make matters worse, the detachment he had left behind in southern Armenia got into difficulties, while his lieutenant in Pontus was heavily defeated by the enemy near Ziela. His own troops also continued to cause him anxiety. Thus he was forced to remain inactive and then retire to guard the Roman province of Asia, while Tigranes and Mithradates set about recovering Pontus and overran Cappadocia.

[1] 15,000 Romans to 80,000 of the enemy is a reasonable estimate.

The trouble which Lucullus had with his men may have been partly due to a certain aristocratic aloofness, and to the fact that as a commander he was something of a martinet. But the greater part of the blame rests with the Roman senate. Many of Lucullus' soldiers had been in the Near East since Sulla's day and were clamoring for their discharge; also, their prolonged stay in Asia Minor in time of peace had undermined their discipline. The senate, instead of sending Lucullus fresh troops and recalling at least some of his veterans, did nothing. The result was that most of what he had achieved between 74 and 69 was undone in the next two years.

To the mass of the Roman people, however, this war in distant lands did not come home very nearly. For them a more real danger was presented by the pirates in the Mediterranean. These pests had increased substantially in numbers and power during the last half century. Since 146 there had been no strong navy in the eastern Mediterranean to keep them in check. From time to time their interference with maritime trade led the Roman government to take action. Thus, in 103 the prætor M. Antonius operated with some effect in southwestern Asia Minor. The occupation of a few bases in that region formed the beginning of the Roman province of Cilicia. Between 78 and 76 P. Servilius expelled pirates from that same district, and they retired to Crete. Two years later M. Antonius, son of the prætor of 103, was sent to that island to stamp out the corsairs; but he proved incompetent. The depredations of the raiders were now more formidable than ever before. Several Roman ships were burnt close to the Italian coast, and grain ships were constantly in danger of capture. While the possibility of a shortage of food, or even of famine, aroused the people, the equestrian class saw themselves confronted with financial ruin if the pirates were not stopped and order restored throughout the Mediterranean area and Anatolia.

At the beginning of 67 the tribune A. Gabinius, came forward with a radical proposal. A man of consular rank was to be appointed to take general charge of operations against the pirates, and, to do so effectively, was to be entrusted with unprecedentedly wide authority and resources, namely, a three-year command with a navy of two hundred vessels and a staff of fifteen lieutenants of prætorian rank to be nominated by himself, a large initial grant from the treasury, and the right to draw further on the financial resources of the state, and, finally, proconsular authority in all Roman territories bordering on the Mediterranean to a distance of fifty miles inland. The senators, like every one else, knew that Pompey was meant, and doubtless realized that there was no other person fit to be entrusted with so difficult a task. But they feared that, by giving him such unlimited authority, they were affording him the means to make himself master of Rome, — a second Sulla without Sulla's sympathy for senatorial government, — since Pompey's association with the *populares* in 71–70 was fresh in their minds. In the senate, we are told, every member save a very junior one, C. Julius Cæsar, voted against the bill; but the enthusiasm of the people was unbounded, and the equites threw all their influence into the scale. Thus the assembly passed the measure, and even voted Pompey larger powers than those stipulated in the original bill. The episode of the Gabinian law has an importance quite apart from its immediate purpose and effect. It was the first striking success of the restored tribunate, and the tribune, whose proposal it was, was not so much the champion of the people, or even of the Popular party, as the tool or agent of Pompey. During the next two decades, the last years during which the office had any importance, the tribunate was successfully used by the military commanders to impose their will upon the people or to further their own ends. Of the noteworthy and influential tribunes during this epoch the only one who, at least at times, followed an independent line, was P. Clodius.

Pompey's appointment was thoroughly justified. Dividing his naval forces into squadrons, and setting them methodically to scour the Mediterranean from west to east, he stamped out the corsairs in less than four months, his final triumph being the crushing defeat which he inflicted on the most formidable body of them near Cape Coracesium in southwestern Asia Minor. To Pompey these operations were only a preliminary to a more glorious task. Early in 66 the tribune C. Manilius proposed that the command against Mithradates and Tigranes be entrusted to Pompey, with powers even more extensive than those conferred by the Gabinian law. If any proof were needed that Pompey knew of Manilius' intention before, and that the tribune was in fact merely acting as Pompey's agent, we could find it in the circumstance that Pompey began his campaign, which needed months of preparations actually carried out in the winter 67–66, as soon as he received official notification of his appointment. In Rome the opposition to Manilius' bill was not nearly so strong as to the bill of the previous year. Some senators openly spoke in favor of it, notably Cicero, whose speech is still extant, and it passed with far less trouble than the measure of Gabinius. Thus Pompey superseded Lucullus in the East. Unavailing efforts were made by the *populares* and *equites* to attack the latter on his return to Rome. He retired from public service to enjoy a life of refined luxury, which his wealth made possible, and to be the patron of letters and the arts.

The immediate task confronting Pompey was not as formidable as his panegyrists subsequently claimed. Mithradates' resources after eight years were woefully reduced; so that after one defeat in Pontus, on the site of the city of Nicopolis afterward founded there by Pompey, he retired to his possessions in the Crimea. His last years were embittered by the revolt of his own son, Pharnaces, and in 63 he committed suicide. Pharnaces was subsequently installed by Pompey as a vassal of Rome.

Tigranes, on his part, was overawed by the power and resources of the Roman commander-in-chief, and made his submission without fighting. He was reinstated on his throne as the client ally of the Roman state. The wild tribes of the Caucasus gave Pompey more trouble. They attacked his army in northern Armenia, and punitive reprisals against them were carried out in 65.

While the military renown won by Pompey in the East was largely undeserved, — it was Lucullus who had directed mortal blows against the power of both Mithradates and Tigranes, with far smaller military resources than his successor, — his work as an administrator and reorganizer, whereby Rome's authority was securely extended to the confines of Parthia, deserves the fullest admiration and respect. Syria was at this time distracted by civil war. Pompey intervened, brought the Seleucid kingdom to an end, and annexed the country as a province. In

Palestine, too, unrest prevailed. After being the subjects of foreign powers — the Chaldæan empire, Persia, and the Seleucids — for centuries, the Jews, under the leadership of the Maccabees, recovered their independence in 142. The later rulers of this house oppressed the people, and Alexander Jannæus, who ruled for twenty-eight years and died in 76, was a bloody tyrant. Thus the unity of the kingdom was disrupted and civil war was rife, when Pompey intervened in 63, and after a three months' siege captured Jerusalem. One of the late rival priest-kings, Hyrcanus, was then installed as ruler of Judæa and tributary vassal of Rome. It devolved on the Roman governor of Syria to keep an eye on this neighboring dependency.

In Asia Minor the province of Cilicia was enlarged and reorganized. The old kingdom of Bithynia, with the addition of the coast of Paphlagonia and western Pontus, became the new province of Bithynia and Pontus. Elsewhere the native rulers were confirmed in their principalities, which they held under Rome's suzerainty. Such were Cappadocia, Paphlagonia, Galatia with eastern Pontus, and Commagene, Gordyene, and Sophene on the northern frontiers of Syria and Mesopotamia. Many new cities were founded, and old ones rebuilt and enlarged, by Pompey's orders. It was a wise policy thus to add to the already numerous urban communities in the eastern provinces. They were left to exercise their own local government, and the generally equitable settlement imposed by Pompey promoted contentment and prosperity among them.

By the annexation of Syria, Rome and Parthia became immediate neighbors. Pompey's treatment of the Parthian king, whose impressive title, king of kings, he refused to recognize, and whom he deprived of territory (Gordyene) to which Parthia had claims, though it produced no immediate ill effects, began that enmity of the Oriental power toward Rome which lasted for centuries, and was on many occasions productive of baneful results to both empires. Whoever reads, in the ancient biographer, the account of Pompey's dealings with Phraates must conclude that the Roman regarded the Parthian king as but one more of the petty kings of the East, instead of as the monarch of a great and powerful empire.[1]

[1] Plutarch, *Pompey*, 38.

During the five years of Pompey's absence in the Mediterranean and the Near East the political struggle in Rome was carried on with intensity. In spite of the anti-optimate legislation of 70, the power of the senate had remained substantially unshaken. The chief office-holders between 70 and 66 were on the senatorial side, and even among the tribunes there were some ready to exert their influence or use their veto against the Popular leaders. The passing of the Gabinian law, followed by the Manilian in the next year, was a serious set-back to the senate; and these measures also introduced a fresh problem into Roman politics. From 66 all parties looked with a greater or less degree of apprehension to the future; for a few years the immediate aim of each was not so much to restrain the other, and to preserve and increase its own power, as to create a means of keeping Pompey in check, when he returned at the head of his victorious legions from the East. Over and above the recognized political groups — *optimates, equites, populares* — there were men of unscrupulous ambition and ruined nobles who, if they could not restore their shattered fortunes or secure their own advancement along constitutional lines, were prepared to resort to violence. In 66, after the consuls elect for the next year had been disqualified for bribery, a conspiracy was formed to assassinate the two men who replaced them, and set up the two unseated candidates in their place on January 1st. The plot was discovered and failed. But, though a senatorial commission was appointed to inquire into the matter, its findings were hushed up. Among those implicated were Cn. Calpurnius Piso and L. Sergius Catilina. The former was, probably through Crassus' influence, sent as propraetor to Spain in 65, where he soon after lost his life in a rising provoked by his extortions.

Scandal actually associated the names of Crassus and a rising young politician, C. Julius Caesar, with this plot. While it is impossible to believe that either would have countenanced open violence and murder, we cannot doubt that they, and especially Caesar, favored anything that weakened the senatorial position and promoted their own interests. Caesar, who was born in 102, came of an old aristocratic family; but his father's sister had been the wife of Marius, his own wife was the daughter of Cinna. It was with the Marian party that Cæsar threw in his lot from the first. Having incurred the displeasure of Sulla in 81, he left Italy and saw his first military service in Asia Minor between 80 and 78. Between 77 and 68 he was partly in Rome, gaining political experience and perfecting his oratorical powers by prosecuting members of the Optimate party, and partly abroad. In 68 he began his official career as quæstor in Further Spain; in 65 he became curule ædile. Though he was by this time recognized as a rising member of the Popular party, and was known to be in the closest touch with Crassus, none saw in him a future rival of Pompey.

Catiline was a man of very different stamp. A member of an old Patrician family, he had been a close supporter of Sulla. In 68 he was prætor, and in the following year went out as governor of Africa. On his return he was accused of extortion and therefore not allowed to stand for the consulship. The conspiracy in which he was involved, as we saw, came to nothing. In 65 his trial came on; but he procured acquittal by bribes, of which his chief accuser seems to have received an ample share. Balked once more in his aim of securing the consulship owing to the postponements incident to his trial, he now strained every nerve to attain his object at the elections held in 64 for the year 63. He had the powerful support of Crassus and Cæsar, as well as Crassus' financial backing. Of the other candidates for the consulship one was Cicero, the other was C. Antonius, an undistinguished person who also had the help of the *populares*. The success of Cicero at the bar and in office was a source of displeasure to many of the senators, who despised him as a political upstart with no family tradition of office behind him. He could, however, rely on the support of the equestrian class, in whose interests he had spoken for the Manilian law, and of a good many of the more sober-minded citizens. As the elections approached, many senators became alarmed at the future, if Catiline were returned. Efforts were made by legislation to check the bribery and corrupt practices which Catiline and his supporters did not scruple to employ. In the end it was shown that he had overreached himself. For, at the election, Cicero received a large measure of support from the senators, for which he could hardly have hoped, and was returned at the head of the poll. C. Antonius became his colleague, having beaten Catiline by a few votes.

Undeterred by the failure of their plans, Crassus and Cæsar worked to procure a leading position for Cæsar in another way. It was a tribune, P. Servilius Rullus, who served as their instrument. Rullus introduced a bill to appoint ten agrarian commissioners to hold office for five years and be entrusted with military authority. The avowed purpose of this commission was to carry out the confiscation and purchase of lands, and the founding of colonies and settlements on a large scale and over a wide area. But its real aim was to create a position for Crassus and Cæsar, who would dominate the commission, little if at all inferior to that exercised by Pompey. Cicero on entering office took the lead in opposing this insidious measure. In four speeches, of which two are wholly and one is partially preserved, he pulverized the arguments of his opponents and forced the bill to be withdrawn. It was some consolation for Cæsar that he succeeded soon after in being elected to the vacant office of *pontifex maximus;* this was a position not only of dignity, but one in which the holder could wield considerable political influence. Another attempt to embarrass the senate over the trial of an aged and disreputable senator, C. Rabirius, also fell flat, largely through Cicero's efforts.

When, in the middle of the year, the elections for 62 came on, Catiline was once more a candidate; but he had not the same support as in the previous year, and a far stronger opposition led by the senior consul to face. Thus he failed again. Having been foiled in the attempt to gain the chief magistracy — which would have been followed by a provincial governorship, enabling him to refill an empty purse — he now elaborated a plot for the subversion of all lawful authority. Among his adherents were many members of old aristocratic families of reduced or ruined fortunes, disbanded Sullan veterans who had failed to make good on the land, descendants of those proscribed by Sulla, and, finally, some Italian communities which were discontented with the settlement made after the Italian war. An insurrection in northern Etruria was planned to begin on October 27th, after a plot to assassinate the senior consul and obtain control of Rome had been carried out. But Cicero received

timely warning, and, denouncing Catiline in the senate, prevailed on the Fathers to pass a *senatus consultum ultimum.*
Catiline left Rome and joined the insurgents at Fæsulæ. A
goodly number of his fellow conspirators, however, remained in
the capital and elaborated further plans for carrying out a
coup d'état.

Cicero, for his part, was on the alert; but it was not till
December 2d that he obtained sufficient evidence to enable him
to arrest the conspirators. On December 5th the fate of these
prisoners was discussed at length in the senate. In spite of
Cæsar's efforts to get life imprisonment substituted for the
death penalty, the senate voted for execution, and on the instructions of the senior consul the sentence was carried out
without delay. A month later the insurrection in Italy was
stamped out, Catiline himself fighting courageously to the last.
It has been the fashion to minimize the importance of the
Catilinarian conspiracy, and with it the service rendered by
Cicero to his country. His contemporaries — all save his political opponents of the Popular party — judged differently;
they were right. The plot was a serious threat to Roman society
and stable government. Cicero, all through those anxious weeks
acted with courage and promptitude. It was due to him that
timely steps were taken to deal with the rising in Etruria, as well
as that the malcontents in Rome were seized at the earliest
possible moment. Cicero had his reward. He was acclaimed
"father of his country" by a grateful senate, and, save in the
last year of his life, his influence was perhaps never greater
than in the months following his brilliant consulship. His
political ideal, an effective coalition between the senatorial and
equestrian orders, in which Pompey, too, would hold the chief
place of honor, was in truth impossible of realization. Such a
coöperation, if difficult to achieve, was not unthinkable. But
Cicero like the rest of his contemporaries had not yet divined
that a completely new form of government was alone adapted
to preserve Rome and the empire.

In 62 the imminent return of Pompey filled all political
parties with anxiety. Cæsar was one of the prætors in that
year and worked hard, if not very successfully, to insure a
union between the *populares* and Pompey. In 61 he went to

Further Spain as governor. His administration seems to have been just and popular with the natives; at the same time he was able subsequently to pay off the heavy debts which he had incurred in previous years, mainly through lavish expenditure calculated to win popularity and the support of the masses. When Pompey landed in Italy at the end of 62, and, disbanding his army, entered Rome in January, 61 as a private citizen, he surprised every one. His refusal to make himself a military autocrat was not, as has often been maintained, due to weakness or lack of spirit. In truth, he does not seem to have thought of one-man rule as the future government of Rome. Rather he envisaged himself as a constitutional statesman, consulted by, and acting in coöperation with, the senate, as one who would occupy the same leading position in the world of politics which he had already won for himself as a military commander. That his aspirations were doomed to failure was due to a variety of causes. He was aloof in his manner and lacking in that easy courtesy with which a Cæsar could mollify even a bitter political opponent. Exceptionally able as an organizer and administrator, he was devoid of that personal magnetism and those arts of diplomacy, tact, and even intrigue, without which no successful political career has ever been possible, least of all at Rome in the first century B.C.

Much blame, however, attaches also to the senate. Most of its members could not master their suspicion of the man who had been able to carry out a great work in the East because of a popular vote; and, with few exceptions — Cicero was one — they were too short-sighted to see that by a right line of action they might win Pompey to their side — a great asset when his tremendous popularity with the people of Rome, Italy, and the eastern provinces is borne in mind. Pompey had carried through sweeping administrative reforms in Anatolia, had made and unmade princes, and generally settled the affairs of Rome there as he saw fit. It is doubtful whether the Manilian law had conferred as wide powers as that, though he may so have interpreted its scope. In any case, having performed a great work, he could expect the immediate ratification of his acts by the senate. Instead, the reactionary element in that august body prevailed, and it was decided to discuss and vote on each of Pompey's acts separately, a tedious process for all concerned, and little short of an insult to Pompey. In the second place, he asked that provision be made for his veterans on their discharge. Again the senate delayed action; in short, it did everything to alienate him, thereby playing into the hands of its political opponents.

Early in 60 Cæsar returned from his province. Whether he had already formulated in his own mind the plan which, if successful, would make him the sole master of the Roman world, or not, we shall never know. But, even to attain the highest constitutional magistracy in the teeth of senatorial opposition, was a task of no mean difficulty, and could only be carried out with powerful support. Conditions in Rome favored his plans. He brought about a reconciliation between Crassus and Pompey. Then a secret and informal coalition was formed between the three. Pompey and Crassus undertook to use all their influence to effect Cæsar's election to the consulship for 59; while he engaged, if elected, to satisfy Pompey's legitimate demands, and — this was at Crassus' request — to reduce by one-third the amount to be paid by the *publicani* for collecting the taxes of Asia. This application had been made by the *equites* to the senate, but had been refused, thus causing disharmony between the two orders. The union between the three most influential men at Rome — the so-called First Triumvirate — gave the death blow at once to senatorial supremacy and to Cicero's cherished union of the Orders. The orator knew the fatal error made by the Optimates in estranging Pompey, but he had been powerless to prevent it. Cæsar tried hard to win Cicero over to the side of the "Triumvirs"; for the active coöperation of the first orator in Rome, and an ex-consul at that, would have been invaluable to them, while a hostile Cicero might prove a serious obstacle to their future plans. But Cicero, to his credit, in view of his political opinions, refused to be won over.

Cæsar was duly elected, receiving as his colleague an optimate, M. Bibulus. During the months between his return and January 1st he was busily engaged in framing an agrarian bill which he brought before the senate at the beginning of his year of office. Though we are ignorant of its details, its general purpose was to provide for the purchase of lands in Italy, on which Pompey's veterans and also some of the urban proletariat could be settled. The cost was to be defrayed partly out of the ordinary sources of revenue, partly by using some of the vast treasure brought back by Pompey from the East. The opposition to the bill in the senate was so consistent that Cæsar brought his measure directly before the assembly, where it was passed. Even then matters did not pass off without some disturbance of the peace. But the senate which had neither military nor police forces at its disposal was impotent, while Cæsar could rely on the presence of Pompey's discharged soldiery. A second bill followed which provided for the distribution of the Campanian *ager publicus* among veterans and the eviction with some compensation of the small farmers settled there. Cæsar had kept his promise to Pompey; but on economic grounds — setting aside all other considerations — it was a bad measure to replace an established and thrifty group of agriculturists by veterans who in the most favorable circumstances would take some time to become efficient farmers. It has been suggested with much probability that Cæsar was unable to obtain sufficient land by purchase, as provided in his first bill, unless he was prepared to pay exorbitantly, because the equestrian class had raised the price of land against him.

The promise to Crassus and the *publicani* was also kept, a bill reducing the price of their contract being passed somewhat later in the year. Of other legislation effected by Cæsar the most important was a bill praised even by his political opponents which aimed at preventing extortion in the provinces. Its details are unknown. The consul meanwhile was not forgetful of his own future. The senate, foreseeing his probable election, had provided that an unimportant province would fall to his share in 58. The tribune P. Vatinius, acting on Cæsar's behalf, introduced a measure before the assembly to assign *Gallia Cisalpina* to Cæsar. This was passed; then the senate, under pressure from Cæsar's supporters and especially Pompey, added the Narbonese province as well. It was an extraordinary command for five years from March 1, 59; initially it carried with it the command of four legions. Thus Cæsar acquired the important military governorship that he coveted. Apart from this, the threat at that time of an invasion into Gaul by the Helvetii and other tribes made special precautions imperative. Cæsar did not leave for his province until the early spring of 58. Before this he became aware that his political supporters in Rome might become the target for senatorial attacks, and especially that efforts would be made to undo his own agrarian legislation. His most dangerous opponent was Cicero, to whom he had made more than one offer of an honorable mission or appointment which would have removed the orator for a time from Rome. But all these invitations were firmly declined; whereupon Cæsar, with the agreement of Pompey and Crassus, took other steps to compass his ends. One of the tribunes for 58, P. Clodius Pulcher, who was by birth a Patrician but had with Cæsar's connivance procured adoption into a Plebeian *gens* in order to be eligible for the tribunate, had a personal grudge against Cicero for the part which the orator had played in the trial of Clodius for sacrilege in 61. Clodius' earlier career suggests that he was unscrupulous and corrupt; he was also extremely able, and Cæsar saw in him a most suitable agent to look after his interests during his own absence in Gaul. Toward the end of March, 58, Clodius, who had an understanding with the two Popular consuls of the year, carried a bill in the assembly outlawing any person responsible for putting a Roman citizen to death without a trial. It was obviously aimed at Cicero and his action toward the Catilinarian conspirators in 63. The orator, who for some time had realized his danger, and debated what course of action he should take when the blow fell, left Rome the day before Clodius' measure came to the vote. He went into exile in Macedonia. Shortly after the passing of the first bill a formal sentence of banishment was voted against him.

Among other acts secured by Clodius was one raising the embargo placed on political clubs and associations by the senate in 64. The gangs of desperadoes and ruffians organized by Clodius and others in the next few years under the name of political clubs intimidated the peaceful inhabitants of the city as well as the senate, and often caused virtual suspension of public business for months at a time. With their help legislation could be forced through the *comitia*, free election of magistrates could be reduced to a farce, and political opponents could be rendered harmless. A younger but embittered member of the senate, M. Porcius Cato, who had taken an important part in the debate on December 5th, 63, and more recently had been prominent in his opposition to Cæsar's legislation, was in 58 designated to go on a special mission to Cyprus. This he was unable to decline, and in consequence he too was absent from the capital for a space.

Cicero's exile lasted actually seventeen months. During that time the real masters of Rome were the gangs organized by Clodius, and then in opposition to him by the tribune T. Annius Milo. The relations between Clodius and Pompey became so strained that the latter, asserting that his life had been threatened, shut himself up for weeks on end. Efforts were repeatedly made by Cicero's friends to effect his recall, and Pompey himself, who had acquiesced in his banishment before, now seems to have regretted his action. But it was not till the end of July, 57, that a decisive vote could be carried in the senate; a few days later the *comitia centuriata* passed the necessary enactment. Cicero, who had already travelled as far as Dyrrachium as he anticipated his recall, reached Rome on September 4th.

The experience of the last few months had shown Pompey that, in the face of organized gangs and the inability of the senate to maintain order, reliance on his personal prestige was a poor substitute for office. A temporary economic crisis in the autumn of 57 enabled him to secure for himself an appointment which was in effect a military command. Through a variety of circumstances there was a scarcity of grain, and prices had soared very high. Riots took place in Rome and the senate was induced to appoint Pompey as *curator annonae* for five years; that is to say, to give him general superintendence of the entire grain supply in the empire, together with the necessary authority in its various harbors. In order that he might perform his very responsible duties he received the proconsular authority and a number of legates. He carried out his new functions with characteristic care, visiting several provinces in person during the winter. The effect of his work was soon seen in the fall in prices.

The situation in Rome, however, did not improve. Pompey's relations with Crassus were strained. In 56 Cato returned from the East and at once made his presence felt in the senate.

Cicero, too, who had at one time thought of retiring from political life, was becoming more confident and indicated his intention of questioning the legality of Cæsar's agrarian legislation of 59. Cæsar, whose first two seasons' campaigns in Gaul had been brilliantly successful, saw the coalition of which he was the author in imminent danger of disruption. He spent the winter months in Cisalpine Gaul. After a preliminary and private meeting with Crassus, he brought both him and Pompey together to a more formal conference at Luca in April, 56. Here he was able to smooth over the disagreements of his colleagues and with them to map out their joint line of action for the ensuing years. Of the various decisions taken by them four are of essential importance. It was agreed that Pompey and Crassus should hold the consulship in 55, their magistracy to be followed by five-year provincial commands. Pompey was to be governor of Spain — both provinces — and Africa, Crassus of Syria. In the second place, Cæsar stipulated that his own command be extended for a further five years, counting from March 1st, 54. Third, while Crassus would proceed in person to his province, Pompey was to remain in the capital and rule his provinces through legates. Finally, the three arrived at a general understanding about the candidates to be run for the more important offices in the next few years.

Against this renewed coalition the senate was more powerless than before. Its unhappiest member was Cicero. For he was constrained not only to abstain from his proposed attack on Cæsar, but a little later to speak on behalf of certain demands made by Cæsar to the senate. His extant speech, *De provinciis consularibus*, is oratorically one of his most impressive efforts, and his expressed admiration for Cæsar's victories in Gaul was genuine — not feigned. Yet, from his letters to his intimate friend, T. Pomponius Atticus, it is clear that he was ashamed at his *volte-face* — so it seemed to the world in general — and very regretful that he had not followed out his earlier intention of abstaining from politics.

The second consulship of Crassus and Pompey is not remarkable for any striking legislation or reforms. Enactments designed to check bribery and the activities of political clubs at election time had little effect. The arrangements regarding the provinces of the "Triumvirs" were legalized by the Trebonian law. In the late autumn Crassus set out for Syria, having made no secret of his intention to take the offensive against Parthia in the next year. Less than two years afterward he brought disaster on his men and on himself. At the battle of Carrhæ in Mesopotamia (beginning of June, 53) his army, save for a small remnant, was annihilated by the Parthians. Shortly afterward Crassus with a few staff officers had an interview with the enemy commander. He and his companions were seized and put to death.

In Rome the year 54 was noteworthy for a large number of political trials, in several of which Cicero appeared as defending counsel. Owing to the pressure exercised by Pompey and Cæsar he was obliged to appear even on behalf of Gabinius and Vatinius whose political conduct he had bitterly attacked on earlier occasions. The violence of the political gangs of Clodius and Milo was constant in 54 and 53. In the former year no elections to the consulship were made at all, and in 53 not till more than half the year had elapsed. The year 52 again opened with an interregnum. Pompey who had been reconciled to Clodius and now condoned his activities, while Milo with his roughs posed as the champion of senatorial interests, made no effort to restore order. It seems clear that his purpose was to let matters drift till the senate was forced into appointing him to the dictatorship or to a similar position, if it did not wish Rome to be given up entirely to anarchy. Early in 52 a crisis was reached. A fight between the rival gangs occurred in which Clodius was killed. Riots followed in Rome in which, among other deeds of violence, the senate house was burnt to the ground. Even the most bitter Optimates now saw that any form of government was better than none at all. On the motion of Bibulus, seconded by Cato, a decree was passed empowering the *comitia centuriata* to elect Pompey sole consul for the year. He entered on office at once and took steps to bring those responsible for Clodius' death to book, and to have a stringent law passed against bribery and corruption. Of the various persons prosecuted in connection with the recent riots Milo was the first. He was found guilty and went into exile. Cicero spoke in his defense but, perhaps for the only time in his life, broke down badly. The extant speech, *Pro Milone*, was not the one delivered in court, but an amplified version for publication. Of the other trials that followed Milo's it is enough to remark that the majority went in favor of the supporters of Milo and the Optimate party.

. By this time the relations between Pompey and Cæsar had become all but openly hostile. Crassus who had always held the balance between them, had perished in 53. Shortly before, Julia, Cæsar's daughter and Pompey's wife, died, and so a personal link between the two men was snapped. Above all, Cæsar's phenomenal achievements in Gaul showed the world that Pompey's position as the first military commander of the age was no longer unchallenged. We cannot wonder at Pompey's jealousy of the younger man. The outcome of their estrangement was that in 52 Pompey was drawn over to the senatorial side and was responsible for legislation, the scope of which left no doubt that the rupture between himself and Cæsar was complete. It can hardly be doubted that the most recent developments in Gaul, which were certainly largely influenced by political conditions in Rome a few months earlier, in their turn reacted on the position in the capital and helped Pompey to reach his momentous decision.

In the forty odd years between Vercellæ and the beginning of Cæsar's governorship the peace of Narbonese Gaul had from time to time been disturbed by tribal insurrections. None of these episodes were, however, of great moment or duration. A more serious situation arose about 62 beyond the frontiers of the Roman province. Several of the more powerful Gallic tribes fell to war, and the Arverni even took the dangerous step of inviting the trans-Rhenish Suevi under their king, Ariovistus, to intervene. But this ambitious chief purposed to found a Suevic kingdom in Gaul, and in 60 he defeated the Aedui and their late enemies the Sequani. About the same time the Helvetii, the southern neighbors of the Suevi, planned a westward migration into Gaul. It was not actually begun till two years later. In view of the general unrest caused by these tribal wars and shifts Cæsar's appointment was singularly opportune. He himself must from the first have seen in the complicated political situation in Gaul a chance to extend

Roman authority over the whole country. He has left us a masterly narrative of his campaigns from 58 to 51, containing, in addition, much valuable if brief information about the organization and customs of the Gallic, and some British and Germanic tribes. Already in the first year of his governorship he showed his military genius by the manner in which he followed up the Helvetii after they had overrun Gallic territory, forced an engagement at the most favorable opportunity, and, after defeating them, compelled them to return to their own territory. This initial success he followed up before the end of 58 by the defeat of Ariovistus, thereby ending that chief's hopes of retaining a permanent footing in Gaul. Wintering in Gaul, Cæsar in the next season's campaigns advanced northward and, partly by fighting, partly by diplomacy, obtained the submission of the Remi, Belgæ, and other tribes in the north and northeast. The Nervi alone fought to the last and were all but annihilated. The year 56 saw the reduction of the tribes inhabiting what is now Brittany, and especially the Veneti, whose territory was near the estuary of the Loire. At the same time Cæsar's lieutenant, P. Crassus, conquered the tribes of the southwest (Aquitania). At the end of the year virtually the whole country had been brought to submission.

Cæsar, however, was fully aware of two future dangers; fresh risings in Gaul and renewed incursions into that country from beyond. Thus two German tribes crossed the Rhine in 55; whereupon Cæsar made an incursion across the river, not with any idea of conquest, but as a demonstration to the tribes there of Roman power. In the same year, but rather late in the season, he crossed over to Britain, where the southern tribes at least were in close communication with their kinsmen in Gaul. A longer and more successful invasion was carried out in 54, Cæsar advancing as far as the Thames and even beyond that river. After some fighting he received the submission of a number of tribes in the southeast of the island. No attempt at annexation was made, and nearly a century passed before a renewed effort to conquer Britain led to permanent occupation. In that interval, from 54 B.C. to 43 A.D., though the islanders were independent, a good deal of Roman influence trickled through, partly through contacts with the rapidly Romanizing provinces of Gaul, partly perhaps through occasional Roman and Italian merchants who found their way across the channel.

During Cæsar's absence in Britain in 54 several Gallic tribes rose in revolt, and Cæsar's lieutenants — among them was Cicero's younger brother, Quintus — narrowly escaped disaster. It was not till the summer of 53 that the land appeared in a fair way to being tranquillized. But appearances were deceptive. The powerful tribe of the Arverni under their chief Vercingetorix in the winter of 53–52 instigated a general insurrection of the Gallic peoples, encouraged by the rumors that reached them that Cæsar's own position with the Roman government had assumed an unfavorable aspect. The odds against which Cæsar was thus forced to fight in 52 and 51 were much greater than any that he had faced in previous years. For now even the Aedui, since many years the faithful allies of Rome, turned against him. After being forced to abandon the siege of Gergovia — one of his very few military failures — Cæsar besieged Vercingetorix in Alesia, and all efforts of other Gallic tribes to relieve the city were unavailing. Finally Vercingetorix surrendered himself as a ransom for his countrymen. This broke the resistance of the Gauls, although some minor operations were still needed in the following months before tranquillity was completely restored. Cæsar then began the settlement and organization of the new provinces; but soon this necessary work was interrupted by the crisis which his own fortunes had reached.

It will now be apparent that when Pompey first acted in open hostility to Cæsar the latter was engaged in the most critical of all his Gallic campaigns. During the course of 52 two measures, sponsored by Pompey and approved by the senate, were passed. The one provided that in future an interval of five years must elapse between tenure of a magistracy in Rome and a governorship in a province, such as till then had followed in the year immediately succeeding. In itself this was an excellent measure, designed effectively to exclude from office men who were only anxious for a consulship or prætorship in order to have a province to plunder the year after. But in its immediate effect it was a direct hit at Cæsar's position. His command expired on March 1st, 49. At the beginning of 52 he had been

legally exempted from personal canvass for the consulship for 48;
and he was relying on being elected in his absence. Moreover,
under the old arrangement all the available magistrates would
have proceeded to their provinces at the beginning of the year;
and so Cæsar, following the practice by which a governor remained in his province until his successor came to take over,
would be able to continue as governor of Gaul until the end of
the year, and then come to Rome as consul. Thus his numerous
political enemies would have no means of attacking him, since
he could not be touched while in office. Then another provincial
command would follow his second tenure of a magistracy. Once
the new law took effect, ex-consuls and ex-prætors of longer
standing would have to be called upon for several years to take
provincial governorships during the four years which would
elapse before a more or less automatic sequence of magistracy and
pro-magistracy had been established. In these circumstances
Cæsar could be relieved on March 1st just as well as at any
other time, and he would then be a *privatus* for nine months.

A second measure, making it compulsory on candidates for
office to conduct a personal canvass, was no less anti-Cæsarian.
Pompey, when challenged on this point, added a rider to the
bill, exempting Cæsar from its provisions. This he had no legal
right to do; but his action shows that he hesitated to break with
Cæsar openly. The years 51 and 50 at Rome witnessed a succession of moves and counter-moves on the part of the senate,
Pompey, and the supporters of Cæsar. The Optimates desired
to force Cæsar's abdication on the date when his command
expired. Pompey, ever reluctant to force the issue when the
crisis was imminent, suggested compromises which satisfied no
one. Thus the end of 50 came and no decision had been reached.
On January 1st a despatch from Cæsar was laid before the senate
in which he promised to resign from his military command if
Pompey would do the same. Several days passed during which
efforts were made by moderate-minded senators — among them
was Cicero, just returned from the governorship of Cilicia which
he had been reluctantly obliged to undertake owing to the need
for viceroys created by Pompey's law of 52 — to bring about an
accommodation. But the counsels of Cato and other unyielding
Optimates prevailed. The senate's reply was that Cæsar must

disband his troops unconditionally, or be declared an outlaw.
The veto interposed on Cæsar's behalf by M. Antonius and
another tribune was set aside, and the two tribunes, whose
personal safety was threatened, fled to their chief who was
awaiting the senatorial reply at Ravenna.

The die was cast, and Cæsar acted with characteristic speed
and decision. Though the troops at his disposal were few at the
moment, they were superbly trained and utterly reliable. The
senate and Pompey had only two legions, which had previously
served under Cæsar, so that their loyalty to their new commander was highly suspect, and a legion of recently levied
recruits. After a few weeks, during which Cæsar seized one
after another of the important points along the east coast route
from northern Italy to Rome, Pompey judged rightly that, with
such resources as he had, Italy was not defensible. He therefore
embarked for Greece with his legions and with many members of
the senate. At the end of March Cæsar, who tried but failed to
prevent Pompey's departure from Brundisium, reached Rome.
In transferring himself to the eastern half of the empire Pompey
took a soldier's decision. But to many the abandonment of
Rome and Italy was tantamount to surrendering at the outset to
a usurper. We can see this point of view, based on purely political
considerations, and ignoring or misunderstanding the military,
which, now that things had gone so far, alone mattered, in the
correspondence of Cicero at this time. The orator remained in
Italy for some months; when Cæsar sought to enlist his support
in the senate he politely but firmly refused. In June he left for
Thessalonica, there to join Pompey and the other senators who
had left Italy.

The task which now confronted Cæsar was one which none
but he or an Alexander or a Napoleon would have tackled.
Apart from Gaul and Italy the Roman empire was in the hands
of his opponents. The three lieutenants of Pompey in Spain
commanded seven legions between them. It was of them that
Cæsar decided to dispose before undertaking his major campaign against Pompey in the East. The Spanish War of 49,
ending in the forced surrender near Ilerda of Afranius and
Petreius after a six weeks' campaign, was one of Cæsar's most
brilliant achievements. He took tremendous risks and on at

least one occasion came near to destruction. But his ready resource and the speed of his movements, which constantly placed his slower opponents at a disadvantage, carried the day. Further Spain, where M. Terentius Varro was in command, was a region where Cæsar's popularity was great, thanks to his equitable government in 61, and its governor was forced to surrender to Cæsar without fighting. By December the conqueror was back in Rome. Early in the new year he crossed with a part of his army from Brundisium to Epirus, leaving M. Antonius to follow with the rest as soon as opportunity offered. This division was necessary because of a shortage of transports, and because the crossing was in any case a matter of grave risk, for a strong senatorial fleet patrolled the Adriatic. His immediate objective was Dyrrachium, which was of vital importance for two reasons: here the Pompeians had accumulated vast stores, and here was the terminal of the main highway connecting the Adriatic coast with Macedonia (the Egnatian Way). Cæsar landed some distance to the south of the city and was able to occupy Oricus and Apollonia. But Pompey arrived with his army from Macedonia in time to prevent the seizure of Dyrrachium. The two commanders now encamped on the River Apsus and remained inactive for a good many weeks. Primarily this was due to the nature of the country and the season of the year. For the low-lying regions were swampy and impassable; while, even by making wide detours inland, the movement of large bodies of troops was extremely difficult. Pompey, furthermore, though commanding a far larger army than Cæsar, was not prepared to attempt a direct assault on his opponent, because so many of his men were half-trained. Cæsar for his part was anxiously awaiting the arrival of Antonius with the rest of his army. Not till the spring was the latter able to elude the senatorial fleet under M. Bibulus — Cæsar's old colleague of 59 — and to land at Nymphæum, lying some way north of Dyrrachium. Pompey should now have prevented a junction between the two divisions of the Cæsarian forces, but he failed to do so. Then he took up his position at Asparagium (Petra), a few miles southeast of Dyrrachium. Here he entrenched himself along the hills for a distance of some fifteen miles. He retained control of Dyrrachium, and his fleet was master of the sea. He could therefore afford to wait while his opponent was bound to feel a constantly increasing difficulty in obtaining supplies.

Cæsar now took a very bold step. Had it succeeded he would have ended the war there and then. He blockaded Pompey in his entrenchments, his own line of circumvallation being about seventeen miles long. In time Pompey was hard pressed for water and forage for his horses; but Cæsar's difficulty to feed his men was even more acute. This fact explains why he weakened his army by sending away detachments of it at a crucial time. One was despatched under Domitius to hold in check or delay the Pompeian reinforcements expected to arrive from Macedonia; another was sent to Greece to win support there for the Cæsarian cause. Finally Cæsar attempted to surprise Dyrrachium. Although he failed in this he was able to cut Pompey's lines of communication with the town. Pompey's reply was a general assault against the southern end of Cæsar's lines where his adversary was weakest. After desperate fighting the attack succeeded and Cæsar was very near ruin. But at night he effected a masterly retirement of all his men, unbeknown to the enemy, and within four days he had marched them safely back to Apollonia. He now decided to cross over into Thessaly, hoping by the threat to Pompey's reinforcements to compel his opponent to follow him. Moreover, once there, the commissariat difficulties would cease. His stratagem succeeded. Pompey followed and took up his position near Larissa, while Cæsar had executed a more difficult march through Epirus and encamped near Pharsalus, after joining forces with Domitius and his detachment. Even now Pompey appears to have hesitated to pit his skill and strength against his adversary. But the clamorous insistence to fight of his senatorial comrades overcame his judgment. On August 9th, 48, a decisive engagement was fought hard by Pharsalus. Cæsar by superb tactics and after a struggle lasting all the day utterly defeated his opponents who were about twice as numerous as his men.[1] Some 15,000 Pompeian soldiers were killed; the rest surrendered to their conqueror. Pompey himself escaped and made his way to

[1] Pompey's army numbered 47,000 foot and 7000 horse; Cæsar's 22,000 infantry and only 1000 cavalry.

Egypt, where he hoped to find support for further operations against his rival. But in Egypt civil war was raging between the young king and his sister and joint ruler, Cleopatra. At the instigation of the king's counsellors, who feared to be drawn into a Roman war, Pompey was murdered on landing.

Cæsar who hastened to Alexandria with only a small force, intending perhaps to effect a meeting with his defeated rival, was greatly troubled at his murder, and is said subsequently to have ordered the execution of the assassins. He stayed nine months in Egypt, intervening in the dispute between the two rulers and their supporters, and being in turn besieged in the eastern district of Alexandria by the Alexandrian mob, whose patriotic rage had been aroused by his interference in Egyptian affairs. Only the timely arrival of his fleet saved Cæsar from disaster. When order was restored, he installed Cleopatra and a younger brother of the queen on the throne of Egypt, but left a garrison of two legions in the country. He himself tarried so long, moreover, that he hazarded his position in the empire. Finally news of a rising in Anatolia organized by Pharnaces of Pontus roused him to action. A single engagement sufficed to bring the client prince to order; it was fought at Ziela in 47. In the West the situation was even more disturbing. Those leaders of the senatorial party who had escaped after Pharsalus, rallied first at Corcyra and then proceeded to northern Africa, there to organize a further formidable stand against the usurper. Some of Cæsar's deputies, moreover, had acted with less wisdom and tact than their master. The Cæsarian governor of Spain had made him self so disliked that he had to be superseded by another; and in Italy and Rome there had been disturbances which M. Antonius had been unable to quiet. Cæsar reached Rome in September, 47, and quickly restored order. In the following spring he defeated the combined Republican and Numidian forces at Thapsus in northern Africa. Of the Republican leaders Cato then committed suicide; several were murdered by Cæsar's troops; a few, among them Labienus and the two sons of Pompey, escaped to Spain. Here they fomented further trouble which compelled the dictator to go to the peninsula in the winter of 46–45. With the defeat of the insurgents at Munda in March, 45, the last resistance to Cæsar collapsed.

Although the task of making himself master of the Roman empire was done, the no less difficult and withal slower process of reorganizing its government had only been begun. From the time that he became master of Italy Cæsar made it clear that a return to Republican government was impossible, and that a new solution must be found. He survived his conquests too short a time to enable us to say with any certainty what his ultimate plans for the government were. But there is little doubt that he himself intended to rule for life, and that the cardinal principle adopted by him was to centralize executive power in a single person, himself. In other words, he founded a military autocracy; and, though a long period of civil war followed his death, his successor, when he had bested all his rivals, built on the foundation laid by his predecessor. For, as we shall see, though the fact was disguised in a variety of ways, Augustus' rule was in essence no less absolute than that of Cæsar. In effectively subordinating the rulers in the provinces to the central authority in Rome, Cæsar broke absolutely with one of the worst features of senatorial government and introduced a system which became fixed under his successor.

Cæsar's power from 49 rested primarily on the dictatorship. To this he was first nominated toward the end of 49, but he held it for only a brief space. At the beginning of 48 he assumed the consulship, and he continued to fill that office every year. After his victory over Pompey he was proclaimed dictator for a year. In 46 the office was bestowed upon him for ten years, and in 45 for life. Already in 48 the tribunician power was decreed to him; thereby he could exercise the veto and other powers of the plebeian magistrates without actually being one of them. Later, censorial power and other rights, such as that of nominating a certain number of magistrates for office, were added. By virtue of the proconsular power, which he held for life, he was the master of Rome's military and naval forces. Between 49 and his assassination on March 15th, 44, Cæsar was not in Rome for more than fifteen months all told. Nevertheless he was responsible for a vast number of reforms and the most varied legislation. He increased the senate to 900, admitting to it both enfranchised Gauls and some of his former soldiers. But the Fathers had ceased to have any authority; they could

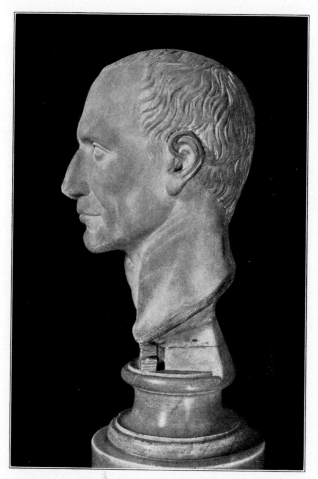

BUST OF JULIUS CÆSAR

Plate 35

only obey the will of Cæsar. So, too, the assemblies continued to meet to carry out their electoral or legislative duties. The republican magistracies were filled yearly, with some irregularities. But *comitia* and magistrates alike were in reality, if not in name, subordinate to the dictator's will. And he did not even strive to uphold the full dignity of the old-established offices. Occasionally they were suspended for considerable periods, and in Cæsar's absence the direction of affairs in Rome and Italy was more often left to prefects specially named by him. At the same time, to meet the demand for more administrative officers, he greatly increased the number of prætors and quæstors elected each year. He tightened up the procedure in the criminal courts, and excluded all but men of the senatorial and equestrian classes from the panels of jurors.

A number of social reforms were noteworthy. Cæsar legislated so as to ease the position of debtors, especially those whose difficulties resulted from the civil war, and imprisonment for debt became obsolete. The rate of interest was limited to a maximum of 12 per cent. Political clubs were suppressed. The number of recipients of free grain was drastically reduced from over 300,000 to 150,000.

Of great importance was Cæsar's colonial policy. His numerous veterans were established partly in Italy, partly in colonies outside its frontiers, especially in southern Gaul. Two foundations of quite exceptional size were made in 46 on the sites of Carthage and Corinth. They provided for large numbers of Rome's excess population. Cæsar was generous with the franchise. He bestowed it on the Transpadane Gauls in 49, and on the people of Gades and some other provincial communities; while partial citizenship, the private without the public rights, was even more freely granted.

The reform which lasted longest of all was that of the Roman calendar, which, carefully worked out by the Greek scientist Sosigenes, came into force on January 1st, 45. This is the calendar still used in the Eastern Church, while our own is the Cæsarian, with a slight correction introduced by Gregory XIII at the end of the sixteenth century. The codification of the Roman law, and a general survey of the geography and resources of the empire were schemes projected by the dictator

which he did not live to carry out. More than a century passed
before a beginning was made with the former vast undertaking.
The latter was carried out by Augustus and his ministers.
Building and engineering enterprises planned by him also lapsed
and remained for his successors to execute in their own way.
Finally he left an incomplete draft of a law which aimed to regu-
larize, with a view to securing a uniform procedure, the election
of municipal senators and magistrates in all the Italian townships, and also provided for a regular ·quinquennial census
in Italy. This draft with other "Acts" was passed into law by
M. Antonius some months after Cæsar's death. A fortunate
chance has preserved for us the version of it set up by the
people of Heraclea in southern Italy.

Toward the end of 45 and during the early months of 44
Cæsar was making elaborate preparations for an expedition
against Parthia. Four days before he was scheduled to depart
from Rome he was assassinated by a body of conspirators
numbering between seventy and eighty. Among the ringleaders
were men who had served with Cæsar since the days of his Gallic
command, and others who had been pardoned by him in 48
and then given office under him. C. Cassius and M. Junius
Brutus belonged to the latter, D. Junius Brutus and C. Tre-
bonius to the former category. They claimed to have freed
Rome from a tyrant, but their act was not only one of ingrati-
tude but of stupendous folly. They had made no plans for the
future, and their belief that with Cæsar's death the old senatorial
oligarchy could at once resume the reins of government, shows
them to have been completely out of touch with the realities of
the political situation.

There is no clear evidence that Cæsar's conduct in the last
year of his life was more despotic or more contemptuous of Republican forms than before, nor yet that he planned to assume a
regal style and title. But his rise to power had been so swift that
men had scarcely had time to realize how his solution of Rome's
problems was the only one. He fell the victim of a small group
of false patriots and petty intriguers. When, seventeen years
later, Octavian began his work of reconstruction, he was more
careful to make allowances for Republican prejudices. But in
one way he had an easier task than Cæsar: the intervening

years of the Second Civil War had not only decimated the upper classes at Rome, but had shown to all the world that the old forms of government really were outworn, and had made all men desirous of one thing above all — peace.

Contrary to their expectation the conspirators found that their action roused no enthusiasm among the people of Rome. The immediate master of the situation was the consul, M. Antonius (Mark Antony), who had long been associated with Cæsar and now planned to supersede him. The only military force on the spot was a small detachment on Tiber island commanded by Cæsar's master of the horse, M. Aemilius Lepidus. With him Antony at once came to an agreement. The consul further strengthened his position by securing all Cæsar's private papers from his widow. Two days after the murder a meeting of the senate was held at which a general amnesty was voted, a piece of temporizing which can have deceived no one. When, shortly afterward, Antony delivered a funeral oration on Cæsar, he excited public indignation so much that the chief assassins found it politic to leave the capital. Meanwhile Cæsar's will had been made public, and it was found that he had designated as his personal heir C. Octavius, his great-nephew and adopted son.[1] The young man was in his nineteenth year, and at the time of Cæsar's death was at Apollonia in Epirus studying oratory and military science. For it had been the dictator's intention that Octavian should accompany him on his eastern campaign. Octavian, when news of the murder reached him, hastened to Italy to claim his inheritance. Much of it had already been spent by Antony, who treated the young man as negligible and at first refused to satisfy his legitimate demands. The senatorial party was led by Cicero, who soon began to take alarm at Antony's arbitrary acts and hoped to use Octavian as a senatorial tool. Antony, to whom Macedonia had been assigned by the senate as his province in 43, soon carried through a wholesale rearrangement of the provincial commands which had been determined before Cæsar's death. C. Antonius was to take the

---

[1] His full name after adoption was C. Julius Cæsar Octavianus; hence he is usually referred to as Octavian. However, when speaking of his career after 27 B.C., when the senate conferred on him the honorific title of Augustus, it is customary to refer to him by that name.

place of Brutus originally named for Macedonia, and Dolabella was to proceed to Syria in place of Cassius. The two chief conspirators were assigned insignificant commands in which they would be powerless to cross Antony's plans. He himself now purposed to take Cisalpine Gaul in place of Decimus Brutus. There he would be near the capital and in a region whose sympathies were strongly Cæsarian. The high-handed manner in which he proceeded to carry out various measures, some of them quite indefensible in themselves, invoking at every turn the authority of Cæsar's "Acts," some of which he had himself more recently forged, made him numerous enemies.

Meanwhile Octavian was unobtrusively laying his plans. He secured the support of many of Cæsar's veterans in Italy; and, when in the autumn Antony summoned the four Macedonian legions to Italy preparatory to using them in Cisalpine Gaul, two of them went over to Octavian. Undeterred, Antony at the end of 44 began operations against Decimus Brutus and besieged him in Mutina. Octavian, whose military force was not inconsiderable, since he had, besides the two Macedonian legions, a good number of Cæsar's veterans from Campania enlisted under him, appeared as champion of the senatorial cause and advanced to Cisalpine Gaul to assist Decimus Brutus. The senate, to whom this development was not over welcome, at the beginning of the new year made him a senator and invested him with pro-prætorian authority. Assigning to the two consuls of 43 the task of making war on Antony, they associated Octavian with them in the command. By the end of April Antony had been defeated, and had retired to Transalpine Gaul to join forces with its governor, Lepidus. The two consuls had lost their lives in the recent fighting, so that Octavian was left in sole charge of eight legions. The senate, thinking that he had served their purpose, now proposed to ignore him and confirm Decimus Brutus in his command in the north. Octavian's answer was to march to Rome at the head of his troops. The senators could only fall in with his demands; on August 2d, they elected him to the consulship with a colleague, Q. Pedius.

Antony in the interval had reached a friendly understanding with Lepidus as well as with the governors of northern Gaul and Further Spain. Their combined forces were such as neither

Brutus nor Octavian could have faced with any chance of success. Octavian had, however, matured his plans. With his own army he met Lepidus and Antony at Bononia, and here the three came to terms. Then they advanced to Rome and had themselves appointed by the assembly as triumvirs, extraordinary commissioners to restore the commonwealth (*tresviri reipublicae constituendae*). Their first act was to take vengeance on political and personal enemies by ordering a proscription, which rivalled, if it did not actually surpass, Sulla's reign of terror. Among the first victims was Cicero who was killed by Antony's emissaries on December 7th, 43. During the last months of his life the great orator had come forward as the noble champion of a lost cause. Minded at one time to join M. Brutus in the East, he partly by accident, partly by design, returned to Rome. There from the end of August, 44, to his death he was the chief figure in the senate. In a series of magnificent speeches — the Philippic orations — he denounced the conduct of Antony and tried to rally the Republican party, fully aware that if Antony should prevail he would pay for his bold harangues with his life.[1]

While the western half of the empire was thus distracted by the rivals for power, Brutus and Cassius had succeeded in establishing themselves after all in the provinces originally assigned to them. Then they collected military and naval forces with which to fight for the Republican cause. The triumvirs decided that Lepidus should remain behind in Italy, while Octavian and Antony crossed to Macedonia where their adversaries had mustered. Late in 42 the two armies confronted one another by Philippi. The operations lasted for the best part of a month. In the first engagement the triumvirs suffered a partial defeat, which was slightly offset by the suicide of Cassius who had been misled by a false report of Brutus' defeat. In the second battle, fought in the middle of November, the Republican forces were routed. Brutus, rather than fall into the hands of his conquerors, imitated the example of the younger Cato. The survivors of the Republican army surrendered to the triumvirs, but the fleet of Brutus and Cassius sailed away and joined Sextus Pompeius in Sicily. This younger

[1] The First Philippic was spoken on September 1st, 44, the Thirteenth on March 20th, 43.

son of Pompey had escaped after Munda; subsequently he had been given a command by the senate against Antony. He had thereupon made himself master of Sicily. Joined by many of those proscribed by the triumvirs and then by the aforesaid naval detachments, he was for years a serious menace to Antony and Octavian.

The settlement of the West was now left to Octavian, while Antony undertook to restore Roman authority in the East. Lepidus for the present remained in nominal charge of Italy; in reality he was little more than a cipher. For ten years, from 42 to the end of 33, Octavian and Antony, in spite of disagreements which more than once threatened to result in civil war, managed to avoid a rupture. Fresh pacts or treaties between them were concluded on several occasions — in 40, in 39, when Sextus Pompeius was for a short time taken into partnership, and again in 37. In 36 Octavian finally disposed of Pompeius, and Lepidus was forced to retire into private life, though retaining the office of *pontifex maximus*. The Roman world was now divided between two men only, but they interpreted their responsibilities and used their power in very different ways.

Octavian ever since 42 had worked steadily to settle Italy and then to consolidate his position in the West. His studied moderation, even toward his political opponents, and his zeal to conciliate all classes resulted in a steady growth of popularity. Stringent steps were taken to suppress lawlessness in Italy, so that its inhabitants, after harassing years of civil conflict and wholesale destruction, might at last follow their several vocations in peace, and an era of reconstruction and renewal of prosperity might begin. Some remission of taxation and of outstanding debts was granted to hasten the economic recovery of the worst victims of the war.

Very different was Antony's progress in the East. As far back as 41 B.C. he had laid oppressive taxation on the Asiatic provinces. In the same year owing to the danger of a Parthian war, he summoned a congress of client princes to Tarsus. Hither also came Cleopatra, and her meeting with Antony had very fatal consequences. From this time infatuation for the queen of Egypt exerted a dominating influence on the Roman. He followed her to Egypt and spent the best part of two years there, a devotee of love and pleasure, neglectful of all affairs of state. Then he returned to the West, and his new agreement with Octavian, followed as it was by his marriage to Octavian's sister, Octavia, seemed to promise not only a renewal of cordial relations with his fellow triumvir but a return to the serious duty of administering the East. Not satisfied, however, he intrigued for a space with Sextus Pompeius, which forced Octavian to come to a fresh understanding in 39. Meanwhile the Parthians had overrun Syria. Antony's able lieutenant, P. Ventidius Bassus, in three campaigns (40–38) expelled the enemy from the Roman province and finally defeated him in Mesopotamia. When at last Antony himself appeared in Syria there was no further need of military action. By 36 Antony, who had left his Roman wife in Italy, had returned to Cleopatra. He now made vast preparations for a war of retaliation on Parthia. His campaign was a complete fiasco. Two years later, however, he attacked Armenia, ostensibly because its king had not lent him adequate support in the Parthian war. He deposed Artavasdes, and then for this inglorious and bloodless achievement he celebrated a magnificent triumph at Alexandria.

His prestige in the West had steadily declined. His defeat by the Parthians, the unprovoked attack on Armenia followed by the celebrations in the Egyptian capital, which seemed a mockery of a genuine Roman triumph, and his general behavior in the East, which was more fitting to an oriental potentate than a Roman commander, made men turn more and more to Octavian as the protector of the empire and the upholder of Roman tradition and ideals. At last news came that Antony had assigned various provinces of the East to the queen of Egypt and her sons, and that her son by Julius Cæsar, Cæsarion, was being proclaimed the true heir of the dictator.

Octavian, who must long since have realized that in the end the sword must decide whether he or his rival should prevail, not only rejoiced that Antony's conduct and misdeeds should be known in Rome and in the West, but declared him openly to be guilty of treason to the Roman state. Nor did he scruple to seize Antony's testament, which had been deposited for safe-keeping with the Vestal Virgins in Rome, and to publish it. Its terms confirmed the earlier rumors concerning Cleopatra and the succession of her children. About the same time Antony repudiated his Roman wife, since he had formally espoused the queen of Egypt. Public indignation in Rome was now intense, and the senate declared war on Cleopatra. At the same time Antony was deprived of his triumviral powers, and his prospective consulship for 31 was declared null and void. Owing mainly to Antony's dilatory conduct, which was of great advantage to Octavian as his military forces were less concentrated and took longer to muster, the decisive action was not fought till 31. On September 2d, the long-standing rivalry between the two triumvirs was brought to an end by Octavian's decisive naval victory at Actium in northwestern Greece. Both Antony and his queen made good their escape to Egypt. Antony's land forces, deserted by their chief, in a few days surrendered to the victor. Octavian spent the winter months in settling, in a preliminary fashion, the Anatolian provinces that had suffered so severely from Antony's misrule. In 30 he proceeded to Egypt and, after some fighting, seized Alexandria. Antony, seeing himself deserted by his men, and in no doubt that his cause was lost, committed suicide. The queen, rather than grace the triumph of Octavian, followed the example of her lover. Egypt was annexed by Octavian, and a prefect, Cornelius Gallus, was installed to govern it. When later this provisional arrangement was changed to one more permanent, the country was treated not as an ordinary province but as the personal domain of the ruler of Rome.

CHAPTER XXVI

THE PRINCIPATE OF AUGUSTUS

> *In my sixth and seventh consulship, after I had extinguished the civil wars, having been put in supreme possession of the whole empire by the universal consent of all, I transferred the republic from my own power into the free control of the senate and Roman people.* — From the autobiographical inscription of Augustus in the temple of Augustus and Rome at Ancyra.

FOR ten years Octavian's authority had rested on his triumviral power. From 31 until 27 B.C. he held the consulship each year. Inasmuch as he exercised supreme control in all the empire after his victory at Actium, his actual power far exceeded that held by any senior magistrate of Republican times. The tribunician power, which his adopted father had already wielded before him, was conferred on Octavian in 36; but for thirteen years he laid little stress on it. Early in 27 he formally abdicated from his extraordinary position, a fact briefly recorded by himself in the memorable words cited at the head of this chapter. The senate voted him the honorary title of Augustus, a word which like its Greek equivalent, *Sebastos*, signified no more than "venerable" or "worthy of respect," but marked him out as taking precedence over all other citizens of the state. He had retained the consulship for 27, and the proconsular power was forthwith bestowed upon him by a grateful senate. It was this last which formed the essential and indispensable foundation of his power, both from 27 to 24, and during the rest of his long life, when the form of his government was somewhat changed in other respects. For it was by virtue of the *proconsulare imperium* that he commanded the military and naval forces of the state, and could exercise authority in the provinces of the empire. For some years after 27 he continued to fill the consulship annually; but in 23 he abandoned this practice. His authority

as civil head of the government thereafter rested on the tribunician power, with which he was formally reinvested year by
year, and by reference to which he now dated the years of his
reign, and on a number of special rights and privileges conferred
upon him. He was enabled to take precedence over all persons,
including the senior magistrates of any given year, in summon-
ing the senate and in proposing motions before it. Authority to
make treaties and to declare war and peace was vested in him.
And, though he made sparing use of the prerogative, he was
entitled to "recommend" candidates for office and for election
to the senate, as well as to raise non-senators to senatorial rank.
The title "princeps," from which is derived the word, principate, as a name for the government of the earlier emperors,
meant no more than first citizen, and in this sense had years
before been used by Cicero of Pompey. No official power
attached to it. When Augustus, as we may now call him, said
in the Ancyra inscription, "I surpassed all in authority," he
expressed very exactly his position as it must have appeared to
men in general. That authority rested on the sum total of the
several powers and prerogatives that we have specified.

The reforms which he gradually effected left no part of the
government untouched. We may begin with his military organization. We have seen how the army reforms of Marius had had
political consequences of the direst kind, and for nearly a century had made the commanders of legions— Sulla, Pompey,
Crassus, Cæsar— the real masters of Rome. The reforms introduced by Augustus resulted in the creation of a standing
army, on the loyalty of which the secure position of the princeps, who was at its head by virtue of his proconsular power,
ultimately rested. The permanent military establishment at
the end of Augustus' long reign consisted of twenty-five legions
(125,000–150,000 men) and an approximately equal number of
auxiliary troops. All were stationed in the provinces. No less
than eight legions were on the Rhine frontier, five in the Danubian provinces, three each in Spain, Syria, and Egypt, two in
Dalmatia, and one in northern Africa. The legionary commander (*legatus legionis*) was a man of senatorial rank; the junior
officers were recruited from the equestrian class. The period of
service for non-commissioned ranks and men was at first six-

teen, and later twenty years, for legionaries, and twenty-five for auxiliaries. The latter were levied from the rural population of the provinces, the former from Italy and urban centres elsewhere. It was a new principle that all the subjects of the Roman empire were liable for military duty. The only soldiers stationed in Italy were the nine cohorts, each a thousand strong, of the Prætorian Guard. They were the imperial body-guard, and as a *corps d'élite* they enjoyed better terms of service and higher pay than the legionaries. Two prefects of equestrian rank were in command of these troops, which in Augustus' time were quartered in several parts of Italy. In Rome itself the only soldiery were the so-called urban cohorts and a body of "watchmen" (*vigiles*). Though organized on a military basis, these in effect formed the police force of the capital. A considerable fleet was also kept up. Besides the two chief naval squadrons, with their headquarters respectively at Misenum and Ravenna, a number of smaller detachments were stationed in non-Italian waters.

To the various elements in the constitution Augustus' attitude was one of tolerance and apparent compromise. The senate, reduced once more to six hundred, in some degree shared with the princeps the heavy burden of administration. The older provinces, in which no disturbances were to be foreseen and consequently no military establishment would normally be required, were senatorial and governed by a proconsul, who usually held office, as formerly, for one year.[1] The old Republican treasury (*aerarium*) continued to be administered by the senate. But the emperor had his own treasury, later called the *fiscus*. Moreover, after 14 B.C. Augustus retained the exclusive right of minting gold and silver currency, the issuing of copper being left to the senate. Since the administration of Italy, and at first of Rome also, devolved wholly on the senate, the expenses connected therewith, such as the cost of public festivals, construction and maintenance of roads, and the upkeep of public buildings fell upon the *aerarium*. But, as we know

[1] The governor of a senatorial province, irrespective of his substantive rank, which might be either that of consul or prætor, was a proconsul. The legates of imperial provinces were all proprætors, again whatever their substantive rank, because they were all viceroys of the emperor. He alone was proconsul of the imperial provinces.

from Augustus' own statement, it was on sundry occasions so near to insolvency that the emperor was obliged to provide heavy subsidies to restore its credit. In course of time, as the senatorial administration of Rome proved inadequate, several new offices were created whose holders replaced the senate and ordinary magistrates in this important sphere. In the absence of the emperor a prefect of the city of senatorial rank was appointed. The *praefectus vigilum* had duties comparable to those of a chief commissioner of police. The regulation of the grain supply was from 6 A.D. entrusted to an imperial official (*praefectus annonae*) of equestrian rank. Even in the government of Italy the hitherto unrestricted control of the senate was in time somewhat reduced. For example, the upkeep of Italian roads was given over to special commissioners (*curatores*).

But, if the senate was deprived of many of the most important functions that it had once exercised, it now received certain compensating duties. As a judicial body it attained to great importance; for it was constituted as a permanent court of justice under the presidency of a consul, which in theory could try any criminal offense but in practice dealt only with offenders of high rank or prominent station. It also enjoyed far wider legislative powers than heretofore, although this fact must not be interpreted to mean a great increase in senatorial authority. For the last word rested with Augustus, who did not as a rule legislate himself, but acted through others, either seeing that the senate passed a decree, or, more rarely, deputing a magistrate to introduce the needful bill before the assembly.

The system of government established by Augustus has been described as a dyarchy, a title implying a division of government between the princeps and the senate. If thereby be meant — though in that case the name is somewhat inaccurate — a division of administrative duties, no exception can be taken to the description. But if it be implied that there was a real partition of power, then it is erroneous. For the absolute authority of Augustus was never at any time in doubt. He commanded the army; his *imperium* was defined as superior to that of all other magistrates in the provinces; so that, if he wished, he could use his authority even in those administered by the senate and its proconsuls. And in every department of government he was able to insure that his will or his wishes were carried out. He chose to disguise the fact that he was an autocrat, and he desired not only that the senate and magistrates should occupy a position of dignity in the state, but that they should bear their share in the vast burden of imperial administration.

The *cursus honorum* of the senatorial magistrates was observed with great strictness. The quæstorship, as had first been instituted by Sulla, qualified the holder for a seat in the senate. But to be eligible for it the candidate must have fulfilled certain specific conditions, in addition to possessing the necessary census qualification. And there were ample administrative functions to perform for the occupants of both the senior and the junior offices. From the equestrian class the emperor obtained the majority of his army officers. To the *equites* also he assigned the duty of acting as jurors in the criminal courts, together with a limited number of less wealthy persons. For senators were now excluded from these courts. To a restricted extent members of the equestrian order were also used for administrative employment. They governed certain provinces; in the imperial provinces ruled by senatorial legates the collection of taxes and administration of finance were partly in their hands.

The Roman assemblies continued to perform their electoral, and to a far less degree their legislative, functions. Actually, since the emperor, by virtue of his tribunician power and his right of nominating candidates for office, could exercise an unrestricted control over their actions, the importance of the *comitia centuriata* and *comitia tributa* even in Augustus' day was nominal rather than real. After his time they rapidly sank into complete insignificance.

No branch of the administration demanded and received more careful attention than finance. To stabilize conditions after the civil wars, and then to secure the revenue to defray the huge expenditure of an imperial state, required not only the most careful economy but an examination of all sources of income and outlay. Augustus on one occasion had thoughts of introducing direct taxation in Italy; but he desisted from his project because it would have met with immense opposition.

Hence the inhabitants of Rome and Italy paid only indirect dues to the exchequer. The more important taxes of which we hear at this time were a 2 per cent tax, later increased to 4 per cent, on the sale of slaves; a 1 per cent tax on merchandise; a 5 per cent tax on manumitted slaves; and a 5 per cent tax on inheritances. The last proved a very copious source of income, and gradually a large procuratorial staff grew up in all parts of the empire to deal with it. There were, further, customs and harbor dues, but the rate levied was not uniform throughout the empire. Far the largest source of revenue, however, was the tribute paid by the provincials. Many cities, especially in the eastern part of the empire, had during the Republic enjoyed special privileges, of which exemption from taxation was the most prized. These *privilegia* were carefully reviewed by Augustus and many adjustments made. The amounts fixed for the poll-tax paid by provincials for themselves and for their slaves, and for the land tax, continued to be regarded as the standard rates by subsequent emperors. Many of the abuses and complaints in the provinces during the Republic had been due to the shifting of responsibility from one person to another, with the result that those best able to pay often escaped lightly and the small farmer was practically ruined. On the instructions of Augustus elaborate calculations, based on a careful census and valuation, were made in the provinces. This full information in the hands of the central administration, combined with more rigorous supervision on the spot, was designed to make the old abuses impossible. An ancient writer, Hyginus, informs us that in the appraisement a distinction was drawn between first and second class arable land, meadows, pasture land, and two types of forest land. The tax to be rendered was fixed according to the particular kind of soil, and was paid in some cases in cash, in others in kind. For wheat the usual rate was one-tenth, for oil and wine one-fifth.

We have already seen that the old *aerarium* continued to exist side by side with the imperial treasury. Augustus also created a special military chest to which he assigned a large capital sum, and to which in future the proceeds of the inheritance tax were paid. Its income was used to pay pensions and gratuities to the soldiers when their time of service had expired.

In Italy, including now *Gallia Cisalpina*, which for purposes of taxation was divided into eleven regions, the old distinction between *coloniae* and *municipia* disappeared, although the separate names continued to survive. The municipal organization was modelled on that of Rome. The government was in the hands of two senior magistrates supported by some junior officials and by a council of one hundred *decuriones*, forming a municipal senate. The magistrates were chosen by an assembly of the townspeople. The capital city also was divided into fourteen regions for their better local administration; the task of general supervision was entrusted to prætors, tribunes, and ædiles.

Much has been made of Augustus' social reforms. Yet often it is peculiarly difficult to ascertain the degree to which they were effective. He strove earnestly by legislation at various times to restrain luxury and licentious conduct, to encourage marriage and the rearing of families, and to regulate more strictly the laws governing divorce. "By the passing of new laws I restored many traditions," he says, "which were falling out of our observance, and in my own person I handed down many ideals which are worthy of imitation by posterity." In his social reforms, as in his efforts to revive the state religion of Rome, he was filled with an intense desire to restore the ideals of morality, family life, and orthodox piety to the gods, which had distinguished Roman society of an earlier age. Much of this legislation was bitterly opposed at the time, and it may well be doubted whether his sumptuary and social enactments were productive of any permanent effect. To restore the Roman religion he revived various priestly offices which had fallen vacant or had not been filled during the civil wars. He was himself a member of several priestly colleges; and, after Lepidus' death in 13 B.C., he assumed the office of *pontifex maximus*, which thereafter became one of the offices invariably filled by the princeps. Many temples in Rome and Italy that had become ruined were rebuilt. New temples of great magnificence were set up, of which the chief was on the Palatine hill in honor of Apollo, the deity whom Augustus regarded as his particular patron. In 17 B.C. took place the impressive celebration of the Secular Games to mark the birth of a new era (*saeculum*). The climax of the religious ritual was reached on the third day with a solemn procession to the Palatine hill and the singing, by a double choir of boys and girls, of a hymn — the extant *Carmen Saeculare* — composed for the occasion by Horace. The great temple of Venus Genitrix in the forum of Julius, and that of Mars Ultor in the forum of Augustus, together with the magnificent altar of Peace erected in the Campus Martius, were further examples of the emperor's lavish expenditure on buildings devoted to the impressive maintenance of the Roman religion.

The reorganization of provincial government and the securing of Rome's frontiers were tasks of Herculean difficulty, the performance of which displays Augustus' genius at its highest. Apart from the division into senatorial and imperial provinces, there were recently acquired countries whose organization demanded the most careful attention. Henceforward there were four Gallic provinces, the old Republican province of *Gallia Narbonensis* and the vast territory conquered by Julius Cæsar, which was now administered as the three provinces of *Gallia Belgica*, *Lugdunensis*, and *Aquitania*. Spain, particularly the tribes of the northwest which had never properly acknowledged Roman authority in the peninsula, caused a good deal of trouble in the early years of the principate. Military intervention was needed on several occasions, and the country was not completely pacified till 19 B.C., when the Cantabrians, the last Spanish tribe to resist, were crushed. Hereafter Spain was divided into three provinces, of which the settled south (*Baetica*) was left to the senate to govern, while *Tarraconensis* and *Lusitania* were entrusted to imperial legates. Some changes were introduced in the East, whereby, for example, Galatia on the death of its ruler in 26 B.C. became a province. Pamphylia, once joined to Galatia, now became a separate administrative region. Smaller adjustments were made from time to time, as native princes in Anatolia died. But Augustus continued the policy of leaving much of the interior of the country in the hands of vassal kings. It was only under his successors that fresh and considerable annexations were made. The treatment of Egypt was in many ways peculiar. It was not an imperial province in the usual sense, that it was administered by the emperor for the Roman people, but the domain of the emperor himself. Though he assumed no kingly title there, Augustus in effect stepped into the place of the Ptolemaic rulers. Hence the actual government was entrusted not to a governor of senatorial rank but to an equestrian prefect, commanding three legions, who was more completely the servant or agent of the princeps. Senators were even forbidden to land in Egypt without the express permission of the emperor. Achaia, which had hitherto been subordinate to the governor of Macedonia, became a separate senatorial province.

A problem of special difficulty was the establishment of a safe frontier on the north and northeast. For, both in the Balkans and the Danubian area, there was an element of serious peril in the half-civilized tribes which occasionally threatened settled provinces like Macedonia, or the Adriatic coast, or even northern Italy. The various operations carried out during Augustus' long life, although they took place at different times, all formed part of a carefully matured plan to advance the northern boundary of the empire to the Danube.

A beginning was made between 35 and 27 B.C. by the conquest of Illyricum. In the same period punitive measures were taken against the peoples to the north of Macedonia. The sequel was that Thrace became a dependent kingdom, a position it retained, in spite of several disturbances calling for military action by Rome, until 46 A.D.; while the district later to become the province of Mœsia seems to have been occupied as a military area. In 11 B.C., this region was again disturbed and a strong hand was needed to put down a rebellion. It is uncertain whether Mœsia attained the full status of a province before the beginning of Tiberius' principate.

The reduction and pacification of the Alpine tribes in 15 B.C. was followed by a Roman advance to the Upper Rhine and the source of the Danube. Then came the annexation of a wide territory, organized shortly after as the two provinces of Rætia and Noricum. A few years later (12–9 B.C.), when serious unrest in Illyricum recurred, the emperor appointed his step-son Tiberius to take charge of the military problems raised. The recalcitrant tribes were gradually subjugated, and Roman authority was advanced as far as the middle Danube. A thorough reorganization of the enlarged Illyrian area followed. Hereafter there were two provinces, Pannonia and Dalmatia, in place of one Illyricum. The headquarters of the Pannonian legions were at Poetovio; but an advance post and military garrison was stationed at Carnuntum on the Danube.

So far the systematic progress of Roman arms northward had been successfully accomplished. The Danube from its source to its estuary formed a frontier which was relatively both secure and easy of defense. The further plans of Augustus, to which the occupation of Rætia and Noricum had been a necessary preliminary, to advance the boundaries of the empire beyond the Rhine, were not attended by the same measure of success. At the time when Tiberius was fully engaged in the Pannonian war, his brother Drusus, who had succeeded him as commander-in-chief of the Rhine legions, began a series of campaigns into the lands east of the Rhine. As a result of three years fighting (12–10 B.C.) all the territory between that river and the Weser was in Roman hands. In 9 B.C. Drusus carried the Roman standards to the Elbe. But in the autumn he died from the results of an accident. He was replaced in the command by his brother whose work in Pannonia was now concluded. Tiberius remained in charge of the Rhine legions during 8 and 7 B.C. During that time he consolidated his brother's conquests as far as possible, but without as yet attempting to create a new province. For some twelve years we hear little of this remote region of the empire. Tiberius had been superseded at the end of 7 B.C. For some years his relations with the emperor were far from cordial. At last in 4 A.D. he was re-appointed to the Rhine command. Several German tribes within the occupied area had recently thrown off their allegiance to Rome, and two seasons of fighting were needed to restore order. At last, in 6 A.D., a grand attack was launched from two sides, from the Rhine and from the Danube, the ultimate purpose being the occupation of the territory between the Upper Elbe and Danube. The Romans would then have had a considerably shorter frontier to defend; at the same time intercommunication between the Danubian provinces in the east and Gaul in the west would have been improved. This ambitious plan was never carried out because an alarming rebellion

broke out in Pannonia, in which more than 200,000 insurgents
are said to have taken part. Little as we know of the new
Pannonian operations of Tiberius, who had on his staff his
young nephew Germanicus, the fact that it took four years to
restore peace and Roman authority in the province shows how
serious a situation had existed.

The war was scarcely over when the emperor received news
of a disaster to Roman arms in Germany. Certain tribes in the
territory held by Rome — chief among them were the Che-
rusci led by their prince Arminius (Hermann) — preparatory
to a general war of liberation, entrapped the Roman general
P. Quinctilius Varus with three legions and six divisions of
auxiliaries in the Teutoburg forest. Of a total of about 20,000
men only the three divisions of cavalry escaped; all the rest
were wiped out. The ignominious character of the disaster
and the loss of the Roman standards shocked the emperor and
Roman society even more than the heavy loss of life. For some
years the Roman government was content to secure the Rhine
frontier from invasion, and acquiesced in the loss of the territory
to the east of the river, which had followed hard on the Varian
disaster. These defensive measures were entrusted to Tiberius,
until in 13 A.D. he was succeeded by Germanicus. For the failing health of Augustus necessitated Tiberius' presence in Rome,
as he had now been adopted and marked out for the succession
to the principate. Between 13 and 16 A.D. Germanicus was
permitted to attempt the reconquest of Germany. In spite,
however, of notable successes which brought the Roman legionaries once more to the banks of the Elbe, the casualties and expenditure entailed seemed to Tiberius, who became emperor
in 14 A.D., too heavy a price to pay for the acquisition of territory which experience had now convinced him might always be
difficult to defend satisfactorily. Germanicus was therefore
recalled, and the Rhine once more marked the limit of Roman
occupation. The command of all the Rhine legions, which had
in the case of the emperor's kinsmen been on several occasions
entrusted to one man, was hereafter regularly divided between
two legates. To these commands the Romans in loose parlance
sometimes applied the name "provincia"; but it must be
clearly understood that the "provinces" of the Upper and

Lower Rhine were military commands, not territorial governorships. The Upper Rhine army had its headquarters at Moguntiacum (Mayence), the Lower Rhine army at Castra Vetera (Xanten). While their primary duty was the defense of the frontier, these eight legions could also be used, if necessary, to insure order in Gaul where no legions were stationed.

CHAPTER XXVII

THE SUCCESSORS OF AUGUSTUS TO THE ACCESSION OF SEPTIMIUS SEVERUS

> *Now at last heart is coming back to us: from the first, from the very outset of this happy age, Nerva has united things long incompatible, imperial rule and liberty; Trajan is increasing daily the happiness of the times; and public confidence has not merely learned to hope and pray, but has received security for the fulfilment of its prayers and even the substance thereof.* — Tacitus, *Agricola*, 3 (Hutton's translation).

FROM the early years of his principate Augustus made it clear that he intended his high office to be hereditary, even though the fiction of election by senate and people were to be maintained. To make the succession sure he purposed to create an associate with himself, who by receiving the proconsular *imperium* and the tribunician power would be marked out as his proper successor, while being subordinate to Augustus during the emperor's lifetime. In his dynastic plans, however, Augustus was singularly unfortunate. Thrice married, he had no son of his own. His only child by his second marriage was a daughter, Julia. His third wife, Livia, was the mother of two sons, Tiberius and Drusus. Finally there was his sister's son, Marcellus. It was this youth who, after being formally adopted by the emperor, was intended to succeed him. He married Julia in 25 B.C., but in 23 he died. The trusted minister of Augustus, M. Vipstanius Agrippa, in 21 wedded the widowed Julia. Two sons, Gaius and Lucius, were born of this union; and so for years the succession seemed secure. But both of Augustus' grandsons died on the threshold of manhood, Lucius in 2 A.D., Gaius in 4 A.D. Augustus' younger step-son had, as we saw, died in 9 B.C.; and so finally his elder step-son, Tiberius, was adopted, although the relations between the two men had never been cordial. In 13 A.D. Tiberius was associated with Augustus in the government of the empire. Next year, after Augustus' death, the sole rule passed without question to him. But the formal election and the conferring of all the necessary powers on the new princeps were duly carried out by senate and people.

At his accession Tiberius (14–37 A.D.,) was a man of mature years, whose military and administrative experience had been profound. Temperamentally he lacked the urbanity of his eminent predecessor. What in the early years of his principate was no more than a certain aloof austerity, generally and with reason attributed to the disappointments and slights endured in earlier life, and contrasting strongly with Augustus' amiable address, toward the end of his career degenerated into suspiciousness and a despotic misuse of power.

As far as the empire was concerned there was little departure under Tiberius from the general policy of Augustus. But at home he introduced several significant constitutional changes. In the first place, the popular assemblies lost whatever importance they had till then retained. The election of magistrates was transferred to the senate. Since the quæstorship qualified a man for a seat in the senate, that august body now became self-elective, subject only to the right of recommending candidates vested in the emperor. The people, like some Homeric *demos*, was asked to approve the senatorial choice. Nor did the assemblies keep their legislative functions in fact. The right to pass laws was not abrogated, but we know of only two enactments during the reign which were passed by the *comitia tributa*. The law-making body was the senate, whose decrees now had full legal force without even a formal ratification by the people.

On a superficial view these changes might be thought to have greatly increased the importance of the senate and to have strengthened the dual government by that body and the princeps. Actually the reverse was true, and Tiberius' rule became increasingly more absolute. The prefecture of the city, which had been an occasional office entrusted by Augustus during his absences from Rome to an experienced and trustworthy member of the senatorial class, was by Tiberius instituted as a permanent office. Thereby sundry administrative duties hitherto performed by the senate or the regular magistrates were handed over to a nominee of the emperor. In the next place, Tiberius took a step of far-reaching consequences when, by moving all the Prætorian cohorts into a permanent camp outside one of the gates of Rome, he introduced the practice of having a body of troops continuously quartered in the capital. This privileged corps of picked men, now united in the same garrison, soon developed the consciousness of power, a process hastened by the exceptional reliance which Tiberius placed in the single prefect to whom he entrusted the command. L. Aelius Sejanus was an *eques* of undistinguished birth. The steps by which he wormed his way into the confidence of Tiberius are withdrawn from our view; but for ten years he was the most powerful man in Rome.

The court of Tiberius, as of his immediate successors, became a hot-bed of intrigue between different members of the imperial family. The emperor, at Augustus' request, had adopted his nephew Germanicus; thus the son of the elder Drusus was indicated as the next holder of the principate. But Germanicus died in 19 A.D., whereupon the emperor worked to secure the succession for his own son, Drusus the younger. Four years later the youth died in mysterious circumstances. The presence of Livia, the emperor's mother, of Agrippina, widow of Germanicus, and of the younger Livia, widow of Tiberius' son Drusus, at the court, and the mutual rivalries and jealousies of these imperious women led Tiberius to lean more and more on the Prætorian prefect. Then, in 26, he retired from Rome, and thereafter resided mainly in the island of Capri. The children of Agrippina were, it is true, adopted by him; but in framing his dynastic plans Tiberius had reckoned without Sejanus. For this man was scheming to grasp the supreme power himself. It was he who, as was divulged after his death, was responsible for the death of the younger Drusus, and he who strained every nerve to remove Agrippina and her children from his path. She had, however, powerful supporters in the senate; the prefect, unchecked by Tiberius, who was weary of intrigues and suspicious of all and sundry, therefore instituted a reign of terror against all who stood in his way. The offense of *maiestas* or treason, which had originally meant any offense that threatened the security of the state, had been interpreted somewhat more widely by Sulla to include not only positive offenses but dereliction of duty on the part of public officials.   The Julian law of Augustus attached a fresh significance to *maiestas*.   For, as the princeps was, as it were, the embodiment of the state, assaults not only on the person but on the dignity and authority of the emperor now constituted the offense.   Augustus himself, though occasionally the target for libellous attacks, was too magnanimous or too conscious of the security of his position to take action against offenders save on the rarest occasions.   His successor was at first hardly less generous in his attitude.

The professional informers (*delatores*) who, as there was no office of public prosecutor, could serve a useful purpose so long as their activity was strictly regulated and false accusations were rigorously punished, obtained under the régime of Sejanus the widest scope for their infamous profession.   Delation was used by the prefect to remove the prominent supporters of Agrippina, and finally Agrippina herself.   While in the last years of his principate Tiberius himself found in it a means of terrorizing the senate.   In 29 the elder Livia died.   The last check on Sejanus' ambitions seemed to be removed by the passing of the woman who had protected Agrippina and her children, besides exercising a deep influence on her own son.   At last, when Sejanus' machinations did not after all progress quite as rapidly as he desired, — in spite of exceptional honors and powers bestowed on him by Tiberius, — he was rash enough to instigate a conspiracy against his master.   This was betrayed to the emperor.   Sejanus was deposed and put to death (31 A.D.). In Rome the remaining years of Tiberius' reign were made hideous by a long catalogue of horrors and prosecutions of prominent men.   Though he named no definite successor to himself, Tiberius in 35 made his nephew Gaius, the youngest son of Germanicus, and his own grandson, Tiberius Gemellus, his joint heirs.   When at last he died early in 37, it was the former prince who, backed by the Prætorian Guard, was duly invested by the senate with the powers appertaining to the principate.

Gaius' short rule (37–41 A.D.) is of little import.   His advent to power was universally acclaimed because men rejoiced at the liberation from a tyrant's rule. And, at first, various salutary measures were passed, including the suppression of informers and of the misuse of the law of treason. Yet, within a year, Gaius embarked on a life of luxurious extravagance. Soon this was followed by the removal of Tiberius Gemellus, and then by persecution of influential and wealthy men. To meet the enormous expenditure caused by useless pomp and the senseless squandering of wealth on his debased pleasures, heavy taxes were imposed in Rome and Italy, which bitterly antagonized the masses who three years before had hailed the elevation of Gaius with delight. A conspiracy, led by several officers of the Prætorian Guard and helped by freedmen in the palace, was more successful than an earlier plot had been. Gaius was murdered at the beginning of 41. The troops who had raised him to the throne, also pronounced his doom. It was they also who led off the emperor's uncle, Claudius, the younger brother of Germanicus, whom they found hiding in the palace, and proclaimed him emperor. The senators had perforce to acquiesce in the choice of the military.

The reign of Claudius (41–54 A.D.) had many notable features. His health was poor and his imperial relatives had always affected to regard him as mentally deficient. Thus, slighted and ignored in earlier life, he had devoted himself to various learned pursuits, and wrote voluminously on historical and antiquarian topics. In reality he proved himself a clement and in many ways an able ruler. It was, however, unfortunate that the indecision of his character allowed him to be unduly influenced by the chief freedmen in the imperial household. Entrusted with the duties of secretary, or of receiving petitions, or of managing the emperor's accounts, these men, whom stronger rulers kept in strict subordination, became the most powerful ministers of Claudius. Nor was the court free from female intrigues, due to the rivalry of the empress Messalina, a woman of unspeakably bad reputation and life, and the younger Agrippina, sister of the late emperor Gaius. Both of these masterly women had their supporters in the palace, and their interests were guarded by one or another of the chief freedmen. Finally, the outrageous conduct of Messalina brought about her downfall and death in 48. In the next year Claudius married his niece, Agrippina, a marriage of near kinsfolk that shocked healthy Roman sentiment. All the efforts of the new empress were devoted to securing the succession for her son by a former marriage, Nero, and ousting Britannicus, the son of Claudius by Messalina. When the emperor passed away in the autumn of 54 — rumor said that he was poisoned by the empress — Agrippina's son attained to the throne because his mother had made sure of the powerful support of the Prætorian prefect, Afranius Burrus. Nero was acclaimed by the Prætorians, and subsequently the usual powers were voted him by the senate.

Apart from the scandals and intrigues of the court circle Claudius' government had been equitable, as well as beneficial to the empire as a whole. The emperor had inclined to take Augustus as his model. Hence, for example, we find the legislative powers of the *comitia* temporarily revived, and note serious efforts to restore to the senate some of the dignity that it had lost under the previous two rulers. So, too, he celebrated the secular games in 47, this year being reckoned the eight hundredth anniversary of the foundation of Rome. In one important respect, however, he very definitely departed from the policy of Augustus. For he bestowed the Roman franchise on many provincial communities, while to the people of Gaul — he himself had been born in Lugudunum — he accorded even more generous treatment. He granted to all those who already enjoyed the private rights of Roman citizenship the further privilege of becoming candidates for Roman magistracies (*ius honorum*).

Nero's principate (54–68 A.D.) seemed to open auspiciously. In view of his youth — he was in his eighteenth year at his accession — the task of government devolved primarily on his two influential advisers, Burrus, and the wealthy and cultured L. Annæus Seneca. Until 62 good government was on the whole the order of the day. The emperor, however, in addition to passing his life in lewdness, was guilty of horrid crimes which his advisers could not or would not prevent. The murder in 55 of Britannicus, whom Nero feared as a possible future rival, was followed four years later by that of his own mother, Agrippina, who had bitterly opposed his projected alliance with the alluring but unprincipled Poppæa Sabina. With the death

of Burrus in 62 the chief restraining influence on the young
emperor disappeared. Seneca, finding his own authority gone,
retired discreetly into private life. Two Prætorian prefects
succeeded Burrus; but only one, Tigellinus, was influential,
and, unlike his predecessor, he encouraged Nero in all his excesses. Extravagance and blood-lust were the key notes of the
last six years of tyrannical rule. Delation and trials for treason
were the order of the day. Many leading men, especially
senators, were done to death to enable the emperor to confiscate
their estates. An accidental fire in Rome in 64 did vast damage,
and the work of rebuilding the destroyed quarters of the city
entailed a heavy outlay. In the following year a conspiracy
was formed to which many notable men were privy. Its timely
discovery saved the emperor; but numerous trials and execu-
tions followed. Among those who perished were Seneca and
the poet Lucan, both of whom anticipated certain condemnation
by suicide. The persecutions in the years that followed became
even more numerous, since Nero was now thoroughly fearful
for his own safety. At last disaffection spread to the provinces
and the provincial armies in Gaul, Spain, and on the Rhine.
Through the intrigues of a new Prætorian prefect — the fate
of Tigellinus is unknown — Nymphidius Sabinus, the Guards
were persuaded to transfer their allegiance to P. Sulpicius Galba,
governor of Spain. Nero fled from Rome; when pursued, he
died by the hand of a faithful servitor rather than fall into the
hands of his enemies. With him the Julian line became extinct.

And now, in the immortal epigram of Tacitus, "a secret of
empire was divulged, that an emperor could be made elsewhere
than in Rome."[1] Between June, 68, and December, 69, three
emperors, each of them the choice of the army or some portion
of it, enjoyed brief periods of power, — Galba, M. Salvius Otho,
and A. Vitellius, the choice of the Rhine legions. But the man
whom the legions of Syria acclaimed, T. Flavius Vespasianus,
not only worsted his rival Vitellius, as Vitellius had worsted
Otho, — Galba had been murdered by Otho's soldiery, — but
was able to maintain his position and found a new line of imperial rulers, the Flavian dynasty (69–96).

Vespasian (69–79 A.D.) was an excellent ruler, who almost at

[1] Tacitus, *Histories*, i, 4.

once associated his elder son, Titus, with himself in the government. The persecutions under Nero, followed by a year and a half of civil war, had alarmingly reduced the older nobility and the senate. Vespasian introduced many new members into the latter body, including some provincials; by conferring patrician rank on many persons he created a new nobility. Many provincial communities received the full or partial franchise, the emperor in this matter imitating the example of Claudius. The careful census of the empire conducted by him had as its primary aim an inquiry into the resources of the whole Roman world. The extreme financial exhaustion, resulting from the events of the past few years, required not only stringent economy but increased revenues. But, though Vespasian in many cases increased taxation, the burden appears to have been equitably distributed. The inclusion of several cities and client states, whose position had hitherto been privileged, in the regular provincial system, brought in additional tribute. The credit of the imperial treasury was completely restored, and Vespasian's reign inaugurated a new period of prosperity in the provinces. The suppression of the Jewish revolt and of a serious rising under Julius Civilis affecting both Gaul and the Rhine district, as well as the energetic measures of the legate of Britain, Petilius Cerealis, showed that the security of Rome's frontiers engaged the earnest attention of the emperor. The senate, though treated with consideration, enjoyed little power. And the somewhat autocratic conduct of Vespasian, coupled with his clearly marked intention to keep the succession within his family, caused some discontentment.

He was succeeded for a brief space by Titus (79–81 A.D.). On his premature death Vespasian's younger son, Domitian (81–96 A.D.), was saluted emperor by the Prætorian Guard. The senate thereupon conferred on him the usual powers, military and civil. Constitutionally Domitian's reign is of great interest, because it was more openly despotic than that of any of his predecessors. His tenure of the consulate each year to 88 A.D., and on several occasions after that date, and the assumption of perpetual censorial power, which gave him direct and undisguised control over the corporate body of the senate and each member thereof, were equivalent to an open disavowal of even a semblance of dyarchy. To the senate it seemed also an affront that a number of *equites* was coöpted into the informal council of the emperor, which under previous rulers had been composed exclusively of persons of senatorial rank.[1] The despotic attitude of the emperor did not go wholly unchallenged. There were members of the senate, convinced adherents of the Stoic philosophy and fanatical admirers of the younger Cato, Brutus, and Cassius, who risked banishment or death by the freedom of speech that they allowed themselves. Such opposition to the government by men unreconciled and irreconcilable to the absolutism of the age, had occurred in the time of Nero and even under Vespasian. We can admire the courage, even while marvelling at the lack of political insight of men who could for one instant believe that Republican government could be revived at all, or, if it could, would be equal to the administration of a vast empire. On Domitian the effect of such opposition was disastrous, the more so as, in the absence of a son of his own, he saw in any prominent man a possible aspirant to supreme power. Suspicious and crafty by temperament, and withal an admirer of Tiberius, he in the later years of his reign resuscitated all the horrors of delation and accusations of *maiestas*. Finally, in 96 A.D., a plot in which the prefects of the Prætorian Guard were implicated was formed, and Domitian perished by the dagger of an assassin. The evils of Domitian's principate, like those of Tiberius' second period, were confined to Rome. The provinces continued to be well governed, and important additions to the empire were made.

Although their prefects had been concerned in Domitian's death, the Prætorian Guard made no effort to choose a successor. M. Cocceius Nerva, an elderly senator who had held the consulship on two occasions, was elected by the senate to fill the imperial office. His brief tenure of power (96–98 A.D.) was universally welcomed as a relief from the tyranny of the preceding reign. In view of his poor health and advanced years Nerva formally adopted a consort who would ultimately suc-

---

[1] It is significant that Domitian permitted or even expected his subjects to address him as *dominus*, a word implying the relations of slave to master. Half a century after his death we already find it used by a subordinate official to his superior.

ceed him. M. Ulpius Traianus was a choice that could hardly have been bettered. He was an experienced soldier of Spanish birth, who at the time of his adoption (October, 97) held the responsible post of legate of the legions on the Upper Rhine. The proconsular *imperium* and tribunician power were conferred on him at the same time. Within three months Nerva passed away; his successor proved to be one of the ablest rulers of the empire. Trajan's successful campaigns, resulting, as they did, in large territorial additions to it, have tended to obscure the excellence of his administration. He was conciliatory to the senate and tolerant of the criticism of members with Republican sentiments. Yet he lessened the administrative functions of that body to a marked degree. For he appointed financial controllers (*curatores*), not only in many of the free cities situated in the imperial provinces, but in the countries governed by the senate, where there had been much mismanagement, and even in Italy. This was a serious encroachment on the powers and responsibilities of the senate. The management of the imperial finances, about which we have little detailed information, appears to have been good. For, even if we allow for the additional revenue which accrued to the imperial treasury through the working of the Dacian gold mines, the war expenditure of his reign was especially heavy, but was met without increasing the taxation of the provinces. In the tenth book of the letters of the younger Pliny we have a highly illuminating series of documents to illustrate the emperor's care for the provinces. Pliny was appointed legate of Bithynia — hitherto a senatorial province — where the inefficiency of the administration would seem to have been particularly flagrant. He carefully audited the income and expenditure of a number of towns, consulting the emperor on a great variety of points, and receiving terse but eminently practical directions in return. The result of Trajan's institution of *curatores* was that the municipalities, both in Italy and in the provinces, lost much of their local autonomy, and passed to an increasing degree — for Trajan's successor continued the policy — under the control of the central authority, especially in matters of finance.

With Hadrian (117–138 A.D.), who was formally adopted by Trajan before his death, we come to an administrator of tran-

scendent ability. In the course of his reign, which, apart from
the Jewish rebellion, was free from serious military undertakings,
Hadrian himself visited every province of the empire, some of
them twice. Of his measures to secure the frontiers of the
empire something will be said in another place. He introduced
important reforms in the army with the object of improving
both tactics and discipline. His broad vision is seen in the
ordinance requiring officers to study the arms and the tactical
evolutions of enemy races with which Roman troops might at
any time be required to fight. By appointing four consular
judges in Italy, he lightened the burdens resting on consuls
and prætors, and speeded up litigation and especially appeal
cases. Since these were matters with which the local magistrates of the municipalities could not deal, the institution of
these circuit judges or judges of appeal hardly meant a limitation of local government. But it could be interpreted as,
in some sense, a further reduction of senatorial authority in
Italy; just as at an earlier date the appointment of a permanent
prefect of the city had reduced the senate's authority in Rome.
Moreover, the distinction between Italy and the provinces,
which had hitherto been so jealously guarded, was perceptibly
disappearing.

Both Julius Cæsar and Augustus had thought of codifying
the law. It was only Hadrian who made a beginning by fixing
once for all the edict of the *praetor urbanus*. The sources of law
under the Republic had been enactments of the assembly and
the edicts of magistrates, all of which had been to a great extent
modelled on the edict of the urban prætor. Under the early
empire decrees of the senate had superseded laws made in the
assembly. But, in addition, the emperor was an important, and
ultimately became the only, source of law. His *placita* included
edicts, judicial decisions, rulings on disputed points, and administrative instructions to provincial officials. Once the
prætorian edict became fixed, — the task was entrusted by
Hadrian to the eminent jurist Salvius Julianus, — no additions
could be made save by an imperial edict or rescript. By this
codification a solid foundation was laid for later collections of
Roman law culminating in the *Corpus Iuris* of Justinian.

Finally we must note Hadrian's sweeping reform, it might

almost be said, creation, of the imperial civil service. The absence of this in any proper sense had been a serious inconvenience under earlier emperors; it became the more acute at the beginning of the second century as the control of the central government over all parts of the empire increased. Hitherto, while senators were appointed as governors and legates, the enormous business at Rome had been carried on mainly by slaves and freedmen of the ruler. At times, particularly under Claudius, the immediate result had been to make these persons inordinately powerful. Hadrian not only entrusted the chief secretaryships in the imperial bureaus to *equites*, — this was not entirely an innovation, — but placed members of the order in numerous responsible posts throughout the provinces, especially in connection with finance and taxation. In this way a regular equestrian *cursus honorum* was evolved, in which the able men could be promoted gradually from some small procuratorship to high offices, like the prefecture of Egypt or one of the chief secretaryships at Rome. Not infrequently, too, as we know from abundant inscriptions, the emperors in the second century bestowed on efficient *equites* tribunician or prætorian rank, thereby enabling them to transfer from the equestrian to the senatorial career. The importance and influence of the *equites* steadily grew through the century, mainly at the expense of the senate. The Prætorian prefect, who, from Hadrian's time, was more and more commonly an eminent jurist, became in time the most important individual in the state after the emperor himself.

A further development, dating from the time of Hadrian, was the separation of civil from military careers. There was again no abrupt alteration. But there are records of men whose advancement was entirely in one sphere or the other. Since specialization made for greater efficiency, the practice became more and more general. One other noteworthy change spread, almost imperceptibly at first, with beneficial results to all concerned. The collection of customs, taxes, and mining royalties by private contractors had continued through the first century of our era, although these men had not, of course, been allowed the latitude which they enjoyed in the later years of the Republic. In the second century direct collection under the control of imperial procurators gradually superseded the older system. How the change was often effected can be seen from inscriptions. One man, who is described in an inscription as a contractor of harbor dues, in a record of somewhat later date appears as an imperial procurator for the same purpose. But it should be added that private contractors are heard of as late as the opening years of the fifth century A.D.

Hadrian's successor, Antoninus Pius, was a middle-aged man when he was adopted by the emperor in 138. He had had varied experience, having been both a consular judge in Italy and pro-consul in Asia, as well as a member of the emperor's council. A few months after the adoption Hadrian died. Antoninus' principate (138–161) was not remarkable for any serious constitutional or administrative alterations. The imperial reorganization effected by Hadrian worked well, and the half century from 117 to 161 perhaps marks the zenith of prosperity in the empire. Antoninus was somewhat more liberal in the amount of responsibility that he permitted to the senate, so that his reign is generally thought to mark a reaction against the absolute government of men like Trajan or Hadrian. It is difficult to estimate whether the greater consideration shown to the Fathers, and their more frequent consultation by the emperor, really amounted to much more than a semblance of increased power. In any case M. Aurelius, the adopted son and son-in-law of Antoninus, though always courteous in his treatment of the senate, followed the example of Hadrian rather than of Antoninus in keeping it in strict subordination to himself. His reign (161–180) was a period of almost constant anxiety for the welfare and safety of the empire. For, besides a war with Parthia, a serious revolt by the governor of Syria, and an epidemic brought from the East by Roman troops, which caused most severe loss of life in Italy and Rome, attacks by Germanic peoples on the northeastern boundaries of the empire necessitated extensive military operations on the Danube front extending over a period of years. M. Aurelius, as will be seen, made the frontier secure once more. But one action of his had consequences of a far more momentous kind than he, with all his statesmanship, could have foreseen. By permitting a large number of Germanic settlers to take up their permanent abode in several of Rome's frontier provinces he introduced a considerable "barbarian" element into the empire. The settlers were military colonists. Personally free, they were nevertheless not permitted to leave the lands allotted to them. They were also required to perform military service. The full significance of the emperor's innovation was not apparent until the following century.

The twelve years' reign of Aurelius' unworthy son, Commodus (180–192), recalled the worst years of Gaius or Nero. The personal excesses and cruelty of this ruler seem to have surpassed even what those earlier experts in vice had been able to achieve. The treasury was exhausted, the government of the empire was neglected, resulting in ominous unrest in various quarters. At last, on the night of December 31, 192, Commodus was assassinated by a small group of conspirators. The empire now passed to a senator, Pertinax; but at the end of three months he was killed by the Prætorian Guard. Their new choice was a wealthy senator, Didius Julianus. Soon he, too, displeased them; and, besides, he was not accepted by the most powerful legates of the provinces. The governor of Pannonia, Septimius Severus, marched to Italy at the head of his troops and seized the throne with little opposition. Before, however, he could regard his own position as secure, he had to worst his rival, the governor of Syria, and several years later to take the field against the legate of Britain.

THE ROMAN EMPIRE

at its Greatest Extent

Under TRAJAN, 98-117 A.D.

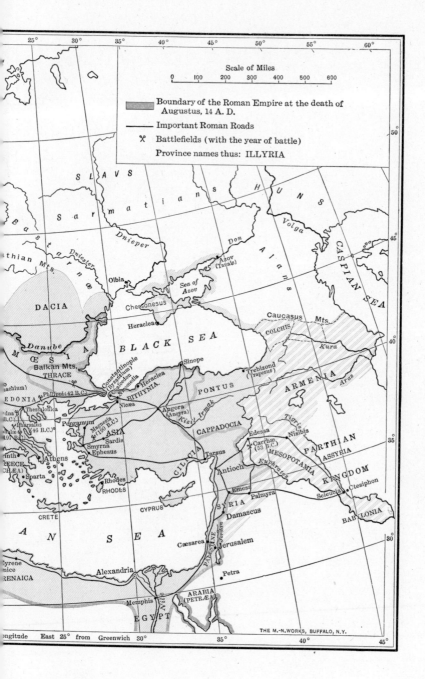

Scale of Miles

0   100   200   300   400   500   600

▓▓▓ Boundary of the Roman Empire at the death of
Augustus, 14 A. D.

──── Important Roman Roads

⚔ Battlefields (with the year of battle)

Province names thus: ILLYRIA

S L A V S

S a r m a t i a n s

H U N S

Volga

B a s t a r n æ

Dnieper

Don

A l a n s

CASPIAN SEA

50°

rthian Mts.

Dniester

Azov
(Tanais)

DACIA

Olbia

Sea of
Azov

Chersonesus

Caucasus   Mts.

COLCHIS

Kura

45°

Danube

Heraclea

B L A C K   S E A

40°

M Œ S I A

Balkan Mts.
THRACE

Sinope

Trebizond
(Trapezus)

Arda

achium)

Constantinople
(Byzantium)
Chalcedon
Nicomedia

Heraclea

PONTUS

ARMENIA

EDONIA

Philippi (42 B.C.)

BITHYNIA

Nicæa

35°

dna
B.C.)
alus
(46 B.C.)
(197 B.C.)

Thessalonica

Pharsalus

Pergamum

Magnesia
(190 B.C.)

ASIA

Angora
(Ancyra)

Kizil Irmak

CAPPADOCIA

Edessa

Carrhæ
(53 B.C.)

Nisibis

Tigris

MESOPOTAMIA

PARTHIAN

ASSYRIA

inth
REECE
HÆA)

Athens

Sardis

Smyrna
Ephesus

Tarsus

CILICIA

Antioch

Euphrates

KINGDOM

Sparta

Rhodes

RHODES

CYPRUS

SYRIA

Emesa

Palmyra

Seleucia

Ctesiphon

BABYLONIA

CRETE

Damascus

A N   S E A

Cæsarea

PALESTINE

Jerusalem

Jordan

30°

yrene
nice
RENAICA

Alexandria

Petra

ARABIA
(PETRÆA)

Memphis

Nile

E G Y P T

THE M.-N.WORKS, BUFFALO, N.Y.

ngitude   East 25° from   Greenwich   30°   35°   40°   45°

CHAPTER XXVIII

ROME'S FOREIGN POLICY AND THE FRONTIERS OF THE EMPIRE IN THE FIRST AND SECOND CENTURIES

> *Held far and wide in awe, let her name spread*
> *To farthest shores, where central stream*
> *Europe divides from Africa,*
> *Where flooding Nile waters the tillage lands.*

> *Whatever bound is set unto the world,*
> *It she shall reach by arms, joying to see*
> *The region where the fires their revels hold,*
> *And where the mists and raining dews.*
> Horace, *Odes* iii, 3 (Garnsey's translation).

THE empire which Augustus left at his death was, as we have seen, a compact whole. The aged emperor is said to have counselled that its boundaries should not be extended. It was perhaps the advice of one weary from half a century of rule; and, even if no ambitions of conquest had stirred his successors, it might prove difficult to follow as the political conditions on Rome's frontiers changed. And, after all, there were some problems which the great administrator had left at least partially unsolved. A brief survey will demonstrate the modifications and extensions of the Roman boundaries in the first two centuries of our era, and at the same time will make clear some of the main lines of Rome's foreign policy.

In the South, Mauretania, corresponding to the modern Algiers and Morocco, which had been left under the rule of client princes by Augustus, was annexed as a province a quarter of a century after his death. A few years later it was for administrative purposes subdivided into two districts, *Caesariensis* and *Tingitana*. During the further course of the first century the greater security of these coast-lands was insured by the conquest of the interior as far as the Atlas mountains, and on the eastern side even beyond, to the borders of the Sahara.

521

In the East no fresh conquests were made in the first century. The military commitments of Rome, however, were there especially heavy. They were necessitated above all by the frequent clashes with Parthia. Augustus' general attitude toward Parthia had been pacific; he had, however, committed himself to the policy of treating Armenia as a client kingdom of Rome. In view of Roman suzerainty over the principalities in Asia Minor, and for the security of her most near-lying provinces, his action was intelligible. But in the sequel this oriental kingdom became a constant source of dispute and hostilities between the two imperial neighbors for more than half a century. Early in Tiberius' reign the intrigues between pro-Parthian and pro-Roman cliques in Armenia led the emperor to intervene. He sent out his nephew, Germanicus, on a special mission to the East. He settled the affairs of the monarchy, reached a friendly agreement with Parthia, and at the same time converted the one-time client kingdom of Cappadocia into a province (17 A.D.). For the greater part of Tiberius' principate peace reigned in the East; but in 34, on the death of the Armenian king whom Rome had sponsored, Parthian intrigues were resumed and Tiberius once more intervened. Under Claudius the relations between Parthia and Rome grew steadily worse; as before, Armenia was the chief cause of contention. The accession of a very able and ambitious prince, Vologases I, to the throne of Parthia in 51 increased the danger to Roman interests in the East. From that year to 66 the Eastern question remained unsettled.

The rather vacillating policy followed by Claudius in the last years of his life was changed under his youthful successor Nero. Acting on the advice of his two chief counsellors, Burrus and Seneca, the emperor appointed the most able military commander of the age, Cn. Domitius Corbulo, to an eastern command in 57. By this man's energetic measures the Parthian nominee was forced from the Armenian throne, and a Roman *protégé* was installed in his place. Vologases, too, was by 61 prepared to come to an accommodation. But the settlement provisionally concluded between him and Corbulo did not meet with the approval of the Roman government. War in the East broke out afresh. Corbulo was temporarily superseded in the chief command, only to be reappointed a year or two later. With an army fifty thousand strong he now forced the submission of Armenia and sufficiently overawed the Parthian monarch that he reopened negotiations. Tiridates, originally a Parthian nominee, was confirmed in his possession of the Armenian throne after having come to Rome and sworn formal allegiance to Nero in person (66). There are grounds for believing that at one time the emperor or his advisers contemplated the annexation of Armenia as a province. Actually the settlement reached in 66 was still on the lines of Augustus' policy. Yet, inasmuch as it endured for nearly fifty years, it may be regarded as satisfactory.

Early in the next century Parthian intrigues recommenced, but negotiations between the oriental potentate and the Dacian Decebalus were abortive. A few years later a new Parthian ruler came to power and the Armenian throne also fell vacant. Chosroes of Parthia intervened to make his own nominee king of the buffer state, an action which Trajan treated as a violation of the pact of 66 and therefore a *casus belli*. A Parthian embassy which met him in Greece on his way to the East was curtly dismissed. Reaching Antioch in 114, he prepared to take the offensive in the spring of 115. A strong contingent of troops transported from Pannonia was added to the seven legions stationed in the eastern provinces. Trajan's military progress was rapid and spectacular. Armenia was forced to submit. Then, while one of his officers attacked Media, the emperor himself overran Mesopotamia, occupied the trans-Tigris region of Adiabene, and finally took Babylon and Ctesiphon. From there he advanced to the Persian gulf. His easy progress in the western territories of the Parthian empire was to a great extent due to the civil dissensions and dynastic struggles which had broken out in Parthia. Trajan conferred the Parthian crown on a son of Chosroes, who for the moment became the vassal of Rome. The territories of Armenia, Mesopotamia, and Adiabene were annexed as Roman provinces, the last under the name of Assyria. But while the emperor was on the lower Tigris he received news of widespread revolts not only in the lands lately conquered, where several Roman garrisons were annihilated, but among the Jewish population of several provinces of the

empire, in Cyprus, Egypt, and Cyrenaica. The resistance in
Mesopotamia was crushed; then the emperor returned to Syria,
and thence began his journey back to Italy where urgent matters
awaited his attention. But on his way he was taken ill and
died within a few days (117), leaving to his successor an empire
troubled by unrest in many parts. Hadrian wisely abandoned
the eastern provinces lately created. The Euphrates became
again the boundary between Parthia and Rome, while Armenia
reverted to its status as a client kingdom.

Once more nearly half a century passed during which Rome
and Parthia were at peace. But at the beginning of M. Aurelius'
reign the Parthian king, Vologases III, sent an army into Armenia, deposed the reigning monarch, and set up a candidate of his
own. Roman officers, for example, in the province of Cappadocia, met with severe defeats, and Rome's prestige in the East
was seriously threatened. The emperor, not underrating the
gravity of the situation, entrusted the conduct of the war nominally to his co-regent, L. Verus, actually to his ablest general,
Avidius Cassius, supported by two other commanders of tried
worth. As the result of three seasons of campaigning (163–165)
Roman authority in Armenia was reëstablished, and a series of
decisive defeats, culminating in the capture and destruction of
Ctesiphon, were inflicted on the chief enemy, Parthia. A portion of northern Mesopotamia (Osroëne) was made into a Roman
dependency; otherwise the emperor sought for no additions to
the empire. The energetic action of Aurelius' generals secured
peace on the eastern frontier for a quarter of a century. At the
beginning of his imperial career Septimius Severus crushed his
rival, Pescennius Niger, governor of Syria (194). A punitive
expedition into Mesopotamia against several peoples which had
sided with Niger followed in 195. Two years later the Parthians, who had abstained from interference in the struggles of two
Roman rivals for power, assumed the offensive. This compelled
Severus to undertake a fresh campaign in the East, where he was
from 198 to 200. By the peace which he ultimately imposed on
Parthia all northern Mesopotamia as far as the river Aborras
(Khabur) was annexed by Rome, the administrative capital of
the new province being at Nisibis.

Thus Severus went beyond what had been done by M. Aurelius and partially reverted to the policy of Trajan. The new frontier, in spite of occasional set-backs, was maintained by Rome for several centuries. It will have become clear that there was in the first and second centuries of our era a marked similarity in the causes of occasional hostilities between the two empires, and not a little in the issue. In the main Rome more than upheld her prestige; she also insured the security of her rich provinces in the East. But the constant maintenance of large bodies of troops there, coupled with the disorganization and sometimes material destruction caused by the not infrequent wars, formed a very heavy liability. Yet we are too ill-informed about many of the details of Rome's Eastern policy to enable us to say whether more drastic action in the East from the first would have reduced or aggravated a difficult problem. The most obvious example of that would have been the annexation of Armenia as a province. But this would have necessitated a serious addition to Rome's military establishment in the East, and the action of Hadrian, perhaps the ablest Roman emperor after Augustus, in abandoning the conquests of Trajan suggests that the drawbacks and possible dangers of a policy of annexation greatly outweighed its real or potential advantages.

A by no means negligible problem for Roman administration in the East was presented by Judæa. The settlement of Pompey, by which that country became a dependent kingdom under Roman protection, endured till 6 A.D. In that year, at the request of a Jewish majority, which was discontented with the rule of Archelaus, son of Herod the Great who had died two years before, Judæa was converted into a province to be administered by an imperial procurator. This official, like the king of Judæa before, was under the general supervision of the governor of Syria. The policy of the Roman government was in general conciliatory toward the Jews, here as in other parts of the empire, until the emperor Gaius, by his foolish demand that the emperor's statue be set up in the synagogues and even in the temple at Jerusalem, provoked a violent outburst of nationalism. Only his death at the critical moment prevented a serious rebellion. His successor installed a native prince as ruler of Judæa in 41; but, when Agrippa died soon after, the country again became a procuratorial province. The difficulties of the

Roman administration were greatly increased by the constant quarrels of the Jews among themselves. Several different factions existed; against the extreme party, the Zealots, who preached opposition to the government and at times resorted to violence, the Roman procurator was on several occasions forced to take military action. Nevertheless, it was not until the last years of Nero's principate that a dangerous situation developed. In 66 the outbreak of disturbances and insurrections in several parts of the country quickly precipitated a general conflict. The Jewish War lasted from that year to 70. Its length was partly due to civil war within the empire, which withdrew Vespasian, who was in command in Judæa in 67 and 68, from the East, and ended in his elevation to the principate; partly to the determined and often heroic resistance offered by the Jews. Vespasian's elder son, Titus, took over the command in 70. By the siege, and after five months the capture, of Jerusalem, whose inhabitants underwent acute privations and unspeakable sufferings, as we can still read in the harassing pages of the Jewish historian Josephus, the war was brought to an end. Jerusalem, including the temple, was in ruins. Cæsarea became a Roman burgess colony, and the tribute hitherto paid by the Jews to the temple at Jerusalem was in future rendered to Rome.

We have already referred to the wide-spread Jewish insurrection in the last year of Trajan's reign. Frightful savagery was let loose against Romans and natives alike, especially in Cyrenaica, and produced ruthless retaliation. Yet the Roman officers deputed to stamp out the unrest in the different provinces had a difficult task. The loss in life during two or three years, particularly in northern Africa, was terrible. About the last organized resistance of the Jews in their own country we know very little, since we have no narrative by an eye-witness, as is the case with the war of 66–70. In 132, after Hadrian had taken steps to found a Roman colony on the site of Jerusalem and planned to build a temple to Jupiter on the site of the Jewish temple, a general rebellion broke out.[1] Peace and order were not apparently reëstablished until 135. From such brief notices as we possess it would seem that the Roman generals

[1] It would appear that the emperor also promulgated an edict against the Jewish practice of circumcision.

proceeded with exceptional harshness, while the Jews fought with the courage of desperation. When all was over more than half a million persons are said to have perished, though this estimate is perhaps exaggerated. Yet the Jewish state had ceased to be. Jerusalem, under the name of Aelia Capitolina, became a Roman colony and flourished greatly for the next century. The official designation of the province hereafter was Syria Palestina.

It was, however, in the North that the most drastic territorial changes were effected during the first two centuries of the Christian era. Augustus is credited with the intention at the beginning of his principate of attempting the conquest of Britain. In a moment of caprice Gaius mustered a large military expedition for the same purpose, only to abandon his project abruptly on the eve of the date set for its departure. It was left to Claudius to begin the incorporation of the island in the empire. Strong reasons must have presented themselves to his mind for embarking on an undertaking which was bound to be very costly in itself, which at the outset can hardly have promised substantial profit to Rome as an offset to the expenditure involved, and which would necessitate an army of occupation, and therefore perhaps an increase in Rome's military establishment. In the main Claudius was concerned for the peace and security of Gaul. The Roman government had taken steps to suppress the Druidic religion and its priests, who were the chief upholders of nationalism and fomenters of anti-Roman feeling in Gaul. The Druids had fled to Britain where their headquarters were on Mona (Anglesey). From there they could still exercise a potent influence not only upon the islanders but on their Gallic kinsmen. Only by military intervention in Britain could the emperor hope to put an end to propaganda and activities subversive of Rome's authority.

In 43 Aulus Plautius, with three legions from the Rhine and one from the Danubian army, landed on the southeastern coast of Britain. In the course of his four-year command he subdued the south and southeast of the island. Roman veterans were settled at Camulodunum (Colchester) which became the headquarters of the Roman administration. The process of Romanization in the conquered area was rapid, and towns similar to Roman *municipia* quickly grew up at Londinium and Verulamium (St. Albans) in the southeast, and soon after at Aquæ Sulis (Bath) and Glevum (Gloucester) in the west. In 47 Ostorius Scapula succeeded Plautius. His main achievement was the defeat of the Iceni in East Anglia and the inclusion of their territory within the Roman province. He also warred against the tribes on the borders of England and Wales, especially the powerful Silures. The next two governors seem not to have attempted any serious enlargement of the province. But in 59 Suetonius Paulinus, an able officer who had already performed valuable services in northern Africa, took over the governorship of Britain. His first objective was northern Wales and Mona, from which he proposed to root out the Druids and their worship once and for all. But, before his work there had been completed, a great rising in East Anglia, provoked largely by the misgovernment of Roman officials, threatened to overthrow Roman authority in the island. Eastern towns like Camulodunum, Londinium, and Verulamium were sacked and burnt, and their inhabitants put to the sword by the infuriated natives led by their queen, Boudicca. Paulinus exacted a bloody retribution; for some eighty thousand of the Iceni and their allies were slaughtered. Thus Roman authority in the southern half of Britain was restored. Within a few years the farthest outposts of Roman occupation appear to have been Deva (Chester) and Lindum (Lincoln).

In 71 Petilius Cerealis took the offensive against the Brigantes in the north. Though the frontier of the province was enlarged, the new territory was still an unsettled zone in which the natives were liable to give trouble at any time. Five or six years later (in 77 or 78) Julius Agricola took over the British command. Of his career and especially his governorship in Britain we possess an admirable account from the pen of his son-in-law, the historian Tacitus. Agricola first finished the subjugation of Wales and Mona, which had perforce been left incomplete by Paulinus. In a second season's campaign he pushed forward in the north as far as the Tyne, at the same time building military roads and constructing forts in the area that he traversed. The year 81 saw him well advanced

ROMAN BRITAIN

SHOWING CHIEF ROMAN ROADS

Scale of Miles

0   25   50   75   100

into southern Scotland.   The Scottish lowlands, too, were
provisionally guarded by advanced posts and by a series of
forts between the Clyde and the Forth.   In the next years
he led his army into the heart of Caledonia.   In 84 he defeated
a great native host at Mons Graupius, a site not yet identified.   His fleet circumnavigated Great Britain, and, in addition
to his obvious intention of essaying the conquest of all Caledonia, he at one time planned an expedition into northern
Ireland.   But the emperor Domitian recalled him in 85.
The northern frontier of the Roman province was thus left
rather indeterminate.   Moreover, the history of the island
during the next thirty years is almost wholly lost to our view.
In 115 a great rising in the north of England occurred in
which the Brigantes were the ringleaders.   Owing to the eastern wars, and then the death of Trajan, some years elapsed before serious steps were taken to reëstablish Roman authority.
By Hadrian's orders a more systematic frontier was devised.
After peace had been restored in northern England — the emperor visited the island in person in 122 — the advance posts
in southern Scotland were abandoned, and a massive wall,
eight feet thick and twenty feet high, was built across from
Solway to the mouth of the Tyne, a distance of about 73 miles.
It was strengthened at intervals by fourteen forts, as well as by
watch-towers at shorter distances along its whole course.   A
military road ran behind the defense, while the frontier was
clearly demarcated by a ditch (*vallum*) running parallel to
and on the southern side of the wall from sea to sea (Plate 36).

The normal headquarters of the three legions stationed in
Britain were at Caerleon, Chester, and York (Eboracum).   The
last was now the administrative capital of the province.   While
all the country south of York flourished, and the communities
there developed a distinctive Romano-British civilization, the
northern portion of the occupied area — from York to the Wall
— retained the character of a military zone, and native disturbances as well as raids by the wild hillsmen of Caledonia were
not infrequent occurrences during the second century.   Early in
the reign of Antoninus Pius the Roman governor, Lollius Urbi-
cus, after some fighting reoccupied the Scottish lowlands, rebuilt
forts of Agricolan date, and constructed a turf wall strengthened

Plate 36

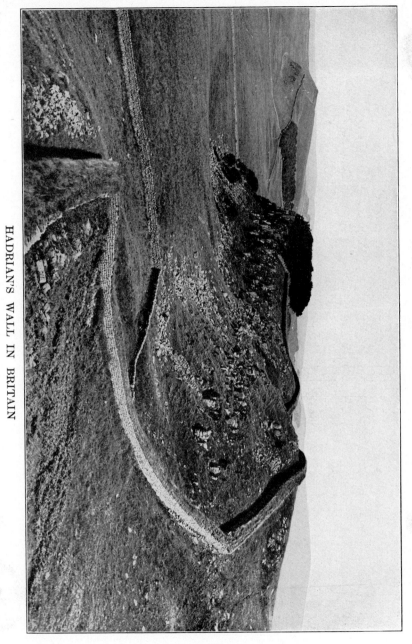

HADRIAN'S WALL IN BRITAIN

by frequent stone forts from Clyde to Forth (143). Though our scanty literary sources are silent, excavations have shown that the northern part of the province remained in an unsettled condition. A great rebellion broke out just after the death of M. Aurelius. Though the military forces stationed in Britain managed to hold their own and prevented the southeast from being overrun, it was more than twenty years before Roman authority in the north was fully restored. From 208 to 211 Severus was in Britain. He not only reconquered lost territory but made a punitive expedition into the north of Scotland. The Wall of Hadrian and many forts and defenses which had been destroyed in the long years of insurrection were thoroughly rebuilt. In consequence of the greater security thus attained the island during the greater portion of the third century enjoyed peace and prosperity, and that at a time when more than one province lying nearer to Italy and Rome was being menaced or ravaged by invaders.

The plan of extending the Roman frontier line beyond the Rhine to the Elbe was definitely abandoned by Tiberius in 16 A.D. Already in Augustus' time, however, some Gallic tribes had settled in the valley of the Neckar and the corner of territory between the Rhine and the upper Danube. They paid a tithe to the Roman government but were exempt from military service; nor was this territory (called *Agri Decumates*) technically included within the empire. The Flavian emperors took steps to organize this region as a military zone. A line of fortification — the so-called *limes Germanicus* — about two hundred miles long was constructed partly by Vespasian, partly by Domitian. It extended from the Taunus to the borders of Rætia, where it joined the hundred miles of defense-works on the north of that province (*limes Raeticus*). Additional forts and a continuous palisade were constructed in the next century by Hadrian. Within this new area a network of good military roads gradually grew up, and the whole region became an important frontier defense-line. Military stations there soon took on the character of towns; trade with the German tribes flourished; and the Roman influences, which thus percolated through among the native peoples outside the Roman area, were far from inconsiderable. Nothing is more certain than that, when several generations later Germanic tribes attacked and crossed the boundaries of the empire, many of them were partially Romanized, or at least familiar with Roman institutions and methods.

The Danubian provinces remained unchanged during the first century, though occasional disturbances in one or other of these demanded the attention and military action of successive Roman emperors. At the beginning of the second century the emperor Trajan took a momentous step. The tribes of Dacia had on several occasions invaded the provinces of Mœsia or Pannonia. In the reign of Domitian they had inflicted serious reverses on Roman troops and captured Roman forts, before their depredations were checked. An inconclusive peace followed, which caused a good deal of resentment in Rome. The next few years were utilized by the Dacian ruler Decebalus to reorganize his subjects for a more energetic assault on the Roman provinces. The menace of a strongly organized and hostile state in the immediate proximity of Pannonia and Mœsia decided Trajan soon after his accession to take the offensive. In the first Dacian War (101–102) he defeated Decebalus in a great engagement at Tapæ and forced him to sue for peace. The Dacian king became a vassal of Rome, the more important strongholds in Dacia were destroyed, and a small Roman army of occupation was left north of the Danube. Decebalus, however, did not abide by the terms of peace. He rebuilt his fortifications and gave other proofs that he was far from ready to accept Roman suzerainty permanently. Trajan, who perhaps at first had had no thoughts of annexation, now saw the need for more drastic action. In two seasons' campaigning (105–106) he completely crushed the resistance of the enemy, and then annexed their country as a province. Four colonies were subsequently founded there. Since in the two wars all but a small fraction of the Dacian people had been wiped out, the emperor repeopled the country with large numbers of settlers from other quarters of the empire. The new province, which for administrative purposes was subdivided later in the second century, prospered exceedingly, and the Roman exchequer derived a large profit from the proceeds of its rich gold mines.

The Danube frontier and its adjacent provinces remained undisturbed for half a century after Trajan's conquests. But the emperor M. Aurelius was called upon to defend those provinces of Rome against a far more formidable attack than any launched by the barbarians before. His operations, called after one of the chief tribes against whom he had to contend, the Two Marcomannic Wars, extended over the best part of twenty years; and, though the brunt of the fighting was in the central section, almost the whole of the Danube frontier was affected at one time or another. At his death the security of Rome's northeastern provinces had been reëstablished; but he did not live to carry out a plan of annexing the regions north of the Danube and west of Dacia, and thereby advancing the Roman boundary well beyond the river.

CHAPTER XXIX

THE ECONOMIC DEVELOPMENT OF THE EMPIRE
c. 100 B.C.–211 A.D.

> *The man who with the sturdy plough upturns the heavy soil; this cheating vintner, soldiers and sailors too who boldly scud o'er every sea, confess they hardships bear with this intent, that in old age they may retire to ease secure, when they have gained enough for life's support.* — Horace, Satires i, 1, 28–32 (Bryce's translation).

THE expansion of trade and industry, which reached its widest extent under the Flavian and Antonine emperors, had begun fully a century and a half earlier. The archæological materials and the inscriptions are most copious for the first and second centuries of our era. But for the hundred years or so before Augustus our information is scanty, so that the origins of many noteworthy developments are very obscure. In the case of tenure and cultivation of the land, both in Italy and in the provinces, our knowledge is uneven for the entire period, being relatively full for certain epochs and specific regions, and all but non-existent for others. We cannot doubt that the great increase in wealth during the second century B.C., and the passing of a large part of the ancient world under the direction of a single state, would have favored a very swift economic growth, given stable political conditions. Instead, the era from the Gracchi to Augustus was one of constant unrest. Civil wars, wars with foreign states, ruthless exploitation of the provincials by the ruling class of Rome and their protected minions, slave risings, and attempted revolutions, these were not the conditions favorable to the intensive cultivation of the arts of peace.

In the last years of the Republic it had become more and more apparent that the growing of field crops in Italy was, save in a few districts, quite unprofitable. Much land, too, had fallen out of cultivation and had become waste-land or at best pasture-land, and the growing of olives and vines, and, on the other hand, stock-raising were alone likely to enable the owner to pay his way. The predominant way of working estates was with slave-gangs, a method which could never produce the best results; yet it was a long time before the Romans realized this. We are poorly informed about the provinces at that date. In the case of Sicily at the time of the prosecution of Verres the Sicilian land consisted partly of large estates, partly of tracts leased out by the government to tenants. The tenants sub-let their land to sub-tenants, and it was these last who performed the actual cultivation. It was this system of tenancy and sub-tenancy which under the empire was more and more adopted in Italy and the provinces. At the end of the first century A.D. the cultivation in northern Italy, as we learn from Pliny, was in the hands of tenant farmers. We cannot however deduce from this that the slave-gang system had ceased entirely. There were in truth several reasons for the limitation of slave labor. We have seen how several slave risings were suppressed by the government. On those occasions enormous numbers perished; moreover, the senate were now no doubt anxious to limit the number of servile workers in any given area. In addition, from Augustus' time there was a far smaller supply of slaves; the huge influx in the previous century had been primarily due to the foreign conquests of Rome. In northern Africa what had once been Carthaginian territory was in the first century B.C. partly owned by Roman citizens and presumably worked by slave labor, partly left in the possession of native tenants, whose taxes were now paid to the Roman quæstor instead of to the Punic authorities.

The reforms of Augustus in the provinces must indirectly have been of great benefit to the farmers there, since they knew what their obligations in the matter of tribute were, and with the advent of a good provincial administration they were protected from the abuses and extortions of an earlier age.

Besides the gradual substitution of a tenant peasantry for slave-gangs on privately owned estates, we must notice the rapid growth in the first two centuries of our era of the imperial domains. A valuable group of inscriptions, dating from the reigns of Trajan, Commodus, and Septimius Severus not only illustrates the working of the imperial estates in northern Africa in the second century, but, since they refer to earlier legislation, seem to show that the system goes back to the time of Vespasian. The tenant (*colonus*) is a small farmer who is usually provided with a certain stock (*instrumentum*), which he is expected to keep in good condition and to return on the expiration of his agreement with the owner. In the case of the African domains we find the estates of the chief tenants worked by slave labor, and a number of smaller farms cultivated by free peasants. These last were required by their contracts to give a certain amount of help each year on the main estates, at the time when the need for extra hands was imperative. Encouragement was also given for *coloni* to put waste-lands under cultivation. In that case they were allowed a certain period free of rent for such reclaimed land. The time varied according to the character of the produce raised — five years in the case of vineyards and fig plantations, ten years in the case of olive orchards. The fact that the peasantry did not hold their farms directly from the emperor but from chief tenants gave rise periodically to abuses. The chief tenants, in league with the imperial procurator, maltreated subtenants or tried to compel them to do labor not specified in their contracts. To the fact that the *coloni* petitioned the emperor for redress, and that instructions were promulgated by him to prevent malpractices in future, we owe this important group of inscriptions.

Much care was taken in Africa to insure an adequate water supply. In addition to aqueducts large tanks were constructed in which the winter rains could be stored for use in the dry months. We even find the hours during which water could be turned into the fields specified, due allowance being made for lands to which the water would have to be pumped. Yet the absence of inventive skill among the Romans is very noticeable. Few improvements were made in the plow; the ground had to be broken up with a hoe, and the ripe grain cut with a hand-sickle. Pliny the Elder mentions a reaping machine, which is also described in detail by a later writer. But, as it had to be propelled from behind by an ox, it was not adapted for use on sloping ground. Also it cut off only the ears, so that all the straw was left standing. Such an implement cannot have been extensively used; nor have we evidence for a general use of the harrow. Where, as under the empire, labor gradually became more difficult to obtain, the only remedy, if the amount of land under effective cultivation was not to decline, would have been the employment of labor-saving devices. Instead there seems to have been little difference in the methods of tilling, plowing, reaping, and so forth followed in the time of Cato the Elder (early second century B.C.) and of the Spanish writer on agriculture, Columella, who flourished in the second half of the first century A.D.

Rome and Italy depended on the provinces for most of their grain. Some continued to be grown in central Italy and in the Po valley; southern Italy was given over to pasturage. The cultivation of the vine and the olive, however, throve, wine and oil being the two main Italian exports. Grain was imported primarily from Egypt, while large quantities came also from Africa. Sicily, which during the Republic had been the chief granary of Rome, in the imperial period grew few field crops and turned to viniculture. Wheat was successfully raised both in Spain and Gaul. Both countries also became great centres of the wine industry before the end of the first century A.D., although the early emperors had tried to restrict the planting of vines there for fear that the Italian wine growers would be adversely affected by provincial competition. In the eastern provinces the cultivation of vine and olive had long been endemic, and continued to thrive.

With regard to the mineral wealth available during the period, it must be remembered that districts which had been highly productive in the Hellenic period had become largely or wholly exhausted. Thus the famous silver mines of Laurium in Augustus' day produced very little ore; a century later they had ceased to be worked altogether. Gold in the imperial era was mined in Spain, in Dalmatia and Mœsïa, and, after Trajan's conquest, in Dacia. Some was also obtained from Arabia Petræa, while Egypt continued to rely for the precious metal on Abyssinia, as she had done for centuries past. The chief source of the silver supply was Spain; some was also procured in southern Gaul and in Dalmatia. Spain, and later Britain, provided lead; tin at this date was chiefly mined in the Spanish peninsula. Iron was found in many parts of the empire; but by far the richest deposits were in Noricum and some districts of Asia Minor.

The raw material for textiles came from many parts of the Roman world. Intensive sheep-rearing was carried on in Asia Minor as it had been in the Greek period. A good deal of wool was still obtained in Italy itself, from the region round Tarentum and the Padus valley. In this, as in so many other undertakings, Gaul rapidly came to the front. But the wool from that country was coarser and not regarded as suitable for the finer fabrics. Flax was raised in Syria and Egypt, and all the more delicate linen came from those countries. But flax-growing was introduced into Gaul with good results. Gaulish linen being coarser than the oriental was mainly used for sails, awnings, and similar articles. Cotton, grown in Egypt and manufactured in the Orient, was chiefly used to mix with silk owing to the scarcity and extremely high cost of the latter.

The development in industry during the period, though remarkable enough, must not be overestimated. From the middle of the second century B.C. specialization in crafts made rapid strides. Where before one heard only of workers in wood (*fabri*), the particular branch in which the craftsman specialized is now indicated. Inscriptions of imperial date furnish us with copious evidence for innumerable kinds of *fabri*, many of whom specialized entirely on the manufacture of two or three, or even a single, luxury article. During the early empire our information for methods of production is fullest for the brick and the pottery industries. In the case of the manufacturies of bricks and tiles in Italy (*figlinae*) we find that the more important had by the second half of the first century A.D. passed into the hands of members of the imperial family and a few rich private owners. The actual management was commonly in the hands of an overseer — freedman or slave; alternatively, the concern might be leased to a contractor. Most of the important buildings in Rome erected or repaired during the latter part of the first and the early years of the second century A.D. were, in so far as bricks and tiles were used, built of bricks from the yards of Domitius Afer and his successors. It is a fortunate circumstance that the bricks were stamped, and so provide the modern archæologist with much valuable information. The most complete stamps give the date, the name of the estate from which the clay was obtained, the name of the manufactory, and the maker of the mould.

The great centre of the ceramic industry in Italy was Arretium. The Arretine pottery was a fine red-glaze ware ornamented with elaborate designs in low relief. The pots were turned out of a mould, and the moulds were commonly stamped with the names of the manufacturer and the workman who made them. Thus it has been possible to arrive at certain very tentative statistics of the number of persons employed in one or two of the best known workshops. The factory of a certain P. Cornelius, which may have employed from eighty to a hundred workmen at a given date seems to have been an exceptionally large undertaking. There is therefore even in the ceramic industry no question of mass production in the modern sense. In the provinces production on a smaller scale, by a master craftsman working with a few helpers, seems to have been the rule. The making of good glazed pottery (the so-called *terra sigillata*) became one of the most flourishing industries in Gaul, and the ware had a wide distribution. When Britain had been included in the Roman empire much of the ware was exported thither; before long it was imitated by the island craftsmen. The chief centres of the manufacture of metal objects in Italy continued to be Etruria and Campania. Campanian bronze bowls have been discovered well beyond the boundaries of the empire, showing that they were used in barter with the natives of those outlying regions. The manufacture of glass was an eastern industry which had long flourished, especially in Alexandria. Toward the end of the Republican period glass-blowing had been introduced into Italy and was successfully carried on in Campania. Under the empire the craft was taken up in the western provinces. Judged by the copious remains, the industry in Gaul became hardly less flourishing than the making of pottery.

The craftsmen in Rome and Italy were largely, perhaps

predominantly, slaves and freedmen, many of them being Greeks or Græco-Orientals. In thoroughly Romanized provinces, like *Gallia Narbonensis*, conditions may have resembled those in Italy. But in the more recently conquered areas — the three Gauls, Britain, and the lands bordering on the Rhine — most of the craftsmen and artisans were free-born natives. In the eastern provinces conditions seem to have varied a good deal; but free craftsmen appear to have been in the majority everywhere.

Great as are the gaps in our knowledge of the economic history of the empire, there is at all events no doubt concerning the volume of commerce carried on throughout the empire and beyond. Already by the time of Augustus numerous good roads provided ample facilities for communication by land. The efficient upkeep of naval squadrons made the Mediterranean safer for sea-traffic than it had been for centuries, and this security continued to the end of the second century. The construction of new roads and the repair of old ones engaged the attention of successive emperors; and, as new territories were added from time to time to the empire, the new highways, constructed in the first instance for military purposes, quickly became avenues for peaceful traffic. The four main arteries of the Italian road system, the *Via Appia*, *Via Aurelia*, *Via Flaminia*, and *Via Aemilia*, besides being connected by many secondary roads, linked up to the chief highways leading to the western provinces and to the Danubian countries. The city of Aquileia at the head of the Adriatic was in imperial days the meeting point of no less than six important routes. From Dyrrachium the *Via Egnatia* threaded its way across to Thessalonica. For the traveller in haste it provided the quickest means of going from Italy to Asia Minor and beyond. In Asia Minor three main roads ran eastward or southeastward from the coast. The most northerly ran from Nicomedia by the valley of the Sangarius to Ancyra, and thence almost due east to Satala and to Armenia beyond. The middle route started from Smyrna and led up the valley of the Hermus to Ancyra. The southern route, which began at Ephesus and followed the Mæander valley, led by way of Iconium and the Cilician gates over the Taurus to northern Syria. From Tarsus in Cilicia, from Syrian Antioch, and from Damascus the merchant and the wayfarer passed by one or other of the routes across the desert to Mesopotamia and the Persian Gulf. Of the routes to the Far East the most used now, as in Hellenistic days, went from Seleuceia down the Tigris to the Gulf and thence by sea to India. But the overland routes also carried much traffic (cf. p. 357). Moreover the northerly route from Phasis, at the eastern end of the Black Sea, through the Caucasian Gates (Dariel Pass) to the Caspian and on through the Oxus valley seems to have been used not a little during the first two centuries of our era. It had the advantage over the other land routes to the Far East that it avoided Parthia.

The importance of Alexandria as a mart and centre of eastern commerce did not decrease in Roman days. The commodities of Arabia, the Somali coast, and southwestern India were landed at one or other of the Red Sea ports — Myos Hormos or Berenice — and then transported on camels across the desert to Coptos. From there they were taken down the Nile to the Egyptian capital. The superlative importance of Alexandria was due to its grain trade — according to one ancient writer the amount exported annually to Rome amounted to twenty million *modii;* to the great trade in luxury articles from the East — precious stones, spices, frankincense, and so forth — which passed through this mart; and to its own flourishing industries, *in primis* the manufacture of linen and of glasswares.

The maritime trade to Italy came chiefly to Puteoli, until Claudius built a new port two miles west of old Ostia. Then much trade was diverted there, and Portus Augusti or Portus Urbis, as it was called, soon rivalled the older port in the Bay of Naples in the volume of its sea-borne trade. The harbor built by Claudius was half a century later enlarged by Trajan. In the Aegean area Ephesus, Smyrna, Byzantium, and Corinth were ports of the first rank. In the western provinces Massilia and Narbo in Gaul, Tarraco and Gades in Spain, enjoyed a similar preëminence. Nor must Arelate on the Rhone and, at a later date, Burdigala (Bordeaux) be omitted from the list. Merchants, Roman and Italian, as well as the natives of Greece and the Near East, were ubiquitous. Of the eighty thousand Romans and Italians massacred in Asia Minor in 88 (cf. p. 452) more than half, perhaps two-thirds, were there for trade and commerce. At the time of the civil war between Cæsar and Pompey many Roman merchants were settled at Corduba and Hispalis in southern Spain. Enterprising traders had found their way into the heart of Gaul even before Cæsar conquered the land. Utica in northern Africa in 46 contained a colony of three hundred Roman merchants. Again we are informed that, at the time of the Pannonian revolt in 6 A.D., a number of Romans settled in that region — their interests must have been mainly commercial — were murdered. Considering how recently the conquest of that area had been effected, we get some notion of the rapidity with which military occupation was followed by commercial exploitation. The same thing is illustrated by the statement of Tacitus that, when the Iceni rose in arms in 61, that is to say, less than twenty years after the first Roman occupation of Britain, many Roman traders resided in Londinium. The abundant inscriptions of imperial date demonstrate over how extended an area merchants of all nationalities plied their calling. The presence of Syrians in such widely separated cities as Naples, Ravenna, Puteoli, Malaga in Spain, and Sirmium in Pannonia proves that they were as active in the western half of the empire as in their own country and the adjacent lands. A Greek inscription from Hierapolis in Phrygia records how Flavius Zeuxis had made no less than seventy-two voyages to Italy by way of Cape Malea. At distant Tomi on the Black Sea, where the poet Ovid passed unhappy years of exile, there was an association of Alexandrian merchants who fostered the cult of their deity Serapis.

The whole tendency during the first two centuries of our era was toward decentralization of trade and industry. New provinces like Gaul were not only quickly able to supply all or most of their own needs, but soon plied a large export trade. And, as the prosperity of the provinces grew apace, that of Italy remained stationary at first and then began to decline. The number of cities, large and small, in the empire of the Antonine age was enormous both in the East and in the West. And it is remarkable how even insignificant urban communities could lavish money on fine buildings and on works of utility like aqueducts and paved streets. It was the civic populations throughout the Roman world which alone shared in the Græco-Roman or Roman culture of the period. The inhabitants of the country districts, which in many parts of the empire comprised a large part of the territory, were backward and could exert no political influence. For the land which the peasantry cultivated, insofar as it was not owned by the state or by the emperor, had for the most part been acquired by the wealthy citizens of towns. It was the town authorities who were held responsible for the punctual payment of the tribute to the imperial procurator, while the voiceless peasantry produced the most important portion of the tribute, namely the grain, of which many thousands of bushels were annually shipped to Rome and Italy.

It is inevitable that, because our knowledge of the economic life of the empire is derived almost wholly from inscriptions and the study of excavated sites, the life of the town-dwellers should alone stand out with some distinctness. Yet, even in the case of the urban populations, it is mainly the governing class, the men of wealth who used much of their riches in making handsome benefactions to their community during their life-time or bequeathing them by will, whose activities and generosity are, as it were, mirrored in the epigraphic and monumental remains. Of the humbler folk, craftsmen, shopkeepers, laborers, whether they were free by birth, freedmen, or slaves, we know little, save what can be learnt from their innumerable associations or guilds.

The association of a number of persons for a particular object, for which there were several Latin terms of which the commonest was *collegium*, was an institution which traditionally went back to the regal days of Rome. With official or state associations, such as the priestly colleges, we are not here concerned, but only with what may be described as professional associations. During the last century of the Republic a good many of these existed. Since they were misused by demagogues for political purposes (cf. p. 474) the government suppressed many of them. Both Cæsar and Augustus forbade all except certain old established guilds, which were politically harmless.

Under the empire, therefore, the permission of the emperor was needed for the formation of a *collegium*. When, however, we survey the enormous number of these associations in the Flavian and Antonine periods, we can see clearly that the law was not strictly enforced. In other words, where no political activities were to be feared and no actions calculated to undermine the authority of the government, there was no interference, even though a *collegium* might technically be "illicit," that is to say, not sanctioned by law. When Trajan suppressed *collegia* in Bithynia, he did so because the province was at that time in a disturbed state and he feared that the guilds might be used for other than social or religious purposes.

Although it has been convenient to use the name "guild" to translate *collegium*, it must be emphasized at the outset that these associations did not, like a medieval guild or a modern trades union, exist for an economic purpose. Some were merely formed so that the members could join periodically in the worship of a common patron deity, or as "burial societies." Indeed, the provision of proper funeral rites and occasional offerings to the dead afterwards were one of the purposes of most of the *collegia*. The members of many of these unions belonged to the poorest class, free and servile. The larger *collegia*, whose members were men of somewhat more substance, and which could boast of wealthy patrons, existed largely for the promotion of social intercourse and occasional recreation. We must not therefore be misled into the belief that, because members of one craft or profession banded together to form a *collegium*, they did so to improve their economic status, to obtain better wages, or even to use the weapon of the strike. The known instances where a number of persons of the same calling stood together to get their economic grievances redressed are so few that we are justified in saying that this use of a *collegium* was accidental.

Large as is the total of collegiate inscriptions there are many trades which are not represented at all. Particularly numerous are the guilds of *fabri*, of persons engaged in the manufacture of various kinds of luxury articles, of shippers and merchants, and of men who performed the civic duty of acting as a volunteer fire-brigade.[1] The bulk of the collegiate inscriptions have been found in the western half of the empire — in Italy, Gaul, the Danubian provinces, Dacia, and, to a less degree, in Spain. Africa, apart from very few towns, was mainly agricultural; hence the absence there of such guilds is not surprising. In the eastern provinces, on the other hand, the more elaborate town and municipal organization, which was often centuries old, made the formation of *collegia* unnecessary. And associations of the Roman type are rare in those regions, though religious unions for the worship of a particular deity, or "actors' unions," like those of the Dionysiac artists, were common enough.

The organization of the *collegia* was modelled on that of the municipalities, and titles of rank which are familiar in the latter appear regularly in the former. The associations, especially the larger ones, invited prominent citizens to become patrons of the guild. The distinction was prized, the patron on his part being expected to give pecuniary support, by gift or bequest, to the *collegium*. His services as an intermediary with the authorities might also be very valuable, if the association became involved in any litigation, or if its rights of property as a corporate body were in danger of being infringed.

From the end of the second century both the upper class in the towns and the *collegia* began to get into difficulties. The holder of a magistracy had always and necessarily been a man of wealth. For, while he received no salary, he was expected to spend considerable sums for the public benefit. As long as the prosperity of the towns remained unimpaired,

---

[1] These were the so-called *centonarii*. The word is derived from *cento*, a felt or patch-work rug; hence the *centonarii* have sometimes been described as makers of these articles. But their chief function, often in conjunction with some others, was what we have stated in the text. The recent discovery of an important inscription of the year 205 from Solva, which refers to certain privileges confirmed to that *collegium*, shows that these men were not felt-rug makers. For the inscription contains a list of 93 members, far too large a number to be engaged in one such trade in a small town. Clearly here the *centonarii* were an association for fire-brigade purposes made up of members of different civil occupations. The inscription was published in the *Jahreshefte* of the Austrian Archæological Institute, xviii (1915), pp. 98 ff.

these financial burdens were readily shouldered by the well-to-do citizens, some of whom expended far more than would normally be expected of them. But once that prosperity declined, what had been a liability, voluntarily and cheerfully undertaken by public-spirited men for the good of the community and for the honor attaching to tenure of public office, became a real imposition, and it became necessary to use compulsion in order to keep the magistracies filled. The Roman government in the third century made the local town councillors (*decuriones*) responsible not only for finding magistrates each year from among themselves, but for collecting the imperial tribute and taxes for the town or district. The *decuriones* were held liable for the total sum assessed, and, if they failed to raise the required amount from among the whole civic body, had to make good the deficiency out of their own pockets. A parallel exploitation by the Roman government was put in force against some of the *collegia*. Those associations whose members exercised a calling connected with the food-supply of the capital — for example, the shippers (*navicularii*) and the millers and bakers (*pistores*) — a calling which they had hitherto plied on the basis of free private contracts with the government, were directly supervised by the imperial authorities, and were required to act for a part of their time in the service of the government. Even the substantial privileges, accorded by the emperors to such guilds as the *collegia* of *navicularii*, cannot have been an adequate compensation for the grave restriction placed upon the free exercise of their trade throughout the year by the obligation of first transporting Rome's grain supply from Alexandria or northern Africa. Toward the end of the third century, as will appear hereafter, a more drastic curtailment of civil liberties began to be enforced.

CHAPTER XXX

LITERATURE, ART, AND RELIGION,
c. 100 B.C.–200 A.D.

> *To them that ask thee, Where hast thou seen the*
> *Gods, or how knowest thou certainly that there be*
> *Gods, that thou are so devout in their worship?*
> *I answer, first of all, that even to the very eye*
> *they are in some manner visible and apparent. Sec-*
> *ondly, neither have I ever seen mine own soul, and*
> *yet I respect and honor it. So then for the Gods,*
> *by the daily experience that I have of their power*
> *and providence towards myself and others, I know*
> *certainly that they are, and I worship them.* —
> M. Aurelius, *Meditations,* xii, 21 (M. Casaubon's
> translation).

THE century from the dictatorship of Sulla to the death of
Augustus witnessed the finest achievement in both prose and
verse of Latin literature. We have seen how all-pervading Hellenic influences had become in the West during the previous
epoch. A knowledge of Greek was in the age of Cicero a necessary accomplishment for every educated man. Indispensable
for those whose business took them to the countries bordering
on the eastern Mediterranean, it was no less essential for the
student of literature, history, rhetoric, or philosophy. Greek
teachers were frequently inmates of wealthy Roman households.
Many Romans finished their education by spending a year or
more in Greek lands attending lectures on philosophy or rhetoric
given by the leading exponents of those subjects. Thus Cicero
was in Athens, Asia Minor, and Rhodes between 78 and 76;
Cæsar as a young man studied rhetoric with Molon of Rhodes,
who also numbered Cicero among his pupils. But, if the great
writers of the period in every branch of literature found inspiration, guidance, and the finest models for their work in Greek
literature, they were no slavish copyists. Combining what they
had learnt with their own Roman traditions and ideals, and

bringing to their task a native vigor that, more often than not, was lacking in Hellenistic literature, they produced masterpieces whose position in the world's literature has remained unchallenged ever since.

In prose the outstanding figure was Cicero. Though some of his works are lost, we still possess more than fifty of his speeches, a vast body of correspondence, and a number of treatises on rhetoric and philosophy. While his orations became the model in that genre of prose for future generations, his treatise *On the Orator*, based as it was partly on a study of earlier writers on the subject, partly on his own unrivalled experience as a speaker, is the profoundest contribution to the theory and practice of education in the Latin language. His letters, which were never intended by him for publication, are not only for that very reason a priceless historical source, but as literature have rarely been equalled and never surpassed. The importance of his philosophical treatises will be explained hereafter.

Among the prose writers contemporary with Cicero we may single out three. C. Sallustius Crispus (86–35 B.C.), after spending a number of years in public life, retired to enjoy an easy existence and devoted himself to historical studies. His two extant books on the war with Jugurtha and on the Catilinarian conspiracy are, in spite of a certain intentional archaism of language, most elegant compositions. Sallust's portrayal of his characters, his skillful narrative, and his incisive epigrams fascinate the reader, who is in danger of forgetting Sallust's limitations as a historical writer. Even in his maturest work, the lost *Histories*, which dealt with the period from 78 to 67 (or 65), and of which only fragments remain, his strong Popular or anti-senatorial bias colored his interpretation.

The *Commentaries* of Julius Cæsar on the Gallic Wars and the First Civil War are models of terse narrative. To the student of ancient warfare they are invaluable; to the general historical inquirer they are an indispensable source of information, though it must never be forgotten that both works aim at justifying the public career of the writer.

M. Terentius Varro (116–28 B.C.) was a man of immense learning and indefatigable industry. A member of the senatorial class who was on Pompey's side in the Spanish War of 49, he

Plate 37

ROMAN TEMPLE AT NEMAUSUS (Nîmes)

ROUND TEMPLE AT TIVOLI

Plate 38

was treated with generosity by Cæsar, but narrowly escaped becoming one of Antony's victims during the proscriptions of 43–42. Most of his life was devoted to study. Of his voluminous writings on the history and antiquities of Rome, and of his *Satires*, which, written partly in verse and partly in prose, treated of literary and philosophical topics as well as of contemporary manners and institutions, fragments alone have survived. The only substantial remains of Varro's literary output are a treatise on farming and a considerable part of a great book on the Latin language. Both are of great value, the latter especially being a storehouse of erudition from which numerous grammarians of a later date drew extensively.

Two poets of the Ciceronian age — both are in the first rank — can be judged from their extant works. Catullus (87–54 B.C.) was the author of some sixty short lyrics, six longer poems in hexameters or elegiacs, and a number of elegiac epigrams. While he was familiar with the poets of the Alexandrian age, his spontaneity and his poetical inspiration raise his finest lyrics — for instance, those to Lesbia, the poem on Sirmio, and that addressed to Septimus — far above any Hellenistic poetry that has survived.

His contemporary, Lucretius (95?–55 B.C.), was a writer of very different stamp. His hexameter poem in six books, *On the Nature of Things*, is an exposition of the philosophy, or, more specifically, the physical theory of Epicurus. Much of the poem is from the nature of the subject dry and unattractive to the general reader. But in his not infrequent digressions and in the introductions to the several books, when he is momentarily freed from the trammels of a philosophic theory, Lucretius rises to poetic heights, especially in his descriptions of natural scenery, which even Vergil has not surpassed.

The new era inaugurated by Augustus, which brought peace to the world, could boast of a galaxy of literary talent. The emperor himself, and more particularly his minister, C. Cilnius Mæcenas, were warm patrons of literature. Among the names that are indissolubly linked with the artistic circle which Mæcenas gathered about him, are some of the greatest in Roman literature. Vergil (70–19 B.C.), the son of a small land-owner, was born near Mantua. As a youth he studied rhetoric and philosophy at Rome. Then during the proscriptions of the Triumvirs he was evicted from his paternal property. In 37, when he was already on friendly terms with Mæcenas, he published his *Eclogues*, ten pastoral poems modelled on the bucolic idylls of Theocritus. These at once established his reputation as a poet and brought him the interest of Octavian. The *Georgics* was a more serious work composed between 37 and 30 — in content a poem in hexameters on husbandry, in spirit a panegyric on country life and the dignity of labor. Then followed the composition of his masterpiece, the *Aeneid*, which was left unrevised by the poet on his death. The *Aeneid* is one of the world's great epics. In the fullest sense it is a national poem, celebrating the history and achievement of Rome and glorifying her lofty mission and that of the Julian house, as the champions of civilization, law, and order.

Horace (65–8 B.C.) was the son of a freedman from Venusia. He, too, suffered in the Second Civil War, but subsequently gained the friendship of Mæcenas and the emperor. In his *Odes* he adapted with infinite skill the lyric metres of Alcæus, Sappho, and other Greek lyric poets, to the statelier genius of the Latin tongue. Their content shows an infinite variety, from the great patriotic odes — for example, the first six of Book III — to charming trifles portraying the simple pleasures of his Sabine farm; from bitter satire on an inconstant mistress to the deeply felt tributes to friends like Mæcenas or Vergil. It is this universal interest in his fellow creatures, coupled with the artistry of his verse and an unsurpassed felicity in language, which has ensured the poet's wide popularity through the ages. His *Satires* and *Epistles*, written in hexameter verse, again deal with many topics. It is in them that he shows himself not alone a skilled depicter of scenes of daily life and a shrewd observer of contemporary manners but a literary critic of no mean order. If Vergil and Horace stand out as the chief poets of the day, there were others, Ovid, Tibullus, Propertius, whose works enjoyed a deserved popularity.

While the Ciceronian Age was the great epoch of Roman oratory, the Augustan could pride itself on its historical writers. The history of Asinius Pollio (76 B.C.–5 A.D.), which covered the tumultuous years from 60 to 42 B.C. is unhappily lost. Pollio appears to have been a man of independent judgment and to have had a high conception of how history should be written. Added to this he was describing an epoch through which he had himself lived and in whose political struggles he had taken some part. But his style was dry and unattractive. Hence a work which had great merits as a historical composition enjoyed little vogue, because its appeal as a work of art was small.

Very different was the vast history composed by Pollio's contemporary, T. Livius (59 B.C.?–17 A.D.). Of its 142 books which traced the history of Rome from its origin down to the latest years of Augustus' principate, only thirty-five have survived.[1] Judged by modern criteria Livy had many defects as a historian. His treatment of chronological and topographical questions is often defective; he is very ignorant of military affairs, herein contrasting strongly with Thucydides and Polybius; and he had little or no experience of public life. Also the manner in which he often used his sources was far from critical. Yet, with all these defects, his work was the greatest historical composition ever produced by a Latin writer. As a work of literary art it is superb; and as a history it is a very great achievement, if we look not so much to details as to the main conception and its bold sweep over the centuries. The reader, seeking to ascertain the progress and causes of Rome's expansion in Italy, or to study the struggle between the Orders and many other broad topics, will find in Livy accounts of these which are true in their main lines even though there may be not a little inaccuracy and some contradictions in details. To have done so much was a great achievement, and Livy's history was, as it were, a national monument that could be set side by side with Vergil's mighty epic.

For nearly half a century after Augustus' death little literature of merit was produced, a circumstance mainly to be explained by the oppressive political conditions at Rome. It is noteworthy how many of the leading writers during the age of Nero and the Flavians were natives of Spain. L. Annæus

---

[1] The surviving portions are books i–x, covering the period from the foundation of Rome to 293 B.C., and books xxi–xlv which deal with the years 218 to 167 B.C.

Seneca (4 B.C.–65 A.D.) achieved success both as a writer of tragedies, in which he was heavily indebted to Euripides, and for his prose writings which are in the main concerned with the ethical teaching of the Stoics. The epic poem on the First Civil War, called *Pharsalia*, by Seneca's nephew Lucan is, in spite of its excessive use of rhetorical devices, a work of passionate vigor and much genuine poetic feeling. Greatly admired in its day, the *Pharsalia* enjoyed wide popularity in the Middle Ages and in more recent times.

In the reign of Domitian we may note two poets: Statius (61–98 A.D.?), who composed two lengthy epics — one of them is a fragment — and a series of shorter poems on various subjects; and Martial (43–100 A.D.), a native of Bilbilis in Spain, whose short epigrams satirized in the most elegant and pointed verse the weaknesses and foibles of his contemporaries. Yet another native of Spain was Quintilian (35–95 A.D.), who, after teaching rhetoric in Rome with outstanding success for a quarter of a century, composed a work on the theory and practice of rhetoric — the *Institutio Oratoria* — which became at once the standard work on the subject. The theory of education which he develops, especially in the opening sections of the book, can still be studied with much profit.

Pliny the Elder (23–79 A.D.), his older contemporary, deserves mention as the compiler of a voluminous work, called the *Natural History*, which is a compendium of the natural sciences and the arts. A man of great erudition, Pliny, unlike his more eminent predecessor, Varro, lacked a critical faculty. Yet his work contains a vast amount of interesting and curious information, which is valuable because the sources he used are mostly lost. Later writers pilfered freely from him; and much of the scientific or pseudo-scientific lore that was purveyed during the earlier Middle Ages in the West, can be traced back ultimately to this writer.

With Tacitus (55–116 A.D.), whose literary activity fell in the reigns of Nerva and Trajan, we come once more to a prose artist of the first rank. Besides his brief treatise on the customs and institutions of the German tribes, and his life of his father-in-law, Julius Agricola, he wrote two large historical works, the one describing the period from 14 to 68 A.D., the other continuing the history of Rome from the death of Nero to 96 A.D. The extant books cover approximately half that period. As a historical author Tacitus has many of the same weaknesses as Livy; thus, for instance his topographical data are too often inaccurate or vague, even where, as for the *Agricola*, he was in the best position to obtain full and precise information. In one important respect he is definitely inferior both to Polybius and to Livy. He, the Roman of senatorial rank, has his interest centred on Italy and, above all, on Rome; he shows but little for the empire as a whole. His two predecessors, though in different ways, conceived the plan of depicting Rome's greatness as a conqueror, and then as a ruler and a civilizing force. If Tacitus' sympathies are with the senatorial order, he has also a passionate desire for freedom of speech. It was the natural reaction from the tyrannical rule of Domitian, which was just over when Tacitus began his historical composition. If his point of view is sometimes narrow and his portraits, while unforgettable for the strength of their lineaments, are drawn with a partisan pen, his moral earnestness, the originality of his thought, and the marvellous felicity and terseness of his diction, which thrills every reader and is the despair of every translator of his pages, have secured for him an abiding place among the greatest writers of prose.

Contemporary with Tacitus were his friend the younger Pliny, whose letters, intended, as they were, for publication, are elegant if somewhat enervated compositions, and the poet Juvenal, who in his *Satires* lashed the vices and follies of his and the preceding ages. Of Suetonius (70–160 A.D.?), who, after a brief spell in the imperial civil service, passed his life in amassing information on the most varied topics, we possess only his biographies of Julius Cæsar and the emperors from Augustus to Domitian. His *Prata*, a diffuse collection of jottings on antiquities and natural science, and a literary history of Rome, have unfortunately not survived.

The Antonine Age, so notable in other ways, displayed a depressing sterility in literary output. An archaistic revival, which sent men back to Cato, Ennius, and other early but less deserving authors, to the neglect of more recent literature, always excepting Vergil and Cicero, permeated the schools and literary coteries alike. But the greatest appeal was made by rhetoric. As a subject it was the one best adapted to fit young men for public life; while the lectures and declamations of the rhetors or Sophists in both Greek-speaking parts of the empire and in the West were an ever popular form of entertainment. Chairs of rhetoric endowed by the imperial treasury or by municipalities were to be found in all the more notable cities. In addition, some of the most esteemed Sophists travelled to different towns to declaim before appreciative audiences. The one Latin writer of note in the second half of the second century, Apuleius, who was born at Madaura in northern Africa, for a time toured in this way giving public recitals. Much of his writing was an attempt to reproduce in Latin the rhetorical displays of the Greek Sophists. At the same time he was endowed with a great deal of poetic talent, and, as has been observed by modern critics, he would, had he lived a century earlier, doubtless have chosen verse as his medium of expression. Of his extant works the *Golden Ass*, or more properly, the *Metamorphoses*, is cast in the form of a fictitious autobiography, and is a strange medley of credible and incredible tales, interspersed with observations on men and manners, and a good deal of mystical pseudo-philosophy.

Of the surviving Greek writers of the first and second centuries A.D. it is sufficient to name Lucian (*c.* 120–200), who, though a native of Samosata in Syria, wrote in the purest Attic Greek, and Plutarch (50–120). Lucian, thoroughly trained in all the devices of the rhetorical schools, in a large variety of short pieces — many of them are in dialogue form — levelled his witty satire not only against the pretensions of sophists and philosophers, but against many aspects of contemporary society. The *Parallel Lives* of Plutarch, portraying the careers of great Greeks and Romans of bygone ages, have an alluring charm which has made them perhaps the most popular work of all ancient literature. The devotee of an eclectic philosophy, in which Platonism predominated, Plutarch also wrote numerous tracts on ethical and philosophico-religious topics.

In the arts, as in literature, Rome's debt to Greece was heavy. But it is as unjust as it is untrue to deny, as has so often been done, all originality to Roman sculpture and architecture. Roman sculpture developed late, and it is only from the time of Augustus that it developed on lines of its own and can satisfactorily be studied. Many of the architectural monuments of the first and second centuries A.D. are adorned with plastic decoration. The great column set up by Trajan in commemoration of his Dacian victories was completely covered with reliefs depicting his two campaigns against the trans-Danubian people. More than fifty years later M. Aurelius erected a similar column, recording pictorially his Marcomannic wars. Though inferior artistically its historical value is hardly less than that of the Trajanic pillar. Perhaps the most striking feature of these reliefs is the skill in portraiture displayed by the artists. Roman legionaries, Dacian soldiers, the warriors of the Marcomanni and Quadi, the barbarians' womenfolk, even the emperors themselves are sculptured with lifelike fidelity. Portraiture in the round, as in relief, is indeed the branch of sculpture in which the Roman artists excelled. The finest examples of portrait busts and statues belong to the Flavian and Hadrianic eras.

In the main the Romans took over their architecture from Greece, while some features developed by them were originally inspired by Etruscan models. But they also elaborated new forms, and showed their skill in the use of the round arch and in concrete construction, which were foreign to Greek architecture. Neither the Doric nor the Ionic orders were much favored by the Romans; all the greater was the popularity of the Corinthian. They perfected the Corinthian capital, using it on shafts that were sometimes left plain, sometimes fluted. Far less pleasing artistically was a Roman invention, the composite capital, which combined the acanthus leaves of the Corinthian with the volutes of the Ionic capital. One of the earliest examples of its use is on the arch of Titus (81 A.D.). Many of the emperors were exceedingly lavish in their expenditure on public buildings, sacred and profane. Besides Augustus we may single out Vespasian, Titus, Trajan, Hadrian, and Septimius Severus.

Roman temples differ in some noteworthy points from the Greek. They were commonly shorter, so that in an extreme example, like the temple of Mars Ultor at Rome, the ground plan was almost square. The ambulatory is often dispensed with wholly or partially, the columns being in part engaged in the wall of the cella. Instead of the three-stepped stereobate favored in Greece, Roman temples have often a much higher substructure. For a typical specimen we may refer to the best preserved of all Roman temples, the so-called Maison Carrée at Nîmes, the ancient Nemausus. It is a hexastyle building raised on a podium twelve feet high, to which a flight of steps gives access at one end. Except for the columns forming the porch the pillars are engaged in the wall of the temple. The building dates from the age of Hadrian (Plate 37). Many of the religious buildings were of immense size, one of the largest being the temple of Venus and Rome. It was begun in 121 A.D. and completed fourteen years later, and had ten columns on the short, and twenty on the long, sides. The Romans also had a fondness for round temples. Of these the most famous is the Pantheon at Rome, which was also built under Hadrian. The span of its great dome is 145½ feet, a central opening giving light to the building. Of small round shrines a good example is the temple of Vesta at Tibur (Tivoli). Eighteen Corinthian columns surrounded the cella, the whole being raised on a podium six feet high (Plate 38).

The first stone theatre in Rome was completed in 52 B.C. Two others were built somewhat later. But the best preserved specimens of Roman theatres are to be found in the provinces, for example at Arausio (Orange) in southern Gaul. More characteristically Roman are the amphitheatres built for the exhibition of those entertainments most popular with all classes of Romans, the gladiatorial fights and wild beast baitings. The finest of all is the Flavian amphitheatre at Rome — the so-called Colosseum. Although much of it has been destroyed by the passage of centuries, it is still the most impressive ruin in Rome. Its shape is oval. On the outside it is divided into four tiers, of which three are pierced by arches and decorated with engaged columns in three orders. On the inside the auditorium was divided into two halves and subdivided into a series of tiers and wedges by vertical and horizontal gangways. There is said to have been a total seating accommodation

Plate 39

THE FLAVIAN AMPHITHEATRE AT ROME

THE TRIUMPHAL ARCH OF CONSTANTINE AT ROME

Plate 40

for between 40,000 and 50,000 persons (Plate 39). Remains of Roman amphitheatres in various states of preservation have been found in all parts of the empire. The latest discovery of such a structure was made at Cærleon in Monmouthshire. Built about 80 A.D., it could, according to the excavator's estimate, seat about 4600 spectators.[1]

Very typical Roman monuments are the triumphal arches, of which many fine specimens have survived in Rome, Italy, and the provinces. Two types were used, one with a single arch, the other with a large central arch flanked by two smaller ones. At Rome the arch of Titus is of the former pattern, those of Septimius Severus and Constantine (Plate 40) of the latter.

Finally, we may note the immense labor and money expended on works of utility, aqueducts, sewers, paved roads, and baths. There were few towns in the empire, as it was in the second century A.D., which were not thoroughly "up-to-date" in all these material adjuncts to civilization.

We have seen how interest in Greek philosophy was stimulated in Rome during the second century B.C., especially by the visit of the three men who at that time presided over three leading schools at Athens (cf. p. 437). Of all the systems the Stoic was the one which won most adherents among educated Romans. For its ethical teaching was peculiarly fitted to appeal to the Roman mind. Interest in philosophy did not wane in the next century. Belief in the Epicurean system, and the conviction that it could free men from the bondage of superstition, impelled Lucretius to compose his great poem. The rigid idealism of the younger Cato and the misguided patriotism of Brutus were both inspired by their Stoic creed. Above all, Cicero devoted much of his leisure to the study of philosophy, and published a number of treatises, designed to present the doctrines of several schools in the Latin language in a more readable form than that presented by the Greek originals. He was himself an eclectic; that is to say, though he claimed primarily to be a disciple of the New Academy, he was not a little influenced by Stoicism and, to a less extent, by the Peripatetics. His treatise on Duty was a free adaptation of a

[1] See *The Year's Work in Classical Studies*, xxi (1928), pp. 88–90.

book by the noted Stoic, Panætius, the some-time friend of the
Scipionic circle. Cicero as a philosopher was not an original
thinker; for that reason his philosophical writings have sometimes been disparaged. Yet the fact remains that, but for them,
we should know far less than we do about post-Aristotelian
philosophy. Also it was Cicero who created a philosophical
terminology in Latin. He was in the best sense of the word a
popularizer.

During the early years of the empire it was adherents of
Stoicism who were most often in the public eye. The followers
of Epicurus took no part in public life and were left to themselves. But, as we saw, much of the opposition to absolute
government from Nero to Domitian came from convinced
Stoics. The Antonine emperors were either more tolerant, like
Hadrian, or else were, like Marcus Aurelius, themselves adherents of this philosophic system. It is noteworthy, too, that
the only philosophical writings of moment were those by Stoics,
the works of Seneca, the ethical precepts of Epictetus (flourished
c. 100–120 A.D.), and the *Meditations* of Marcus Aurelius. A
sect, which after centuries in obscurity, revived under the early
empire was the Cynics. Their asceticism, and the exhorta-
tions to their fellow-men to return to the simple life of nature,
gave them the character of religious missionaries rather than
philosophers. The best of them won the admiration of the
disciples of other schools; for we find Seneca and Pætus Thrasea,
a Stoic of exemplary life, admiring the Cynic Demetrius. The
number of their adherents was not small. Yet there were some
who used philosophy as a cloak for something far less admirable.
Much of the hostile criticism levelled against the Cynics,
and to a less degree against the Stoics, was to the effect that
their outward austerity, befitting a philosopher, was merely a
mask for their disreputable conduct in private life. The
grotesque side of Cynicism, as exemplified in some of its followers, ragged dress, an unkempt and dirty appearance, and
ostentatious poverty, which nevertheless did not shrink from
begging and parasitism, made normal men dislike and scoff
at philosophers as a class, and led them to condemn the genuine
and pure-living disciples and teachers, who were many, in
company with the charlatans, who were relatively few.

But, after all, philosophy or an ethical system appealed only to a minority, the highly-educated class. The mass of the population looked elsewhere for spiritual comfort or emotional satisfaction. The state religion of Rome was by now little more than a formal iteration of ceremonies and sacrifices. All the efforts of Augustus had failed to infuse living interest or appeal into the worship of the old gods. For political ends the emperor no doubt acted wisely; and some of his successors, notably Antoninus and M. Aurelius, followed his example in reviving old rites, keeping the priestly colleges filled, and themselves, with other members of the imperial family, taking their part in the elaborate ceremonials. The nine hundredth anniversary of Rome (147 A.D.) was used by Antoninus to revive belief in the state religion. But he and M. Aurelius failed, even as Augustus had done. Of great importance for political ends was the cult of Rome and Augustus. The personification of cities and deification of rulers was no novelty in the eastern provinces. Instances are not lacking of divine honors being paid to eminent Romans of the Republican era by Greek communities. In Egypt and Syria the absolute authority of the monarch had long been acknowledged by his subjects by according him deification. Augustus fostered this imperial cult, in which his name was associated with the personified mistress of the world, not only in the East but in the West. Only in Italy the emperor declined such honors, which would have been inconsistent with his character as chief citizen and chief magistrate of a constitutionally governed state. Yet, even in Italy, many of the towns chose from among the wealthy freedmen a college of priests, called *Augustales*, whose duty it was to offer periodical sacrifice for Augustus. The deification of the dead was unobjectionable to Roman as to Greek sentiment. Augustus had decreed the deification of Julius Cæsar in 42 B.C.; he himself was similarly honored after his death. In future it was only emperors like Tiberius, Nero, or Domitian, whose rule had been bad, or at least odious to the governing classes, to whom this distinction was denied.

Conformity to the state religion, and especially to the imperial cult, presented no difficulties to the vast majority of Rome's citizens and subjects. The educated class could find spiritual or intellectual satisfaction in the tenets of the philosophers. The rest, in so far as they felt the need of religious experience, turned to one or other of the many cults which at different times had been transplanted from the East to the West. It was these that gave an outlet for the emotions, and by their picturesque and often symbolic ritual, followed after a period of probation by more mystic celebrations, gave men the solace for which they craved. We must confine ourselves to a few that are best known.

The cult of the Mother Goddess of Ida (see p. 435), though long restricted officially to those who were not Roman citizens, had many adherents. By the time of Claudius the last day of the great spring festival (March 22–27) of the goddess had become a general carnival, and probably participation in the rites was by that time open to all in Rome. Many years later, when a conspiracy against Commodus, timed to take place at the time of that same festival, was discovered, Commodus offered thanks to the Great Mother, and the people followed suit for the safety of the emperor. The circumstance shows how universally accepted the cult then was.

The worship of the Egyptian divinities, Isis and Serapis, had found its way to Italy in late Republican times. The earliest trace of it in Rome belongs to the time of Sulla. The attitude of the government was, however, much more hostile to it than to the worship of the Magna Mater. Several efforts were made to suppress the cult of Isis, and shrines of the goddess were destroyed. It was one thing to label it a "base superstition" and quite another to eradicate it. It continued to have its devotees, and Augustus was content to forbid the rites within the city walls. Tiberius proceeded more drastically and once more sought to suppress the cult. The Flavian and Antonine emperors were tolerant. Finally, from the end of the second century, the worship of Isis received the adherence of more than one emperor, for example, of Commodus and Caracallus.

The worship of the Persian Mithras reached the West much later. Although there is no reason to disbelieve Plutarch's statement that Mithraism became known in Italy about 66 B.C., it cannot have made much progress in the West at this time. In some of the eastern provinces it had long had its adherents.

Only toward the end of the first century A.D. did it become more wide-spread in the western portions of the empire. The poet Statius had some definite information about the cult, since he refers to two important features of it, the use of mountain caves by the worshippers and the greatest exploit of Mithras during his earthly career. The cult now spread very rapidly. Mithraic monuments of the second and third centuries abound in the Danubian provinces, the military area along the Rhine, the *Agri Decumates*, and, to a less extent, in Britain. It was the soldiers, legionaries as well as auxiliaries, who were the most numerous adherents of Mithraism. The mystery and austerity of the several grades of initiation through which the worshippers had to pass, the sense of fellowship attained by the initiated through the common bond of these secret trials and ceremonies, the emphasis laid in the Mithraic theology, and especially in the heroic achievements of Mithras himself, on all the manly virtues, endurance, courage, and obedience, and finally the promise of a future life — these were essential features of the Mithraic religion which insured its wide popularity with that very portion of the population, the fighting men, whose importance and influence steadily grew from the time of the Antonines onwards.

We have previously noted that the Roman emperors on the whole treated the Jews within the empire with forbearance, though Vespasian, Titus, and Hadrian suppressed the national aspirations of that people in Judæa with severity. The Christians were at first regarded by the Romans as no more than a Jewish sect of little importance. The Founder of the religion had been crucified in the reign of Tiberius by order of the procurator of Judæa, after the Jewish Sanhedrin had found Him guilty of blasphemy. But the earliest followers of Jesus of Nazareth continued to make converts; then from Judæa Christianity spread to communities in Asia Minor and beyond. By the time of Claudius there was already a small Christian community in Rome; but, as we have said, the Roman authorities do not appear to have regarded it as other than a Jewish sect. From this obscurity the Christians were dragged at the time of the great fire of Rome (64 A.D.). The conflagration is now generally believed to have been due to an accident; but Nero himself was suspected of being responsible for it, acting on a tyrant's mad whim. Popular indignation was diverted from himself to the Christians in Rome, who were unpopular because they kept to themselves and took no part in the ordinary life and pleasures of the Roman populace. Many Christians were done to death on this occasion; yet it was not a religious persecution in the proper sense of the term. The execution of certain Christians in Rome by Domitian in 95 A.D. rests on the slenderest evidence, and may indeed be apocryphal. There is better proof for some persecutions about that time in Asia Minor. For Trajan's principate we possess somewhat fuller information, thanks to the correspondence between Pliny and the emperor regarding the Christian communities of Bithynia. These had all the outward marks of a religious *collegium* to Roman eyes, and, not having the sanction of the government, were illicit and liable to be suppressed. The unpopularity of the Christians with their fellow townsmen, due to the aloofness to which we have already referred, and sometimes also to their proselytizing zeal, as well as to a common belief that their meetings were secret because abominable practices were perpetrated by them, was liable to lead to disturbances of the peace. When Trajan ordered the suppression of associations in Bithynia, the ban naturally fell also on the Christians. Pliny was much puzzled; for, as he tells his master, the crimes attributed to the Christians had no foundation in fact. The worst that could be said about them was that they were distinguished by an incurable "obstinacy." The emperor instructed his legate that, if Christians were brought before him, admitted their faith, and refused to recant, they must be punished. But Pliny is neither to seek out Christians nor to take proceedings against them on the strength of anonymous accusations. The official Roman attitude, then, was not to prosecute this religion for its own sake — indeed few governments have been more tolerant than the Roman toward every variety of creed — but because the adherents of Christianity alone were believed to be politically dangerous, or else the unwitting cause of riots and civil strife. The policy of Hadrian and of Antoninus was similar to that of Trajan. The central government, moreover, began to realize that no danger to the state was to be anticipated from the Christians.

Meantime the number of converts continued to grow. In

the second half of the second century there were many Christian communities in all parts of the Near East. Alexandria, too, was an important centre of the cult. A considerable colony of Christians was settled in southern Gaul; Rome and Italy contained not a few; and even in Spain there was a goodly number before the end of the century. In the reign of M. Aurelius the position of the Christian communities grew less favorable. The chief danger to which they had hitherto been exposed was not official action against them by the emperor but proceedings instituted by provincial governors, consequent on anti-Christian demonstrations in the towns, accompanied by violence and rioting. M. Aurelius himself sanctioned legal proceedings against Christians in several parts of the empire, the worst persecution being at Lugdunum in Gaul. Refusal to recant was punished by death. Yet in justice to the Roman government it must be said that officials often tried to be lenient. Thus, in 180, when trouble of the usual sort had arisen in Africa, some Christians were tried before the Roman proconsul at Carthage. He sought to persuade the defendants to perform the necessary act of sacrifice to the emperor. Then, when they refused, he granted them thirty days in which to reconsider their decision. Only then, when they still adhered to their faith, was their execution carried out.

Persecutions were in abeyance for a while after M. Aurelius' death. But though the government was tolerant, popular agitation still brought trouble on the Christians from time to time. A disaster, like the severe earthquake in Cappadocia (235), by which whole towns were laid in ruins, or plagues, or famines were attributed by popular superstition to the anger of the gods at the "abominable Christian sect," and persecutions resulted. The emperor Decius adopted a new principle, when he instituted a methodical persecution of the Church (250–251) for the purpose of destroying it utterly. Every effort was made, by the use of torture and long imprisonment, to get the ordinary worshippers to recant; while many of the heads of the Church paid for their staunch faith with their lives. Wholesale flights into the remoter parts of the empire gave to the persecution the appearance of momentary success. Actually, though some of its members recanted, and some were martyred, the Church as a whole was strengthened by persecution. The Christian communities had long since ceased to be recruited only from the humblest classes of society. Many men of substance or in prominent stations were now adherents of the faith. A further persecution in 257, ordered by Valerian, was followed by a period of toleration which lasted till the opening years of the fourth century.

During the late second and the whole of the succeeding century, when there was an almost complete absence of pagan literature, Greek and Roman, — what little there was was undistinguished — the only vital literature produced was the work of Christian writers. Christian Apologists, who sought to make clear to a wider public the position and doctrines held by them and their co-religionists, began to appear from the time of Hadrian on. The beautiful dialogue, called *Octavius*, by Minucius Felix, in which the chief charges brought against the Christians are refuted and the superiority of the Christian faith over the pagan cults set forth, was probably composed before the end of M. Aurelius' reign.[1] The third century produced a series of Christian writers of note whose works were composed in Latin. Tertullian, Cyprian, and Arnobius — all of them born in northern Africa — defended the Christian doctrines with impressive eloquence, and the first-named especially did not hesitate to condemn with passionate violence the corrupt manners and pleasures of contemporary paganism.

Till the advent of these Christian Latin authors, Greek had been the language in which all the earlier Christian literature, beginning with the epistles of St. Paul, had been composed. By the third century a considerable body of Christian writings in Greek had accumulated. The summit of achievement was reached by Origen (c. 185–254), one of the greatest minds of all time. He was a profound scholar and a philosophic mind, whose voluminous writings, though later looked at askance because their orthodoxy was suspect, were of immense value to Christian scholars of the next generations. His famous *Hexapla*, which was a great contribution toward securing a sound recension of the Old Testament, and his commentaries on the Scriptures, in

[1] Some critics, however, hold that the dialogue was not written till the beginning of the third century.

which acute criticism based on deep learning is found side by side with bold interpretation, prove him second to none of the Fathers in originality; while in erudition he was surpassed, if at all, by Jerome alone.[1]

[1] The six versions given side by side in the *Hexapla* were the Hebrew text, four different Greek versions, of which the earliest was that which we now refer to as the Septuagint, and the Hebrew version in Greek characters.

CHAPTER XXXI

THE CRISIS OF THE EMPIRE IN THE THIRD CENTURY AND THE RESTORATION OF DIOCLETIAN AND CONSTANTINE

> *Constantine Augustus, having assumed the government, made it his first care to restore the Christians to the exercise of their worship and to their God; and so began his administration by reestablishing the holy religion.* — Lactantius, *On the Death of the Persecutors,* 24.

SEPTIMIUS SEVERUS, who came from an equestrian family and was born in the province of Africa, sought to increase the dignity of himself and his house by assuming the name of Antoninus, borne by the great emperors of the second century. Yet he never rid himself of a frank contempt of Rome and Italy and their inhabitants; nor had he any regard for the constitutional forms which had always been kept alive so far, even when they were most openly flouted. His government was undisguisedly a military autocracy. Being a strong man and an able soldier, he restored order in the empire, and secured the frontiers, for example, in the East and in Britain. His increase, by three new legions, of the military establishment was justified by the perils of the time, but it added a fresh burden to the exchequer. The fact that one of these legions was stationed in Italy near the capital seemed to emphasize the purely military basis of imperial power. The old Prætorian Guard was disbanded by him and replaced by a new guard regiment recruited from the Danubian legions. Severus' expenditure on wars and on the reconstruction of the defenses of the empire (cf. p. 531) was heavy; in addition, he spent lavishly on public buildings in Rome and elsewhere. At the same time it must be admitted that he had acquired enormous wealth by the defeat of his rivals in the East and West and the subsequent confiscation of their properties, as well as from the spoils of the Parthian war.

The senatorial *aerarium* ceased to be of any importance. The emperor, on the other hand, instituted a new financial department, the *res privata* or privy purse of the emperor. Thus there existed side by side two imperial departments of finance; the one receiving the public revenues of the empire, the other, though strictly the private fortune of the emperor, enriched by the confiscations already named, as well as by the proceeds of new acquisitions made by Severus. The *res privata* thus became fully as important as the *fiscus*.

The senate sank into complete insignificance, the more so as important posts, especially the higher military appointments, were increasingly bestowed on equestrians. The Prætorian prefect, who was generally a distinguished jurist, acted in the emperor's absence as president of the imperial council, and became the chief judge of appeals, besides having supreme criminal jurisdiction over the greater part of Italy.

With Severus' death in 211 the weakness of his autocratic régime became at once apparent. He was succeeded by his two sons, Caracallus and Geta; but the latter was soon assassinated at the instance of his brother. Caracallus is chiefly known for the cruelty and infamy of his life, and for the enactment, called, as the name Antoninus was retained by him, the *constitutio Antoniniana*, which made all the provincials, save those who were, like the barbarians in the frontier provinces, dependents not free men, Roman citizens. We cannot assume that he took this step from any considerations of justice or high statesmanship, although it appears in itself to be the logical conclusion to the rapid increase in the number of fully enfranchised persons which characterized the empire of the Antonines. Caracallus' purpose was to increase the revenue, especially by the operation of the tax on inheritances, to which only Roman citizens were liable, and which he augmented from five to ten per cent. The wealth acquired he squandered on his pleasures or used to keep the soldiers in a good humor by lavish gifts.

With his murder in 217 we enter on a period of sixty-seven years, during which twenty-nine emperors filled the throne of the Cæsars. After the brief reigns of Macrinus and the profligate Elagabalus the rule of the young Alexander Severus (222–235 A.D.,) marked a brief reaction from military despotism. The authority of the senate, at least as an advisory council, grew during a few years, a situation recalling the days of the earlier Antoninus. The attacks of northern barbarians were a preliminary warning of what was to occur more intensively in the years to follow. But the most momentous event at this time took place in the empire of Rome's powerful neighbor in the East. The Arsacid house, whose princes had ruled over Parthia for more than four and a half centuries, was overthrown by the Persian Ardashir, the founder of the so-called Sassanian dynasty, which was destined to survive till the days of the Arab conquests in the seventh century. The new ruler followed up his domestic triumph by an assault on the Roman provinces of Mesopotamia, Cappadocia, and Syria. After a short war peace was made in 233 without any territorial loss to Rome. But the sequel showed that this settlement was no more than provisional.

After the death of Alexander Severus there came a period of virtual anarchy in the empire. The soldiers became more and more uncontrollable. Recruited, as the majority of them was, from the frontier provinces, many were wholly uncouth, others had received no more than the thinnest veneer of Roman civilization. Hardy fighters they may have been; but they were unamenable to discipline, and they realized their power in making and unmaking emperors, according as the pay and booty that they received were satisfactory or not. The more settled countries of the empire suffered from them, from the enormous burdens of taxes imposed by successive rulers, and from the attacks of foreign peoples, which now began in earnest, and no longer imperilled merely the boundaries of the empire but its fairest provinces.

The Persian attacks in the East culminated in a great offensive launched in 256. Syria was overrun, Antioch was captured, and a Roman emperor, Valerian, was taken captive. Simultaneously in the northeast the Goths and other tribes got possession of the Black Sea ports, and thence made devastating raids on the Aegean coast-lands and on Greece. Whole provinces ceased to acknowledge the rule of the emperors of Rome. Gaul, together with Britain and Spain, was united into a Gallic empire by Postumus in 258, who assumed the imperial title after he had repulsed a great body of Frankish invaders. He maintained his independent realm for a decade. In the East the ruler of Palmyra, Odænathus, who had grown powerful, allied himself with Rome, and did valuable service in defeating Persian attacks on Mesopotamia.

It was above all the work of two emperors, Claudius (268–270) and Aurelian (270–275) that restored the unity of the empire. The former won a great victory over the Goths at Naissus (Nish in Modern Serbia) in 269. Aurelian with tremendous energy tackled foe after foe. In the North he crushed successively the Alamanni, the Vandals, and the Goths. But he also decided to abandon the province of Dacia, as being too difficult an outpost of empire to defend. The surviving settlers there were transported to the lands lying south of the Danube. The widowed queen of Palmyra, Zenobia, and her son, having proclaimed their independence, Aurelian secured their submission to himself by force of arms. Zenobia lived to grace the conqueror's triumph at Rome. Her city soon rebelled once more, and was then levelled to the ground by the Roman emperor. Finally, a year before his death, Aurelian recovered Spain, Gaul, and Britain.

After several able but short-lived rulers, the imperial power passed to C. Valerius Aurelius Diocletianus in the autumn of 284. He too, like so many of his predecessors, was the choice of the army; but unlike them he ruled for two decades. Then he abdicated, lived in pleasant retirement for several years, and died a natural death. It is due to him, and to his successor Constantine, that the Roman empire in the West, and with it Roman civilization there, survived for nearly two centuries. And when at last it collapsed, the Germanic conquerors had learnt much of Roman government and culture, while their rulers were very far from being the rude and illiterate barbarians that they have sometimes been represented. Moreover, the eastern half of the empire was destined to be the centre of a high civilization and a bulwark against powerful oriental aggressors for more than a thousand years.

Diocletian, then, is not unworthy to be named after Augustus and Hadrian, even if to him the security of the government and the maintenance of a strong army were the two objects to which all else must be sacrificed, even at the price of reducing a majority of his subjects to a condition little better than that of serfs. Realizing that the efficient government of so vast an empire, now constantly threatened by foreign enemies, was beyond the compass of a single ruler, he associated with himself as co-emperor, Maximian. Somewhat later these two *Augusti* nominated two *Caesares* — this was now the usual title of the successor or "heir-apparent" to the throne — who would not only take their share of responsibilities immediately, but would ultimately succeed Diocletian and Maximian. Thus the supreme government was divided between these four rulers; but, as the *Caesares* were subordinate to the *Augusti*, there was no fourfold partition of the empire. The Orient, including Egypt and Thrace, was ruled by Diocletian; Africa, Italy, Rætia, and Spain by Maximian. The Cæsar Galerius was responsible for the Danubian provinces and the Balkan peninsula, apart from Thrace; while the other Cæsar, Constantius, administered Gaul, and Britain after 296.[1]

The provinces were subdivided into smaller administrative units, to which the old name, however, continued to be applied. Of these new *provinciae* there were one hundred and one. Thirteen dioceses, some of which corresponded approximately to the provinces of an earlier day in extent, while others were appreciably larger, formed greater governmental areas, each containing a certain number of provinces.[2] It is worth while noting that this subdivision of the older *provinciae* at the end of the third century was not wholly an innovation. A few such changes had been made from time to time before, notably by Septimius Severus; but they had been confined to single examples at a time, and no reorganization of the entire empire

[1] The island had recently undergone vicissitudes. Raids from Caledonia in 275 and sea-raids by the Saxons in 287 on the southeastern coast threatened the prosperity and safety of the province. The Roman commander Carausius now assumed the title of emperor and governed the island from 288 to 294. Murdered by one of his staff, his authority passed for two years to the assassin Allectus. But in 296 Constantius recovered Britain, and it became again an integral part of the empire.

[2] Cf. Map 15. Some further developments and changes were made in the course of the fourth century, whereby the number of dioceses was increased to fourteen and the total of provinces to 120. Above all were four prefectures, each including several dioceses. Each prefecture was governed by a Prætorian prefect.

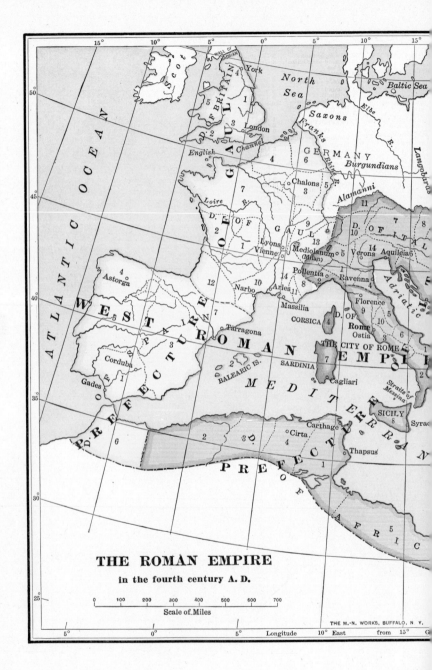

THE ROMAN EMPIRE

in the fourth century A. D.

Scale of Miles

0 100 200 300 400 500 600 700

THE M.-N. WORKS, BUFFALO, N. Y.

Longitude 10° East from 15°

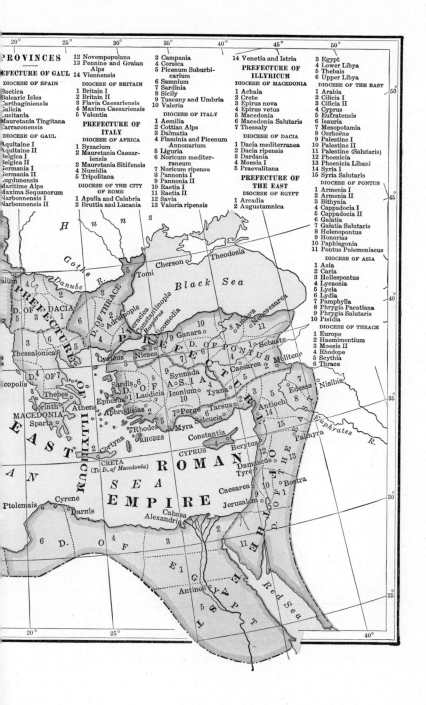

PROVINCES

PREFECTURE OF GAUL

DIOCESE OF SPAIN

Baetica
Balearic Isles
Carthaginiensis
Galicia
Lusitania
Mauretania Tingitana
Tarraconensis

DIOCESE OF GAUL

Aquitaine I
Aquitaine II
Belgica I
Belgica II
Germania I
Germania II
Lugdunensis
Maritime Alps
Maxima Sequanorum
Narbonnensis I
Narbonnensis II

12 Novempopulana
13 Pennine and Graian Alps
14 Viennensis

DIOCESE OF BRITAIN

1 Britain I
2 Britain II
3 Flavia Caesariensis
4 Maxima Caesariensis
5 Valentia

PREFECTURE OF ITALY

DIOCESE OF AFRICA

1 Byzacium
2 Mauretania Caesariensis
3 Mauretania Sitifensis
4 Numidia
5 Tripolitana

DIOCESE OF THE CITY OF ROME

1 Apulia and Calabria
2 Bruttia and Lucania

3 Campania
4 Corsica
5 Picenum Suburbicarium
6 Samnium
7 Sardinia
8 Sicily
9 Tuscany and Umbria
10 Valeria

DIOCESE OF ITALY

1 Aemilia
2 Cottian Alps
3 Dalmatia
4 Flaminia and Picenum Annonarium
5 Liguria
6 Noricum mediterraneum
7 Noricum ripense
8 Pannonia I
9 Pannonia II
10 Raetia I
11 Raetia II
12 Savia
13 Valeria ripensis

14 Venetia and Istria

PREFECTURE OF ILLYRICUM

DIOCESE OF MACEDONIA

1 Achaia
2 Crete
3 Epirus nova
4 Epirus vetus
5 Macedonia
6 Macedonia Salutaris
7 Thessaly

DIOCESE OF DACIA

1 Dacia mediterranea
2 Dacia ripensis
3 Dardania
4 Moesia I
5 Praevalitana

PREFECTURE OF THE EAST

DIOCESE OF EGYPT

1 Arcadia
2 Augustamnica

3 Egypt
4 Lower Libya
5 Thebais
6 Upper Libya

DIOCESE OF THE EAST

1 Arabia
2 Cilicia I
3 Cilicia II
4 Cyprus
5 Eufratensis
6 Isauria
7 Mesopotamia
8 Osrhoëne
9 Palestine I
10 Palestine II
11 Palestine (Salutaris)
12 Phoenicia
13 Phoenicia Libani
14 Syria I
15 Syria Salutaris

DIOCESE OF PONTUS

1 Armenia I
2 Armenia II
3 Bithynia
4 Cappadocia I
5 Cappadocia II
6 Galatia
7 Galatia Salutaris
8 Helenopontus
9 Honorias
10 Paphlagonia
11 Pontus Polemoniacus

DIOCESE OF ASIA

1 Asia
2 Caria
3 Hellespontus
4 Lycaonia
5 Lycia
6 Lydia
7 Pamphylia
8 Phrygia Pacatiana
9 Phrygia Salutaris
10 Pisidia

DIOCESE OF THRACE

1 Europe
2 Haemimontium
3 Moesia II
4 Rhodope
5 Scythia
6 Thrace

had been attempted. In the new scheme the distinction between Italy and the provinces finally disappeared. The inhabitants of Italy had to pay the land-tax, like the provincials, and Italy was included with the other countries in the territorial reorganization. Only the inhabitants of the city of Rome continued to enjoy a more privileged position. On the other hand, the administrative capitals of the two *Augusti* and the two *Caesares* were Nicomedia, Sirmium, Milan, and Trèves or York; so that Rome ceased to be the centre of government of all, or even a part of, the empire. It was Diocletian's intention to keep the civil government absolutely distinct from the military. In practice this rigid separation was not invariably carried through. But, in the main, the distinction between the two spheres of activity was kept by him and by his successors.

The military reforms introduced at the end of the third century were even more radical than the alterations in the administrative system. Numerically the army was increased; its inner organization and the distribution of its parts were changed fundamentally. The troops stationed along the frontiers (called now *limitanei* or *riparii*) were reduced in number, and performed only defensive duties. Large reserve armies were kept at a number of strategically important points in the interior of the empire, whence they could be most expeditiously and effectively moved to the nearest war zones in case of hostile attack, or mobilized when the emperor embarked himself on an offensive campaign. These troops were known as *comitatenses*. Although the name "legion" survived, it was now applied to a much smaller unit than before. Very notable was the great increase in the mounted branch of the service, so that the total cavalry strength was considerably in excess of what had been available during the early empire. To the able and devoted soldier a career of steady advancement was opened up. From service with the *comitatenses* — occasionally even a soldier of the frontier force might advance to responsible positions — he might win promotion to the special body of palace troops (*palatini*), who formed the emperor's body-guard. Later he might attain to the status of an officer commanding a troop; and then, having, as we should say, reached commissioned rank, he might hope that even the highest military appointments would ultimately come within his grasp. In practice much depended on the favor of his superiors; for, without it, he had little chance of being put in charge of a large detachment, still less of becoming a *dux*, as the commander of an army corps now came to be called.

Thus two elaborate systems, a military and an administrative, were developed. Each required for its efficient working an enormous *personnel;* and the members of the military and the civil services formed a privileged class, or, as it might be called, a new aristocracy. At the court itself Diocletian introduced an intricate ceremonial and strict etiquette — his successors developed this still further — which were frankly modelled on the procedure favored at oriental courts. The emperor who is described as "most sacred lord" (*dominus sacratissimus*), whose subjects are "slaves" (*servi*), whose rescripts are signed by the sacred hand (*sacra manu*), and who is referred to as "thy divinity" (*numen tuum*), has the closest affinity with the Sassanian prince on the Persian throne; he bears no resemblance at all to the Princeps or first citizen of the empire of the preceding centuries. In keeping with this new absolute monarchy was the creation of numerous titles of nobility. Here again the successors of Diocletian elaborated a practice which he kept within moderate limits.

The finances of the state and the economic condition of the empire, when Diocletian took over the supreme control, were pitiful. The decline had been rapid ever since the time of Septimius Severus. The appalling extravagances of Caracallus, and still more of Elagabalus, had brought Rome to the verge of bankruptcy. By the strictest economy, personal and public, Alexander Severus and his advisers were able to effect a temporary improvement. But, after his death, the downward descent was more rapid than before. As a modern writer has remarked, "where a modern state has recourse to borrowing, the ancient as a last resort depreciated the currency." Successive emperors made abundant use of this expedient, the worst period of financial chaos being reached under Gallienus (253–268). His "silver" issues were base metal covered with the thinnest wash of silver. It is difficult to understand how commercial intercourse, except of the simplest and most restricted kind, was possible when the exchange medium was constantly sinking. To increase the hardship for the citizens of the empire, the treasury, while it issued base coin and paid in it, refused to accept it in payment from the provincials, who were required to render their tribute in kind or else in precious metal. Of the predecessors of Diocletian only one, Aurelian, appears to have made a serious effort at improvement, by calling in the worthless coins in circulation and issuing a somewhat better silver currency.

Diocletian made various experiments with the monetary units; but, besides causing a good deal of distress, his changes did not secure stability. Thus it was natural that it should become the general custom to pay salaries to state officials, and wages to soldiers, in rations or kind. When, later on, Constantine introduced a gold standard and succeeded in putting the currency on a sound basis, this more convenient form of reckoning payments was widely readopted.[1]

When Diocletian thoroughly revised the system of taxation in the Roman world, he carried out a reform that was indeed enduring, but in the long run caused the pauperization of the empire. The heaviest burden was the land-tax, which, in the shape of produce, was levied on the basis of an assessment in which land, head of cattle, and human labor were ingeniously equated. Reassessments were at first made quinquennially, later, only every fifteen years. Besides this a tax was imposed on all trades, while special taxes were levied from the senatorial class and from the municipal *decuriones*. Even this did not exhaust the liabilities placed on the subjects of the emperor. The quartering of troops and officials in towns at the expense of the inhabitants, and the upkeep of the imperial post, were most irksome impositions.[2]

---

[1] The gold *solidus* of Constantine was worth about three dollars (twelve shillings).

[2] The imperial post was first instituted by Augustus. It consisted in keeping available vehicles or horses at stages along the great high roads, so that the emperor and his messengers could proceed at the most expeditious rate from the capital to the provinces. The cost of upkeep had always devolved on the provincials, and might at any time become a burden if excessive use were made of the institution. Hadrian and Antoninus both gave some alleviation, by partly defraying the cost of maintenance out of the *fiscus*. Under the later empire, when the facilities of

In 301 Diocletian issued an edict to regulate prices and wages in the empire, or at least in the eastern half of it. It begins with a long preamble, the gist of which is as follows: The emperors aver that they can no longer contemplate with indifference the shameless avarice which is responsible for excessively high prices. Neither plentiful imports nor good harvests avail to lower prices, because the dealers regard such plenty as detrimental to their own speculations. This high cost is especially bad in the districts where troops are stationed; the price of commodities has risen fourfold or even eightfold, so that a soldier has to spend all he has merely to buy the necessaries of life. The emperors then say that all they have decided to do is to fix the maximum price, beyond which it shall not be legal to charge. The severest penalties attach to transgressions. Finally there is a general exhortation to observe the ordinance, and so help to better the condition of the empire. There then follows a long list of the maximum prices to be charged for various raw materials and manufactured articles; also the maximum wages to be paid to various classes of workers, including what we should term professional men, are fixed. Although considerable portions of the edict are lost, what remains throws a valuable light on the economic condition and resources of the empire at the opening of the fourth century. We see the great variety in food products, and an even greater diversity in manufactured articles. But for the purpose for which it was intended the edict was a complete fiasco, as it deserved to be. It is indeed astonishing that so able an administrator should have promulgated so unpractical an order. Its crudities — we might well say, absurdities — are many. The wages of professional teachers are so fixed that an obscure beginner receives as much as what we should now call a professor with an international reputation. No difference in price is made whether goods are delivered wholesale or disposed of retail in small quantities. Moreover, there is no allowance for a natural fluctuation in prices, dependent on a variety of circumstances; the prices are fixed to remain in perpetuity. Actually the edict lapsed on the retirement of Diocletian. Yet in the

the imperial post were conceded to large numbers of imperial officials, the burden became intolerable.

four years that it remained in force it caused much misery. Riots occurred in a number of places, which were suppressed with great severity. Real or supposed transgressors were savagely punished. Thus, in addition to making the economic situation worse than before, it was the means of destroying many lives.

Diocletian and Maximian retired into private life in 306. The former's work seemed to crumble to pieces at once; for the two *Caesares*, Galerius and Constantius, now become emperors, and the new *Caesares*, so far from carrying on the government of the empire in amity, fell to warring between themselves. Fresh partitions of the empire were made, only to be rendered abortive by renewed hostilities. By the end of 313 the empire was divided between Constantine, the son of Constantius, and Licinius. Eleven years later, in 324, Constantine, at the end of two years of fighting with Licinius, whom he twice decisively defeated, became sole emperor and remained so until his death in 337.

In the organization and management of the army, and in his civil administration, Constantine followed the system inaugurated by Diocletian, and further developed it. So, too, the new methods of taxation remained in force. But we must also notice certain legislative acts which curtailed the liberties of a large section of the population.

Reference was made in an earlier chapter to the barbarians who were settled by M. Aurelius in some of Rome's frontier provinces. These settlers, known as *inquilini*, apart from their obligation to military service, differed in one important respect from the tenant peasantry (*coloni*). For, while the latter had a terminable contract with the owner of the land or else with a chief tenant, the *inquilini* were not permitted to leave the soil which they cultivated; in other words, they were in a partial state of serfdom. The process by which these originally distinct types of cultivator gradually approximated, so that in the end there was no difference between them save in name, is far from clear, and in any case lies outside the scope of this work. The Diocletianic system of taxation at all events accelerated the process considerably. For the purposes of the assessment it was immaterial what the tiller's legal status might be. For the unit of calculation was a day's work of a male agricultural worker; so that it did not matter whether he was a free *colonus*, a slave *colonus,* or an *inquilinus.* Hence for the purposes of taxation we may say that the worker on the land merely represented one part of the estate. In 332 Constantine issued an edict that no *colonus* should have the right to leave his tenancy, and severe penalties attached to attempted desertion, and also to harboring any runaway peasant. Many additional enactments respecting the peasantry were passed by later emperors during the fourth century, which tightened the bonds by which the farming population was tied to the soil more closely, and increased the penalties for breaking the law. It is therefore hardly permissible to describe all the agricultural workers of the empire as serfs until the end of the fourth or the beginning of the fifth century. But the edict of Constantine was the first measure to give legal authority to conditions which had existed here and there in practice years before.[1] Through a variety of causes a sub-tenant must often have become bound to the estate on which he was working, whether through debt or by hereditary association — the son following the father's occupation on the land through several generations — or through some other cause. Had Constantine's enactment introduced a wholly new and unfamiliar principle, it is difficult to believe that such an innovation would have been accepted without wide-spread riots and disturbances, even by a people as cowed and war-weary as the inhabitants of the Roman empire at the opening of the fourth century.

But it was not only the agriculturists to whom the principle of compulsion was applied. It was natural that the *collegia* connected with the food-supply — the *navicularii* and *pistores* — should receive the particular attention of the emperor. It was also natural that in these occupations and in the majority of trades the son should generally follow his father's calling. For, after all, the son inherited the ships or the workshop of his father — not to speak of that more intangible, though none the less real, something, inherited ability for an art or craft; and the continuance of the father's trade was therefore both the most obvious and likely to be the most profitable course.

[1] In some parts of the empire, Egypt, northern Africa, and parts of Asia, many agricultural workers were in fact bound to the soil in the third century.

Diocletian had required the shippers by law to transport the grain-supply free to the capital, and had made their whole possessions surety for this. Once that had been done they were, of course, free to carry on private trade. But, already in 315, we find both the *navicularii* and the *pistores* referred to as hereditary corporations. A principle thus established by a despotic government was not likely to remain restricted to one or two groups of citizens. We find the "hereditary" principle applied to the great middle class, the *decuriones* of the towns, who were held responsible for the collection of tribute and taxes, and who were now bound to remain in their order. This arbitrary course was first instituted by law by two edicts of Constantine, promulgated in 325 and 326 respectively. We cannot here follow the further process of this compulsory principle. Suffice it to say that gradually during the fourth century every trade and calling that was of any importance to the government was treated in the same way. A man was bound to his calling and could not marry outside his guild. And, both in the fourth and in the fifth centuries, numerous ordinances were passed to prevent desertions and the consequent diminution of this or that guild or class. The fact that so much legislation was needed is sufficient proof that, in spite of the harshest penalties, many attempts were made to escape from the effects of this iron rule.

Two events of Constantine's reign stand out above all others: the placing of Christianity on the same footing with other religions in the empire, and the foundation of a new capital. During the last years of Diocletian's rule, and for several years to follow, there had been carried out the most severe persecution of the Christians that had yet occurred. At first Christians were excluded from the privileges of citizenship; then church property was destroyed or confiscated, and many heads of the Church were arrested. These measures were succeeded by more active persecution of individuals. In the regions administered by Galerius and Maximian a reign of terror was instituted; wholesale imprisonments were made; torture and death awaited all those who did not disown their religion by making sacrifice to the emperor and the pagan deities. In Gaul, on the other hand, where Constantius was in control, although there was some destruction of property, there was not the same amount of organized persecution. The proceedings against the Christians lasted sporadically in certain parts of the empire until 313. But from that date Christianity was officially recognized as one of the lawful cults, and the principle of religious toleration was vindicated by Constantine in the edict promulgated at Milan in February, 313. Licinius some months later followed suit in the eastern half of the empire; but he himself remained a pagan to the end.

The attitude of Constantine to the Christian religion, and his motives — to cite freely from the edict — "in assuring both to Christians and to all the free exercise of the religion of their choice," have been widely disputed. It has been held that his purpose was political. But, as the total number of Christians at this date amounted to less than half the entire population of the empire, while in Constantine's half of it the proportion of Christians to pagans was a good deal less, this thesis cannot satisfactorily be maintained. It is probable that the ancient tradition, which made him the subject of a sudden conversion, is in the main correct, even if the narrative of that occurrence has been overlaid with many miraculous details. Already by 312 he had introduced as his military standard the *labarum*, the symbol being a combination of the cross and the two initial letters of the name, *Christos*. When in that same year a statue was set up in his honor by the Roman senate, he caused a cross to be placed in its hand. Before long the cross appears on some of the imperial coins, though not yet in a prominent place. After 324 the *labarum* became a regular type on all the Constantinian issues. As his reign progressed his zeal was intensified and became more open. He even intervened in disputes within the Church; then in 325 he summoned to Nicæa the famous council of bishops at which were defined the articles of orthodox faith, and the tenets of Arius and his followers were condemned as heretical. Four years earlier the emperor had conferred a great boon on the Christian communities when he permitted legacies to be left to the Church. Even more momentous was his action in granting to bishops judicial authority to give decisions in civil actions and disputes. It is true that Constantine himself did not receive baptism until he was on his deathbed. But in this he was only acting in accordance with a common practice of the time, explained by the belief that baptism washed away all sins committed during a man's life-time up to the moment when he received the sacrament.

The most important aspect of Constantine's policy towards the Church was that he assigned to her a recognized place within the elaborate organization of the state. Many years were still to elapse before all pagan cults were suppressed and Christianity had become the universal religion of the empire. But, save during the brief reign of Julian (360-363), Christianity was the official faith of the emperors. The ultimate development in the two halves of the empire was different. In the East the emperors remained the effective heads not only of the temporal state but of the Church. In the West the Church under the bishop of Rome, her organization modelled on that of the Roman state, was not only the spiritual mistress of the world, but, exerting an immense political power, remained for centuries the only stable temporal institution, the while the western empire passed away, and the kingdoms carved out of its wide territories by the northern invaders rose and fell.

In considering the establishment of a new capital in the eastern portion of the empire, called after its founder, Constantinople, we must distinguish between the purpose and significance of the event at the time, and its importance when viewed in historical perspective. Begun before the end of 324, the building of the new city on the site of ancient Byzantium was sufficiently far advanced on May 11, 330 for the emperor to carry out its solemn dedication. Let it be granted that the site was, as indeed it had always been, singularly advantageous for trade, and that, as it was situated on the European-Asiatic frontier, its political was commensurate with its economic value. It was nevertheless the fact that, when Constantinople was built, the dangers threatening the empire were in the West, not in the East — on the middle Danube and on the Rhine, not on the Parthian front or even from the direction of Scythia — ; nor could the new capital hope to rival Alexandria commercially. It is also true that the new foundation proved to be of world-historic importance, and became, after the disruption of the Roman empire, the centre of that eastern, or Byzantine, empire which, enduring many assaults, only succumbed finally to the Turkish aggressor in the fifteenth century of our era (1453). But it is obviously idle to believe that Constantine acted as he did because he envisaged even dimly the future greatness of the metropolis named after him. To attribute to him such prescience would imply a miracle greater than even his most credulous contemporaries would have believed. Thus we are driven to seek a less weighty reason for his act. The ecclesiastical historian Eusebius, in narrating the foundation of Constantinople, represents the emperor's action as a thank-offering to God for the striking victory over his rival Licinius. We may well believe that this was one motive which impelled Constantine. Coupled with it was the desire to have a new Christian capital in place of old Rome, whose leading families, and all of whose traditions, were still predominantly pagan. Thus the construction of Constantinople would be the outward and visible sign of the union of Church and State with which Constantine's name must ever be associated.

The new capital was modelled on Rome. Its government was similarly organized; its inhabitants were privileged like those of Rome. That they might receive free grain, the produce of Egypt was hereafter earmarked for the use of Constantinople, while Rome had to depend on the harvests of northern Africa. Like the Romans the citizens of Constantinople received not only free bread, but the free entertainment of the beast and circus shows.

During the age of Diocletian and Constantine there continued to be a great output in plastic works of art, though their artistic merits may be much less than those of an earlier epoch, and especially in architecture. Both emperors built extensively, as witness the sumptuous baths at Rome which bore Diocletian's name, the great palace erected by the same ruler at Salona (Spalato) in Dalmatia, the great triumphal arch of Constantine in Rome (Plate 40), some of whose sculptural adornment was taken from an earlier monument of Trajanic date, and, finally, the building of the new capital on the Bosphorus. But in literature the only name of importance is that of the Christian writer Lactantius (c. 260–340) whose *Divine Institutions* is a monument of pure latinity, modelled on Cicero, as well as a theological work of enduring value.

EPILOGUE

THERE is no sharp division between the Ancient World and the Middle Ages, and the basic fact of historical continuity makes any separation of consecutive epochs, whatever their dissimilarities, false, or at least no more than a convention and a convenience. Yet much reason exists for concluding a survey of Ancient History with the death of Constantine, surnamed the Great. His work, and that of Diocletian, reëstablished the Roman empire. But it is a changed world in which the striking features, autocracy, the sharp cleavage between the aristocracy, whether civil or military, and the producing classes, predial serfdom, retrogression to a natural economy, triumphant Christianity, mark the beginning of a new era and have little in common with the society and institutions of the past. So, too, the prolonged struggles in the western empire against the ever-growing number of its northern enemies, which ended in its dismemberment and the rise of the barbarian kingdoms of Vandal, Goth, Frank, and Lombard, form the prelude to the study of the Middle Ages rather than an epilogue to the study of the Ancient World.

One great contribution the declining empire had still to make, a contribution of paramount importance to western civilization, which has lasted to the present day, the codification of Roman law. In the first half of the fifth century the great body of edicts known as the Theodosian Code, and covering the period from Constantine to Theodosius II, was compiled by order of the last named emperor. A century later Justinian caused a more comprehensive compilation to be made. The *Corpus iuris civilis*, collected by Trebonian and other jurists, comprised the Code, in which were contained all the imperial edicts and constitutions; the *Digest*, a huge collection of abstracts from the works of earlier jurists, designed to elucidate and amplify the Code; and the *Institutes*, which was a handbook of Roman law derived largely from the earlier work of Gaius (end of the second century A.D.).

In the realm of thought and letters the pagan world could

still produce some works of marked distinction, if not of genius, — the history of Ammianus Marcellinus, the writings of the. Sophist Libanius, and of the emperor Julian, the philosophy of the Neo-Platonists, of whom the earliest and greatest, Plotinus, belongs to the preceding era, and the poetry of Ausonius and Claudian. Nevertheless, the intellectual life of the fourth and fifth centuries, as mirrored in the schools of Constantinople, Athens, Antioch, Carthage, or Burdigala, in spite of its superficial brilliance was a sterile, indeed a dying thing. For its participants were, to borrow a happy phrase from Matthew Arnold, in "a state of moral indifferency without intellectual ardor." The great names in these centuries are those of Christian scholars, thinkers, and preachers — Ambrose, Jerome, Augustine, in the West, Athanasius, Eusebius, Basil, the two Gregories, of Nazianzus and Nyssa, John Chrysostom, in the East. Pagan culture supplied them with the instruments of their calling — the training in literary form, rhetorical art, and dialectic method — ; but their inspiration, and the vigor and freshness of their writings, were the outcome not of a decaying civilization but of a new faith.

In conclusion, if the question be asked why the empire declined and finally collapsed, the reply must be that no single cause can account for so thorough an overthrow. Nothing but the synchronism of many adverse factors can explain the downfall of a structure so mighty and founded on such ancient and enduring foundations. The constantly increasing pressure of Rome's enemies, the economic régime outlined in the preceding chapter, which pauperized the rural and the urban populations alike for the sake of an unproductive bureaucracy and army, the steady decline of the old stock within the empire and its replacement by barbarian blood, the relaxation of moral fibre and pessimistic outlook engendered by the political and economic conditions, Christianity, which could only build anew after the old pagan traditions and institutions had been undermined and then destroyed — these were among the potent causes for the disruption of an empire that had endured for a span of time vastly greater than any empire before or since — six centuries.

SELECT BIBLIOGRAPHY

THE following bibliography makes no pretense to offer more than a brief selection of works dealing with ancient history and civilization, or with special aspects thereof. For full bibliographical information the reader is referred to the *Cambridge Ancient History*. Seven volumes of this have appeared to date, the latest being devoted to the Hellenistic Age and to the history of Rome from the beginning down to 218 B.C. In the *Social and Economic History of the Roman Empire* by M. Rostovtzeff will be found exhaustive references to the vast literature on imperial Rome.

For new publications appearing year by year the student should consult the *Annual Bulletin of Historical Literature* of the English Historical Association, in which the first section is assigned to Ancient History, and *The Year's Work in Classical Studies*, published by the Classical Association, which regularly contains chapters on Greek and Roman history. In the *Journal of Egyptian Archaeology* bibliographical articles by various specialists are issued periodically, recording new works on Egypt from the earliest times down to the beginning of the Byzantine period.

A. GENERAL HISTORIES AND WORKS OF REFERENCE

Cambridge Ancient History. *In progress.* Vols. 1 to 7 (Cambridge University Press, 1923–28) and Vols. 1 and 2 of Plates have appeared to date.

Cavaignac, E. *Histoire de l'Antiquité.* Vols. 1 to 3 (Paris: de Boccard, 1913–20).

Daremberg, C. V. and Saglio, E. *Dictionnaire des antiquités grecques et romaines.* (Paris: Hachette, 1877–1919.)

Gercke, A. und Norden, E. *Einleitung in die Altertumswissenschaft.* Ed. 2, 1914; Ed. 3, 1921 — . (Leipzig: Teubner.)

Kubitschek, J. W. *Grundriss der antiken Zeitrechnung.* (Munich: Beck, 1928.)

Lübker, F. H. C. *Reallexikon des klassischen Altertums.* Ed. 8, 1914. (Leipzig: Teubner).

Meyer, E. *Geschichte des Altertums.* Vols. 1 to 5. Vol. 1, two parts, in the third edition (1910–13), together with *Nachtrag: die ältere Chronologie Babyloniens, Assyriens und Aegyptens* (1925). Vol. 2, part 1 (1928). Vols. 3 to 5 (1901–02). (Stuttgart: Cotta.)

Pauly-Wissowa-Kroll. *Realenzyklopädie des klassischen Altertums.* *In progress.* So far there has appeared A to Mantike; RA to Sparsus; also four *Supplementbände* (1903–24). This is an indispensable work of reference for any detailed study of classical antiquity. (Stuttgart: Metzler.)

Rostovtzeff, M. *History of the Ancient World.* Vols. 1 and 2 (Oxford University Press, 1926–27). Vol. 1 is devoted to the Orient and Greece, Vol. 2 to Rome.

B. Chapter I

Burkitt, M. C. *Prehistory.* (Cambridge University Press, 1921.)

Childe, V. G. *The Aryans.* (London: Kegan, Paul; New York: Knopf, 1926.)

Childe, V. G. *The Dawn of European Civilization.* (London: Kegan, Paul; New York: Knopf, 1925.)

Déchelette, J. *Manuel d'archéologie préhistorique* 1. (Paris: Picard, 1908.)

Ebert, M. *Reallexikon der Vorgeschichte. In progress.* (Berlin: de Gruyter.) This valuable dictionary is nearing completion. To date Vols. 1 to 12 (A to Südliches Afrika) have appeared; also 13, part 1 (Südostbaltikum to Südrussland) and 14, parts 1 to 4 (Uckermark to Wirtschaft).

Forrer, R. *Reallexikon.* (Stuttgart: Spemann, 1907.)

Hoernes, M. *Natur und Urgeschichte des Menschen.* Vols. 1 and 2 (Vienna: Hartleben, 1909).

Hoernes, M. and Menghin, O. *Urgeschichte der bildenden Kunst.* (Vienna: Schroll, 1925.)

Keith, A. *The Antiquity of Man.* Ed. 2, 1925 (Philadelphia: Lippincott).

Macalister, R. A. S. *Textbook of European Archaeology:* Vol. 1. *The Palaeolithic Period.* (Cambridge University Press, 1921.)

MacCurdy, G. G. *Human Origins.* Vols. 1 and 2 (New York: Appleton, 1924).

Moret, A. *From Tribe to Empire.* (London: Kegan, Paul; New York: Knopf, 1926.)

Myres, J. L. *The Dawn of History.* (London: Williams and Norgate; New York: Holt, 1911 and reprints.)

Osborn, H. F. *Men of the Old Stone Age.* (New York: Scribners, 1916.)

C. Chapters II–V

Breasted, J. H. *Ancient Records of Egypt.* Vols. 1 to 5 (University of Chicago Press, 1906–07).

Breasted, J. H. *History of Egypt.* Ed. 2, 1909 (New York: Scribners).

Cowley, A. *The Hittites.* (Oxford University Press, 1926.)

Delaporte, L. *La Mésopotamie; les civilisations babylonienne et assyrienne.* (Paris: Renaissance du livre, 1923.)

Erman, A. *Life in Ancient Egypt.* (Macmillan, 1894). This is an English translation of the first German edition of this work. A new and greatly revised edition of the German original appeared in 1925, entitled *Aegypten.* (Tübingen: Mohr.)

Garstang, J. *The Land of the Hittites.* Ed. 2, 1929 (London: Constable.)

Hall, H. R. *The Ancient History of the Near East.* Ed. 6, 1926 (London: Methuen).

Harper, R. F. *Assyrian and Babylonian Literature.* (New York: Appleton, 1901.)

Harper, R. F. *The Code of Hammurabi.* (University of Chicago Press, 1904.)

Hogarth, D. G. *The Ancient East.* (London: Williams and Norgate; New York: Holt, 1914.)

Hogarth, D. G. *Kings of the Hittites.* (Oxford University Press, 1926.)

Jastrow, M. *The Civilization of Babylonia and Assyria.* (Philadelphia: Lippincott, 1915.)

King, L. W. *History of Babylonia.* (London: Chatto and Windus, 1919.)

King, L. W. *History of Sumer and Akkad.* (London: Chatto and Windus, 1923.)

Maspero, G. *The Dawn of Civilization: Egypt and Chaldæa.* (London: S. P. C. K., 1910.)

Meissner, B. *Babylonien und Assyrien.* Vols. 1 and 2 (Heidelberg: Winter, 1920–25). This is now the best and most detailed treatment of the ancient cultures of Mesopotamia.

Meyer, E. *Reich und Kultur der Chethiter.* (Berlin: Curtius, 1914.)

Petrie, W. M. F. *Arts and Crafts in Ancient Egypt.* (London: P. Davies, 1923.)

Petrie, W. M. F. *Social Life in Ancient Egypt.* (London: Constable, 1923.)

Rogers, R. W. *History of Babylonia and Assyria.* (New York: Abingdon Press, 1915.)

Smith, S. *The Early History of Assyria to 1000 B.C.* (London: Chatto and Windus, 1928.)

Wiedemann, A. *Das alte Aegypten.* (Heidelberg: Winter, 1920.)

Wreszinski, W. *Atlas zur altaegyptischen Kulturgeschichte. In progress.* (Leipzig: Hinrichs.)

D. Chapter VI

Atkinson, T. D. and others. *Excavations at Phylakopi in Melos.* (London and New York: Macmillan, 1904.)

Chadwick, H. M. *The Heroic Age.* (Cambridge University Press, 1912.)

Dörpfeld, W. *Troja und Ilion.* Vols. 1 and 2 (Athens: Beck und Barth, 1902).

Dussaud, R. *Les Civilisations préhelléniques.* Ed. 2, 1914 (Paris: Geuthner).

Evans, A. J. *The Palace of Minos. In progress.* Vol. 1, 1921; Vol. 2, parts 1 and 2, 1928. (London and New York: Macmillan.)

Fimmen, D. *Die Kretisch-mykenische Kultur.* Ed. 2, 1921 (Leipzig: Teubner).

Glotz, G. *The Aegean Civilization.* (London: Kegan, Paul; New York: Knopf, 1927.) The French original of this book appeared in 1923.

Hall, H. R. *The Civilization of Greece in the Bronze Age.* (London: Methuen, 1928.)

Leaf, W. *Troy.* (London and New York: Macmillan, 1912.)

Leaf, W. *Homer and History.* (London and New York: Macmillan, 1915.)

Maraghiannis, G. and others. *Antiquités crétoises. In progress.* (Candia: Maraghiannis.)

Murray, G. G. *The Rise of the Greek Epic.* Ed. 3, 1924 (Oxford University Press).

Nilsson, M. P. *The Minoan-Mycenean Religion and its Survival in Greek Religion.* (Oxford University Press, 1927.)

Ridgeway, W. *The Early Age of Greece.* (Cambridge University Press, 1901.)

Rose, H. J. *Primitive Culture in Greece.* (London: Methuen, 1925.)

Seymour, T. D. *Life in the Homeric Age.* (London and New York: Macmillan, 1907.)

Wace, A. J. B. and Thompson, M. *Prehistoric Thessaly.* (Cambridge University Press, 1912.)

Xanthoudides, S. A. *The Vaulted Tombs of Mesará.* Translated by J. P. Droop. (London: Hodder and Stoughton, 1924.)

Important articles will also be found in the cyclopædias of Pauly-Wissowa-Kroll and of Ebert, cited under A and B above.

E. CHAPTERS VII, VIII, AND XII

Baynes, N. H. *Israel amongst the Nations.* (London: Student Christian Movement, 1927.)   An admirable survey with valuable bibliographical annotations.

Browne, E. G. *Literary History of Persia,* Vol. 1 (London: Fisher, Unwin, 1906).

Driver, S. R. *An Introduction to the Literature of the Old Testament.* Ed. 9, 1913 (Edinburgh: Clark).

Huart, C. *La Perse antique.* (Paris: Renaissance du livre, 1925.)

Kittel, E. *Geschichte des Volkes Israel,* Vol. 1 Ed. 5, 1923; Vol. 2 Ed. 4, 1922 (Gotha: Perthes).

Macalister, R. A. S. *The Philistines.* (Oxford University Press, 1914.)

Meyer, E. *Die Israeliten und ihre Nachbarstämme.* (Halle: Niemeyer, 1906.)

Olmstead, A. T. *History of Assyria.* (New York: Scribners, 1923.)

Peake, A. S. *The Bible.* (London: Hodder and Stoughton, 1914.)

Peake, A. S. (editor). *The People and the Book.* (Oxford University Press, 1925.)   A series of essays on the Old Testament by various scholars.

Prasek, J. V. *Geschichte der Meder und Perser.* Vols. 1 and 2 (Gotha: Perthes, 1906–09).

Sellin, E. *Geschichte des Israelitisch-jüdischen Volkes,* Vol. 1 (Leipzig: Quelle und Meyer, 1924).

Stade, B. *Die Entstehung des Volkes Israel.* (Giessen: Ricker, 1899.)

Sykes, P. M. *A History of Persia.* Vols. 1 and 2 (London and New York: Macmillan, 1915).   Vol. 1 treats of the history of Persia to the Arab conquest. The work is provided with two admirable maps.

Wellhausen, J. *Prolegomena to the History of Israel.* (London: Black, 1885.)

See also the works of Hall, Meissner, Rogers, and Smith, listed under C.

F. CHAPTERS IX, X, AND XIII–XVI

Beloch, J. *Griechische Geschichte.* Vols. 1 to 4 (Berlin: de Gruyter, 1914–27).

Bilabel, F. *Die Ionische Kolonisation.* (Leipzig: Dieterich, 1920.)

Botsford, G. W. *Hellenic History.* (London and New York: Macmillan, 1922.)

Bury, J. B. *History of Greece to the death of Alexander.* Ed. 2, 1922 (London and New York: Macmillan).

Busolt, G. *Griechische Geschichte.* Vols. 1 to 3 (Gotha: Perthes, 1893–1904).

Busolt, G. *Griechische Staatskunde.* Vols. 1 and 2. Ed. 3 (Munich: Beck, 1920–26).

Cary, M. *The Documentary Sources of Greek History.* (Oxford: Blackwell, 1927.) A brief but excellent introduction to the subject.

Casson, S. *Macedonia, Thrace, and Illyria.* (Oxford University Press, 1926.)

De Sanctis, G. *Atthis: Storia della repubblica ateniese.* (Turin: Bocca, 1912.)

Ferguson, W. S. *Greek Imperialism.* (New York: Houghton Mifflin, 1913.)

Fowler, W. W. *The City State of the Greeks and Romans.* (London and New York: Macmillan, 1893.)

Francotte, H. *L'Industrie dans la Grèce ancienne.* Vols. 1 and 2 (Brussels: Société Belge de librairie, 1901–02).

Freeman, E. A. *History of Sicily.* Vols. 1 to 4 (Oxford University Press, 1891–94).

Gardner, P. *History of Ancient Coinage, 700–300 B.C.* (Oxford University Press, 1918.)

Glotz, G. *Histoire de la Grèce: des origines aux guerres médiques.* (Paris: Presses Universitaires de France, 1926.)

Glotz, G. *Le Travail dans la Grèce ancienne.* (Paris: Alcan, 1920.) An English translation appeared in 1926 under the title *Ancient Greece at Work.* (London: Kegan, Paul; New York: Knopf.)

Grote, G. *History of Greece.* New Ed. (London: Murray, 1884).

Greenidge, A. H. J. *Handbook of Greek Constitutional History.* (London and New York: Macmillan, 1902.)

Grundy, G. B. *The Great Persian War.* (London: Murray, 1901.)

Grundy, G. B. *Thucydides and the History of his Age.* (London: Murray, 1911.)

Hasebroek, J. *Staat und Handel im alten Griechenland.* (Tübingen: Mohr, 1928.)

Head, B. V. *Historia Numorum.* Ed. 2 (Oxford University Press, 1911).

Heitland, W. E. *Agricola: A Study of Agriculture and Rustic Life in the Greco-Roman World.* (Cambridge University Press, 1921.)

Hill, G. F. *Historical Greek Coins.* (London: Constable, 1906.)

Holm, A. *Geschichte Siziliens im Altertum.* Vols. 1 to 3 (Leipzig: Engelmann, 1870–98).

Minns, E. H. *Scythians and Greeks.* (Cambridge University Press, 1913.)

Myres, J. L. *The Political Ideas of the Greeks.* (London: Arnold, 1927.)

Ormerod, H. A. *Piracy in the Ancient World.* (London: Hodder and Stoughton, 1924.)

Pöhlmann, R. von. *Geschichte der sozialen Frage und des Sozialismus in der antiken Welt.* Ed. 3 (Munich: Beck, 1925).

Rostovtzeff, M. *Iranians and Greeks in South Russia.* (Oxford University Press, 1922.)

Schömann, G. F. and Lipsius, J. H. *Griechische Altertümer.* (Berlin: Weidmann, 1897–1902.)

Ure, P. N. *The Origin of Tyranny.* (Cambridge University Press, 1922.)

Vinogradoff, P. *Outlines of Historical Jurisprudence.* Vol. 2 (Oxford University Press, 1922).

Whibley, L. (editor). *A Companion to Greek Studies.* Ed. 3 (Cambridge University Press, 1916).

Whibley, L. *Greek Oligarchies.* (Cambridge University Press, 1896.)

Zimmern, A. E. *The Greek Commonwealth.* Ed. 4 (Oxford University Press, 1924).

G. CHAPTERS XI AND XVII

Anderson, W. J. and Spiers, R. P. *The Architecture of Ancient Greece.* (London: Batsford, 1927.)

Barker, E. *Greek Political Theory: Plato and his Predecessors.* (London: Methuen, 1918.)

Blass, F. *Die Attische Beredsamkeit.* Vols. 1 to 3. Ed. 2 (Leipzig: Teubner, 1890–93).

Burnet, J. *Early Greek Philosophy.* Ed. 3 (London: Black, 1920).

Burnet, J. *Greek Philosophy: Part 1.* (London and New York: Macmillan, 1914.)

Bury, J. B. *The Ancient Greek Historians.* (London and New York: Macmillan, 1909.)

Buschor, G. *Greek Vase Painting.* (London: Chatto and Windus, 1921.)

Christ, W. von. *Geschichte der Griechischen Literatur.* Ed. 6 revised by W. Schmid. Vols. 1 and 2 (Munich: Beck, 1920–24).

Collignon, M. *Histoire de la sculpture grecque.* Vols. 1 and 2 (Paris: Didot).

Croiset, A. and M. *Histoire de la littérature grecque.* Vol. 1, Ed. 3 (1909); Vol. 2, Ed. 2 (1898); Vol. 3, Ed. 3 (1914); Vol. 4, Ed. 2 (1899); Vol. 5 (1899). (Paris: Fontemoing.)

D'Ooge, M. *The Acropolis of Athens.* (London and New York: Macmillan, 1908.)

Farnell, L. R. *The Cults of the Greek States.* Vols. 1 to 5 (Oxford University Press, 1896–1909).

Flickinger, R. *The Greek Theater.* Ed. 3 (University of Chicago Press, 1926).

Freeman, K. J. *Schools of Hellas.* Ed. 3 (London and New York: Macmillan, 1922).

Gardiner, E. N. *Olympia.* (Oxford University Press, 1925.)

Gardner, E. A. *Ancient Athens.* (London and New York: Macmillan, 1902.)

Gardner, E. A. *Handbook of Greek Sculpture.* Ed. 2 (Macmillan, 1915).

Gardner, E. A. *Six Greek Sculptors.* (London: Duckworth, 1910.)

Gomperz, T. *The Greek Thinkers.* Vols. 1 to 4 (London: Murray, 1901–12).

Haig, A. E. *The Attic Theatre.* Ed. 3 (Oxford University Press, 1907).

Jaeger, W. *Aristoteles.* (Berlin: Weidmann, 1923.)

Jebb, R. C. *The Attic Orators.* Vols. 1 and 2 (London and New York: Macmillan, 1893).

Livingstone, R. W. (editor). *The Legacy of Greece.* (Oxford University Press, 1922.) A series of essays by different hands.

Murray, G. G. *History of Greek Literature.* (London: Heinemann, 1902.)

Nilsson, M. P. *A History of Greek Religion.* (Oxford University Press, 1925.)

Pfuhl, E. *Meisterwerke Griechischer Zeichnung und Malerei.* (Munich: Bruckmann, 1924.)

Pickard-Cambridge, A. W. *Dithyramb, Tragedy, and Comedy.* (Oxford University Press, 1927.)

Poulsen, F. *Delphi.* (London: Gyldendal, 1920.)

Ridgeway, W. *The Origin of Tragedy.* (Cambridge University Press, 1910.)

Ross, W. D. *Aristotle.* (London: Methuen; New York: Scribners, 1923.)

Taylor, A. E. *Plato: The Man and his Work.* (London: Methuen; New York: Kennerley, 1927.)

Tucker, T. G. *Life in Ancient Athens.* (London and New York: Macmillan, 1906.)

Walters, H. B. *History of Ancient Pottery.* Vols. 1 and 2 (London: Murray, 1905).

H. CHAPTERS XVIII AND XIX

Beloch, J. *Griechische Geschichte.* Vol. 4. See under F.

Bevan, E. and Mahaffy, J. P. *A History of Egypt under the Ptolemaic Dynasty.* (London: Methuen, 1927.)

Bevan, E. *The House of Seleucus.* Vols. 1 and 2 (London: Arnold, 1902).

Bevan, E. *Stoics and Sceptics.* (Oxford University Press, 1913.)

Bouché-Leclerq, A. *Histoire des Lagides.* Vols. 1 to 4 (Paris: Leroux, 1903–07).

Bouché-Leclerq, A. *Histoire des Séleucides.* Vols. 1 and 2 (Paris: Leroux, 1913–14).

Bury, J. B. and others. *The Hellenistic Age.* Ed. 2 (Cambridge University Press, 1925). Four suggestive essays on the political history, the literature, the philosophy, and the economic conditions of the Hellenistic Age.

Cardinali, G. *Il Regno di Pergamo.* (Rome: Loescher, 1906.)

Ferguson, W. S. *Greek Imperialism.* See under F above.

Ferguson, W. S. *Hellenistic Athens.* (London and New York: Macmillan, 1911.)

Freeman, E. A. *History of Federal Government.* Ed. 2 revised by J. B. Bury. (Macmillan, 1893.)

Heath, T. L. *Aristarchus of Samos.* (Oxford University Press, 1913.)

Heath, T. L. *History of Greek Mathematics.* Vols. 1 and 2 (Oxford University Press, 1921).

Hicks, R. D. *Stoic and Epicurean.* (London and New York: Longmans, 1910.)

Hogarth, D. G. *Philip and Alexander of Macedon.* (London: Murray, 1897.)

Jouguet, P. *L'Impérialisme macédonien et L'hellénisation de l'Orient.* (Paris: Renaissance du livre, 1926.)

Kaerst, J. *Geschichte des Hellenismus.* Vols. 1 and 2 (Leipzig: Teubner, 1917–26).

Niese, B. *Geschichte der Griechisch und Makedonischen Staaten.* Vols. 1 to 3 (Gotha: Perthes, 1893–1903).

Powell, J. U. and Barber, E. A. *New Chapters in the History of Greek Literature.* (Oxford University Press, 1921.)

Rostovtzeff, M. *A Large Estate in Egypt in the Third Century.* (University of Wisconsin Press, 1922.)

Rostovtzeff, M. *The Economic Policy of the Pergamene Kings.* See in *Anatolian Studies presented to Sir W. M. Ramsay.* (Manchester University Press, 1923.)

Schnebel, M. *Die Landwirtschaft im Hellenistischen Aegypten.* (Munich: Beck, 1925.)

Singer, C. *Greek Biology and Greek Medicine.* (Oxford University Press, 1922.)

Susemihl, F. *Geschichte der Griechischen Literatur in der Alexandrinerzeit.* Vols. 1 and 2 (Leipzig: Teubner, 1891–92).

Tarn, W. W. *Antigonus Gonatas.* (Oxford University Press, 1913.)

Tarn, W. W. *Hellenistic Civilisation.* (London: Arnold, 1927.)

Wendland, P. *Die Hellenistisch-römische Kultur.* (Tübingen: Mohr, 1912.)

Wilcken, U. und Mitteis, L. *Grundzüge und Chrestomathie der Papyruskunde.* Vols. 1 to 4 (Leipzig: Teubner, 1912).

Zeller, E. *The Stoics, Epicureans, and Sceptics.* (London: Longmans, 1880.)

See also the works of Whibley listed under F, and of Blass, Christ-Schmid, and Croiset listed under G.

I. CHAPTERS XX–XXII, XXIII (PART), XXIV AND XXV

Bailey, C. (editor). *The Legacy of Rome.* (Oxford University Press, 1923.) A series of essays by different hands.

Boak, A. E. R. *History of Rome.* Revised edition. (London and New York: Macmillan, 1929.)

Boissier, G. *Cicero and His Friends.* (Putnams; the latest reprint of this book is dated 1925.)

Botsford, G. W. *The Roman Assemblies.* (London and New York: Macmillan, 1909.)

Ciaceri, E. *Storia della Magna Grecia.* (Rome: Albrighi, 1927.)

Davidson, J. L. S. *Cicero.* (London: Putnams; 1894 and several reprints.)

De Sanctis, G. *Storia dei Romani.* (Turin: Bocca, 1907–23.) *In progress.* So far Vols. 1 to 4, part 1, of this very important work have appeared, covering the history of Rome from the beginnings to the early years of the second century B.C.

Ducati, P. *Etruria antica.* Vols. 1 and 2 (Turin: Paravia, 1925.)

Fell, R. A. L. *Etruria and Rome.* (Cambridge University Press, 1924.)

Ferrero, G. *The Greatness and Decline of Rome.* Vols. 1 to 5 (London: Heinemann, 1907–09). A brilliant work, in which, however, many conclusions should be received with caution.

Fowler, W. W. *Social Life at Rome in the Age of Cicero.* (London and New York: Macmillan, 1909.)

Frank, T. *Economic History of Rome.* Ed. 2 (Baltimore: Johns Hopkins University Press, 1927).

Frank, T. *A History of Rome.* (New York: Holt, 1923.)

Frank, T. *Roman Imperialism.* (London and New York: Macmillan, 1914.)

Greenidge, A. H. J. *A History of Rome from 133 B.C. to 69 B.C.* (London: Methuen, 1905.) Only the first volume of this excellent work was published; it contains an admirable summary of economic conditions in Italy before the Gracchi, and treats in detail of the years from 133 to 104 B.C.

Greenidge, A. H. J. *Roman Public Life*. (London and New York: Macmillan, 1901.)

Gsell, S. *Histoire ancienne de l'Afrique du Nord*. Vols. 1 to 8 (Paris: Hachette, 1914–28).

Heitland, W. E. *Agricola*. See under F above.

Heitland, W. E. *The Roman Republic*. Vols. 1 to 3. Ed. 2 (Cambridge University Press, 1923).

Hill, G. F. *Historical Roman Coins*. (London: Constable, 1909.)

Holleaux, M. *Rome et la Grèce et les monarchies hellénistiques au IIIe siècle avant J. C.* (Paris: de Boccard, 1921.)

Holmes, T. R. *Caesar's Conquest of Gaul*. Ed. 2 (Oxford University Press, 1911).

Holmes, T. R. *The Roman Republic and the Founder of the Empire*. Vols. 1 to 3 (Oxford University Press, 1923). In spite of its title this work deals only with the last century of the Republic. For the political and especially the military history of that age it is indispensable.

Holmes, T. R. *The Architect of the Roman Empire*. (Oxford University Press, 1928.) A continuation of the previous work, covering the period from 44 to 27 B.C.

Homo, L. *L'Italie primitive et les débuts de l'impérialisme romain*. (Paris: Renaissance du livre, 1925.)

Homo, L. *Les Institutions politiques romaines*. (Paris: Renaissance du livre, 1927.)

Jones, H. S. *A Companion to Roman History*. (Oxford University Press, 1912.)

Jullian, C. *Histoire de la Gaule*. Vols. 1 to 8 (Paris: Hachette, 1908–26).

MacIver, D. R. *Villanovans and Early Etruscans*. (Oxford University Press, 1924.)

MacIver, D. R. *The Early Iron Age in Italy*. (Oxford University Press, 1927.)

MacIver, D. R. *The Etruscans*. (Oxford University Press, 1928.) This is a brief but good popular account of the Etruscans. The two preceding works by the same author are large and fully illustrated; they are indispensable for the study of the early civilizations of Italy.

Marsh, F. B. *The Founding of the Roman Empire*. Ed. 2 (Oxford University Press, 1927).

Meltzer, O. und Kahrstedt, U. *Geschichte der Karthager*. Vols. 1 to 3 (Berlin: Weidmann, 1879–1913).

Meyer, E. *Caesar's Monarchie und das Principat des Pompeius.* Ed. 2 (Stuttgart: Cotta, 1919).

Mommsen, T. *History of Rome.* Vols. 1 to 4 (London and New York: Macmillan, 1895).

Ormerod, H. A. *Piracy, etc.* See under F. above.

Peet, T. E. *The Stone and Bronze Ages in Italy and Sicily.* (Oxford University Press, 1909.)

Pelham, H. F. *Outlines of Roman History.* (London: Rivington, 1893 or later reprints.)

Petersson, T. *Cicero: a Biography.* (University of California Press, 1920.)

Poulsen, F. *Etruscan Tomb Paintings.* (Oxford University Press, 1922.)

Rosenberg, A. *Einleitung und Quellenkunde zur Römischen Geschichte.* (Berlin: Weidmann, 1921.)

Sandys, J. E. (editor). *Companion to Latin Studies.* Ed. 2 (Cambridge University Press, 1913).

J. Chapter XXVI–XXIX

Abbott, F. F. and Johnson, A. C. *Municipal Administration in the Roman Empire.* (Princeton University Press, 1927.)

Barrow, R. H. *Slavery in the Roman Empire.* (London: Methuen, 1928.)

Bouchier, E. S. *Spain under the Roman Empire.* (Oxford: Blackwell, 1914.)

Bouchier, E. S. *Syria as a Roman Province.* (Oxford: Blackwell, 1916.)

Bury, J. B. *Student's Roman Empire.* (London: Murray, 1893 and many reprints; New York: American Book Co.)

Chapot, V. *Le Monde romain.* (Paris: Renaissance du livre, 1927.) A succinct but excellent survey of the empire and its resources during the first three centuries of our era.

Charlesworth, M. P. *Trade-routes and Commerce of the Roman Empire.* (Cambridge University Press, 1924.)

Cheesman, G. L. *The Auxilia of the Roman Imperial Army.* (Oxford University Press, 1914.)

Collingwood, R. G. *Roman Britain.* (Oxford University Press, 1923.) Brief but excellent.

Dessau, H. *Geschichte der Römischen Kaiserzeit. In progress.* Vol. 1 (1924) deals with Augustus, Vol. 2, part 1 (1927) with the emperors from Tiberius to Vitellius. (Berlin: Weidmann.)

Dill, S. *Roman Society from Nero to Marcus Aurelius.* (London and New York: Macmillan, 1904.)

Duff, A. M. *Freedmen in the Roman Empire.* (Oxford University Press, 1928.)

Frank, T. See under I above.

Gardthausen, V. E. *Augustus.* Two volumes in six parts. (Leipzig: Teubner, 1891–1904.)

Haverfield, F. *Ancient Town-planning.* (Oxford University Press, 1913.)

Haverfield, F. *The Roman Occupation of Britain.* Ed. 2 (Oxford University Press, 1924).

Haverfield, F. *The Romanization of Roman Britain.* Ed. 4 (Oxford University Press, 1923).

Henderson, B. W. *The Life and Principate of the Emperor Nero.* (London: Methuen, 1903.)

Henderson, B. W. *Civil War and Rebellion in the Roman Empire, 68-70 A.D.* (London and New York: Macmillan, 1908.)

Henderson, B. W. *Five Roman Emperors.* (Cambridge University Press, 1927.) The emperors in question are Vespasian, Titus, Domitian, Nerva, and Trajan.

Henderson, B. W. *The Life and Principate of the Emperor Hadrian.* (London: Methuen, 1923.)

Hirschfeld, O. *Die kaiserlichen Verwaltungsbeamten bis auf Diocletian.* Ed. 2 (Berlin: Weidmann, 1905).

Jones, H. S. See under I.

Jullian, C. See under I.

Liebenam, W. *Städteverwaltung im römischen Kaiserreich.* (Leipzig: Duncker und Humboldt, 1900.)

Marquardt, K. J. *Römische Staatsverwaltung.* Vols. 1 to 3. Ed. 2 (Leipzig: Hirzel, 1881–85).

Mattingly, H. *Roman Coins.* (London: Methuen, 1928.)

Milne, J. G. *A History of Egypt under Roman Rule.* Ed. 2 (London: Methuen, 1925).

Mommsen, T. *Roman Provinces.* Ed. 2 (London and New York: Macmillan, 1909).

Mommsen, T. *Römisches Staatsrecht.* Vols. 1 to 3. Ed. 3 (Leipzig: Hirzel, 1887).

Norden, E. *Die germanische Urgeschichte in Tacitus' Germania.* Ed. 2 (Leipzig: Teubner, 1922).

Paribeni, R. *Optimus Princeps.* Vols. 1 and 2 (Messina: Principato, 1927). A detailed study of the life and times of Trajan.

Parker, H. M. D. *The Roman Legions.* (Oxford University Press, 1928.)

Parvan, V. *Dacia.* (Cambridge University Press, 1928.)

Reid, J. S. *Municipalities of the Roman Empire.* (Cambridge University Press, 1913.)

Rostovtzeff, M. *Social and Economic History of the Roman Empire.* (Oxford University Press, 1926.) See the remarks at the beginning of this bibliography.

Sandys, J. E. See under I above.

Schiller, H. *Geschichte der römischen Kaiserzeit.* Vols. 1 and 2 (Gotha: Perthes, 1883–87). A new edition of this work is in preparation.

Shuckburgh, E. S. *Augustus.* (London: Fisher, Unwin, 1903.)

Stein, A. *Der römische Ritterstand.* (Munich: Beck, 1927.) A valuable study of the Equestrian Order during the empire.

Warmington, E. H. *The Commerce between the Roman Empire and India.* (Cambridge University Press, 1928.)

K. CHAPTERS XXIII (PART) AND XXX

Anderson, W. J. and Spiers, R. P. *The Architecture of Ancient Rome.* (London: Batsford, 1927.)

Arnold, E. V. *Roman Stoicism.* (Cambridge University Press, 1911.)

Bardenhewer, O. *Geschichte der altkirchlichen Literatur.* Vols. 1 to 4. Ed. 2 (Freiburg i. B.: Herder, 1902–24).

Cagnat, R. L. V. and Chapot, V. *Manuel d'Archéologie romaine.* Vols. 1 and 2 (Paris: Picard, 1916-20).

Carter, J. B. *The Religious Life of Ancient Rome.* (Boston and New York: Houghton Mifflin, 1911.)

Cichorius, K. *Die Reliefs der Trajansäule.* Vols. 1 and 2 and two Vols. of plates (Berlin: Reimer, 1896–1900).

Cruttwell, C. T. *History of Roman Literature.* Ed. 6 (London: Griffin, 1898).

Cumont, F. *Afterlife in Roman Paganism.* (Oxford University Press, 1922.)

Cumont, F. *The Mysteries of Mithra.* (London: Open Court Co., 1910.)

Cumont, F. *Oriental Religions in Roman Paganism.* (London: Open Court Co., 1911.)

Duchesne, L. M. O. *Early History of the Christian Church.* Vols. 1 to 3 (London: Murray, 1909–24).

Duff, J. W. *A Literary History of Rome.* Vol. 1. Ed. 6 (1927). Vol. 2 (London: Fisher, Unwin, 1927).

Fowler, W. W. *The Roman Festivals.* (London and New York: Macmillan, 1899; reprint 1908.)

Fowler, W. W. *The Religious Experience of the Roman People.* (Macmillan, 1911.)

Fowler, W. W. *Roman Ideas of Deity.* (Macmillan, 1914.)

Gwynn, A. *Roman Education from Cicero to Quintilian.* (Oxford University Press, 1926.) A useful bibliography will be found on pp. 253–256.

Halliday, W. R. *The Pagan Background of Christianity.* (London: Hodder and Stoughton, 1925.)

Harnack, A. *Mission und Ausbreitung des Christentums in den ersten drei Jahrhunderten.* Ed. 4 (Leipzig: Hinrichs, 1923). The English translation, being a version of the first German edition, is out of date.

Labriolle, P. de. *Histoire de la littérature latine chrétienne.* Ed. 2 (Paris: Les Belles Lettres, 1924).

Mackail, J. W. *Latin Literature.* (London: Murray, 1895 or reprints.)

Mau, A. *Pompeii.* (Translated by F. W. Kelsey.) Ed. 2 (London and New York: Macmillan, 1902).

Merrill, E. T. *Essays in Early Christian History.* (London and New York: Macmillan, 1924.)

Meyer, E. *Ursprung und Anfänge des Christentums.* Vols. 1 to 3 (Stuttgart: Cotta, 1921–23).

Peter, H. *Die Geschichtliche Literatur über die Römische Kaiserzeit bis Theodosius I.* (Leipzig: Teubner, 1897.)

Petersen, E. and others. *Die Marcussäule.* One volume and atlas of plates. (Munich: Bruckmann, 1896.)

Schanz, M. von. *Geschichte der Römischen Literatur.* Ed. 3, three parts in five volumes (Munich: Beck, 1907–22). A fourth, revised edition of part 1 by C. Hosius appeared in 1927.

Strong, Mrs. A. *Roman Sculpture.* (London: Duckworth, 1907.)

Teuffel, W. S. *Geschichte der Römischen Literatur.* Ed. 6 (Leipzig: Teubner, 1910–16). The English translation of this work is antiquated.

Wickhoff, F. *Roman Art.* (London: Heinemann, 1900.)

L. CHAPTER XXXI

Cambridge Mediaeval History. Vol. 1 (Cambridge University Press, 1911).

Dopsch, A. *Grundlagen der Europäischen Kulturentwicklung.* Vol. 1. Ed. 2 (Vienna: Seidel, 1923).

Firth, J. B. *Constantine the Great.* (London and New York: Putnams, 1923.)

Gibbon, E. *The Decline and Fall of the Roman Empire.* The edition of this classic by J. B. Bury (London: Methuen, 1896) should be used.

Lot, F. *La Fin du monde antique et le début du moyen âge.* (Paris: Renaissance du livre, 1927.)

Rostowzew, M. *Studien zur Geschichte des Römischen Kolonats.* (Leipzig: Teubner, 1910.)

Schwartz, E. *Kaiser Constantin und die Christliche Kirche.* (Leipzig: Teubner, 1913.)

Seeck, O. *Geschichte des Untergangs der antiken Welt.* Vols. 1 to 6 (Stuttgart: Metzler, 1897–1921).

Stein, E. *Geschichte des Spätrömischen Reiches.* Vol. 1 (Vienna: Seidel, 1928).

INDEX